THE **ESSENTIAL HISTORY** OF
BLACKBURN ROVERS

FOREWORD BY RONNIE CLAYTON

MIKE JACKMAN

First published in 2001
by HEADLINE BOOK PUBLISHING
for WHSmith, Greenbridge Road, Swindon SN3 3LD

1 3 5 7 9 10 8 6 4 2

ISBN 0 7553 1022 5

Design by designsection, Frome, Somerset.
Photographs supplied by EMPICS apart from: Howard Talbot pages 4, 8, 29, 32, 46, 48, 49, 55, 69, 73, 74, 76, 78, 79, 80, 83, 86, 90, 92, 95, 96, 99, 101, 103, 104, 106, 109, 113, 115, 116, 118, 119, 120, 122, 125, 128, 132, 133, 134, 139, 146; Anne Barry pages 140, 143, 144, 145, 147, 153, 158, 159, 162, 165, 167, 168, 169, 172, 176; Blackburn Library pages 13, 19, 30, 35, 36, 37, 40, 64; Reed Northern Newspapers pages 10, 15, 18, 61

The author would like to thank Amelia Jackman, Harry Jackman, John Williams, Ronnie Clayton, Julian Flanders, Derek Jones, Howard Talbot, Anne Barry, Mike Davage, Jim Creasy and Louise Cassell

Printed and bound in Great Britain by Clays Ltd, St Ives PLC, Bungay, Suffolk

HEADLINE BOOK PUBLISHING
A division of Hodder Headline
338 Euston Road
London NW1 3BH

www.headline.co.uk
www.hodderheadline.com

Contents

Foreword
By Ronnie Clayton

Blackburn Rovers has been my life since 1949 and I have enjoyed every minute of it. Today, I still watch the team every week and a bad result still hurts just as much as it did when I was playing. For me there is no finer ground than Ewood Park, nor finer club than Blackburn Rovers.

I first came to Blackburn when I was 14 years old and signed for the club at the same time as my brother, Ken. In those days, I had to sweep up around the ground, clean the bath, make sure the boots were all immaculate and, most important of all, put dubin on the footballs. As strange as it might seem, I loved every minute of it. However, my favourite part came at the end of the day when I would get to use the gym for an hour or so.

I was just 16 years old when I made my first-team debut but I was fortunate in that we had a lot of good professionals to look after me. Ronnie Suart, the old Blackpool full back, took me under his wing and had a great influence on me. Of course, for a couple of years I had to limit my football because of National Service. When I returned to the first team I was fortunate enough to be in a very good side. The older players looked after me on the pitch and if I strayed out of position they were quick to tell me. They were exciting times and I got so nervous that I often couldn't sleep before a match.

After several near misses, you can imagine my delight when we finally won promotion at Charlton Athletic in April 1958. That game was one of the highlights of my career. We appeared to be coasting it at 4-1 and then, suddenly, Charlton scored a couple of goals and it was panic stations. We managed to hang on and by the time I got back to the dressing room I was shaking like a leaf.

Ronnie Clayton, left, served Blackburn Rovers with great distinction over 20 years, and made 665 appearances for the club between 1949 and 1969.

I was fortunate to play with some great players during my time at Ewood Park, although I genuinely believe that Bryan Douglas was one of the greatest. He had such a big heart and never shirked a tackle. He was wonderful in possession and I used to tell him to keep the ball for five minutes so that I could have a rest. He was that good.

I still go to the games with Duggie and it gave us both a great thrill to see the club capture the Premier League Championship in 1994-95. Today, I'm still working at Ewood Park, taking groups of supporters on tours around the ground. I just love chatting to people about Blackburn Rovers. It has always been a family club and I can't begin to describe the joy it has brought to me. As I said, I've enjoyed every minute I've been here.

Ronnie Clayton

Ken and Ronnie Clayton, who teamed up as half backs regularly through the late 1950s leading up to the promotion season of 1957-58. Injury sadly put paid to Ken's career but Ronnie went on from strength to strength to appear 665 times for the Rovers in a distinguished career.

Chapter One: 1875-88
Formation and Early Years

Even at the opening of the 21st century, the mention of the name of Blackburn conjures up images of cobbled, smoky terraced streets dwarfed by factory chimneys. It is the image of a Lowry landscape that never changes. Yet the Blackburn of today is far removed from the stereotype picture of a traditional mill town, and nowhere is that better exemplified than at Ewood Park. Today's visitor to the home of Blackburn Rovers will find a modern stadium that hosts restaurants and conference facilities and boasts a seven-days-a-week operation. In neighbouring Ribble Valley, an impressive training complex caters for the senior professionals while nearby is a multi-million-pound academy for nurturing some of the finest young talent in the country. Yet, Blackburn Rovers garners the majority of its support not from some vast city conurbation, but from its old industrial heartland.

The success of Blackburn Rovers today is due to the passion and vision of the late Jack Walker, a local boy made good, who continued the traditions of those who founded the club in 1875. Herein lies the whole history of Blackburn Rovers. While its support has often been drawn from a working class proletariat, its leadership has often been in the hands of those who belong to a different stratum of society. Yet both have happily coexisted to keep Blackburn Rovers at the forefront of the national game.

The 17 men who gave birth to Blackburn Rovers at a meeting at the St Leger Hotel in Blackburn, in November 1875, could hardly be described as proletarian. These men belonged to that class of society that revelled in money, power and influence. The result was that Blackburn Rovers was able to emerge from the myriad of local football clubs to become the one dominant force in the town. However, when John Lewis, Arthur Constantine and the others formed the club there could have been little thought given to what the future might hold. The public school background soon became evident when it was decided to model the club colours on those of the Old Malvernians who sported a quartered shirt. However, instead of the traditional green it was decided to opt for a Cambridge blue.

Early officials at the club included Walter Duckworth, a former pupil of Clitheroe Grammar School, who became club secretary, while Lewis was treasurer. Thomas Greenwood, another member of a prominent local family,

John Lewis, one of the founders of Blackburn Rovers in 1875.

was appointed captain, while two of his brothers, Harry and Doctor, would also play for the club. The scholastic profession was represented by J.T. Sycelmore, a master at Blackburn Grammar School. The son of the vicar of Blackburn, A.L. Birch, was also a member of the team while Richard Birtwistle belonged to one of the leading cotton manufacturing families in Blackburn. The report of the first game that the club played, at Church, was carried in *The Blackburn Times* on 18 December 1875 in just a few lines. The only detail given was that Richard Birtwistle had scored the Blackburn goal in a 1-1 draw. No teams were given but it is widely believed that the Blackburn side comprised: Thomas Greenwood, Jack Baldwin, Fred Birtwistle, Arthur Thomas, J.T. Sycelmore, Walter Duckworth, John Lewis, Thomas Dean, Arthur Constantine, Harry Greenwood and Richard Birtwistle.

Search for a Ground

At this time, Blackburn Rovers was little more than a sporting club for young gentlemen, and without a ground to call their home the players played all their fixtures on the grounds of their opponents. In the 1876-77 season, the club opted to rent a piece of farmland at Oozehead on the western side of town. This was a fairly rudimentary piece of land that required several turf-covered planks to cover a large pool of water in the field.

As well as hosting fixtures at Oozehead, the club played games at Pleasington and it was on the field near The Butler's Arms Inn that tragedy struck on a Saturday afternoon in December 1877. A match between Blackburn Rovers and Preston Rovers was halted in the most dramatic of circumstances. One of the Preston team, a man named Henry Smith, was seen to collapse after running for about 100 yards. He was carried into The Butler's Arms and stimulants were administered. Before qualified medical help could arrive, Smith had passed away with a suspected heart attack.

Within weeks of the tragedy at Pleasington the club had found a new home at the Alexandra Meadows Cricket Ground in Blackburn. The first game in these new surroundings was held on 2 January 1878 against Partick Thistle. The visit of such illustrious opponents drew a crowd not only from Blackburn but also the surrounding area. An added attraction was the first appearance for the Rovers of Albert Neilson Hornby. Popularly known as 'Monkey', Hornby was a member of a family that owned cotton mills in the Brookhouse area of Blackburn. He was a natural athlete and local hero as he excelled at cricket, rugby, soccer and athletics. In 1867, he had first appeared for the Lancashire County Cricket Club and would eventually go on to appear in 292 matches for the Red Rose county. He would also captain his country and feature in three test matches. Interestingly, the visiting team included Fergie Suter, a man who would later play a prominent role in the history of Blackburn Rovers. Two goals from Dick Birtwistle helped the Rovers to a 2-1 victory over their Scottish opponents and thus enabled them to make their first mark on the national football map.

The Birth of Blackburn Olympic

The summer provided the club with a further opportunity for progress when John Lewis was invited to a meeting at The Volunteer Inn, Bromley Cross, to discuss the formation of a Lancashire Football Association. In September 1878, a meeting was held at the Co-operative Hall in Darwen with Blackburn Rovers just one of 23 clubs involved in the birth of this new organization.

Another event in 1878 that was to have a major impact on Blackburn Rovers was the formation of Blackburn Olympic. This new club was the result of an amalgamation between the Black Star and the James Street clubs of the town and, with the patronage of Sidney Yates of the local iron foundry, Blackburn Rovers now had a serious rival within the town.

The 1878-79 season saw the Rovers continue to embark upon a number of ambitious ventures. In November, a match was played under electric lamps at the Alexandra Meadows against Accrington. A crowd of around 6,000 gathered to watch a game that was played under a rudimentary floodlighting system. The ground was illuminated by the Gramme light, one light being fixed at the east end of the ground and one at the west end. Each lamp was affixed to a scaffold that was some 30-40 feet above ground level, and the lamps were reputed to have 6,000 candle power. The ball was painted white to offer better visibility and as well as the crowd in the ground, a big group gathered to watch in the neighbouring park overlooking the ground.

A severe blow to the ambitions of the club came in February 1879 when the long-anticipated meeting between the Rovers and the Olympic took place at Alexandra Meadows. In what was described as 'One of the fastest and

Team circa 1878-79.
T. Greenwood (10),
D. Greenwood (11),
Haworth (12),
Thomas (13),
F. Birtwistle (8),
Baldwin (9),
H. Ibbotson (umpire),
J. Duckworth (2),
Dean (3),
R. Birtwistle (4),
Lewis (5),
Hargreaves (6),
W. Duckworth (7).

finest games ever played in Blackburn', the Rovers succumbed to a 3-1 defeat. Although the Olympic players appeared physically frailer than those of the Rovers, their speed of thought and movement left the home side looking lacklustre by comparison. The local press wrote that the Olympic '...now takes rank as one of the best, if not the best, club in town'.

Overcoming this dent to local pride, the Rovers embarked on competitive football for the first time during the 1879-80 season. On 11 October 1879, the club played its first competitive cup match when a 1-1 draw was gained at Enfield in the first round of the Lancashire Cup. The replay produced a 5-1 win. On 1 November 1879, the club made its debut in the FA Cup when the Tyne Association Football Club visited Alexandra Meadows to lose 5-1. While the club made impressive progress in the Lancashire Cup, the national competition produced a third-round exit at Nottingham Forest. The Rovers had tried to get this tie postponed as they were without several of their first-team regulars. Unfortunately, Forest insisted that the game should be played and the Rovers slumped to a 6-0 defeat.

The Professionalism Debate Begins

It was during these cup-ties that the Rovers began to look to Scotland to bolster their squad for cup games. The second-round FA Cup-tie with Darwen in December 1879 had seen Hugh McIntyre, the former Partick Thistle and Glasgow Rangers player, make his debut for the Rovers. The following month, he reappeared for the club together with Peter Campbell, another player with links to Glasgow Rangers, for the visit of Turton in the third round of the Lancashire Cup. The Turtonians lodged a formal protest about the involvement of McIntyre and Campbell but the Lancashire Association allowed the match result, a 2-1 win to the Rovers, to stand. This was the first of several confrontations that would involve the Rovers with regard to imported players. The debate about professionalism was about to be ignited, and for the next five years the name of Blackburn Rovers would be at the forefront of the dispute over the employment of paid professionals.

The 1879-80 season ended in disappointment when the Lancashire Cup was lost in a controversial final with Darwen. In the build-up to the game Darwen officials lodged a complaint about the presence of Monkey Hornby in the Blackburn team. They argued that Hornby was not a regular member of the Blackburn side so was ineligible to play in the final. Blackburn countered with the accusation that one of the Darwen players, a man named Kirkham, was also of dubious qualification, and that if Hornby was to be banned then so should the Darwen man. The debate raged and at one point the Rovers threatened to withdraw from the competition. Fortunately, wiser counsel prevailed and the game was eventually played at Darwen on 20 March 1880 to 10,000 spectators. The Rovers didn't include Hornby but Kirkham appeared for the home side who enjoyed a 3-0 win. Five days prior to this game the Rovers had been honoured with its first international recognition when Fred Hargreaves made his England debut against Wales at Wrexham.

The 1880-81 season was to be dominated by more bickering between Blackburn Rovers and Darwen as relations between the two clubs descended into little more than tribal warfare. The new campaign began with Hugh McIntyre, now the host of The Castle Inn in Blackburn, ensconced in the Rovers team. He was to be joined in the Blackburn ranks by Fergie Suter, the old Partick Thistle player, who had spent the previous season with Darwen.

The Darwen officials were incensed when they learnt that Suter had thrown in his lot with the Rovers and immediately accused the Blackburn committee of offering improved terms to Suter to get him to switch his allegiance to the Rovers. However, as professionalism was illegal, it was a difficult argument for the Darwen club to pursue. Although they had always vehemently denied making payments to Suter themselves, it had not gone unnoticed that the Scottish stonemason had quickly given up his previous trade on moving to Lancashire. He had been heard to complain that the local stone was rather too hard to work with.

Shortly after the start of the new campaign, a third Scot arrived at Alexandra Meadows in the form of Jimmy Douglas, a terrier-like inside forward who had been awarded a Scottish cap while with Renton. With the three Scottish players in the team, the Rovers enjoyed some impressive results during the early stages of the 1880-81 season, and the supporters witnessed some explosive goal scoring during this period. However, there were explosions of a different sort on 27 November 1880 when Darwen visited Alexandra Meadows for a game that was to end in a riot.

The flames of fire had been fanned by Darwen officials before the game when they announced that they would be represented by men who were 'Darwen born and bred', an obvious slur on the three Scots in the Blackburn team. A crowd of 10,000 assembled and on several occasions encroached onto the playing area. The visitors took the lead but John Duckworth equalized before half-time. However, it was in the second period that the fireworks began and, ironically, it was Suter who was at the centre of the storm. The second half had barely begun when Suter clashed with Marshall of Darwen. The two players were separated but the crowd on the grandstand side of the ground flocked onto the field. Events got out of hand and the game was stopped as the pitch became engulfed in supporters with many of the Blackburn contingent lifting their players shoulder high and carrying them off the pitch in triumph. Acts of vandalism followed, including in the Darwen dressing room where one mirror was stolen and another smashed.

A season that had produced many thrilling friendly victories provided little cheer in the cup competitions. The Rovers made a second-round exit from the FA Cup on an icy pitch at Alexandra Meadows. The Sheffield Wednesday team that beat the Rovers 4-0 wore 'leather-headed nails' on the soles of their boots. It proved a smart move as the Blackburn players found it hard to keep their feet on the treacherous surface, let alone play football.

The Lancashire Cup provided some consolation with 15 goals being scored in the first three rounds and none conceded. Unfortunately, the fourth round brought another clash with Darwen. This time the internecine conflict began before a ball was kicked, with both clubs arguing about the date of the game. With no compromise in sight, the Lancashire Association, who had had enough of the petty bickering, ejected both clubs from the competition.

FA Cup Disappointment

The 1881-82 season began with a 13-3 win over Great Harwood and ended with the club claiming to be the premier team in England. The season also saw the club move from its base at Alexandra Meadows to a new home at Leamington Street. However, it was progress in the FA Cup that dominated the season. The team was still built around the three Scottish players, but the club could now boast four English internationals in Doc Greenwood, Fred

Lancashire Cup-winning team from 1882, from left to right: back row – D.H. Greenwood, Howorth, J. Hargreaves, Suter, W. Duckworth (umpire); middle – J. Duckworth, McIntyre, Sharples, F. Hargreaves, Strachan, Avery; front – Brown, Douglas.

and Jack Hargreaves and Jimmy Brown. Further changes were made with the introduction of Tot Strachan to the forward line and the promotion of Roger Howorth to first-team goalkeeper. Strachan, who had joined the club from Witton, was to form a lively partnership with Brown in attack. The Lancashire Cup found them at their devastating best and the first-round win over Kirkham brought four goals for Brown and three for Strachan as 14 goals were scored without reply. The second round brought a 10-1 win over Clitheroe with even Howorth managing to score. Accrington Wanderers lost 7-0 in the third round and a 6-0 win over Church gave the Rovers a semi-final place.

Progress was equally emphatic in the national competition with a 9-1 win over Blackburn Park Road in the first round, a 6-2 victory over Bolton Wanderers in the second and in the third a home tie with Darwen resulted in a 5-1 win, but again the tie was surrounded with acrimony and was only played after the intervention of the Football Association. A place in the semi-final was achieved when Wednesbury Old Athletic lost 3-1 at the Leamington ground.

The Lancashire Cup semi-final enabled the Rovers to re-establish local supremacy with a 6-1 win over Blackburn Olympic. However, the FA Cup semi-final against Sheffield Wednesday proved a more difficult affair and the Rovers had to settle for a replay after a goalless affair at Huddersfield. The second game was played at Whalley Range, Manchester, and on this occasion the Rovers simply overran the men from Yorkshire and recorded a 5-1 win. When the Rovers faced the Old Etonians at the Kennington Oval, they became the first provincial club to reach this stage of the competition. However, the presence of the three Scotsmen, and the air of professionalism that pervaded the club, meant few outside of Blackburn wished them well in their bid to capture the trophy. Ironically, all three of the Scots had found nominal employment within the town. McIntyre remained licensee of The Castle Inn while Suter had found employment in the textile industry as a tape sizer. Douglas had gone to work in the iron foundry of W. & J. Yates.

The game produced an intriguing clash of styles. Rovers favoured their normal dribbling game while their opponents opted for a quicker approach with several long balls played directly into the heart of the Blackburn defence. The Rovers looked strangely out of sorts and the Old Etonians enjoyed victory by the narrowest of margins when Anderson scored the only goal of the game. Fortunately, the club found some solace in the capture of the Lancashire Cup after a 3-1 win over Accrington at Burnley in April 1882.

After the euphoria of the FA Cup final, the 1882-83 season was one of pure anti-climax. A major blow came at the start of the campaign when Doc Greenwood announced his intention to withdraw from the team. The former England international went on to make just a handful of appearances for the Rovers during that campaign, while the role of partnering Suter at full back went to Joe Beverley who had been enticed from Blackburn Olympic. Another setback came in November 1882 when Fred Hargreaves, the Blackburn captain, was forced to sit out the remainder of the season when his knee gave way in a match at Aston Villa. There was talk of him making a comeback as a goalkeeper but Hargreaves was to have played his last match for the club.

The loss of Greenwood and Hargreaves was compounded by an early exit from the FA Cup at the hands of Darwen. Although local pride was restored when the Rovers beat their old rivals in the final of the Lancashire Cup, it was Blackburn Olympic who delivered a hammer blow. The Olympic, having won through to the FA Cup final, exacted revenge on the Old Etonians and returned to Lancashire with the trophy that the Rovers craved so dearly. Rovers outwardly congratulated their rivals on becoming the first provincial club to win the competition, but it was a devastating blow to the club.

The new season brought key changes. The goalkeeping position was now entrusted to Herbie Arthur while Jimmy Forrest retained the place he had won following the injury to Fred Hargreaves. Joe Sowerbutts was promoted from the second team to fill one of the places in the forward line. The 1883-84 season opened with a string of impressive results as the Rovers again established themselves as the leading club in the area. Yet, at a time when the debate over professionalism continued to reverberate throughout the game, the Blackburn committee decided to ruffle a few more feathers in its quest to make the Rovers the leading team in the country. On 2 February 1884, the Blackburn team that faced Darwen in a friendly fixture contained a new face from Scotland in the shape of John Inglis. The former Scottish international had previously played against Blackburn with Glasgow Rangers and he made an impressive goal-scoring debut in the 8-0 win over Darwen. However, when the Blackburn committee announced that Inglis was to appear in future important cup-ties, there was uproar in the town.

National and local press condemned the move but the committee remained unrepentant, and seven days after his debut he helped the club overcome Upton Park in the fifth round of the FA Cup. With a place in the semi-final assured, the protests began to fade and few objections were heard when the Rovers beat Notts County 1-0 to reach the final. The Nottingham club immediately objected to the presence of Inglis in the Blackburn team, claiming that his inclusion was not in the spirit of the competition. However, although Inglis still resided in Glasgow, where as a mechanic he was reported to have earned 25 shillings a week, there was no evidence to prove that he was receiving financial inducements to travel down and turn out for the Rovers. The objection was dismissed and Inglis was selected as part of the team that was to face Queens Park at the Kennington Oval on 29 March 1884.

The meeting of the top two teams either side of the border meant the match was billed as an international affair. The Scottish club had two goals disallowed for offside before Sowerbutts put the Rovers into the lead, and Forrest added a second shortly afterwards. Christie pulled a goal back but the trophy returned to Lancashire for the second successive season, this time with Blackburn Rovers. The following month, Blackburn Olympic were beaten in the replay of the Lancashire Cup final.

Nat Walton, a member of the FA Cup-winning side of 1886.

There was now no doubt as to who was the dominant force, not only in Blackburn but in the whole of Britain.

Cup Domination Continues

The next two years saw the club continue to dominate the national competition. The FA Cup final, held on 4 April 1885, saw a rematch between Blackburn and Queens Park at the Kennington Oval. Although Inglis had ceased to be involved with the club at the end of the previous campaign, the Rovers still retained the services of Suter, McIntyre and Douglas – the Scottish triumvirate that had served the club so well. The march to the Oval had been launched in the most impressive of circumstances at home to Rossendale. The 11-0 win remains a record for the club in a

first-class fixture, and other rampant performances followed with an 8-0 demolition of Romford in the fourth round and a 5-1 thrashing of the Old Carthusians in the semi-final. The second meeting with Queens Park produced a 2-0 win, the goals coming from Brown and Forrest and, once again, this was followed by the retention of the Lancashire Cup.

The 1885-86 season was once more dominated by the quest to retain the FA Cup, although there were doubts as to the capability of the team to capture the trophy for the third successive season. The competition opened with a 2-0 win over the unfancied Clitheroe, and the second round produced another unimpressive display with a single goal win against Oswaldtwistle Rovers. Fortunately, the team found its form in the later rounds and reached the semi-final. However, the meeting with Swifts at Derby produced a tighter affair and the Rovers only reached the final by the narrowest of margins, winning 2-1.

The meeting with West Bromwich Albion at the Kennington Oval on 3 April 1886 was a fairly dire spectacle ending in a goalless draw. As a result, the FA Cup final left the capital for the first time with

Blackburn Rovers dominated the FA Cup in the mid 1880s, winning from 1984-1986. These cigarette cards show the 1883-84 (top) and 1885-86 (bottom) winning teams.

the replay being held in the Midlands at the County Cricket Ground in Derby. The Blackburn committee made one change to the team that had played at the Oval, and Nat Walton was recalled at the expense of the young Joe Heyes. The latter had been somewhat overawed by the Oval, and a strangely timid performance by his colleagues had hardly inspired confidence in him.

The Rovers Turn Professional

The Blackburn team that ran out at Derby was a far more confident outfit, and goals from Sowerbutts and Brown enabled the club to carve a niche in the record books by winning the trophy for a third successive season. Although Blackburn Rovers continued to be a formidable force in the game, there were signs that this domination was on the wane. The FA Cup apart, the 1885-86 season had been something of a disappointment. The 60-match first-team programme had resulted in 25 defeats. This was a disappointing return for the club during the first season of legalized professionalism. The Rovers had been quick to register themselves as professionals and a total of £615 was spent on the payment of wages during the 1885-86 campaign.

The 1886-87 season kicked off with news that Jimmy Brown, who had postponed retirement plans 12 months earlier, had now decided to call it a day in order to concentrate on his legal career. However, Joe Beverley, who had left the Rovers to return to his beloved Olympic in the summer of 1884, was once more recruited to fill one of the full-back places. The Blackburn committee also persuaded Billy Townley to accompany him on the short journey from the Olympic to the Rovers. While the results remained respectable, there were a number of worrying signs. Preston North End inflicted a series of crushing defeats on their neighbours – two games being lost by a 6-1 margin, a third resulting in an 8-2 defeat – while the first round of the Lancashire Cup ended in a 7-1 defeat for the Rovers. The greatest blow to prestige came in the FA Cup with elimination in the second round. The club had been handed a walkover in the first round when Halliwell was scratched from the competition, and the second round produced a 2-2 draw away to Scottish club Renton. A crowd of 6,000 gathered at the Leamington ground to watch the home team slip to an unexpected 2-0 defeat. With interest in the cup competitions removed, the remainder of the campaign proved uninspiring, a disappointing end to Scot Hugh McIntyre's association as he hung up his boots at the end of the season.

The last season of friendly football produced a new strikeforce at Blackburn in the shape of Jack Southworth and Edgar Chadwick. The latter was an extremely gifted youngster, while the former had slightly more experience, having performed for several clubs, including Blackburn Olympic. Once again,

50 Greatest Players

FERGIE SUTER Full back

Born: Glasgow, 21 November 1857

Joined Blackburn: 1880   **From:** Darwen

Debut: 30 October 1880 v Sheffield
Providence, FA Cup

Appearances: 39   **Goals:** 3

Left Blackburn: 1889 (retired)

Honours won with Blackburn: FA Cup winner
1884, 1885, 1886

A stonemason by trade, Fergie Suter found
employment in a local cotton mill during his
association with Blackburn Rovers. Many
believed that this was an employment of
convenience and that his true occupation
during his stay was 'professional footballer'
although professionalism was illegal until 1885. Prior to joining the Rovers, he had played
with Partick Thistle and Glasgow Rangers before coming to Lancashire to appear with
Turton and then Darwen. It would appear that some kind of remuneration was received
from both of these clubs before he left Darwen for 'personal reasons' to come to the
Rovers. A quick, tough-tackling full back, Suter was noted for his ability to clear the ball
while under pressure and was also useful in the air. When first at Blackburn he partnered
Doc Greenwood, the epitome of the English amateur, at full back. He later enjoyed a
fruitful partnership with Joe Beverley, another English international. He won three FA Cup-
winners' medals but his career was over by the time the Football League began in 1888.
His only appearance in league football came as a stand-in goalkeeper in 1888.

the 1887-88 season was one of indifferent performances. Only the FA Cup
appeared to capture the imagination of both players and spectators alike.
Unfortunately, interest in this competition came to an end in January 1888
when the club slumped to a 2-1 defeat at Derby Junction in a sixth-round tie.
Although Blackburn Olympic had faded from the scene, the Rovers were to face
a new challenge for local supremacy when the Witton club faced the Rovers on
2 January 1888 in a match that was billed as the championship of Blackburn.
A 4-2 win enabled the Rovers to retain its position as the premier club in the
town, but further blows to prestige came when Witton beat the Rovers in a
benefit match for Jimmy Douglas. To add insult to injury, Witton then invited
Derby Junction to Blackburn and beat the Rovers' cup conquerors 3-0.

Chapter Two: 1888-1905
First Steps in the Football League

The formation of the Football League in 1888 drew a line under any prospective challenge to the supremacy of Blackburn Rovers within the immediate vicinity of the town. Rovers were now among an elite group of 12 clubs who organized a series of matches, home and away, against each other, that would bring an end to the chaos that often surrounded friendly matches. Following the advent of professionalism, the game itself would now be run on a professional basis. Membership of this elite group was essential for the development of the Rovers, but club officials were reluctant to lose the more lucrative friendly fixtures, so the club committed itself to a frenetic schedule of league, cup and friendly engagements during the 1888-89 season.

The summer of 1888 brought several important changes to the playing personnel. The previous season had witnessed a benefit game for Fergie

FA Cup-winning team, 1890. From left to right: back row – Jack Southworth, John Southworth, R. Birtwistle (umpire), Horne, Dewar; middle – Lofthouse, Campbell, Forbes (captain), Walton, Townley; front – Barton, Forrest.

Suter, and the long-serving Scot was no longer in contention for a full-back spot when the league competition began. Indeed, his only league appearance for the Rovers came at Deepdale against Preston North End in December 1888 when he filled the goalkeeping position. Fortunately, Tom Mitchell, the Blackburn secretary, was able to sign an excellent replacement from Vale of Leven – John Forbes. The summer also brought the return to Blackburn of Herbert Fecitt, who had left the club 12 months earlier to join Accrington. Edgar Chadwick departed to Everton soon after. Another familiar face re-joining the ranks was Jimmy Brown who came out of retirement to aid the Rovers. However, the former cup-winning captain found that the intervening years had taken their toll, and he was restricted to a peripheral role in the first season of league football.

In truth, the Rovers were ill-equipped to make an assault on the league title and, besides, everyone connected with the club still favoured the FA Cup as the most prominent competition. The Rovers opened the league programme a week later than the rest and the crowd at the Leamington ground witnessed a thrilling 5-5 draw with Accrington. Preston North End went on to record the first league and cup double and the Rovers achieved their own respectability with a fourth-place finish and a place in the semi-finals of the FA Cup. Defeat by Wolves prevented an all-Lancashire Cup final.

The Cup Returns to Blackburn

The second season of league football was marred by the lack of a first-class goalkeeper. After six try-outs only Jack Horne lived up to expectations. The club improved its league position by one place and won the FA Cup for the fourth time. The 6-1 victory over Sheffield Wednesday set a new record for an FA Cup final, and Billy Townley also claimed a place in the record books by becoming the first man to score a hat-trick in the final. The Rovers donned white dress shirts, hurriedly acquired from a London outfitters, after it was discovered that Sheffield Wednesday were to play in blue and white stripes.

The summer of 1890 brought a new problem for the Rovers when the landlord of the Leamington ground decided to ask for a rise in the rent. It was time to look for a new home and one was found in the Ewood area of the town. Ewood Park had originally opened as a sports ground in 1882, and various activities had taken place at that site since. Indeed, Blackburn Rovers had played four friendly matches at a ground called 'Ewood Bridge' in April 1882, and it is believed that this was the ground to which the club returned in 1890. A sum of £1,000 was spent to update the ground and the opening match on 13 September 1890 was a goalless draw with Accrington.

Great Matches

THE FOOTBALL LEAGUE	**Leamington Ground, 15 September 1888**	
Blackburn Rovers 5	**Accrington 5**	**Attendance: 5,000**
Jack Southworth	Kirkham 2	
Beresford	Holden	
Townley 2	Chippendale	
Fecitt	James Southworth (o.g.)	

The opening of Blackburn's Football League campaign was a goal bonanza. After just five minutes the visitors had taken the lead when former Rovers' favourite Joe Lofthouse floated a cross that Herbie Arthur misjudged. Before the Blackburn custodian could collect, he was met by the physical presence of John Kirkham who bundled both Arthur and ball into the net. Within three minutes, the Rovers had responded with a goal of their own after Herbert Fecitt found Jack Southworth and the Rovers' leading marksman beat Jack Horne in the Accrington goal. Southworth became a thorn in the side of 'Th' Owd Reds' defence and near the 20-minute mark the Rovers took the lead when a fierce Southworth shot was saved by Horne, but the ball fell kindly to the feet of Billy Townley who presented the ball for Jimmy Beresford to head home. Accrington's Lofthouse prodded and probed for an opening and it was from his splendid cross that Holden snatched the equalizer. More Accrington pressure brought another two goals. With half-time approaching, a shot from Townley reduced the arrears for Blackburn. In the second half, Townley levelled the scores with Accrington's players appealing for offside. With just 15 minutes remaining, Jimmy Southworth became the first Blackburn player to score an own goal in a league match. With three minutes remaining, Beresford forced a brilliant save from Horne who couldn't hold the ball and Fecitt forced the ball over the line to end Blackburn's first taste of the Football League.

Blackburn Rovers: Arthur, Beverley, James Southworth, Forrest, Almond, Douglas, Beresford, Walton, Jack Southworth, Fecitt, Townley

Accrington: Horne, Stevenson, McLellan, Haworth, Chippendale, Pemberton, Lofthouse, Bonar, Kirkham, Holden, Wilkinson

Referee: Mr Hindle

Once again, the 1890-91 season provided the club with mixed fortunes in league and cup competitions. The club slipped to sixth in the league, but the FA Cup was retained after Notts County were beaten in the final. Jimmy Forrest collected his fifth FA Cup-winner's medal that day, and thus ensured his own niche in the history of the competition.

Although the 1891-92 season proved a major disappointment – ninth in the league and a second-round exit from the FA Cup – the next few seasons told a similar story. Respectable league positions were complimented with exciting cup runs that twice took the club to the semi-final stage. Sadly, Wolves prevented the Rovers from making a final appearance in 1892-93 and the following season saw Notts County pip the Rovers for a place in the final.

Standards Decline at Ewood Park

Playing personnel began to show considerable changes as Tom Mitchell tried to rekindle the old winning formula. The controversial departure of Tom Brandon for Sheffield Wednesday in the summer of 1891 saw the arrival of Mick McKeown from Glasgow Celtic as his successor. McKeown was surprisingly released after only one season as the club sent Mitchell back to Scotland to look for new talent. Geordie Anderson and Harry Marshall proved inspired signings but many failed to sparkle.

The team that won the 1890-91 FA Cup.

The biggest blow came in August 1893 when goal machine Jack Southworth joined Everton. Further changes saw the return of Tom Brandon and the retirement of Johnny Forbes. The latter continued to serve the club as a member of the committee and as a director.

Finishes of fourth in 1893-94, fifth in 1894-95 and eighth in 1895-96 only helped mask the decline in the standard of football. The loss of Southworth was keenly felt during the 1894-95 campaign, and only Harry Chippendale managed to record double figures in league goals. The club suffered a further blow when Marshall was injured and restricted to just two league appearances. His injury was so severe that he returned to his native Scotland with his career in England seemingly at an end.

The club ended the 1896-97 campaign in 14th place with Tom Mitchell resigning as secretary in October to be replaced by Joseph Walmsley who had to make a speedy transition from cotton mill manager to football club secretary. A former player with Blackburn Olympic, Walmsley was a shrewd businessman and a good judge of a player but had stepped into a cauldron of unrest. Players were accused of lacking fitness and desire, and the committee stood accused by the local press of failing to do anything about the slide into mediocrity. The final straw was when captain Geordie Anderson was hauled before the committee and suspended until he improved his fitness. Minor club Chorley held the Rovers on two occasions in the

Lancashire Senior Cup, before finally being overcome, showing how far standards had fallen.

Perhaps the brightest moment in a desperate season came on 3 April 1897 when a young Bob Crompton made his debut for the club in a friendly game against Darwen. It was said that, 'Crompton played a hard game, and he showed promise of making a good man.' However, Crompton was Blackburn's future while it was the immediate present that was of more concern.

The 1897-98 campaign was an unmitigated disaster from beginning to end. A total of 28 players were used in 30 First Division games, but no matter how they were shuffled the result was usually the same. The final 14 games produced ten points as Blackburn finished the campaign one place off the bottom. As a result, the club was condemned to play in the test match series to decide if it would retain its First Division status, or suffer the ignominy of relegation.

Not even the threat of relegation could galvanize the players into raising their game. Defeat by Burnley in the first two games of the four-match series virtually condemned the club to relegation. Indeed, the Rovers had been so desperate that Harry Marshall returned on loan from Hearts to play for the club, while Geordie Anderson was recalled from New Brighton Tower, where he had spent the season. Peter Turnbull and Josh Hargreaves also returned

50 Greatest Players

JIMMY BROWN Centre forward

Born: Blackburn, Lancashire, 31 July 1862

Joined Blackburn: 1876; 1888

Debut: 1 November 1879 v Tyne Association, FA Cup

Appearances: 36   **Goals:** 29

Left Blackburn: 1886; 1889 (retired on each occasion)

Honours won with Blackburn: FA Cup winner 1884, 1885, 1886; 5 England caps

Jimmy Brown, a speedy, and most effective dribbler, was the diminutive skipper who led the club to FA Cup glory in the 1880s. Brown became a prolific goalscorer, notching up four goals on two occasions in the FA Cup, and also registered the first hat-trick for Blackburn in that competition in the 7-2 win over Sheffield Providence in October 1880. The first of his five England caps was gained while he was still a teenager. He had begun his involvement with Blackburn while articled to a solicitor and retired after the 1886 FA Cup triumph to concentrate on his legal career. He was lured back for the inaugural Football League season but loss of form meant just four appearances. Brown came out of retirement for a third time in August 1890 to help guide the younger players.

A team from 1892-93. From left to right: back – Anderson, Dewar; second – Murray, Forbes, Marshall; third – Dodd (linesman), Walton, Hunter (trainer); front – Mann, Sawers, Southworth, Hall, Bowdler.

to familiar surroundings, as club officials put its faith in the old guard to try and save them. A 4-3 win over Newcastle United proved academic when the 'Magpies' won the return game 4-0 and thus sent the Rovers down.

Fate intevened to help lift the club in the guise of Burnley Football Club who proposed that the First Division should be enlarged which meant that both Newcastle United and Blackburn Rovers won a place in the new top flight. Ironically, the resolution was passed by the Football League despite the opposition of John Lewis, co-founder of the Rovers, who voted against the proposal. Rovers made the most of the last-minute reprieve and the 1898-99 campaign brought a revival of fortunes. Bob Crompton was installed at left back, to partner Tom Brandon, while Geordie Anderson returned on a permanent basis. The inexperienced pairing of John Moreland and Daniel Hurst operated on the left flank of the attack, while Tom Jackson, a relative unknown from Padiham, was entrusted with leading the forward line. With the likes of Tom Booth and Ben Hulse fulfilling the promise they had shown the previous season, the outlook at Ewood Park suddenly appeared brighter.

New Century, New Start

The dawn of the 20th century brought further comings and goings to the club as officials strove to re-establish the club as a force in the First Division. The club was enjoying better luck in the transfer market, particularly with the arrival of Jimmy Moir in the summer of 1900. Plucked from reserve-team football at Celtic, Moir became the outstanding player of the season but Celtic quickly recalled him when the season was ended, having shrewdly only allowed him to leave on an extended loan deal.

As well as Moir, the club could now boast the services of players like Peter Somers, a talented goalscorer from Celtic, in another loan arrangement in February 1900, and Walt Whittaker, an experienced custodian who came from Reading in February 1900. The club was also prepared to place its faith in young local talent, thus Bob Haworth and 'Kelly' Houlker continued to occupy prominent places in the team, while Bob Crompton became the outstanding defender of his generation. Another star performer was Fred Blackburn who won his first England cap in March 1901 when he scored one of the goals in a 2-2 draw with Scotland at Crystal Palace.

The 1900-01 season was overshadowed by the death of Queen Victoria and disaster struck in the FA Cup. Of the 32 clubs involved in the first round, the Rovers could boast the most impressive record while opponents Woolwich Arsenal had the worst. The Rovers travelled to London only to return 2-0 losers. A fourth place finish to the 1901-02 campaign sadly proved to be something of a false dawn and the Blackburn squad was seriously weakened during the 1902 close season when Somers returned to Scotland. A further blow occurred when Houlker, who had just won his first England cap, moved into the Southern League with Portsmouth. This move in particular brought intense criticism of the club with suggestions that the

50 Greatest Players

JACK SOUTHWORTH   Centre forward

Born: Blackburn, Lancashire, December 1866

Joined Blackburn: 1887   **From:** Blackburn Olympic

Debut: 5 November 1887 v Blackburn Olympic, FA Cup

Appearances: 132   **Goals:** 121

Left Blackburn: 1893   **For:** Everton

Honours won with Blackburn: FA Cup winner 1890, 1891; 3 England caps

At the age of 12, Jack Southworth formed a club named Inkerman Rangers. Spells with other clubs followed, including Chester and Blackburn Olympic, before he arrived at Ewood Park for the final season of pre-league football. Southworth was a fleet-footed centre forward whose goal-scoring exploits made him a popular figure. Apart from his electrifying pace, Southworth had a number of other assets to his game. He was also an astute playmaker and his passing ability enabled him to create numerous opportunities for colleagues. He was also a great ball winner in the tackle. However, it was his eye for goal that made him a national figure and led to the winning of three England caps while with Blackburn. His love of music dominated his life after football and for 30 years he was a member of the Pier Pavilion Orchestra in Llandudno.

directors lacked sufficient ambition to retain the services of their best players. However, few of the Blackburn faithful could have predicted the calamities that were to befall their team during the 1902-03 season. When it was over, the club had avoided relegation by the narrowest of margins, and the local press had no doubts as to where the blame lay.

Directors Take the Blame

'The directorate have worked in their own peculiar style this season, and they are undoubtedly to blame for many things. They have signed plenty of useless men, and few good ones,' railed the correspondent of *The Blackburn Times* in his summation of the campaign. However, there were a number of factors that led to such a disastrous campaign, and injuries to key players certainly played a significant part. A wrenched knee kept Bob Crompton out of action for several weeks, while Bob Haworth suffered an injury at Bury in October that would keep him on the sidelines for the rest of the season. Also, several of the new players didn't perform as expected.

'Tiny' Joyce was installed as the new keeper and was immediately plunged into a whirlpool of self-doubt. His wanderings from the penalty area became increasingly eccentric, and his misjudgement of crosses put a huge strain on his colleagues. He conceded 34 goals in 14 games before being discarded in

50 Greatest Players

JIMMY FORREST Half back

Born: Blackburn, Lancashire, 24 June 1864

Joined Blackburn: 1883 **From:** Witton

Debut: 20 November 1883 v Southport, FA Cup

Appearances: 195 **Goals:** 7

Left Blackburn: 1895 **For:** Darwen

Honours won with Blackburn: FA Cup winner 1884-86, 1890-91; 11 England caps

Jimmy Forrest made his first appearance for the club in the friendly with Wednesday Old Athletic on 27 January 1883 and 14 months later was named in the England team that beat Wales 4-0 at Wrexham. Forrest went on to win a total of 11 caps. However, it was in the FA Cup that he made his biggest impact. On 21 March 1891, he was a member of the Blackburn team that beat Notts County in the FA Cup final and collected his fifth FA Cup-winners' medal with the club. He was the only member of the successful cup-winning teams of the mid-1880s to enjoy a lengthy career in the Football League and would have extended his run in the side but for a dispute with the committee. Latterly, he became a director of the club, a position he held until his death in December 1925.

1901-02, left to right: back – Walmsley (sec), McIvor, Whittaker, McClure, Hardy, Crompton, Walton (trainer), A. Blackburn, Ball, Dewhurst, Bryant, Haworth, Hunter, F. Blackburn; front – Whittaker, Somers, Houlker, Morgan, Gate.

favour of Billy McIver. Neil Logan was dismissed by commentators as being 'lethargic', while Billy Bow proved unequal to the task of replacing Somers. George Robertson, a close-season signing from Clyde, also failed to make much impression, and was restricted to just ten league outings.

Rumours of a Conspiracy

Before the end of April whispers started circulating about a conspiracy to keep Blackburn in the First Division, at the expense of Grimsby Town. The second relegation spot had been a battle between the Rovers and Grimsby and eyebrows had first been raised when, with just four games left to play, the Rovers visited Bury on Good Friday and returned with an unlikely point. The following day the team travelled to Middlesbrough and was soundly thrashed before visiting Everton on Easter Monday. With a point separating them from Grimsby, the game was of paramount importance. A brace of goals from Adam Bowman, together with a strike from Fred Blackburn, gave the visitors a comfortable 3-0 win. Safety was assured the following Saturday when Newcastle United were beaten 3-1 at Ewood Park.

The word in Grimsby was that the Lancashire clubs had conspired to prevent the Rovers from being relegated, and doubts were cast over the results against Bury and Everton. An official inquiry was held but although no evidence of collusion could be found, the inquiry suspended Joseph Walmsley from any further involvement with football. With no other evidence against any other Blackburn official the result against Everton was allowed to stand. The table remained unaltered and the Rovers survived.

Walmsley continued to plead his innocence and insisted that any remarks he had made had been of a jocular nature and never intended to be a serious attempt at match fixing. Those within the town who knew him never doubted his honesty and it was a severe blow to the club to lose the services of such a hardworking administrator. In July 1903, the club appointed Robert Middleton, a former Rotherham Town, Darwen and Blackpool secretary, as his successor. There was to be no dramatic improvement in fortunes but rather a period of consolidation over the next few years. A poor end to the 1903-04 campaign almost put the club back in trouble, but a 2-0 win over Middlesbrough in the penultimate match of the season enabled the club to finish in 15th place, two points out of the relegation zone. The following season saw the club up in 13th position, but still only three points away from relegation.

Middleton continued to rebuild the team and a number of astute signings were made. Billy Bradshaw, a young attacking half back, was secured from Accrington Stanley and given a place in the first team. Doubts about McIver's lack of inches persisted and Bob Evans, the experienced Welsh international, was signed to take over goalkeeping duties. In a bid to add more firepower, the club looked to Adam Bowman, a bustling young Scottish player who was just beginning to break into the senior team at Everton. The summer of 1904 brought a major surprise with the acquisition of Sam Wolstenholme from Everton. That the Ewood Park board was prepared to bring in a current England international sent a wave of renewed optimism around the town.

Team group from 1903-04. From right to left: back – Bowman, Evans, Walton, McDonald, McClure; middle – Whittaker, Smith, Crompton, Monks, Blackburn; front – Dewhurst, Bradshaw.

Chapter Three: 1905-19
Cotton Delivers the Title

Although no one knew it at the time, a defining moment in the club's fortunes occurred on 28 March 1905 when Lawrence Cotton was elevated to the position of chairman. Cotton, a local businessman with interests in the textile trade, began to use his business acumen and financial muscle to rejuvenate the ailing club. Cotton immediately put in place a programme for the systematic upgrading of the facilities at Ewood Park. In 1905, the Darwen end (with a capacity of 12,000) was covered at a cost of £1,680. The following year, the new chairman oversaw the construction of the Nuttall Street grandstand that opened on New Year's Day 1907. Cotton continued to improve the ground during the summer of that year and he ended up with a stadium that could boast a capacity of 40,000.

While the redevelopment of Ewood Park became the main priority in the immediate aftermath of Cotton becoming chairman, he also ensured that money was available for strengthening the team. Billy Davies was brought from Wrexham in April 1905 to lead the Ewood attack, while Wattie Aitkenhead, an industrious inside forward, was signed from Partick Thistle. There were also several smaller signings that would have a significant impact on the club in later years. Arthur Cowell joined the Rovers from Nelson and established himself as the perfect foil for Bob Crompton at full back. Perhaps the most significant signing during this period was the £25 invested in the signature of Eddie Latheron. Latheron was unknown outside of the Grangetown club for which he played, but he would go on to win two championships while with Blackburn, and feature in the England team.

Lawrence Cotton was made chairman in March 1905 and brought success and prosperity to the Rovers.

One of the upgrading schemes for the ground that chairman Lawrence Cotton implemented was the construction of the Nutall Street stand, opened New Year's Day 1907.

Throughout this period of change the club had to settle for a place in mid-table, but the 1908-09 season brought a welcome upturn in fortunes and a fourth place finish in the table. The following season proved even better with the club finishing in third place, albeit eight points behind the champions, Aston Villa.

The team was continually evolving, and the 1908-09 season brought Jimmy Ashcroft, the Woolwich Arsenal and England goalkeeper, to Ewood Park to replace Bob Evans. Another full back had been added to the squad in Tommy Suttie, a rugged defender who came from Leith Athletic and would have been a regular at any other club. However, at Ewood Park he had to settle as back-up to the accomplished teaming of Crompton and Cowell, although for periods between 1907 and 1909 he actually kept Cowell out of the team. A new half-back line was now beginning to emerge with Albert Walmsley – who had been signed from Darwen in May 1904, but who had not made his league debut until October 1907 – now being seen on a more regular basis.

The centre-half position was filled by George Chapman who had arrived from Raith Rovers in August 1908, while Billy Bradshaw retained his place at left half. However, although Latheron, Davies and Aitkenhead had emerged as the strongest inside trio, the wing positions continued to cause problems. Billy Garbutt and Walter Anthony filled these berths for much of the time between 1908 and 1910, but the former was coming to the end of his career while the latter often flattered to deceive, despite having the ability to send in pinpoint crosses without seeming to break stride.

The club suffered a setback in 1910-11, only finishing in 12th position in the First Division. The club had also lost the services of George Chapman, who had returned to Scotland to join Rangers. His replacement was Percy Smith who, having turned 30, was regarded as coming to the closing stages of his career when he was signed from Preston North End in May 1910. What made this move all the more unlikely was that Smith had been signed as cover for the forward positions, having led the line at Deepdale for many seasons before drifting into the back division. However, although he didn't win a regular place in the Ewood half-back line until November 1910, once he did so it was clear that he was the perfect foil for Walmsley and Bradshaw.

While the league form was disappointing, the Rovers found their form in the FA Cup and reached the semi-final. Alas, despite being firm favourites, the team didn't do themselves justice and slumped to a 3-0 defeat at the hands of Bradford City.

The 1910-11 season was also noteworthy in that under the watchful eye of Lawrence Cotton, the club broke the British transfer record when a fee of £1,800 was paid to Falkirk for the services of Jock Simpson in January 1911. Simpson was a flying outside right, a man whose game was built on the simple premise of pushing past the full back and then sprinting past him before sending in an accurate cross. In April, a fee of £900 was invested in Joe Clennell, a young inside forward, who was still learning his trade at Blackpool, and whose signing was regarded as a sound investment in the future of the club.

Champions at Last

The 1911-12 season began with a change in goal as Alf Robinson had edged ahead of Ashcroft following a close-season tour of Austria and Hungary. Robinson had been signed from Gainsborough Trinity in May 1911 following concerns about the health and fitness of Ashcroft. Crompton and Cowell continued as full backs with Suttie able to cover for either man. Walmsley, Smith and Bradshaw proved a formidable half-back line, both defensively and in supporting the attack.

In October 1911, the club strengthened their hand by persuading George Chapman to return from Rangers and take his place in the centre of defence. The forward line now had Simpson on the right flank and Anthony on the opposite wing. Aitkenhead and Clennell shared the inside-left duties while Latheron and Johnny Orr, who had joined the club from Scottish junior football in January 1908, rotated the inside-right position. Billy Davies had started a number of early-season games at centre forward but it was clear that his best days were now behind him. For a couple of games, the Ewood management tried Percy Smith – who had lost his place to Chapman, in his old role as leader of the attack – but without much success. Eventually, it was decided to put Smith back into the centre-half position and move Chapman into the forward line.

The Rovers managed to cling to the coat-tails of Newcastle United and Aston Villa, who had set the pace early on in the campaign. However, the middle part of the season found the Rovers at the top of their game and during a period of three months they remained unbeaten, and collected 17 points from a possible 22. While Chapman was not the most aesthetically pleasing centre forward ever to don the colours, he had the pace and power to trouble defenders. Yet, although he managed to notch up nine goals in 23 league games, he never really looked like a viable long-term solution to what had become a problem position.

The visit to Everton in April 1912 saw the Rovers produce a truly championship performance against one of their main rivals for the title. After a goalless first 45 minutes, the Rovers turned on the power and cruised to a 3-1 win. A narrow 1-0 win against Oldham Athletic, two days later, put the Rovers in a strong position to capture their first championship title.

The 1911-12 championship team from left to right: back row – Simpson, Latheron, Chapman, Aitkenhead, Anthony; middle row – Walmsley, Smith, Bradshaw, Middleton (sec); front row – Crompton (captain), Robinson, Cowell.

However, there was still a hiccup before the trophy was finally captured. The team travelled to London to face Woolwich Arsenal on 22 April 1912, and returned on the wrong end of a 5-1 thumping. Nerves were calmed three days later when West Bromwich Albion visited Ewood Park for a game that was to clinch the title. A brace of goals from both Aitkenhead and Clennell gave the Rovers a 4-1 win, and the First Division championship.

It was rather ironic that the Rovers should capture the championship by defeating West Bromwich Albion, for it was the Baggies who had knocked them out of the FA Cup at the semi-final stage, just a few weeks earlier. The semi-final had gone to a replay and Albion had won by the narrowest of margins with just a single-goal victory. Sadly, the Rovers had created numerous chances in both games but had been woefully inept at finishing them off.

Investment Reaps Rewards

There was no doubt a huge feeling of satisfaction in the Ewood boardroom as the investment of Lawrence Cotton finally reaped its just reward. There was also financial reward for lifting the title as the league receipts at Ewood Park had risen from £7,185 4s 6d the previous season to an impressive £9,432 6s 4d. As First Division champions, the Rovers were due to face the champions of the Southern League during the 1912-13 season in the FA Charity Shield. However, it was decided to bring the match forward so that the proceeds could go to the Titanic Relief Fund. The match against Queens Park Rangers was played at White Hart Lane on 4 May 1912, in front of a crowd of 7,111. Although Rangers took the lead, it was the Rovers who looked the better team. Two goals from Wattie Aitkenhead were sufficient to win the game and bring the curtain down on a wonderful season.

Hopes of retaining the championship foundered in mid-season when December 1912 brought a succession of injuries and a run of five successive defeats. Robbed of the services of Crompton, Cowell, Smith, Bradshaw, Davies and Orr, plus one or two of their possible replacements, the team lost vital ground in the championship race.

In a bid to revive their flagging fortunes, Cotton and his fellow directors again turned to the transfer market. In January 1913, the club broke the British transfer record when Danny Shea was signed from West Ham United for a fee of £2,000. Shea, who had scored 111 goals in 179 Southern League games for the Hammers, was a talented inside forward. It was hoped he would work well with Simpson on the right flank. A further addition to the squad was made that month when a fee of £1,000 was paid for Joe Hodkinson, Glossop's talented outside left.

With the forward line strengthened, the team returned to winning ways, but had lost too much ground to make much impression in the championship race. The season ended with the club standing in fifth place in the table with 45 points, only four points less than the previous campaign when they had won the title. Furthermore, the away record of 20 points had only been bettered during the 1908-09 season. The addition of Shea and Hodkinson had certainly pepped up the attack, with 36 goals being scored in the final 15 games and, indeed, Shea notched up a dozen goals from his 15 league outings.

The close season brought a tour of the continent with games being played in Hungary, Austria and Germany during the month of May 1913. At the same time, work began back at Ewood Park to further improve the facilities at the ground. Archibald Leitch, who had been responsible for the design of the Nuttall Street stand, now brought forward his plans for a new stand on

50 Greatest Players

EDDIE LATHERON Inside forward

Born: Grangetown, Middlesbrough, 1887

Joined Blackburn: 1906   **From:** Grangetown

Debut: 22 December 1906 v Middlesbrough

Appearances: 303   **Goals:** 120

Left Blackburn: Killed in World War I

Honours won with Blackburn: Division 1 championship 1912, 1914; 2 England caps

The horror of war touched Ewood Park in October 1917 when news was brought back to Blackburn of the death of Eddie Latheron. One of the heroes of the championship-winning sides of 1912 and 1914, the memory of his special talent would continue to glow in the hearts of the Blackburn public long after the guns had been silenced. Latheron had joined the Rovers from his native Grangetown in 1906 for £25, and what a bargain he proved to be. Just 5ft 5ins tall, he had a speed of thought and quickness of eye that enabled him to open up the tightest of defences. Comfortable on either side of the field, he was an accomplished goalscorer and a gifted playmaker with an unquenchable enthusiasm and dogged tenacity that appealed to the public. Capped twice by England, he was at the peak of his powers when war broke out and was forced to spend the 1915-16 season playing with Blackpool as the Rovers closed down for the campaign. He returned to Ewood Park the following year and appeared for the last time on 17 March 1917 when he scored one of the goals that helped to gain a 2-2 draw with Bury at Ewood Park. Five days later he marched off to war.

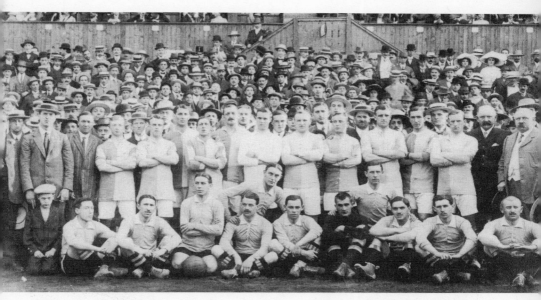

In May 1913, the Rovers went on a close-season tour through Hungary, Austria and Germany. From left to right, Blackburn players standing: Latheron, Orr, Smith, Clennell, Crompton, Robinson, Cameron, Anthony, Walmsley, Aitkenhead, Davies.

the Riverside section of the ground. The new stand, which was partly double-decker in design, cost an estimated £7,000 and provided seats for some 3,000 spectators. The stand also provided covered accommodation for a further 9,000 standing supporters, and brought the total capacity of the Riverside area to 20,650. By the time that all the ground improvements had been completed, the reported capacity of Ewood Park stood at 70,866.

Champions Again

The only new addition to the squad for the advent of the 1913-14 season was Alex Bell, a veteran half back who had given stalwart service to Manchester United for many years. Bell had made 278 league appearances for United and helped the club to two league championships, in 1908 and 1911, as well as the FA Cup win of 1909. However, he came to Blackburn in the knowledge that he would be nothing more than an understudy to the existing half-back line of Walmsley, Smith and Bradshaw. The real problem for the club revolved around the centre-forward position. Several men had been tried the previous season, without success, and Chapman, for all his faults in this position, remained the best option. Cotton assured shareholders during the summer that no stone would be left unturned in the search for the

After their championship-winning heroics of the 1913-14 season, a very dapper looking team take time to relax in the comfortable surroundings of a hotel lounge.

right man, and that a considerable sum of money would be available to purchase such a player.

However, the right man continued to elude the club, and the season began with Chapman leading the attack. Fortunately, the rugged Scot displayed excellent early-season form as the Rovers opened the new campaign with seven wins from the first eight games. Sadly, Chapman's form began to dip, and both Joe Clennell and Wattie Aitkenhead failed to take the opportunity to establish themselves in the centre-forward role.

In January 1914, the club accepted an offer of £1,500 from Everton for the services of Clennell. With both Chapman and Aitkenhead offering nothing more than workmanlike qualities as leader of the attack, the lack of a genuine centre forward was a concern for all at Ewood Park. The need to resolve the problem became imperative when the club fell victim to Manchester City in the third round of the FA Cup. The result saw yet another new transfer record established when the club paid £2,500 to Heart of Midlothian for Percy Dawson.

Although Dawson took time to settle in the English game, sufficient points were already in the bag to enable the Rovers to mount a serious championship challenge. As others began to fade, the Rovers claimed sufficient points to secure the title with a goalless draw at Newcastle United on 10 April 1914.

Having won the championship twice in three years, there was no doubt that the club now stood at the pinnacle of English football. However, as celebrations continued, storm clouds began to gather over Europe, but the outbreak of war on the eve of the 1914-15 season had surprisingly little impact on the start of the new campaign.

Once again, hopes of retaining the championship were severely hit by injuries. Dawson was injured at Middlesbrough on 19 December 1914 and missed the next ten games, while a serious knee injury to Shea, sustained on New Year's Day, kept him out of action for the remainder of the season. Questions were also beginning to be asked of the half-back line, with Smith not getting any younger and Bradshaw struggling to maintain the standards he had set earlier in his career. A major upset occurred in the FA Cup when Swansea inflicted a 1-0 defeat on the Rovers at the Vetch Field in a first-round tie. With a deficit of almost £9,000, there was an understandable reluctance to turn to the chequebook to try to solve the mounting problems.

The War Years

In truth, the appetite for the game was beginning to wane as the full horrors of what was occurring across the Channel began to filter back to Lancashire and the rest of the country. Although the club ended the final season of peacetime football in third place, there was little cause for celebration. War in Europe would have lasting ramifications on British society, and Blackburn Rovers would not be immune from the fallout. Although no one realized it at the time, it would be another 80 years before the club could again claim to be at the pinnacle of the English game.

The summer of 1915 had seen the Football League suspend its activities and replace the normal league structure with two regional sections.

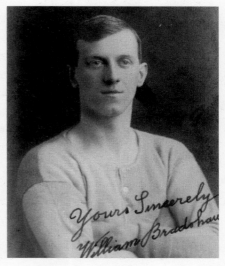

Billy Bradshaw holds the record for the most penalties scored while at Blackburn – 20 in the league and two in the FA Cup.

50 Greatest Players

BOB CROMPTON Right back

Born: Blackburn, Lancashire, 26 September 1879

Joined Blackburn: 1896   **From:** Blackburn Trinity

Debut: 10 April 1897 v Stoke, League

Appearances: 608   **Goals:** 14

Left Blackburn: 1920 (retired)

Honours won with Blackburn: Division 1 championship 1912, 1914; 41 England caps

When Bob Crompton first appeared for the club in a friendly match against Darwen on 3 April 1897, he received very favourable reviews in *The Blackburn Times* which turned out to be well founded as he must undoubtedly rank as the greatest 'Rover' of them all. His first three league appearances were made at centre half before he was switched with great success to the left-back spot in September 1898. In March 1900, he was moved to the opposite flank and it was as a right back that he became a national figure. He made his international debut on 3 March 1902, and for the next 12 years he became the automatic choice for his country at right back. He became the first professional player to captain England and went on to establish a new appearance record at international level with 41 appearances for his country.

Crompton became the dominant figure at Ewood Park during the early part of the 20th century for as a captain he was not only an excellent tactician but also an inspirational leader of men. Crompton was a resolute defender who had the advantage of a powerful build and great physical strength, but would never take unfair advantage of an opponent. Rarely beaten in the air or on the ground, Crompton was the rock on which two championship-winning teams were built at Ewood Park. The outbreak of war resulted in Blackburn Rovers suspending operations for the 1915-16 season and Crompton plied his trade with Blackpool before returning to make 32 appearances in wartime football for the Rovers. He made just two more appearances for the club in 1919-20 before bringing down the curtain on a long and illustrious playing career.

Set amid the carnage of trench warfare, there was growing unease about the continuation of professional football. The directors of Blackburn Rovers, aware of the prevailing local climate, announced that they would suspend all activities for the 1915-16 season. The result was that several of the players had to offer their services to other clubs, so Bob Crompton spent the season with Blackpool, along with Eddie Latheron, George Chapman and Joe Hodkinson. Burnley gave opportunities to Arthur Cowell, Albert Walmsley and Johnny Orr, while Tommy Suttie contented himself with appearances for Accrington

Stanley. Both Alex Bell and Billy Bradshaw settled for more humble surroundings in the Lancashire Combination with Blackburn Trinity.

With the advent of conscription came a change of heart by the directors of the club. A couple of friendly matches were arranged towards the end of the 1915-16 season, and the following campaign brought participation in the regional competition. However, with many of the team now in the army, the wartime game provided very poor entertainment for those who watched it. Numerous juniors were called into the ranks and on more than one occasion the club had to turn to its opponents to borrow a player or two to make a team. A visit to Stoke on 10 November 1918 saw the need to borrow a goalkeeper named Underwood, and a left back called Tompkins. Neither man was able to provide much help to a particularly weak Blackburn team, and the home team enjoyed a rather farcical 16-0 win.

Older players were also brought out of retirement to give a helping hand, thus the Blackburn faithful were able to witness Kelly Houlker, who had first joined the Rovers in August 1894, and Billy McIver, who was first seen at Ewood in July 1901, ply their trade yet again on the football pitch. However, the desperation of the situation was perhaps best illustrated when Edgar Chadwick, who had played for the club way back in 1887, made an

---

50 Greatest Players

BILLY BRADSHAW Half back

Born: Padiham, Lancashire, April 1884

Joined Blackburn: 1903   **From:** Accrington Stanley

Debut: 12 September 1903 v Wolverhampton Wanderers, League

Appearances: 457   **Goals:** 51

Left Blackburn: 1920   **For:** Rochdale

Honours won with Blackburn: Division 1 championship 1912, 1914; 4 England caps

In an era when brawn often dominated the ebb and flow of a game, Billy Bradshaw stood out like a beacon in a fog-bound harbour. His natural athleticism and perceptive reading of the game meant that he rarely had to expend energy in the tackle in order to gain possession. He would merely read the game and intercept the ball before it reached its intended target. However, once in possession Bradshaw was a mightily dangerous opponent. He was renowned for his passing ability and rarely gave the ball away. His probing of the opposing defence was a major factor in the two championship triumphs of 1912 and 1914. Capped on four occasions for England, his career was severely disrupted by the advent of World War I. Although he returned to Blackburn for the 1919-20 season, he left the club in April 1920 to become player-manager at Rochdale.

50 Greatest Players

DANNY SHEA Inside forward

Born: Wapping, London, 6 November 1887

Joined Blackburn: 1913 **From:** West Ham United

Debut: 25 January 1913 v Notts County, League

Appearances: 108 **Goals:** 69

Left Blackburn: 1920 **For:** West Ham United

Honours won with Blackburn: Division 1 championship 1914;

2 England caps, 2 England victory international appearances

Blackburn Rovers broke the British transfer record when the club paid £2,000 to capture Danny Shea from West Ham United. The player himself was reputed to have collected around £550 for agreeing to move Ewood Park. Unfortunately, his arrival came too late for the club to retain the championship trophy that had been captured the previous season. However, the 1913-14 campaign saw Shea revel among the highly-priced forwards that had been assembled at to Ewood Park. The second game of the season brought him four goals in the 6-2 thrashing of Liverpool, and he collected a further two hat-tricks during the course of the campaign.

While his 28 goals played a major part in the winning of the championship, it was his all-round wizardry that enthralled the Blackburn faithful. His guile created an endless string of opportunities for colleagues while opponents found him almost ghostlike in the way in which he appeared to drift past them. Sadly, what should have been his most productive years at Ewood Park were lost to the war, and Shea made only a handful of wartime appearances for the club. Although no longer the player he had been it was still a shock when the club agreed to allow him to return to West Ham United in May 1920.

appearance for the Rovers in November 1916, some nine years after his last appearance in the Football League.

Nor could Ewood be immune to the tragedy of war, and on 14 October 1917, a German shell extinguished the life of Eddie Latheron. The loss of such a gifted young man (he was survived by a widow and young son), graphically illustrated the human toll of the years between 1914 and 1918. There were, of course, less serious casualties of war in that several of the players were unable to revive their careers when football recommenced in 1919. All professional athletes have a limited time in which to pursue their passion and, unfortunately, the war years robbed many of what should have been their most productive years.

Chapter Four: 1919-36
Reconstruction, Glory and Decline

The aftermath of war echoed around the corridors of Ewood Park long after the guns had fallen silent. The championship years were now a distant memory of a different time and place. The world changed between 1914 and 1918 and Ewood Park was not immune to those changes. The loss of Latheron was immense and others, too, were unable to return. Medical advice had forced Wattie Aitkenhead into premature retirement, while Jock Simpson was unable to resume his career due to injuries received while playing wartime football with Falkirk. Although Bob Crompton, Arthur Cowell and Billy Bradshaw made a valiant effort to resume their careers, the sands of time had run out for them too. After 22 league appearances, Bradshaw accepted a player-manager position with Rochdale. Cowell was restricted to one appearance before injury forced him onto the backroom staff. Even the legendary Crompton had to succumb to the inevitable, and his final appearance for the Rovers came at Bradford on 23 February 1920. A business career would beckon Crompton, although his affair with Blackburn Rovers was far from over.

Another significant change had occurred in February 1919 when Lawrence Cotton had stepped down from his position as chairman, due to his increasing civic duties. In 1917, he had become the Mayor of Blackburn and, in 1919, he had been made an Alderman. Fortunately, with his brother Clement installed as chairman, Lawrence Cotton accepted the opportunity to become the club's first president.

A period of reconstruction was clearly needed and the 1919-20 season brought a succession of new players as the directors tried to find a winning formula. A total of 39 players were used in the first postwar season, but the club could manage no better than 20th place in the table. The FA Cup also produced little cheer, with a first-round exit at the hand of Wolves. Although many of the new faces were disposed of with almost indecent haste, a number of key signings were made during that campaign. Ronnie Sewell arrived from Burnley to take over the goalkeeping duties, while David Rollo, an Irish international full back, proved a shrewd investment. Frank Reilly, who arrived from Falkirk, showed himself to be a fiercely competitive centre half, while Jimmy McKinnell, an acquisition from Queen of the South, displayed a great deal of youthful zest at half back. However, it was the signing of experienced professionals like Ernie Hawksworth and Norman Rodgers that revitalized the forward line. The loss of Latheron and Simpson, coupled with the waning powers of Shea, had seriously undermined the attacking options at the club.

The 1920-21 season brought a slight improvement with a mid-table finish, but yet another first-round exit from the FA Cup. The evolution of the team continued and the departure of Danny Shea in May 1920 proved something of a surprise. Fortunately, Hodkinson and Dawson still remained from the pre-war team to add their experience to the more youthful faces that were

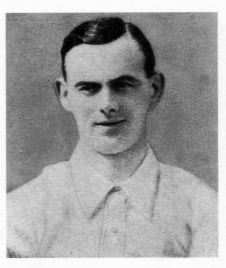

Left back Fred Duckworth won two England victory international caps in 1919.

springing up around them. Sadly, the 1920-21 campaign also marked the end of an era at Ewood Park with the death of Lawrence Cotton in May 1921. His loss to the club was further compounded when his brother, Clement, decided the time had come to resign as chairman.

Under New Management

The early part of the 1921-22 campaign merely underlined the need for further strengthening of the senior squad. The opening 14 games produced a miserly three wins, and it was clear that the club was bereft of inside forwards who had the capability to create and take goal-scoring opportunities. The directors were again forced to dig deep and enter the transfer market to acquire the services of such men. In November 1921, a deal was negotiated with Celtic for the transfer of Jock McKay, a reserve player who had joined the Scottish club in June 1919. He had scored on his debut for Celtic and was regarded as a player of great potential but, fortunately, the Scottish club had a glut of such players. In January 1922, a second inside forward was signed but, on this occasion, the directors went for a little more experience in the form of Johnny McIntyre from Sheffield Wednesday. Like McKay, McIntyre was a Scot who had served his apprenticeship north of the border, with Partick Thistle, before moving south to join Fulham in February 1917.

In February 1922, the directors embarked on a new policy by employing a full-time manager. They chose the vastly experienced Jack Carr, a former

Newcastle United and England international, who had spent many years on the backroom staff at St James's Park. The directors made no secret of the fact that they were prepared to back the new manager with financial support, and a 15th-place finish at the end of the season suggested that they would have to be true to their word if an improvement was to be made. The boardroom certainly contained a wealth of football experience with former players Jimmy Forrest, Johnny Forbes and Bob Crompton now directors of the club.

The summer of 1922 brought the unlikely acquisition of Dickie Bond from Bradford City. While the need for new blood on the right flank was clear, it was less obvious why the club opted to bring in a player who had already celebrated his 38th birthday. For half a season he strove manfully to turn back the clock, but the club was finally forced to look elsewhere for a long-term solution to the right-wing problem. In March 1923, the club signed Jack Crisp for a fee of £3,175, from West Bromwich Albion where he had won a championship medal in 1919-20.

Cup of Shame

Thankfully, the 1922-23 campaign did provide one glorious memory on the pitch when McIntyre scored four goals in a five-minute spree against Everton in September 1922. That 5-1 win was one of the few highlights in another bitterly disappointing season. Fourteenth place in the First Division was a slight improvement on the previous year, but the FA Cup provided the club with one of its most embarrassing moments. Having held lowly South Shields, of the Third Division North, to a goalless draw at the Horsley Hill Stadium, the Rovers approached the replay with great confidence. Incredibly, the Rovers managed to snatch defeat out of the jaws of victory when the visitors scored with what was virtually their only shot of the game. Even then the goal, scored after 14 minutes, was a fortunate one as a shot from Jack Smith was struck with so much venom that Sewell allowed the ball to slip through his hands and into the net. The victory must have been particularly sweet for Robert Faulkner on the South Shields right wing as he had been one of the many players who were discarded by the Rovers at the end of the 1919-20 season.

The result of another indifferent campaign was more upheaval in the ranks. Veteran wingers Bond and Hodkinson bade farewell to the club as Crisp and Jack Byers, who was signed from Huddersfield Town, were entrusted with the wide positions. Percy Dawson was another old favourite to say his goodbyes during the summer of 1923 but, in this case, the club had no ready-made replacement for the veteran centre forward. Instead, it was decided to gamble on Ted Harper, an untried youngster, signed from Sheppey United.

An eighth place finish in the league and 18 goals for Harper were reasons for satisfaction at the end of the 1923-24 season. Sadly, the FA Cup again provided the club with further humiliation when the Rovers visited Crystal Palace to play the Corinthians in a first-round tie. The heavy conditions and slippery long grass proved something of a handicap to the Rovers, and the team were unable to get the ball down and play their usual style of football. Corinthians took the lead with an unspectacular goal from Doggart, and the Blackburn attack contrived to spurn a number of golden opportunities. Once again, a familiar face enjoyed the experience of putting his former club to the sword. This time it was Benjamin Howard Baker (who had been a reserve centre half at Ewood Park before being converted to a goalkeeper in the Central League team) who was able to celebrate after keeping a clean sheet.

Clement Cotton, the former chairman, collapsed and died shortly after being told of the 1-0 defeat, while watching a reserve match at Ewood Park. Matters went from bad to worse when the players arrived back in Blackburn. A fracas between Tom Wylie and Byers developed into a public brawl between the two players. This shameful incident resulted in Byers being suspended and then transferred to West Bromwich Albion within a fortnight. Wylie was absolved of all blame and allowed to continue his career with the Rovers.

On the Cup Trail Again

After two disastrous seasons of FA Cup football, the 1924-25 campaign brought a change of fortune for the club and its supporters. A place in the FA Cup semi-final was more in keeping with club traditions and, to a certain extent, obscured the fact that the league season had been disappointingly poor. Once again, the problems revolved around goal scoring with Harper, after his splendid debut season, blighted by the inconsistency of youth. The solution was again found north of the border, and a fee of £4,000 was paid to Falkirk for Syd Puddefoot, the former West Ham United inside forward. Although 30, and considered by some to be approaching the end of his career, he put a little more pep into what had become an increasingly lacklustre attack at Ewood Park.

The irony was that as the club struggled to find a win in the league, with only two of the final 13 league matches being won, performances in the cup became increasingly confident. A Jock McKay goal had been sufficient to enable the Rovers to overcome Oldham Athletic in the first round. The second round was even tighter, with the Rovers being held at Ewood Park to a goalless draw by Portsmouth before both clubs played out another goalless affair at Fratton Park. The third game was played at Highbury and, once again, the margin between the teams was wafer thin. A Jack Crisp goal was sufficient to earn a place in the third round and a meeting with Tottenham Hotspur at White Hart Lane. Goals from Joe Hulme and McKay were enough to force a replay. The Rovers enjoyed a 3-1 win over Tottenham at Ewood Park to set up a local derby with Blackpool in the sixth round. A crowd of 60,011 saw Puddefoot score the only goal of the game and put Blackburn into yet another FA Cup semi-final. Unfortunately, the meeting with Cardiff City at Meadow Lane, Nottingham, proved a major disappointment, considering that the Rovers had drawn opponents who were thought to be the weakest of the four remaining teams. The Welsh team based their play on making the most of the windy conditions, and a number of high balls were hoisted into the heart of the Blackburn defence who inexplicably got an attack of the jitters and failed to deal with balls that bounced and bobbled in the danger areas. Ultimately, the Rovers slipped to a 3-1 defeat, with a goal from McKay being scant consolation for a terribly disappointing performance.

Harper Strikes Gold

The 1925-26 season was about the rejuvenation of one man – Ted Harper. He didn't feature in the opening three games of the season, all of which were lost, however, he celebrated his recall for the trip to Newcastle United with five goals in a 7-1 win, and thus began a fairytale season. In all other respects, it was a fairly insignificant campaign as Rovers came 12th in the league and suffered a fourth-round exit in the FA Cup, but Harper made it special. He scored 43 goals from 37 league appearances which at the time set a new record for the Football League and established a club record that is never likely to be broken. Harper was well served by the cunning of Puddefoot, who was able to exploit changes in the offside law to provide a succession of chances for the young centre forward. The two young wingers, Hulme and Arthur Rigby, both provided him with crosses that begged to be finished, which Harper duly did. His game may have lacked finesse, but he knew how to find the back of the net, and in 1925-26 he was the deadliest marksman in the First Division.

Sadly, the club suffered a major setback on 1 September 1925 with the death of Robert Middleton, the long-serving club secretary. Rather than appoint a successor the directors were more than happy to ask Jack Carr to add the secretarial duties to his managerial ones.

The following season enabled Harper to prove that he was not just a one-season wonder. A total of 35 goals from 39 league games proved that the previous season had been no fluke. However, the 1926-27 season was not a memorable one. An 18th-place finish in the First Division was largely due to a poor finish to the campaign that brought just five points from the final 11 games. Once again, the FA Cup provided little cheer with another embarrassing exit, this time at the hands of lowly Southport of the Third Division North.

Crompton Takes Over

The defining moment of the season came in December 1926 when Jack Carr resigned his position as secretary-manager. Carr, who had proved to be an extremely proficient administrator, was highly regarded by the directors and his loss was a severe blow to the club. While the appointment of Carr had been generally seen as a success, the directors resisted the temptation to appoint a successor from outside of the ranks of Ewood Park. Instead, it was agreed that Bob Crompton would take over as honorary manager. The directors then appointed Arthur Barritt, formerly a member of the office staff at Burnley, to take over the secretarial duties at Blackburn.

Crompton had spent his first few months at the helm trying to strengthen the playing squad. Tommy McLean arrived from St Johnstone to fill an inside-forward role, while John Whyte, a half back, was also signed from the same club. As the season came to an end, the manager again returned to Scotland for Bill Rankin, a rugged centre half from Dundee. However, a significant loss occurred in January 1925 when Joe Hulme moved to Arsenal.

It was clear that Crompton had his own ideas and, as a result, long-serving players like Ronnie Sewell and David Rollo were both made available for transfer while Jock McKay was sold to Middlesbrough. Crompton settled on Jock Crawford as his goalkeeper with the unlikely duo of Jock Hutton and Herbert 'Taffy' Jones as full backs. The rotund Hutton and the slightly built Jones were the perfect combination. During the course of the season, the strongest half-back line to emerge was Healless, Rankin and Aussie Campbell, a tireless worker who had been at the club since February 1923.

In attack, the loss of Hulme had finally been solved with the arrival of

Aussie Campbell, a tireless worker in the half-back line, seen here after a battling performance in the 1928 FA Cup final.

George Thornewell from Derby County in December 1927. On the opposite flank, Arthur Rigby continued to enhance his reputation, having won five England caps during 1927. Inside-forward positions were retained by Puddefoot and McLean while the season had started with Harper continuing to plunder goals. However, in October 1927 an offer was accepted from Sheffield Wednesday for Harper, and Crompton then utilized the pace of Tom Mitchell, signed as an outside left from Stockport County in February 1926, through the middle. Although big and strong, Mitchell didn't really have sufficient aggression to make a success of the position. In the latter stages of the season, the manager gave Jack Roscamp, a tigerish half back, a run in the centre-forward slot.

More FA Cup Glory

While the league position of 12th showed a significant improvement, it was the FA Cup that again captured the public imagination. The team looked completely at ease as the likes of Newcastle United, Exeter City, Port Vale and Manchester United were overcome en route to a semi-final meeting with Arsenal. However, the team went into the clash against the Gunners at Leicester as underdogs. The Ewood cause was not helped by the loss of McLean, which necessitated the inclusion of Peter Holland, a player who had been at the club for nine years but who had never really been regarded as a first choice. Against all expectations, the Rovers took the lead when Roscamp raced clear of the defence to calmly put the ball into the net. A splendid rearguard action followed to give the Rovers the narrowest of victories and a place at Wembley.

Although at full strength, the Rovers were given little chance of overcoming the highly-fancied Huddersfield Town at Wembley. The Yorkshire club was still chasing the title and it was therefore a major surprise when the Rovers captured the trophy by a 3-1 margin. It brought some welcome relief to a season that had been overshadowed by personal tragedy at Ewood Park. The whole of Blackburn had been shocked by the news of the death of Bobby Marshall, a promising young full back, on 3 January 1928. Marshall, who was the regular left back for the second string, had been injured while playing for the Rovers in a Central League match at Bloomfield Road on Boxing Day. He had collided with an opponent but, while he had been forced to leave the pitch, the injury was not thought to be serious. After the match, he had left with his fiancée for a nearby house in which they were staying. During the night he was taken ill with abdominal pains and was rushed to Blackpool Victoria Hospital were he was operated on. His condition appeared to improve before he entered what proved to be a terminal decline. Before the

Great Matches

FA CUP FINAL   **Wembley, 21 April 1928**
Blackburn Rovers 3   **Huddersfield Town 1**   **Attendance: 92,041**
Roscamp 2   Jackson
McLean

According to the pundits of the day there could only be one winner of this game, and it wasn't Blackburn Rovers. Huddersfield Town were challenging for the First Division title while the Rovers occupied a more lowly aspect of the table. Within the opening minute the Rovers made a complete nonsense of those predictions. Syd Puddefoot and George Thornewell worked the ball upfield for centre forward Jack Roscamp to chase. Roscamp, a converted half back, was suddenly faced with Barkas blocking his way to goal. With breathtaking impudence he chipped the ball over the defender. His touch had been a little strong and the ball appeared destined to float into the arms of the waiting Billy Mercer in goal. Unperturbed, Roscamp dipped his right shoulder and headed for the keeper who was about to collect the ball while standing on the line. From the resultant collision the ball squirmed from Mercer's grasp and entered into the goal with the keeper following closely behind it.

The Rovers continued to enjoy plenty of possession during the early stages and after 22 minutes the Ewood Park team notched up a second goal. This proved to be a more orthodox affair with Arthur Rigby finding Tommy McLean with a perfect cross who fired a scorcher past the statuesque Mercer. In the second half, Huddersfield made a tactical switch and moved Scottish international Alex Jackson from the wing to occupy a more central position. The move was sufficient to ruffle the Blackburn defence and it was Jackson who fired a goal for Huddersfield. With Huddersfield pouring forward the Blackburn defence stood firm. Five minutes from time the Rovers finally clinched the game when Roscamp hit a low shot into the net and the final whistle brought scenes of great joy among the Blackburn players and supporters as the game finished as one of the major shocks of the season.

Blackburn Rovers: Crawford, Hutton, Jones, Healless, Rankin, Campbell, Thornewell, Puddefoot, Roscamp, McLean, Rigby
Huddersfield Town: Mercer, Goodhall, Barkas, Redfern, Wilson, Steele, Jackson, Kelly, Brown, Stephenson, Smith
Referee: T.G. Bryan (Willenhall)

Harry Healless collects the FA Cup after the shock victory against Huddersfield.

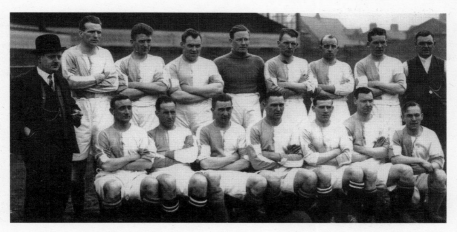

*Team members of the 1927-28 FA Cup-winning season. From left to right: back row –
Barritt (sec), Rankin, Roxburgh, Hutton, Crawford, Campbell, Jones, Mitchell, Atherton
(trainer); front row – Thornewell, Puddefoot, Roscamp, Healless, McLean, Rigby, Holland.*

month was out, the club received a further blow with the death of Johnny
Forbes. The former Scottish full back had been a director at Ewood Park for
some 31 years and, before that, had been a member of the club committee.

The 1928 FA Cup final success ought to have provided the club with a
platform on which to build future prosperity but, unfortunately, reality
turned out to be a much bleaker affair. There were, of course, financial
benefits from the Wembley success and these, coupled with money from the
Harper transfer, enabled further improvements to be made. A concrete wall
was erected around the pitch and there was sufficient money to allow the
Riverside stand to be re-roofed. Aware that the Wembley triumph had been
secured with two goals from a converted half back playing as a centre
forward, the directors were quick to strengthen the forward division. Thus,
a deal was struck with Bristol City that brought Albert Keating and Clarrie
Bourton to Ewood Park. Keating, a strong and purposeful inside forward,
had been the main target with Bourton very much an unknown quantity and
more of a gamble.

In the event, the 1928-29 season became a tale of 'What might have been.'
Although the league campaign got off to a dismal start, with two crushing
away defeats, results were quickly turned round. Between 13 October and 3
November 1928, the club occupied the top spot and, with progress being
made in the FA Cup, there was every prospect of a successful season. The
sixth-round meeting with Bolton Wanderers at Ewood Park ended in a 1-1
draw, and was watched by a record crowd of 62,522. The replay at Burnden

50 Greatest Players

TED HARPER Centre forward

Born: Sheerness, Kent, 22 August 1901

Joined Blackburn: 1923; 1933   **From:** Sheppey United; Preston North End

Debut: 25 August 1923 v Chelsea, League

Appearances: 177   **Goals:** 122

Left Blackburn: 1927; 1935   **For:** Sheffield Wednesday; retired

Honours won with Blackburn: 1 England cap

During the glorious 1925-26 campaign, Harper bagged 43 league goals in 37 appearances. At the time this was not only a club record, which it still is, but also a new Football League record. His first season at Ewood Park brought 18 goals from 42 appearances but when the goals dried up the following season he appeared destined to remain in the backwater of Central League football. Only three defeats in the opening three games of the 1925-26 campaign earned him a recall for the visit to Newcastle United on 9 September 1925. On that day he scored five goals in a 7-1 win and his career suddenly took off. Fed by the astute passing ability of Syd Puddefoot, Harper proved a revelation and on 17 April 1926 he made his debut for England. Sadly, his game had too many shortcomings for him to be regarded as an international player but at club level he was one of the most lethal exponents of goal scoring of his era. He scored prolifically at other clubs before he returned to Blackburn in November 1933 and when he hung up his boots in May 1935 he joined the coaching staff where he remained until May 1948.

Park attracted another huge attendance at 65,295, but it was the Wanderers who took the honours by a narrow 2-1 margin.

The league campaign simply fell apart after the defeat by Bolton. Only two league games out of 13 were won after the FA Cup exit. During this period, public interest simply evaporated and the final home game of the season, a local derby with Burnley, drew a crowd of just 5,461. This was a far cry from the record crowd that had squeezed into Ewood Park for the cup-tie with Bolton Wanderers, a crowd that had produced record receipts of £4,772. The receipts for the Burnley game were reported to have been £248 – clearly insufficient to sustain a successful First Division club.

Gloomy Times at Ewood Park

The feeling among the Blackburn public was that a chance of glory had been missed through lack of investment. Injuries had robbed the club of the services of key players at different times in the season, and several others suffered a dip in form. Once again, the attack bore the brunt of criticism over the closing months of the campaign. Of the new men, Keating was largely undistinguished, while Bourton proved a revelation early in the season, only to fade away as the season died. He bagged 12 goals in his first 13 league games and then failed to score in the remaining 15 games that he played in. Seventh place in the league and reported profits of £6,048 were all the club had to show for 1928-29. However, with several weaknesses in the squad to fill, coupled with declining attendances, it was clear that problems lay ahead.

Fortunately, those problems didn't surface during a 1929-30 campaign that brought an improvement of one place in league standing. The problems in front of goal were finally remedied with a league total of 99, creating a new record for goals scored in a season. Bourton, who had spent the first half of the campaign playing Central League football, was recalled in December and ended the season as the leading goalscorer on 21. Puddefoot and McLean reached double figures from the inside-forward positions, as did Arthur Groves, who had filled the inside-left berth for a spell earlier in the campaign, before being sold to Everton. The fifth player to record double figures that campaign was Arthur Cunliffe, the discovery of the season. Cunliffe had graduated through the ranks at Ewood and was given an extended run on the left wing during the second half of the campaign. Another new face in the Ewood team that season was Jack Bruton, who joined the club from Burnley in December 1929 for a club record fee of £6,500.

Crompton Departs

A combination of intrigue, accusation and self-destruction were the key elements that filled the 1930-31 season. However, while internal conflict roamed the corridors of Ewood Park unabated, there was a more serious cloud that hung over East Lancashire. It was the shadow of a trade depression that had begun to tighten its grip on the old industrial heartland. The vast army of unemployed had little money for anything, let alone football, and if

Tom McLean was a consistent goalscorer during the late 1920s and early 1930s.

50 Greatest Players

JACK ROSCAMP Half back/Forward

Born: Blaydon, 8 August 1901

Joined Blackburn: 1922   **From:** Wallsend

Debut: 29 September 1923 v West Bromwich Albion, League

Appearances: 250   **Goals:** 44

Left Blackburn: 1932   **For:** Bradford City

Honours won with Blackburn: FA Cup winner 1928

But for the 1928 FA Cup final, the career of Jack Roscamp might not have stood out in the record books. Much of his early career at Blackburn had been spent as a hard-working half back who was not a regular choice for the first team. The whole-hearted Roscamp was not the most skilful of men but compensated for this with a physical no-nonsense approach. The departure of Ted Harper, and lack of any suitable replacement, resulted in Roscamp being tried as centre forward. His robust approach suited the slot and he scored many important goals in the FA Cup run of 1927-28. However, it was his performance at Wembley in April 1928 that finally carved his niche in the history of Blackburn Rovers. Against the highly-fancied Huddersfield Town he scored in the first minute to rock the favourites before clinching the trophy with a third goal just five minutes from time.

they were to be enticed through the turnstiles the club had to provide an exciting brand of football.

With the loss of nearly £5,000 over the previous 15 months, the directors had little option but to call a halt to any involvement in the transfer market. Indeed, the only newcomer to Ewood Park during the summer of 1930 was Frank Britton, a young half back from Bristol Rovers, who had been snapped up on a free transfer.

Incredibly, with an economic crisis on their very doorstep, both players and officials at Ewood Park became consumed with petty jealousies and internal bickering. The ultimate act of self-destruction was brought about by a totally misguided demonstration of player power that resulted in the removal of Bob Crompton from his position as honorary manager. A number of people at Ewood Park were reportedly ill at ease with the autocratic style of Crompton, yet he had ensured that the club remained a dominant force in the First Division and, of course, had masterminded a Wembley triumph in the FA Cup. An astute tactician, Crompton made no secret of the fact that he felt the team required an injection of pace. He firmly believed that the successful clubs of the future would need to play the game at an increased tempo. However, he had an ageing squad at Ewood Park, and not everyone was anxious to play in a team where speed would play a dominant role.

Matters came to a head on the eve of a trip to London to face Chelsea in the fifth round of the FA Cup. The chairman received a letter that was reputedly signed by a number of the senior players in which concern was expressed at the management style of Crompton. On learning of the letter, the manager wasted no time in withdrawing from all playing affairs and left things to Mo Atherton, the long-serving trainer. The team crashed 3-0 at Stamford Bridge and their league form remained patchy until the end of the season. Crompton, while still a director, continued to keep a discreet distance from the players. However, Crompton's 34-year association with the club was soon to come to an end. The shareholders opted to inflict a mortal wound on the club by voting to oust Crompton from the board of directors. It was a decision that the club would rue in years to come.

The Recession Hits Hard

While Crompton awaited his fate at the hands of the shareholders, the directors had decided to hand the managerial duties over to Arthur Barritt,

---

50 Greatest Players

SYD PUDDEFOOT Inside forward

Born: West Ham, London, 17 October 1894

Joined Blackburn: 1925   **From:** Falkirk

Debut: 7 February 1925 v Arsenal, League

Appearances: 277   **Goals:** 87

Left Blackburn: 1932   **For:** West Ham United

Honours won with Blackburn: FA Cup winner 1928; 2 England caps

Syd Puddefoot had had considerable experience with West Ham United and Falkirk before arriving at Ewood Park in February 1925. Although aged 30, and thought to be approaching the veteran stage of his career, the Rovers had to find a fee of £4,000 to bring him to Lancashire. It proved a wise investment as he was a naturally-gifted ball player whose greatest asset was his vision to create goal-scoring opportunities for his colleagues with passes of pinpoint accuaracy. The change in the offside law enabled him to create chances galore for Ted Harper in his glorious record-breaking 1925-26 season, while he helped himself to ten goals in that year. He could always be relied upon to chip in with his fair share of goals. Capped twice by England while at Ewood Park, he was a key member of the 1928 FA Cup-winning team and went on to give excellent service to the club over seven years.

the club secretary. He inherited a fairly healthy situation, as both the reserves and the 'A' team had enjoyed successful seasons in the Central League and West Lancashire League, respectively. Although the first team required strengthening, the club's overdraft had continued to rise, and Barritt found himself with very little room to manoeuvre financially. The only signing he was able to make was that of Ernie Thompson from Bath City, and the new man duly took his place at centre forward on the opening day of the new season. Sheffield Wednesday visited Ewood Park that day and, although Thompson registered a goal on his debut, an inept performance resulted in a 6-1 defeat for the Rovers.

The club continued to feel the icy blast of economic depression that had engulfed the area. Receipts for league games dropped by £2,200 to £9,203, and the directors were forced to sell players to maintain any kind of stability. Thus Bill Rankin, Les Bruton, Syd Puddefoot and Jack Roscamp departed as the directors put their faith in younger men. Despite the crippling financial plight, the directors sanctioned the signing of Ronnie Dix from Bristol Rovers for £3,000. Dix was a much sought-after property and it was a real coup for the Rovers to be able to bring him to Ewood Park.

In finishing 15th in 1932-33, the club had improved the league standing of the previous season by one place. However, there had been some ominous defeats that suggested the following campaign would find them fighting against relegation. The heaviest of these reversals came at Arsenal in

Jack Bruton was a tireless playmaker down the right flank for the Rovers through the 1930s, creating many shooting opportunities for others, and a few for himself, too.

50 Greatest Players

HARRY HEALLESS Half back

Born: Blackburn, Lancashire, 10 February 1893

Joined Blackburn: 1915   **From:** Blackburn Trinity

Debut: 20 October 1919 v Sheffield United, League

Appearances: 399   **Goals:** 14

Left Blackburn: 1933 (retired)

Honours won with Blackburn: FA Cup winner 1928; 2 England caps

The story of Harry Healless was the classic tale of the local boy who climbed the ranks of his beloved football club, captained them to FA Cup glory and collected England caps into the bargain. Having played for several junior clubs in the town he joined the Rovers as an amateur in April 1915 and made his debut in a wartime game against Manchester City. An 8-0 defeat was hardly an auspicious start and in the immediate postwar years young talent became a disposable item at Ewood Park as the playing pack was constantly shuffled. Not the most skilful of performers, there was a tenacity about Healless that enabled him to be used in a variety of positions. His strong running, tough tackling and relentless work ethic endeared him to the powers that be. He eventually won a place in the half-back line and proved proficient in all three positions. His proudest moment was when he climbed the steps of Wembley to collect the FA Cup in April 1928. He remained with the club until he retired in 1933 to embark upon a coaching career with the club. In 1935, he moved to Holland as coach to the Alemio club before returning to Lancashire a couple of years later to play junior football with Haslingden Grange. He returned to the coaching staff at Ewood in 1951 to leave when Johnny Carey became manager in 1953.

Captain Harry Healless holds the FA Cup aloft at Wembley after the famous victory in the 1928 final.

February 1933 when the Rovers were crushed 8-0. Once again, only the form of the forward line had kept the Rovers away from perilous waters. Dix proved a sound investment with 14 goals to his name, only three less than leading goalscorer, Ernie Thompson. Cunliffe, who had won two England caps during the course of the season, continued to give impressive displays on the left flank, and also chipped in with 14 goals. On the opposite flank, although not prolific in terms of goals, Bruton continued to be a constant source of danger.

Once again, the club was not immune to off-the-field controversy. In January 1933, the Ewood faithful were rocked by the news that Mo Atherton, the man who had trained the championship team of of 1914 and the FA Cup-winning side of 1928, had ended his association with the club. Within 24 hours of walking out of Ewood Park he had been installed as trainer of Grimsby Town. Another familiar face to leave the club, albeit in less controversial circumstances, was Jock Hutton who ended his contract by mutual consent in March 1933, at the end of a long and successful career.

Familiar Faces Depart

The departures that ignited the greatest unrest occurred in the closing week of the campaign when Dix and Cunliffe were both sold to Aston Villa for a miserly fee of £8,500. The reaction of the Blackburn public to this decision was one of intense hostility. However, Arthur Barritt defended the move and

---

50 Greatest Players

JACK BRUTON Outside right

Born: Westhoughton, Bolton, 21 November 1903

Joined Blackburn: 1929   **From:** Burnley

Debut: 7 December 1929 v Leeds United, League

Appearances: 345   **Goals:** 117

Left Blackburn: 1943 (retired)

It took a club record fee of £6,500 to persuade Burnley to part with Jack Bruton in December 1929. In signing this former miner the Rovers captured a supreme athlete who matched dynamic pace with the probing thoughtfulness of a natural schemer. Bruton, who had won three England caps while with Burnley, was also blessed with an eye for goal and despite playing on the right wing was a regular goalscorer. He also had the knack of staying fit, missing only one league game between 1931 and 1935. Throughout the 1930s he provided a constant threat down the right flank although, at times, the quality of support he received was lacking. By the time the club won the Second Division title in 1938-39, the former England winger had been replaced by Billy Rogers. Bruton became a member of the backroom staff during the war years and filled various posts before becoming assistant to Will Scott in 1947. When ill health forced Scott to resign, the directors had no hesitation in giving the manager's job to Bruton in December 1947. Sadly, he was unable to revive flagging fortunes and in May 1949 he was relieved of his duties. He later managed Bournemouth between 1950 and 1956, and in August 1961 he renewed his links with Ewood Park in a scouting role.

---

accused the public of not supporting the club in sufficient numbers, pointing out that gate receipts had plummeted and were insufficient to support a First Division club. The acrimony continued and appeared to receive support from within the club when the vice chairman, Alderman W.H. Grimshaw, resigned. It was in this hostile atmosphere that the Annual General Meeting was held in June 1933. The outcome was a club that was clearly divided, and one that had lost touch with the public that supported it.

Striker Ernie Thompson broke his leg in a 7-1 win over Wolves in November 1933.

The existing chairman, J.W. Walsh, only just received sufficient votes for him to reclaim his seat on the board. Alderman Grimshaw raised his opposition to the sale of the best young players, while another director, Walter Tempest, made it quite clear that he would invest no further money and would sell any player if a reasonable price could be negotiated. Within a week, Walsh resigned as chairman and Tempest found himself in the hot seat.

Matters on the field during the 1933-34 campaign improved despite the handicap of losing key players to injury. Billy Gormlie was hurt in the game against Chelsea on 11 October 1933, and such was the extent of the injury that the goalkeeper never again appeared for the club. A few weeks later Ernie Thompson broke his leg in pursuit of his fourth goal in the game with Wolves, a game that the Rovers won 7-1, at Ewood Park. To fill the void, the directors turned to an old Ewood favourite and signed Ted Harper – now nearing the end of his career – from Preston North End. For half a season he managed to roll back the years and ended the campaign with 15 goals from 22 league appearances.

The season was one of truly Jekyll and Hyde proportions when it came to results. At home, the team remained unbeaten in the league programme with 16 wins and five draws. However, away from Ewood Park it was a totally different story with only six points coming from 21 matches. As the financial climate continued to tighten, there was much relief at an eighth-place finish in the First Division.

The economic recession that gripped East Lancashire continued to have an adverse affect on gate receipts during the 1934-35 campaign. Matters were made worse with a wretched run of bad weather that did little to entice the public from their homes. In fairness, the quality of the football on offer at Ewood Park was rather inferior to that of the previous season. A tendency to over-experiment with formations led to a number of inconsistent performances. The directors found sufficient funds to strengthen the squad in mid-season with the acquisition of Jack Beattie from Wolves, and Norman Christie from Huddersfield Town. While the former added a little extra sparkle to the attack, the latter helped to steady a rocky defence.

Blackburn Slide into Division Two

As the club flirted with danger at the wrong end of the table, an apathetic public continued to turn its back on Ewood Park. Fifteenth place ensured First Division football for another year, but there could be no doubt about the direction in which things were heading. The irony of relegation, when it finally arrived in 1935-36, was that Aston Villa, another founder member of the Football League, should accompany the Rovers into the Second Division. Indeed, some solace could be taken from the fact that Villa enjoyed greater wealth and better gates than Blackburn and yet, they too, had not been immune to the fluctuating fortunes of football.

Surprisingly, the club had made its best start to a campaign since the war, with four wins coming from the opening five games. However, a 7-2 reverse at Sunderland, in the latter part of September, triggered a slide that became unstoppable. As results worsened, Arthur Barritt continually reshuffled his limited resources, but to no avail. Moments of hope – a 4-1 win over Manchester City in October and a 5-1 win over Aston Villa in December – were quickly extinguished by a succession of heavy defeats, the worst being 8-1 reversals at Wolves and West Bromwich Albion.

The tension on the field was mirrored in the corridors of power at Ewood Park as relations between the directors and Arthur Barritt worsened. There were thought to be several issues of policy over which the directors and Barritt differed, but team selection was believed to be a particularly delicate issue. In March 1936, the secretary-manager announced his intention to resign and he duly left Ewood Park on 11 April 1936, following a goalless draw with Sheffield Wednesday. Defeat at Liverpool two days later virtually condemned the club to relegation, and wins against Portsmouth and Aston Villa proved to be academic. Defeat at Chelsea on the last day of the season finally brought an end to First Division football at Ewood Park.

Chapter Five: 1936-53
A New Era After the War

Following the departure of Arthur Barritt, the directors had decided not to appoint another secretary-manager but had merely given the secretarial duties to Reg Taylor, an experienced administrator who had occupied a similar position with Preston North End. Arthur Cowell continued to look after the players on a day-to-day basis in his role of trainer-coach. However, team selection remained solely in the hands of the directors. The opening months of the 1936-37 season found the Rovers struggling to make much impact on the Second Division. A lack of firepower continued to haunt the club, with the bulk of the early-season goals coming from Jack Bruton on the right wing. As the club continued to slide, the football correspondent of *The Blackburn Times* launched a blistering attack on the administration of the Rovers. This particular newspaper had long championed the cause of Bob Crompton, and felt that most of the problems that now afflicted the club were largely due to the dismissal of the former director from his position as honorary manager.

A majority of the Ewood faithful no doubt agreed with the views expressed by the newspaper when it claimed: 'The recruitment, development and blending of players is the job of specialists, and the sooner the responsibility is solely placed in such hands the better.' To most supporters this was a thinly veiled plea to the club to restore Crompton to the helm at Ewood Park.

Such a plan was anathema to the directors at that time and, instead, they appointed Taylor to the position of secretary-manager towards the end of October 1936. The move did little to appease an increasingly disenchanted public, while results on the pitch continued to be inconsistent. The season reached its nadir in January 1937 when the club faced Accrington Stanley at Ewood Park in the third round of the FA Cup. The Rovers gave a debut to Nathan Fraser and, although the young forward was fairly ineffective, he did manage to score the second goal for Blackburn in a 2-2 draw.

The replay brought more changes to the team with Fraser left out and Jack Lee, a local amateur and Oxford Blue, given his debut. A Charlie Calladine goal had given the Rovers the lead before Bob Mortimer equalized for Stanley and sent the game into extra-time. A minute before half-time in the extra period, Mortimer gave Stanley the lead and, five minutes from the end, a goal by Walter Rivers sealed the win for the Peel Park Club.

This defeat galvanized the directors into action. Prior to the game with Stanley, the club had signed Billy Guest from Birmingham and, soon afterwards, Len Butt and Jock Wightman both arrived from Huddersfield Town. All three made their debuts in a goalless draw with Norwich City just three days after the Accrington debacle. It was the start of a sequence that resulted in just four defeats in the final 18 games of the season. The whole atmosphere around Ewood Park changed as despair finally gave way to hope.

The club had only finished 12th in the Second Division, and the policy of selling good players continued unabated, yet there was cause for optimism. The fee received for Jimmy Gorman, who had been sold to Sunderland in January 1937, had been reinvested in the likes of Butt and Wightman. The end-of-season run had included a record 9-1 win over Nottingham Forest at Ewood Park in April 1937. The gloom appeared to be lifting and there was a genuine belief that at long last there might be light at the end of the tunnel.

Crompton Returns

Sadly, that light was quickly extinguished. The 1937-38 season was a campaign of struggle and the club faced the very real danger of dropping into the Third Division North. Ironically, the team played some of the most entertaining football seen at Ewood Park for some time, but results continued to go against them. The FA Cup brought a third-round exit at the hands of Tottenham Hotspur, and by March 1938 it became clear that the club was in severe danger of losing the fight against relegation. Drastic measures were clearly called for and the directors, backed into a corner, had little option but to bow to public pressure and seek out Bob Crompton. The former director had managed Bournemouth & Boscombe Athletic for a brief period between June 1935 and February 1936. Although he had been quite successful, he had returned to Blackburn but kept a dignified silence on the happenings at Ewood Park.

The directors asked Crompton to return to Ewood Park in an unofficial capacity for the final month of the season. His brief was to help Taylor in any way that he could over the vital final few games. His reappearance coincided with a 2-1 win over Bury, on 2 April 1938, the first win that the team had enjoyed since the beginning of March. His presence was sufficient to inspire the players to win four and draw one of the remaining eight games. The points gained were enough to lift the club to 16th place and ensure survival in the Second Division.

Wisely, the directors acted quickly to make Crompton the club manager and leave the secretarial duties in the capable hands of Taylor. However, hopes that this might ensure a peaceful Annual General Meeting were quickly dashed. A loss of £5,256 1s 8d on the season had brought the debts to £26,309 7s 2d, and a bitter attack on the directors was launched by Albert Cowell, Crompton's former full-back partner.

Cowell had been on the coaching staff at Blackburn for many years before being dismissed during the 1936-37 season. Although he was now a member of the staff at Wrexham, the plight of the Rovers was close to his heart. He was quick to condemn the directors for selling a number of talented young players and then spending too much money on inferior replacements. It was a point that many of the Ewood faithful could agree with, indeed, the new manager let it be known that he was not entirely unsympathetic to this view. Crompton let it be known that in his opinion the future of the club would have to revolve around the introduction of younger players. He offered no short-term solutions to appease the increasingly frustrated supporters, but merely asked for time, patience and support while these young players established themselves in the first team.

The 1938-39 season was the campaign that proved that Crompton really was blessed with the Midas touch. He took a squad of players that had barely escaped relegation and turned them into a championship-winning team. While capturing the Second Division title, he also masterminded a run in the FA Cup that took the club to the sixth round. This revived memories of the golden days when Crompton, as captain, led his troops on the pitch and lifted two championship crowns.

The 1938-39 team that won the Second Division title. From left to right: back row – Bob Crompton (manager), Crook, Pryde, Whiteside, Baron, Chivers, Lanceley; front row – Rogers, Butt, Weddle, Clarke, Langton.

Without the resources to attempt any major rebuilding of the playing squad, Crompton signed a few key individuals and then instilled a collective team spirit and will to win among the players. He snapped up Jack Weddle, the veteran Portsmouth centre forward, to lead the attack, and signed Albert Clarke from Birmingham to play alongside Weddle in attack. The other inside-forward position was occupied by Len Butt who had been a constant source of goals since his transfer from Huddersfield Town.

Back in the Top Flight

On either side of this explosive trio of goalscorers the manager turned to youth. Billy Guest became a fixture on the right flank, while Bobby Langton established himself on the left wing. Behind this forward line the manager used Frank Chivers, Bob Pryde and Arnold Whiteside as his settled half-back line. The full backs were Billy Hough and Walter Crook for the majority of the season, until Ernest Lanceley replaced the injured Hough for the last 11 games. Behind them the manager relied on the steady reliability of Jimmy Barron between the posts.

Only 19 players were used during the campaign and, for the most part, the team remained unchanged as stability proved to be the key to success. If the style of football was rather rudimentary, few of the Ewood crowd complained. The manager selected tactics that suited the players available, and how they revelled in what Crompton preached. The accent was on a direct style that produced 94 goals and 25 victories. The public of Blackburn responded and the crowds that had long since deserted the club began to return to Ewood Park.

The euphoria of promotion and the expectation of First Division football continued to be overshadowed during the summer of 1939 by the threat of war in Europe. However, the season got underway in August and the Rovers travelled to Portsmouth for a game that was played in a strangely muted atmosphere. The team then travelled to London to face Arsenal at Highbury and, once again, the game reflected the lack of appetite for the game that the public showed. Both games were lost, 1-2 and 0-1, respectively, but the whole exercise seemed of academic importance. On 2 September 1939, the Rovers drew with Everton in a game which, in any other circumstances, might well have been described as a thrilling affair. However, the following day, war was declared and the Football League immediately called a halt to proceedings until after the hostilities.

The club then embarked on a series of friendly fixtures until the North West Regional League was started towards the end of October. Fortunately,

Bob Pryde made 525 appearances for the Rovers. He was a dominant and influential figure during his 16-year stay at the club.

the standard of football was far superior to that which was seen during World War I. A succession of guest players, usually professionals who were stationed near Blackburn, appeared for the club between 1939 and 1945. As well as a variety of guest players, the team also contained one or two familiar faces from the first-team squad as well as a number of the club's younger players.

However, for the League War Cup competition of 1939-40, the manager was able to call upon the services of the majority of his first-team squad. Indeed, only young Langton was missing from the team that reached the War Cup final that season. The Rovers met West Ham United at Wembley in June 1940 in front of 43,000 spectators but, unfortunately, they returned to Lancashire without the cup as a Sam Small goal clinched victory for the Hammers. After the match, the Blackburn party gathered at the Great Northern Hotel for a celebratory banquet before going their separate ways. Sadly, this would be the last gathering of the 1938-39 championship squad as war would again take its toll on Ewood Park, just as it had for an earlier generation.

The first casualty of war proved a major shock, as it was perhaps the least expected. Bob Crompton collapsed shortly after watching the Rovers beat Burnley at Ewood Park, on 15 March 1941, and died that same evening. The loss of the great man was a tremendous blow to the club and left Ewood Park with a gaping hole at its heart. Two of the men who gained championship medals under Crompton also failed to survive the conflict. Frank Chivers was killed in a mining accident in April 1942, while Albert Clarke was killed in action with his regiment in 1944.

Life, however, had to go on, and it was left to Reg Taylor to try to lead the club through the difficult wartime seasons. The acquisition of well-known guests kept interest alive, and the club also signed one or two players on a

Great Managers – 1926-31 & 1938-41

BOB CROMPTON

The most famous player in the history of Blackburn Rovers enjoyed two successful spells as manager. He took charge of the team for the first time following the resignation of Jack Carr in December 1926. At the time he was a director of the club so took the title of 'honorary manager'. In 1926-27, the Rovers came 18th in the First Division. Under Crompton the standings gradually improved until the club finished sixth in 1929-30. His greatest achievement during his first spell in charge was victory in the 1928 FA Cup final. Ironically, this had been the trophy that Crompton had most wanted to win as a player and yet was the one honour that eluded him during his playing career. His reign as 'honorary manager' ended controversially in February 1931 with a revolt by some of the players. Always a forward thinker, Crompton believed that the game would become quicker in the future and would require players who could pass the ball accurately at a faster tempo. This was not the sort of game that a number of his ageing squad felt comfortable with and, as the team was preparing for a fifth-round FA Cup-tie with Chelsea, the chairman announced that he had had a letter from players highlighting a number of grievances. Crompton withdrew from all managerial duties and in March 1931 received the ultimate snub when he failed to win re-election as a director. Without Crompton the Rovers endured difficult times and suffered relegation for the first time in the club's history. In June 1935, Crompton became manager of Bournemouth & Boscombe Athletic. After eight months he had returned to Blackburn.

By March 1938, Blackburn Rovers was a club in crisis and appeared destined to drop into the Third Division North. Under severe pressure the directors invited Crompton back to the club. Crompton offered his services to assist secretary-manager Reg Taylor. The move worked and relegation was avoided, at which point the directors installed Crompton as manager and allowed Taylor to concentrate on administrative matters. Within a season Crompton led the Rovers to the Second Division championship in 1938-39 when the team won 25 league games to create a new club record. The outbreak of war resulted in the suspension of the Football League after just three games but Crompton remained at Ewood Park to supervise the wartime activities. On 15 March 1941, Crompton watched the Rovers defeat Burnley 3-2 at Ewood Park. Tragically, later that same evening, the greatest Rover of them all collapsed and died.

more permanent basis to bring some stability to the team. The most notable signing during the wartime period was that of Herman Conway from West Ham United. Conway, who had appeared against the Rovers in the 1940 War Cup final, went on to make 134 wartime appearances for the Rovers, but declined the chance to stay at Ewood Park for the final season of wartime football. Instead, he moved to Southend United in order to continue his building trade interests.

From Tragedy Comes Hope

The 1945-46 season brought some semblance of normality with the club featuring in a 42-game Football League North competition. With a return to the traditional competitions earmarked for the 1946-47 season, the directors turned their attention to appointing a successor to Bob Crompton. Finally, the choice was made and lengthy negotiations began with Eddie Hapgood, the former Arsenal and England full back. Hapgood had been a key figure in the phenomenally successful Arsenal team of the 1930s, and the directors obviously hoped that his vast experience would help stabilize the club in the immediate postwar years.

Hapgood took up his position on 1 January 1946 and then used the remainder of the campaign to assess the players at his disposal. The new manager was even forced to make a couple of appearances himself as the season ended in a disappointing fashion. Twenty-first in the league and an early exit from the FA Cup suggested that the new manager would struggle to make much impact at Blackburn. It was therefore no surprise that he should return to Highbury and ask Horace Cope, his former playing colleague, to join him at Ewood Park as first-team trainer. On the eve of the 1946-47 season, he again returned to Highbury to persuade his old club to part with George Marks, an England wartime international goalkeeper, who was highly regarded by the new manager. In March 1946, he snapped up Jack Smith, an experienced centre forward who had seen action with both Newcastle United and Manchester United.

The euphoria surrounding the championship-winning side of 1938-39 was but a distant memory. The death of Crompton had somehow drawn a line in the sand in the history of Blackburn Rovers. As the players assembled for pre-season training in the summer of 1946, they did so in the knowledge that a new era was about to dawn at Ewood Park. The 1946-47 season proved a baptism of fire for Eddie Hapgood. With limited funds with which to strengthen his playing resources, he was forced to shuffle a squad that contained ageing pre-war players and a number of raw and untried youngsters. The jewel in the crown was Bobby Langton, whose impressive early-season form had been rewarded with an England cap in September 1946.

Seventeenth place reflected the transitional nature of a season that had seen a number of established faces usurped by younger men. The evolution had been far from peaceful and in January 1947 Walter Crook asked to be placed on the transfer list. The captain of the 1938-39 promotion-winning team made no secret of a conflict of interests with the manager and in May 1947 he left Ewood Park to join Bolton Wanderers despite the fact that Hapgood was no longer at the club.

The Departure of Hapgood

The parting of the ways between manager and club arrived during the opening months of 1947. Faced with the very real danger of relegation the directors found the money to embark on a sortie into the transfer market. A new club record was established when a £10,000 fee was paid to bring centre forward Jock Weir from Hibernian in January 1947. Shortly afterwards, a similar amount was paid to capture winger Jackie Oakes from Queen of the South. The directors also invested £6,000 in Frank McGorrighan, a play-making inside forward from Hull City.

The rift between the manager and his employers became apparent when Hapgood insisted that he had not chosen the new arrivals. It therefore came as no great surprise when the manager tendered his resignation on 19 February 1947. The directors asked Horace Cope to hold the fort until a new manager was appointed. However, there was still to be one final key acquisition that would ensure the survival of the club. In late February, the club finally landed the veteran Alec Venters from Third Lanark, almost a decade after attempts had first been made to lure the wily playmaker to Ewood Park. The infusion of his mature guile into the attack provided his colleagues with sufficient opportunities to enable the Rovers to escape from the clutches of relegation. Indeed, his silky skills were about all that illuminated a particularly gloomy season. In April 1947, as the season was drawing to a close, the directors announced the appointment of Will Scott, the Preston North End secretary and former trainer, as the new manager of Blackburn Rovers.

Survival that season had been built on a solid defence and the ability to perform away from Ewood Park. Indeed, the majority of the better performances during that campaign came in the eight wins that the team enjoyed while on the road. However, despite the indifferent form shown in home games, the Blackburn public poured into Ewood Park and lifted the average attendance to 26,367. This postwar boom compared favourably with the average of 18,262 that had been recorded during the 1938-39 season.

The club was again thrown into chaos after only three games of the 1947-48 season. The new manager was struck down with ill health and forced to take a period of leave from Ewood Park. The playing affairs were now put in the hands of Jack Bruton who, since the end of his playing career, had been part of the administrative team at Ewood Park. When Scott returned the directors appointed Bruton as assistant to the manager and shortly afterwards the former Blackburn winger was short-listed for a managerial position with Manchester City. Fortunately, he decided to withdraw his name from consideration in order to remain at Ewood Park.

Like Hapgood before him, Scott put his faith in the younger players at the club. He replaced Weir (who had failed to live up to expectations) with young Verdi Godwin, while the likes of Bob Tomlinson, George Higgins, Les Cook and Jimmy Baldwin were all given a chance to prove their worth with extended runs in the first team. However, no matter how the pack was

50 Greatest Players

WALTER CROOK Left back

Born: Whittle-le-Woods, Lancashire, 28 April 1912

Joined Blackburn: 1931   **From:** Blackburn Nomads

Debut: 19 March 1932 v Liverpool, League

Appearances: 350   **Goals:** 2

Left Blackburn: 1947   **For:** Bolton Wanderers

Honours won with Blackburn: Division 2 championship 1939; 1 England wartime cap

Crook graduated through the ranks at Ewood Park and finally, after another rare call to first-team duty on 22 December 1934, his name remained on the first-team sheet until the end of the 1938-39 season. During that campaign, he captained the team to the Second Division championship. He played at Wembley in the 1940 War Cup final and, although military service detained him through much of the war, he made 113 wartime appearances for the club. When the Football League kicked off again Crook was back in his familiar role at left back. By appearing in the first 17 games of the 1946-47 season, he took his number of consecutive league appearances to 208, a club record, even though it took some 12 years to complete. A tough tackler, his natural aggression made him a great favourite with the crowd at Ewood Park. He joined Bolton Wanderers in May 1947 but injury forced him into premature retirement. He then embarked on a highly successful coaching career in Holland although managerial stints in England were less successful. After 18 years on the backroom staff of Preston North End, he finally left football.

shuffled, consistency remained an elusive quality and the deterioration in results began to have a detrimental affect on the health of the manager. On 9 December 1947, following two heavy defeats against Middlesbrough and Sheffield United, Scott decided that his health could no longer stand the strain and he tendered his resignation.

Bruton in Control

The directors moved quickly to install Bruton as the new manager and in turn the former Ewood favourite inspired an upturn in results. Just when it seemed that the club would pull clear of relegation, the team suffered an inexplicable loss of form. Only one of the last ten games was won and as a result a return of five points from a possible 20 sent the club spiralling into the Second Division. The failure to find a younger version of Venters (the veteran having returned to Scotland as his form wavered) and a goal-scoring centre forward were two of the main factors that brought about relegation. In defence there were major concerns regarding the full-back positions, although the emergence of Bill Eckersley on the final day of the season would prove part of the solution to this particular problem.

50 Greatest Players

BOB PRYDE Centre half

Born: Methil, 25 April 1913

Joined Blackburn: 1933   **From:** St Johnstone

Debut: 21 October 1933 v Chelsea, League

Appearances: 525   **Goals:** 22

Left Blackburn: 1949   **For:** Wigan Athletic

Honours won with Blackburn: Division 2 championship 1939

Bob Pryde arrived at Ewood Park in May 1933 and the tall, slim defender was to stay for 16 years and become one of the dominant figures of his generation at the club. Initially, he struggled to find consistency, but once his game matured he became one the leading figures of the 1938-39 Second Division championship team. During the war, when Pryde ought to have enjoyed his best years, he was a figure of continuity at Ewood Park. He made 180 wartime appearances for the Rovers but still found time to guest for other clubs. When peace was restored he continued to be a dominant force at the heart of a struggling team. Despite relegation back to the Second Division in 1947-48, Pryde continued to provide leadership and hope for a dispirited team. Always keen to go out while still at the top, Pryde announced his retirement at the end of the 1948-49 season.

Inside forward Les Graham slots the ball home from the penalty spot past Ernie Gregory of West Ham United on 9 September 1950. Blackburn went on to lose 3-1.

The summer of 1948 brought some much needed transfer activity as Bruton attempted to rebuild his shattered squad. George Marks was allowed to leave the club with the manager opting to use Stan Hayhurst in goal. Eckersley was given the left-back berth and Bruton signed David Gray from Preston North End to fill the other full-back spot. The ageing Bob Pryde continued at centre half with the youthful exuberance of Baldwin and Eric Bell utilized in the half-back positions. Relegation from the top flight inevitably led to the departure of Langton and his move to Preston North End brought winger Jackie Wharton to Ewood Park from Manchester City. Don Carter, a close-season signing from Bury, was another player who operated on the flanks and who was seen as a possible successor to Langton. The goal-scoring problems were solved with the arrival of Dennis Westcott from Wolverhampton Wanderers and the manager also had Les Graham and Eddie Crossan, who had arrived from Ireland the previous season, at his disposal to fill the inside-forward positions.

The influx of new faces ought to have enabled the Rovers to mount a serious promotion challenge, but the 1948-49 season was a bitterly disappointing affair. Indeed, the spectre of the Third Division North hung over the club for a time in a topsy-turvy season. An awful start was followed by improved results, if not performances. Ironically, when performances improved, during the second half of the season, results faltered.

The Bestall Years

In May 1949, the directors decided to take action to arrest the aura of decline that had enveloped the club. As a result, both Jack Bruton and Horace Cope were sacked. The parting of the ways was far from amicable with the former manager claiming directorial interference in team selection. Fortunately, these claims did little to dissuade prospective candidates from showing an interest in the job, and the directors eventually appointed Jackie Bestall, the former Grimsby Town and England international, as the new manager. His backroom team consisted of Jack Weddle and Jock Wightman, both popular and familiar faces at Ewood Park. However, another familiar figure bade farewell to the club when the veteran Bob Pryde accepted the player-manager's job at Wigan Athletic. Pryde began strengthening the Wigan squad by signing Arnold Whiteside, his long-time colleague at Ewood Park.

The new manager was quick to promote players from within to fill the void left by Pryde. Bill Holt became the automatic choice at centre half while Ron Suart, who had been signed from Blackpool in September 1949, had to be content with a peripheral role during his first season at Ewood Park. Once

50 Greatest Players

ERIC BELL Half back

Born: Bedlington, 13 February 1922

Joined Blackburn: 1945   **From:** Blyth Shipyard

Debut: 31 August 1946 v Portsmouth, League

Appearances: 370   **Goals:** 9

Left Blackburn: 1957 (retired)

Eric Bell arrived at Ewood Park to participate in the final season of wartime football. However, unlike so many other youngsters who came and went during the wartime game, Bell would remain a prominent member of the first-team squad for the next decade. At his best as a tenacious half back, Bell was also versatile enough to operate at left back, inside forward and outside left. Always a loyal servant, Bell was the type of player who rarely caught the eye. His was the unspectacular role, the solid reliable performer who won the ball and gave it to the playmakers. He narrowly missed international selection and when he finally hung up his boots he became involved with the coaching of the youth team before graduating to trainer of the Central League team. Under his guidance the team won the Central League on two occasions in the mid-1960s.

50 Greatest Players

EDDIE QUIGLEY Inside forward

Born: Bury, 13 July 1921

Joined Blackburn: 1951   **From:** Preston North End

Debut: 17 November 1951 v Birmingham City, League

Appearances: 166   **Goals:** 95

Left Blackburn: 1956   **For:** Bury

Eddie Quigley served Blackburn Rovers as a player, manager and scout over 30 years. When he arrived at Blackburn he was approaching the veteran stage of his career and looked rather overweight, having the brawn that one often associates with defenders of that era. However, he was blessed with a remarkable football brain. He was an astute tactician and exquisite playmaker. He raked long, accurate crossfield passes with minute precision. It was a skill that enabled him to dismantle the tightest of defences. To this he added a potent shot that he unleashed whenever the opportunity arose. In the 1954-55 season he scored 28 goals in 40 appearances. He left Blackburn in August 1956 to join Bury but returned in October 1966 as assistant manager to Jack Marshall. In February of the following year he became caretaker manager before being appointed manager in April 1967. During his tenure the club maintained a challenging position in the Second Division without ever really threatening to win promotion. Always the master tactician, Quigley maximized a small squad to its full potential but success remained elusive. He departed the club in 1971 but returned in 1979 as chief scout, a position he held until May 1981.

again, the Rovers had appointed a manager who was eager to nurture young talent. However, Bestall was keen to encourage youth development at all levels and therefore a number of promising young players arrived at Ewood Park to play with the junior teams at the club. During the period that Bestall was in charge the likes of Ronnie and Ken Clayton, together with Bryan Douglas, all began their development through the junior ranks.

However, while the Clayton brothers and Douglas would be part of a brighter future, the manager struggled to make an immediate impression on the first team. Sixteenth place in the Second Division and a third-round exit from the FA Cup provided little joy for the Ewood faithful. A further blow came in February 1950 with the departure of Dennis Westcott to Manchester City and his loss to the club was keenly felt. Despite the fact that he wasn't at the club for the final 13 matches of the campaign, he was still the only player to reach double figures in terms of goal scoring.

50 Greatest Players

BOBBY LANGTON Winger

Born: Burscough, 8 September 1918

Joined Blackburn: 1937; 1953 **From:** Burscough Victoria; Bolton Wanderers

Debut: 10 September 1938 v Swansea Town, League

Appearances: 262 **Goals:** 74

Left Blackburn: 1948; 1956 **For:** Preston North End; Ards

Honours won with Blackburn: Division 2 championship 1939; 7 England caps

Bobby Langton had two spells with Blackburn Rovers. In his first incarnation he was a flying winger who used the exuberance of youth to race past defenders before sending in a pinpoint centre. He was also a dangerous raider when it came to goal scoring and he was noted for cutting inside the full back and unleashing a ferocious shot at goal. He won a Second Division championship medal in 1939 and in the 1946-47 season his exhilarating performances were rewarded with England international caps. Relegation to the Second Division resulted in Langton leaving Ewood Park to join Preston North End in August 1948. His second incarnation at Blackburn began in September 1953 when he returned as a totally different player from the one that had previously roamed Ewood Park. Gone was the electrifying pace and in its place was a player who used craft and guile to open up opposing defences. He was still a potent threat in front of goal and 1954-55 saw him help the club to score 114 league goals, with Langton's own tally standing at a respectable 13. He finally left Blackburn in June 1956 to play out his time in Ireland before returning to England to embark on a coaching career in non-league football.

There was very little optimism around Ewood Park at the start of the 1950-51 season, indeed, the common view was that the club would do well to avoid being involved in another fight against relegation. Yet the season opened with three wins and by late autumn the club was sitting comfortably among the leading pack. During February and March 1951 the Rovers dallied in second place in the table and thoughts began to turn to promotion. However, a depressing sequence of results during the latter part of March ended all hopes of First Division football, although sixth place was a vast improvement on the previous season. In truth, the club was still lacking in certain areas but there was no doubt that Bestall was slowly beginning to have an impact on the club.

One point from the opening eight games of the 1951-52 season represented the worst start to a season that the club had experienced and virtually ended all hope of promotion before summer had given way to autumn. Indeed, by mid-November the club was in serious trouble with a meagre haul of just six points from a possible 32. During this disastrous spell the manager was forced to make a succession of signings to try and shore up his flagging team. In September 1951, he signed Willie Kelly from Airdrie to fill the centre-half berth, and Albert Nightingale soon followed to provide a little more guile to the inside-forward positions. Added pace was given to the flanks with the arrival of Alec Glover from Luton Town. However, it was the acquisition of goalkeeper Reg Elvy and inside forward Eddie Quigley that signalled the start of a much-needed revival. In total, the club spent something in the region of £53,000 to stave off relegation and provide a platform for an improved second half of the season. Another significant change brought Harry Healless back to Ewood Park to take charge of coaching.

A run of seven successive victories between December and February lifted the club in every sense, and as league fortunes improved the club embarked on the FA Cup trail, a journey that would lead to its 14th appearance at the semi-final stage of the competition. Although the league position continued to improve it was the FA Cup campaign that caught the imagination of the public. The competition really came alight when 52,900 crowded into Ewood Park to witness the sixth-round meeting with Burnley. Goals from Nightingale, Bill Holmes and Glover gave the Rovers a 3-1 victory and ensured that the majority of supporters went home happy.

The semi-final found the Rovers against Newcastle United, the cup holders, and once again the men from Lancashire rose to the occasion. The first game at Hillsbrough ended in a goalless draw, despite the fact that the Rovers enjoyed dominant spells during the match. The replay at Elland Road was a slightly different affair due to the fact that both Suart and Holmes were missing from the Blackburn line-up. The aerial power of Suart in defence was particularly missed and it was perhaps no coincidence that George Robledo should have given Newcastle the lead with a headed

Goalkeeper Reg Elvy's consistency earned him 156 consecutive appearances between November 1951 and April 1955.

Tommy Briggs signs during the 1952-53 season. He was too late to make an impression at this stage of the campaign but went on to become an influential player in forthcoming seasons at the club. He scored 143 goals in 204 appearances.

goal. A typically powerful shot from Quigley brought the Rovers onto an equal footing and the men from Ewood Park began to pour forward in search of a winning goal. Sadly, the Newcastle defence stood firm and the Magpies won the game with a disputed penalty from Bobby Mitchell.

The league campaign ended with the Rovers in 14th position in the Second Division. However, the form shown during mid-season and throughout the cup run suggested that brighter times were ahead for the club. The season had also seen the emergence of Ronnie Clayton from the youth ranks, while the new signings merely underlined the fact that money spent wisely could hasten a return to the top flight.

Sadly, the patience of supporters was once again tested to the full during the 1952-53 campaign. The first half of the season was a period of utter dejection as the team once more hovered in the lower regions. Bestall was again required to enter the transfer market to kick-start the campaign, and the arrival of Tommy Briggs, who was signed with Bill Smith from Birmingham City, provided a little impetus to proceedings. Unfortunately, the revival came too late to make any real difference with regard to promotion and the club had to settle for ninth place in the table.

Chapter Six: 1953-60
Enter the Quiet Irishman

Although Bestall had managed to stabilize the club, the First Division looked as far away as ever. Younger players had started to graduate to the first team but consistency remained the Achilles' heel. Amid rumours of unrest, the directors and Bestall agreed that a parting of the ways would be of mutual benefit for both parties. Rather than appoint an established manager the directors decided to offer the job to Johnny Carey, the Manchester United stalwart who was coming to the end of a long and illustrious playing career.

'Attractive soccer that wins matches' was to be the philosophy around which he based his tactics during his time at Ewood Park. Initially, he had to make do with what he had inherited in terms of the playing staff as there was little money available for an influx of new players. Although there were one or two early blips – an 8-0 defeat at Lincoln City in August 1953 being the biggest – Carey quickly changed the whole atmosphere around the club. He placed the emphasis on teamwork and he instilled a new sense of purpose among the players who were encouraged to play a more refined game that revolved around accurate ground passing rather than a big kick up field.

It was a time of mixed fortunes for the Rovers and the downside was typified by Dave Whelan's broken leg in the 1960 FA Cup final – a disastrous affair from start to finish.

The team from the 1954-55 season when Blackburn Rovers scored 114 goals, including the 9-0 win against Middlesbrough. Left to right: back row – R. Clayton, Suart, Briggs, Elvy, Bell, Kelly; front row – Mooney, Crossan, Eckerlsey, Quigley, Langton.

Even the defenders were asked to adopt this more sophisticated style. During the course of the campaign, the new manager made two significant signings that enabled him to strengthen his attacking options. Firstly, he brought Bobby Langton back to the club from Bolton Wanderers and, although obviously older and a little slower, the former Ewood favourite provided a constant flow of ammunition to Briggs and Quigley. Carey's other major acquisition was the capture of Frank Mooney from Manchester United to play on the opposite flank to Langton. Although Carey's first season at Ewood Park was to ultimately end in disappointment, with a third-place finish, the transformation that had occurred in just 12 months was remarkable.

Goals Galore

The 1954-55 campaign continued in the same fashion with the team committed to an attacking style of play that caught the public imagination. A total of 114 league goals were scored with a 9-0 win over Middlesbrough and an 8-3 win over Bristol Rovers that saw Briggs score seven goals. The whole of the forward line gorged themselves with Mooney picking up 16, Crossan 18, Briggs 33, Quigley 28 and Langton 13. Although the ultimate prize of promotion remained tantalizingly out of reach, the club finished sixth, and the Ewood faithful had been treated to an outstanding season of football.

Entertainment remained high on the agenda during the 1955-56 season. However, there were still nagging doubts as to whether the team was really good enough to clinch a promotion place. Concern was growing about Reg Elvy's failing eyesight and use of contact lenses, and while Eckersley continued to dominate the left-back position there was no clear choice on the opposite flank. Bill Smith and Ken Taylor had proved competent while the arrival of Republic of Ireland of international Tommy Clinton from Everton offered further options in this area. The Clayton brothers were largely automatic choices at half back although the introduction of Mick McGrath towards the end of the season offered a further option at half back. Earlier in the season, Carey had replaced Willie Kelly with Eric Binns at centre half but had later been compelled to recall the ageing Scottish defender. The only major change in the attack came with the introduction of Bryan Douglas on the right wing.

Although the club achieved fourth place, the 1955-56 season lacked the explosive nature of the previous campaign. Deficiencies in the team had to be addressed and Carey didn't shy away from the drastic pruning needed. 1956-57 became a season of transition as Carey began to rebuild while trying to challenge for promotion. The task proved too great and the Rovers ended another campaign on the fringe of a promotion. However, if another fourth-

---

50 Greatest Players

EDDIE CROSSAN Inside forward

Born: Londonderry, 17 November 1925

Joined Blackburn: 1947   **From:** Derry City

Debut: 31 January 1948 v Sunderland, League

Appearances: 302   **Goals:** 74

Left Blackburn: 1957   **For:** Tranmere Rovers

Honours won with Blackburn: 3 Northern Ireland caps

The mercurial talents of Eddie Crossan first burst upon Ewood Park during the death throes of the club's fall from the First Division in 1947-48. He left the club at the start of the 1957-58 season, a campaign that would see the club recapture a place in the top flight. However, if the bulk of his football was played in the Second Division there was nothing second rate about his footballing qualities. His brilliant close control and mesmeric dribbling left many an opponent trailing in his wake. However, he had the unique ability to enthral, delight and frustrate all at the same time. His game was one of contradictions – many of his 74 goals were memorable efforts but he is also remembered as the player who most frequently squandered short-range chances. His talents were perfect for the style of football adopted by Johnny Carey and he was undoubtedly at his peak in the 1954-55 season when he notched up 18 of the 114 goals scored during that campaign.

place finish was disappointing, the seeds of future success had been sown. A successor to Elvy was found in Harry Leyland who, after being released by Everton, had found his way to Tonbridge. Carey stepped in to divert him to Ewood Park before he could make an appearance for the non-league outfit. In November 1956, he signed Matt Woods from the Goodison Park club to fill the vacancy at centre left that the declining powers of Kelly had created.

There were also key changes to the personnel in the forward line with Ally MacLeod being signed in the summer of 1956 to replace the ageing legs of Langton on the left flank. The season also saw the emergence of Roy Vernon who had graduated through the junior ranks and made a dozen league appearances in the previous campaign. Another figure to emerge from the Central League team was young Peter Dobing and he and Roy Vernon claimed the inside-forward places. A major setback occurred when Ken Clayton broke his leg in the game against Middlesbrough in April 1957. However, the manager was fortunate to have an exciting prospect in McGrath to act as cover and the young Irishman grabbed the opportunity to become a permanent fixture.

Promotion at Last

The new season began with one win, three draws and a defeat, yet Carey's young thoroughbreds soon got into their stride and led the table during parts of October and November before slipping away in mid-season. However, the lack of a traditional centre forward was becoming an issue as Dobing had had to be moved from his favoured inside-forward slot to fill the void vacated by Briggs. The former golden boy of Ewood Park was coming to the end of his career and was no longer the dominant number nine of old. In March 1958, he was allowed to move to Grimsby Town as the manager pulled off another transfer masterstroke. With the transfer deadline looming, and the threat of yet another promotion fade-out imminent, the manager paid £15,000 to bring Tommy Johnston to Ewood Park from Leyton Orient.

Johnston was a player of similar ilk to Briggs yet, against all expectations, *Ken and Ronnie Clayton, regulars in the half-back positions throughout 1956-57.*

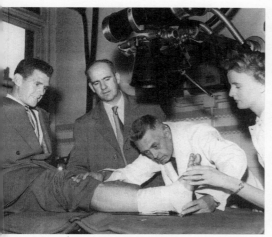

Concerned manager Johnny Carey oversees the examination of Ronnie Clayton's injury.

the manager declined to use Johnston as a swashbuckling opportunist but instead he was allowed to become the footballing general of the attack. Under his tutelage, Roy Vernon and Peter Dobing blossomed and in the 11 games that featured Johnston a total of 40 goals were scored as the Rovers embarked on a promotion-winning sequence of results. These 11 games produced nine wins, one draw and just one defeat.

The club was also engaged in a successful run in the FA Cup. Away wins over Rotherham United and Everton were followed by a victory over Cardiff City, after a replay. The sixth round produced a monumental tussle with Liverpool at Ewood Park but goals from Ronnie Clayton and MacLeod proved sufficient to edge the Rovers into a semi-final meeting with Bolton Wanderers at Maine Road. Sadly, a Blackburn team kitted out in an unfamiliar strip of black and white stripes lost by the odd goal in three.

Promotion was only confirmed on the final day of the season when the Rovers visited The Valley to play Charlton Athletic in a game that would decide who accompanied West Ham United into the First Division. It proved a nerve-wracking affair for the 56,435 at the ground and the thousands waiting nervously back in Blackburn. After 61 minutes, the Rovers appeared to be destined for top-flight football after two goals from Dobing and one apiece from Vernon and Douglas had given the team a 4-1 lead. However, the last 15 minutes produced a thrilling fightback before the Rovers could finally celebrate a 4-3 win and promotion.

The First Division appeared to hold no fears for the men from Ewood Park as the team opened the 1958-59 campaign with a 5-1 win at Newcastle United. This was followed with two 5-0 home wins against Leicester City and Tottenham Hotspur, respectively. Johnston, who many had felt would find the top flight beyond his capabilities, answered his critics with five goals in these opening three games. Sadly, reality belatedly arrived at Ewood Park and, after this initial success, the club went nine games without a win before registering a fourth victory, a 4-1 home win over Preston North End. Unfortunately, by the time Preston visited Ewood Park the club had lost its manager to Everton. Eager to retain the services of Carey the Blackburn directors offered to match the terms that the Goodison Park club had put to the Rovers' manager. However, Carey, who had always operated without a contract at Ewood Park, decided to accept the long-term contract that was on offer on Merseyside, but he readily agreed to postpone his departure until the Rovers had found a successor. Dally Duncan, who had been manager of Luton Town since 1947, was the man given the unenviable task of following Carey. He appeared to have the ideal credentials for the Blackburn post as he had proved himself capable of building a successful squad with a limited budget. The new manager quickly stabilized the club in the First Division and led the team to a comfortable mid-table position.

Dally Duncan Takes Over

Duncan had soon been required to demonstrate his managerial skills with several issues coming to the fore during the opening months of his reign. The declining influence of Johnston meant that the manager readily agreed to allow him to return to Leyton Orient in February 1959. Duncan initially promoted Jack Swindells from the Central League team and the youngster celebrated a dream debut with the winning goal against Portsmouth in February 1959. However, he was clearly far from the finished article and the void left by Johnston was once again filled by moving Peter Dobing into the centre spot.

When Newcastle United rejected overtures from the Ewood Park club to sign Bill Curry, the Blackburn manager looked to the south coast for a possible alternative. The player who had aroused so much attention was Derek Dougan, a player that the Rovers had been interested in before he moved to Portsmouth. On that occasion the Blackburn club had been unable to reach agreeable terms with his employers at Distillery. However, this time the club moved swiftly to seal his move from Fratton Park to Lancashire.

Away from the first team the highlight of the 1958-59 season was

Three key members of the 1957-58 promotion-winning side. From the left, Roy Vernon, Tommy Johnston and Ally MacLeod.

Great Matches

FOOTBALL LEAGUE DIVISION TWO		The Valley, 26 April 1958
Charlton Athletic 3	**Blackburn Rovers 4**	**Attendance: 56,435**
Lucas	Dobing 2	
Firmani	Vernon	
Hewie (pen)	Douglas (pen)	

A long and arduous season had seen both clubs fighting for promotion but after 41 matches the fixture list provided a tense last-day showdown with Charlton only needing a draw for second place. Within minutes the Blackburn defence failed to clear the ball and when Johnny Summers whipped in a cross Fred Lucas buried his header. Stuart Leary then fluffed a golden opportunity when left unmarked in the Blackburn penalty area. The Rovers eventually began to claw their way back, largely due to the endeavours of Ronnie Clayton and Mick McGrath. On 23 minutes, the teams were on level terms when young striker Peter Dobing headed the ball into the net.

Charlton now began to feel the strain and Blackburn's second goal came on 35 minutes when Bill Eckersley played a superbly weighted long ball down the left wing for the energetic young legs of Dobing to chase and slot past keeper Willie Duff. On 42 minutes, the Blackburn fans were again celebrating when Roy Vernon unleashed a vicious left-foot drive past Duff. Soon afterwards, the unlucky keeper fumbled the ball and dropped it at the feet of Tom Johnston who moved for the ball and was pulled back. The referee pointed to the spot and Bryan Douglas stroked the ball home for a 4-1 lead. With 15 minutes remaining an Eddie Firmani header beat Leyland and on 84 minutes Matt Woods handed Charlton a lifeline when he conceded a penalty with a clumsy challenge. South African John Hewie stepped up to slot the ball past Leyland. With Woods at the heart of the action the Rovers managed to hold out for the final five minutes to bring ecstatic celebrations from the Ewood fans.

Charlton Athletic: Duff, Firmani, Townsend, Hewie, Ufton, Kiernan, Werge, Lucas, Leary, White, Summers

Blackburn Rovers: Leyland, Whelan, Eckersley, R. Clayton, Woods, McGrath, Douglas, Dobing, Johnston, Vernon, MacLeod

Referee: L. Callaghan (Glamorgan)

undoubtedly the capture of the FA Youth Cup. A two-legged victory over West Ham United was just reward for a squad that contained future internationals of the calibre of Keith Newton, Mike England and Fred Pickering. A further cause for celebration at the end of the first season back in the top flight was that the club made a profit of £25,000, money that enabled the Rovers to erect a floodlight system.

The 1959-60 season was a story of amazing contrasts. An appearance at Wembley in the FA Cup final ought to have been the highlight of the year but it merely masked the storm clouds that engulfed Ewood Park. Prior to Christmas the club seemed on course to build upon the foundations that had been laid 12 months earlier. However, the first four months of 1960 proved disastrous for all concerned with the club. The year began with unrest in the camp, largely revolving around Roy Vernon and his strained relationship with Dally Duncan. The matter was only resolved when the Welshman left Ewood Park in February 1960 to join his mentor, Johnny Carey, at Everton.

Ironically, the loss of one of the most gifted inside forwards that the club had possessed actually lifted morale for a time and enabled the club to continue with its impressive run in the FA Cup. However, while cup results kept interest alive, the bread and butter league programme disintegrated. In the last 18 First Division matches only three games were won and two drawn – the rest were lost. Eight points from a possible 36 might well have cost the club its place in the First Division but for the points harvested during the autumn and early winter period. In an attempt to halt this alarming slide the club paid £25,000, a club record fee, to sign Chris Crowe from Leeds United.

50 Greatest Players

TOMMY BRIGGS Centre forward

Born: Chesterfield, 27 November 1923

Joined Blackburn: 1952　　**From:** Birmingham City

Debut: 29 November 1952 v Bury, League

Appearances: 204　　**Goals:** 143

Left Blackburn: 1958　　**For:** Grimsby Town

Tommy Briggs had already gained a reputation as a fearsome marksman before he arrived at Ewood Park in November 1952 but Briggs and Blackburn Rovers was a marriage made in heaven. With Carey's commitment to attacking football Briggs couldn't help but prosper. Like Ted Harper before him, Briggs was not the most technically skilled of predators but when it came to putting the ball in the back of the net he had few equals. During each of four Second Division campaigns, between 1953-54 and 1956-57, Briggs scored over 30 goals on each occasion. Briggs was already 29 when he arrived at Ewood Park but age proved no barrier to goal scoring. In 1954-55, the club recorded 114 league goals and Briggs was responsible for 33 of them. However, he could also create opportunities for others and when the club recorded its record league win, 9-0 over Middlesbrough on 6 November 1954, Briggs was not on the scoresheet. A couple of months later he made up for it when he bagged seven goals in the 8-3 win over Bristol Rovers at Ewood Park.

The fact that Crowe, a talented inside forward, was cup-tied showed how desperate the situation had become at Ewood Park. In fact, the player rarely gave glimpses of the value placed upon his head and he made just five appearances as the club struggled against relegation.

Cup of Mixed Fortunes

However, while the league form went from bad to worse the club could seemingly do no wrong in the cup. Although it required two games to pass Sunderland in the third round, the 4-1 victory in the replay at Ewood Park was a fairly comfortable affair. In the fourth round, only an extremely late goal from Mick McGrath prevented the Rovers from going out at home to Blackpool. Once again, the replay proved to be a much easier affair with two goals from Dobing and one from Dougan giving the Rovers a 3-0 win.

In view of the appalling league form, a fifth-round trip to Tottenham Hotspur offered little in the way of cheer for the Ewood faithful. Yet, once again, the team rose to the occasion and romped to a 3-1 win. This set up a sixth-round local derby meeting with Burnley. With only 17 minutes to go, and a 3-0 deficit to pull back, the cup dream appeared to have evaporated. It was then that the Rovers produced the performance of the season and clawed their way back into the game. A fairly harmless Peter Dobing effort

Peter Dobing fires a shot past Bill Foulkes and a Manchester United defence that has drafted in some canine help. Dobing scored another 103 goals in 205 appearances.

struck the boot of Alex Elder and flew up onto his hand. The intent was debatable but the referee pointed to the spot. A bewildered Burnley team watched Bryan Douglas accept the gift and bring some respectability to the score. Three minutes later a 25-yard drive from Dobing found the back of the net and suddenly the Turf Moor crowd groaned a collective sigh of dismay.

The sustained Blackburn pressure began to cause the Burnley defence to falter. Ronnie Clayton provided inspirational leadership as he drove his team forward. Both physically and mentally the balance of power had shifted dramatically and four minutes from the end the Rovers gained an unlikely equalizer. A shot by Clayton fell to the feet of McGrath in a crowded penalty area. The Irish international simply swung his foot at the ball to send it goalwards. Fortunately, he sliced the shot and Adam Blacklaw was left stranded in the Burnley goal as the ball rolled across the line.

The replay attracted a crowd of 53,839 who witnessed a virtuoso performance from Bryan Douglas. The Burnley defence had no answer to his skills but the Blackburn attack failed to capitalize on his hard work. As extra-time began, any nagging doubts that the Rovers would fail to prosper from their superiority disappeared with goals from Dobing and MacLeod. The semi-final took the Rovers to Maine Road, Manchester, for a meeting with

50 Greatest Players

ROY VERNON Inside forward

Born: Ffynnongroew, nr Holywell, Flintshire, 14 April 1937

Joined Blackburn: 1954   **From:** Mostyn YMCA

Debut: 3 September 1955 v Liverpool, League

Appearances: 144   **Goals:** 52

Left Blackburn: 1960   **For:** Everton

Honours won with Blackburn: 9 Wales caps, 1 Wales Under-23 cap

When Roy Vernon left Ewood Park in February 1960 he was one of the finest inside forwards to ever wear the blue and white shirt of the Rovers. He was a magnificent talent. Pencil thin, yet incredibly durable, Vernon was a combination of predator and playmaker. When striking the ball he employed only subtle backlift and gave defenders little opportunity to block the impending thunderbolt, and the power of his shooting, particularly when striking a dead ball, had few equals. His mentor at Ewood Park was Johnny Carey who seemed able to coax the genius from Vernon while being able to control his fiery temperament. His career at Blackburn began to falter after Carey departed for Everton and Dally Duncan took over as manager. The former Luton Town boss and Vernon continually clashed and it was no surprise when Vernon joined Carey at Goodison Park.

Great Matches

FA CUP SIXTH ROUND   Turf Moor, Burnley, 12 March 1960

Burnley 3   Blackburn Rovers 3   Attendance: 51,501

Pilkington	Douglas (pen)
Pointer	Dobing
Connelly	McGrath

Rovers played eight games before reaching the sacred twin towers but none of those eight games were as difficult as this titanic clash with Burnley at Turf Moor. The game was still without a goal at half-time although the Rovers had enjoyed plenty of possession. Early in the second period the game would totally change complexion. It was the majestic Jimmy McIlroy who instigated the opening goal with a wonderful crossfield pass that found Brian Pilkington lurking in a dangerous position. The Burnley winger sent a rasping right-foot shot wide of Harry Leyland's left hand and into the net at the angle of crossbar and post. The goal came against the run of play but worse was to follow for the Rovers. McIlroy slipped a ball through a huddle of Blackburn defenders for Ray Pointer to turn it into the net. When Connelly hit the deftest of chip-shots into the net, with just 15 minutes remaining, the home side appeared to be in an unassailable position. However, it was at that moment that fate gave the Rovers a helping hand. A fairly harmless looking shot by Peter Dobing appeared to be going wide when it hit the boot of defender Alex Elder, flew up and struck his hand. To the consternation of the Burnley players and supporters the referee awarded the most dubious of penalties. Bryan Douglas gladly accepted the gift and reduced the arrears.

Three minutes later the whole game was turned on its head when Douglas turned provider and found Dobing with a typically astute piece of play. However, as Dobing was 25-yards from goal there appeared little danger until he suddenly unleashed a thunderbolt that beat Blacklaw. The game was completely transformed and as the Rovers grew in confidence the Burnley defence began to panic.

The Rovers poured forward in search of an equalizer which arrived four minutes from the end when Ronnie Clayton blasted a shot towards the Burnley goal. It flew into a mass of bodies before Mick McGrath swung his foot at the ball which hit the inside of the post and rolled into the net. The unlikeliest of fight-backs was complete. The replay was another tight affair but two late goals gave the Rovers the win and clinched a place in the FA Cup semi-final.

Burnley: Blacklaw, Angus, Elder, Seith, Miller, Adamson, Connelly, McIlroy, Pointer, Robson, Pilkington

Blackburn Rovers: Leyland, Bray, Whelan, R. Clayton, Woods, McGrath, Bimpson, Dobing, Dougan, Douglas, MacLeod

Referee: J.W. Hunt (Portsmouth)

Sheffield Wednesday. A brace of goals from Derek Dougan gave the Rovers a 2-1 win in front of 74,135 spectators and sent the club to its first Wembley final since 1940, and its first FA Cup final since 1928. Yet for all the success in the cup, the league form remained lamentable. The good humour of the Blackburn faithful had been sorely tested but Wembley would merely add insult to injury. Rumours with regard to ticket distribution caused major unrest among supporters and many of the long-time fans became permanently alienated as they found themselves unable to obtain tickets.

On the eve of the final against Wolverhampton Wanderers, Derek

Harry Leyland, Ally MacLeod, Bryan Douglas and Ronnie Clayton prepare for the ill-fated 1960 FA Cup final by playing the Wembley board game.

Dougan handed in a transfer request amid fears that he was not fit to play at Wembley. He passed a late fitness test but for large parts of the game was little more than a passenger. Matters were worsened when Dave Whelan broke his leg in a clash with Norman Deeley. Just a minute earlier a McGrath own goal had given Wolves the lead. A brace of goals from Deeley enabled Wolves to coast to a 3-0 win. As a spectacle the game had been ruined by the injury to Whelan and the incapacity of Dougan, and the rugged tackling employed by Wolves did little to lighten the gloomy mood of Blackburn supporters. The only comfort from the whole sorry episode was that the cup run had generated sufficient money to allow for a cantilever roof to be erected at the Blackburn end of the ground. Ewood Park was now covered on all four sides.

A close-season tour of Germany did little to ease the growing pressure on Dally Duncan and stories of poor club discipline merely increased the speculation regarding his future at Blackburn. The directors clearly felt that it was time for a change but Duncan had the security of a long-term contract. In a move reminiscent of the removal of Jackie Bestall, the directors asked Duncan to resign. The canny Scot was in no mood for compromise and declined the directorial request that he should fall on his sword. As a result, the board had little option but to sack him and begin the search for a replacement.

Chapter Seven: 1960-66
Disappointment and Relegation

When the 1960-61 season began, the club found itself in the unenviable position of having no manager at the helm. The man who had been earmarked for the position was Jack Marshall, the manager of Fourth Division Rochdale. However, he was unable to take up his managerial duties at Ewood Park until the Spotland Road directors had found a suitable replacement. Thus the season was already six games old before Marshall was able to take control. He arrived at a club that was still in turmoil following the previous disastrous campaign. Many of the supporters, who had been alienated by the Wembley debacle, failed to reappear at Ewood Park when the new season began, and many would never return. The average attendance for 1959-60 stood at 27,299 but by the end of the 1960-61 season this had fallen alarmingly to just 19,344.

The new manager was also faced with a number of injury problems that prevented him from selecting a settled side. Senior professionals like Harry Leyland and Bill Eckersley were struggling with injury, and both were clearly coming to the end of their Ewood Park careers. The manager was resigned to the loss of Dave Whelan following his Wembley injury, while John Bray, his full-back partner, was also confined to the sidelines with injury. Meanwhile, the future of Wembley rebel Derek Dougan was a topic of constant speculation while Peter Dobing had a growing list of admirers who were willing to take him from Ewood Park.

The Lifting of the Maximum Wage

That the Rovers should finish the season in eighth place, the club's highest standing for 27 years, was a tremendous endorsement of the decision to appoint Marshall. Yet the failure to revive public enthusiasm remained a mystery. Admittedly, the Rovers had suffered a major embarrassment in December 1960 when Wrexham eliminated the club from the newly-formed Football League Cup. However, another run in the FA Cup, when the club reached the fifth round, ought to have rekindled interest. That it didn't was a major concern to the club, particularly as the Professional Footballers' Association was committed to the abolition of the maximum wage. At that time the players were able to earn a maximum of £20 a week during the season, and £17 in the summer. With the prospect of industrial action by the players hanging over the game, Reg Taylor (the Blackburn secretary) predicted that clubs would have difficulty in maintaining the current size of playing staffs if the players were successful. Clearly, clubs in the industrial towns of Lancashire, with limited gate revenue, would be at a disadvantage if limits on the maximum wage were lifted. Nonetheless, Harry Leyland, a member of the PFA executive, spelt out the other side of the argument succinctly when he said: 'Our wages and conditions at Ewood Park compare favourably with those of any club in the country, but we are fighting for a principle.'

On 9 January 1961, the maximum wage was abolished, and within the month the players celebrated a victory over their contracts. The game would change forever and nowhere would that be more clearly demonstrated than in the county of Lancashire. The 1960-61 season saw Blackburn, Blackpool, Bolton Wanderers, Burnley and Preston North End all enjoying First Division football, and each club boasting a number of international stars. Eleven years later all of these clubs would be out of the top flight and some, including the Rovers, would have tasted Third Division football. While those problems belonged to the future, the present was not exactly trouble free for

50 Greatest Players

BILL ECKERSLEY Left back

Born: Southport, 16 July 1925

Joined Blackburn: 1947   **From:** High Park

Debut: 1 May 1948 v Manchester United, League

Appearances: 432   **Goals:** 21

Left Blackburn: 1961 (retired)

Honours won with Blackburn: 17 England caps

Eckersley joined the professional ranks in March 1948 and was given his senior debut with the club already doomed to relegation but the following season he was an ever-present. On 2 July 1950, he made his England debut against Spain in the opening round of the World Cup finals in Brazil. He appeared an almost frail figure on the left flank of the Blackburn defence but rarely can the club have had a more tenacious competitor. He combined pace and poise and was never ruffled. A popular and respected figure at the club, he was the natural choice for captain. His international career was brought to a premature end by the visit of the Hungarians to Wembley in November 1953 and his later years at Ewood Park were dogged by injury. He retired at the end of 1960-61 and a crowd of 21,000 turned up at Ewood Park to bid him an emotional farewell. Following his untimely death in October 1982, his ashes were scattered over Ewood Park.

the manager. As he still enjoyed the honeymoon period in the job the manager agreed to sell Peter Dobing to Newcastle United for a fee of £40,000. However, the deal collapsed when the player expressed his reluctance to move. Another deal collapsed when Marshall attempted to unload Chris Crowe to Preston North End. A fee of £27,500 was agreed when the Deepdale club had a last-minute change of heart.

Marshall was clearly unhappy with the firepower at his disposal and towards the end of the campaign he opted to use Fred Pickering, the reserve left back, at centre forward. The move proved more successful than the manager could have hoped for with the raw, but enthusiastic, youngster grabbing seven goals in his ten appearances in the No. 9 shirt. However, the real discovery of the season was Andy McEvoy, a reserve inside forward, who was transformed into an outstanding half back, so much so that he was capped for the Republic of Ireland.

The Rebuilding Begins

The summer of 1961 was a busy one for the manager as he supervised a number of comings and goings to his playing staff. Both Dobing and Dougan finally left Ewood Park with the former joining Manchester City while the latter moved to Aston Villa. Also on his way out of Ewood Park was Ally MacLeod who returned to Scotland to join Hibernian. Marshall proved to be the ideal man to have at the helm at a time when the game was in transition. He was a shrewd operator in the transfer market, and he used the money that had been accrued wisely in bringing several new faces to the club.

The summer had seen Harry Leyland bow out to join Tranmere Rovers, and on the eve of the new campaign the manager pulled off a major coup by signing Fred Else, a former England 'B' international, from Preston North End. With the emergence of Pickering the manager settled for just one new acquisition to his strikeforce and that was Ian Lawther, Sunderland's hard-working inside forward who had been capped by Northern Ireland. To replace MacLeod on the left flank the manager signed another Irish international, Joe Haverty, the diminutive Arsenal and Republic of Ireland winger.

Once again, the apathy of the Blackburn public continued towards the club as was clearly indicated by an attendance of 18,428 for the opening fixture against Cardiff City. This was the smallest opening-day attendance at Ewood Park since before World War II. The uninspiring form displayed by Lawther and Haverty did little to entice the supporters back, and the former was axed after only two games. Fortunately, he returned to form fairly quickly and ended the season with a respectable 14 goals from 37 league

Bryan Douglas slides the ball past the great Gordon Banks from the penalty spot. Blackburn went on to win the match against Leicester City 2-0 on 20 October 1962.

appearances. Sadly, Haverty's decline was rather more serious. He retained his place for the opening 13 games of the season before giving way to Roy Isherwood and then Barrie Ratcliffe. Haverty, who returned to the team late in the season, was placed on the transfer list at his own request.

The 1961-62 season was a rather disappointing affair after the promise of the previous campaign. Sixteenth position in the First Division reflected the lack of consistency that the team had displayed throughout the year. However, once again, the cup games saw the players raise their game to a new height. The Football League Cup brought early-season excitement with Eddie Thomas scoring all four goals in a 4-0 win over Bristol Rovers in a second-round replay at Ewood Park. Having progressed to the semi-final stage of the competition, it was a bitter blow to prestige when the team succumbed to Rochdale over two legs. The FA Cup campaign also ended on a disappointing note with defeat at home to Fulham in a sixth-round replay.

On the brighter side, the club had successfully introduced younger players like Keith Newton, Mike England and John Byrom into the team, and towards the end of the campaign the manager was able to sign Bobby Craig, from Sheffield Wednesday, a player who the manager had been tracking all season. Another player who had caught Marshall's eye was rather closer to home. The manager had noted the performances of Mike Ferguson in the Accrington Stanley forward line and when that club folded he moved quickly to bring him to Ewood Park. The summer of 1962 was uneerily quiet on the transfer front as the manager happily settled to work with the squad that he had at his disposal. The arrival of Mike Harrison from Chelsea in September 1962 was the only addition to the squad that was made throughout the campaign.

For three-quarters of the season, the team appeared to be drifting aimlessly and once again the public of Blackburn gave little indication that its appetite for the game was returning, but there were special moments that stood out. A ten-goal thriller with Arsenal at Ewood Park produced a hard-earned point, and the following week the team travelled to West Bromwich Albion and returned with a 5-2 win. Otherwise, much of the football had been surprisingly drab. Fortunately, the final quarter of the season provided a complete contrast as the team suddenly clicked into another gear.

The forwards became rampant in their quest for goals and ended the season with 79 league goals, more than in any season since promotion in 1957-58. The fulcrum of the attack was, again, Bryan Douglas who was used as both a winger and inside forward during the course of the season. The other success in the front rank was Fred Pickering who, despite looking out of his depth on occasions, managed to score 28 goals in all competitions.

50 Greatest Players

PETER DOBING Forward

Born: Manchester, 1 December 1938

Joined Blackburn: 1955   **From:** Crewe Rangers

Debut: 29 September 1956 v Bristol City, League

Appearances: 205   **Goals:** 104

Left Blackburn: 1961   **For:** Manchester City

Honours won with Blackburn: 7 England Under-23 caps

Peter Dobing belongs to that elite band of footballers who have appeared in 500 or more league games and notched up 200 goals. What makes Dobing remarkable is that after 205 appearances and 104 goals he was still only 22 when he left Blackburn. Even more extraordinary was the fact that he was able to combine his career in professional football with his National Service and still produce these outstanding statistics. A well-built and energetic youngster, his main attributes were pace and power. He loved to run at defenders and was never afraid to unleash a powerful shot. He could occupy either inside-forward or centre-forward positions with equal aplomb, although it was in the former that he was seen at his best. He was still a teenager when he hit 20 goals from 34 appearances during the promotion campaign of 1957-58 and he looked even better in the top flight. His 24 goals from 40 appearances in 1958-59 included a hat-trick and five two-goal performances.

Keeper Fred Else manages to tip the ball away from the feet of deadly Dennis Law on 2 March 1963. The game against Manchester United finished in a 2-2 draw.

The season ended with a 3-0 win over Tottenham Hotspur at Ewood Park and the game marked the end of the Blackburn career of Matt Woods. After amassing 307 league and cup appearances, the colossus at the heart of the defence left to start a new life in Australia.

Rarely can the club have endured such a season of disappointment as that of 1963-64. It was a classic case of from riches to rags as the club let slip a golden opportunity to clinch the championship. Particularly painful was that the Rovers sold Fred Pickering to Everton, who were one of the main rivals for the title, just as the club was approaching the last lap of the campaign.

Marshall's Misfits

With the Rovers finishing seventh, it was a far cry from the heights that were scaled in the first half of the campaign. Marshall, who was known throughout the game as 'Jolly Jack', certainly brought a smile to the faces of the fans during the opening months of the 1963-64 campaign. He had assembled a team that became known as 'Marshall's Misfits' because of his happy knack of successfully moving players from their original positions. Keith Newton, Mike England, Andy McEvoy and Fred Pickering were perfect examples of this.

Title pretensions were there for all to see when Tottenham Hotspur were demolished 7-2 at Ewood Park on 7 September 1963. With Douglas pulling the strings, the Rovers completely overwhelmed the all-star line up from White Hart Lane. The chief executioner that day was Andy McEvoy who

Marshall, having converted him into a half back, transferred back into the front division with dramatic effect. Four goals came from the Irishman that day to illustrate how Marshall had turned him into a goalpoacher supreme.

The twin spearhead of Pickering and McEvoy wrought havoc with the best of defences, thanks to the subtle playmaking of Douglas. With Ferguson and Harrison offering a permanent threat from the flanks, the Ewood outfit became a force to be reckoned with in the First Division. Between 9 November and Boxing Day the Rovers won seven and drew one of a sequence of eight games. Unfortunately, the season reached its peak for the Rovers at Upton Park on Boxing Day when they romped to an 8-2 win with Pickering and McEvoy notching up hat-tricks. Two days after the victory at Upton Park the Hammers visited Ewood and won 3-1.

League form suddenly became patchy and the FA Cup delivered a major shock when the Rovers slumped to a 3-1 defeat at Oxford United. In a bid to shore up the squad, the Rovers paid £10,000 for Walter Joyce, a utility player from Burnley. However, it was then that the directors were rocked with a transfer request from Fred Pickering. Having found himself on the fringe of the England team, the Blackburn number nine wanted to maximize his earnings at the height of his career. The directors were reluctant to meet his wage demands and felt that it would be in the club's best interests to place Pickering on the transfer list. Everton were quick to pounce, and on 10 March 1964 the player moved to Goodison Park for a fee of £80,000.

To fill the void left by Pickering the Rovers moved swiftly to sign George Jones, a promising young forward, who was playing Second Division football with Bury. The 18-year-old England youth international signed at 2pm on 13 March 1964 and then dashed down to Birmingham so that he could make his first appearance that evening at St Andrew's. He made a dream debut, despite the fact that he arrived at the ground only seven minutes before the kickoff, and scored one of the goals that helped to give the Rovers a share of the spoils in a 2-2 draw.

In a bizarre quirk of fate, the week after the Birmingham game the visitors to Ewood Park were none other than Everton. The game was of vital importance as both clubs were chasing a championship dream. A tense affair was made all the more bitter by the return of Pickering, and he quickly incurred the displeasure of the crowd and referee with a crude challenge on Mike England that earned him a booking. However, England and his colleagues managed to keep Pickering subdued throughout the match. With Roy Vernon (another former Ewood favourite) suspended, Everton's attack was not up to its usual potency. Twice the Rovers struck the woodwork

50 Greatest Players

MATT WOODS Centre half

Born: Skelmersdale, 1 November 1931

Joined Blackburn: 1956   **From:** Everton

Debut: 24 November 1956 v Middlesbrough, League

Appearances: 307   **Goals:** 3

Left Blackburn: 1963   **For:** Hakoah (Australia)

Matt Woods must rank as one of the best buys that Blackburn Rovers have ever made. For a paltry £6,000 the club acquired a colossus, a centre half who displayed the grit and determination that inspired colleagues and captured the hearts of supporters. He joined Everton as a youngster in November 1949 but had made just eight league appearances before moving to Blackburn. He was the fearless lynchpin of the famous half-back line of Clayton, Woods and McGrath, three players who epitomized what being a model professional was all about. An ever-present during the promotion campaign of 1957-58, Woods was regarded as one of the finest uncapped centre halves of his generation. He had the knack of being able to intimidate opponents who were physically bigger than himself and strength, perfectly timed tackles and sound positional play were at the core of his game. He retired from the English game at the age of 32 and emigrated to Australia where he played for the Hakoah club.

before Douglas finally opened the scoring. However, from that moment on, fate decreed that the points would go elsewhere. Against the run of play, the Evertonians equalized and five minutes from time a Mike Harrison goal was wrongly ruled out because of offside. The travesty was complete in the last minute when Derek Temple scored to win the game for Everton.

The defeat, and the manner of it, proved an enormous disappointment for all at Ewood Park. The remainder of the season was nothing more than total anti-climax. The Everton game was the first of five successive defeats as the team fell apart at the seams. As the season came to a close, there was a genuine belief that Jones, who had been bought to replace Pickering, was more suited to the role of inside forward. As the club were already well served in this department, it made the need for a swashbuckling No. 9 all the more urgent.

William Westall, the long-time football correspondent of *The Blackburn Times*, summed up the 1964-65 campaign with unerring accuracy when he described it as 'another dish of sweet and sour' as the club finished in tenth position in the First Division. There were sparkling goal feasts throughout

Fred Pickering switched from full back to centre forward to become a deadly striker.

the season, with four goals being scored on six occasions, while the team managed five in a further four matches. Yet in the League Cup, the same team allowed Workington to score five at Ewood Park, and inflict a highly embarrassing defeat on the club. There were games that provided splendid entertainment for the Ewood public, and yet there were other home games that were shoddy in the extreme. Even the supporters proved to be increasingly fickle in their support of the club. The visit of Manchester United on 3 April 1965 produced a gate of 29,363, and yet just a couple of weeks earlier only 8,990 turned up for the visit of West Ham United.

The first-team squad was strengthened in March 1965 with the arrival of George Sharples from Everton, but there was much criticism about the lack of experienced reserves to step into the senior team. Ironically, the club had been grooming several young players from the North East in the reserves and such was their success at this level that the club captured the Central League title for the first time in the club's history.

Humiliated and Relegated

The 1965-66 season was a complete fiasco. While some of the factors that led to relegation were within the scope of the club to affect, there were others that left officials impotent. When all these factors were put together, they resulted in a season that saw the club embarrassingly stranded at the foot of the table with a meagre haul of just 20 points. A short pre-season tour of Holland produced two excellent performances with the Rovers beating Blauw-Wit FC 5-1 and GVAV Groningen 4-0. However, when the team returned to Lancashire it found Blackburn in the grip of a polio epidemic. There was no alternative but to cancel the opening league fixtures and, as a result, the club found itself playing 'catch-up' throughout the season.

Anchored at the foot of the table from the beginning, and becoming increasingly short of match practice, it was perhaps not surprising that the first eight games produced just one win and seven defeats. Another telling factor in these defeats was that Bryan Douglas missed the first seven games of the season due to injury. Deprived of his scheming qualities, the forward line had a look of paucity about it with only McEvoy providing any real threat. When Douglas returned for a five-match sequence in late September and early October the team offered a little more threat to the opposition, and enjoyed a memorable 4-1 win against Burnley at Turf Moor. In a bid to find extra firepower, Jack Marshall had been forced to move Mike England into the centre-forward position for the game at Burnley, and the Welsh international responded with the opening goal.

The experiment with England continued until January 1966, but while his presence in the attack offered a greater physical threat, his

Johnny Byrom scored 25 goals from 40 league games in the 1964-65 season.

absence from defence put a greater strain on the rest of the back four. Marshall had been left with little option but to give youth its chance, and Dick Mulvaney was promoted to fill the gap left by England at the heart of the defence. Other youngsters were also given their chance, with Billy Wilson coming in at full back and Malcolm Darling being given his opportunity in the forward line on the right wing. The introduction of Darling allowed Mike Ferguson to move to inside forward to replace Douglas, who had finally succumbed to a long-term cartilage injury.

While the mercurial Ferguson was a formidable opponent on his day, the loss of Douglas was a devastating blow to the club. The loss of the midfield

50 Greatest Players

MIKE ENGLAND MBE Centre half

Born: Greenfield, North Wales, 2 December 1941

Joined Blackburn: 1957   **From:** School

Debut: 3 October 1959 v Preston North End, League

Appearances: 184   **Goals:** 21

Left Blackburn: August 1966   **For:** Tottenham Hotspur

Honours won with Blackburn: 20 Wales caps, 11 Wales Under-23 caps

At Ewood Park, Mike England developed into one of the finest, most versatile central defenders of his generation. His early senior appearances found him switching between wing half, centre half and full back. He possessed all the qualities of an outstanding defender – he was commanding in the air, had deceptive speed, was strong in the tackle and sound in his positional play. However, he was also blessed with an adroit touch that enabled him to control the ball in an instant and his distribution was almost radar-like in its accuracy. During the 1965-66 campaign he displayed other qualities when asked to play as a makeshift centre forward for several months, and he celebrated his first game in this position with the opening goal in a 4-1 win at Burnley. Following relegation, he moved to Tottenham Hotspur and went on to appear in over 300 league games for the White Hart Lane club. During his career he won FA Cup, League Cup and UEFA Cup winners' medals and represented Wales on 44 occasions.

genius had an immediate affect on the form of McEvoy and Byrom as goalscorers. Chances became few and far between and both players suffered a crisis of confidence in league games. Indeed, McEvoy found himself being used as a half back during mid-season as the manager shuffled the pack in search of an elusive winning combination. For a time, George Jones looked like he might be an unlikely saviour but, after scoring nine goals in nine games, injury forced him out of the picture.

A 4-2 win over Newcastle United at Ewood Park in early November suggested that all was not lost, and there were impressive wins against Nottingham Forest and Northampton Town at Ewood before Christmas. Unfortunately, the team was unable to put a run of results together and these isolated victories did little to lift the club away from the danger zone.

If McEvoy and Byrom were a disappointment in the league their form in the FA Cup was almost dazzling by comparison. In reaching the sixth round of the competition, McEvoy notched up six goals from the same number of games while Byrom hit seven goals in five matches. However, when the club

Keith Newton played over 350 times for Blackburn and collected 19 full England caps.

slipped to a 2-1 home defeat to Sheffield Wednesday, in the sixth round, the goals once again began to dry up.

Desperate to strengthen his squad, Marshall failed in a bold move to bring Terry Hennessey, Birmingham City's Welsh international midfield star, to Ewood Park. Other innovative moves to strengthen his attacking options also failed with Huddersfield Town rejecting a bid to take Allan Gilliver from Leeds Road to lead the Blackburn attack. Attempts to sign Colin Bell from Bury and Wyn Davies from Bolton Wanderers also met with disappointment. In a last-ditch bid to add some badly needed punch to his lacklustre attack the manager bought Martin Britt, an England youth international, from West Ham United in March 1966. Britt was a little-known reserve at West Ham who, ironically, had made his debut for the Hammers against the Rovers in May 1963.

The situation was too far gone for the inexperienced Britt to have any real affect on it. He was dropped after three games and although he was quickly recalled his eight appearances failed to produce a goal. The last 13 league games brought one win and 12 defeats as the club surrendered its First Division life in the meekest of circumstances. Indeed, 18 of the last 21 matches were lost and it was little wonder that crowds fell alarmingly. The average home attendance of 13,513 was the lowest recorded since 1934-35.

Chapter Eight: 1966-75
The Road to Oblivion

While the rest of the nation spent of the summer of 1966 enthralled by the World Cup, the thoughts of the ever-dwindling band of Blackburn fans were preoccupied with relegation. Although the directors decided to keep faith with the manager, they were reluctant to offer him a new contract. Fortunately, Marshall didn't make an issue of this and offered to continue without any long-term security. Both manager and directors were keen to make use of the money that they had tried to spend during the previous campaign. Thus, while Alf Ramsey plotted to capture the Jules Rimet trophy, Jack Marshall began to rebuild his shattered Blackburn team. The news that Mike England had stated his wish to remain in the First Division meant that the club, at some point during the summer, would be assured a sizeable cheque.

It was hardly surprising that the first signature he obtained was that of a goalscorer. Having failed to capture Allan Gilliver from Huddersfield Town during the previous campaign, the manager wasted no time in returning to Leeds Road to succeed where he had failed before. The tall and strongly-built centre forward was seen as the ideal man to lead the attack and it was

Andy McEvoy takes on Norwich's Kevin Keelan in a 0-0 draw on 22 October 1966.

hoped that he would form an effective partnership with McEvoy. The position of goalkeeper was one that had become a matter of urgency following the decision of the club to release Fred Else on a free transfer. The man chosen to fill the position was John Barton, a former deputy to Else at Preston North End. Having made his debut for Preston as a 16-year-old, Barton had found it impossible to win a regular spot at Deepdale, as first Else and then Alan Kelly restricted his senior outings. He had made just 48 appearances for Preston in seven seasons and therefore jumped at the opportunity of establishing himself at Ewood Park.

The third summer signing was Barrie Hole from Cardiff City. A regular member of the Welsh international team, Hole was regarded as one of the finest attacking midfield players in Britain. Unfortunately, he wasn't to have the opportunity to play alongside Mike England, his Welsh team-mate. On the eve of the new campaign the Rovers accepted an offer in the region of £95,000 from Tottenham Hotspur for their talented centre half. In the wake of England's World Cup triumph optimism even pervaded the terraces of

50 Greatest Players

MICK McGRATH Half back

Born: Dublin, 7 April 1936

Joined Blackburn: 1954   **From:** Home Farm

Debut: 28 April 1956 v Nottingham Forest, League

Appearances: 312   **Goals:** 12

Left Blackburn: 1966   **For:** Bradford

Honours won with Blackburn: 18 Republic of Ireland caps

Mick McGrath was a model professional throughout his career. As one third of the famous half-back line of Clayton, Woods and McGrath, his niche in the history of Blackburn Rovers is assured. Although he tended to be a more defensive half back, thereby allowing Ronnie Clayton to surge forward and support the attack, McGrath notched up a couple of vital goals during the FA Cup run of 1960-61, before having the misfortune to concede an own goal at Wembley. Originally spotted while playing with Home Farm, he was groomed in the Central League team before getting his opportunity when Ken Clayton broke his leg. He made the left-half spot his own and was an ever-present during the successful promotion campaign of 1957-58. A player who always gave 100 per cent, McGrath was also a remarkably consistent performer and retained his first-team place until March 1965. On 6 November 1965, he became the first Blackburn player to be substituted under the new rule that allowed an injured player to be replaced. He won 18 full caps for the Republic of Ireland while with the Rovers.

Winger Mike Harrison blasts the ball past Bury's Chris Harker from the penalty spot in a match that Blackburn went on to win 2-1 on 8 October 1966.

Ewood Park, and early season results suggested that this optimism might be well founded. Five of the first seven league games were won and a sixth produced a point. However, following a 4-1 home win against Cardiff City the wheels began to fall off the promotion wagon. A trip to Wolves – strongly fancied to challenge the Rovers for promotion – ended in a worrying 4-0 defeat.

The response from the Ewood boardroom was to sanction the transfer of John Connelly from Manchester United for a fee in the region of £40,000. This was a major coup as Connelly had featured for England in the opening game of the World Cup finals. Although he was to lose his place, due to a tactical reshuffle, he was still very much in the international eye. Indeed, just days before joining the Rovers he had been the star of the Football League team that enjoyed a 12-0 win over the Irish League at Home Park, Plymouth. Connelly himself had scored two goals, and although he had had offers from both First Division Blackpool and Burnley, he rejected them for Ewood Park.

While the capture of Connelly delighted the Ewood faithful, there were other problems facing Marshall that threatened to undermine a promotion push. George Sharples, who had lost his place to Hole, requested a transfer and Andy McEvoy had talks with the manager about his future. Marshall was also required to persuade Dave Holt, Mulvaney's understudy at centre half, from quitting the game altogether. In October, the club was faced with a transfer request from George Jones, another player who found himself on the fringe of first-team activities. With Dick Mulvaney absent from the team following a perforated eardrum the manager attempted to exchange Jones for George Kinnell, the Oldham Athletic centre half, but the deal collapsed. The absence of Mulvaney gave both Holt and Ben Anderson a chance to

50 Greatest Players

ANDY McEVOY Half back/Inside forward

Born: Dublin, 15 July 1938

Joined Blackburn: 1956   **From:** Bray Wanderers

Debut: 20 April 1959 v Luton Town, League

Appearances: 213   **Goals:** 103

Left Blackburn: 1967   **For:** Limerick

Honours won with Blackburn: 17 Republic of Ireland caps

When he arrived, McEvoy was regarded as little more than a workmanlike inside forward, although he did mark his senior debut with a brace of goals. He was gradually converted into an attacking half back, but was largely restricted to the role of understudy. McEvoy's career at Blackburn was finally transformed when Jack Marshall decided that the player should revert to his former inside-forward role. The closing stages of 1962-63 saw the manager experiment with him as a strike partner for Fred Pickering. The switch saw him become a goalscorer supreme. His lightning quick speed of thought and movement, coupled with his deadly finishing, made him the perfect foil for the more physical Pickering. In 1963-64, he hit 32 goals from 37 league games to finish as the club's leading marksman and became the first player since Tommy Briggs, in 1956-57, to hit the 30-goal mark for the club. The following season found McEvoy with a new partner, John Byrom, but his eye for goal remained undiminished. His 29 goals enabled him to become the First Division's joint-leading goalscorer alongside no less a marksman than Jimmy Greaves.

claim a place alongside Ronnie Clayton in the centre of defence. Neither made a lasting impression on the manager and hence his decision to turn to Sharples. Although the former Evertonian was more familiar with the traditional half-back role, he quickly formed an effective partnership with Clayton.

The greatest problem facing the manager was the loss of Allan Gilliver through a back injury that turned out to be a slipped disc. While the player underwent surgery, the Rovers entered negotiations with Huddersfield Town regarding the fitness of the player at the time of his move to Ewood Park. The matter was taken to the Football League and a commission ruled that the Yorkshire club should repay some £18,000 of the fee paid for Gilliver. The case was to have far-reaching affects as it led to stringent medical examinations becoming a routine part of any transfer deal. Problems continued to mount for the manager. No matter how he juggled his resources, he found that good results continued to be elusive. Between 17 September and 5 November 1966, a sequence of nine games produced just one win.

It was towards the end of this sequence that the directors decided to make a major change to the backroom staff. Former Ewood favourite, Eddie Quigley, was invited to rejoin the club in the role of chief coach. Quigley, who was the manager of Stockport County at the time, requested the title of assistant manager before agreeing to make the switch. The directors were only too happy to agree to his wishes. In announcing the return of Quigley, the directors gave assurances with regard to the future of existing staff members Jimmy Gordon and Eric Bell. However, Quigley was given complete control of coaching throughout the club.

The Return of Quigley

Quigley took up his duties on 31 October 1966 and immediately began to tinker with the tactics that the team employed. Always an astute tactician, Quigley felt that with Douglas and Hole in midfield the team required a little more aggression in the middle of the park. He opted to give Douglas a free role and ask Walter Joyce to move from full back and employ his no-nonsense approach to tackling in the midfield. He used Joyce as a man marker with the simple instruction to stop the key playmaker in the opposition from functioning. It was a job that Joyce was well suited to.

Despite the serious injury to Gilliver the club parted company with George Jones in November 1966, allowing him to return to Bury. This left the Ewood

attack perilously threadbare, so Quigley recommended that the club should purchase Frank Lord from his former club. The Stockport centre forward was approaching the twilight of a career that had largely been spent in the lower divisions. His no frills approach had been particularly effective at that level and he had a reputation for being a good header of the ball. Sadly, the move to Second Division football came rather too late in his career to be a success and after just one goal in ten games he was axed. At the end of the season he joined the coaching staff to look

Eddie Quigley discusses tactics with mutton-chop-whiskered striker, Jim Fryatt.

after the junior players before embarking on his travels again to try and revive his playing career with Chesterfield in August 1967. A disappointing exit from the FA Cup, at the hands of Carlisle United, increased the pressure on Jack Marshall who was facing mounting criticism about the inability of the team to make much impact on the promotion race. During the course of the campaign, Marshall had had to appease a growing number of players who had become unsettled at the club. Disenchanted with the situation in which he found himself, Marshall tendered his resignation and left Ewood Park on 10 February 1967.

The directors immediately installed Quigley as caretaker manager and the players responded with a sequence of results that took the club into the heart of the promotion race. The key fixture in this battle was the clash at Ewood Park on Easter Saturday between the Rovers and second-placed Coventry City. In front of a crowd of 26,380, the promotion dream died as the Rovers committed football suicide. Things began to go astray when Ferguson became embroiled in a scuffle with Dietmar Bruck, the Coventry full back, before half-time. The referee took the view that Ferguson had used an elbow on his opponent and ordered him from the field. Within five minutes of the restart a Ronnie Rees cross was floated into the Blackburn area. John Barton failed to collect and in a flash Bobby Gould pounced to bundle the ball into the net. This was the first league goal that the team had conceded at Ewood Park since the 2-2 draw with Portsmouth on 5 November 1966. It was enough to burst the promotion bubble and the Rovers ended the season in fourth place.

Striker Don Martin, centre, was one of the only shining lights of the dismal 1967-68 season, here seen with Malcolm Darling, left, being denied by Carlisle keeper, Alan Ross.

50 Greatest Players

MIKE FERGUSON Outside right/Midfield

Born: Burnley, 9 March 1943

Joined Blackburn: 1962   **From:** Accrington Stanley

Debut: 18 August 1962 v Ipswich Town, League

Appearances: 249   **Goals:** 36

Left Blackburn: 1968   **For:** Aston Villa

Mike Ferguson was possibly one of the most gifted players of his era, but he could also be totally frustrating and was prone to the odd lapse of discipline on the field. If the complete package was flawed, his brilliance was beyond question. 'Fergie' arrived at Blackburn in an unusual fashion following the demise of Accrington Stanley. He was actually training with Burnley when he became the target of both the Rovers and Preston North End. Fortunately, Jack Marshall located him more quickly than Jimmy Milne, the Preston boss. Originally an inside forward, Marshall converted him into an outside right and he blossomed into a tricky individualist. Ferguson revelled in the attacking style of football that Marshall preached and as a natural crowd pleaser he scored many memorable goals. The pick of the bunch was undoubtedly at Aston Villa in September 1964 when he beat six defenders, calmly walked around the goalkeeper and then put the ball into the net. The other side of the Ferguson coin was seen at Ewood Park on Easter Saturday 1967 when he contrived to get himself sent off in a vital promotion clash with Coventry City that the Rovers went on to lose.

The directors had appointed Quigley as manager on 19 April 1967, and the summer was spent trying to strengthen the squad for yet another promotion push. Although the manager had earmarked Fred Pickering, (the former Ewood favourite) as his main transfer target, he launched a bid for Tony Leighton, the Huddersfield Town forward, and John Coddington, a vastly experienced centre half who had been at Huddersfield since September 1953. While Coddington agreed to leave Leeds Road, Leighton refused because he was reluctant to move his home into the Blackburn area. Another move that was successfully completed was the capture of Adam Blacklaw from Burnley. The former Scottish international keeper was a veteran of 318 First Division games for the 'Clarets'. Throughout the summer, the proposed move for Pickering continued to rumble on until the Rovers dramatically withdrew from the deal with the result that the player moved to Birmingham City.

The 1967-68 season was yet another bitterly disappointing campaign. After a bright start the team was well placed for promotion, but the second half of the season resulted in them fading from the picture. Once again, a lack of goals was the main problem. In 1966-67, the team had managed to score just 56 goals and an identical total in 1967-68 condemned the club to eighth position in the table. Unfortunately, the fade-out had occurred earlier than 12 months previously and the final weeks of the season found a general mood of apathy envelop Ewood Park. As the crowds had drifted away, the only redeeming feature had been the form of Don Martin, a talented centre forward who had been signed from Northampton Town in February 1968. Although not suggesting that he might be the prolific goalscorer that was so urgently required, he displayed outstanding football qualities.

Second Division football, and the continual ebb of support, meant that the club began the 1968-69 campaign with a reported loss of £84,723. While the directors refuted claims that Keith Newton would be sold to cover the losses, some general housekeeping was required. The emergence of Stuart Metcalfe enabled the club to sell Mike Ferguson to Aston Villa for £50,000, while Ben Anderson, a reserve centre half, who had enjoyed a modicum of success as a makeshift centre forward, was sold to Bury for £10,000. In September 1968, a further £60,000 was received when Aston Villa snapped up Barrie Hole. The only new face at Ewood Park during the summer of 1968 was Les Chappell, the Rotherham United forward who arrived in a straight swap for Allan Gilliver.

The season began with the team again taking up a prominent position among the promotion-chasing pack. Once again, a lack of goals threatened to undermine any realistic hope of making it to the top flight. On only three occasions did the team manage to register more than one

Adam Blacklaw appeared 110 times for the Rovers, here seen collecting a cross as centre half John Coddington looks on.

50 Greatest Players

RONNIE CLAYTON Wing half

Born: Preston, Lancashire, 5 August 1934

Joined Blackburn: 1949   **From:** School

Debut: 25 April 1951 v Queens Park Rangers, League

Appearances: 665   **Goals:** 16

Left Blackburn: 1969   **For:** Morecambe

Honours won with Blackburn: 35 England caps, 6 England Under-23 caps

Ronnie Clayton was the epitome of the perfect club professional. His illustrious career cannot be measured in medals – by staying loyal to the Ewood Park outfit he missed out on those – but he captured the hearts of the Blackburn public. Like Crompton before him, Clayton not only captained the Rovers but also went on to become the England skipper. A total of 35 England caps illustrated the esteem in which he was held nationally as well as locally. A powerful wing half, Clayton was a dominant presence in the 1957-58 promotion-winning team. He arrived at Ewood in the summer of 1949 with his younger brother Ken and, by the mid-1950s, both occupied half-back positions in the Ewood first team. While Ken's career was ended by injury, Ronnie went from strength to strength. Strong in the tackle and good in the air, Clayton was an outstanding defender. However, he also possessed a natural athleticism that enabled him to drive the team forward from midfield. Whatever role he was asked to undertake the man simply oozed class. During his later years at the club he dropped into the centre of the back four and played the role of centre back as if he had been born for the position.

goal in the opening 12 league fixtures. It was in a bid to remedy this that £25,000 was paid to Stockport County for Jim Fryatt in October 1968. Like Frank Lord before him, the moustachioed, mutton-chop-whiskered Fryatt had built up a reputation in the lower divisions. The burly striker was particularly powerful in the air and his debut resulted in a 3-1 away win at Bury. While always a constant threat in the opposition area, Fryatt, like Martin, seemed better suited to creating chances rather than snapping them up. He managed just three goals in 24 league games while Martin notched up ten goals in 38 league outings.

The failure in front of goal began to sap the confidence of the team and long before the end of the campaign the club found itself in freefall. Sufficient points had been garnered earlier in the campaign to avoid relegation but the season ended with the Rovers in 19th place in the Second Division – the lowest placing in the history of the club at that point. It was a tragic way for two of the club's greatest servants, Ronnie Clayton and Bryan Douglas, to bow out as both had announced their intentions to retire.

The 1968-69 season proved to be something of a watershed in the history of the Rovers. In January 1969, the club announced a change to the management structure at the club with Johnny Carey returning to Ewood Park in the role of administrative manager. The idea behind the move was to allow Eddie Quigley to spend more time on the coaching field and less on administrative matters. The summer of 1969 was a busy one for the managerial duo following the disastrous season. Since relegation from the First Division in 1966, the Rovers had been caught up in a whirlpool of despair that seemed intent on pulling the club down. In a bid to rid the club of the shackles of stagnation, the directors sanctioned the signing of Allan Hunter from Oldham Athletic, Ken Knighton from Preston North End and Brian Hill from Huddersfield Town. The total cost of this new infusion of talent was said to be in the region of £100,000. A further change saw the departure of Jimmy Gordon as first-team trainer and the promotion of Brian Birch, the

50 Greatest Players

BRYAN DOUGLAS Winger

Born: Blackburn, Lancashire, 27 May 1934

Joined Blackburn: 1952   **From:** Lower Darwen Youth Club

Debut: 4 September 1954 v Notts County, League

Appearances: 503   **Goals:** 115

Left Blackburn: 1969   **For:** Great Harwood

Honours won with Blackburn: 36 England caps, 5 England Under-23 caps

As a boy, growing up in the shadow of the Ewood Park floodlights, Bryan Douglas had one ambition and that was to play for his beloved Blackburn Rovers. He signed professional forms in April 1952, but 'Duggie', as he was popularly known, not only achieved his dream but went on to become one of the outstanding figures in the history of the club. A winger in the mould of Stan Matthews and Tom Finney, he had an immaculate touch for instant control. This skill, coupled with a sleight of foot and perfect balance, empowered him to mesmerize defenders with his dribbling. International honours came his way as he became recognized as one of the finest players of his generation. Douglas could operate on the flank or at inside forward as he had an innate sense of when to pass the ball and when to take on an opponent. Once the poker-faced maestro had decided to beat a defender he could take the ball to within touching distance of his opponent before jinking his way past. It was impossible to over-estimate his importance to the team, as demonstrated in the relegation season of 1965-66 when Douglas was sidelined for all but 16 games.

Bryan Douglas appeared 503 times for the Rovers and was an immense figure in the history of the club.

youth coach, to the position of chief coach. The club appeared to undergo a professional transformation with the new coach putting his charges through a testing pre-season regime.

The team also underwent a major tactical switch to the 4-3-3 formation, with Stuart Metcalfe and Eamonn Rogers linking with Knighton in midfield. Behind them Hunter slotted into the middle of the back four alongside Dick Mulvaney, with Keith Newton and Billy Wilson operating at full back. The vastly experienced Blacklaw remained in goal with Barton being retained as his deputy. If a weakness remained it was in the front division, with Martin asked to be the spearhead, flanked by John Connelly and Hill.

Although reservations remained about goal scoring, the season opened brightly with three wins and two draws. Once again, the autumn found the club among the leading candidates for promotion. There appeared to be a new belief in the squad and by Christmas the First Division appeared to beckon. Unfortunately, the club had been unable to win back the crowds in sufficient numbers to ease the financial position at Ewood Park. In December 1969, the club finally accepted an offer for Keith Newton, an England international and a player who had been on the transfer list at his own request. The departure of Newton for Everton proved to be the signal for the start of another inexplicable decline.

With little money available, it had been a surprise when £30,000 was invested in the purchase of Roger Jones, an England Under-23 international goalkeeper from Bournemouth, and supporters would have to wait before discovering how wisely this money had been spent as Jones suffered a serious groin injury in only his fourth game for the club and was ruled out for the remainder of the campaign.

A depressingly familiar slump in fortunes resulted in the Rovers finishing the season in eighth position. The close season merely reflected the quandary in which the club now found itself – in need of quality players but without the fan base from which to finance them. The final game of the 1969-70 season had seen the attendance drop to just 7,336. Grasping the nettle the directors found sufficient funds to allow Quigley to buy Jimmy Kerr from Bury who was an immensely talented midfield player and a much sought-after commodity. His quality was reflected in the fee of £60,000, a new club record for the Rovers. However, with all of the financial resources earmarked for Kerr, the manager had to shop in the bargain basement department for his other new players.

A swap was arranged with Norwich City that took Malcolm Darling to Carrow Road in exchange for Bryan Conlon, a tall, raw-boned No. 9 whose record was hardly one of prolific goal scoring. The final acquisition for the senior squad was Alex Russell, a neat and tidy midfield man, who came from Southport in exchange for reserve full back, Laurie Calloway. In view of the pattern of previous seasons, a good start followed by a dramatic collapse,

50 Greatest Players

KEITH NEWTON Full back

Born: Manchester, 23 June 1941

Joined Blackburn: 1958   **From:** Spurley Hey Youth Club

Debut: 19 September 1960 v Chelsea, League

Appearances: 357   **Goals:** 10

Left Blackburn: 1969   **For:** Everton

Honours won with Blackburn: 19 England caps, 4 Under-23 caps

Keith Newton was a product of the youth system at Blackburn. Originally a gangling inside forward, Newton played at both centre half and left half during his time with the youth team. Although he made his senior debut at left half, the 1961-62 season found him as first-choice left back. Tall and athletic, Newton developed into a cultured, attacking full back. He had the pace to track the speediest of wingers and was immaculate in the tackle. Exceptionally good in the air, Newton also possessed the ability to read the game and anticipate a problem before it arose. The arrival of Walter Joyce and the emergence of Billy Wilson saw Newton switched to right back and he was soon collecting England honours at Under-23 level. He gained his first full cap against West Germany in February 1966 and was unfortunate to miss out on the squad for that summer's World Cup finals. He remained at Blackburn following relegation to the Second Division and was sufficiently versatile to be used in midfield on occasions. He became a regular in the England team during the late 1960s and in December 1969 he finally left Ewood to join Everton.

alarm bells began to ring when the team won just one of the opening 13 league games. The situation was made worse by the fact that Martin had broken his ankle in the third game of the campaign. The manager had also had to make do without Kerr for the opening five matches due to injury. The former Bury player would again be sidelined after only 11 appearances with an injury that would force him into premature retirement.

A difference of opinion over tactics between Brian Birch and Eddie Quigley had resulted in the former leaving Ewood Park for a coaching appointment in Turkey on the eve of the new season. This had led to the promotion of Ken Waterhouse to the post of trainer-coach from his post with the Central League team. However, harmony on the coaching staff did not last long. In October, the directors acted to try to arrest the slide by asking Quigley to swap duties with Johnny Carey. Within a week there was further turmoil when Waterhouse left the club to take a management position with non-league Morecambe. Thus, just two months after taking charge of the second string at Ewood Park, Arthur Proudler found himself promoted to senior coach. The arrival of Carey was broadly welcomed by the Ewood faithful, particularly by those who remembered his earlier stint at the club. However, times had changed and by mid-season the team had only three victories to its name. Nor were the corridors of power immune to the shifts of fortune. In January 1971, William Bancroft, at 39, became the youngest chairman in the club's history.

The new chairman soon found himself fighting for the very existence of the club and, as a result, he made it plain that there would be no money available to strengthen the squad. The seriousness of the financial situation meant that the club had no option but to sell Ken Knighton to Hull City for £60,000. A small amount of money was given to Carey to try and find a saviour who could prevent the impending drop into the Third Division. Carey opted to bring Fred Pickering back into the fold and snapped him up from Blackpool for a moderate fee. Unfortunately, there was to be no happy return for the prodigal son. Plagued by injury and weight problems, Pickering had little chance to resurrect the ailing club. On 27 April 1971, a 2-0 defeat at Queens Park Rangers consigned Blackburn Rovers to the Third Division for the first time in the club's history. On 1 May, a meagre crowd of 3,971 gathered at Ewood Park to witness the 'last rites' as the season came to an end with a draw against Bristol City. To complete a miserable campaign, the Rovers were forced to seek re-election to the Central League.

Three weeks after dropping to the Third Division the club was rocked by a financial bombshell. The club had suffered a loss of £51,178 during the course of the season and the balance deficit now stood at £81,604. The once proud club was in dire need of rejuvenation. As a first step towards recovery the directors sacked the two managers. Quigley vigorously defended his record at Ewood Park and pointed out that he had had no control over the sale of players. He also highlighted the lack of stability at the club. The fact that he had worked with four different chairmen in the previous three years and had also had four different trainer-coaches during a similar period told its own story.

It was entirely fitting that a young chairman should elect to appoint the youngest manager in the history of the club. However, in enticing Ken Furphy away from Watford, the directors had secured not only a young tracksuit manager, but one who had plenty of experience of managing in the lower divisions. Prior to leading Watford into the Second Division, and an

Great Managers – 1953-58 & 1970-71

JOHNNY CAREY

Johnny Carey had enjoyed a glittering playing career with Manchester United and by the time he quit the club to take control at Ewood Park he had been capped 36 times, winning caps for both the Republic and Northern Ireland, and had captained Manchester United to FA Cup success in 1948. In 1949, he had been voted Footballer of the Year and in 1951-52 he led United to the league championship. When he arrived at Ewood Park he announced that he wanted his team to play attractive, attacking football that won matches, and took charge of his own coaching. The progression from successful player to manager is not always an easy journey but for Carey the transition seemed effortless. For four seasons this quiet, pipe-smoking Irishman provided the Blackburn public with a brand of attacking football that produced goals galore. One of his greatest assets was his ability to blend the right players together, and he made a number of shrewd raids into the transfer market without incurring much expense. He was quick to realize that Tommy Briggs required service if he was to plunder the goals that Carey demanded, so he captured two wingers offering very different qualities in Frank Mooney and Bobby Langton.

In 1954-55, the team scored 114 league goals but still failed to gain the ultimate prize of First Division football. After three successive failures to gain promotion, Carey began to rebuild his side during the 1956-57 season. His later teams were built around the exciting young talent that was beginning to blossom at Ewood Park, thus Ronnie Clayton, Bryan Douglas, Peter Dobing and Roy Vernon became the cornerstones of the team. Added to these were a number of other astute signings and Carey hadn't forgotten his roots as a number of young Irish players arrived also, with the most notable being Mick McGrath and Andy McEvoy. Carey finally guided the club to promotion in 1957-58 but the following season he was persuaded to leave Ewood Park to take charge of Everton. He returned to manage playing affairs in October 1970, unfortunately with less success.

Roger Jones saves as Dick Mulvaney looks on shortly before relegation in 1971. Blackburn went on to lose 2-0 against Carlisle on 2 February 1971.

appearance in the FA Cup semi-final, he had been player-manager at Workington. Indeed, he had masterminded the Cumbrian club's victory at Ewood Park in the Football League Cup in 1964-65 at a time when the Rovers were still basking in First Division football.

Within a week of his arrival, the manager sacked coach Arthur Proudler and announced that he would take charge of coaching the senior squad. Richard Dinnis was given the reserve team to look after while Jimmy Kerr took charge of the juniors. The emphasis was clearly on youth and this was reflected in the selection of two 18-year-olds – Gerry MacDonald and David Bradford – for the opening game of the season.

The Furphy Revolution

The season itself evolved into various stages with the opening weeks finding Furphy testing the strengths and weaknesses of his squad. It soon became clear that there was more of the latter than the former as only four points were gained from five games. A mediocre start to the League Cup campaign merely emphasized the need for change and on 9 September 1971 the manager began his Ewood revolution. The first stage of this radical rebuilding resulted in the departure of Allan Hunter to Ipswich Town in exchange for £60,000 and Bobby Bell. At the same time the manager returned to his former club to sign Terry Garbett for £16,000. The campaign then entered a transitional phase that brought a further nine new faces to the club, albeit that one, Terry Shanahan, was only on loan. In the opposite direction the manager used Eamonn Rogers in a swap deal with Charlton Athletic for Barry Endean while Graham Moseley, the third-choice goalkeeper, was sold to Derby County on his 18th birthday for £20,000. The biggest surprise came with the departure of Bobby Bell a fortnight after joining! The manager sold him to Crystal Palace for £50,000 and made a profit of £30,000 for the club.

It was hardly surprising that results should continue to suffer during this period of instability. The Rovers entered November with just three wins behind them and the prospect of a long, hard winter fighting relegation. However, it was the final piece in Furphy's jigsaw that was to transform the season. Mid-November brought the arrival of John McNamee, a big, broad, burly Scot from Newcastle United. Furphy had found a centre half of the old school, one who, although lacking fitness and mobility, had enough presence to inspire those around him. He also knew how to physically intimidate opposing forwards – the Blackburn defence was no longer a soft touch.

With McNamee holding the defence together, and Tony Field, a successful buy from Southport, proving a deadly goalmouth predator, the club ended the season in a comfortable mid-table position. While tenth in the Third Division may have been a fall from grace in terms of its illustrious past, the fact remained that the club had stopped the rot. There was now a platform on which to build for the future. Incredibly, the first season of Third Division football had seen the club produce a profit of £34,959, the first profit that the club had recorded for several years.

An end-of-season-tour of Czechoslovakia provided Furphy with the opportunity for further fine-tuning of his squad. It was on this tour that Ben Arentoft, a Danish international midfielder who had struggled to cope with the rough and tumble of the Third Division, emerged as a classy left back. The tour also provided Barry Endean, a player who'd been struck down with injury and illness, the chance to prove his worth to the manager.

The 1972-73 season opened with just one point from three games. As a result, the manager wasted no time in signing Kit Napier from Brighton & Hove Albion to add to the firepower at his disposal. He also signed Dave Turner, an experienced midfielder, from Brighton. A couple of weeks later Furphy pulled off a major coup by signing John O'Mara from Brentford for £30,000. The lanky striker had been the target of several First Division clubs but had been persuaded that a slumbering giant was about to reawaken at Ewood Park. Unfortunately, that giant still required a gentle prod to get it moving as three times between mid-August and October the team was anchored at the foot of the table. However, the revival, when it came, was dramatic and at the end of the season the club missed out on promotion by a mere three points. Ironically, 12 months later the third-place finish that the Rovers achieved would have gained promotion as the Football League changed its rules during the summer of 1973.

Once again, the club made a disappointing start when the 1973-74 season opened with three wins and six defeats during the first nine league games. However, Furphy again motivated his slow starters to respond in a positive manner and the next nine league games produced six wins and three draws. Contact was again made with the promotion places when the club was rocked by the bombshell that Furphy was quitting to take charge of Sheffield United. Although Bill Bancroft offered to match the terms offered by the Yorkshire club, he couldn't overcome Furphy's desire to manage in the First Division. When Furphy left, Richard Dinnis took over as caretaker manager.

Champions at Last

The loss of Furphy and the delay in appointing a successor proved a serious dent to promotion hopes. Although Dinnis did an excellent job to maintain

continuity, the club found itself in limbo. However, on 14 January 1974, it was announced that Gordon Lee, the Port Vale manager, would take up the position of manager while Dinnis would remain on the coaching staff. Lee was well versed in operating on a shoestring and had won promotion with Vale in 1971. During the latter stages of 1973-74, it became clear that Lee was far from impressed with the squad that he had inherited. Handicapped by injuries and suspensions the manager settled for mid-table respectability but many on the terraces were disappointed with 13th place in the Third Division.

The summer of 1974 brought another metamorphosis at Ewood Park as the team that Furphy built was dismantled and replaced with men of Lee's own choosing. Any lingering doubts among the Ewood

John McNamee (right) became a rock in the defence in 1971 after the slide into Division Three. John O'Mara jumps with him.

faithful with regard to the new manager were dispelled during an opening run that brought just one defeat in the first 12 league games. By combining new signings Ken Beamish, Graham Oates and Graham Hawkins with the likes of Stuart Metcalfe and Tony Parkes, the manager found a winning combination. However, a real masterstroke was the decision to revive the flagging career of Don Martin. Although he was approaching veteran status, Martin, who had either been completely ignored by Furphy or asked to play in the centre of defence, returned to his more familiar role in the attacking line-up. He was rejuvenated to such an extent that he ended the season as the leading goalscorer.

Lee proved himself ready to make tough and controversial decisions and for the first half of the season he put John Waddington ahead of Derek Fazackerley in the pecking order to partner Hawkins in the centre of defence. The early season acquisition of Andy Burgin, a left back from Halifax Town, further strengthened a back four that was proving difficult to break down. Indeed, it wasn't until December 1974 that the first real blip occurred when Hereford United pulled off an unlikely 6-2 win over the Rovers at Edgar Street. Fazackerley returned to the defence as did the team to winning ways.

It wasn't until February 1975 that supporters had genuine cause for concern with regard to the promotion drive. A 1-0 home defeat at the hands of Peterborough United was made all the more painful by the fact that Jimmy Mullen broke his leg in the game. Three days later the club was toppled from the top of the table following defeat at second-placed Plymouth

In the vital promotion-clinching clash against Plymouth Argyle on 15 February 1975, Mike Hickman scored two vital goals, here seen steering one past Jim Furnell.

Great Matches

FOOTBALL LEAGUE DIVISION THREE   Ewood Park, 15 February 1975

Blackburn Rovers 5   **Plymouth Argyle 2**   Attendance: 17,818

Blackburn	Plymouth
Beamish	McAuley
Martin 2	Delve
Hickman 2	

Eleven days earlier the two sides had met at Home Park and the Rovers had lost by the odd goal in three. This had been their second defeat in three days and as a result Plymouth had leapfrogged above them to head the Third Division table. The visitors took the lead after 15 minutes when Hugh McAuley put Plymouth ahead and two minutes after the breakthrough John Delve met a corner and back-headed the ball into the Blackburn net while the Rovers' defence stood still. Despondency deepened when Jim Furnell saved a Don Martin penalty. On the brink of half-time, Martin made amends by sending a cross into the Plymouth goalmouth which Graham Oates headed back across the face of the goal where Ken Beamish stooped to head the ball into the empty net.

In the second half the Rovers midfield began to dominate. Metcalfe crossed to Beamish at the far post who sent his header to the opposite post where Martin planted the ball in the roof of the net.

Gordon Lee stood on the touchline and waved his troops forward. Within two minutes of Martin's goal, Mike Hickman pounced to poke the ball past the advancing Furnell – the Rovers were in the lead. Hickman and Beamish chased and harried defenders as error after error was made. A through ball caught the Plymouth back line static and appealing in vain for offside. Beamish shot, Furnell saved and Hickman slotted the rebound into the back of the net. The visitors were still reeling from this when Hickman hit an angled cross-shot past the stranded Furnell for Martin to calmly tap it over the line shortly before the referee signalled the end of one of Ewood Park's finest afternoons.

Blackburn Rovers: Jones, Heaton, Burgin, Metcalfe, Hawkins, Fazackerley, Beamish, Oates, Hickman, Parkes, Martin

Plymouth Argyle: Furnell, Hore, Burrows, Saxton, Green, Delve, Randell, Johnson, Mariner, Rafferty, McAuley

Referee: K. MacNally (Ellesmere Port)

Argyle. The response of the manager was to sign Mike Hickman from Grimsby Town. The new man made an immediate impact on his debut when he came off the bench and scored in a 2-1 win over Bury at Gigg Lane.

The week after the win at Bury brought Plymouth to Ewood Park for a vital top-of-the-table clash. The match developed into a real test of character when the Rovers found themselves two goals down early on. With the

Great Managers – 1974-75

GORDON LEE

Gordon Lee only spent a season and half at Ewood Park but it proved sufficient time for him to leave an indelible mark on the club. In Lee, the directors had found a man who was well versed in surviving, indeed, prospering on a shoestring budget. Prior to moving to Lancashire, he had occupied the managerial position at Port Vale and gained promotion for the 'Valiants' despite a lack of financial resources. When Lee arrived at Ewood Park, in January 1974, he inherited a squad that was still in contact with the promotion places. However, the manager appeared less convinced that promotion was a realistic possibility and began to experiment with the players at his disposal. The manager had his own ideas about how the game should be played and he clearly felt that not all of the players shared his beliefs. In a bid to raise funds he sold a host of players and his first incoming transfer was Pat Hilton on a free transfer from Brighton & Hove Albion. Curiously, the next signing was Ken Beamish, another Brighton player, but on this occasion Lee was forced to pay £25,000 to get his man – the largest fee that he had paid in his managerial career.

Ken Beamish and Gordon Lee celebrate after Blackburn win promotion in 1975.

Lee spent his money wisely and the summer of 1974 saw all newcomers repay him with valuable contributions towards the capture of the Third Division championship. However, Lee's greatest strength was how he motivated players to give extraordinary performances, and in turn the players he favoured had the utmost respect for the man. The boys of 1974 responded to the work ethic that Lee instilled and he became the first manager at Ewood to lead a team to championship success since Bob Crompton in 1938-39.

manager urging his players on from the touchline the Rovers responded in emphatic fashion. One goal was clawed back before half-time before the second period became a rout as the Rovers swamped their visitors from the West Country and ran out winners by a margin of 5-2. Promotion was clinched with a home win over Chesterfield and eight days later an emphatic 4-1 win away at Port Vale virtually wrapped things up. The title was duly claimed a couple of days later when a goalless draw against Wrexham was played out in front of 21,290 ecstatic fans at Ewood Park.

Chapter Nine: 1975-81
The Turbulent Years

Within weeks of the euphoria of the championship celebrations the bottom dropped out the Rovers' world. News that the club was £221,000 in the red was compounded by the loss of another manager. Once again, the directors found that they were unable to overcome the lure of the First Division and had little choice but to watch Gordon Lee depart for Newcastle United. At 34, Jim Smith became the youngest manager in the club's history when he was appointed in June 1975. Smith had cut his managerial teeth with non-league Boston United before enjoying a successful period at the helm of Colchester United. With Richard Dinnis joining Lee at Newcastle United, there was a complete overhaul of the backroom staff at Ewood. Norman Bodell was appointed assistant manager and coach while John Pickering arrived from Halifax Town to look after the second string and youth-team players.

The 1975-76 season was the centenary season of Blackburn Rovers but there was precious little to celebrate. After a bright start to the campaign the team quickly found itself faced with a real battle to retain Second Division status. The new manager was handicapped by the loss of Mick Heaton, Andy Burgin, Graham Hawkins and Ken Beamish through injury while Don Martin, nearing the end of his career, was allowed to return to Northampton Town. Two other members of the championship team also bade an early farewell to Ewood Park with Mike Hickman moving to Torquay United and Pat Hilton to Gillingham. Funds were found for the manager to return to Colchester and sign Bobby Svarc, but as the striker was coming into his best form an injury brought an end to his season.

On 8 November 1975, the club celebrated its centenary when Bolton Wanderers visited Ewood Park for a league game. A crowd of 24,430 witnessed a goal by Graham Oates that earned a valuable point.

Roger Jones, Bill Eckersley and Mick Heaton at the club's centenary celebrations.

The new manager took advantage of the loan system to prop up his ailing side. Gordon Hindson arrived from Luton Town in October and impressed the Ewood crowd with his old-fashioned wing play. Bill Bancroft was quick to point out that the club was not in a position to finance major signings and Hindson returned to Luton Town with the club unable to offer him a permanent contract.

It was a major blow when manager Gordon Lee left for First Division Newcastle.

Financial Tightrope

With so little money available the manager had to make sure that whoever he signed would make a significant improvement on his existing squad. One player who the manager would have liked for his squad was Geoff Hutt of Huddersfield Town. The left back spent three months on loan with the Rovers but had to return to Leeds Road because the Rovers couldn't afford the £8,000 fee.

50 Greatest Players

JOHN CONNELLY Winger

Born: St Helens, 18 July 1938

Joined Blackburn: 1966   **From:** Manchester United

Debut: 24 September 1966 v Ipswich Town, League

Appearances: 164   **Goals:** 39

Left Blackburn: 1970   **For:** Bury

John Connelly was simply an old-fashioned winger. He was quick, equally effective on either flank, a splendid crosser and had an eye for goal. These qualities earned him championship medals with Burnley and Manchester United as well as 20 England caps. It was a major coup for the Rovers to lure him to Ewood Park in September 1966. Two months earlier he had been a member of the England team that had opened the World Cup finals with a goalless draw against Uruguay at Wembley. Connelly rejected the opportunity to stay in the First Division with either Burnley or Blackpool in favour of agreeing to a £40,000 move from Old Trafford to Ewood Park. During the four seasons he spent at Blackburn, he continued to enthral the supporters with his exciting brand of wing wizardry. He was also a prominent threat in front of goal and was the top league scorer for the club in 1966-67, and joint top scorer in 1968-69.

Fortunately, funds were found later in the season for the manager to capture two veteran wingers – Dave Wagstaffe from Wolves and Gordon Taylor from Birmingham City. The arrival of the two experienced campaigners compensated for the loss of Roger Jones and Graham Oates who both joined Gordon Lee at Newcastle as the transfer deadline approached. Wagstaffe had first arrived at the club in January on a one-month loan arrangement but a lack of funds had prevented the manager from making the deal permanent. With the funds from the Newcastle deal he was able to add Wagstaffe and Taylor to his depleted squad at a vital time. The key game in the closing weeks of the season came at Bolton when the Rovers visited Burnden Park and produced a scintillating performance. A goal from John Waddington was enough to win the game and from that moment the goals began to flow and relegation fears eased with the club finishing 15th.

After beginning the 1976-77 season with an opening day win over Bolton Wanderers, the Rovers lost the next four games. They were also humbled in the League Cup by lowly Stockport County, managed by former Rovers boss, Eddie Quigley. At the start of the season the chairman had issued a warning

50 Greatest Players

FRED PICKERING Centre forward

Born: Blackburn, Lancashire, 19 January 1941

Joined Blackburn: 1956; 1971   **From:** School; Blackpool

Debut: 10 October 1959 v Leicester City, League

Appearances: 158   **Goals:** 74

Left Blackburn: 1964; 1972   **For:** Everton; released

Honours won with Blackburn: 3 England Under-23 caps.

Blackburn born and bred, it was only natural that Fred Pickering should opt to join his local club after leaving school. In those days, Pickering was a left back who was steady rather than spectacular. In 1959, Jack Marshall opted to experiment with Pickering at centre forward in reserve-team matches. He made his senior debut in this position in a 4-1 win over Manchester City at Ewood Park on 18 March 1961 and his two goals were sufficient to earn him a regular first-team spot. The 1962-63 season saw him bag 23 goals from 36 league appearances. He had developed into a powerful, strong-running target man and he struck up a deadly partnership with Andy McEvoy. With Bryan Douglas prompting from midfield, the pace and power of Pickering proved too hot to handle for many defenders. He became unsettled at Blackburn and in March 1964 he completed a move to Everton for a fee in the region of £80,000. He returned to Blackburn in March 1971 but the reunion wasn't a success and his contract was terminated in early 1972.

Graham Oates was a useful midfielder but followed Gordon Lee to Newcastle.

that Second Division survival would not be easy for a club with limited resources and even the most optimistic of fans was now forced to agree. In a bid to boost a flagging forward line the manager brought John Byrom back to the club and the veteran managed to add another five goals to his Ewood league tally before being released at the end of the campaign.

Twelfth position represented a slight improvement, albeit a small one, on the previous campaign. Throughout the season the team had played some attractive football but without any real punch in the final third of the field. Sammy Chung, manager of promoted Wolves, made a telling comment when he was quoted as saying that, 'If Blackburn had my two strikers, they would be up there with us now.' Sadly, with the club heavily in debt, the manager could only experiment with the players already at his disposal.

The season saw the emergence of several of the younger players and the likes of Paul Bradshaw, John Bailey and Kevin Hird all became regulars in the first team. The season also saw the club enter the record books when Dave Wagstaffe became the first Football League player to receive a red card, being sent off for dissent in the away game with Orient on 2 October 1976.

Once again, the only new arrivals at Ewood Park during the summer of 1977 came courtesy of free transfers. The manager snapped up John Curtis, a right back from Blackpool, while a more influential signing proved to be the capture of Noel Brotherston from Tottenham Hotspur. The manager also invited Jack Lewis to spend a week of pre-season training with the club but then had difficulty trying to find the £20,000 fee that Grimsby Town wanted for his services. Reluctantly, Smith had to allow Lewis to return to Blundell Park until a compromise could be agreed upon. The player only missed one game of the season before Smith was able to negotiate a deal. Lewis, a former Welsh Under-23 international, had been on the fringe of full international honours for some time and was seen by Smith as the perfect replacement for Bobby Svarc. Another major signing occurred during the

50 Greatest Players

JOHN McNAMEE Centre half

Born: Coatbridge, 11 June 1941

Joined Blackburn: 1971   **From:** Newcastle United

Debut: 26 November 1971 v Tranmere Rovers, League

Appearances: 57   **Goals:** 10

Left Blackburn: 1972 (retired)

Although McNamee only appeared on 57 occasions, he made a lasting impact. Rarely can there have been such an unlikely hero as this rugged Scot. Playing on borrowed time, his body had been ravaged by age and injury, Blackburn proved to be his 'last hurrah'. The basement and oblivion were beckoning until McNamee was installed at the heart of defence. He took Derek Fazackerley, a young and inexperienced defender, under his wing and tutored him in the art of defending. In return the energetic youngster was more than happy to cover more ground to hide McNamee's lack of mobility. McNamee was of the 'old school' where centre halves prevented their keepers from being flattened by oncoming forwards. Roger Jones benefited from this human shield and became a better keeper. There was little subtlety about the granite-like Scot and he relished the challenge of a physical contest against a burly No. 9. He was the final piece in the jigsaw of new players that Ken Furphy assembled during the autumn of 1971 to help take the club to mid-table security.

early weeks of the campaign when the club signed Glenn Keeley from Newcastle United to add to an already impressive array of central defenders.

With the youthful exuberance of Hird and Bailey driving forward from the full-back positions, and the wily cunning of Wagstaffe on the left-hand side of midfield, the Rovers began to climb the table. By November, there was real hope that a sustained promotion challenge might be maintained. The only reservation that remained was regarding the strikeforce. Once more, the manager was forced to use the loan system and for a short period over Christmas the arrival of Keith Fear boosted the front line. The player that the manager really wanted to sign was Steve Kindon, the former Burnley front runner who was playing with Wolves. Unfortunately, financial constraints meant that he had to look elsewhere to supplement his depleted resources. In February 1978, he signed John Radford (the former Arsenal centre forward) from West Ham United for a fee in the region of £35,000.

Radford enjoyed an impressive debut against Oldham Athletic and scored the opening goal in a 4-2 win over the Latics. However, a draw at Charlton Athletic and a home defeat by Bristol Rovers virtually ended any realistic chance of gaining promotion. Within 48 hours of the Bristol defeat the club was dealt a shattering blow when Jim Smith announced that he was to leave to become the manager of Birmingham City.

The 172 Days of Jim Iley

The directors put Norman Bodell in temporary command although it was understood that as soon as a replacement was found Bodell would follow Smith to Birmingham. With just four games of the season remaining, the directors announced the appointment of Jim Iley, the Barnsley manager, as the new man at the helm. As a player, Iley had sampled life at the top with successful spells at Tottenham Hotspur, Nottingham Forest and Newcastle United. However, as a manager he had had to settle for the more modest surroundings of Peterborough United and Oakwell. In finishing the season in fifth position in the Second Division, the club achieved its highest league standing since the 1966-67 season. Furthermore, the club had made a profit of £110,648 that enabled the directors to drastically reduce the club's debts.

The new manager acted swiftly to make changes to the backroom staff and after promoting John Pickering to assistant manager he appointed Bobby Kennedy, the former Manchester City stalwart and Bradford City manager, to the post of reserve-team coach. While the financial situation had improved,

50 Greatest Players

ROGER JONES Goalkeeper

Born: Upton-on-Severn, 8 November 1946

Joined Blackburn: 1970   **From:** Bournemouth

Debut: 20 January 1970 v Millwall, League

Appearances: 277

Left Blackburn: 1976   **For:** Newcastle United

Honours won with Blackburn: Third Division championship 1975

During his six years with the club Jones proved himself to be one of the finest goalkeepers that had ever represented Blackburn Rovers. Although not the tallest of men, standing an inch under six feet, Jones had a natural athleticism that enabled him to make a string of world-class saves. Much of his time at Blackburn was spent in the Third Division otherwise he might well have progressed at international level beyond the England Under-23 caps that he won at Bournemouth. Jones was a keeper who dominated his area and his judgement of crosses was impeccable. He maintained an ever-present record during the Third Division championship season of 1974-75 before moving to Newcastle United in March 1976 to be reunited with Gordon Lee, his former Ewood boss.

Chelsea keeper Peter Borota throws himself at a shot from Noel Brotherston. Blackburn went on to draw the match 1-1 on 18 October 1980.

there was still little money for new players and the manager was forced to spend the summer hunting for bargains. He snapped up Peter Morris on a free transfer from Preston North End while John Aston, the former Manchester United star, arrived for a modest fee from Mansfield Town. Another modest outlay brought Martin Fowler from Huddersfield to strengthen the midfield.

On the eve of the season the supporters received the devastating news that Dave Wagstaffe was leaving to join Blackpool following contractual problems. Rightly or wrongly, the Ewood faithful blamed the manager for the loss of the popular 'Waggy' and it became the first of a series of blows that would quickly undermine the manager's position at Ewood Park.

From start to finish the 1978-79 season was a complete shambles. From the moment that Dave Gregory, a loan signing from Stoke City, opted to leave Ewood Park in favour of Third Division Bury, the manager appeared to be living on borrowed time. Iley, who had begun the season with hopes of promotion, found himself out of a job after eight league games. He had lasted 172 days and his sacking came four days after the directors had sanctioned the signing of Joe Craig from Celtic and Alan Birchenall from Memphis Rogues.

Relegation Beckons

The team was put in the hands of John Pickering while the directors turned their attentions to finding a new manager. Unfortunately, there appeared to be no obvious candidates for the job and, in the meantime, matters on the field simply got worse. Only one of the opening ten league games was won and the best efforts of the directors to make a quick appointment came to nothing. In December, the club appointed John Radford as player-coach in the hope that his experience might be of use to Pickering. While the league form continued to slide, the team gave one its best performances in the unlikely surroundings of Anfield. Although the third-round FA Cup-tie was lost, the players heartened their supporters with a valiant display.

On 9 February, the directors decided to appoint Pickering as manager and give him a short-term contract until the end of the season. This vote of confidence in Pickering came at a time when the team was in the middle of a run that would create a new club record. Unfortunately, it was a record that no one at Ewood Park wanted as the team went 16 games without a single league win. To provide support for Pickering the directors appointed Jimmy Armfield, the former Bolton and Leeds United manager, as 'honorary chief executive'. The move was all the more ironic for the fact that Armfield had already rejected the opportunity to become manager following the sacking of Iley. There were also changes at directorial level when Bill Bancroft was put out of action by illness. Although he remained a prominent member of the board, he was succeeded by Derrick Keighley as chairman.

In a last-ditch attempt to avoid the drop to the Third Division the directors allowed Pickering to enter the transfer market. A fee of £40,000 was paid to Birmingham City for Mick Rathbone, while a similar fee went to Manchester City for Russell Coughlan. However, the biggest signing was that of Duncan McKenzie from Chelsea who cost a reported £80,000, a new club record. The money to cover the cost of this influx of new players came from the sale of Kevin Hird to Leeds United for a fee of £375,000, the most that the Rovers had ever received for a player. Ultimately, the moves proved too little too late and defeat at home to Newcastle United on 25 April 1979 officially confirmed the club's relegation to the Third Division. There were still four games to be played and, with their fate already sealed, the players responded with four wins. The final match of the season ended in scenes of high emotion as fans invaded the pitch at the end to chant their support for John Pickering.

A New Direction

While there was no doubting Pickering's popularity, the directors were looking to take the club forward in a different direction and on 15 May 1979 it was announced that the club would not be renewing the contract of Pickering and that the search had begun for yet another new manager. The

50 Greatest Players

TONY PARKES　Midfielder

Born: Sheffield, 5 May 1949

Joined Blackburn: 1970　　　**From:** Buxton Town

Debut: 5 September 1970 v Swindon Town, League

Appearances: 409　　　**Goals:** 46

Left Blackburn: 1982 (retired)

Honours won with Blackburn: Third Division championship 1975

Tony Parkes has remained a loyal servant of Blackburn Rovers for over 30 years and in so doing has won a place in the hearts of the Blackburn faithful. He arrived at Ewood Park as a young, rather raw-looking centre forward from Buxton Town who was given his chance during the relegation season of 1970-71. However, it was as an industrious midfield player that he made his mark and it was the management style of Gordon Lee that brought the best out of him. Parkes epitomized Lee's philosophy for the game in that he combined hard work and total commitment with an abundance of skill. Although used primarily as a defensive type of midfield player, who covered any gaps that arose, Parkes never lost the goalscorer's instincts in the penalty area. He had the ability to drift unnoticed into the box and throughout his career he scored a number of vital goals. Parkes helped the Rovers to climb out of the Third Division for a second time in 1979-80, while becoming increasingly involved in the coaching of younger players. A badly broken leg in February 1980 ended his playing career and led to a full-time move to the coaching staff. Since then he has served the club with distinction in various capacities and has occupied the post of caretaker manager on no fewer than five occasions.

decision to appoint Howard Kendall as player-manager was a dramatic move away from the previous policy of plucking aspiring young managers from the lower divisions. Although he had enjoyed a glittering playing career, Kendall arrived at Ewood Park with no previous managerial experience. After coming to prominence with Preston North End he had spent the most fruitful part of his playing career with Everton before serving Birmingham City and Stoke City. At Stoke he had occupied the role of player-coach and had helped City win promotion to the First Division during the 1978-79 season.

Before he had time to settle into his new role he found himself in the unenviable position of having to negotiate the transfer of John Bailey to Everton for £300,000. It was little wonder that he found morale at the club was low following the loss of Second Division status and the departure of the talented young full back. Kendall's own excursions into the transfer market

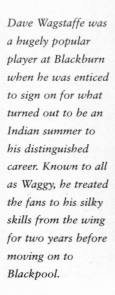

Dave Wagstaffe was a hugely popular player at Blackburn when he was enticed to sign on for what turned out to be an Indian summer to his distinguished career. Known to all as Waggy, he treated the fans to his silky skills from the wing for two years before moving on to Blackpool.

proved to be of a fairly modest nature. He plucked Jim Arnold from non-league Stafford Rangers and then signed Stuart Parker from Sparta Rotterdam. The signing of Arnold was the biggest surprise as the former England semi-professional international goalkeeper had no previous league experience and was 29 when he made his debut in the Football League on the opening day of the season. Hopes that Kendall would quickly restore the club to a higher status soon evaporated as the team made an appalling start to the new campaign. One win was recorded in the opening ten league games and interest in the League Cup ended with an emphatic 6-1 defeat at Nottingham Forest.

Languishing in the lower reaches of the Third Division prompted Kendall to act swiftly to plug the gaps in his fragile team. However, both of his new acquisitions, Jim Branagan from Huddersfield Town and Andy Crawford from Derby County, were plucked from the relative obscurity of Central League football.

50 Greatest Players

DAVE WAGSTAFFE Winger

Born: Manchester, 5 April 1943

Joined Blackburn: 1976; 1979   **From:** Wolverhampton Wanderers; Blackpool

Debut: 17 January 1976 v Bristol City, League

Appearances: 92   **Goals:** 9

Left Blackburn: 1978; 1980   **For:** Blackpool; retired

Dave Wagstaffe ended a long and illustrious career with a glorious Indian summer at Ewood Park. 'Waggy', as he was popularly known, first arrived at Blackburn in January 1976 on a month's loan from Wolves. He quickly endeared himself to supporters who had been starved of genuine class for so long. Although age had blunted his speed, he had developed other facets to his game to compensate for the loss. His wily experience was now at the forefront of his weaponry and, of course, he still retained his magical left foot that could pass a ball the length and breadth of the pitch with unerring accuracy. Attempts to bring him to Blackburn on a permanent basis finally succeeded in March 1976 and for two years he treated the Ewood faithful to a virtuoso performance of wing play. He adopted a deeper role that allowed the youthful John Bailey to surge past him and make attacking runs from left back. From this withdrawn role he was able to pepper long-range passes to all quarters of the field. He was released when Jim Iley took over as manager and moved to Blackpool. In March 1979, although almost 36, Wagstaffe returned to Blackburn when John Pickering signed him in an attempt to save the club from relegation. Unfortunately, he was injured in his second game which effectively ended his career.

Late autumn and early winter brought a gradual climb up the table as the manager began to steady the ship. As well as building a platform from which to launch a promotion bid, the early rounds of the FA Cup were also successfully negotiated. Kendall had also changed his backroom staff with Mick Heaton, the former captain, being promoted to first-team coach from his role with the Central League team. The watershed for Kendall was an away fixture at Grimsby on 12 January 1980. Two goals from Duncan McKenzie proved sufficient to give the Rovers a 2-1 win and so began a run of 15 games that brought 14 wins and a draw. Between mid-January and early April a total of 29 from a possible 30 points were taken as the team put itself into the heart of the promotion race.

Kendall had found a winning combination and was sufficiently experienced not to tinker with it. Arnold had dispelled all fears about his lack of experience and proved himself to be a goalkeeper of the highest calibre. The back four of Jim Branagan, Glenn Keeley, Derek Fazackerley and Mick Rathbone was probably the finest defensive unit outside of the First Division. During that amazing run of 15 games this miserly defence conceded only four goals. Kendall himself was the main driving force in midfield, although he received excellent support from Tony Parkes. Once again, Noel Brotherston operated on the right flank and contributed seven vital goals from this position. The manager had wisely elected to release Duncan McKenzie from a normal midfield role and allow him to roam more freely. It was a move that wrought havoc with Third Division defences as most had no answer to the subtlety displayed by McKenzie. He bagged a dozen league goals for himself and created countless other chances for his colleagues. While McKenzie probed from deeper positions, it was Simon Garner and Andy Crawford who evolved as the main attacking spearhead of the team. Crawford, in particular, proved a revelation and scored 18 goals in 36 league games.

Success in the league was mirrored in the FA Cup with First Division Coventry City falling to a giant-killing act at Ewood Park in the fourth round. The fifth round produced two thrilling games with Aston Villa before the Rovers succumbed to a single goal defeat. While the successful run in the FA Cup brought the club back into the national headlines, it was promotion that was the main goal of the season. This was finally clinched at Gigg Lane in the penultimate game of the season when the Rovers celebrated a 2-1 win in front of a large number of Blackburn Rovers fans who had made the short trip to nearby Bury.

Pipped at the Post

The summer of 1980 brought little change to the playing personnel at Ewood Park. The manager signed Hull City's long-serving full back, Roger De Vries, to strengthen his left-sided defenders, while Micky Speight was signed from Sheffield United to add a little more muscle in midfield. In view of the club's recent past, the 1980-81 season ought to have been a cause for celebration but, ultimately, it merely gave rise to the deepest despondency. By the end of the campaign the supporters had seen their team pipped for promotion to the First Division on goal difference, and then watched another talented manager walk out to join a top club.

Once again, as had happened so often in the past since 1965-66, promotion hopes were holed by a lack of goals. However, injuries and off-the-field disputes also played their part in preventing the Rovers from celebrating successive promotions.

Great Managers – 1979-81

HOWARD KENDALL

Howard Kendall faced a daunting task when he arrived at Ewood Park in July 1979. Blackburn Rovers had just been relegated to the Third Division and John Bailey, the club's outstanding full back, was on his way to Everton. Kendall hadn't picked the easy option in starting his managerial career with Blackburn Rovers. His appointment was something of a gamble for the Rovers. Not only had he no previous managerial experience but he also had no experience of Third Division football. The appointment also broke new ground as he was the first player-manager in the club's history. The opening months of the 1979-80 campaign were difficult ones, despite spending in the region of £90,000 on four new players. The men he selected were largely unknown, with Jim Arnold coming from Stafford Rangers, Stuart Parker from Sparta Rotterdam, Jim Branagan from Huddersfield and Andy Crawford from Derby. By Christmas the club was mid-table but showing signs of potential. Kendall then coaxed an amazing run from his players that brought 29 points from a possible 30 to propel them into the promotion race.

Kendall had tightened his defence and from this solid base he built his promotion-winning team. Duncan McKenzie responded magnificently to the management style of Kendall and produced some scintillating form. Kendall was also able to exert influence on the team from his position in midfield. He also opted to change the backroom staff and promoted Mick Heaton to first-team coach while Tony Parkes took charge of the reserves while continuing to remain a key member of the senior team. At the end of his first season in management the Rovers gained promotion to the Second Division after finishing runners-up to Grimsby Town. In his second season at the club he took the Rovers to the brink of the First Division. Only goal difference prevented the Rovers from enjoying two successive promotions. Ultimately, it was a lack of goals that prevented Kendall from taking the club into the top flight, coupled with the loss of Noel Brotherston to injury just after the transfer deadline had passed. At the end of the 1980-81 season Kendall was offered the managerial position at Everton and, with the Merseyside club being so close to his heart, he bade farewell to Ewood Park.

The 1980-81 season started brightly with seven wins and two draws from the opening nine games. However, during this phase the club had been rocked by a transfer request from Andy Crawford. The player began to suffer from indifferent form and Kendall had little option but to axe him from the team. Gradually, opponents began to find a way of nullifying the Blackburn attack with the result that goals began to dry up. Fortunately, the rock-solid defence that Kendall had moulded remained firm, an impressive

23 clean sheets were kept, and this helped to ensure that the club kept in contact with the promotion pack. Unfortunately, too many games were drawn with the team failing to score on no fewer than 16 occasions. The 11 goalless draws of the season proved to be a record.

Financial worries eventually led to the departure of Duncan McKenzie to Tulsa Roughnecks while Kendall was able to bring Viv Busby, the former Sunderland and Fulham striker, in the opposite direction. With little money available with which to strengthen the squad it was imperative that key players remained free from injury, but sadly this proved not to be the case. A major set-back occurred in February when Tony Parkes broke his leg, an injury that would prove sufficiently serious to curtail his playing career. Another blow came just two days after the

Viv Busby scores in a 3-1 win against Sheffield Wednesday on 14 March 1981.

transfer deadline had elapsed when Noel Brotherston was ruled out for the remainder of the campaign.

Even in the closing weeks of the season the team had chances to establish themselves in a promotion place. Unfortunately, goalless draws at home to Notts County and Bolton Wanderers, together with a similar scoreline at Preston North End, meant that the club entered the last match of the season knowing that even a win would not be enough to guarantee promotion. Although the Rovers won their final game, a typically tight 1-0 win at Bristol Rovers, victory for Swansea City at Preston meant that the Rovers had to settle for fourth place, missing promotion on goal difference.

Six days after the end of the season it was announced that Kendall, who earlier in the campaign had rejected overtures from Crystal Palace, was to leave Blackburn to become manager of Everton. The manager also took Mick Heaton with him to Goodison and so the search for a new management team began once more at Ewood Park.

Chapter Ten: 1981-91
The Nearly Men

The man who was given the unenviable task of following Howard Kendall was Bob Saxton, the manager of Plymouth Argyle. Saxton was under no illusions about the size of his task and readily acknowledged that finishing fifth would be seen as failure. The new manager was quick to surround himself with a backroom staff that he knew well from Home Park, thus Jim Furnell arrived to be given the job of reserve-team manager, while Harold Jarman replaced Eddie Quigley, the former Ewood favourite, who had been acting as chief scout with the Rovers. Tony Long came in as physiotherapist to replace Jack Cunnington and one change that found favour with everyone at the club was the appointment of Tony Parkes as first-team coach.

There were changes on the field too. Kendall had returned to his old club to prize Jim Arnold away for a fee of £200,000 – he had cost the club £25,000 two years earlier making this a remarkable piece of business. In his place Saxton signed Terry Gennoe from Southampton for £60,000, while an identical sum was spent on Ian Miller, a winger from Swindon. In November, the manager paid another sizeable fee to Wolves for Norman Bell.

Ultimately, the team was never quite good enough to clinch a promotion spot. The best part of the campaign coincided with the four months that

Bob Saxton with his new squad after taking control in the summer of 1981. He was given very little financial support but managed to keep the team in the Second Division through turbulent times.

Kevin Arnott spent on loan at the club. The Rovers lacked resources to buy the Sunderland midfielder on a permanent basis and after he left the team won only two of the final ten league games. The final seven matches produced four points and saw the club finish in tenth position.

Towards the end of the 1981-82 season the club gained a new chairman when Bill Fox stepped up from vice chairman and immediately outlined the financial problems facing the club. The manager would only be given funds for players if the attendances increased, and in future there would be a direct correlation between income through the turnstiles and money spent on players. This didn't make the new chairman popular with the crowd but it ensured that the Rovers survived in the Second Division at a time when other clubs in the area were plummeting into the lower divisions.

Careful Financial Planning

The financial constraints meant that only two new faces arrived at Ewood Park during the summer of 1982. Colin Randell, a midfield player who Saxton had worked with at Plymouth, joined the club from Home Park for £40,000. A more modest outlay was required to sign Vince O'Keefe from Torquay United to act as understudy for Gennoe. Unfortunately, the 1982-83 season was one that was dominated by the financial gloom that had descended

upon the club. The manager again used the loan system to bring Kevin Arnott to the club for three months. This was a player that Saxton wanted to sign but, because of the lack of funds, he had had to watch the former Sunderland midfielder join Sheffield United the previous summer.

In view of the constraints that the club was operating under there was general satisfaction that mid-table respectability was again achieved. While 11th might have brought little cheer to the fans, the harsh realities of football suggested this was some

Simon Garner bursts through the defence and shoots home against Wimbledon in a 2-0 victory on 29 September 1984.

achievement. Other clubs throughout the area were struggling with Burnley and Bolton Wanderers both relegated to the Third Division and Preston North End to the Fourth Division. The waters may have been choppy but the stewardship of Fox and Saxton had at least kept the ship afloat.

Once again the summer of 1983 was a fairly quiet affair on the transfer front for Blackburn Rovers. Chris Thompson arrived from Bolton Wanderers to provide some support for Norman Bell and Simon Garner in attack, and he was called upon to replace the injured Bell in the opening game of the season. Sadly, the injury that Bell received was sufficiently serious to end his playing career. However, as one career came to an end, the careers of two of the younger players at the club were launched during the 1983-84 season with the debuts of Simon Barker and Mark Patterson. Barker ousted Randell from midfield and Patterson was given an extended run on the left wing.

In difficult circumstances the manager continued to make progress and led the team to a highly satisfactory sixth position in the table. Simon Garner, who had scored 22 league goals the previous season, continued to develop into one of the most dangerous marksmen outside of the First Division. He topped the scorers with 19 league goals and recorded all five in a 5-1 win over Derby County at Ewood Park in September 1983.

With the sole addition of Jimmy Quinn to the squad the Rovers began the 1984-85 season in splendid fashion. The form of Thompson and Garner meant that Quinn had to sit on the bench until mid-December 1984. When Derek Fazackerley scored the winning goal, a penalty, against Carlisle United on 23 December 1984, he gave the Rovers a four-point lead at the top of the table. A 2-1 win over Leeds United at Ewood Park on Boxing Day was greeted with euphoria so it was all the more distressing for the fans when the wheels came off the promotion wagon as the team appeared to run out of steam. Vital points were dropped at Ewood Park to both Oxford United and Manchester City, major rivals for promotion. Suddenly, the goal-scoring trio of Thompson, Garner and Quinn found it increasingly difficult to find the net. The manager refused to panic and kept faith with the men who had taken the club into such a promising position. With just six games left to be played, four of which were at home, promotion seemed a real possibility. However, three defeats ended the dream and left the club in fifth positon.

Despite the disappointment of the previous campaign the manager continued to work with the same group of players during the 1985-86 season. However, after a bright start, the team began to struggle for results and the club suddenly found itself embroiled in a relegation battle. After beating Leeds United on Boxing Day the team only registered one more win before facing Sheffield United at Ewood Park on 19 April 1986. As the team had not won one of the previous ten games, there was little cause for optimism among the 4,736 fans who appeared lost in the vast empty spaces of Ewood Park. Mark Patterson marked the occasion with his first league hat-trick and helped the Rovers to an unlikely 6-1 win. Suddenly, there was just a glimmer of hope, even though this was almost extinguished the following week when the team crashed 3-0 at Charlton Athletic.

A torrential downpour led to the postponement of the game with Grimsby Town on Saturday 3 May 1985 which meant that the match had to be hurriedly rearranged for Monday. Everyone knew what was required: a win would ensure safety. Quite a few of the 7,600 that assembled at Ewood had barely settled into position when Garner put the Rovers ahead after 42 seconds. Though the Mariners equalized the Rovers played like a team that knew their own destiny and a goal from Dave Hamilton and a Simon Barker penalty ensured a 3-1 win and the continuation of Second Division football.

Saxton Leaves Ewood Park

The prolonged flirtation with relegation in the previous campaign led to a reassessment of the playing squad during the summer of 1986. Although fiercely loyal to the players who had served him so well, Bob Saxton was given the money to make a couple of additions to his armoury. Chris Price, an attacking right back, came from Hereford United, while Scott Sellars, a left-sided midfield player, arrived from Leeds United.

The 1986-87 season began with three straight wins as the addition of Price and Sellars provided a fresh impetus to the team. Indeed, the third of these games produced an impressive 6-1 victory over Sunderland at Ewood Park in which Simon Garner notched up four goals. Sadly, this period was simply the lull before the storm. After the bright opening the Rovers then recorded just one win from the next 17 league games.

The home form in particular became embarrassingly poor as the disenchantment on the terraces took its toll on the players. Jimmy Quinn, who two seasons earlier had been welcomed as a possible saviour, became the focus of abuse for the frustrated supporters. In truth, the unrest on the terraces had been growing since the latter stages of the 1984-85 campaign when many believed that a glorious opportunity for promotion had been squandered. As Christmas approached, and relegation loomed, the manager took the bold step of allowing Quinn to return to Swindon Town. In his place he signed Paul McKinnon from Sutton United. Although he had previously played in

European football, with Malmo FF, and had enjoyed a successful career in the semi-professional game, he had yet to appear in the Football League.

McKinnon made his debut in a 3-0 defeat at Sunderland four days before Christmas. This left the Rovers one point and one place above Huddersfield Town who where anchored at the foot of the table. By a twist of fate the Yorkshire outfit visited Ewood Park on Boxing Day for a game that was of vital importance for both clubs. The game opened with an early exchange of goals and then became a predictably tense affair. When it looked as if the Rovers would have to settle for a point Simon Barker had the misfortune to score an own goal. The 88th minute goal was a devastating blow and a belated Christmas present to the men from Leeds Road.

In the wake of the defeat the players reiterated their loyalty to the manager and accepted responsibility for the present predicament. Bill Fox, a great supporter of the manager, was finally compelled to bring the curtain down on the reign of Bob Saxton at Ewood Park. The chairman rightly praised the excellent work of a manager who had kept the Rovers in the Second Division, often in the higher reaches, while at the same time having few resources with which to strengthen his squad. During his stay he had brought in £475,000 from transfers while only £343,000 had been spent on new players. These

---

50 Greatest Players

STUART METCALFE Midfield

Born: Blackburn, Lancashire, 6 October 1950

Joined Blackburn: 1966; 1982 **From:** School; Carolina Lightning

Debut: 27 April 1968 v Cardiff City, League

Appearances: 451 **Goals:** 26

Left Blackburn: 1980; 1983 **For:** Carlisle United; retired

Honours won with Blackburn: Third Division championship 1975

Stuart Metcalfe was capped by England at youth level and went on to give outstanding service to his local club. He signed schoolboy forms in March 1964 and became an apprentice in June 1966 before turning professional in January 1968 by which time he had already helped the club to win the Central League title in 1966-67. Originally an outside right, he later graduated with great success into a central midfield player, although the instincts of a winger always remained with him and he loved to run at defenders with the ball. He was at his best during the 1970s when he formed an effective midfield partnership with Tony Parkes. Metcalfe was a creative playmaker whose intuitive passing could prise open the meanest of defences. He also bagged some vital goals, particularly during the Third Division championship season of 1974-75.

figures merely underlined the dilemma in which the manager had found himself. In helping the club to survive financially he had been unable to rebuild an ageing team. This had led to a sequence of results that ultimately cost him his job. The manager's lot at Ewood Park was not for the faint hearted.

Following the dismissal of Saxton the directors put Tony Parkes in charge of playing affairs with Jim Furnell acting as his assistant. As so often happens, a change of manager brought a change in fortune and the Rovers enjoyed a mini-revival. The directors allowed the temporary manager to sign Sean Curry, a diminutive striker from Liverpool, for a modest fee. Although eliminated from the FA Cup during this period the Rovers enjoyed a narrow 4-3 win over Oxford United to reach the quarter-finals of the Full Members' Cup.

Don Mackay Takes Over

Following a 1-0 win over Oldham Athletic on 31 January 1987, the directors announced the appointment of Don Mackay, the former Dundee and Coventry City manager, as the new man at the helm of Ewood Park. He had

---

50 Greatest Players

DEREK FAZACKERLEY Central defender

Born: Preston, Lancashire, 5 November 1951

Joined Blackburn: 1969   **From:** School

Debut: 23 February 1971 v Hull City, League

Appearances: 689   **Goals:** 26

Left Blackburn: 1987   **For:** Chester City

Honours won with Blackburn: Third Division championship 1975

Derek Fazackerley remained a fairly anonymous face outside of Ewood Park until he became coach to the England team under Kevin Keegan. However, at Blackburn he is the player who made a record number of appearances. He was a model professional and a consistent defender who came to prominence during the darkest period in the history of club. He was forced to establish himself in the physically demanding world of Third Division football at a time when a number of other young players disappeared without trace. He had an experienced tutor in John McNamee during those formative days. Graham Hawkins, another experienced campaigner, continued his education in 1974-75 when the Third Division championship was won. 'Faz' was highly regarded as a traditional, tough-tackling defender who had a commanding presence in the air. He was also electrifyingly quick which enabled him to cover his colleagues at the back. Calm and collected under pressure, if his game had a flaw it was his distribution of the ball. However, his strengths far outweighed any weaknesses and his presence was always a threat at set-pieces.

Tony Parkes managed playing affairs before Don Mackay took over in January 1987.

also held coaching positions in England and Denmark and left the backroom staff of Glasgow Rangers to take the Blackburn job.

Under Mackay the team continued to build on the progress that Tony Parkes, who had reverted to assistant manager, had earlier inspired. However, it was the Full Members' Cup that gave the manager the platform on which to make his mark. An emphatic 3-0 win over Chelsea in the quarter-final began to reawaken interest in the club.

The victory over Chelsea had been marred by the loss of Mick Rathbone with a broken leg, and this resulted in the manager making his first excursions into the transfer market. To cover the loss of Rathbone he brought Chris Sulley from Dundee United, initially on loan and then in a permanent deal. He also revisited his former club, Dundee, to sign a young reserve player named Colin Hendry for £30,000. The blond-haired youngster could play at centre forward or centre half but he was unknown outside of Dundee. Both Sulley and Hendry made their debuts for the club in the semi-final of the Full Members' Cup when Ipswich Town visited Ewood Park on 11 March 1987. Both gave assured performances in a game that the Rovers won 3-0 to book a trip to Wembley for the final.

While the Full Members' Cup may have been scorned by many, it provided the opportunity for 28,000 Blackburn fans to journey to London for a Wembley final for the first time since 1960. After so many years of frustration and disappointment the Blackburn faithful finally had something to rekindle their passion for the club. The game was played on Sunday 29 March 1987 and was certainly not the greatest spectacle that Wembley had staged. For 85 minutes the Rovers found themselves on the back foot against a Charlton Athletic team that tried to live up to its First Division status. However, Vince O'Keefe was in inspired form in the Blackburn goal and was able to repel the waves of Charlton attacks before the Rovers grabbed the lead. The hero of the hour was Colin Hendry who hit a screaming shot into the net to give the Rovers a 1-0 lead just five minutes from the end. The team

Simon Barker, left, and Ian Miller hold the Full Members' Cup aloft after victory. This was Blackburn's first trip to Wembley since 1960 and the ecstatic crowds were overjoyed to go home with the silverware after a screamer from new boy, Colin Hendry.

received an ecstatic ovation from the huge Blackburn contingent that had made the journey south. The following day thousands flocked to the Town Hall to welcome the players back at the civic reception. Blackburn, it appeared, had been reborn as a football town.

The success in the Full Members' Cup was mirrored by an improvement in the league that enabled the club to finish in 12th position. The new manager continued to encourage renewed interest in the club with a spending spree. Ally Dawson, a Scottish international defender, was signed from Glasgow Rangers for £50,000 while Howard Gayle arrived from Stoke City to pep up the forward line. The signing of Gayle was seen as something of a gamble as he had gained a reputation for being difficult to handle at Liverpool. He'd since had spells with Birmingham and Sunderland as well as a period in America before moving to Stoke. The signing of Nicky Reid from Manchester City was seen as a major capture as he could operate in defence or midfield.

The new-look team took time to gel with the opening ten games of the 1987-88 season providing three wins and two draws but five defeats. However, after three successive defeats at the end of these ten games, the team earned a 1-1 draw at Aston Villa on 30 September 1987 and embarked on a 23-match unbeaten run. In the midst of this run the manager shocked the football world by securing the services of Steve Archibald from Barcelona on a six months loan arrangement. The capture of the former Tottenham Hotspur and Scotland international striker caught the public imagination and the average home gate virtually doubled in size following his arrival.

He made his debut on 19 December 1987 and helped the Rovers to a 2-0 win over Birmingham City at Ewood Park. On 20 February 1988, he scored two goals in a top-of-the-table clash with Aston Villa at Ewood. The 3-2 win that the Rovers secured took the club to the top of the table and was the seventh successive victory that the team had enjoyed. Promotion was again the sole topic of conversation among the Blackburn faithful.

The promotion push faltered slightly during March and in response the manager pulled off another major acquisition. He persuaded Argentinian World Cup star Ossie Ardiles to move to Ewood Park from Tottenham Hotspur for the final few weeks of the campaign. Mackay's idea behind the loan move was to reunite Ardiles with Archibald in the hope that the two could spur the Rovers to promotion.

Mackay's bold gamble deserved a better reward than fate delivered. Ardiles was injured on his debut and had to sit out the next two games that saw vital points lost to Oldham Athletic and Shrewsbury Town. However, with five games remaining, promotion was still very much in their own hands. Although only one of those games was lost, draws against Swindon Town and Reading at home condemned the club to the play-offs.

Having finished in fifth position the Rovers had to face Chelsea, 19th in the First Division, in the semi-final stage. Handicapped by the loss of Archibald, and with Ardiles deemed only fit enough for a place on the bench, the odds seemed stacked against the Rovers. In glorious May sunshine the Rovers slipped to a 2-0 defeat at Ewood Park in front of a crowd of 16,598. Three days later the team travelled to London for the second leg but, despite the inclusion of Archibald and Ardiles, the deficit proved too great and the team went down to a 4-1 defeat on the night, losing 6-1 on aggregate.

Garner Breaks the Record

The summer of 1988 brought the expected departures of Archibald and Ardiles. However, failure to gain promotion also resulted in the sale of Chris Price to Aston Villa for £150,000, while Simon Barker joined Queens Park Rangers in a record-breaking £400,000 deal. The club also lost Mark Patterson who joined Preston North End for a more modest return of £20,000. To cover these losses the manager paid Scunthorpe United £40,000 for Mark Atkins, a young full back who was seen as a natural replacement for Price. Another £40,000 was paid for midfielder Tony Finnigan from Crystal Palace while another midfield player, Ronnie Hildersley, arrived from Preston North End on a free transfer. The manager varied his attacking options by signing Andy Kennedy from Birmingham City for £50,000.

A lack of star names didn't prevent the club from mounting another serious promotion challenge. The highlight of the season came on 15 April 1989, the day of the horrific Hillsborough tragedy, when Simon Garner scored a hat-trick in the 4-0 demolition of Manchester City at Ewood Park. The significance of the win was that Garner's first goal equalled Tommy Briggs' record of 140 league goals for the club while the second put Garner at the head of the list of all-time goalscorers for Blackburn Rovers.

The team finished the campaign in fifth position and thereby guaranteed another crack at the play-offs. Once again, the club hosted the first leg of the semi-final with Watford being the opponents. A goalless draw meant that the Rovers had it all to do when they travelled to Vicarage Road for the second leg. Fortunately, a Simon Garner goal proved sufficient to earn the Rovers a draw and ensure passage into the two-legged final on the away goals rule.

Roared on by a crowd of 16,421 the Rovers established a 3-1 lead over Crystal Palace in the first leg of the play-off final. Two goals from Howard Gayle and one from Simon Garner put the Rovers firmly in the driving seat. Indeed, the club could have been in an even stronger position had not Gayle

50 Greatest Players

GLENN KEELEY Centre half

Born: Barking, Essex, 1 September 1954

Joined Blackburn: 1976   **From:** Newcastle United

Debut: 28 August 1976 v Cardiff City, League

Appearances: 430   **Goals:** 24

Left Blackburn: 1987   **For:** Oldham Athletic

Honours won with Blackburn: Full Members' Cup winner 1987

Glenn Keeley was still relatively inexperienced when he arrived at a club that already possessed three proven central defenders in Graham Hawkins, John Waddington and Derek Fazackerley, and it took time for him to win over the Ewood faithful. His early days with the club proved to be testing as his game was littered with rash tackles. Fortunately, Keeley displayed a steely grit that enabled him to develop into an outstanding central defender. The supporters began to warm to his aggressive style and christened him 'Killer' Keeley. Under the tutelage of Howard Kendall, he acquired other facets to his game and formed a successful partnership with Fazackerley at the heart of the defence. In November 1982, he followed Kendall to Everton, on a month's loan, but returned to Blackburn after being sent off in the Merseyside derby. In March 1987, he became the first Blackburn captain since Harry Healless, in 1928, to lead his team to victory in a Wembley final, lifting the Full Members' Cup.

Simon Garner holds the Blackburn record for the highest aggregate league goalscorer.

missed from the penalty spot. However, the fans who travelled to Selhurst Park in the hope of celebrating a long-awaited return to the top flight returned bitterly disappointed. In the white-hot atmosphere of a highly partisan Selhurst Park the Rovers team simply crumbled. Aided and abetted by some favourable refereeing decisions, the home side took the game into extra-time before delivering the killer blow.

A hat-trick of play-off appearances resulted from finishing the 1989-90 season in fifth place. However, unlike the previous two campaigns, there was little cause for optimism as the season had been a fairly dreary affair. Reaching the play-offs said more about the mediocrity of the division rather than the potential of the Rovers. Once again, the manager had managed to capture the national headlines with the signing of Frank Stapleton from Le Havre during the summer. In January 1990, the manager persuaded Kevin Moran, Stapleton's former Old Trafford colleague, to move to Ewood Park from Sporting Gijon. Unfortunately, a contract dispute resulted in Colin Hendry clashing with the manager and being left out of the team for a time before eventually moving to Manchester City. The loss of such a talented young player brought renewed accusations about the club lacking ambition.

Although younger players like David May, Keith Hill, Craig Skinner, Lenny Johnrose and Jason Wilcox were introduced, the most consistent performers remained the old guard. At 37 years old, Terry Gennoe continued to be an outstanding goalkeeper, while Moran and Stapleton showed that class has a permanency that age doesn't tarnish. After the excitement of the previous season the play-offs turned out to be a huge disappointment for all concerned at Ewood Park. The first leg of the play-off semi-final brought Ossie Ardiles back to Blackburn in his role as manager of Swindon Town. It

50 Greatest Players

TERRY GENNOE Goalkeeper

Born: Shrewsbury, 16 March 1953

Joined Blackburn: 1981   **From:** Southampton

Debut: 29 August 1981 v Sheffield Wednesday, League

Appearances: 334

Left Blackburn: 1992 (retired)

Terry Gennoe took over between the sticks from the popular Jim Arnold at the start of the 1981-82 season. He dominated his area and his commanding figure rose to claim crosses with ease. Gennoe was athletic and agile, his bravery was unquestioned, and in 1984-85 fellow professionals nominated him as a member of the PFA Second Division team of the season. Injury plagued his career and he was unfortunate to miss the 1987 Full Members' Cup final. In 1988-89 he established a new record for goalkeeping appearances for Blackburn Rovers but injury on the opening day of the 1990-91 season brought a long and illustrious career to an end. Gennoe remained at Ewood Park, combining his work as a goalkeeping coach with that of the club's education officer.

proved a happy return for the Argentinian as his Swindon side enjoyed a 2-1 win. The game at the County Ground saw Swindon record another 2-1 win and so ended the Ewood promotion dreams for yet another year.

The 1990-91 season was one of pure anti-climax after the promotion challenges of the previous three years. The summer had brought little in the way of transfer activity apart from the club agreeing a new record transfer to bring Kevin Richardson to the club from Watford. While Richardson was valued at £250,000, the deal involved Andy Kennedy moving in the opposite direction, and as the striker was valued at £190,000 it meant that the Rovers got the talented young midfielder for £60,000. The only other capture of note brought a third former Old Trafford favourite to Ewood Park in the form of Mike Duxbury. The veteran England international, who could operate in defence or midfield, was signed on a free transfer.

New Management Brings Hope

Unfortunately, the cracks that had begun to appear during the previous campaign now began to widen. A series of injuries to key players underlined the threadbare nature of the playing squad. Terry Gennoe was injured in the opening match of the season and didn't reappear for the rest of the campaign, while Simon Garner and Scott Sellars were both stricken by hernia problems that required surgery. No fewer than eight senior players were ruled out for up to three months during the course of the season as injuries literally began to cripple the club. The manager turned to the loan market and thus Mark Grew came from Port Vale to cover the loss of Gennoe while Jim Beglin, the former Liverpool and Republic of Ireland international, was brought from Leeds United for a month. Other players to spend short periods at the club included Bernard Gallagher from Aston Villa, Phil Starbuck from Nottingham Forest and Jason Beckford from Manchester City. The manager also looked abroad to strengthen his resources and Lars Frisch was brought from AFG Arhus to take part in a Central League match before being sent back to Denmark.

Perhaps the strangest deal brought Claus Reitmaier from Austrian club Wiener SC for a trial that saw him keep goal in the Zenith Data Systems tie against Everton at Ewood Park on 18 December 1990. The German keeper could do little to prevent the Merseyside club from winning 4-1 but gave an impressive display considering the situation in which he found himself. The manager chose not to sign him and the player returned to Austria. Ironically, he moved into German football shortly afterwards and spent the next decade as one of the leading keepers in the Bundesliga.

Peter Shilton of Plymouth Argyle collects before Mark Atkins gets a chance to shoot. David Speedie was to go on and score a hat-trick in a 3-1 win on 2 May 1992.

145

Businessman Jack Walker, shortly after he took control of the club in January 1991.

By the end of 1990 the club found itself in a perilous position at the foot of the table. It was at this point that the Rovers signed goalkeeper Bobby Mimms from Tottenham Hotspur for £250,000. This was the most that the club had ever paid for a player in a strictly cash deal. However, on 12 January 1991, defeat at Newcastle United left the Rovers floundering in 20th position, a mere four points ahead of bottom-placed Hull City.

It was while the club was looking into the abyss that a saviour appeared. On 17 January 1991, Jack Walker took control of Blackburn Rovers with the full support of the existing board. A life-long supporter of the Rovers, the Jersey-based multi-millionaire had started his business career in Blackburn in the humblest of circumstances but, with his brother Fred, had gone on to create the Walker Steel empire that he was reported to have sold for £330 million. When he took control at Ewood Park he was still active in various businesses but was determined to turn around the fortunes of his beloved Rovers. On his arrival at Ewood he expressed his full confidence in the existing board. 'I know some of the Rovers' performances have been abysmal and I fully understand why the supporters are fed up,' said Mr Walker. He explained that chairman Bill Fox and manager Don Mackay had put their energies into keeping the club viable but that now was the time to begin to invest in the team.

The first stage in this investment had come with the signing of Bobby Mimms, and on the day that Mr Walker took control a further £750,000 was spent on bringing Steve Livingstone and Tony Dobson from Coventry City. Both were players that Mackay knew well, having signed them as apprentices for Coventry. Although both were only 21, they had gained First Division experience and made a major contribution to the revival of Blackburn during the second half of the 1990-91 season. Livingstone hit nine goals in 18 appearances while Dobson gave a number of assured performances in the centre of defence. While a finishing place of 19th could hardly be construed as success, the Rovers at least lived to fight another day.

Chapter Eleven: 1991-97
The Walker Revolution

With the massive financial support of Jack Walker the summer of 1991 found Don Mackay searching at the highest level for players, although attempts to land Gary Lineker, Paul Stewart, Mike Newell and Teddy Sheringham were fruitless. The manager was able to persuade Scottish international Stuart Munro to leave Glasgow Rangers for £350,000 while Steve Agnew, a talented midfield player, was signed from Barnsley for £750,00 – a club record fee at the time. On the eve of the season the manager landed his first big-name player with the arrival of David Speedie from Liverpool in a £500,000 deal. Expectation levels soared among the Ewood faithful as the 1991-92 season began. It was therefore all the more disappointing when the season got off to a stuttering start. Just one point was collected from the opening three games and the club was knocked out of the Rumbelows Cup by Hull City.

On 2 September 1991, the club announced that Don Mackay's four-and-a-half-year reign was at an end. While the directors placed on record their appreciation of his work, it was clear that a change of direction was needed. Once again, Tony Parkes inspired a steady improvement that provided a platform for the promotion challenge that was to come, while Jack Walker set about pursuing the man he wanted to lead his Ewood revolution.

Kenny Dalglish Arrives

On 12 October 1991, the national football media assembled at Ewood Park to hear the news that Jack Walker had been successful in his quest as he announced that Kenny Dalglish had agreed to become manager of Blackburn Rovers. An astounded news corps also learned

David Speedie was the first big-name signing after Jack Walker's arrival.

that Ray Harford, the former Wimbledon and Luton Town manager, had agreed to become assistant manager. The new management team announced that they would keep the existing backroom staff, with Tony Parkes being given the title first-team coach.

Straight after the news conference, Dalglish and Harford watched their new charges, under the stewardship of Parkes, demolish Plymouth Argyle 5-2 at Ewood. However, during the early weeks of the new regime results were mixed and both Dalglish and Harford became acutely aware of the need to add new blood to the squad if promotion was to become a reality.

The first new arrival was Blackpool's diminutive left back, Alan Wright, who cost £500,000, but the second signing really captured the imagination of the Blackburn public. Colin Hendry returned from Manchester City for £700,000 to form a tight defensive partnership with Kevin Moran. The third new arrival epitomized the outside world's changing attitude to Blackburn Rovers. During the close season, Don Mackay had attempted to lure Mike Newell from Everton without success. However, when Dalglish approached Newell he quickly agreed to become Blackburn's first seven-figure signing at £1.1 million. The end of November brought an end to spending with the acquisition of Aston Villa's veteran midfielder, Gordon Cowans. The former England international occupied the pivotal position in the centre of midfield. With Moran marshalling the defence, and Speedie utilizing his vast experience to play havoc with opposing defences, the Rovers finally had an experienced spine to the team.

Tragically, as the team was moving into top gear, the club was rocked by the death of Bill Fox, club chairman and president of the Football League. The life-long supporter was to miss the better times that lay ahead after all his assistance with keeping the club afloat during financially difficult times.

Points and players continued to come as the club began to pull away at the top of the Second Division. Another familiar face returned to Ewood Park in the form of Chris Price who rejoined the club from Aston Villa. Other new players to join the Ewood revolution were Tim Sherwood from Norwich City and Roy Wegerle from Queens Park Rangers. A thrilling 3-1 win

Mike Newell wasn't keen on moving to Blackburn initially, but once Dalglish arrived, he jumped on board.

50 Greatest Players

NOEL BROTHERSTON Winger/Midfielder

Born: Belfast, 18 November 1956

Joined Blackburn: 1977   **From:** Tottenham Hotspur

Debut: 20 August 1977 v Notts County, League

Appearances: 381   **Goals:** 54

Left Blackburn: 1987   **For:** Bury

Honours won with Blackburn: 27 Northern Ireland caps, 1 Under-21 cap

Noel Brotherston was the perfect example of how a successful career can sometimes be resurrected after the disappointment of a free transfer. Groomed in the junior ranks at White Hart Lane, he had made only one senior appearance for Tottenham before being released in the summer of 1977. Fortunately, Jim Smith had spotted his potential and offered him a contract at Ewood Park. The red-headed winger was a bundle of tricks who could operate on either flank but didn't rely on pure pace to beat an opponent. Skill and trickery were the tools of his trade and he paraded these on a world stage as he helped Northern Ireland qualify for the 1982 World Cup finals in Spain. Nor was he simply a creator of chances, for Brotherston possessed the instincts of a striker in and around the penalty box, while also being capable of unleashing a thunderbolt of a shot from distance. Despite his undoubted ability, Brotherston remained a quiet, unassuming family man who was completely unaffected by the fame he achieved.

over Newcastle United on 15 February 1992 was gained at a cost. While a brilliant hat-trick from David Speedie put the Rovers in a comfortable position at the top of the table, Mike Newell suffered a broken leg.

Suddenly, the wheels came off the promotion wagon. Only one of the next 12 games was won as the club slipped out of the automatic promotion places. Attempts to remedy the situation were made by signing Duncan Shearer, Swindon Town's leading goalscorer, and Matt Dickins, a young goalkeeper from Lincoln City. Shearer scored on his debut but the match was still lost, while the only appearance that Dickins made ended in a personal disaster with the young keeper misjudging a lob in the final minute of a match against Wolves at Ewood Park. The error presented the visitors with a 2-1 win and four days later the Rovers lost a sixth successive match when Leicester City, a promotion rival, left Ewood Park with maximum points.

With four games left there was a real danger that the club wouldn't make the play-offs. However, Newell was rushed back into the team to visit Tranmere Rovers and scored one of the goals, from the spot, that gave the

Rovers a valuable point. He scored again in the next match, a vital 2-1 win over Millwall at Ewood Park. However, the Rovers travelled to Plymouth Argyle on the last day of the campaign knowing that only a victory would guarantee a play-off place. With Argyle needing to win to avoid relegation it promised to be a tense affair. Fortunately, David Speedie was at his best and notched up a hat-trick to ensure that the season was extended for another month.

Wembley Joy

Within the first 15 minutes of the first leg of the play-off semi-final a familiar picture began to unfold at Ewood Park. After raising the hopes of supporters, the team gave a stuttering performance in a play-off game. Already 2-0 down, to goals from Marco Gabbiadini and Tommy Johnston, there appeared little hope of a recovery until Scott Sellars shot home after 35 minutes. On the stroke of half-time euphoria swept through Ewood Park when Mike Newell launched an unstoppable shot towards the Derby goal. The second half found Blackburn at their brilliant best and two goals from David Speedie ensured that the players left Ewood Park to an electrifying reception. With a 4-2 lead there was genuine optimism that a Wembley final beckoned. However, when Andy Comyn gave Derby the lead, after 23 minutes of the second leg, those hopes began to waver. Fortunately, nerves were calmed after the half-time interval. A corner kick saw the ball spin into the air on the Derby goalline. As others paused, Kevin Moran launched himself at the ball and bundled his way past defenders to head the ball over the line. Although Derby pulled a goal back through Ted McMinn the Rovers hung on to reach the play-off final.

Rarely can a game of football have had such importance attached to its outcome as that between the Rovers and Leicester City as the break up of the Football League and the formation of the Premier League for the 1992-93 season, with all its envisaged financial rewards, put enormous pressure on both teams. The importance of the occasion was reflected in the tense affair that was played out on a baking hot Spring Bank Holiday Monday.

The match turned on a controversial refereeing decision just before the interval. David Speedie clashed with Steve Walsh in the penalty area and referee George Courtney had no hesitation in awarding a penalty, despite frantic appeals by the Leicester players. The irony was that this was the same referee who had been in charge of that infamous clash with Crystal Palace a few years earlier. On the stroke of half-time, Mike Newell calmly strode up and placed his shot into the net. The second half produced the expected onslaught from a desperate Leicester, but although Newell missed another

Great Matches

FOOTBALL LEAGUE SECOND DIVISION PLAY-OFF FINAL Wembley, 25 May 1992
Blackburn Rovers 1   Leicester City 0   Attendance: 68,147
Newell (pen)

This epic battle was played out on a baking May Bank Holiday. The telling moment of the
first 45 minutes came on the stroke of half-time. Mike Newell challenged for a high ball
in the Leicester City area with the result that the ball fell kindly for David Speedie. The
Scottish international cleverly nutmegged Steve Walsh and was then fouled by the
Leicester skipper. The referee had no hesitation in pointing to the spot despite the
desperate pleas of the Leicester players. Mike Newell sent Carl Muggleton the wrong way
to give the Rovers the lead. The second half opened with a barrage of Leicester attacks
and it required some last-ditch defending from Alan Wright and Colin Hendry to keep the
scoreline intact. However, driven by the tireless Mark Atkins the midfield began to take
control of the game. With just five minutes remaining Atkins burst through only to be
brought down by Muggleton. Once again, Newell was entrusted with the responsibility
but this time the keeper redeemed his error and turned Newell's penalty onto a post.
However, it was the Rovers who finished the stronger of the two sides and when the final
whistle blew Wembley erupted. It was entirely fitting that the Blackburn players should
put on their traditional blue and white shirts before climbing the Wembley steps.
Blackburn Rovers: Mimms, May, Hendry, Moran, Wright, Price, Atkins, Cowans, Sellars
(Richardson), Newell, Speedie
Leicester City: Muggleton, Mills, Whitlow, Hill, Walsh, James (Gee), Thompson, Grayson,
Wright, Ormondroyd, Russell
Referee: G. Courtney (Spennymoor)

*Being founder
members of the
Football League,
it was a touch of
historical symmetry
that victory ensured
that the Rovers
became founder
members of the
newly-formed
Premier League.*

penalty, Blackburn held on until the final whistle and Wembley erupted to the roar of the Blackburn supporters.

At the insistence of Kenny Dalglish, the privilege of leading the team out fell to Tony Parkes, the loyal servant who had been with the club since its darkest days in the early 1970s. At the end the players swapped yellow shirts for traditional blue and white before mounting the steps to claim the trophy. The following day the streets of the town were crowded with fans celebrating the end of a 26-year exile from the top flight. Players and officials returned to the town for a civic reception and the loudest cheer from the waiting crowds was reserved for Jack Walker.

Record Transfer

The summer of 1992 brought a renewed influx of players to Ewood Park as the management planned for life among the elite. The first new signing was a fairly modest capture with Lee Makel switching from Newcastle United. The talented young midfielder was viewed as an excellent prospect for the future. Dalglish then set a new club record when he paid £1.2 million for Middlesbrough winger, Stuart Ripley. However, within weeks of Ripley's arrival this fee had been dwarfed by the £3.3 million deal that brought Alan Shearer to Ewood Park from Southampton. The England Under-21 centre forward was rated as an outstanding prospect and the Rovers were required to smash the British transfer record to capture him. To the consternation of the supporters the manager was also forced to part with David Speedie as the Saints insisted that Blackburn's leading scorer should replace Shearer at the Dell.

The arrival of expensive new players meant Duncan Shearer and Lee Richardson both made the journey to Scotland to join Aberdeen while Paul Shepstone also went north of the border to link up with Motherwell. Other moves took Scott Sellars back to Leeds United for £800,000, Chris Sulley joined Port Vale on a free transfer and Simon Garner, Blackburn's favourite son, moved to West Bromwich Albion for £30,000.

Under the astute leadership of Dalglish and Harford the club adapted to life at the top. On 3 October 1992, Norwich City, sitting at the top of the table, visited Ewood Park and left on the wrong end of a 7-1 thrashing. Two goals apiece from Alan Shearer and Roy Wegerle, together with goals from Tim Sherwood, Gordon Cowans and Stuart Ripley, put the Rovers at the top of the Premier League. Dalglish kept the club in the top six throughout the season.

Once again, he freshened his squad with new faces at strategic phases of the campaign. Nicky Marker, a utility defender and midfield man, was signed early in the season while January brought two more defenders to the club in the Scandinavian pair of Henning Berg and Patrik Andersson. Norwegian international Berg was signed from Lillestrom, while Swedish international Andersson arrived from Malmo FF. On the eve of the transfer deadline the manager allowed Steve Livingstone to move to Chelsea as part of the deal that brought left back Graeme Le Saux to Ewood for £650,000. A further £1.5 million was spent in signing Kevin Gallacher, Coventry City's Scottish international forward, with Roy Wegerle moving in the opposite direction.

The season, however, was to have its disappointments. The biggest blow came in January with news that Alan Shearer, who had scored 16 goals in 21 league appearances, had succumbed to a cruciate ligament injury. There was also disappointment at the end of two very successful cup runs. Having progressed to the semi-final of the Coca-Cola Cup, and the sixth round of the FA Cup, the club was ordered to play their sixth-round replay away to Sheffield United 48 hours after visiting Sheffield Wednesday in the second leg of the Coca-Cola Cup semi-final. With the team already behind 4-2 from the first leg the manager fielded a slightly weakened team for the visit to Wednesday but, even so, the team was unlucky to lose 2-1. The match with Sheffield United proved a pulsating cup-tie that went to extra-time before ending 2-2. The result was decided by penalties and the Rovers lost 5-3.

The acquisition of Gallacher and Le Saux ensured that the disappointment of the cup defeats did not transfer itself to the league programme. The Rovers finished the season with eight wins from their final 11 games to ensure a

It was a great day for the Rovers when Alan Shearer was signed for a record £3.3 million.

50 Greatest Players

SIMON GARNER Forward

Born: Boston, 23 November 1959

Joined Blackburn: 1976   **From:** Boston United

Debut: 29 August 1978 v Exeter City, League Cup

Appearances: 570   **Goals:** 194

Left Blackburn: 1992   **For:** West Bromwich Albion

Honours won with Blackburn: Full Members' Cup winner 1987

The record books show that on 15 April 1989, the second of Simon Garner's three goals against Manchester City broke Tommy Briggs's aggregate record of 140 league goals. However, what the record books don't reflect is that he was a player who enjoyed mixing with the people who paid to watch him play football, and this endeared him to the supporters. Garner won a regular first-team place during the second half of the 1979-80 season and notched up six goals as the club gained promotion from the Third Division.

Throughout the 1980s Garner was the scourge of Second Division defenders as he built up a fearsome reputation as a penalty-box predator. Garner had all the assets required of a top-class finisher in that he was fast, had an eye for goal and was clinical in his finishing, particularly when faced with a one-on-one situation with the goalkeeper. During his time at the club he gave a number of memorable performances but among his best was a five-goal haul against Derby County at Ewood Park in September 1983.

---

fourth place finish. The progress that the Rovers made during the first 18 months of the reign of Kenny Dalglish was undeniable. From Second Division mid-table mediocrity to knocking on the door of European football was a huge achievement. In finishing fourth in the inaugural Premier League campaign of 1993-94 the Rovers claimed their highest league position for 78 years.

Chasing the Title

The manager resisted the temptation to spend more during the summer of 1993, contenting himself with the modest acquisition of Andy Morrison, a sturdy young defender from Plymouth Argyle. Surgery on Alan Shearer had proved successful and, under the watchful eye of physiotherapist Mike Pettigrew, his rehabilitation went well. The manager refused to rush him back into action and the young striker had to spend the opening weeks of the 1993-94 season on the bench. Although he played on 29 August 1993 to score his first goal of the season, and rescue a point away to Newcastle, it was the latter part of September before he returned to the starting line-up.

Tim Sherwood, the inspiring captain that lifted the Premiership trophy in 1995.

While the summer had been quiet on the transfer front Dalglish finally opened the chequebook during the early stages of the new campaign. In September 1993, he paid Sheffield Wednesday £2.7 million for Paul Warhurst, a versatile player who could play in defence, midfield or attack. Always on the lookout for promising young talent, Dalglish also snapped up Ian Pearce, a promising young defender from Chelsea. In October, the manager splashed out another £2.75 million to sign David Batty, Leeds United's combative little midfield player, while November brought goalkeeper Tim Flowers from Southampton for £2 million.

Tragically, Warhurst broke his leg in only his fifth game but the other signings blended quickly into the new-look team. Flowers replaced Bobby Mimms in goal while Henning Berg and Graeme Le Saux made the full-back positions their own. The club was in the fortunate position of being able to pick any two from three outstanding central defenders in Kevin Moran, David May and Colin Hendry. The form of these three meant that the club quickly dispensed with the services of Patrik Andersson, a world-class defender, who found it difficult to adjust to English football. The Ewood midfield was now centred around Tim Sherwood and David Batty, with Stuart Ripley and Jason Wilcox operating on the flanks. In attack, Alan Shearer led the line with Kevin Gallacher and Mike Newell in support.

Christmas 1993 found the Rovers in third position in the table some 14 points behind leaders Manchester United. To all intents and purposes, the race for the championship was over. Meanwhile, Blackburn fans could bask in the new surroundings of two imposing new stands that had been built at the Blackburn and Darwen ends of the ground. In January 1994, the old Nuttall Street stand was demolished as the final stage of redevelopment began.

The cup competitions of 1993-94 provided little of the excitement of the previous year with a fourth-round exit from the Coca-Cola Cup at the hands of Tottenham Hotspur at White Hart Lane. The FA Cup provided a further shock with a surprise home defeat by Charlton Athletic in a fourth-round replay. However, while interest in the cup competitions came to an early end, the Rovers launched an unlikely pursuit of Manchester United. By 2 April 1994, when United visited Ewood Park, the margin between the two clubs had been cut to just three points. With the Rovers enjoying a nine-point lead over third-placed Arsenal, the title race was clear cut.

Ground restrictions, due to the development work, meant that very few United fans gained access to an Ewood Park that had become an intimidating arena. The fireworks began in the second half when Shearer opened the scoring with a header that beat Peter Schmeichel. As United tried desperately to retrieve the situation they were struck by the classic sucker punch. A long ball from Stuart Ripley exposed the United defence and freed Shearer who went on to blast the ball past a startled Schmeichel for a 2-0 victory. Unfortunately, after clawing back a 16-point lead, the Rovers were unable to go on and claim the title. However, in finishing second, the club had enjoyed

50 Greatest Players

DAVID SPEEDIE Striker

Born: Glenrothes, 20 February 1960

Joined Blackburn: 1991   **From:** Liverpool

Debut: 17 August 1991 v Portsmouth, League

Appearances: 43   **Goals:** 26

Left Blackburn: 1992   **For:** Southampton

Honours won with Blackburn: Second Division play-off winner 1992

Few players can have made the same impact at a club in 12 months as that made by David Speedie in 1991-92. He arrived at Ewood Park from Liverpool on the eve of the season, costing £500,000, and was the only 'big' name to agree to a move to Blackburn prior to the arrival of Kenny Dalglish. Ironically, Speedie had been the former Liverpool manager's final signing before announcing his retirement from Anfield. Throughout the 1991-92 campaign, his fiery nature and endless enthusiasm made him a great favourite at Ewood Park. A goalmouth predator, with an eye for the spectacular, he collected two hat-tricks during the course of the campaign and rarely gave defenders a moment's rest. His tigerish tackling was usually seen only in defenders. Speedie also had a football brain and was able to turn a seemingly harmless situation into one of threat. His last-day hat-trick against Plymouth Argyle ensured a place in the play-offs while his two goals against Derby County gave the team something to defend in the semi-final second leg. At Wembley, Speedie won the penalty that took Blackburn to the Premier League.

Henning Berg was hugely influential in Blackburn's championship bid and holds 45 international caps for Norway.

its most productive season of league football since 1913-14 when the championship was last held at Ewood Park. The club won a place in the UEFA Cup, the first time that the Rovers had secured a place in a European competition. Alan Shearer's remarkable comeback earned him the Footballer of the Year award from the Football Writers' Association.

Into Europe

As the 1993-94 campaign came to an end the club was hit by the news that a contract dispute had led to the loss of David May to Manchester United. A further blow came with the retirement of Kevin Moran. Although the defensive resources had been seriously depleted it was in attack that the manager looked to strengthen his options. Once again, the club broke the British transfer record to sign England Under-21 striker Chris Sutton from Norwich for £5 million. To provide more options in the wide midfield positions the manager paid £300,000 for Australian international Robbie Slater from Lens FC. However, as the pre-season games got under way the need for defensive cover was clear. As a result, the manager turned to Tony Gale, a veteran of over 500 league games, who had been released by West Ham United at the end of the previous campaign. Gale appeared for the club against Celtic in a friendly and then lined up in the centre of defence for the FA Charity Shield at Wembley against Manchester United. As United had won the double the previous season the Rovers received a special invitation to meet the Old Trafford side by virtue of finishing second in the league.

Shorn of long-term injury victims Kevin Gallacher, Paul Warhurst and David Batty, together with Alan Shearer, Mike Newell and Chris Sutton, it was a very much under-strength team that Jack Walker proudly led onto the Wembley pitch. Once again, Dalglish had insisted that the honour of leading the team out should go to someone other than himself and everyone agreed that there was no more fitting candidate. A 2-0 defeat at Wembley had little affect on the team when the Premiership season began. The combination of

50 Greatest Players

KEVIN MORAN Centre half

Born: Dublin, 29 April 1956

Joined Blackburn: 1990   **From:** Sporting Gijon (Spain)

Debut: 27 January 1990 v Stoke City, League

Appearances: 173   **Goals:** 12

Left Blackburn: 1994 (retired)

Honours won with Blackburn: 24 Republic of Ireland caps; Second Division play-off winner 1992

When he came to Ewood Park Moran was a few months away from his 34th birthday and appeared to be just another short-term buy on the part of manager Don Mackay. However, Moran proved an inspirational signing and played a major part in leading the club into the Premier League. While some doubted that he would be able to cope with the pace of top-flight football, Moran quickly proved them wrong. He used his vast experience to organize his fellow defenders into an effective unit and his impeccable positional play ensured that he was rarely caught out. His rugged tackling and powerful heading was the rock on which Kenny Dalglish built his defence for the first two seasons of Premier League football. During this time Moran remained a regular in the Republic of Ireland squad and went with them to America for the 1994 World Cup finals.

Sutton and Shearer, tagged the SAS by the media, quickly settled into a potent force. The only blip during the opening months of the new campaign came with the unexpected defeat by Swedish part-timers Trelleborgs FC in the UEFA Cup. After losing by a single goal at Ewood Park the Rovers travelled to Sweden determined to rectify the situation. Although the Swedish club had equalized a goal from Chris Sutton, the Rovers appeared destined for the next round when Alan Shearer found the back of the net late in the game. However, in the closing minutes the Swedish club snatched an equalizer that gave them a 3-2 aggregate win.

With the stadium finally completed, a full house of 30,263 witnessed a thrilling 3-2 win over Liverpool on 15 October 1994. This was the biggest Ewood Park crowd for over 28 years. Progress continued to be made during the late autumn and in November the Rovers hit the top of the table. Once again the league developed into a head-to-head battle with Manchester United. An early exit from the FA Cup, at the hands of Newcastle, enabled the Rovers to concentrate their energies in pursuit of the league.

Away wins over Everton and Queens Park Rangers, in early April, enabled the Rovers to enjoy a lead of eight points over the team from Old Trafford. Once again, the manager had taken the opportunity to strengthen the squad for the final push. He paid Southampton £1.45 million for full back Jeff Kenna and brought Dutch international midfield player Richard Witschge from Bordeaux on loan until the end of the season. With the finishing line in sight the Rovers began to feel the pressure. A last-minute goal robbed them of maximum points at Leeds on Easter Saturday and two days later Manchester City inflicted a shock 3-2 home defeat on the Rovers. In a crowded fixture schedule the team reappeared at Ewood Park just three days later to struggle to a 2-1 win over Crystal Palace. The goals in this game came from the unlikely duo of Jeff Kenna and Kevin Gallacher, making his first appearance since his badly broken leg of the previous season. Tragically, Gallacher suffered another leg fracture in this game. The win over Palace did little to calm the nerves and a visit to relegation-threatened West Ham United produced another unexpected defeat.

Premiership Champions

With two games left it was vital that the Rovers beat Newcastle United at home if their title hopes were to be kept alive. On the 50th anniversary of VE Day, a crowd of 30,545 crammed into Ewood as an Alan Shearer goal gave the Rovers three vital points. However, while Shearer grabbed the headlines with his 33rd goal of the season, it was Tim Flowers who ensured the points came to Blackburn with a string of outstanding saves. The crowd roared its approval on the final whistle as the fans hijacked the VE Day celebrations and launched their own victory at Ewood party.

Two days later a disputed penalty gave Manchester United a narrow victory over Southampton and ensured that the championship chase would go to the last day. The Rovers still retained a two-point lead at the top of the table but faced a difficult

Chris Sutton, above, and Alan Shearer became known as the 'SAS' as their potent pairing propelled Blackburn to the title.

last-day trip to Anfield. With Manchester United highly fancied to win at West Ham United in their last match the emphasis was on the Rovers to win.

After 20 minutes all seemed to be going well as Alan Shearer gave a lively Rovers the lead. Within minutes there was more cause for celebration with news that West Ham had taken the lead against United. Unfortunately, fate decreed that the final 45 minutes would be a tortuous affair for all connected with Ewood Park. On 64 minutes, John Barnes grabbed an equalizer for Liverpool and shortly after news came through that Manchester United had levelled their match. As the game drifted into injury time the Rovers received what appeared to be a mortal blow. Jamie Redknapp hit a thunderous free kick from the edge of the area into the back of the net. For a moment Blackburn players and supporters stood in stunned silence. However, before the enormity of the goal could be digested news came from Upton Park that sent the whole of Anfield into delirium. Manchester United, despite constant pressure, had failed to find a way past the gallant Ludek Miklosko. After a wait of 80 years Blackburn Rovers were again the champions.

The Liverpool fans joined with Blackburn supporters in saluting the new champions. Tim Sherwood was presented with the trophy as Jack Walker shed a tear. The manager and benefactor stood side by side with the trophy on the Anfield pitch as the crowd roared its approval. The following evening the team made a triumphant return to Ewood Park for the formal presentation of the trophy in front of a full house.

An ecstatic Blackburn celebrate claiming the Premiership crown in the 1994-95 season.

Great Matches

FA PREMIER LEAGUE

Anfield, Liverpool, 14 May 1995

Liverpool 2   Blackburn Rovers 1
Barnes   Shearer
Redknapp

Attendance: 40,014

This was the most important match that Blackburn Rovers had played for over 80 years as the destination of the championship crown depended on it. A draw or a defeat would hand the title to Manchester United if the team from Old Trafford were victorious in their final match at West Ham United. The game began slowly but the supporters were soon celebrating as Alan Shearer scored the opening goal after 20 minutes. The jubilant Blackburn crowd had more cause for celebration with the news that West Ham United were also a goal to the good. In the second half neither side carried too much threat to the opposing goal but after 64 minutes Barnes steered home a low cross from Mark Kennedy. News that United had also got themselves on level terms did little to ease the pressure. With the scorelines level at both Anfield and Upton Park the tension became unbearable. As the game moved into injury time Liverpool were awarded a free kick just outside of the Blackburn penalty area. Jamie Redknapp's strike flew into the top corner of the net. The faces of the Blackburn supporters seemed frozen in time. Within a split second the horror turned to joy as news filtered through that Manchester United had been held at Upton Park. The championship crown belonged to Blackburn.

Liverpool: James, Thomas, Scales (Matteo), Harkness, Babb, McManaman, Barnes, Redknapp, Kennedy, Fowler, Clough

Blackburn Rovers: Flowers, Berg, Pearce, Hendry, Le Saux, Ripley, Sherwood, Batty, Kenna, Shearer, Sutton

Referee: D. Elleray (Harrow-on-the-Hill)

On that night of celebration Kenny Dalglish had been presented with the Carling Premiership Manager of the Year award, but six weeks later he announced his intention to step down from the day-to-day rigours of management. In a bid to cause as little disruption as possible, the directors appointed Dalglish to the newly-created position of director of football while Ray Harford stepped up to become the manager.

Managerial Reshuffle

Having won the title the club chose not to embark on any major signings during the summer of 1995. Instead, the manager arranged for Robbie Slater to move to West Ham United as part of a deal that brought Mattie Holmes to Ewood Park. The only other departure during the summer was that of

The hard work has finally paid off for Graeme Le Saux (left), Colin Hendry and Tony Parkes (centre) and Tim Flowers (right). They really were the champions.

Tony Gale who, having won a championship medal at the end of a long career, was allowed to return south to join Crystal Palace on a free transfer.

The players appeared to suffer a reaction to winning the championship and the 1995-96 campaign opened in disappointing fashion. Only four points were gained from the opening six league games as the club suddenly found itself in the lower reaches of the table. The opening of the European Champions' League also started with a defeat at home to Spartak Moscow.

Prior to the start of the European campaign the manager had appointed Derek Fazackerley as first-team coach. He had been a prominent member of the backroom staff at Newcastle United but welcomed the chance to return to Blackburn. Following Harford's promotion, Tony Parkes had stepped up to assistant manager. As the league campaign continued to falter, particularly away from Ewood Park, the manager turned, belatedly, to the transfer market. The midfield was strengthened by Billy McKinlay from Dundee United and Lars Bohinen from Derby County. Harford later gave himself extra attacking options with the signing of Graham Fenton, an England Under-21 international, from Aston Villa, and the defence was bolstered by the arrival of Chris Coleman from Crystal Palace in December 1995. Another new face in December was that of Swedish international Niklas Gudmundsson who initially signed on extended loan from Halmstad before making the move permanent. Prior to the transfer deadline the club paid

Manchester City £3.2 million for Garry Flitcroft who was sent off within a couple of minutes of his debut against Everton on 30 March 1996.

The influx of so many new faces meant another period of transition but during the second half of the season the club began to climb the table. Indeed, there was still a chance of qualifying for European football right up to the last day of the season. The narrow margin between success and failure was clearly exemplified by the club's experiences in the European Champions' League. Some elements of the national media targeted the club for what amounted to little more than public ridicule for their performances in the competition. Even allowing for the fact that the club was still a relative novice in European football, the criticism seemed overly harsh. While it was true that the club did not help its own cause at times, particularly when David Batty and Graeme Le Saux came to blows with each other in Moscow, the mounting attacks seemed extreme. If the team had beaten Legia Warsaw at Ewood Park then the Rovers would have qualified for the quarter-finals.

The fall-out from the Moscow fracas continued to rumble until David Batty was transferred to Newcastle United at the end of February 1996 for a fee of £3.75 million, a new club record for an outgoing transfer. Sadly, it was to mark the break up of the championship team.

The season ended with the Rovers in seventh position which, considering the fact that injuries had robbed the club of Kevin Gallacher and Graeme Le Saux for long periods, appeared a satisfactory conclusion to a difficult campaign. Alan Shearer, who scored 30 league goals for the third successive season, missed the final games as the Rovers allowed him to have minor surgery to ensure his fitness for Euro 96. On a more positive note, the season had seen Mike Newell register a hat-trick in the European Championship match against Rosenborg, while Graham Fenton scored two memorable goals late in the season that went some way to depriving Newcastle United of the championship. However, the best team performance of the season came on the day that the revamped Ewood Park was officially opened on 18 November 1996. On that day the Rovers rattled seven past Nottingham Forest without reply to underline the strength that still remained at Ewood.

Following the Euro 96 championships the national media was filled with speculation regarding the future of Alan Shearer. All at Ewood Park made it clear that the club had no intention of parting with the England striker, indeed, Ray Harford was busy trying to build a new strikeforce around his magical No. 9. To that end, the club signed Georgious Donis from Panathinaikos under the Bosman ruling as the Greek winger, nicknamed 'The Train' because of his speed, was out of contract. Unfortunately, Harford was thwarted in his attempts to bring French striker Christophe Dugarry to the club to partner Shearer.

Shearer Leaves for Newcastle

When Shearer returned from holiday he requested a meeting with officials of the club and a desperate bid was made to retain the services of the England centre forward. The persuasive tongue of Jack Walker appeared to have talked Shearer into remaining at the club and at one point it was reported that he had been offered the position of player-manager with Ray Harford happy to revert to his former coaching role. Ultimately, however, the player's wish to return to his roots with Newcastle United proved too strong and on 29 July 1996 the news broke that the club had reluctantly sold Alan Shearer to Newcastle for a world-record fee of £15 million.

A blanket of gloom descended on the whole town immediately following the departure of Shearer. Ironically, the club also said goodbye to Mike Newell who departed for Birmingham City and when Chris Sutton was injured in a pre-season friendly the attacking resources looked rather threadbare. An opening day loss at Ewood Park to Tottenham Hotspur did not auger well for the new campaign and it was not long before the club was embroiled in a traumatic battle against relegation. Before August was out the club had not only lost its most potent weapon in attack but had also parted company with Kenny Dalglish. His role as director of football had been a rather nebulous affair and the termination of his position at the club appeared to be the logical progression of things. Sadly, Ray Harford became an increasingly isolated figure at the helm as public confidence in the manager began to wane.

When the club played host to Stockport County in the third round of the Coca-Cola Cup the Rovers were bottom of the league with just three points from nine matches. A shambolic performance against Stockport ended in defeat and the only goal of the game encapsulated the misfortunes that had befallen the club. A long throw was launched towards the near post where players were already gathered ready to clear the ball. Suddenly, Tim Flowers decided to come out and punch the ball but only succeeded in knocking the ball against the back of Tim Sherwood's head and it rebounded over the line. Three days later Ray Harford offered his resignation and the board reluctantly accepted it. The manager had become a victim of circumstance but in resigning had offered the club an opportunity to rectify the situation before it became too late.

Tony Parkes made the familiar walk to the manager's office to assume caretaker duties while the club looked for Harford's replacement. However, the club was in no hurry to make an appointment as Jack Walker and his

Great Managers – 1991-95

KENNY DALGLISH

Most of the national media were sceptical as to whether Jack Walker would be able to tempt Dalglish out of retirement at a time when Blackburn Rovers was regarded as a perennial Second Division club, residing in an ageing stadium. However, his persuasive tongue and Dalglish's own desire to prove himself away from the familiar surroundings of Anfield led to his appointment on 12 October 1991. Dalglish invited Ray Harford, the former Luton Town and Wimbledon manager, to join him as his assistant and the two men, backed by Jack Walker, lifted the club from mid-table to become red-hot favourites to win the Second Division championship. The arrival of new faces such as Colin Hendry, Mike Newell, Tim Sherwood and Roy Wegerle helped the promotion drive but when the team faltered Dalglish kept his nerve and guided them to promotion via the play-offs.

Next Dalglish began to build a team that could compete at the highest level. He sold the popular David Speedie to capture Alan Shearer for a British record fee of £3.3

million, and the young striker looked on the manager as the perfect role model. Dalglish guided the club to fourth position during the inaugural season of the Premier League and then claimed the runners-up spot in 1993-94. During that campaign he brought Paul Warhurst, David Batty and Tim Flowers to the club, and the summer of 1994 brought Chris Sutton from Norwich City for £5 million. The 1994-95 season saw Blackburn win the championship for the first time in 80 years and it was perhaps fitting that it should have been clinched on the final day of the season at Anfield. Dalglish thus made his mark in the history books by winning a championship title with two different clubs.

Kenny Dalglish transformed the fortunes of Blackburn Rovers in just four years, and won the Premiership crown in 1995.

directors scoured Europe looking for the right man. In the interim, Parkes did his usual meticulous job at the helm and gradually hauled the club off the bottom of the table. In December 1996, the Rovers announced that Sven Goran Eriksson would take over the club in the summer when his contract with Sampdoria ended. Chairman Rob Coar announced that Eriksson would sign a three-year contract, with Parkes controlling team affairs until then.

The impending appointment of Eriksson was a real coup for the club and the news was broadly welcomed. However, as Parkes continued to inspire the team to climb away from the bottom of the table there were increasing rumours that the Swede was having a change of heart. In February it was announced that Eriksson had contacted the club and officially requested permission to withdraw from his agreement citing personal reasons for wishing to remain in Italy, and the Rovers quickly looked elsewhere for a replacement. In the end Jack Walker returned to the man who he had approached before Eriksson, namely Roy Hodgson of Inter Milan. Hodgson had originally resisted offers to take over at Ewood but when the club returned he immediately accepted. Tony Parkes would continue as manager until the new manager took control in the summer.

Parkes Ensures Survival

While the off-the-field shenanigans occupied the minds of the fans, Parkes and the players got on with the job of ensuring that Hodgson arrived at a Premier League club in the summer. In his bid to save the club Parkes had jettisoned the unpredictable Donis in favour of a midfield consisting of Billy McKinlay, Tim Sherwood and Garry Flitcroft. Sherwood proved an inspirational captain as he led the team from the front. With other areas of the team in disarray, the goalkeeper and defence stood firm. Flowers continued to keep the promising Shay Given at bay with outstanding performances. Henning Berg and Colin Hendry began to develop into a powerful central defensive combination and suddenly Rovers had became a tough unit to crack.

It was in attack that the team continued to struggle. Although Chris Sutton and Kevin Gallacher reached double figures there was little support from elsewhere with new signing Per Pedersen proving particularly disappointing. A 4-1 win over Sheffield Wednesday on 22 April 1997 virtually guaranteed Premier League survival and a goalless draw at home to Middlesbrough officially made the Rovers safe. It was ironic that Middlesbrough should provide the point required for safety as earlier in the season they had refused to play at Ewood Park because of an injury crisis. The powers-that-be took a dim view of such behaviour and deducted three points from their total. Ultimately, this proved sufficient to condemn Middlesbrough to relegation.

As a token of appreciation for the tremendous work that he had done on behalf of the club, Jack Walker made a special presentation to Tony Parkes before the last game of the season at Ewood Park. He was also rewarded with a Carling No. 1 award during the summer which is given to individuals who have made an outstanding contribution to the national game. None at Blackburn would deny his contribution to the Rovers during 1996-97.

Chapter Twelve: 1997-2001
Souness to the Rescue

After the traumas of the previous season Roy Hodgson made an immediate impact at Ewood Park. With his vast knowledge of continental football it came as no surprise that the majority of his signings came from abroad. Anders Andersson, whom he had previously signed for Malmo FF, arrived from the Swedish club. Another Swedish international to be signed was striker Martin Dahlin, who joined the club from AS Roma, while French full back Patrick Valery was signed from Bastia. A player who Hodgson had managed while in charge of the Swiss national side was signed when Stephane Henchoz agreed a move from Hamburg SV. The fifth new face to arrive at Ewood Park was goalkeeper John Filan, an Australian international who was signed from Coventry to provide experienced back-up to Tim Flowers.

In September, the manager signed another experienced Norwegian international when Tore Pedersen joined for £500,000 from the German club St Pauli, and Northern Ireland international goalkeeper Alan Fettis from Nottingham Forest after Shay Givens had left for Newcastle looking for first-team football. A new face that the manager introduced to the backroom staff at Ewood Park was Arnaldo Longaretti, an experienced fitness coach who had worked with several top Italian clubs.

Swedish striker Martin Dahlin was one of Roy Hodgson's international imports.

Hodgson Makes an Impact

Other familiar faces to depart Ewood Park during the summer included Henning Berg and Graeme Le Saux who were both subject to £5 million moves and joined Manchester United and Chelsea, respectively. Graham Fenton, Nicky Marker, Mattie

50 Greatest Players

ALAN SHEARER Striker

Born: Newcastle, 13 August 1970

Joined Blackburn: 1992 **From:** Southampton

Debut: 15 August 1992 v Crystal Palace, League

Appearances: 171   **Goals:** 130

Left Blackburn: 1996   **For:** Newcastle United

Honours won with Blackburn: 25 England caps; Premiership championship 1995

Alan Shearer was the greatest goalscorer of his era. Kenny Dalglish paid a British record fee of £3.3 million for him and he was rewarded with goals in abundance. Shearer missed several months of his first season with a cruciate ligament injury but his determination to regain his fitness brought him all the rewards the game could offer. A championship medal in 1995, the Football Writers' Association Player of the Year award 1993-94, the Professional Footballers' Association Footballer of the Year award 1995 and 25 England caps all came his way during his four years at Ewood Park. He was idolized by the fans as a more athletic version of Ted Harper or Tommy Briggs. His game was based on pace and power and yet he possessed an ability to shield the ball from defenders and thereby bring other players into the action. His greatest gift was his ability to score goals from all areas of the pitch – he was powerful in the air and lurked around the penalty area to snap up the merest half chance. He was always happy to accept a tap-in but was also capable of scoring with the rocket-like power of his shooting. He reached the 30 goals mark in three successive seasons and became the first player to score 100 Premier League goals. His move to Newcastle United in 1996 for £15 million rocked the town.

Holmes, Paul Warhurst and Niklas Gudmundsson were all allowed to leave by the new manager as he began to reshape the squad.

The quality of the football played by the Rovers during the opening months of Hodgson's reign proved a revelation. The second game of the season produced a comprehensive 4-0 away win at Aston Villa while the third match brought a 7-2 demolition of Sheffield Wednesday at Ewood Park. Sadly, in that game, the manager lost John Filan for virtually the rest of the season with a badly broken arm. As Christmas approached, the club was in second place in the league just four points behind Manchester United. The players had responded magnificently to the new methods that Hodgson had introduced. This included all-day training sessions with the fitness of each player continually monitored. Unfortunately, the nagging doubts about the depth of quality of the squad came to the fore during a disappointing second half of the season. In the end, only a late goal from Chris Sutton on the last day of the season produced a win over Newcastle United that ensured European qualification. It was the least that Hodgson and his players deserved.

Having seen his side fade during the latter part of the previous season Roy Hodgson again looked to strengthen his squad during the summer of 1998. However, his first sortie into the transfer market was taken with a view to the future with the signing of 17-year-old Jimmy Corbett from Gillingham. The manager added experience to his defence by taking Darren Peacock (available under the Bosman ruling) from Newcastle United. Sebastian Perez, a player who could operate at either full back or in midfield, was signed from Corsican outfit Bastia. The former French Under-21 star cost the Rovers £3 million and was keen to join the club after talking to Patrick Valery, his former team-mate at Bastia. Ironically, within weeks of Perez arriving in Blackburn, Valery had made the journey in the opposite direction to rejoin the Corsican club. The Rovers also bade farewell to Stuart Ripley and James Beattie who both left Ewood Park to head for Southampton.

However, the deal that really captured the headlines was when the Rovers

paid £7.25 million for Kevin Davies from Southampton. An England Under-21 international, Davies had initially come to prominence in the 1996-97 season when he helped Chesterfield reach the FA Cup semifinal. This had earned him a move to Southampton in the summer of 1997 for £700,000. Now, just 12 months later and despite missing half of the previous campaign through injury, he had cost the Rovers a new record fee.

On the eve of the season, with preparations for the new campaign well advanced, the club was rocked by a transfer request from Colin Hendry. He was about to start his testimonial season but wanted to return to Scotland and was not interested in remaining with the

Roy Hodgson brought experience to the defence with Newcastle's Darren Peacock.

Brian Kidd took over as manager after the departure of Roy Hodgson.

Rovers. Despite the best efforts of Blackburn officials, the player held firm to his decision to return to Scotland, citing family reasons. With Hendry departing for Glasgow Rangers for a fee in the region of £4 million, the manager had to move swiftly to replace him. Ironically, the player chosen was Christian Dailly who appeared at Ewood Park on the opening day of the season playing for Derby County. The following week he was in the Blackburn team at Leeds United after a £5 million move.

The Hendry saga had hung over the club's pre-season preparations and once the campaign got under way the manager found his squad decimated by injuries. Matters became so desperate that Martin Taylor, a promising young central defender, made his debut as a substitute against Olympique Lyonnais in France. However, such was the chronic injury situation surrounding his forward players that Hodgson was forced to use Taylor as a centre forward.

The injuries began to impact on results in the league and by early November the club was again fighting relegation. Hodgson again entered the transfer market and Oumar Konde, a 19-year-old Swiss Under-21 international midfielder, was signed from FC Basle, while Dario Marcolin, an experienced Italian midfielder, came on an extended loan deal from Lazio. An initial fee of £3.75 million was paid for Nathan Blake, Bolton Wanderers' Welsh international centre forward after Dion Dublin rejected an approach.

However, there was growing unrest in the Blackburn camp and the manager and Tim Sherwood clashed after Tottenham Hotspur made an abortive raid to sign the Ewood skipper. On 21 November 1998, the Rovers slipped to the bottom of the table when Southampton, the club already occupying bottom spot, came to Ewood Park and inflicted a 2-0 defeat on the Rovers. After the game a special news conference was called at which it was announced that the Rovers had parted company with Roy Hodgson. Just a few months earlier he had been touted as a possible England manager but somehow the mixture of this most erudite of managers and Blackburn Rovers did not quite gel. Although hamstrung by a mounting injury list, it was the failure of his expensive signings, particularly Kevin Davies, that gradually undermined the manager's credibility. His subsequent career on the continent proved that, whatever his failings at Blackburn, he was still one of Europe's most respected and successful coaches.

Brian Kidd Appointed

Tony Parkes took control once more but on this occasion it was for only the briefest of periods. Jack Walker had already identified the man he wanted and on 5 December 1998 Brian Kidd, the Manchester United assistant manager, was introduced to the crowd as the new manager before the home game with Charlton Athletic. Although he was not supposed to officially take control until after the game he spent virtually the entire match on the touchline shouting instructions to his new charges. After the more phlegmatic and studied approach of Hodgson the overly-animated Kidd found favour with many fans at Ewood.

As with the final months of the Hodgson reign, the new manager dipped heavily into the war chest that Jack Walker provided. Kidd immediately added to his backroom staff by appointing former Old Trafford colleague Brian McClair to the coaching staff. However, the appointment of McClair meant the

Jason McAteer was signed from Liverpool for his skills in central midfield.

axe for Derek Fazackerley. The first new signing also had Old Trafford links in that Keith Gillespie had served his apprenticeship under Kidd before leaving Manchester for Newcastle United. Kidd agreed a £2.3 million fee to bring the winger from St James's Park to Blackburn. Other big money signings soon followed with Ashley Ward joining from Barnsley for £4.25

The tenacious Lee Carsley was signed from Derby in 1999 to strengthen the midfield.

million and Matt Jansen from Crystal Palace and Jason McAteer from Liverpool, both for £4 million. With an eye to the future the manager also invested a potential £2.6 million in a couple of youngsters from St Mirren in Burton O'Brien and David McNamee. Both teenagers then returned to Scotland to spend the remainder of the season on loan with their former club.

Results under the enthusiastic Kidd began to improve and by the time Sheffield Wednesday visited Ewood Park the club was up to 16th position in the table. However, by this point the club had lost captain Tim Sherwood who finally moved to Tottenham Hotspur. While there had been a certain amount of turbulence about his departure, the fact remained that the former skipper's influence was badly missed on the field. Sheffield Wednesday, also struggling at the wrong end of the table, romped to a 4-1 win and in so doing triggered a slump.

The loss of midfield general Sherwood severely weakened the midfield and the manager seemed strangely reluctant to utilize the experience of Dario Marcolin, preferring to opt for the youth of David Dunn to partner Jason McAteer in central midfield. With just eight games remaining, and the club still deeply embroiled in the relegation battle, the manager paid out £3.375 million to capture Derby County's midfield bulldog, Lee Carsley. The Republic of Ireland international was the type of tenacious individual that had been sorely missed in the middle of the park.

Rovers Head For Division One

Unfortunately, the situation was too far gone for Carsley to make any difference and the team performances over the final few weeks of the season suggested that the players already sensed that the game was up. Perhaps the worst performance of the season was reserved for the most important game of the campaign. The visit of already-relegated Nottingham Forest to Ewood

Park on 8 May 1999 was a game that had to be won. The Ewood Park crowd responded to the pleas of the club to roar the team on to victory but the response on the field suggested that the pressure had finally got to many of the players. After the match, a distraught manager accused his players of being 'rubber dinghy men'. The final nail in the Rovers' coffin was delivered by Manchester United, the club that Kidd had left the previous December. A goalless draw was sufficient to send the Rovers into the First Division while United went on to win the treble.

In view of the manager's comments following the Nottingham Forest game the supporters expected to see a substantial change of personnel at Ewood Park during the summer. However, the changes proved to be of a more minimal nature. As expected, Dario Marcolin was allowed to return to Italy

---

50 Greatest Players

COLIN HENDRY Defender

Born: Keith, 7 December 1965

Joined Blackburn: 1987; 1991   **From:** Dundee; Manchester City

Debut: 11 March 1987 v Ipswich Town, Full Members' Cup

Appearances: 408   **Goals:** 35

Left Blackburn: 1989; 1998   **For:** Manchester City; Rangers

Honours won with Blackburn: 35 Scotland caps; Premiership championship 1995

Colin Hendry was a virtual unknown when he arrived in 1987 from Dundee. When he left for the first time in November 1989 he had captured the hearts of the Blackburn faithful. By the time he left for a second time in August 1998 he had become a legend – Blackburn's very own 'Braveheart'. When he scored the only goal of the Full Members' Cup final at Wembley he was a raw centre forward who made up for his lack of finesse with a whole-hearted approach. When he moved to centre half he delighted supporters with his rampaging charges up field but, while his bravery was unquestioned, there was a naivety about his play that comes with the rashness of youth.

The fans were crestfallen when he left for Manchester City and when Kenny Dalglish brought him back in November 1991 he was welcomed like a prodigal son. Under Dalglish and Harford the rough edges of his game were soon smoothed over and in Kevin Moran he had an excellent tutor in the finer arts of defending. His contribution to the championship season of 1994-95 was immense and he was selected for the PFA Premiership team of that season. It came as a major shock to everyone when on the eve of his testimonial season he announced that he wished to return to his native Scotland.

and Oumour Konde, who had made just one substitute appearance for the club, left to play in Germany with SC Frieburg. Liverpool quickly moved in to sign Stephane Henchoz for £3.5 million after the Swiss international indicated that the First Division was not for him. On the eve of the season the club also allowed Tim Flowers to move to Leicester City, as the former England international had become unsettled with the role of back-up to John Filan. However, the biggest departure from Ewood Park was that of Chris Sutton who moved to Chelsea for around £10 million. The manager added three experienced men to his squad in Republic of Ireland international goalkeeper Alan Kelly from Sheffield United, full back Simon Grayson from Leicester City and central defender Craig Short from Everton.

After the opening two games produced a single point the manager arranged a deal that took Kevin Davies back to Southampton and brought Egil Ostendstad to Ewood Park. However, no matter how Kidd shuffled the pack

50 Greatest Players

TIM SHERWOOD Midfielder

Born: St Albans, 6 February 1969

Joined Blackburn: 1992   **From:** Norwich City

Debut: 22 February 1992 v Middlesbrough, League

Appearances: 300   **Goals:** 32

Left Blackburn: 1999   **For:** Tottenham Hotspur

Honours won with Blackburn: Premiership championship 1995

While there was nothing pretentious or pompous about Sherwood, there was no mistaking the imperious attitude that came from the knowledge that he excelled in his role as a midfield general. This attitude might not always have endeared him to the general public but the true professional knew its real worth. Kenny Dalglish, following the retirement of Kevin Moran, had no hesitation in handing Sherwood the captaincy and watched him flourish with the added responsibility. His crowning moment came at Anfield in May 1995 when he lifted the Premiership trophy. When Sherwood arrived at Blackburn in February 1992, he had found it difficult to establish himself until after promotion was won at Wembley via the play-offs. The player was obviously more suited to a higher level and under the tutelage of Dalglish and Harford he matured into one of the outstanding midfield players in the Premiership. Never one to dwell unnecessarily on the ball, Sherwood kept the play moving, feeding both his wingers, usually Stuart Ripley and Jason Wilcox, as well as prompting Alan Shearer with precision passes that bisected the tightest of defences. He was a constant threat in the opposition penalty area having the knack of being able to glide into the danger area without an accompanying marker.

the team simply failed to make an impact on the First Division. Other new faces followed with Steve Harkness joining from Benfica and Per Frandson making the short move from Bolton Wanderers while Kevin Gallacher was surprisingly allowed to move to Newcastle United. With the Rovers being seen as the team that everyone wanted to beat, each game became a battle and by the time Queens Park Rangers arrived at Ewood Park on 2 October 1999 the Rovers had only won three of their 13 league games. Far from challenging for promotion the club was in 18th place in the table, three points off the bottom and 14 points from top-placed Manchester City.

When Queens Park Rangers inflicted a 2-0 defeat on the Rovers there was growing unrest among supporters who had continued to remain loyal to the club despite the alarming fall from grace. Four days after the defeat by Rangers both Brian Kidd and Brian McClair were summoned from the training ground at Brockhall to a meeting at Ewood Park. The outcome was that the contracts of both men were terminated and Tony Parkes was yet again put in charge of the team. Like Hodgson before him, Kidd had paid the price for failing to get results, despite spending around £30 million on new players. Sadly, too many of the new recruits didn't perform for Kidd.

Graeme Souness took charge in March 2000 with one aim in mind: promotion.

Although he spent heavily, the manager also recouped £27 million – much of what he spent – by selling a number of established stars. Unfortunately, fans felt that the players who left were better than those who were signed and results tended to lend credence to the argument.

Parkes did his usual effective job as stand-in manager and got the results that lifted the team into a mid-table position. In early December, Jack Walker and the directors offered the manager's position to Parkes until the end of the season. The new manager, with Terry Darracott moving up from the reserves to coach the first-team squad, celebrated his first game in charge with a 3-1 win over Bolton Wanderers that put the Rovers within range of the play-off places. It was at this point that the Rovers accepted an offer of £3.7 million from Leeds United for Jason Wilcox. Sadly, a sustained challenge failed to materialize. A run of four games from late January through February produced one point and undermined any realistic hope of getting closer to the teams at the top.

Enter Souness

In March the club appointed its third manager of the season when Graeme Souness was invited to take control. Another backroom shake-up saw Tony Parkes revert to his assistant manager's role while Phil Boersma arrived with Souness to assist him with the first team. The new manager had a fairly dramatic effect on the team with three successive wins reviving the faint hope that a dramatic dash for the play-offs could yet be made. However, defeat at Wolverhampton ended these hopes and the manager used the remaining five

50 Greatest Players

TIM FLOWERS Goalkeeper

Born: Kenilworth, 3 February 1967

Joined Blackburn: 1993   **From:** Southampton

Debut: 6 November 1993 v Queens Park Rangers, League

Appearances: 217

Left Blackburn: 1999   **For:** Leicester City

Honours won with Blackburn: 10 England caps; Premiership championship 1995

The record-breaking signing of Tim Flowers was to prove a wise investment as the former Southampton custodian played a major role in capturing the Premiership crown for the Rovers. He had previously spurned the opportunity to join Liverpool, as he was determined to join the Ewood revolution. He arrived at Blackburn with over 250 league games behind him and was approaching the peak of his career.

After moving to Lancashire he received his first England international cap against Brazil in the summer of 1993 and then became a regular in the England squad. He was a hugely popular figure with the Blackburn supporters who immediately took to his enthusiastic approach to the game. A fierce competitor, Flowers was an excellent shot stopper and confident in his command of the penalty area. Always quick to act as a sweeper behind his back four, Flowers made a significant contribution to the winning of the Premiership crown in 1994-95. Indeed, his man-of-the-match performance against Newcastle United at Ewood Park on 8 May 1995 was one of the finest displays of goalkeeping ever seen by a Blackburn custodian.

league games to assess the quality of his new playing staff. Having finished the season in 11th position in the First Division, it was clear that the manager had a major job on his hands if he was to restore the club to its former glory. However, of more concern to everyone connected with the club was that Jack Walker was waging a war against serious health problems.

The summer of 2000 brought three new faces to Ewood Park with full backs John Curtis being signed from Manchester United for £1.5 million and Stig Inge Bjornebye arriving from Liverpool for £300,000. The largest fee was paid for Barnsley midfield star Craig Hignett who was the subject of a £2.25 million deal. Unfortunately, the latter was injured in pre-season training and spent the early weeks of the season sidelined.

An opening-day win over Crystal Palace was quickly overshadowed by the shattering news that Jack Walker had lost his gallant fight for life on Thursday 17 August 2000. The death of the club's 71-year-old benefactor was mourned not just by the followers of the club but by the whole of Blackburn. In the days following news of his loss the area around the Jack Walker stand became a sea of flowers as the people of Blackburn paid their respects to a man who, despite his wealth, never lost the common touch. Jack Walker was a man of the people and the people of Blackburn mourned the loss of one of their own. Jack Walker had no need of the limelight and poured millions into the club without thought of personal gain. His only wish was for Blackburn Rovers to be successful – truly a man who came to give rather than take. In rebuilding the stadium, in investing millions in a training complex for the players and a state-of-the-art academy complex for the youngsters, Jack Walker left the club and the supporters a legacy which will always be remembered.

The visit of Norwich City on 26 August 2000 was an emotional affair the like of which Ewood Park had never witnessed before. Prior to the match thousands gathered in hushed silence among the floral tributes that surrounded the Jack Walker stand. When a moving tribute to Jack Walker was screened prior to the match its end was greeted with a standing ovation from all sides of the ground. The Blackburn players laid flowers in the centre circle and Norwich City laid a bouquet in respect of a football man. In such circumstances it was little wonder that the Blackburn players found it difficult to concentrate on the game. However, a 3-2 win was the type of tribute Jack Walker would have appreciated and the manager immediately issued a challenge to his players to win promotion in the memory of a man who had given so much to so many others.

On the football field the manager looked to strengthen his squad and brought Henning Berg back to Ewood Park on a three months loan

It was a shrewd move when Graeme Souness signed up veteran Mark Hughes.

arrangement. Kabia Diawara, the former Arsenal forward, was brought on loan from Paris Saint Germain but was dispatched after a month as not being the type of player that Souness wanted. Although early results were promising, a controversial home defeat by Watford caused a minor slump that wasn't brought to an end until the club won at Wimbledon in mid-October. By this time, the club was 11th in the table, 14 points behind second-placed Watford and 18 points behind leaders Fulham.

'Sparky' Boosts the Squad

Souness shrewdly secured the signing of the vastly experienced Mark Hughes. With a number of highly-talented young players at his disposal the manager was well aware that, although almost 37 years of age, the Welsh international manager would be a steadying influence on his team. Furthermore, despite his age, he was still an outstanding target man who could harry defences into submission. The manager's judgement reaped immediate dividends when Sparky scored two goals on his debut against Grimsby Town on 21 October 2000.

With the team now steadily climbing the table November proved another busy month for the manager on the transfer front. After work permit problems were ironed out the manager signed Brad Friedel from Liverpool to be his number one goalkeeper. Although this was no reflection on Alan Kelly and John Filan, who had shared the duties up to that point, the manager was a great admirer of the experienced American international, having previously worked with him at Galatasaray in Turkey. While Friedel came on a free transfer, an initial fee of £1.35 million was paid for the Sheffield United front runner, Marcus Bent. A player with aggression and pace, Bent was also a consistent goalscorer for the Yorkshire club.

November also saw the club celebrate its 125th anniversary with the football authorities granting the club special permission to use a different strip for the game against Wolverhampton Wanderers on 18 November 2000. The match was the highlight of a special weekend of celebrations at Ewood Park and before the game there was a parade of former stars that included players from six different decades.

As well as the long-awaited fixture with Burnley, the month of December saw another arrival at Ewood Park with Alan Mahon from Sporting Lisbon. The former Tranmere youngster arrived at Blackburn on loan for the remainder of the season and was immediately given a place on the bench for the trip to Turf Moor. On the eve of the clash with Burnley the manager also signed Henning Berg on a permanent basis. The first meeting between the arch rivals in 17 years proved to be a joyous occasion for all Blackburn supporters. Goals from Jason McAteer and a first goal for Marcus Bent ensured that one part of East Lancashire enjoyed a very merry Christmas.

50 Greatest Players

HENNING BERG Defender

Born: Eidsvell, Norway, 1 September 1969

Joined Blackburn: 1993; 2000   **From:** SK Lillestrøm; Manchester United

Debut: 2 February 1993 v Crystal Palace, League

Appearances: 239   **Goals:** 5

Left Blackburn: 1997   **For:** Manchester United

Honours with Blackburn: 45 Norway caps; Premiership championship 1995

Although a central defender, Berg was utilized by Kenny Dalglish at right back and developed into one of the finest attacking full backs in the Premier League. He made 40 league appearances – more than any other player – during the championship season of 1994-95, and was one of the unsung heroes of the team. The quiet, thorough professional was an excellent reader of the game and was never ruffled under pressure with his perfect timing making tackling seem almost an art form. He left Ewood Park in August 1997 to join Manchester United for £5 million but became a victim of the rotation system. Although he a won a championship medal in 1998-99 he returned to Ewood Park in 2001 as a vital ingredient of the promotion-winning team of 2000-2001. Hugely popular with the supporters, during the summer of 2001 Berg claimed Bob Crompton's record as the most capped player in the history of the club.

When another local rival succumbed at Ewood Park in January 2001, this time Preston North End slipped to a 3-2 defeat, the Rovers found themselves third, just two points behind second-placed Bolton Wanderers. As the club prepared for the vital few months to come, the manager again added a familiar face to the squad when he signed Eyal Berkovic on loan from Celtic. It was Souness who had first brought the Israeli international to Britain when he was manager of Southampton and he was of the firm belief that this intricate playmaker would prove a telling addition to his squad. The manager also signed Marc Keller, West Ham United's former French international wide player, on a short-term contract to the end of the season.

The team embarked on a successful run in the FA Cup while keeping up the pressure on Bolton Wanderers in the league. A trip to Premiership Derby County for a fourth-round replay produced an impressive 5-2 win and proved a massive boost to confidence. After a slight blip at Nottingham Forest, which brought an end to a 13-match unbeaten run, the Rovers struck a psychological blow over Bolton Wanderers in the fifth round of the FA Cup. Although Garry Flitcroft had been dismissed early in the game the Rovers had left the Reebok Stadium unbeaten. Three days later the team travelled to Watford and completed a 1-0 win over another promotion rival.

However, on this occasion it was the Rovers who enjoyed a significant advantage after Watford had two players sent off before half-time.

Three days after the Watford victory the Rovers returned to the Reebok Stadium for a vital clash with Bolton Wanderers. After a fairly even first half the Rovers grabbed the lead just before the interval, thanks to Marcus Bent. However, the second half became a one-way procession as the Rovers dominated to come away 4-1 winners, with goals from David Dunn, Matt Jansen and Craig Hignett.

West Bromwich Albion became the next promotion rival to lose to the

The speedy Marcus Bent up front proved an important addition to the strikeforce.

Great Managers – 2000-present

GRAEME SOUNESS

Within 14 months of taking charge at Ewood Park, Graeme Souness had joined an elite band of managers who had won promotion with the club. Although the club languished in mid-table of the First Division there was little doubting the enthusiasm and wealth of experience that Souness brought to the job. Like Kenny Dalglish before him, Souness had won all the honours that the game could offer during his playing career with Liverpool. As player-manager of Glasgow Rangers he won four successive league titles and four league cups before returning to Anfield, to succeed Dalglish, where he underwent triple heart-bypass surgery, but returned to management with his passion undiminished. His subsequent managerial career took in spells with Galatasaray in Turkey, Southampton, Italian club Torino and Benfica in Portugal. On arriving at Blackburn he forged a new management team with Phil Boersma, who he brought to the club, and Tony Parkes.

Although three successive victories followed his appointment, promotion was beyond his grasp so he used the remainder of the season to assess the quality of the squad. During the summer he acquired new faces in John Curtis, Stig Inge Bjornebye and Craig Hignett. However, when early season form began to waver he again moved to strengthen his squad with the acquisition of Henning Berg, Mark Hughes, Brad Friedel, Marcus Bent and Alan Mahon. Later in the campaign he added the experience of Eyal Berkovic and Marc Keller. Yet, despite these signings, Souness was always careful to stress the need for keeping within the bounds of a sensible financial structure. He was also quick to promote younger players from the academy and homegrown talent flourished under Souness. During the 2000-2001 season it became clear that the manager had restored the unity that had proved so successful during the reign of Kenny Dalglish. The pride that had seeped away from Ewood Park returned and so too did the optimism. In Graeme Souness the club had found a man with the experience and desire to take Blackburn Rovers into a new era, while the manager had found a club that allowed him to concentrate on football rather than balance sheets. A marriage made in heaven.

Rovers before Bolton were beaten again in the FA Cup replay at Ewood Park. Both sides fielded slightly weakened sides as eyes were firmly kept on promotion. Three days after beating Bolton the Rovers travelled to Highbury for a game that was little more than an interruption to the promotion campaign. There were few among the Ewood faithful who were surprised that Souness chose to rest Jansen and Damien Duff, as another vital promotion clash was coming at Birmingham four days later. Indeed, the 3-0 defeat at Highbury did little to damage the confidence of players or fans.

Great Matches

FOOTBALL LEAGUE DIVISION TWO	**Ewood Park, 1 April 2001**
Blackburn Rovers 5 **Burnley 0**	**Attendance: 23,515**

Short
Davis (o.g.)
Jansen 2
Hignett

April Fools' Day presented Burnley with the perfect opportunity to halt the promotion bandwagon that was gathering pace at Ewood Park. However, the Rovers were in no mood to let slip the wonderful position that they had fought hard to achieve. The Blackburn fans didn't have long to wait before the Burnley defence was breached. Dunn shot from the edge of the box and Craig Short stuck out a foot and diverted it past two stranded defenders. On 28 minutes, after a refereeing decision that played advantage, Short kept a tricky ball in play and fired a shot-cum-cross across the Burnley goal. The ball struck Davis on the inside of his left boot to deflect into the goal.

Brad Friedel, Blackburn's giant American goalkeeper, pulled off a miraculous save to deny Burnley their one chance and with two goals behind them the Rovers began the second period at an increased tempo. The pace was clearly telling on a Burnley side containing a number of senior professionals. The young legs of the Blackburn side began to run them ragged. On 55 minutes, Matt Jansen banged a Marcus Bent cross past Mihopoulos with ease to put the Rovers three ahead, then fired home the fourth goal after 70 minutes when he raced clear after playing a perfect one-two with Alan Mahon. The fifth goal arrived on 82 minutes when a clever ball by Mark Hughes gave Craig Hignett the chance to drive the ball home. Burnley manager Stan Ternent put the positions of the clubs into perspective when he said, '...we're a million miles away financially from Blackburn Rovers and that shows on the football field'.

Blackburn Rovers: Friedel, Curtis, Berg (Hughes), Short, McAteer (Hignett), Dunn, Flitcroft, Mahon, Duff (Bjornebye), Jansen, Bent

Burnley: Mihopoulos, Thomas, Davis, Cox, Weller, Little, Ball (Payton), Cook, Branch (Smith), Taylor, Moore (Armstrong)

Referee: A. Butler (Notts)

Marcus Bent with goalscorer Craig Short and David Dunn after the opening goal.

Matt Jansen scores the only goal of a game that sends Blackburn back to the Premiership.

An electrifying performance in beating Birmingham 2-0 quickly erased the memory of losing to Arsenal as the Rovers now become the in-form team of the Division. This was confirmed on 1 April 2001 when Burnley came to Ewood Park determined to wipe out the memory of the defeat that they had suffered earlier in the season. The Rovers simply ran Burnley ragged and the 5-0 win lifted the club into second place in the table for the first time since the opening week of the season.

Promotion Celebrations

The Rovers and Bolton Wanderers were neck and neck until the end of the season with the Rovers unable to shake off the men from the Reebok Stadium. The Rovers appeared to have gained an advantage after Berkovic inspired the team to an impressive 4-1 victory over Grimsby Town at Blundell Park. However, Bolton responded with a win, at Barnsley, on the Saturday to keep the pressure on the Rovers who faced Portsmouth at Ewood Park the following day. After a fairly nervous affair the Rovers restored their four-point advantage thanks to a 3-1 win, although it needed a Scott Hiley own goal to put the Rovers on level terms after Portsmouth had taken a shock lead.

When Bolton won at Wolverhampton Wanderers on the final Tuesday of the league campaign it meant that the Rovers had to win at least one of their remaining two matches to ensure promotion. However, away fixtures against Preston North End and Gillingham were not the easiest of places to visit when points were required. On Wednesday 2 May 2001, the Rovers visited Deepdale and emerged victorious after a thrilling match that kept Ewood fans on the edge of their seats. A Matt Jansen header on 72 minutes was sufficient to win the game and send the Rovers back into the Premiership amid jubilant scenes of celebration.

After the match the manager and players all paid tribute to the one man who wasn't there to enjoy the occasion. Skipper Garry Flitcroft removed his shirt to reveal a t-shirt that carried the simple message 'Jack This is 4 You'. It was a sentiment that every Blackburn fan shared. Graeme Souness stood in front of the media to pay his own tribute to the man who was Mr Blackburn Rovers.

'I'm sure Jack will be looking down on us and he'll probably be on his second bottle of expensive Bordeaux by now. He'll be drinking it all to himself knowing him,' said Souness. 'But, as I've said many times,' he added, 'this football club is all about Jack Walker – the stadium we have, the training ground we have, the academy we have, and the wages the club pays.

And it's only because of one man that all this was possible. That is something we are all very grateful for and we must never forget that. There will never, ever be another Jack Walker, and this is for him.'

Thanks to the generosity of Jack Walker the club can look forward to a future of continued prosperity. The link between the football club, the community and successful local businessmen remains unbroken. For 125 years Blackburn Rovers has been the focal point of a proud industrial community and, as it looks to a new future in the Premiership, long may it remain so.

Jack Walker, who made Blackburn Rovers a proud team again, here with the hard-earned championship trophy of 1995.

THE ESSENTIAL HISTORY OF
BLACKBURN ROVERS

CLUB STATISTICS

The Blackburn Rovers Directory

Origins
- Founded: 1875
- First entered the FA Cup: 1879-80
- Founder members of the Football League in 1888
- Founder members of the Premier League in 1992
- Grounds: 1875 all matches played away; 1876 Oozehead Ground & Pleasington Cricket Ground; 1877 Alexandra Meadows Cricket Ground; 1881 Leamington Road; 1890 Ewood Park
- Limited Company: 1897

Honours
- FA Carling Premiership champions: 1994-95
- Runners-up: 1993-94
- Division 1 champions: 1911-12, 1913-14
- Runners-up Division 1 – promoted: 2000-01
- Division 2 champions: 1938-39
- Runners-up Division 2 – promoted: 1957-58
- Play-off winners: 1991-92
- Division 3 champions: 1974-75
- Runners-up Division 3 – promoted: 1979-80
- FA Cup winners: 1884-86, 1890, 1891, 1928
- FA Cup finalists: 1882, 1960
- Full Members' Cup winners: 1987
- FA Youth Cup winners: 1959
- FA Youth Cup finalists: 1998, 2001

Records
- Record victory: 11-0 v Rossendale United (h), FA Cup Round 1, 13 October 1884
- Record league win: 9-0 v Middlesbrough (h), Division 2, 6 November 1954
- Record away league win: 8-2 v West Ham United, Division 1, 26 December 1963
- Record league defeat: 0-8 v Arsenal (a), Division 1, 25 February 1933; 0-8 v Lincoln City (a), Division 2, 29 August 1953
- Record home defeat: 1-7 v Notts County, the Football League, 14 March 1891; 1-7 v Middlesbrough, Division 1, 29 November 1947
- Most points gained in a season (2pts): 60 (1974-75)
- Fewest points gained in a season (2pts): 20 (1965-66)
- Most points gained in a season (3pts): 91 (2000-01)
- Fewest points gained in a season (3pts): 35 (1998-99)
- Most senior appearances: Derek Fazackerley 689 (686+3) (1969-87)

- Most league appearances: Derek Fazackerley 596 (593+3) (1969-87)
- Most consecutive league appearances: Walter Crook 208 (1934-46)
- Most FA Cup appearances: Ronnie Clayton 56 (1949-69)
- Most Football League Cup appearances: Derek Fazackerley 38 (1969-87)
- Most collective league goals in a season: 114, Division 2, 1954-55
- Most collective hat-tricks in a season: 8, Division 1, 1963-64
- Most individual hat-tricks in a season: 5 – John Southworth (1890-91), Andy McEvoy (1963-64), Alan Shearer (1995-96)
- Most league goals in a season: Ted Harper 43, Division 1, 1925-26
- Most league goals in a match: 7, Tommy Briggs, v Bristol Rovers (h), won 7-2, Division 1, 5 February 1955
- Most league goals in aggregate: 168, Simon Garner (1978-92)
- Most capped player (with club): Henning Berg (Norway) 45 caps
- Youngest league player: Harry Dennison, aged 16 years, 155 days v Bristol City (h), Division 1, 8 April 1911
- Oldest player: Bob Crompton, aged 40 years, 150 days, v Bradford (a), Division 1, 23 February 1920
- Record transfer fee paid: £7,250,000 for Kevin Davies from Southampton, June 1998
- Record transfer fee received: £15 million for Alan Shearer from Newcastle United, July 1996
- Record attendance at Ewood Park: 62,522 v Bolton Wanderers, FA Cup Round 6, 2 March 1929.

Record League Sequences
- Successive wins: 8 (1979-80)
- Successive draws: 5 (1973-74), (1975-76)
- Successive defeats: 7 (1965-66)
- Successive matches without defeat: 23 (1987-88)
- Successive matches without a win: 16 (1978-79)
- Successive matches without defeat from the start of a season: 10 (1913-14), (1989-90)
- Successive matches without a win from the start of a season: 11 (1996-97)

50 Greatest Players

The list before you is purely the personal indulgence of the author. It contains the names of players who I consider to have made a fundamental contribution to the history of Blackburn Rovers. Apologies to anyone whose favourites are not included but football is a game of opinions. However, I still believe that the majority of the 50 men below would figure somewhere on everybody's list of all-time greats.

No. 1 Bob Crompton (Right back) – 608 appearances, 14 goals. Without question he was the greatest 'Blackburn Rover' of all time. He captained two championship-winning sides and skippered his country. Crompton later served the club as a director and then manager. (See pages 38 and 64)

No. 2 Ronnie Clayton (Right half) – 665 appearances, 16 goals. A former England captain who served Blackburn Rovers with great distinction for 20 years. Second only to Crompton in the order of merit at Ewood Park. (See page 107)

No. 3 Bryan Douglas (Forward) – 503 appearances, 115 goals. Duggie could ply his wizardry on the right wing or at inside forward. From the same mould as Stan Matthews and Tom Finney, Douglas possessed wonderful dribbling skills. (See page 108)

No. 4 Alan Shearer (Centre forward) – 171 appearances, 130 goals. A prolific goalscorer whose 34 league goals fired Blackburn to the Premiership crown in 1994-95. (See page 168)

No. 5 Derek Fazackerley (Defender) – 689 appearances, 26 goals. A reliable defender, Fazackerley appeared in 596 league games, a club record. (See page 138)

No. 6 Simon Garner (Forward) – 570 appearances, 194 goals. A deadly predator in the penalty area, Garner set a new club record by scoring 168 league goals during his time at Ewood Park. (See page 154)

No. 7 Jimmy Forrest (Half back) – 195 appearances, 7 goals. An outstanding half back in the early days of the club, he won five FA Cup-winners' medals with the Rovers and later served as a director. (See page 26)

No. 8 Bill Eckersley (Left back) – 432 appearances, 21 goals. A classy full back who won 17 England caps and proved to be a hugely popular figure at Ewood Park. (See page 88)

No. 9 Harry Healless (Half back) – 399 appearances, 14 goals. Captain of the FA Cup-winning team of 1928, Healless gave outstanding service as a player and later returned to Ewood Park as a coach. (See page 55).

No. 10 Billy Bradshaw (Half back) – 457 appearances, 51 goals. A member of two championship teams at Ewood Park, Bradshaw was an expert penalty taker with 22 successful spot kicks to his name. (See page 39)

No. 11 Jimmy Brown (Centre forward) – 36 appearances, 29 goals. Brown was a prolific goalscorer in pre-league days. He won three FA Cup-winners' medals and five England caps. (See page 23)

No. 12 Eddie Latheron (Inside forward) – 303 appearances, 120 goals. A key figure in the championship-winning sides of 1912 and 1914, Latheron was at the peak of his career when he became one of the fallen of World War I. (See page 34)

No 13 Bob Pryde (Centre half) – 525 appearances, 22 goals. A formidable defender, Pryde was at the heart of the defence for over a decade. (See page 68)

No. 14 Tommy Briggs (Centre forward) – 204 appearances, 143 goals. Briggs hit 30 goals a season for four consecutive seasons in the mid-1950s. In February 1955, he bagged seven in a match against Bristol Rovers. (See page 82)

No. 15 Colin Hendry (Defender) – 408 appearances, 35 goals. Blackburn's very own 'Braveheart'. One of Blackburn's best-ever defenders and a man whose bravery was beyond question. (See page 173)

No. 16 Tim Sherwood (Midfield) – 300 appearances, 32 goals. Captain of the championship-winning side of 1995, outstandingly creative in midfield. (See page 174)

No. 17 Keith Newton (Full back) – 357 appearances, 10 goals. A supremely talented attacking full back who won 19 England caps while at Blackburn. (See page 110)

No. 18 Danny Shea (Inside forward) – 108 appearances, 69 goals. The Rovers smashed the British transfer record to sign Shea for £2,000 and he then helped the club to win the championship in 1914. He was a hugely talented goalscorer. (See page 40)

No. 19 Andy McEvoy (Inside forward/half back) – 213 appearances, 103 goals. McEvoy was seen at his best as a penalty-box predator in the 1960s – also a proficient attacking half back. (See page 102)

No. 20 Terry Gennoe (Goalkeeper) – 334 appearances. Terry was brilliant between the posts between 1981 and 1990. Holds the record for the greatest number of league appearances as the Rovers' goalkeeper. (See page 144)

No. 21 Tony Parkes (Midfield) – 409 appearances, 46 goals. An industrious midfield player who went on to give the club outstanding service in a variety of backroom roles. (See page 127)

No. 22 Jack Bruton (Outside right) – 345 appearances, 117 goals. A speedy winger who could score goals, and had a spell as manager at Ewood Park. (See page 56)

No. 23 Jack Southworth (Centre forward) – 132 appearances, 121 goals. Southworth was a prolific goalscorer during the fledgling days of the Football League. (See page 25)

No. 24 Syd Puddefoot (Inside forward) – 277 appearances, 87 goals. An immensely gifted individual who acted as playmaker in the 1928 FA Cup-winning side. (See page 53)

No. 25 Eddie Quigley (Inside forward) – 166 appearances, 95 goals. An exquisite playmaker who was also a consistent goalscorer. Quigley later had several backroom roles at Ewood Park including a spell as manager. (See page 71)

No. 26 Noel Brotherston (Winger/Midfield) – 381 appearances, 54 goals. Able to operate on both flanks, Brotherston established himself as a Northern Ireland international with his tricky wing play. (See page 149)

No. 27 Henning Berg (Defender) – 239 appearances, 5 goals. Enjoyed two successful spells with the club, winning the Premiership title in 1995 and promotion in 2001, this classy defender is the club's most capped player. (See page 179)

No. 28 Ted Harper (Centre forward) – 177 appearances, 122 goals. A terrific goalscorer who hit 43 league goals during the 1925-26 season to create a new club record. (See page 50)

No. 29 Matt Woods (Centre half) – 307 appearances, 3 goals. Woods was a permanent fixture in the centre of defence for almost seven seasons. (See page 94)

No. 30 Mick McGrath (Half back) – 312 appearances, 12 goals. Republic of Ireland international who, although used as a defensive half back, scored some vital goals for the Rovers. (See page 100)

No. 31 Tim Flowers (Goalkeeper) – 217 appearances. An outstanding goalkeeper who performed heroics to help the Rovers lift the 1995 championship crown. (See page 176)

No. 32 Walter Crook (Left back) – 350 appearances, 2 goals. Tough-tackling full back who made 208 consecutive league appearances. (See page 67)

No. 33 Stuart Metcalfe (Midfield) – 451 appearances, 26 goals. A creative midfield player, Metcalfe loved to run at defenders with the ball and was capable of scoring spectacular goals. (See page 137)

No. 34 Peter Dobing (Forward) – 205 appearances, 104 goals. An exciting young goalscorer, Dobing scored 20 league goals during the promotion campaign of 1957-58. (See page 91)

No. 35 Kevin Moran (Centre half) – 173 appearances, 12 goals. Moran was a veteran Republic of Ireland international who captained the team to promotion via the play-offs and helped establish the club in the Premier League. (See page 158)

No. 36 Roy Vernon (Inside forward) – 144 appearances, 52 goals. A creative playmaker, also capable of scoring goals – a colossal talent. (See page 84)

No. 37 Bobby Langton (Winger) – 262 appearances, 74 goals. He enjoyed two spells at Ewood Park and was a great favourite with supporters. (See page 72)

No. 38 Mike England (Centre half) – 184 appearances, 21 goals. England was a footballing centre half who was not only excellent in defence but also creative in his use of the ball. (See page 97)

No. 39 David Speedie (Forward) – 43 appearances, 26 goals. A genuine cult figure at Ewood Park who played a major role in winning promotion via the play-offs in 1991-92. (See page 156)

No. 40 Fred Pickering (Centre forward) – 158 appearances, 74 goals. A former full back converted into a powerful centre forward who consistently found the back of the net. (See page 121)

No. 41 Glenn Keeley (Centre half) – 430 appearances, 24 goals. Keeley was a tough central defender who captained the team at Wembley in the 1987 Full Members' Cup final. (See page 142)

No. 42 Mike Ferguson (Forward) – 249 appearances, 36 goals. Fergie was an enormous talent who could enthral crowds with his wizardry. (See page 105)

No. 43 Eddie Crossan (Forward) – 302 appearances, 74 goals. A mercurial talent who had fantastic dribbling skills and an eye for goal. (See page 77)

No. 44 Dave Wagstaffe (Winger) – 92 appearances, 9 goals. On the wing Waggy was a master. At Ewood he enjoyed a glorious Indian summer. (See page 129)

No. 45 Roger Jones (Goalkeeper) – 277 appearances. An athletic goalkeeper who was capable of world-class saves, an ever-present in the 1975 Third Division championship team. (See page 124)

No. 46 John McNamee (Centre half) – 57 appearances, 10 goals. McNamee was a rugged centre half who helped to shore up the defence during the dark days of the early 1970s. (See page 123)

No. 47 Eric Bell (Left half) – 370 appearances, 9 goals. A loyal servant to the club who went on to become a member of the backroom staff. (See page 70)

No. 48 Jack Roscamp (Half back/Forward) – 250 appearances, 44 goals. Roscamp was a genuine utility player who was the hero of the 1928 FA Cup final. (See page 52)

No. 49 John Connelly (Winger) – 164 appearances, 39 goals. A fleet-footed winger who could operate on either flank, and a useful goalscorer. (See page 120)

No. 50 Fergie Suter (Full back) – 39 appearances, 3 goals. Widely acknowledged as the first professional employed by the club, holder of three FA Cup-winners' medals. (See page 18)

Results and Tables

Opponents played at home are in capitals and appear in upper and lower case for away games. The 'other' category in League & Cup Appearances includes promotion play-offs and the Charity Shield only.

Key: round – Rd; replay – R; second replay – 2R; leg – L; first leg – 1L; final – F; semi-final – SF; semi-final first leg – SF/1L; quarter-final – QF

Seasons 1875-81

Friendlies 1875-76

DATE	OPPONENTS	SCORE	GOALSCORERS
Dec 11	Church	D 1-1	
Jan 15	Cob Wall	D 0-0	
Mar 4	Church	D 0-0	

Friendlies 1876-77

DATE	OPPONENTS	SCORE
Nov 25	DARWEN	D 0-0
Mar 17	St George's	L 0-1

Friendlies 1877-78

DATE	OPPONENTS	SCORE
Nov 17	Clitheroe	Won*
Nov 24	Darwen	L 0-4
Dec 8	PRESTON ROVERS‡	D 0-0
Dec 15	St George's	D 0-0
Jan 2	PARTICK THISTLE	W 2-1
Jan 5	Church	D 0-0
Jan 12	TURTON†	D 0-0
Jan 19	Darwen	D 0-0
Jan 26	CLITHEROE	L 0-1
Feb 1	Cob Wall	L 0-1
Mar 2	Cob Wall	L 0-1

*Actual result unknown.
‡This game was abandoned when a Preston player collapsed and died.
†This game was abandoned.
Records show that two games were also played against Sheffield although the dates are unknown. In the first game the result was disputed whilst the second game ended in a 1-1 draw.

Friendlies 1878-79

DATE	OPPONENTS	SCORE
Oct 5	Church	W 2-0
Oct 19	Manchester Wanderers	L 0-4
Oct 26	EAGLEY	W 2-0
Nov 2	DARWEN	L 0-1
Nov 4	ACCRINGTON	W 3-0
Nov 9	Partick Thistle	L 0-2
Dec 7	MANCHESTER WANDERERS	D 1-1
Dec 14	Macclesfield Rangers	W 4-0
Dec 14	ACCRINGTON	W 4-1
Jan 1	Sheffield	L 0-3
Jan 2	PARTICK THISTLE	L 2-4
Jan 11	Darwen	Won*
Jan 18	MACCLESFIELD RANGERS	Draw‡
Feb 15	BLACKBURN OLYMPIC	L 1-3
Feb 22	Accrington	W 3-1
Feb 29	MANCHESTER WANDERERS	W 3-1†
Mar 8	SHEFFIELD	D 1-1
Mar 22	Blackburn Olympic	D 0-0
Mar 29	Accrington	W 5-1
Apr 12	Darwen	W 3-1

*Actual result unknown. ‡Actual result unknown. †Some sources record the score as 2-2.

Lancashire Cup 1879-80

Oct 11	Enfield	(Rd1)	D 1-1
Oct 23	ENFIELD	(R)	W 5-1
Dec 13	BOLTON WANDERERS	(Rd2)	W 4-0
Jan 10	TURTON	(Rd3)	W 2-1
Mar 6	ACCRINGTON	(SF)	W 3-1
Mar 20	Darwen	(F)	L 0-3

In the fourth round Blackburn received a bye.

FA Cup 1879-80

Nov 1	TYNE ASSOCIATION	(Rd1)	W 5-1 Brown 2, Lewis, Duckworth 2
Dec 6	DARWEN	(Rd2)	W 3-1 Brown 2, Hargreaves J.
Jan 31	Nottingham Forest	(Rd3)	L 0-6

Friendlies 1879-80

DATE	OPPONENTS	SCORE	GOALSCORERS
Sep 20	Blackburn Park Road	W 4-0	
Oct 4	Accrington	W 3-2	
Oct 18	BLACKBURN OLYMPIC	W 4-1	
Oct 25	GLASGOW RANGERS	L 1-4	
Nov 8	Darwen	D 1-1	
Nov 15	ATTERCLIFFE	L 2-3	
Nov 22	MANCHESTER WANDERERS	W 2-0	
Dec 20	BLACKPOOL ST JOHN'S	D 1-1	
Dec 20	Blackburn Association	D 1-1	
Dec 27	Nottingham Forest	D 1-1	
Jan 2	VALE OF LEVEN	L 0-4	
Jan 3	SCOTCH CANADIANS	L 0-8	
Jan 17	Manchester Wanderers	W 3-1	
Jan 31	Attercliffe	D 3-3	
Feb 7	STOKE	D 3-3	
Feb 21	TURTON	W 4-2	
Mar 13	BLACKBURN OLYMPIC	W 8-2	
Mar 27	Blackburn Olympic	L 0-1	
Mar 29	BANGOR	W 2-1	
Mar 30	NOTTINGHAM FOREST	W 5-0	
Apr 3	DARWEN	L 0-3	

Friendlies 1880-81

DATE	OPPONENTS	SCORE
Sep 25	Hibernian	L 2-5
Sep 27	Edinburgh University	W 5-1
Oct 2	ACCRINGTON	W 3-2
Oct 9	BOLTON WANDERERS	W 7-0
Oct 16	Blackburn Olympic	W 2-0
Oct 25	MANCHESTER WANDERERS	W 9-0
Nov 1	GLASGOW RANGERS	D 0-0
Nov 13	TURTON	W 8-0
Nov 20	WEDNESDAY STROLLERS	W 10-1
Nov 27	DARWEN*	D 1-1
Dec 11	BLACKBURN OLYMPIC	W 4-0
Dec 25	Nottingham Forest	W 4-0
Jan 1	DUMBARTON	L 1-4
Jan 3	HEART OF MIDLOTHIAN	W 2-1
Jan 8	SHEFFIELD PROVIDENCE	W 7-1
Jan 15	NOTTS COUNTY	W 3-1
Jan 29	Aston Villa	L 3-4
Feb 5	Notts County	W 7-3
Feb 7	Clapham Rovers	W 7-1
Feb 8	London Pilgrims	W 6-0
Feb 12	CHURCH	W 7-0
Feb 19	Manchester Wanderers	W 9-0
Mar 1	BLACKBURN OLYMPIC	W 3-2
Mar 5	ACCRINGTON	W 4-1
Mar 7	Glasgow Rangers	W 5-4
Mar 12	NOTTINGHAM FOREST	D 3-3
Mar 19	Glasgow Rangers	L 1-2
Mar 26	Preston North End	W 16-0
Apr 2	Bolton Wanderers	W 5-3
Apr 9	SHEFFIELD WEDNESDAY	W 7-3
Apr 16	HIBERNIAN	W 4-2
Apr 18	ASTON VILLA	W 3-0
Apr 23	DUMBARTON	W 4-0
Apr 30	Bolton & District	W 12-1

*This game was abandoned.

Lancashire Cup 1880-81

Nov 6	BRADSHAW	(Rd1)	W 6-0
Dec 4	CLITHEROE ST MARY'S	(Rd2)	W 3-0
Jan 22	Turton	(Rd3)	W 6-0

Blackburn and Darwen were excluded in the fourth round when they couldn't agree on a date for the match.

FA Cup 1880-81

Oct 30	SHEFFIELD PROVIDENCE	(Rd1)	W 6-2 Hornby, Brown 3, Birtwistle R., Hargreaves F.W.
Dec 18	SHEFFIELD WEDNESDAY	(Rd2)	L 0-4 (Rd 4)

Seasons 1881-84

Friendlies 1881-82

DATE	OPPONENTS	SCORE	GOALSCORERS
Sep 3	Great Harwood	W 13-3	
Sep 7	Church	W 8-0	
Sep 20	Eagley	W 5-2	
Sep 24	Accrington	W 3-2	
Sep 27	Blackburn Park Road	W 14-0	
Oct 1	Bolton Wanderers	D 2-2	
Oct 8	BLACKBURN OLYMPIC	W 4-1	
Oct 15	Manchester Wanderers	W 1-0	
Oct 17	BEITH	W 6-0	
Oct 22	NOTTS COUNTY	W 10-1	
Oct 31	GLASGOW RANGERS	D 2-2	
Nov 12	Walsall Town Swifts	W 3-1	
Nov 21	ASTON VILLA	W 7-2	
Dec 10	JAMESTOWN	W 4-3	
Dec 17	LONDON PILGRIMS	W 3-0	
Dec 24	Nottingham Forest	W 2-0	
Dec 26	QUEENS PARK	D 2-2	
Dec 31	DUMBARTON	W 5-1	
Jan 2	THIRD LANARK	W 6-0	
Jan 14	Blackburn Olympic	W 3-0	
Feb 4	WALSALL TOWN SWIFTS	W 3-0	
Mar 1	WITTON	W 6-1	
Mar 11	Aston Villa	W 4-1	
Mar 18	Darwen	W 5-0	
Apr 1	ACCRINGTON	W 3-0	
Apr 8	HIBERNIAN	D 4-4	
Apr 16	VALE OF LEVEN	L 0-2	
Apr 22	Glasgow Rangers	D 2-2	
May 15	BLACKBURN OLYMPIC	W 12-1	

Lancashire Cup 1881-82

Nov 5	KIRKHAM	(Rd1)	W	14-0
Nov 26	Clitheroe	(Rd2)	W	10-1
Jan 7	ACCRINGTON W.	(Rd3)	W	7-0
Jan 28	CHURCH	(Rd4)	W	6-1
Feb 25	Blackburn Olympic	(SF)	W	6-1
Apr 15	Accrington*	(F)	W	3-1

*Played at Turf Moor, Burnley.

East Lancashire Charity Cup 1881-82

May 26	Darwen	(SF)	W	4-1
Aug 7	BLACKBURN OLYMPIC*	(F)	L	2-5

*The final was held over until the start of the 1882-83 season.

FA Cup 1881-82

Oct 29	BLACKBURN PARK ROAD	(Rd1)	W	9-1	Brown 2, Douglas, Wilson o.g., Avery 2, o.g., Hargreaves J., Strachan
Nov 19	BOLTON WANDERERS	(Rd2)	W	6-2	Avery, McIntyre 2, Brown 2, Sharples
Jan 30	DARWEN	(Rd4)	W	5-1	Hargreaves J. 2, Strachan, Duckworth 2
Feb 11	WEDNESBURY OLD ATH.	(Rd 5)	W	3-1	Lofthouse, Avery, Strachan
Mar 6	Sheffield Wednesday*	(SF)	D	0-0	
Mar 15	Sheffield Wednesday‡	(R)	W	5-1	Hargreaves J., Avery, Douglas, o.g., Suter
Mar 25	Old Etonians†	(F)	L	0-1	

*Played at Huddersfield. ‡Played at Manchester.
†Played at the Kennington Oval. The club received a bye in the third round.

Lancashire Cup 1882-83

Oct 2	EVERTON	(Rd1)	W	8-0
Dec 9	WITHNELL	(Rd2)	W	12-0
Jan 6	ASTLEY BRIDGE	(Rd3)	W	3-0
Jan 29	HALLIWELL	(Rd4)	W	4-0
Feb 17	Padiham	(Rd 5)	W	5-1
Mar 17	Bolton Wanderers*	(SF)	W	4-1
Mar 31	Darwen	(F)	W	3-2

*Played at Darwen.

East Lancashire Charity Cup 1882-83

Apr 7	DARWEN	(SF)	W	2-0
May 2	Blackburn Olympic*	(F)	W	6-3

*Played at Darwen.

FA Cup 1882-83

Oct 23	BLACKPOOL ST JOHN'S	(Rd1)	W	11-1	Suter, Barton 3, Duckworth 2, Brown 4, Avery
Dec 2	Darwen	(Rd2)	L	0-1	

Friendlies 1882-83

DATE	OPPONENTS	SCORE	GOALSCORERS
Aug 26	Witton*	W 5-3	
Sep 5	Preston North End	W 13-2	
Sep 9	Padiham	W 5-1	
Sep 11	Blackburn & District‡	W 5-1	
Sep 23	Liverpool	W 10-1	
Sep 30	Leeds Association	W 12-0	
Oct 7	Blackburn Olympic	W 4-1	
Oct 14	WEDNESBURY OLD ATHLETIC	W 2-0	
Oct 21	NOTTINGHAM FOREST	W 6-0	
Oct 28	ACCRINGTON	W 1-0	
Oct 30	GLASGOW RANGERS	D 1-1	
Nov 4	Queens Park	D 3-3	
Nov 11	Notts County	L 1-7	
Nov 18	SHEFFIELD WEDNESDAY	W 2-1	
Nov 27	Aston Villa	W 3-2	
Dec 4	CAMBRIDGE UNIVERSITY	W 4-0	
Dec 26	WALSALL TOWN SWIFTS	L 2-3	
Dec 30	DUMBARTON	L 1-3	
Jan 1	VALE OF LEVEN	W 4-1	
Jan 2	GLASGOW RANGERS	D 1-1	
Jan 15	ST MIRREN	W 3-2	
Jan 20	BLACKBURN OLYMPIC	W 3-0	
Jan 27	Wednesbury Old Athletic	D 1-1	
Feb 3	ASTON VILLA	L 3-4	
Feb 6	Nottingham Forest	D 0-0	
Feb 10	LONDON PILGRIMS	W 14-0	
Mar 10	Glasgow Rangers	W 3-2	
Mar 19	OXFORD UNIVERSITY	L 1-4	
Mar 24	THIRD LANARK	W 6-1	
Mar 26	EDINBURGH UNIVERSITY	W 6-2	
Apr 5	QUEENS PARK	D 1-1	
Apr 9	Manchester & District	L 2-4	
Apr 14	Bolton Wanderers	L 3-6	
Apr 16	Sheffield Wednesday	W 1-0	
Apr 23	Accrington	W 3-0	
Apr 28	WITTON	W 5-2	

*Played at Southport. ‡Played at Bradford.

Lancashire Cup 1883-84

Oct 22	BLACKPOOL STH SHORE	(Rd1)	W	11-1
Nov 12	LOWER DARWEN	(Rd2)	W	8-0
Dec 13	WITHNELL	(Rd3)	W	5-0
Jan 28	DARWEN OLD W.	(Rd4)	W	2-1
Feb 26	ACCRINGTON	(Rd 5)	D	0-0
Mar 8	ACCRINGTON	(R)	W	6-3
Mar 15	WITTON	(SF)	D	1-1
Mar 19	WITTON	(R)	W	4-1
Mar 22	Blackburn Olympic*	(F)	D	1-1
Apr 19	Blackburn Olympic‡	(R)	W	2-1

*Played at Preston. ‡Played at Darwen.

East Lancashire Charity Cup 1883-84

Apr 26	ACCRINGTON	(SF)	D	1-1
May 10	Accrington*	(R)	L	1-2

*Played at Padiham.

FA Cup 1883-84

Nov 20	SOUTHPORT	(Rd1)	W	7-0	Douglas 2, Lofthouse, Duckworth, Sowerbutts, Avery 2
Dec 1	Blackpool South Shore	(Rd2)	W	7-0	Avery 2, Suter, Sowerbutts 2, Douglas, McIntyre
Dec 24	PADIHAM	(Rd3)	W	3-0	Brown, Connell o.g., Strachan
Jan 19	STAVELEY	(Rd4)	W	5-1	Brown 4, Sowerbutts
Feb 9	Upton Park	(Rd 5)	W	3-0	Inglis, Lofthouse 2
Mar 1	Notts County*	(SF)	W	1-0	Lofthouse
Mar 29	Queens Park‡	(F)	W	2-1	Brown, Forrest

*Played at Birmingham. ‡Played at the Kennington Oval.

Friendlies 1883-84

DATE	OPPONENTS	SCORE	GOALSCORERS
Sep 1	Astley Bridge	W 8-0	
Sep 8	Accrington	W 5-2	
Sep 15	Padiham	W 4-1	
Sep 22	Church	W 4-0	
Sep 29	Dumbarton	L 1-2	
Oct 6	BLACKBURN OLYMPIC	W 3-1	
Oct 13	NOTTS COUNTY	W 4-1	
Oct 27	Sheffield Wednesday	L 0-2	
Nov 3	BOLTON WANDERERS	D 0-0	
Nov 8	BLACKBURN OLYMPIC	D 2-2	

Seasons 1884-86

Nov 10	Darwen	W 6-0
Nov 17	West Bromwich Albion	W 1-0
Nov 19	ASTON VILLA	L 0-1
Nov 24	Accrington	W 3-1
Dec 3	Walsall Town Swifts	W 2-1
Dec 15	CAMBRIDGE UNIVERSITY	L 2-3
Dec 22	Nottingham Forest	D 2-2
Dec 29	Blackburn Olympic	W 4-2
Dec 31	HEART OF MIDLOTHIAN	W 5-0
Jan 1	DUMBARTON	W 2-1
Jan 2	LONDON WELSH	D 1-1
Jan 5	Glasgow Rangers	W 2-1
Jan 12	WALSALL TOWN SWIFTS	W 5-0
Feb 2	DARWEN	W 8-0
Feb 16	ACCRINGTON	W 2-0
Feb 23	Preston North End	L 2-3
Mar 3	Aston Villa	W 2-1
Mar 17	GLASGOW RANGERS	W 4-1
Apr 12	Preston North End	D 0-0
Apr 14	VALE OF LEVEN	L 0-2
Apr 29	SHEFFIELD WEDNESDAY	W 3-1

Lancashire Cup 1884-85

Sep 27	WITHNELL	(Rd1)	W 8-2
Oct 25	Preston Zingari	(Rd2)	W 2-1
Nov 29	DARWEN ROVERS	(Rd3)	W 4-1
Jan 31	Rawtenstall	(Rd4)	D 2-2
Feb 14	RAWTENSTALL	(R)	W 4-1
Apr 11	Bolton Wanderers*	(SF)	L 1-5
Apr 18	Blackburn Olympic‡	(F)	W 2-1

*Bolton were later disqualified. ‡Played at Deepdale, Preston.

East Lancashire Charity Cup 1884-85

Apr 25	ACCRINGTON	(SF)	L 0-1

FA Cup 1884-85

Oct 13	ROSSENDALE	(Rd1)	W 11-0	Barton 3, Sowerbutts 2, Fecitt 4, Birtwistle, Brown
Dec 6	BLACKBURN OLYMPIC	(Rd2)	W 3-2	Fecitt 2, Sowerbutts
Dec 22	WITTON	(Rd3)	W 5-1	Forrest, Brown, Sowerbutts, Lofthouse, Fecitt
Jan 19	ROMFORD	(Rd4)	W 8-0	Rostron, Fecitt 2, Douglas, Sowerbutts 2, Champney o.g., Webster o.g.
Feb 21	West Bromwich Albion	(Rd 6)	W 2-0	Lofthouse, Douglas
Mar 7	Old Carthusians*	(SF)	W 5-1	Brown 2, Sowerbutts 2, Lofthouse
Apr 4	Queens Park†	(F)	W 2-0	Forrest, Brown

*Played at Nottingham. †Played at the Kennington Oval. In the fifth round Blackburn received a bye.

Friendlies 1884-85

DATE	OPPONENTS	SCORE	GOALSCORERS
Aug 25	BLACKBURN PARK ROAD	W 3-1	
Sep 1	Blackburn Park Road	L 0-1	
Sep 3	Low Moor	W 2-0	
Sep 6	Great Lever	L 2-4	
Sep 13	Church	D 2-2	
Sep 20	Witton	W 5-1	
Sep 27	Burnley	W 4-2	
Oct 4	WALSALL TOWN SWIFTS	W 5-0	
Oct 11	SHEFFIELD PARK GRANGE	W 17-0	
Oct 18	DARWEN	W 4-1	
Oct 23	Heart of Midlothian	W 1-0	
Oct 25	NOTTINGHAM FOREST	W 3-1	
Nov 1	Aston Villa	L 1-2	
Nov 8	Vale of Leven	L 0-2	
Nov 15	ACCRINGTON	W 1-0	
Nov 17	NOTTS RANGERS	W 4-0	
Nov 22	SHEFFIELD WEDNESDAY	W 3-1	
Nov 24	ASTON VILLA	W 5-4	
Nov 29	Notts County	W 3-2	
Dec 13	Bolton Wanderers	L 2-3	
Dec 15	CORINTHIANS	L 1-8	
Dec 20	Sheffield Wednesday	D 1-1	
Dec 26	HEART OF MIDLOTHIAN	W 6-0	
Dec 27	Accrington	L 0-2	
Jan 1	DUMBARTON	W 2-0	
Jan 3	GLASGOW RANGERS	D 0-0	
Jan 10	Darwen	D 0-0	
Jan 17	OLD WESTMINSTERS	W 9-1	
Jan 24	Blackburn Olympic	D 4-4	

Feb 2	Derby County	W 4-3
Feb 7	Great Lever	D 2-2
Feb 23	BLACKBURN OLYMPIC	L 1-4
Feb 28	Nottingham Forest	L 0-3
Mar 14	Everton	W 2-1
Mar 21	NOTTS COUNTY	W 2-0
Mar 23	Burnley	L 1-5
Mar 28	BLACKBURN OLYMPIC	D 2-2
Apr 6	VALE OF LEVEN	W 1-0
Apr 8	CORINTHIANS	L 1-2
Apr 22	Glasgow Rangers	W 4-3
Apr 23	St Bernards	L 0-2
May 4	Manchester & District	W 2-0
May 11	GREAT LEVER	W 2-1
May 16	Blackburn Olympic	L 0-3
May 18	BOLTON WANDERERS	L 1-4

Lancashire Cup 1885-86

Oct 10	LOSTOCK HALL	(Rd1)	W 4-0
Nov 7	Hurst	(Rd2)	W 6-0
Dec 26	Church	(Rd4)	W 3-2
Mar 6	PRESTON NORTH END*	(SF)	L 2-4
Apr 17	Bolton Wanderers‡	(F)	L 0-1

*Preston, having fielded ineligble players, were scatched from the competition while the match was in progress. ‡Played at Deepdale, Preston. In the third round Blackburn received a bye.

East Lancashire Charity Cup 1885-86

May 17	Blackburn Olympic	(SF)	W 2-0
May 22	ACCRINGTON	(F)	W 2-1

FA Cup 1885-86

Oct 24	Clitheroe	(Rd1)	W 2-0	Strachan, Douglas
Nov 21	OSWALDTWISTLE ROVERS	(Rd2)	W 1-0	McIntyre
Dec 5	DARWEN OLD W.	(Rd3)	W 6-1	Sowerbutts 2, Brown 2, Fecitt, Lofthouse
Jan 23	STAVELEY	(Rd4)	W 7-1	Lofthouse 2, Fecitt 2, Walton 2, Sowerbutts
Feb 27	Brentwood	(Rd 6)	W 3-1	Fecitt, Walton 2
Mar 13	Swifts*	(SF)	W 2-1	Walton, Strachan
Apr 3	West Bromwich Albion†	(F)	D 0-0	
Apr 10	West Bromwich Albion‡	(R)	W 2-0	Sowerbutts, Brown

*Played at Derby. †Played at the Kennington Oval. ‡Played at Derby. In the fifth round Blackburn received a bye.

Friendlies 1885-86

DATE	OPPONENTS	SCORE	GOALSCORERS
Aug 15	Aston Villa	L 0-2	
Aug 22	Witton	W 3-1	
Aug 29	Astley Bridge	W 2-0	
Sep 3	WITTON	D 1-1	
Sep 5	Everton	W 4-0	
Sep 12	Padiham	D 1-1	
Sep 19	Queens Park	L 1-7	
Sep 19	Blackburn Olympic	W 3-1	
Sep 26	ASTON VILLA	W 2-1	
Oct 3	BURNLEY	D 2-2	
Oct 10	Accrington	L 1-2	
Oct 17	Darwen	D 2-2	
Oct 19	Burnley	D 1-1	
Oct 31	NOTTS COUNTY	L 1-3	
Nov 2	Burslem Port Vale	D 1-1	
Nov 10	Stoke	W 1-0	
Nov 14	Nottingham Forest	L 0-4	
Nov 16	Lincoln City	W 1-0	
Nov 23	GREAT LEVER	L 0-1	
Nov 28	DERBY COUNTY	W 3-2	
Dec 7	Great Lever	L 1-4	
Dec 12	BLACKBURN OLYMPIC	L 3-4	
Dec 14	BURNLEY	L 0-2	
Dec 16	CORINTHIANS	L 0-6	
Dec 19	Aston Villa	W 3-1	
Dec 25	Preston North End	L 0-1	
Dec 26	QUEENS PARK	L 0-3	
Dec 28	Derby County*	D 1-1	
Jan 1	PRESTON NORTH END	L 0-1	
Jan 2	BLACKBURN OLYMPIC	W 2-0	
Jan 6	Bolton Wanderers	L 3-5	
Jan 9	Notts County	L 0-4	
Jan 16	GREAT LEVER	W 3-1	
Feb 1	Burslem Port Vale	D 1-1	
Feb 6	Burnley	L 0-1	
Feb 8	Staveley	D 2-2	
Feb 13	Preston North End	L 1-4	
Feb 20	BOLTON WANDERERS	L 1-2	

Seasons 1886-88

Mar 20	Bolton Wanderers	L 2-5	
Mar 27	DARWEN	W 4-2	
Mar 27	Great Lever	L 2-6	
Apr 21	Glasgow Rangers	L 3-4	
Apr 22	Hibernian	L 0-3	
Apr 24	THIRD LANARK	W 3-2	
Apr 26	VALE OF LEVEN	D 1-1	
May 1	PADIHAM	W 2-1	
May 8	WEST BROMWICH ALBION	W 5-2	
May 10	Aston Villa	L 1-2	
May 25	Accrington‡	L 1-2	
May 31	PRESTON NORTH END	D 0-0	

*This match was abandoned. ‡Played at Rochdale.

Friendlies 1886-87

DATE	OPPONENTS	SCORE	GOALSCORERS
Aug 28	Witton	W 2-0	
Sep 4	Halliwell	L 2-8	
Sep 6	Hyde	W 8-0	
Sep 11	Preston North End	L 1-6	
Sep 13	Burslem Port Vale	W 2-1	
Sep 18	Blackburn Olympic	W 3-0	
Sep 25	ACCRINGTON	L 0-2	
Oct 2	PRESTON NORTH END	L 1-6	
Oct 16	BOLTON WANDERERS	W 6-2	
Oct 23	DARWEN	L 1-4	
Oct 27	Gainsborough Trinity	W 6-1	
Nov 6	Darwen	L 0-2	
Nov 8	Bolton Wanderers	L 4-5	
Nov 13	Blackburn Olympic	D 1-1	
Nov 15	Burnley	W 1-0	
Nov 27	Stoke	W 3-1	
Dec 11	Grimsby Town	D 1-1	
Dec 13	CORINTHIANS	L 2-3	
Dec 18	Halliwell	L 1-4	
Dec 18	Northwich Victoria	W 4-0	
Dec 25	DARWEN	W 2-1	
Dec 27	ACCRINGTON	W 1-0	
Dec 28	Derby County*	L 0-2	
Jan 1	VALE OF LEVEN	W 2-1	
Jan 3	COWLAIRS	L 0-1	
Jan 15	EVERTON	D 0-0	
Jan 22	Burnley	L 0-4	
Jan 24	BURNLEY	W 1-0	
Jan 29	Accrington	W 2-1	
Feb 5	Bolton Wanderers	D 2-2	
Feb 7	PRESTON NORTH END	W 2-0	
Feb 12	Everton	D 1-1	
Feb 14	BOLTON WANDERERS	L 1-5	
Feb 19	Darwen	L 1-3	
Feb 21	Burslem Port Vale	L 1-6	
Feb 22	Notts County	D 2-2	
Feb 26	Preston North End	L 2-8	
Mar 5	NOTTS JARDINES	W 5-1	
Mar 12	ASTON VILLA	D 3-3	
Mar 19	Derby County	L 1-2	
Mar 26	ACCRINGTON	D 2-2	
Apr 2	BURNLEY	L 0-2	
Apr 8	DARWEN	W 5-1	
Apr 9	VALE OF LEVEN	D 1-1	
Apr 11	DUMBARTON	W 3-0	
Apr 16	Bootle	L 1-3	
Apr 18	Burnley	L 1-2	
Apr 23	Accrington	L 0-1	
Apr 30	Aston Villa	L 0-2	
May 9	WITTON	L 1-3	
May 12	Newton Heath & District	D 1-1	
May 14	Newton Heath	L 0-1	
May 23	Blackburn Park Road	W 2-0	
May 30	West Bromwich Albion	L 0-3	

*This match was abandoned.

Lancashire Cup 1886-87

Oct 9	Preston North End	(Rd1) L 1-7	

East Lancashire Charity Cup 1886-87

May 7	Darwen	(SF) W 3-0	
May 21	Accrington	(F) L 0-1	

FA Cup 1886-87

Nov 20	Renton	(Rd2) D 2-2*	Walton, Unknown
Dec 4	RENTON	(R) L 0-2	

*After extra-time. In the first round Blackburn had a walkover as Halliwell scratched from the competition.

Friendlies 1887-88

DATE	OPPONENTS	SCORE	GOALSCORERS
Aug 27	Blackburn Park Road	L 2-4	
Sep 3	Halliwell	W 3-2	
Sep 5	Burslem Port Vale	W 5-3	
Sep 10	BURNLEY	W 3-2	
Sep 17	Hurst	W 7-2	
Sep 19	Boston & District	W 9-2	
Sep 20	Bootle	W 2-1	
Sep 24	BLACKBURN OLYMPIC	W 3-2	
Oct 8	Dumbarton	D 2-2	
Oct 15	BURY	W 10-1	
Oct 22	WEST BROMWICH ALBION	W 7-6	
Oct 29	NOTTS COUNTY	D 4-4	
Nov 12	Sunderland	W 2-0	
Nov 19	Corinthians	L 1-6	
Dec 10	Notts County	L 2-4	
Dec 17	BLACKBURN OLYMPIC	L 1-2	
Dec 24	WOLVERHAMPTON W.	D 1-1	
Dec 26	DARWEN	W 6-3	
Dec 27	DERBY COUNTY†	L 0-2†	
Dec 31	HEART OF MIDLOTHIAN	W 5-3	
Jan 2	Witton	W 4-2	
Jan 14	PRESTON NORTH END	L 3-4	
Jan 23	Burslem Port Vale	W 5-1	
Feb 4	Preston North End	L 0-7	
Feb 11	Blackburn Olympic	W 8-2	
Feb 18	Bolton Wanderers	L 1-4	
Feb 25	Cliftonville	W 6-2	
Mar 3	HALLIWELL	W 10-1	
Mar 5	WITTON	L 3-4	
Mar 10	Accrington	L 3-7	
Mar 17	ASTON VILLA	L 4-6	
Mar 24	Darwen	W 5-2	
Mar 28	Middlesbrough	D 2-2	
Mar 31	Vale of Leven	W 3-2	
Apr 2	DUMBARTON	W 2-1	
Apr 3	CORINTHIANS	W 1-0	
Apr 7	BOLTON WANDERERS	W 6-0	
Apr 14	ACCRINGTON	L 1-2	
Apr 16	Manchester Welsh	L 0-2	
Apr 21	Aston Villa	L 0-2	
Apr 28	Burnley	L 1-3	
May 5	West Bromwich Albion	L 1-2	
May 9	Accrington	W 4-3	
May 21	Cumberland*	W 6-0	
May 21	Bolton Wanderers**	L 2-4	
May 22	Scotch Crusaders‡	D 2-2	

†Match agreed upon as a draw owing to the state of the pitch. *Played at Keswick. **Played at Chester. ‡Played at Whitehaven.

Lancashire Cup 1887-88

Oct 1	Manchester Association	(Rd1) W 11-0	
Nov 19	Irwell Springs	(Rd2) D 1-1	
Dec 3	Irwell Springs	(R) W 5-1	
Jan 21	PRESTON NORTH END	(Rd3) L 3-4	

East Lancashire Charity Cup 1887-88

May 19	Blackburn Olympic	(SF) W 5-2	
Jun 9	ACCRINGTON	(F) D 3-3	

FA Cup 1887-88

Nov 5	Blackburn Olympic	(Rd2) W 5-1	Rushton, Chadwick, Gill o.g., Southworth, Townley
Nov 26	Accrington	(Rd3) W 3-1	Chadwick 2, Walton
Jan 7	Darwen	(Rd5) W 3-0	Heyes, Southworth, Townley
Jan 28	Derby Junction	(Rd6) L 1-2	Southworth

In the first round Blackburn had a walkover as Bury scratched from the competition. In the fourth round Blackburn received a bye.

Season 1888-89

Football League

DATE	OPPONENTS	SCORE	GOALSCORERS	ATTENDANCE
Sep 15	ACCRINGTON	D 5-5	Jack Southworth, Beresford, Townley 2, Fecitt	5,000
Sep 22	WEST BROMWICH ALBION	W 6-2	Townley, Walton 2, Jack Southworth, Fecitt 2	8,000
Sep 29	Wolverhampton W	D 2-2	Jack Southworth 2	5,000
Oct 6	Notts County	D 3-3	Fecitt, Townley, Walton	5,000
Oct 13	Aston Villa	L 1-6	Walton	5,000
Oct 20	WOLVERHAMPTON W	L 2-2	Haresnape, Unknown	6,000
Oct 27	STOKE	W 5-2	Walton 2, Jack Southworth, Townley, Fecitt	3,000
Nov 3	Burnley	W 7-1	Beresford, Forrest, Fecitt 2, Jack Southworth 3	3,000
Nov 10	EVERTON	W 3-0	Almond, Walton, Opp o.g.	6,000
Nov 17	ASTON VILLA	W 5-1	Jack Southworth 3, Fecitt 2	9,000
Nov 24	Derby County	W 2-0	Jack Southworth, Fecitt	3,000
Dec 1	Stoke	L 1-2	Beresford	5,000
Dec 8	BOLTON WANDERERS	D 4-4	Townley 2, Beresford, Stothert	7,000
Dec 15	NOTTS COUNTY	W 5-2	Jack Southworth, Unknown 4	4,000
Dec 22	West Bromwich Albion	L 1-2	Fecitt	1,000
Dec 29	Preston North End	L 0-1		9,000
Jan 12	PRESTON NORTH END	D 2-2	Walton, Fecitt	12,000
Jan 19	Accrington	W 2-0	McLeilan o.g., Jack Southworth	4,000
Jan 26	Bolton Wanderers	L 2-3	Walton, Jack Southworth	7,000
Feb 4	BURNLEY	W 4-2	Jack Southworth 2, Townley, Walton	2,000
Mar 30	Everton	L 1-3	Whittaker	4,000
Apr 15	DERBY COUNTY	W 3-0	Mitchell 2, Haresnape	4,000

FA Cup

DATE	OPPONENTS		SCORE	GOALSCORERS	ATTENDANCE
Feb 2	Accrington	(Rd1)	D 1-1	Unknown	3,000
Feb 9	ACCRINGTON	(R)	W 5-0	Haresnape 2, Walton, Townley, Barton	8,000
Mar 2	ASTON VILLA	(Rd3)	W 8-1	Haresnape 3, Jack Southworth 4, Opp o.g.	12,000
Mar 16	Wolverhampton W.*	(SF)	D 1-1	Haresnape	15,000
Mar 23	Wolverhampton W.*	(R)	L 1-3	Townley	9,900

*Played at the Alexandra Ground, Crewe.
In the second round Swifts scratched from the competition.

League & Cup Appearances

PLAYER	LEAGUE	CUP COMPETITION FA CUP	TOTAL
Almond, W.	21	5	26
Arthur, W.J.H.	15	5	20
Barton, J.	5	1	6
Beresford, J.	12	1	13
Beverley, J.	8		8
Brown, J.	4		4
Douglas, J.	21	5	26
Duerden, J.	2		2
Fecitt, H.L.	17	5	22
Forbes, J.	16	5	21
Forrest, J.H.	19	5	24
Haresnape, R.	9	4	13
Holden, W.	1		1
McOwen, W.A.	5		5
Mitchell, T.	1		1
Porter, W.S.	1		1
Southworth, Jack	21	5	26
Southworth, James	19	4	23
Stothert, J.	1		1
Suter, F.	1		1
Townley, W.	19	5	24
Walton, N.	20	5	25
Whittaker, B.	4		4

Goalscorers

PLAYER	LEAGUE	CUP COMPETITION FA CUP	TOTAL
Southworth, Jack	17	4	21
Fecitt, H.L.	12		12
Walton, N.	10	1	11
Townley, W.	8	2	10
Haresnape, R.	2	6	8
Beresford, J.	4		4
Mitchell, T.	2		2
Almond, W.	1		1
Forrest, J.H.	1		1
Stothert, J.	1		1
Whittaker, B.	1		1
Barton, J.		1	1
Opps' o.gs.	2	1	3
Unknown	5	1	6

Fact File

Blackburn Rovers became founder members of the Football League with Accrington, Aston Villa, Bolton Wanderers, Burnley, Derby County, Everton, Notts County, Preston North End, Stoke, West Bromwich Albion and Wolverhampton Wanderers.

SECRETARY: Thomas Mitchell
TOP SCORER: Jack Southworth
BIGGEST WIN: 8-1, 2 March 1889, v Aston Villa, FA Cup Round 3
HIGHEST ATTENDANCE: 15,000, 16 March 1889, v Wolverhampton Wanderers, FA Cup semi-final
MAJOR TRANSFERS IN: John Forbes from Vale of Leven
MAJOR TRANSFERS OUT: Edgar Chadwick to Everton

Final Football League Table

		P	W	D	L	F	A	PTS
1	PRESTON NE	22	18	4	0	74	15	40
2	ASTON VILLA	22	12	5	5	61	43	29
3	WOLVERHAMPTON W	22	12	4	6	50	37	28
4	BLACKBURN R	22	10	6	6	66	45	26
5	BOLTON W	22	10	2	10	63	59	22
6	WBA	22	10	2	10	40	46	22
7	ACCRINGTON	22	6	8	8	48	48	20
8	EVERTON	22	9	2	11	35	46	20
9	BURNLEY	22	7	3	12	42	62	17
10	DERBY CO	22	7	2	13	41	61	16
11	NOTTS CO	22	5	2	15	40	73	12
12	STOKE	22	4	4	14	26	51	12

Season 1889-90

Football League

DATE	OPPONENTS	SCORE	GOALSCORERS	ATTENDANCE
Sep 7	Everton	L 2-3	Campbell 2	12,000
Sep 14	WOLVERHAMPTON W.	W 4-3	Campbell, Walton, Unknown 2	10,000
Sep 21	DERBY COUNTY	W 4-2	Lofthouse, Jack Southworth 2, Campbell	5,000
Sep 28	Accrington	D 2-2	Walton, Lofthouse	6,000
Oct 19	ASTON VILLA	W 7-0	Townley 2, Jack Southworth, Forrest, Campbell, Walton, Lofthouse	7,000
Oct 26	BURNLEY	W 7-1	Jack Southworth, Campbell 2, Walton 2, White o.g, Unknown	4,000
Nov 2	PRESTON NORTH END	L 3-4	Campbell, Jack Southworth 2	15,000
Nov 9	Bolton Wanderers	L 2-3	Walton, Lofthouse	6,000
Nov 16	NOTTS COUNTY	W 9-1	Walton 3, Unknown, Jack Southworth 3, Campbell, Townley	6,000
Nov 23	ACCRINGTON	W 3-2	Lofthouse, Campbell, Forbes	8,000
Nov 30	WEST BROMWICH ALBION	W 5-0	Jack Southworth 4, Townley	6,600
Dec 7	Preston North End	D 1-1	Campbell	12,000
Dec 21	BOLTON WANDERERS	W 7-1	Jack Southworth 2, Walton 4, Lofthouse	6,000
Dec 23	Stoke	W 3-0	Lofthouse 2, Campbell	unknown
Dec 26	Wolverhampton W.	W 4-2	Townley, Jack Southworth, Lofthouse, o.g.	19,000
Dec 28	EVERTON	L 2-4	Campbell, Jack Southworth	12,000
Jan 4	STOKE	W 8-0	Jack Southworth 4, Campbell 2, Lofthouse, Brandon	4,000
Jan 11	West Bromwich Albion	L 2-3	Barton, Jack Southworth	5,100
Feb 8	Derby County	L 0-4		5,000
Feb 18	Notts County	D 1-1	Lofthouse	4,000
Feb 22	Burnley	W 2-1	Walton, Townley	7,000
Mar 31	Aston Villa	L 0-3		6,000

FA Cup

DATE	OPPONENTS		SCORE	GOALSCORERS	ATTENDANCE
Jan 18	SUNDERLAND	(Rd1)	W 4-2*	Townley 2, Campbell, Barton	10,000
Feb 1	GRIMSBY TOWN	(Rd2)	W 3-0	Almond, Ogilvie o.g., Jack Southworth	3,000
Feb 15	Bootle	(Rd3)	W 7-0	Walton 3, Jack Southworth 2, Forbes, Townley	4,000
Mar 8	Wolverhampton W.†	(SF)	W 1-0	Jack Southworth	14,788
Mar 29	Sheffield Wednesday‡	(F)	W 6-1	Townley 3, Walton, Jack Southworth, Lofthouse	20,000

*After extra-time. †Played at the Racecourse Ground, Wrexham.
‡Played at the Kennington Oval.

League & Cup Appearances

PLAYER	LEAGUE	CUP COMPETITION FA CUP	TOTAL
Arthur, W.J.H.	4		4
Almond, W.	7	2	9
Barton, J.	15	3	18
Brandon, T.	22	3	25
Campbell, H.	22	5	27
Dewar, G.	17	5	22
Doig, J.E.	1		1
Douglas, J.	7		7
Fecitt, H.L.	1		1
Forbes, J.	22	5	27
Forrest, J.H.	21	5	26
Horne, J.K.	2	3	5
Lofthouse, J.M.	18	5	23
McCallum, N.	2		2
McOwen, W.	9	1	10
Paul, A.G.	1	1	2
Southworth, James	2	2	4
Southworth, Jack	22	5	27
Townley, W.	20	5	25
Walton, N.	21	5	26
Waring, W.	1		1
Wilkie, T.	5		5

Goalscorers

PLAYER	LEAGUE	CUP COMPETITION FA CUP	TOTAL
Southworth, Jack	22	5	27
Walton, N.	14	4	18
Campbell, H.	15	1	16
Lofthouse, J.M.	11	1	12
Townley, W.	6	6	12
Barton, J.	1	1	2
Forbes, J.	1	1	2
Brandon, T.	1		1
Forrest, J.H.	1		1
Almond, W.		1	1
Opp's o.gs.	2	1	3
Unknown	4		4

Fact File

Billy Townley became the first man to score a hat-trick in the FA Cup final when he notched up three goals against Sheffield Wednesday.

SECRETARY: Thomas Mitchell

TOP SCORER: Jack Southworth

BIGGEST WIN: 9-1, 16 November 1889, v Notts County, Football League

HIGHEST ATTENDANCE: 20,000, 29 March 1890, v Sheffield Wednesday, FA Cup final

MAJOR TRANSFERS IN: Tom Brandon from St Mirren, Henry Campbell from Renton, George Dewar from Dumbarton

Final Football League Table

		P	W	D	L	F	A	Pts
1	PRESTON NE	22	15	3	4	71	30	33
2	EVERTON	22	14	3	5	65	40	31
3	BLACKBURN R	22	12	3	7	78	41	27
4	WOLVERHAMPTON W	22	10	5	7	51	38	25
5	WBA	22	11	3	8	47	50	25
6	ACCRINGTON	22	9	6	7	53	56	24
7	DERBY CO	22	9	3	10	43	55	21
8	ASTON VILLA	22	7	5	10	43	51	19
9	BOLTON W	22	9	1	12	54	65	19
10	NOTTS CO	22	6	5	11	43	51	17
11	BURNLEY	22	4	5	13	36	65	13
12	STOKE	22	3	4	15	27	69	10

Season 1890-91

Football League

DATE	OPPONENTS	SCORE	GOALSCORERS	ATTENDANCE
Sep 6	Derby County	L 5-8	Southworth 3, Walton, Whitehead	4,500
Sep 13	ACCRINGTON	D 0-0		10,000
Sep 27	WOLVERHAMPTON W.	L 2-3	Southworth, Haydock	5,000
Oct 4	Preston North End	W 2-1	Southworth, Walton	10,000
Oct 11	SUNDERLAND	W 3-2	Southworth 2, Lofthouse	10,000
Oct 18	Burnley	W 6-1	Walton 2, Southworth 2, Barton, Lofthouse	10,000
Oct 25	PRESTON NORTH END	W 1-0	Southworth	18,000
Nov 1	Sunderland	L 1-3	Walton	14,000
Nov 8	EVERTON	W 2-1	Dewar, Southworth	15,000
Nov 15	Notts County	W 2-1	Lofthouse, Southworth	11,000
Nov 22	BURNLEY	W 5-2	Townley, Walton 2, Unknown, Southworth	4,000
Nov 29	Everton	L 1-3	Southworth	11,000
Dec 6	ASTON VILLA	W 5-1	Southworth 3, Campbell, Lofthouse	5,000
Dec 13	Aston Villa	D 2-2	Southworth 2	4,000
Dec 20	WEST BROMWICH ALBION	W 2-1	Southworth, Townley	5,500
Dec 26	Wolverhampton W.	L 0-2		10,000
Jan 3	DERBY COUNTY	W 8-0	Hall 4, Southworth 3, Townley	3,000
Mar 4	Accrington	W 4-0	Southworth 3, Fecitt	unknown
Mar 7	BOLTON WANDERERS	L 0-2		7,000
Mar 9	West Bromwich Albion	L 0-1		2,700
Mar 14	NOTTS COUNTY	L 1-7	Dewar	7,000
Mar 28	Bolton Wanderers	L 0-2		12,000

FA Cup

DATE	OPPONENTS		SCORE	GOALSCORERS	ATTENDANCE
Jan 24	Middlesbrough Ironopolis	(Rd1)	W 3-0	Hall 2, Stevenson o.g.	7,000
Jan 31	CHESTER	(Rd2)	W 7-0	Southworth 3, Hall, Townley, Taylor o.g., Unknown	3,000
Feb 14	WOLVERHAMPTON W.	(Rd3)	W 2-0	Baugh o.g., Fletcher o.g.	16,000
Feb 28	West Bromwich Albion*	(SF)	W 3-2	Southworth, Hall, Unknown	21,774
Mar 21	Notts County**	(F)	W 3-1	Dewar, Southworth, Townley	23,000

*Played at the Victoria Ground, Stoke. **Played at the Kennington Oval.

League & Cup Appearances

PLAYER	LEAGUE	CUP COMPETITION FA CUP	TOTAL
Almond, W.	4		4
Barton, J.	18	5	23
Brandon, T.	17	5	22
Campbell, H.	17	4	21
Dewar, G.	22	5	27
Douglas, J.	3		3
Fecitt, H.L.	3		3
Forbes, J.	22	5	27
Forrest, J.H.	21	5	26
Garstang, H.	3		3
Gow, J.	15	3	18
Hall, C.	14	5	19
Haydock, J.	2		2
Lofthouse, J.M.	20	5	25
Lowe, J.	2		2
Pennington, R.	5	2	7
Southworth, Jack	18	5	23
Townley, W.	16	5	21
Walton, N.	18	1	19
Whitehead, W.	2		2

Goalscorers

PLAYER	LEAGUE	CUP COMPETITION FA CUP	TOTAL
Southworth, Jack	26	5	31
Hall, C.	4	4	8
Walton, N.	7		7
Townley, W.	3	2	5
Lofthouse, J.M.	4		4
Dewar, G.	2	1	3
Barton, J.	1		1
Campbell, H.	1		1
Fecitt, H.L.	1		1
Haydock, J.	1		1
Whitehead, W.	1		1
Opps' o.gs.		4	4
Unknown	1	2	3

Fact File

On 13 September 1890, Blackburn Rovers staged their opening game at Ewood Park.

SECRETARY: Thomas Mitchell
TOP SCORER: Jack Southworth
BIGGEST WIN: 8-0, 3 January 1891, v Derby County, Football League
HIGHEST ATTENDANCE: 23,000, 21 March 1891, v Notts County, FA Cup final

Final Football League Table

		P	W	D	L	F	A	Pts
1	EVERTON	22	14	1	7	63	29	29
2	PRESTON NE	22	12	3	7	44	23	27
3	NOTTS CO	22	11	4	7	52	35	26
4	WOLVERHAMPTON W	22	12	2	8	39	50	26
5	BOLTON W	22	12	1	9	47	34	25
6	BLACKBURN R	22	11	2	9	52	43	24
7	SUNDERLAND	22	10	5	7	51	31	23
8	BURNLEY	22	9	3	10	52	63	21
9	ASTON VILLA	22	7	4	11	45	58	18
10	ACCRINGTON	22	6	4	12	28	50	16
11	DERBY CO	22	7	1	14	47	81	15
12	WBA	22	5	2	15	34	57	12

SUNDERLAND TWO POINTS DEDUCTED FOR FIELDING AN INELIGIBLE PLAYER.

Season 1891-92

Football League

DATE	OPPONENTS	SCORE	GOALSCORERS	ATTENDANCE
Sep 5	Aston Villa	L 1-5	Hall	6,000
Sep 12	NOTTS COUNTY	W 5-4	Lofthouse, Townley 2, Southworth, Dewar	7,000
Sep 19	Everton	L 1-3	Southworth	15,000
Sep 26	BURNLEY	D 3-3	Southworth 2, Walton	4,000
Oct 3	West Bromwich Albion	D 2-2	Chippendale 2	6,000
Oct 10	WOLVERHAMPTON W.	W 2-0	Hall, Southworth	5,000
Oct 17	Darwen	W 5-3	Hall 2, Southworth 2, Lofthouse	10,000
Oct 24	PRESTON NORTH END	L 2-4	Southworth, Walton	10,000
Oct 31	Bolton Wanderers	L 2-4	Southworth 2	11,000
Nov 7	SUNDERLAND	W 3-1	Southworth 2, Townley	6,000
Nov 9	Stoke	W 1-0	Hall	5,000
Nov 14	Preston North End	L 2-3	Southworth, Walton	14,000
Nov 21	BOLTON WANDERERS	W 4-0	Southworth 3, Townley	7,000
Nov 28	Wolverhampton W.	L 1-6	Townley	3,000
Dec 5	EVERTON	D 2-2	Campbell, Walton	4,000
Dec 12	Burnley	L 0-3		5,000
Dec 19	Notts County	D 2-2	Southworth 2	6,000
Dec 25	DARWEN	W 4-0	Almond, Townley, Southworth 2	3,000
Dec 26	ACCRINGTON	D 2-2	Walton, Townley	3,000
Jan 2	DERBY COUNTY	L 0-2		2,000
Feb 27	Accrington	L 0-1		3,000
Mar 5	ASTON VILLA	W 4-3	Townley 2, Dewar, Lofthouse	6,000
Mar 12	WEST BROMWICH ALBION	W 3-2	Chippendale 2, Dewar	6,000
Mar 19	STOKE	W 5-3	Chippendale 2, Townley, Southworth, Walton	2,000
Mar 26	Derby County	D 1-1	Southworth	5,000
Apr 16	Sunderland	L 1-6	Hall	10,000

FA Cup

Jan 16	DERBY COUNTY	(Rd1) W 4-1	Southworth 4	10,000
Jan 30	West Bromwich Albion	(Rd2) L 1-3	Townley	12,135

League & Cup Appearances

PLAYER	LEAGUE	CUP COMPETITION FA CUP	TOTAL
Almond, W.	21	2	23
Arthur, W.J.H.	18	2	20
Barton, J.	2		2
Campbell, H.	24	2	26
Chippendale, H.	8		8
Cockshutt, J.W.	1		1
Dewar, G.	16	1	17
Douglas, J.	3		3
Forbes, J.	24	2	26
Forrest, J.H.	23	1	24
Hall, C.	15	2	17
Hartley, D.	4		4
Haydock, J.	4	2	6
Horne, W.E.	7		7
Lofthouse, J.M.	13		13
McKeown, T.M.	19	2	21
Pennington, R.	1		1
Sanderson, G.A.	3	1	4
Southworth, Jack	24	1	25
Smith, A.	7		7
Stringfellow, J.	4		4
Townley, W.	22	2	24
Walton, N.	23	2	25

Goalscorers

PLAYER	LEAGUE	CUP COMPETITION FA CUP	TOTAL
Southworth, Jack	22	4	26
Townley, W.	10	1	11
Chippendale, H.	6		6
Hall, C.	6		6
Walton, N.	6		6
Dewar, G.	3		3
Lofthouse, J.M.	3		3
Almond, W.	1		1
Campbell, H.	1		1

Fact File

William Horne, who made seven appearances in 1891-92, was one of three goalkeeping brothers. John Kay Horne had played for Blackburn in the 1890 FA Cup final while Dick Horne had been a stalwart with Accrington in the days before the Football League began.

SECRETARY: Thomas Mitchell

TOP SCORER: Jack Southworth

BIGGEST WIN: 4-0, 21 November 1891, v Bolton Wanderers, Football League; 25 December 1891, v Darwen, Football League

HIGHEST ATTENDANCE: 5,000, 19 September 1891, v Everton, Football League

MAJOR TRANSFERS IN: Michael McKeown from Glasgow Celtic

Final Football League Table

		P	W	D	L	F	A	Pts
1	SUNDERLAND	26	21	0	5	93	36	42
2	PRESTON NE	26	18	1	7	61	31	37
3	BOLTON W	26	17	2	7	51	37	36
4	ASTON VILLA	26	15	0	11	89	56	30
5	EVERTON	26	12	4	10	49	49	28
6	WOLVERHAMPTON W	26	11	4	11	59	46	26
7	BURNLEY	26	11	4	11	49	45	26
8	NOTTS CO	26	11	4	11	55	51	26
9	BLACKBURN R	26	10	6	10	58	65	26
10	DERBY CO	26	10	4	12	46	52	24
11	ACCRINGTON	26	8	4	14	40	78	20
12	WBA	26	6	6	14	51	58	18
13	STOKE	26	5	4	17	38	61	14
14	DARWEN	26	4	3	19	38	112	11

Season 1892-93

Football League Division 1

DATE	OPPONENTS	SCORE	GOALSCORERS	ATTENDANCE
Sep 3	NEWTON HEATH	W 4-3	Southworth, Hall 2, Chippendale	4,000
Sep 10	Wolverhampton W.	L 2-4	Chippendale 2	6,000
Sep 17	EVERTON	D 2-2	Almond, Southworth	9,000
Sep 24	Sunderland	L 0-5		8,000
Oct 1	ACCRINGTON	D 3-3	Bowdler, Chippendale, Southworth	6,000
Oct 8	Preston North End	L 1-2	Hall	10,000
Oct 15	SHEFFIELD WEDNESDAY	L 0-2		3,000
Oct 22	Derby County	L 0-3		5,000
Oct 29	PRESTON NORTH END	D 0-0		7,000
Nov 5	Newton Heath	D 4-4	Bowdler, Hall, Sawers, Mann	10,000
Nov 12	WOLVERHAMPTON.W.	D 3-3	Hall 2, Southworth	7,000
Nov 19	Sheffield Wednesday	W 3-0	Southworth 2, Bowdler	8,000
Nov 26	BOLTON WANDERERS	W 3-0	Southworth 2, Sawers	7,000
Dec 3	Burnley	D 0-0		9,000
Dec 10	Aston Villa	L 1-4	Chippendale	6,000
Dec 17	BURNLEY	W 2-0	Bowdler, Southworth	7,000
Dec 24	NOTTS COUNTY	W 1-0	Sawers	5,000
Dec 26	West Bromwich Albion	W 2-1	Sawers, Unknown	7,000
Dec 31	NOTTINGHAM FOREST	L 0-1		3,000
Jan 2	Accrington	D 1-1	Anderson	8,000
Jan 7	DERBY COUNTY	D 2-2	Gillespie, Sawers	5,000
Jan 14	Notts County	D 0-0		5,000
Jan 28	WEST BROMWICH ALBION	W 2-1	Sawers, Horton o.g.	2,300
Feb 11	ASTON VILLA	D 2-2	Sawers 2	3,000
Feb 25	STOKE	D 3-3	Sawers 2, Anderson	3,000
Mar 11	Nottingham Forest	W 1-0	Chippendale	5,000
Mar 18	Bolton Wanderers	L 1-2	Sawers	6,000
Mar 31	SUNDERLAND	D 2-2	Bowdler, Campbell	12,000
Apr 1	Everton	L 0-4		14,000
Apr 3	Stoke	D 2-2	Taylor, Southworth	8,000

FA Cup

Jan 21	NEWTON HEATH	(Rd1)	W 4-0	Campbell 2, Sawers 2	7,000
Feb 4	NORTHWICH VICTORIA	(Rd2)	W 4-1	Bowdler, Campbell, Sawers, Southworth	3,000
Feb 18	SUNDERLAND	(Rd3)	W 3-0	Southworth 2, Bowdler	26,000
Mar 03	Wolverhampton W.*	(SF)	L 1-2	Taylor	25,000

*Played at the Town Ground, Nottingham.

League & Cup Appearances

PLAYER	LEAGUE	CUP COMPETITION FA CUP	TOTAL
Almond, W.	5		5
Anderson, G.E.	22	4	26
Arthur, W.J.H.	3		3
Bowdler, J.C.H.	22	4	26
Campbell, H.	23	4	27
Chippendale, H.	20	1	21
Dewar, G.	30	4	34
Forbes, J.	20	3	23
Forrest, J.H.	20	1	21
Gillespie, M.	6		6
Hall, C.	13		13
Hargreaves, A.	2		2
Hartley, D.	2		2
Mann, G.W.	2		2
Marshall, H.J.H.	20	4	24
Murray, J.W.	30	4	34
Pennington, R.	2		2
Sanderson, G.A.	1		1
Sawers, W.	24	4	28
Smith, W.A.	1		1
Southworth, Jack	23	4	27
Taylor, W.	10	3	13
Walton, N.	28	4	32
Whitehead, W.	1		1

Goalscorers

PLAYER	LEAGUE	CUP COMPETITION FA CUP	TOTAL
Sawers, W.	11	3	14
Southworth, Jack	10	3	13
Bowdler, J.C.H.	5	2	7
Chippendale, H.	6		6
Hall, C.	6		6
Campbell, H.	1	3	4
Anderson, G.E.	2		2
Taylor, W.	1	1	2
Almond, W.	1		1
Gillespie, M.	1		1
Mann, G.W.	1		1
Opps' o.gs.	1		1
Unknown	1		1

Fact File

John Murray had been a regular in the Sunderland team that won the Football League championship in 1891-92 and was an ever-present in his first season at Blackburn.

SECRETARY: Thomas Mitchell

TOP SCORER: Bill Sawers

BIGGEST WIN: 4-0, 21 January 1893, v Newton Heath, FA Cup Round 1

HIGHEST ATTENDANCE: 26,000, 18 February 1893, v Sunderland, FA Cup Round 3

MAJOR TRANSFERS IN: George Anderson from Leith Athletic, John Murray from Sunderland, Harry Marshall from Heart of Midlothian

Final Division 1 Table

		P	W	D	L	F	A	PTS
1	SUNDERLAND	30	22	4	4	100	36	48
2	PRESTON NE	30	17	3	10	57	39	37
3	EVERTON	30	16	4	10	74	51	36
4	ASTON VILLA	30	16	3	11	73	62	35
5	BOLTON W	30	13	6	11	56	55	32
6	BURNLEY	30	13	4	13	51	44	30
7	STOKE	30	12	5	13	58	48	29
8	WBA	30	12	5	13	58	69	29
9	BLACKBURN R	30	8	13	9	47	56	29
10	NOTTINGHAM F	30	10	8	12	48	52	28
11	WOLVERHAMPTON W	30	12	4	14	47	68	28
12	SHEFFIELD W	30	12	3	15	55	65	27
13	DERBY CO	30	9	9	12	52	64	27
14	NOTTS CO	30	10	4	16	53	61	24
15	ACCRINGTON	30	6	11	13	57	81	23
16	NEWTON HEATH	30	6	6	18	50	85	18

Football League Division 1

DATE	OPPONENTS	SCORE	GOALSCORERS	ATTENDANCE
Sep 2	Darwen	W 3-2	Townley, Campbell H. Chippendale	8,000
Sep 9	SHEFFIELD WEDNESDAY	W 5-1	Chippendale 2, Marshall, Campbell H., Hargreaves	6,000
Sep 16	Bolton Wanderers	L 1-2	Hargreaves	8,000
Sep 23	WOLVERHAMPTON W.	W 3-0	Chippendale, Whitehead 2	6,000
Sep 30	Sheffield Wednesday	L 2-4	Hargreaves 2	8,000
Oct 7	PRESTON NORTH END	W 1-0	Whitehead	12,000
Oct 14	Everton	D 2-2	Hargreaves 2	15,000
Oct 21	SUNDERLAND	W 4-3	Townley 2, Chippendale, Anderson	10,000
Oct 28	Stoke	L 1-3	Townley	5,000
Nov 4	ASTON VILLA	W 2-0	Whitehead, Hall	6,000
Nov 11	Preston North End	W 1-0	Townley	11,000
Nov 18	BURNLEY	W 3-2	Chippendale, Whitehead, Townley	3,000
Nov 25	Nottingham Forest	D 0-0		5,000
Dec 2	BOLTON WANDERERS	L 0-1		5,000
Dec 9	Sunderland	W 3-2	Sorley, Chippendale, Doig o.g.	10,000
Dec 16	EVERTON	W 4-3	Townley 2, Chippendale, Sorley	10,000
Dec 23	Burnley	L 0-1		13,000
Dec 25	DARWEN	W 4-1	Hall, Sorley 2, Whitehead	8,000
Dec 26	Wolverhampton W.	L 1-5	Townley	15,500
Jan 6	West Bromwich Albion	L 1-2	Campbell H.	2,024
Jan 13	WEST BROMWICH ALBION	W 3-0	Chippendale, Hall, Anderson	6,000
Jan 15	SHEFFIELD UNITED	W 4-1	Chippendale, Haydock 2, Calvey	3,000
Feb 3	NOTTINGHAM FOREST	W 6-1	Calvey 2, Haydock, Chippendale 3	5,000
Mar 3	Sheffield United	L 2-3	Campbell H., Anderson	8,000
Mar 12	Newton Heath	L 1-5	Hargreaves	5,000
Mar 23	DERBY COUNTY	L 0-2		7,000
Mar 24	Aston Villa	L 1-2	Sorley	18,000
Mar 26	NEWTON HEATH	W 4-0	Hargreaves 2, Haydock, Chippendale	5,000
Mar 31	Derby County	L 2-5	Townley, Haydock	4,000
Apr 14	STOKE	W 5-0	Whitehead 2, Marshall, Sorley 2	2,000

FA Cup

Jan 27	West Bromwich Albion	(Rd1)	W 3-2	Calvey, Chippendale, Forrest	10,243
Feb 10	Newton Heath	(Rd2)	D 0-0*		18,000
Feb 17	NEWTON HEATH	(R)	W 5-1	Calvey, Chippendale, Haydock, Whitehead 2	5,000
Feb 24	Derby County	(Rd3)	W 4-1	Haydock 3, Townley	15,500
Mar 10	Notts County**	(SF)	L 0-1		20,000

*After extra-time. **Played at Bramall Lane, Sheffield.

League & Cup Appearances

PLAYER	LEAGUE	CUP COMPETITION FA CUP	TOTAL
Anderson, G.E.	26	5	31
Brandon, T.	13	5	18
Calvey, M.	6	5	11
Campbell, H.	12		12
Campbell, W.C.	1		1
Chippendale, H.	27	5	32
Dewar, G.	24	3	27
Forbes, J.	2		2
Forrest, J.H.	25	2	27
Hall, C.	25	2	27
Hargreaves, J.	17		17
Haydock, J.	7	4	11
MacFarlane, R.	2		2
Marshall, H.J.H.	29	5	34
Murray, J.W.	28	5	33
Ogilvie, A.	21	5	26
Sorley, J.	14		14
Townley, W.	20	4	24
Watts, C.	9		9
Whitehead, J.	22	5	27

Goalscorers

PLAYER	LEAGUE	CUP COMPETITION FA CUP	TOTAL
Chippendale, H.	14	2	16
Townley, W.	10	1	11
Whitehead, J.	8	2	10
Hargreaves, J.	9		9
Haydock, J.	5	4	9
Sorley, J.	7		7
Calvey, M.	3	2	5
Campbell, H.	4		4
Anderson, G.E.	3		3
Hall, C.	3		3
Marshall, H.J.H.	2		2
Forrest, J.H.		1	1
Opps' o.gs.	1		1

Fact File

Tom Brandon returned to Ewood Park in December 1893 after helping Sheffield Wednesday reach the Football League.

SECRETARY: Thomas Mitchell

TOP SCORER: Harry Chippendale

BIGGEST WIN: 6-1, 3 February 1894, v Nottingham Forest, Division 1

HIGHEST ATTENDANCE: 20,000, 10 March 1894, v Notts County, FA Cup semi-final

MAJOR TRANSFERS IN: Tom Brandon from Sheffield Wednesday, Adam Ogilvie from Grimsby Town

MAJOR TRANSFERS OUT: Jack Southworth to Everton

Final Division 1 Table

		P	W	D	L	F	A	PTS
1	ASTON VILLA	30	19	6	5	84	42	44
2	SUNDERLAND	30	17	4	9	72	44	38
3	DERBY CO	30	16	4	10	73	62	36
4	BLACKBURN R	30	16	2	12	69	53	34
5	BURNLEY	30	15	4	11	61	51	34
6	EVERTON	30	15	3	12	90	57	33
7	NOTTINGHAM F	30	14	4	12	57	48	32
8	WBA	30	14	4	12	66	59	32
9	WOLVERHAMPTON W	30	14	3	13	52	63	31
10	SHEFFIELD U	30	13	5	12	47	61	31
11	STOKE	30	13	3	14	65	79	29
12	SHEFFIELD W	30	9	8	13	48	57	26
13	BOLTON W	30	10	4	16	38	52	24
14	PRESTON NE	30	10	3	17	44	56	23
15	DARWEN	30	7	5	18	37	83	19
16	NEWTON HEATH	30	6	2	22	36	72	14

Season 1894-95

Football League Division 1

DATE	OPPONENTS	SCORE	GOALSCORERS	ATTENDANCE
Sep 1	LIVERPOOL	D 1-1	Hall	12,000
Sep 8	Sheffield Wednesday	L 1-4	Chippendale	15,000
Sep 15	STOKE	W 6-0	Stuart, Whitehead 2, Hall 3	7,000
Sep 22	Liverpool	D 2-2	Stuart, Whitehead	14,000
Sep 29	SHEFFIELD WEDNESDAY	W 3-1	Wade 2, Chippendale	8,000
Oct 6	Preston North End	D 1-1	Whitehead	12,000
Oct 8	Sheffield United	L 0-3		5,000
Oct 13	BOLTON WANDERERS	W 2-1	Whitehead, Haydock	7,000
Oct 20	EVERTON	W 4-3	Hall, Haydock 2, Whitehead	15,000
Oct 27	PRESTON NORTH END	D 1-1	Haydock	12,000
Nov 3	Bolton Wanderers	W 3-1	Chippendale, Anderson, Stuart	5,000
Nov 10	SUNDERLAND	D 1-1	Hall	13,000
Nov 17	BURNLEY	W 1-0	Chippendale	7,000
Nov 24	Everton	L 1-2	Hall	20,000
Dec 1	ASTON VILLA	L 1-3	Stuart	10,000
Dec 8	Aston Villa	L 0-3		5,000
Dec 15	Sunderland	L 2-3	Cleghorn, Haydock	10,000
Dec 22	WEST BROMWICH ALBION	W 3-0	Cleghorn 2, Anderson	1,200
Dec 26	SHEFFIELD UNITED	W 3-2	Whitehead 2, Walton	4,000
Dec 29	Nottingham Forest	W 3-2	Chippendale 2, Sorley	5,000
Jan 1	NOTTINGHAM FOREST	D 0-0		10,000
Jan 5	SMALL HEATH	W 9-1	Sorley, Chippendale 3, Killean 3, Gordon, Anderson	2,000
Jan 12	Burnley	L 1-2	Killean	10,000
Jan 26	West Bromwich Albion	L 0-2		3,000
Feb 23	Wolverhampton W.	D 3-3	Hargreaves 2, Haydock	6,000
Mar 2	Small Heath	D 1-1	Chippendale	5,000
Mar 23	WOLVERHAMPTON W.	W 5-1	Gordon, Killean, Anderson, Chippendale 2	4000
Apr 6	Derby County	D 0-0		2,000
Apr 12	DERBY COUNTY	D 0-0		4,000
Apr 13	Stoke	L 1-5	Hargreaves	8,000

FA Cup

DATE	OPPONENTS		SCORE	GOALSCORERS	ATTENDANCE
Feb 2	Burton Wanderers	(Rd1)	W 2-1	Haydock 2	3,000
Feb 16	Everton	(Rd2)	D 1-1	Forrest	20,000
Feb 20	EVERTON	(R)	L 2-3	Kelso o.g., Gordon	20,000

League & Cup Appearances

PLAYER	LEAGUE	CUP COMPETITION FA CUP	TOTAL
Anderson, G.E.	28	3	31
Brandon, T.	28	3	31
Chippendale, H.	30	3	33
Cleghorn, T.	28	3	31
Dewar, G.	14		14
Forrest, J.H.	19	3	22
Gordon, P.	12	3	15
Hall, C.	12		12
Hargreaves, J.	8	2	10
Haydock, J.	21	3	24
Killean, E.	16	1	17
Marshall, H.J.H.	2		2
Murray, J.W.	27	3	30
Ogilvie, A.	30	3	33
Sorley, J.	12	1	13
Stuart, J.	13		13
Wade, J.J.	1		1
Walton, W.E.	1		1
Whitehead, J.	28	2	30

Goalscorers

PLAYER	LEAGUE	CUP COMPETITION FA CUP	TOTAL
Chippendale, H.	12		12
Whitehead, J.	8		8
Haydock, J.	6	2	8
Hall, C.	7		7
Killean, E.	5		5
Anderson, G.E.	4		4
Stuart, J.	4		4
Cleghorn, T.	3		3
Gordon, P.	2	1	3
Hargreaves, J.	3		3
Sorley, J.	2		2
Wade, J.J.	2		2
Walton, W.E.	1		1
Forrest, J.H.		1	1
Opps' o.gs.		1	1

Fact File

Jimmy Forrest, who won five FA Cup-winners' medals with Blackburn, made his final league appearance for the club against Derby County on the 6 April 1895.

SECRETARY: Thomas Mitchell
TOP SCORER: Harry Chippendale
BIGGEST WIN: 9-1, 5 January 1895, v Small Heath, Division 1
HIGHEST ATTENDANCE: 20,000, 24 November 1894, v Everton, Division 1; 16 February 1895, v Everton, FA Cup Round 2; 20 February 1895, v Everton, FA Cup Round 2 replay
MAJOR TRANSFERS IN: Peter Turnbull from Burnley

Final Division 1 Table

		P	W	D	L	F	A	Pts
1	SUNDERLAND	30	21	5	4	80	37	47
2	EVERTON	30	18	6	6	82	50	42
3	ASTON VILLA	30	17	5	8	82	43	39
4	PRESTON NE	30	15	5	10	62	46	35
5	BLACKBURN R	30	11	10	9	59	49	32
6	SHEFFIELD U	30	14	4	12	57	55	32
7	NOTTINGHAM F	30	13	5	12	50	56	31
8	SHEFFIELD W	30	12	4	14	50	55	28
9	BURNLEY	30	11	4	15	44	56	26
10	BOLTON W	30	9	7	14	61	62	25
11	WOLVERHAMPTON W	30	9	7	14	43	63	25
12	SMALL HEATH	30	9	7	14	50	74	25
13	WBA	30	10	4	16	51	66	24
14	STOKE	30	9	6	15	50	67	24
15	DERBY CO	30	7	9	14	45	68	23
16	LIVERPOOL	30	7	8	15	51	70	22

The Essential History of Blackburn Rovers

Football League Division 1

DATE	OPPONENTS	SCORE	GOALSCORERS	ATTENDANCE
Sep 7	Sunderland	L 1-2	Haydock	10,000
Sep 14	NOTTINGHAM FOREST	W 2-0	Haydock, Tierney	6,000
Sep 21	Everton	W 2-0	Anderson, Whitehead	20,000
Sep 28	ASTON VILLA	D 1-1	Chippendale	15,000
Oct 5	BURNLEY	W 1-0	Chippendale	3,000
Oct 12	PRESTON NORTH END	W 3-0	Hargreaves 2, Whitehead	12,000
Oct 19	Aston Villa	L 1-3	Welford o.g.	17,000
Oct 26	SUNDERLAND	L 2-4	Chippendale, Whitehead	8,000
Nov 2	Preston North End	D 1-1	Chippendale	12,000
Nov 9	WOLVERHAMPTON W.	W 3-1	Haydock, Turnbull 2	3,000
Nov 23	SHEFFIELD WEDNESDAY	W 2-1	Wilkie, Chippendale	4,000
Nov 30	Bolton Wanderers	D 1-1	Brandon	8,000
Dec 7	BOLTON WANDERERS	W 3-2	Killean, Turnbull 2	5,000
Dec 14	Wolverhampton W.	W 2-1	Whitehead, Turnbull	5,000
Dec 28	Nottingham Forest	L 2-4	Chippendale, Haydock	4,000
Jan 1	EVERTON	L 2-3	Haydock, Turnbull	20,000
Jan 4	BURY	L 0-2		7,000
Jan 11	Sheffield Wednesday	L 0-3		10,000
Jan 25	SHEFFIELD UNITED	W 1-0	Wilkie	3,000
Feb 17	WEST BROMWICH ALBION	W 1-0	Wilkie	5,000
Feb 22	DERBY COUNTY	L 0-2		10,000
Feb 29	Small Heath	L 1-2	Hargreaves	6,000
Mar 7	Sheffield United	D 1-1	Turnbull	5,000
Mar 21	SMALL HEATH	W 2-1	Haydock, Hargreaves	5,000
Apr 3	STOKE	W 3-1	Haydock, Chippendale, Whitehead	4,000
Apr 4	Stoke	L 0-3		6,000
Apr 11	Derby County	D 0-0		8,000
Apr 13	Burnley	L 0-6		5,000
Apr 25	Bury	L 0-2		2,000
Apr 29	West Bromwich Albion	L 2-3	Hargreaves, Wilkie	500

FA Cup

Feb 1	WEST BROMWICH ALBION	(Rd1) L 1-2	Turnbull		8,000

League & Cup Appearances

PLAYER	LEAGUE	CUP COMPETITION FA CUP	TOTAL
Anderson, G.E.	28	1	29
Brandon, T.	27	1	28
Chippendale, H.	27	1	28
Cleghorn, T.	17		17
Dewar, G.	27	1	28
Hargreaves, J.	13		13
Hannah, G.	3		3
Haydock, J.	24	1	25
Killean, E.	19	1	20
Murray, J.W.	24	1	25
Ogilvie, A.	30	1	31
Parkinson, J.	1		1
Porter, W.S.	5		5
Tierney, T.T.	9		9
Turnbull, P.	25	1	26
Walton, W.E.	4		4
Wilkie, J.	19	1	20
Whitehead, J.	27	1	28
Yarwood, J.	1		1

Goalscorers

PLAYER	LEAGUE	CUP COMPETITION FA CUP	TOTAL
Turnbull, P.	7	1	8
Chippendale, H.	7		7
Haydock, J.	7		7
Hargreaves, J.	5		5
Whitehead, J.	5		5
Wilkie, J.	4		4
Anderson, G.E.	1		1
Brandon, T.	1		1
Killean, E.	1		1
Tierney, T.T.	1		1
Opps' o.gs.	1		1

Fact File

Jimmy Forrest finally ended his association with Blackburn Rovers following a disagreement with the committee of the club. He joined neighbouring Darwen in October 1895.

SECRETARY: Thomas Mitchell
TOP SCORER: Peter Turnbull
BIGGEST WIN: 3-0, 12 October 1895, v Preston North End, Division 1
HIGHEST ATTENDANCE: 20,000, 21 September 1895, v Everton, Division 1; 1 January 1896, v Everton, Division 1
MAJOR TRANSFERS IN: John Wilkie from Partick Thistle
MAJOR TRANSFERS OUT: Jimmy Forrest to Darwen, Jack Sorley to Burton Swifts, Thomas Cleghorn to Liverpool

Final Division 1 Table

		P	W	D	L	F	A	Pts
1	ASTON VILLA	30	20	5	5	78	45	45
2	DERBY CO	30	17	7	6	68	35	41
3	EVERTON	30	16	7	7	66	43	39
4	BOLTON W	30	16	5	9	49	37	37
5	SUNDERLAND	30	15	7	8	52	41	37
6	STOKE	30	15	0	15	56	47	30
7	SHEFFIELD W	30	12	5	13	44	53	29
8	BLACKBURN R	30	12	5	13	40	50	29
9	PRESTON NE	30	11	6	13	44	48	28
10	BURNLEY	30	10	7	13	48	44	27
11	BURY	30	12	3	15	50	54	27
12	SHEFFIELD U	30	10	6	14	40	50	26
13	NOTTINGHAM F	30	11	3	16	42	57	25
14	WOLVERHAMPTON W	30	10	1	19	61	65	21
15	SMALL HEATH	30	8	4	18	39	79	20
16	WBA	30	6	7	17	30	59	19

Season 1896-97

Football League Division 1

DATE	OPPONENTS	SCORE	GOALSCORERS	ATTENDANCE
Sep 1	WEST BROMWICH ALBION	L 1-2	Whitehead	3,000
Sep 5	LIVERPOOL	W 1-0	Stuart	5,000
Sep 12	Bolton Wanderers	D 0-0		2,000
Sep 19	SHEFFIELD WEDNESDAY	W 4-0	Tierney, Wilkie, Chippendale, Dewar	6,000
Sep 26	Wolverhampton W.	D 1-1	Tierney	5,000
Oct 3	BURNLEY	W 3-2	Dewar, Anderson (pen), Chippendale	9,000
Oct 10	Preston North End	L 1-3	Wilkie	10,000
Oct 17	BOLTON WANDERERS	W 1-0	Chippendale	10,000
Oct 24	Liverpool	L 0-4		10,000
Oct 31	PRESTON NORTH END	L 0-4		14,517
Nov 7	Burnley	W 1-0	Campbell	5,000
Nov 14	NOTTINGHAM FOREST	D 0-0		2,000
Nov 21	Derby County	L 0-6		7,000
Nov 28	ASTON VILLA	L 1-5	Campbell	7,000
Dec 12	Nottingham Forest	L 1-2	Wilkie	2,000
Dec 19	Sunderland	W 1-0	Chippendale	2,000
Dec 25	SUNDERLAND	L 1-2	Haydock	12,000
Dec 26	West Bromwich Albion	L 0-1		8,000
Dec 28	Sheffield Wednesday	L 0-6		unknown
Jan 2	WOLVERHAMPTON W.	W 2-0	Owen o.g., Wilkie	5,000
Jan 9	Sheffield United	L 0-7		1,000
Jan 16	DERBY COUNTY	W 5-2	Wilkie 2, Hargreaves, Nicol, Booth (pen)	6,000
Feb 6	SHEFFIELD UNITED	L 1-3	Haydock	5,000
Feb 20	BURY	L 1-2	Proudfoot	4,000
Mar 6	EVERTON	W 4-2	Campbell, Proudfoot 2, Nicol	6,000
Mar 13	Everton	W 3-0	Proudfoot 2, Wilkie	10,000
Mar 20	STOKE	W 2-1	Rowley o.g., Chippendale	7,000
Mar 27	Bury	L 0-3		4,000
Apr 10	Stoke	L 0-1		3,000
Apr 17	Aston Villa	L 0-3		15,000

FA Cup

Jan 30	SHEFFIELD UNITED	(Rd1)	W 2-1	Booth, Dewar	9,000
Feb 13	WOLVERHAMPTON W.	(Rd2)	W 2-1	Wilkie, Dewar	8,000
Feb 27	Everton	(Rd3)	L 0-2		16,000

League & Cup Appearances

PLAYER	LEAGUE	CUP COMPETITION FA CUP	TOTAL
Anderson, G.E.	27	3	30
Booth, T.E.	22	3	25
Brandon, T.	27	3	30
Campbell, J.	28		28
Chippendale, H.	22	3	25
Crompton, R.	2		2
Devlin, H.	1		1
Dewar, G.	24	3	27
Hargreaves, J.	14	3	17
Haydock, J.	8	3	11
Houlker, A.E.	17		17
Joy, W.J.	3		3
Killean, E.	26	3	29
Nicol, T.	16	3	19
Ogilvie, A.	27	3	30
Porter, W.S.	1		1
Proudfoot, J.	7		7
Sherrington, J.	1		1
Stuart, J.	2		2
Tierney, T.T.	11		11
Whitehead, J.	8		8
Wilkie, J.	27	3	30
Wilmington, T.	9		9

Goalscorers

PLAYER	LEAGUE	CUP COMPETITION FA CUP	TOTAL
Wilkie, J.	7	1	8
Chippendale, H.	5		5
Proudfoot, J.	5		5
Dewar, G.	2	2	4
Campbell, J.	3		3
Haydock, J.	2		2
Nicol, T.	2		2
Tierney, T.T.	2		2
Booth, T.E.	1	1	2
Anderson, G.E.	1		1
Hargreaves, J.	1		1
Stuart, J.	1		1
Whitehead, J.	1		1
Opps' o.gs.	2		2

Fact File

Bob Crompton made his league debut for the club at Stoke on 10 April 1897.

SECRETARY: Thomas Mitchell/Joseph Walmsley

TOP SCORER: John Wilkie

BIGGEST WIN: 4-0, 19 September 1896, v Sheffield Wednesday, Division 1

HIGHEST ATTENDANCE: 16,000, 27 February 1897, v Everton, FA Cup Round 3

MAJOR TRANSFERS IN: John Campbell from Partick Thistle, Tom Nicol from Burnley, John Proudfoot from Partick Thistle

MAJOR TRANSFERS OUT: Peter Turnbull to Glasgow Rangers

Final Division 1 Table

		P	W	D	L	F	A	Pts
1	ASTON VILLA	30	21	5	4	73	38	47
2	SHEFFIELD U	30	13	10	7	42	29	36
3	DERBY CO	30	16	4	10	70	50	36
4	PRESTON NE	30	11	12	7	55	40	34
5	LIVERPOOL	30	12	9	9	46	38	33
6	SHEFFIELD W	30	10	11	9	42	37	31
7	EVERTON	30	14	3	13	62	57	31
8	BOLTON W	30	12	6	12	40	43	30
9	BURY	30	10	10	10	39	44	30
10	WOLVERHAMPTON W	30	11	6	13	45	41	28
11	NOTTINGHAM F	30	9	8	13	44	49	26
12	WBA	30	10	6	14	33	56	26
13	STOKE	30	11	3	16	48	59	25
14	BLACKBURN R	30	11	3	16	35	62	25
15	SUNDERLAND	30	7	9	14	34	47	23
16	BURNLEY	30	6	7	17	43	61	19

Season 1897-98

Football League Division 1

DATE	OPPONENTS	SCORE	GOALSCORERS	ATTENDANCE
Sep 4	Derby County	L 1-3	Hall	5,000
Sep 11	BOLTON WANDERERS	L 1-3	Campbell	10,000
Sep 18	Stoke	L 1-2	Hulse	6,000
Sep 25	ASTON VILLA	W 4-3	Campbell 2, Proudfoot, Briercliffe	10,000
Oct 2	Everton	D 1-1	Wilkie	6,000
Oct 4	Sheffield United	L 2-5	Wilkie, Booth	7,000
Oct 9	PRESTON NORTH END	W 1-0	Proudfoot	11,628
Oct 16	Nottingham Forest	L 1-3	Proudfoot	7,000
Oct 23	SHEFFIELD WEDNESDAY	D 1-1	Proudfoot	6,000
Oct 30	Preston North End	W 4-1	Campbell, Trainer o.g., Wilkie, Hulse	10,000
Nov 13	Sheffield Wednesday	L 1-4	Proudfoot	6,000
Nov 20	SHEFFIELD UNITED	D 1-1	Campbell	6,000
Nov 27	DERBY COUNTY	D 1-1	Briercliffe	5,000
Dec 11	Aston Villa	L 1-5	Wilkie	22,000
Dec 18	Liverpool	W 1-0	Proudfoot	8,000
Dec 25	SUNDERLAND	W 2-1	Booth, Briercliffe	16,000
Dec 26	West Bromwich Albion	D 1-1	Campbell	7,000
Jan 1	EVERTON	D 1-1	Booth (pen)	17,000
Jan 8	LIVERPOOL	W 2-1	Briercliffe, Campbell	6,000
Jan 15	NOTTINGHAM FOREST	D 1-1	Wilkie	4,000
Feb 5	WEST BROMWICH ALBION	L 1-3	Briercliffe	5,000
Feb 26	WOLVERHAMPTON W.	L 2-3	Proudfoot 2	6,000
Mar 5	Notts County	D 0-0		6,000
Mar 12	Sunderland	L 1-2	Wilkie	16,000
Mar 19	BURY	D 1-1	Briercliffe	4,000
Apr 2	Wolverhampton W.	L 2-3	Booth, Proudfoot	4,000
Apr 8	STOKE	D 1-1	Booth	8,000
Apr 9	NOTTS COUNTY	L 0-1		6,000
Apr 14	Bolton Wanderers	W 2-1	Hargreaves, Booth	unknown
Apr 16	Bury	L 0-1		10,000

Test Matches

Apr 21	BURNLEY	L 1-3	Briercliffe	8,000
Apr 23	Burnley	L 0-2		12,000
Apr 28	NEWCASTLE UNITED	W 4-3	Blackburn, Hurst 2, Anderson	1,000
Apr 30	Newcastle United	L 0-4		14,000

FA Cup

Jan 29	Everton	(Rd1) L 0-1		12,000

League & Cup Appearances

PLAYER	LEAGUE	TEST MATCHES	CUP COMPETITION FA CUP	TOTAL
Anderson, G.E.	2	4		6
Ball, W.H.	17			17
Blackburn, F.	3	2		5
Booth, T.E.	29	3	1	33
Bradbury, J.J.L.	2			2
Brandon, T.	29	3	1	33
Briercliffe, T.	26	1	1	28
Campbell, J.	27	2	1	30
Carter, J.	16	4	1	21
Chambers, P.	7			7
Crompton, R.	1			1
Garstang, J.	1			1
Glover, J.W.	23	1	1	25
Hall, G.	1			1
Hargreaves, J.	2	2		4
Houlker, A.E.	11	3	1	15
Hulse, B.	23	3		26
Hurst, D.J.	2	2		4
Jackson, J.T.	1	2		3
Killean, E.	27	3	1	31
Knowles, A.	14			14
Leaver, W.			1	1
Marshall, H.J.H.	2	4		6
Mills, A.	2	1		3
Moreland, J.	2	1		3
Proudfoot, J.	29	1	1	31
Tierney, T.T.	1			1
Turnbull, P.	1			1
Wilkie, J.	29	2	1	32

Goalscorers

PLAYER	LEAGUE	TEST MATCHES	CUP COMPETITION FA CUP	TOTAL
Proudfoot, J.	9			9
Campbell, J.	7			7
Briercliffe, T.	6	1		7
Booth, T.E.	6			6
Wilkie, J.	6			6
Hulse, B.	2			2
Hurst, D.J.		2		2
Hall, G.	1			1
Hargreaves, J.	1			1
Anderson, G.E.		1		1
Blackburn, F.		1		1
Opps' o.gs.	1			1

Fact File

Having finished bottom of the group following the Test Matches, Blackburn were only saved from relegation by the decision to extend the number of clubs in the First Division.

SECRETARY: Joseph Walmsley

TOP SCORER: John Proudfoot

BIGGEST WIN: 4-0, 30 October 1897, v Preston North End, Division 1

HIGHEST ATTENDANCE: 22,000, 11 December 1897, v Aston Villa, Division 1

MAJOR TRANSFERS IN: James Carter from Millwall Athletic

MAJOR TRANSFERS OUT: John Proudfoot to Everton

Final Division 1 Table

		P	W	D	L	F	A	Pts
1	SHEFFIELD U	30	17	8	5	56	31	42
2	SUNDERLAND	30	16	5	9	43	30	37
3	WOLVERHAMPTON W	30	14	7	9	57	41	35
4	EVERTON	30	13	9	8	48	39	35
5	SHEFFIELD W	30	15	3	12	51	42	33
6	ASTON VILLA	30	14	5	11	61	51	33
7	WBA	30	11	10	9	44	45	32
8	NOTTINGHAM F	30	11	9	10	47	49	31
9	LIVERPOOL	30	11	6	13	48	45	28
10	DERBY CO	30	11	6	13	57	61	28
11	BOLTON W	30	11	4	15	28	41	26
12	PRESTON NE	30	8	8	14	35	43	24
13	NOTTS CO	30	8	8	14	36	46	24
14	BURY	30	8	8	14	39	51	24
15	BLACKBURN R	30	7	10	13	39	54	24
16	STOKE	30	8	8	14	35	55	24

Season 1898-99

Football League Division 1

DATE	OPPONENTS	SCORE	GOALSCORERS	ATTENDANCE
Sep 1	Everton	L 1-2	Hulse	12,000
Sep 3	Nottingham Forest	W 1-0	Jackson	17,000
Sep 10	BOLTON WANDERERS	W 4-1	Jackson, Hurst, Hulse, Anderson	7,000
Sep 17	Derby County	D 0-0		5,000
Sep 24	WEST BROMWICH ALBION	W 4-1	Jackson 2, Hurst, Moreland	4,000
Oct 1	BURY	D 0-0		12,000
Oct 8	Sheffield Wednesday	W 2-1	Hulse, Moreland	8,000
Oct 15	SUNDERLAND	W 3-2	McNeill o.g., Jackson, Anderson	15,000
Oct 22	Wolverhampton W.	L 1-2	Jackson	5,000
Oct 29	EVERTON	L 1-3	Moreland	14,000
Nov 5	Notts County	L 3-5	Hurst 2, Hulse	6,000
Nov 12	STOKE	W 4-1	Hurst, Anderson, Moreland 2	5,000
Nov 19	Aston Villa	L 1-3	Moreland	24,000
Nov 26	Burnley	L 0-2		12,000
Dec 3	Sheffield United	D 1-1	Hulse	7,000
Dec 10	NEWCASTLE UNITED	W 4-2	Hulse 2, Hurst 2	5,000
Dec 17	Preston North End	D 1-1	Jackson	4,000
Dec 24	LIVERPOOL	L 1-3	Jackson	6,000
Dec 26	Burnley	L 0-2		20,000
Dec 31	NOTTINGHAM FOREST	D 3-3	Booth, Hurst, Hulse	4,000
Jan 2	NOTTS COUNTY	W 6-0	Crompton, Houlker, Hulse, Hurst, Haworth, Anderson	4,000
Jan 7	Bolton Wanderers	W 2-0	Hurst, Jackson	7,000
Jan 14	DERBY COUNTY	W 3-0	Briercliffe, Hurst, Jackson	6,000
Jan 21	West Bromwich Albion	L 2-6	Hulse, Hurst	1,957
Feb 4	SHEFFIELD WEDNESDAY	W 2-0	Anderson, Hurst	5,000
Feb 14	Bury	L 2-3	Williams, Anderson	4,000
Feb 18	WOLVERHAMPTON W.	D 2-2	Anderson, Booth	4,500
Mar 11	Stoke	W 1-0	Hulse	10,000
Mar 18	ASTON VILLA	D 0-0		10,000
Apr 1	SHEFFIELD UNITED	W 2-1	Blackburn, Briercliffe	10,000
Apr 3	Sunderland	W 1-0	Hulse	15,000
Apr 8	Newcastle United	L 0-1		12,000
Apr 15	PRESTON NORTH END	D 2-2	Hurst, Blackburn	6,000
Apr 22	Liverpool	L 0-2		20,000

FA Cup

Jan 28	Liverpool	(Rd1) L 0-2		14,000

League & Cup Appearances

PLAYER	LEAGUE	CUP COMPETITION FA CUP	TOTAL
Anderson, G.E.	26	1	27
Blackburn, F.	9		9
Booth, T.E.	33	1	34
Brandon, T.	32	1	33
Briercliffe, T.	16	1	17
Brown, C.	1		1
Carter, J.	27	1	28
Chambers, P.	26		26
Crompton, R.	33	1	34
Evans, L.	2		2
Garstang, J.	3		3
Glover, J.W.	2		2
Haworth, R.	16	1	17
Houlker, A.E.	8	1	9
Hulse, B.	34	1	35
Hurst, D.J.	31	1	32
Jackson, J.T.	25	1	26
Knowles, A.	1		1
Moreland, J.	18		18
Thompson, R.	6		6
Williams, W.	24		24
Wilson, T.C.	1		1

Goalscorers

PLAYER	LEAGUE	CUP COMPETITION FA CUP	TOTAL
Hurst, D.J.	14		14
Hulse, B.	12		12
Jackson, J.T.	10		10
Anderson, G.E.	7		7
Moreland, J.	6		6
Blackburn, F.	2		2
Booth, T.E.	2		2
Briercliffe, T.	2		2
Crompton, R.	1		1
Haworth, R.	1		1
Houlker, A.E.	1		1
Williams, W.	1		1
Opps' o.gs.	1		1

Fact File

Ben Hulse was the only ever-present in the Ewood squad.

SECRETARY: Joseph Walmsley

TOP SCORER: Daniel Hurst

BIGGEST WIN: 6-0, 2 January 1899, v Notts County, Division 1

HIGHEST ATTENDANCE: 24,000, 19 November 1899, v Aston Villa, Division 1

MAJOR TRANSFERS IN: Bill Williams from Everton

MAJOR TRANSFERS OUT: George Anderson to New Brighton Tower, John Wilkie to Glasgow Rangers

Final Division 1 Table

		P	W	D	L	F	A	Pts
1	ASTON VILLA	34	19	7	8	76	40	45
2	LIVERPOOL	34	19	5	10	49	33	43
3	BURNLEY	34	15	9	10	45	47	39
4	EVERTON	34	15	8	11	48	41	38
5	NOTTS CO	34	12	13	9	47	51	37
6	BLACKBURN R	34	14	8	12	60	52	36
7	SUNDERLAND	34	15	6	13	41	41	36
8	WOLVERHAMPTON W	34	14	7	13	54	48	35
9	DERBY CO	34	12	11	11	62	57	35
10	BURY	34	14	7	13	48	49	35
11	NOTTINGHAM F	34	11	11	12	42	42	33
12	STOKE	34	13	7	14	47	52	33
13	NEWCASTLE U	34	11	8	15	49	48	30
14	WBA	34	12	6	16	42	57	30
15	PRESTON NE	34	10	9	15	44	47	29
16	SHEFFIELD U	34	9	11	14	45	51	29
17	BOLTON W	34	9	7	18	37	51	25
18	SHEFFIELD W	34	8	8	18	32	61	24

Season 1899-1900

Football League Division 1

DATE	OPPONENTS	SCORE	GOALSCORERS	ATTENDANCE
Sep 2	MANCHESTER CITY	W 4-3	Hulse, Crook, Hurst, Crompton	10,000
Sep 9	Sheffield United	L 0-3		15,000
Sep 16	NEWCASTLE UNITED	L 2-3	Blackburn F., Hulse	6,000
Sep 23	Aston Villa	L 1-3	Hulse	20,000
Sep 30	LIVERPOOL	W 2-0	Haworth, Crook	7,000
Oct 7	Burnley	L 0-1		12,855
Oct 14	PRESTON NORTH END	W 3-0	Whittaker A. 3	7,000
Oct 21	Nottingham Forest	L 2-3	o.g., Hurst	8,000
Nov 4	Stoke	L 0-2		4,000
Nov 11	SUNDERLAND	L 1-2	Law	5,000
Nov 25	EVERTON	W 3-1	Hurst, Blackburn F., Hulse	7,000
Dec 2	Wolverhampton W.	L 0-4		7,000
Dec 9	Derby County	W 2-0	Dewhurst, Blackburn F.	8,000
Dec 16	BURY	W 3-2	Haworth, Blackburn F., Hulse	4,000
Dec 23	Notts County	L 1-5	Briercliffe	5,000
Dec 30	Manchester City	D 1-1	Booth	10,000
Jan 1	BURNLEY	W 2-0	Dewhurst, Briercliffe	14,000
Jan 13	Newcastle United	L 1-4	Whittaker A.	12,000
Jan 20	ASTON VILLA	L 0-4		7,000
Feb 3	Liverpool	L 1-3	Blackburn F.	6,000
Feb 27	Glossop North End	L 2-4	Anderson, Hulse	4,000
Mar 3	GLOSSOP NORTH END	D 2-2	Whittaker A. 2	5,000
Mar 5	NOTTINGHAM FOREST	W 2-1	Somers, Whittaker A. (pen)	4,000
Mar 10	STOKE	W 3-0	Dewhurst, Blackburn F., Whittaker A.	5,000
Mar 24	WEST BROMWICH ALBION	W 2-0	Briercliffe, Blackburn F.	5,026
Mar 31	Everton	D 0-0		10,000
Apr 2	West Bromwich Albion	L 0-1		3,342
Apr 7	WOLVERHAMPTON W.	W 2-1	Dewhurst, Blackburn F.	4,000
Apr 13	SHEFFIELD UNITED	D 3-3	Somers, Hulse, Whittaker A.	13,000
Apr 14	DERBY COUNTY	W 2-0	Whittaker A., Hulse	9,000
Apr 16	Sunderland	L 0-1		6,000
Apr 25	Bury	L 0-2		2,000
Apr 28	NOTTS COUNTY	W 2-0	Blackburn F., Whittaker A.	5,000
Apr 30	Preston North End	L 0-2		4,000

FA Cup

Jan 27	Portsmouth	(Rd1) D 0-0		11,000
Feb 1	PORTSMOUTH	(R) D 1-1*	Hulse	5,000
Feb 5	Portsmouth†	(2R) W 5-0	Blackburn F. 3, Hulse 2	10,000
Feb 17	Preston North End	(Rd2) L 0-1		14,000

*After extra-time. †Played at Villa Park, Birmingham.

League & Cup Appearances

PLAYER	LEAGUE	CUP COMPETITION FA CUP	TOTAL
Anderson, G.E.	19	1	20
Blackburn, A.	2		2
Blackburn, F.	32	4	36
Booth, T.E.	27	4	31
Brandon, T.	21	4	25
Briercliffe, T.	14	2	16
Coupe, T.	1		1
Crook, A.J.	9		9
Crompton, R.	34	4	38
Dewhurst, J.	19	4	23
Hardy, A.	9		9
Haworth, R.	29	4	33
Houlker, A.E.	24	4	28
Hulse, B.	28	4	32
Hurst, D.J.	20	4	24
Knowles, A.	16	4	20
Law, J.	3		3
McClure, S.	7		7
O'Brien, J.	1		1
Somers, P.	14		14
Swift, E.	2		2
Thompson, R.	3		3
Waring, C.	1		1
Whittaker, A.	19	1	20
Whittaker, W.	13		13
Williams, W.	7		7

Goalscorers

PLAYER	LEAGUE	CUP COMPETITION FA CUP	TOTAL
Blackburn, F.	9	3	12
Whittaker, A.	11		11
Hulse, B.	8	3	11
Dewhurst, J.	4		4
Briercliffe, T.	3		3
Hurst, D.J.	3		3
Crook, J.A.	2		2
Haworth, R.	2		2
Somers, P.	2		2
Anderson, G.E.	1		1
Booth, T.E.	1		1
Crompton, R.	1		1
Law, J.	1		1
Opps' o.gs.	1		1

Fact File

Final day defeat at Deepdale meant Preston North End retained First Division status at the expense of Burnley while Rovers avoided the drop by three points.

SECRETARY: Joseph Walmsley
TOP SCORER: Fred Blackburn
BIGGEST WIN: 5-0, 5 February 1900, v Portsmouth, FA Cup Round 1 second replay
HIGHEST ATTENDANCE: 20,000, 23 September 1899, v Aston Villa, Division 1

Final Division 1 Table

		P	W	D	L	F	A	Pts
1	ASTON VILLA	34	22	6	6	77	35	50
2	SHEFFIELD U	34	18	12	4	63	33	48
3	SUNDERLAND	34	19	3	12	50	35	41
4	WOLVERHAMPTON W	34	15	9	10	48	37	39
5	NEWCASTLE U	34	13	10	11	53	43	36
6	DERBY CO	34	14	8	12	45	43	36
7	MANCHESTER C	34	13	8	13	50	44	34
8	NOTTINGHAM F	34	13	8	13	56	55	34
9	STOKE	34	13	8	13	37	45	34
10	LIVERPOOL	34	14	5	15	49	45	33
11	EVERTON	34	13	7	14	47	49	33
12	BURY	34	13	6	15	40	44	32
13	WBA	34	11	8	15	43	51	30
14	BLACKBURN R	34	13	4	17	49	61	30
15	NOTTS CO	34	9	11	14	46	60	29
16	PRESTON NE	34	12	4	18	38	48	28
17	BURNLEY	34	11	5	18	34	54	27
18	GLOSSOP	34	4	10	20	31	74	18

Season 1900-01

Football League Division 1

DATE	OPPONENTS	SCORE	GOALSCORERS	ATTENDANCE
Sep 1	Liverpool	L 0-3		15,000
Sep 8	NEWCASTLE UNITED	D 0-0		10,000
Sep 15	Sheffield United	L 1-2	Blackburn	10,000
Sep 22	MANCHESTER CITY	W 1-0	Haworth	10,000
Sep 29	Bury	W 1-0	Ross o.g.	4,000
Oct 6	NOTTINGHAM FOREST	L 1-3	Oldham	4,000
Oct 13	SHEFFIELD WEDNESDAY	D 2-2	Morgan, Whittaker A.	3,000
Oct 20	Stoke	L 0-2		6,000
Oct 27	WEST BROMWICH ALBION	D 1-1	Morgan	4,000
Oct 29	Aston Villa	D 3-3	Bryant 3	14,000
Nov 3	Everton	D 0-0		12,000
Nov 10	SUNDERLAND	L 0-1		4,000
Nov 17	Derby County	L 0-4		7,000
Nov 24	BOLTON WANDERERS	W 2-0	Somers, Dewhurst	4,000
Dec 1	Notts County	L 1-2	Morgan	6,000
Dec 8	Preston North End	L 1-4	Blackburn	5,000
Dec 15	Wolverhampton W.	D 2-2	Morgan 2	5,000
Dec 22	ASTON VILLA	D 2-2	Blackburn 2	5,000
Dec 29	LIVERPOOL	W 3-1	Dewhurst 2, Whittaker A.	5,000
Jan 1	PRESTON NORTH END	W 3-1	Dewhurst, Whittaker A. 2	12,000
Jan 5	Newcastle United	L 0-1		15,000
Jan 12	SHEFFIELD UNITED	W 1-0	McClure	6,000
Jan 19	Manchester City	W 3-1	Bryant, Haworth, Somers	6,000
Feb 16	Sheffield Wednesday	D 1-1	Opp o.g.	5,000
Feb 23	STOKE	W 3-2	Whittaker A., Capewell o.g., Somers	5,000
Mar 2	West Bromwich Albion	D 1-1	Bryant	5,000
Mar 9	EVERTON	W 2-1	Whittaker A., Bryant	6,000
Mar 16	Sunderland	L 0-2		10,000
Mar 23	DERBY COUNTY	W 1-0	Morgan	6,000
Mar 30	Bolton Wanderers	L 0-1		5,000
Apr 6	NOTTS COUNTY	L 0-2		6,000
Apr 8	Nottingham Forest	W 1-0	Whittaker A.	10,000
Apr 13	BURY	L 0-2		5,000
Apr 20	WOLVERHAMPTON W.	W 2-0	McClure, Whittaker A.	4,000

FA Cup

Feb 9	Woolwich Arsenal	(Rd1) L 0-2		11,000

League & Cup Appearances

PLAYER	LEAGUE	CUP COMPETITION FA CUP	TOTAL
Blackburn, F.	30	1	31
Blackshaw, J.	2		2
Bryant, W.	15		15
Crompton, R.	24	1	25
Dewhurst, J.	26	1	27
Hardy, A.	25		25
Haworth, R.	33	1	34
Hosie, J.	3		3
Houlker, A.E.	32	1	33
Kelly, M.	3		3
McClure, S.	16	1	17
Moir, J.G.	32	1	33
Morgan, H.	26	1	27
O'Brien, J.	2		2
Oldham, W.	9		9
Platt, P.	1		1
Somers, P.	31	1	32
Tomlinson, J.	1		1
Whittaker, A.	30	1	31
Whittaker, W.	33	1	34

Goalscorers

PLAYER	LEAGUE	CUP COMPETITION FA CUP	TOTAL
Whittaker, A.	8		8
Bryant, W.	6		6
Morgan, H.	6		6
Blackburn, F.	4		4
Dewhurst, J.	4		4
Somers, P.	3		3
Haworth, R.	2		2
McClure, S.	2		2
Oldham, W.	1		1
Opps' o.gs.	3		3

Fact File

Jimmy Moir was undoubtedly the discovery of the season after impressing in the pre-season trials. Moir, on loan from Celtic, ousted the more established men and only missed two games before being recalled to Glasgow at the end of the campaign.

SECRETARY: Joseph Walmsley

TOP SCORER: Arnold Whittaker

BIGGEST WIN: 3-1, 29 December 1900, v Liverpool, Division 1; 1 January 1901, v Preston North End, Division 1; 19 January 1901, v Manchester City, Division 1

HIGHEST ATTENDANCE: 15,000, 1 September 1900, v Liverpool, Division 1; 5 January 1901, v Newcastle United, Division 1

Final Division 1 Table

		P	W	D	L	F	A	Pts
1	LIVERPOOL	34	19	7	8	59	35	45
2	SUNDERLAND	34	15	13	6	57	26	43
3	NOTTS CO	34	18	4	12	54	46	40
4	NOTTINGHAM F	34	16	7	11	53	36	39
5	BURY	34	16	7	11	53	37	39
6	NEWCASTLE U	34	14	10	10	42	37	38
7	EVERTON	34	16	5	13	55	42	37
8	SHEFFIELD W	34	13	10	11	52	42	36
9	BLACKBURN R	34	12	9	13	39	47	33
10	BOLTON W	34	13	7	14	39	55	33
11	MANCHESTER C	34	13	6	15	48	58	32
12	DERBY CO	34	12	7	15	55	42	31
13	WOLVERHAMPTON W	34	9	13	12	39	55	31
14	SHEFFIELD U	34	12	7	15	35	52	31
15	ASTON VILLA	34	10	10	14	45	51	30
16	STOKE	34	11	5	18	46	57	27
17	PRESTON NE	34	9	7	18	49	75	25
18	WBA	34	7	8	19	35	62	22

Season 1901-02

Football League Division 1

DATE	OPPONENTS	SCORE	GOALSCORERS	ATTENDANCE
Sep 7	NEWCASTLE UNITED	D 0-0		6,000
Sep 14	Aston Villa	D 1-1	McClure	22,000
Sep 21	SHEFFIELD UNITED	W 2-1	Somers, Dewhurst	7,000
Sep 28	Nottingham Forest	L 0-3		7,000
Oct 5	BURY	L 0-3		4,000
Oct 12	Grimsby Town	L 1-2	Somers	7,000
Oct 19	Stoke	D 2-2	Meredith o.g., Blackburn F.	10,000
Oct 26	EVERTON	W 3-1	Dewhurst, McClure, Gate	10,000
Nov 2	Sunderland	L 2-3	Whittaker A., Morgan	12,000
Nov 9	SMALL HEATH	W 3-1	Whittaker A., McClure, Blackburn F.	4,000
Nov 16	Derby County	D 1-1	Whittaker A.	7,000
Nov 23	SHEFFIELD WEDNESDAY	W 2-0	Somers, Dewhurst	4,000
Nov 30	Notts County	L 0-3		7,000
Dec 7	BOLTON WANDERERS	W 2-0	Somers, Dewhurst	6,000
Dec 14	Manchester City	D 1-1	Whittaker A.	10,000
Dec 21	WOLVERHAMPTON W.	W 2-0	Dewhurst 2	4,000
Dec 25	GRIMSBY TOWN	W 2-0	Dewhurst, Blackburn F.	10,000
Dec 28	Liverpool	L 0-1		12,000
Jan 1	NOTTINGHAM FOREST	W 1-0	Somers	17,000
Jan 4	Newcastle United	W 3-0	Whittaker A., Somers, Dewhurst	12,000
Jan 11	ASTON VILLA	W 4-0	Whittaker A. 2, Dewhurst, Morgan	20,000
Jan 18	Sheffield United	L 1-4	Dewhurst	20,000
Feb 15	STOKE	W 6-1	Morgan 3, Dewhurst 2, Houlker	5,000
Feb 22	Everton	W 2-0	Dewhurst, Somers	10,000
Mar 1	SUNDERLAND	L 0-1		20,000
Mar 8	Small Heath	L 0-2		17,000
Mar 22	Sheffield Wednesday	W 1-0	Morgan	10,000
Mar 28	Bury	L 0-2		16,000
Mar 29	NOTTS COUNTY	W 4-2	Blackburn F. 2, Bryant 2 (2 pens)	5,000
Mar 31	Wolverhampton W.	L 1-3	Morgan	9,000
Apr 5	Bolton Wanderers	L 0-4		7,000
Apr 12	MANCHESTER CITY	L 1-4	Dewhurst	3,000
Apr 19	DERBY COUNTY	W 3-1	Dewhurst 2, Somers	2,000
Apr 26	LIVERPOOL	D 1-1	Whittaker A.	2,000

FA Cup

Feb 1	DERBY COUNTY	(Rd1) L 0-2		15,000

League & Cup Appearances

PLAYER	LEAGUE	CUP COMPETITION FA CUP	TOTAL
Ball, W.H.	3		3
Blackburn, A.	2		2
Blackburn, F.	31	1	32
Bryant, W.	10		10
Crompton, R.	31	1	32
Darroch, J.	17	1	18
Dewhurst, J.	34	1	35
Eastham, J.B.	8		8
Gate, W.H.	4		4
Hardy, A.	8		8
Haworth, R.	34	1	35
Hindle, H.	1		1
Houlker, A.E.	29	1	30
Hoyne, J.	2		2
McClure, S.	31	1	32
McIver, W.	28	1	29
Morgan, H.	28	1	29
Russell, J.	1		1
Somers, P.	31	1	32
Swarbrick, J.	2		2
Whittaker, A.	33	1	34
Whittaker, W.	6		6

Goalscorers

PLAYER	LEAGUE	CUP COMPETITION FA CUP	TOTAL
Dewhurst, J.	16		16
Somers, P.	8		8
Whittaker, A.	8		8
Morgan, H.	7		7
Blackburn, F.	5		5
McClure, S.	3		3
Bryant, W.	2		2
Gate, W.H.	1		1
Houlker, A.E.	1		1
Opps' o.gs.	1		1

Fact File

Bob Crompton won his first England cap on 3 March 1902 in a 0-0 draw with Wales in Wrexham.

SECRETARY: Joseph Walmsley

TOP SCORER: Jack Dewhurst

BIGGEST WIN: 6-1, 15 February 1902, v Stoke, Division 1

HIGHEST ATTENDANCE: 22,000, 14 September 1901, v Aston Villa, Division 1

Final Division 1 Table

		P	W	D	L	F	A	Pts
1	SUNDERLAND	34	19	6	9	50	35	44
2	EVERTON	34	17	7	10	53	35	41
3	NEWCASTLE U	34	14	9	11	48	34	37
4	BLACKBURN R	34	15	6	13	52	48	36
5	NOTTINGHAM F	34	13	9	12	43	43	35
6	DERBY CO	34	13	9	12	39	41	35
7	BURY	34	13	8	13	44	38	34
8	ASTON VILLA	34	13	8	13	42	40	34
9	SHEFFIELD W	34	13	8	13	48	52	34
10	SHEFFIELD U	34	13	7	14	53	48	33
11	LIVERPOOL	34	10	12	12	42	38	32
12	BOLTON W	34	12	8	14	51	56	32
13	NOTTS CO	34	14	4	16	51	57	32
14	WOLVERHAMPTON W	34	13	6	15	46	57	32
15	GRIMSBY T	34	13	6	15	44	60	32
16	STOKE	34	11	9	14	45	55	31
17	SMALL HEATH	34	11	8	15	47	45	30
18	MANCHESTER C	34	11	6	17	42	58	28

Season 1902-03

Football League Division 1

DATE	OPPONENTS	SCORE	GOALSCORERS	ATTENDANCE
Sep 1	MIDDLESBROUGH	L 0-1		3,000
Sep 6	Liverpool	L 2-5	Whittaker 2	15,000
Sep 13	SHEFFIELD UNITED	W 2-0	Dewhurst, Boyle o.g.	8,000
Sep 20	Grimsby Town	L 1-4	Morgan	5,000
Sep 27	ASTON VILLA	L 0-2		10,000
Oct 4	Nottingham Forest	L 0-2		10,000
Oct 11	BURY	L 0-3		6,000
Oct 18	DERBY COUNTY	L 2-4	McClure, Whittaker (pen)	10,000
Oct 25	Sunderland	D 2-2	Morgan, Logan	20,000
Nov 1	STOKE	D 1-1	Morgan	6,000
Nov 8	EVERTON	W 3-2	McClure, Dewhurst, Whittaker	3,000
Nov 15	SHEFFIELD WEDNESDAY	W 2-1	Dewhurst, Logan	7,000
Nov 22	West Bromwich Albion	L 3-5	Morgan, Robertson, Whittaker	12,134
Nov 29	NOTTS COUNTY	L 1-2	Morgan	7,000
Dec 6	Bolton Wanderers	W 2-1	Whittaker, Monks	10,000
Dec 20	Newcastle United	L 0-1		10,000
Dec 25	SUNDERLAND	L 0-2		2,000
Dec 26	Stoke	W 2-0	Dewhurst 2	20,000
Dec 27	Wolverhampton W.	L 0-2		6,000
Jan 1	WOLVERHAMPTON W.	W 1-0	Whittaker (pen)	20,000
Jan 3	LIVERPOOL	W 3-1	Bow, Monks, Whittaker	7,000
Jan 10	Sheffield United	L 1-2	Dewhurst	10,000
Jan 17	GRIMSBY TOWN	W 2-0	Blackburn, Bow	10,000
Jan 24	Aston Villa	L 0-5		17,000
Jan 31	NOTTINGHAM FOREST	D 2-2	Whittaker (pen), Monks	10,000
Feb 14	Derby County	L 0-1		8,000
Mar 14	Sheffield Wednesday	D 0-0		10,000
Mar 21	WEST BROMWICH ALBION	W 1-0	Blackburn	10,354
Mar 28	Notts County	L 0-4		2,000
Apr 4	BOLTON WANDERERS	W 4-2	Bowman, McClure, Monks, Watson	7,000
Apr 10	Bury	D 1-1	Whittaker (pen)	13,000
Apr 11	Middlesbrough	L 0-4		7,000
Apr 13	Everton	W 3-0	Bowman 2, Blackburn	9,000
Apr 18	NEWCASTLE UNITED	W 3-1	Bowman 2, McClure	9,000

FA Cup

Feb 7	SHEFFIELD WEDNESDAY	(Rd1)	D 0-0		8,000
Feb 12	Sheffield Wednesday	(R)	W 1-0	Monks	25,000
Feb 21	Derby County	(Rd2)	L 0-2		15,000

League & Cup Appearances

PLAYER	LEAGUE	CUP COMPETITION FA CUP	TOTAL
Birchall, J.	9		9
Blackburn, F.	26	2	28
Bow, W.	18	3	21
Bowman, A.	7		7
Crompton, R.	28	3	31
Derbyshire, J.E.	11		11
Dewhurst, J.	33	3	36
Eastham, J.B.	22	3	25
Haworth, R.	7		7
Hindle, H.	1		1
Jones, T.R.	11	1	12
Joyce, J.W.	14		14
Logan, N.	22		22
McClure, S.	33	3	36
McIver, W.	20	3	23
Monks, A.	19	3	22
Morgan, H.	23		23
Riley, T.	5		5
Robertson, G.	10	3	13
Swarbrick, J.	13	1	14
Watson, L.P.	9	2	11
Whittaker, A.	33	3	36

Goalscorers

PLAYER	LEAGUE	CUP COMPETITION FA CUP	TOTAL
Whittaker, A.	10		10
Dewhurst, J.	6		6
Bowman, A.	5		5
Morgan, H.	5		5
Monks, A.	4	1	5
McClure, S.	4		4
Blackburn, F.	3		3
Bow, W.	2		2
Logan, N.	2		2
Robertson, G.	1		1
Watson, L.P.	1		1
Opps' o.gs.	1		1

Fact File

A match-fixing scandal rocked Ewood Park and resulted in the departure of Joseph Walmsley from the club.

SECRETARY: Joseph Walmsley

TOP SCORER: Arnold Whittaker

BIGGEST WIN: 3-0, 13 April 1903, v Everton, Division 1

HIGHEST ATTENDANCE: 25,000, 12 February 1903, v Sheffield Wednesday, FA Cup Round 1 replay

MAJOR TRANSFERS IN: Jack Birchall from Blackpool, Lionel Watson from Manchester City, Billy Bradshaw from Accrington, George Robertson from Clyde, Adam Bowman from Everton

Final Division 1 Table

		P	W	D	L	F	A	Pts
1	SHEFFIELD W	34	19	4	11	54	36	42
2	ASTON VILLA	34	19	3	12	61	40	41
3	SUNDERLAND	34	16	9	9	51	36	41
4	SHEFFIELD U	34	17	5	12	58	44	39
5	LIVERPOOL	34	17	4	13	68	49	38
6	STOKE	34	15	7	12	46	38	37
7	WBA	34	16	4	14	54	53	36
8	BURY	34	16	3	15	54	43	35
9	DERBY CO	34	16	3	15	50	47	35
10	NOTTINGHAM F	34	14	7	13	49	47	35
11	WOLVERHAMPTON W	34	14	5	15	48	57	33
12	EVERTON	34	13	6	15	45	47	32
13	MIDDLESBROUGH	34	14	4	16	41	50	32
14	NEWCASTLE U	34	14	4	16	41	51	32
15	NOTTS CO	34	12	7	15	41	49	31
16	BLACKBURN R	34	12	5	17	44	63	29
17	GRIMSBY T	34	8	9	17	43	62	25
18	BOLTON W	34	8	3	23	37	73	19

The Essential History of Blackburn Rovers

Football League Division 1

DATE	OPPONENTS	SCORE	GOALSCORERS	ATTENDANCE
Sep 1	Everton	L 1-3	Bowman	13,000
Sep 5	BURY	D 2-2	Whittaker (pen), Dewhurst	8,000
Sep 12	Wolverhampton W.	L 0-1		8,000
Sep 19	Nottingham Forest	W 1-0	Bowman	6,000
Sep 26	SHEFFIELD WEDNESDAY	D 0-0		10,000
Oct 3	Sunderland	L 0-2		8,000
Oct 10	WEST BROMWICH ALBION	W 2-0	Whittaker, Bowman	10,057
Oct 17	Small Heath	L 1-2	Dunkley	11,000
Oct 24	EVERTON	L 0-2		10,000
Oct 31	Stoke	L 2-6	Watson 2	10,000
Nov 7	DERBY COUNTY	W 2-1	Watson 2	10,000
Nov 14	Manchester City	L 0-1		20,000
Nov 21	NOTTS COUNTY	W 3-0	Dewhurst, Whittaker (pen), Watson	5,000
Nov 28	Sheffield United	D 2-2	Dewhurst, Whittaker	7,000
Dec 5	NEWCASTLE UNITED	W 4-0	Pentland 3, Watson	8,000
Dec 12	Aston Villa	W 3-2	Dewhurst, Watson 2	18,000
Dec 19	MIDDLESBROUGH	D 1-1	Dewhurst	15,000
Dec 25	STOKE	W 2-0	Watson, McClure	25,000
Dec 26	Liverpool	W 2-1	Pentland 2	20,000
Dec 28	West Bromwich Albion	L 1-2	McClure	19,554
Jan 1	NOTTINGHAM FOREST	W 3-1	Watson 2, Pentland	10,000
Jan 2	Bury	L 0-3		10,000
Jan 9	WOLVERHAMPTON W.	D 1-1	Whittaker	4,500
Jan 23	Sheffield Wednesday	L 1-3	Pentland	16,000
Jan 30	SUNDERLAND	L 1-3	Bowman	8,000
Feb 13	SMALL HEATH	D 1-1	Bowman	2,000
Mar 12	MANCHESTER CITY	L 2-5	Bowman, Watson	12,000
Mar 19	Notts County	L 2-4	Watson, Dewhurst	7,000
Mar 26	SHEFFIELD UNITED	W 3-0	Dewhurst, Thickett o.g., Blackburn	7,000
Apr 2	Newcastle United	L 1-2	Blackburn	20,000
Apr 9	ASTON VILLA	L 0-3		5,000
Apr 11	Derby County	L 0-3		4,000
Apr 16	Middlesbrough	W 2-0	Bowman, Watson	12,000
Apr 23	LIVERPOOL	L 2-3	Dewhurst, Crompton (pen)	4,000

FA Cup

Feb 6	LIVERPOOL	(Rd1) W 3-1	Watson, Dewhurst 2	10,000
Feb 20	NOTTINGHAM FOREST	(Rd2) W 3-1	Dewhurst, Bowman, Blackburn	12,000
Mar 5	Derby County	(Rd3) L 1-2	Dewhurst	14,432

League & Cup Appearances

PLAYER	LEAGUE	CUP COMPETITION FA CUP	TOTAL
Birchall, J.	2		2
Blackburn, F.	33	3	36
Bow, W.	2		2
Bowman, A.	17	3	20
Bradshaw, W.	31	3	34
Cameron, J.	2		2
Crompton, R.	32	3	35
Dawson, A.	1		1
Dewhurst, J.	32	3	35
Duckworth, T.C.		1	1
Dunkley, A.E.	4		4
Eastham, J.B.	18	1	19
Evans, R.O.	27	3	30
Haworth, R.	3		3
McClure, S.	26	3	29
McDonald, J.	1		1
McIver, W.	7		7
Moir, J.G.G.	14		14
Monks, A.	5		5
Pentland, F.B.	18		18
Riley, T.	16	2	18
Smith, G.	24	3	27
Watson, L.P.	31	3	34
Whittaker, A.	28	2	30

Goalscorers

PLAYER	LEAGUE	CUP COMPETITION FA CUP	TOTAL
Watson, L.P.	14	1	15
Dewhurst, J.	8	4	12
Bowman, A.	7	1	8
Pentland, F.B.	7		7
Whittaker, A.	5		5
Blackburn, F.	2	1	3
McClure, S.	2		2
Crompton, R.	1		1
Dunkley, A.E.	1		1
Opps' o.gs.	1		1

Fact File

Robert Middleton, the former Blackpool secretary, was appointed as the new secretary at Ewood Park in July 1903.

SECRETARY: Robert Middleton

TOP SCORER: Lionel Watson

BIGGEST WIN: 4-0, 5 December 1903, v Newcastle United, Division 1

HIGHEST ATTENDANCE: 25,000, 25 December 1903, v Stoke, Division 1

MAJOR TRANSFERS IN: John Cameron from St Mirren, Jimmy Moir from Glasgow Celtic, Bob Evans from Wrexham

Final Division 1 Table

		P	W	D	L	F	A	Pts
1	SHEFFIELD W	34	20	7	7	48	28	47
2	MANCHESTER C	34	19	6	9	71	45	44
3	EVERTON	34	19	5	10	59	32	43
4	NEWCASTLE U	34	18	6	10	58	45	42
5	ASTON VILLA	34	17	7	10	70	48	41
6	SUNDERLAND	34	17	5	12	63	49	39
7	SHEFFIELD U	34	15	8	11	62	57	38
8	WOLVERHAMPTON W	34	14	8	12	44	66	36
9	NOTTINGHAM F	34	11	9	14	57	57	31
10	MIDDLESBROUGH	34	9	12	13	46	47	30
11	SMALL HEATH	34	11	8	15	39	52	30
12	BURY	34	7	15	12	40	53	29
13	NOTTS CO	34	12	5	17	37	61	29
14	DERBY CO	34	9	10	15	58	60	28
15	BLACKBURN R	34	11	6	17	48	60	28
16	STOKE	34	10	7	17	54	57	27
17	LIVERPOOL	34	9	8	17	49	62	26
18	WBA	34	7	10	17	36	60	24

Season 1904-05

Football League Division 1

DATE	OPPONENTS	SCORE	GOALSCORERS	ATTENDANCE
Sep 3	Bury	W 2-0	Birchall, Smith	10,000
Sep 10	ASTON VILLA	W 4-0	Smith 2, Watson, Bowman	18,000
Sep 17	STOKE	W 4-0	Smith, Whittaker 2 (1 pen), Watson	15,000
Sep 24	Nottingham Forest	L 2-5	Watson, Bradshaw	13,000
Oct 1	SHEFFIELD WEDNESDAY	L 0-1		12,000
Oct 8	Sunderland	L 1-2	Watson	15,000
Oct 15	WOOLWICH ARSENAL	D 1-1	Bowman	10,000
Oct 22	Derby County	D 1-1	Pentland	12,000
Oct 29	EVERTON	W 1-0	Whittaker	15,000
Nov 5	Small Heath	L 0-2		12,000
Nov 12	MANCHESTER CITY	W 3-1	Dewhurst 2, Bradshaw	10,000
Nov 19	Notts County	L 1-2	Crompton (pen)	5,000
Nov 26	SHEFFIELD UNITED	L 2-4	Bradshaw, Bowman	10,000
Dec 3	Newcastle United	L 0-1		20,000
Dec 10	PRESTON NORTH END	D 1-1	Bowman	25,000
Dec 17	Middlesbrough	L 1-2	Wolstenholme	10,000
Dec 24	WOLVERHAMPTON W.	W 3-0	Bowman, Jones o.g., Dewhurst	5,000
Dec 26	SUNDERLAND	W 2-1	Bowman 2	24,000
Dec 31	BURY	L 0-2		15,000
Jan 2	DERBY COUNTY	W 3-1	Bradshaw 2, Dewhurst	6,000
Jan 7	Aston Villa	L 0-3		8,000
Jan 14	Stoke	L 0-4		5,000
Jan 21	NOTTINGHAM FOREST	D 0-0		5,000
Jan 28	Sheffield Wednesday	W 2-1	Bowman 2	10,000
Feb 11	Woolwich Arsenal	L 0-2		15,000
Feb 25	Everton	L 0-1		23,000
Mar 4	SMALL HEATH	L 1-4	Bowman	5,000
Mar 11	Manchester City	L 1-2	Crompton (pen)	12,000
Mar 18	NOTTS COUNTY	W 1-0	Bowman	7,000
Mar 25	Sheffield United	L 1-3	Bowman	6,000
Apr 1	NEWCASTLE UNITED	W 2-0	Crompton (pen), Dewhurst	8,500
Apr 8	Preston North End	D 0-0		13,000
Apr 15	MIDDLESBROUGH	L 0-2		4,000
Apr 22	Wolverhampton W.	L 0-2		8,000

FA Cup

Feb 4	SHEFFIELD WEDNESDAY	(Rd1) L 1-2	Blackburn	20,723

League & Cup Appearances

PLAYER	LEAGUE	CUP COMPETITION FA CUP	TOTAL
Bennett, J.W.	1		1
Birchall, J.	21	1	22
Blackburn, F.	28	1	29
Bowman, A.	31	1	32
Bradshaw, W.	33	1	34
Cameron, J.	34	1	35
Crompton, R.	27		27
Dewhurst, J.	25	1	26
Duckworth, T.C.	1		1
Evans, R.O.	4		4
McClure, S.	10		10
McIver, W.	30	1	31
Moir, J.	18	1	19
Oliver, A.	2		2
Pentland, F.B.	27	1	28
Riley, T.	1		1
Smith, G.	21		21
Watson, L.P.	15	1	16
Whittaker, A.	17		17
Wolstenholme, S.	28	1	29

Goalscorers

PLAYER	LEAGUE	CUP COMPETITION FA CUP	TOTAL
Bowman, A.	12		12
Bradshaw, W.	5		5
Dewhurst, J.	5		5
Smith, G.	4		4
Watson, L.P.	4		4
Crompton, R.	3		3
Whittaker, A.	3		3
Birchall, J.	1		1
Pentland, F.B.	1		1
Wolstenholme, S.	1		1
Blackburn, F.		1	1
Opps' o.gs.	1		1

Fact File

The signing of Sam Wolstenholme, then an England international, proved a major transfer coup for the Rovers. He represented England against Ireland and Wales during the course of the 1904-05 season.

SECRETARY: Robert Middleton
TOP SCORER: Adam Bowman
BIGGEST WIN: 4-0, 10 September 1904, v Aston Villa, Division 1; 17 September 1904, v Stoke, Division 1
HIGHEST ATTENDANCE: 25,000, 10 December 1904, v Preston North End, Division 1
MAJOR TRANSFERS IN: Sam Wolstenholme from Everton

Final Division 1 Table

		P	W	D	L	F	A	Pts
1	NEWCASTLE U	34	23	2	9	72	33	48
2	EVERTON	34	21	5	8	63	36	47
3	MANCHESTER C	34	20	6	8	66	37	46
4	ASTON VILLA	34	19	4	11	63	43	42
5	SUNDERLAND	34	16	8	10	60	44	40
6	SHEFFIELD U	34	19	2	13	64	56	40
7	SMALL HEATH	34	17	5	12	54	38	39
8	PRESTON NE	34	13	10	11	42	37	36
9	SHEFFIELD W	34	14	5	15	61	57	33
10	WOOLWICH ARSENAL	34	12	9	13	36	40	33
11	DERBY CO	34	12	8	14	37	48	32
12	STOKE	34	13	4	17	40	58	30
13	BLACKBURN R	34	11	5	18	40	51	27
14	WOLVERHAMPTON W	34	11	4	19	47	73	26
15	MIDDLESBROUGH	34	9	8	17	36	56	26
16	NOTTINGHAM F	34	9	7	18	40	61	25
17	BURY	34	10	4	20	47	67	24
18	NOTTS CO	34	5	8	21	36	69	18

The Essential History of Blackburn Rovers

Football League Division 1

DATE	OPPONENTS	SCORE	GOALSCORERS	ATTENDANCE
Sep 2	ASTON VILLA	D 1-1	Bradshaw	10,000
Sep 4	Stoke	L 0-3		6,000
Sep 9	Liverpool	W 3-1	Bowman 2, Davies	15,000
Sep 16	SHEFFIELD UNITED	W 2-1	Bradshaw, Pentland	14,000
Sep 23	Notts County	D 1-1	Davies	8,000
Sep 30	STOKE	W 3-0	Davies, Bowman, Birchall	25,000
Oct 7	Bolton Wanderers	L 0-1		24,000
Oct 14	WOOLWICH ARSENAL	W 2-0	Davies, Chadwick	10,000
Oct 21	Wolverhampton W.	L 1-2	McClure	6,000
Oct 28	Sunderland	L 0-3		10,000
Nov 4	BIRMINGHAM	W 5-1	Bowman 2, Birchall, Whittaker, Davies	10,000
Nov 11	Everton	L 2-3	Bowman, Davies	12,000
Nov 18	DERBY COUNTY	W 3-0	Davies, Bowman, Chadwick	10,000
Nov 25	Sheffield Wednesday	W 1-0	Bradshaw	10,000
Dec 2	NOTTINGHAM FOREST	D 1-1	Bowman	12,000
Dec 9	Manchester City	D 1-1	Robertson	16,000
Dec 16	BURY	W 3-0	Davies, Robertson 2	10,000
Dec 23	Middlesbrough	D 1-1	Robertson	12,000
Dec 30	Aston Villa	W 1-0	Robertson	8,000
Jan 1	NEWCASTLE UNITED	W 1-0	Davies	30,000
Jan 6	LIVERPOOL	D 0-0		10,000
Jan 20	Sheffield United	W 2-0	Robertson, Whittaker	16,000
Jan 27	NOTTS COUNTY	L 1-3	Dawson	14,000
Feb 3	Preston North End	L 1-2	Davies	16,000
Feb 17	Woolwich Arsenal	L 2-3	Wilson, Davies	8,000
Feb 24	WOLVERHAMPTON W.	W 3-1	Bowman 3	3,500
Mar 3	SUNDERLAND	L 0-3		10,000
Mar 17	EVERTON	L 1-2	Robertson	10,000
Mar 24	Derby County	W 2-1	Smith o.g., Dawson	3,000
Mar 31	SHEFFIELD WEDNESDAY	W 1-0	Dawson	10,000
Apr 2	BOLTON WANDERERS	W 4-1	Robertson, Manson 2, Bowman	5,000
Apr 7	Nottingham Forest	W 2-1	Robertson, Bowman	8,000
Apr 13	PRESTON NORTH END	L 1-2	Bowman	29,000
Apr 14	MANCHESTER CITY	D 1-1	Bowman	12,000
Apr 21	Bury	L 0-5		2,000
Apr 23	Birmingham	L 0-3		10,000
Apr 28	MIDDLESBROUGH	D 1-1	Bradshaw	5,000
Apr 30	Newcastle United	L 0-3		12,000

FA Cup

Jan 13	Stoke	(Rd1) L 0-1		15,500

League & Cup Appearances

PLAYER	LEAGUE	CUP COMPETITION FA CUP	TOTAL
Birchall, J.	6		6
Bowman, A.	32	1	33
Bradshaw, W.	36	1	37
Burton, J.H.	1		1
Cameron, J.	7		7
Chadwick, M.	28	1	29
Cowell, A.	33	1	34
Crompton, R.	36	1	37
Cunliffe, T.	1		1
Davies, W.	26	1	27
Dawson, A.	10		10
Evans, R.O.	35	1	36
France, H.	3		3
McAllister, T.	2		2
McClure, S.	21		21
McIver, W.	3		3
Manson, R.	10		10
Moir, J.G.	13	1	14
Pentland, F.B.	6		6
Robertson, J.	26	1	27
Smith, G.	13		13
Whittaker, A.	36	1	37
Wilson, J.	3		3
Wolstenholme, S.	31	1	32

Goalscorers

PLAYER	LEAGUE	CUP COMPETITION FA CUP	TOTAL
Bowman, A.	15		15
Davies, W.	11		11
Robertson, J.	9		9
Bradshaw, W.	4		4
Dawson, A.	3		3
Birchall, J.	2		2
Chadwick, M.	2		2
Manson, R.	2		2
Whittaker, A.	2		2
McClure, S.	1		1
Pentland, F.B.	1		1
Wilson, J.	1		1
Opps' o.gs.	1		1

Fact File

Blackburn remained unbeaten at home until Notts County recorded a 3-1 win at Ewood Park on 27 January 1906.

SECRETARY: Robert Middleton

TOP SCORER: Adam Bowman

BIGGEST WIN: 5-1, 4 November 1905, v Birmingham, Division 1

HIGHEST ATTENDANCE: 30,000, 1 January 1906, v Newcastle United, Division 1

MAJOR TRANSFERS IN: Billy Davies from Wrexham

MAJOR TRANSFERS OUT: Jack Dewhurst to Brentford

Final Division 1 Table

		P	W	D	L	F	A	Pts
1	LIVERPOOL	38	23	5	10	79	46	51
2	PRESTON NE	38	17	13	8	54	39	47
3	SHEFFIELD W	38	18	8	12	63	52	44
4	NEWCASTLE U	38	18	7	13	74	48	43
5	MANCHESTER C	38	19	5	14	73	54	43
6	BOLTON W	38	17	7	14	81	67	41
7	BIRMINGHAM	38	17	7	14	65	59	41
8	ASTON VILLA	38	17	6	15	72	56	40
9	BLACKBURN R	38	16	8	14	54	52	40
10	STOKE	38	16	7	15	54	55	39
11	EVERTON	38	15	7	16	70	66	37
12	WOOLWICH ARSENAL	38	15	7	16	62	64	37
13	SHEFFIELD U	38	15	6	17	57	62	36
14	SUNDERLAND	38	15	5	18	61	70	35
15	DERBY CO	38	14	7	17	39	58	35
16	NOTTS CO	38	11	12	15	55	71	34
17	BURY	38	11	10	17	57	74	32
18	MIDDLESBROUGH	38	10	11	17	56	71	31
19	NOTTINGHAM F	38	13	5	20	58	79	31
20	WOLVERHAMPTON W	38	8	7	23	58	99	23

Season 1906-07

Football League Division 1

DATE	OPPONENTS	SCORE	GOALSCORERS	ATTENDANCE
Sep 1	Aston Villa	L 2-4	Bowman, Whittaker	40,000
Sep 8	LIVERPOOL	D 1-1	Robertson	18,000
Sep 15	Bristol City	L 0-3		18,000
Sep 22	NOTTS COUNTY	L 0-2		11,000
Sep 29	Sheffield United	L 0-3		10,000
Oct 6	BOLTON WANDERERS	L 2-3	Martin 2	10,000
Oct 13	Manchester United	D 1-1	Bowman	20,000
Oct 20	STOKE	W 3-1	Robertson, Martin, Holford o.g.	12,000
Oct 27	DERBY COUNTY	W 5-1	Chadwick, Martin, Wilson, Whittaker Robertson	15,000
Nov 3	Sunderland	L 0-1		11,000
Nov 10	BIRMINGHAM	W 1-0	Martin	10,000
Nov 12	Stoke	D 1-1	Whittaker	5,000
Nov 17	Everton	L 0-2		10,000
Nov 24	WOOLWICH ARSENAL	L 2-3	Bracegirdle 2	12,000
Dec 1	Sheffield Wednesday	L 1-3	Martin	9,000
Dec 8	BURY	W 4-1	Bowman, Martin, Whittaker, Robertson	10,000
Dec 15	Manchester City	D 0-0		12,000
Dec 22	MIDDLESBROUGH	W 4-1	Martin 2, Robertson, Whittaker	9,000
Dec 25	NEWCASTLE UNITED	W 4-0	Whittaker 2, Latheron, Martin	35,000
Dec 26	Preston North End	L 0-1		35,000
Dec 29	ASTON VILLA	W 2-1	Martin, Dawson	10,000
Jan 1	PRESTON NORTH END	D 1-1	Bradshaw	35,000
Jan 5	Liverpool	W 2-0	Chadwick, Bracegirdle	18,000
Jan 19	BRISTOL CITY	L 0-1		15,000
Jan 26	Notts County	W 2-1	Martin, Latheron	8,000
Feb 9	Bolton Wanderers	L 2-5	Martin, Latheron	10,000
Feb 16	MANCHESTER UNITED	L 2-4	Whittaker, Wilson	5,000
Mar 2	Derby County	W 3-2	Chadwick, Martin 2	10,000
Mar 9	SUNDERLAND	W 2-1	Latheron, Wilson	6,000
Mar 16	Birmingham	L 0-2		10,000
Mar 29	SHEFFIELD UNITED	D 1-1	Aitkenhead	10,000
Mar 30	Woolwich Arsenal	L 0-2		20,000
Apr 1	Newcastle United	L 1-3	Martin	35,000
Apr 6	SHEFFIELD WEDNESDAY	L 0-2		6,000
Apr 8	EVERTON	W 2-1	Chadwick, R. Crompton	5,000
Apr 13	Bury	D 0-0		7,000
Apr 20	MANCHESTER CITY	W 4-0	Martin, Robertson 3	5,000
Apr 27	Middlesbrough	W 1-0	Bracegirdle	10,000

FA Cup

Jan 12	MANCHESTER CITY	(Rd1) D 2-2	Aitkenhead, Wolstenholme	20,000
Jan 16	Manchester City	(R) W 1-0	Martin	30,000
Feb 2	TOTTENHAM HOTSPUR	(Rd2) D 1-1	Martin	24,963
Feb 7	Tottenham Hotspur	(R) D 1-1*	Bracegirdle	29,000
Feb 11	Tottenham Hotspur†	(2R) L 1-2	Latheron	18,000

*After extra-time. †Played at Villa Park, Birmingham.

League & Cup Appearances

PLAYER	LEAGUE	CUP COMPETITION	TOTAL
		FA CUP	
Aitkenhead, W.A.C.	16	2	18
Birchall, J.	1		1
Bowman, A.	12		12
Bracegirdle, E.	16	5	21
Bradshaw, W.	32	5	37
Cameron, J.	19	2	21
Chadwick, M.	22		22
Cowell, A.	28	4	32
Crompton, G.E.	3		3
Crompton, R.	28	5	33
Davies, W.	4		4
Dawson, A.	7		7
Evans, R.O.	29	5	34
France, H.	1		1
Hand, J.	2		2
Harvey, A.	1		1
Heywood, J.	3		3
Houlker, A.E.	5		5
Latheron, E.G.	14	4	18
McIver, W.	9		9
Martin, J.	36	5	41
Robertson, J.	36	5	41
Stevenson, H.	2		2
Suttie, T.	1		1
Whittaker, A.	31	5	36
Wilson, J.	30	3	33
Wolstenholme, S.	30	5	35

Goalscorers

PLAYER	LEAGUE	CUP COMPETITION	TOTAL
		FA CUP	
Martin, J.	17	2	19
Robertson, J.	8		8
Whittaker, A.	8		8
Bracegirdle, E.	4	1	5
Latheron, E.G.	4	1	5
Chadwick, M.	4		4
Bowman, A.	3		3
Wilson, J.	3		3
Aitkenhead, W.A.C.	1	1	2
Bradshaw, W.	1		1
Crompton, R.	1		1
Dawson, A.	1		1
Wolstenholme, S.		1	1
Opps' o.gs.	1		1

Fact File

Blackburn enjoyed a 4-0 Christmas Day win over Newcastle United at Ewood Park but at the end of the season it was the Magpies who were crowned as champions.

SECRETARY: Robert Middleton
TOP SCORER: Jack Martin
BIGGEST WIN: 5-1, 27 October 1906, v Derby County, Division 1
HIGHEST ATTENDANCE: 40,000, 1 September 1906 v Aston Villa, Division 1
MAJOR TRANSFERS IN: Wattie Aitkenhead from Partick Thistle

Final Division 1 Table

		P	W	D	L	F	A	Pts
1	NEWCASTLE U	38	22	7	9	74	46	51
2	BRISTOL C	38	20	8	10	66	47	48
3	EVERTON	38	20	5	13	70	46	45
4	SHEFFIELD U	38	17	11	10	57	55	45
5	ASTON VILLA	38	19	6	13	78	52	44
6	BOLTON W	38	18	8	12	59	47	44
7	WOOLWICH ARSENAL	38	20	4	14	66	59	44
8	MANCHESTER U	38	17	8	13	53	56	42
9	BIRMINGHAM	38	15	8	15	52	52	38
10	SUNDERLAND	38	14	9	15	65	66	37
11	MIDDLESBROUGH	38	15	6	17	56	63	36
12	BLACKBURN R	38	14	7	17	56	59	35
13	SHEFFIELD W	38	12	11	15	49	60	35
14	PRESTON NE	38	14	7	17	44	57	35
15	LIVERPOOL	38	13	7	18	64	65	33
16	BURY	38	13	6	19	58	68	32
17	MANCHESTER C	38	10	12	16	53	77	32
18	NOTTS CO	38	8	15	15	46	50	31
19	DERBY CO	38	9	9	20	41	59	27
20	STOKE	38	8	10	20	41	64	26

Season 1907-08

Football League Division 1

DATE	OPPONENTS	SCORE	GOALSCORERS	ATTENDANCE
Sep 2	BURY	W 1-0	Robertson	14,000
Sep 7	ASTON VILLA	W 2-0	Robertson, Martin	20,000
Sep 14	Liverpool	L 0-2		15,000
Sep 21	MIDDLESBROUGH	W 2-0	Latheron, Martin	20,000
Sep 28	Sheffield United	L 2-4	Martin 2	12,000
Oct 5	CHELSEA	W 2-0	Martin, Whittaker	10,000
Oct 12	Nottingham Forest	L 2-3	Ferguson, Chadwick	14,000
Oct 19	MANCHESTER UNITED	L 1-5	Davies	30,000
Oct 26	Newcastle United	L 0-3		28,000
Nov 2	Bolton Wanderers	L 1-3	Bradshaw	7,000
Nov 9	BIRMINGHAM	W 1-0	Latheron	14,000
Nov 16	Everton	L 1-4	Robertson	12,000
Nov 23	SUNDERLAND	W 4-2	Robertson, Martin 2, Latheron	10,000
Nov 30	Woolwich Arsenal	L 0-2		7,500
Dec 2	Chelsea	L 0-1		18,000
Dec 7	SHEFFIELD WEDNESDAY	W 2-0	Latheron, Davies	8,000
Dec 14	Bristol City	D 2-2	Davies 2	12,000
Dec 21	NOTTS COUNTY	D 1-1	Manson	10,000
Dec 26	Preston North End	D 1-1	Bradshaw	27,000
Dec 28	Manchester City	L 0-2		22,000
Jan 1	PRESTON NORTH END	D 1-1	Latheron	30,000
Jan 4	Aston Villa	D 1-1	Crompton R.	15,000
Jan 18	Middlesbrough	L 0-3		15,000
Jan 25	SHEFFIELD UNITED	D 3-3	Davies, Walmsley, Robertson	8,000
Feb 8	NOTTINGHAM FOREST	D 3-3	Linacre o.g., Davies 2	8,000
Feb 15	Manchester United	W 2-1	Aitkenhead, Davies	15,000
Feb 29	BOLTON WANDERERS	W 3-2	Davies 2, Martin (pen)	10,000
Mar 7	Birmingham	D 1-1	Walmsley	5,000
Mar 14	EVERTON	W 2-0	Davies, Anthony	10,000
Mar 21	Sunderland	L 0-4		15,000
Mar 23	NEWCASTLE UNITED	D 1-1	Latheron	15,000
Mar 28	WOOLWICH ARSENAL	D 1-1	Bracegirdle	12,000
Apr 4	Sheffield Wednesday	L 0-2		8,000
Apr 6	LIVERPOOL	L 1-3	Whittaker	8,000
Apr 11	BRISTOL CITY	W 4-1	Crompton E. 2, Latheron 2	8,000
Apr 17	Bury	D 1-1	Crompton E.	13,000
Apr 18	Notts County	W 2-0	Crompton E. 2	12,000
Apr 25	MANCHESTER CITY	D 0-0		10,000

FA Cup

Jan 11	Leicester Fosse	(Rd1)	L 0-2		13,749

League & Cup Appearances

PLAYER	LEAGUE	CUP COMPETITION FA CUP	TOTAL
Aitkenhead, W.A.C.	7		7
Anthony, W.	11		11
Bracegirdle, E.	24		24
Bradshaw, W.	19	1	20
Burton, J.H.	3		3
Cameron, J.	2		2
Cameron, W.S.	3		3
Chadwick, M.	1		1
Cowell, A.	10		10
Crompton, G.E.	8		8
Crompton, R.	33	1	34
Davies, W.	19	1	20
Evans, R.O.	9		9
Ferguson, J.	9		9
Heywood, J.	11	1	12
Houlker, A.E.	20	1	21
Kyle, A.	3		3
Latheron, E.G.	26	1	27
McIver, W.	29	1	30
Manning, J.	4		4
Manson, R.	6		6
Martin, J.	21		21
Orr, J.	1		1
Robertson, J.	16	1	17
Stevenson, H.	23	1	24
Suttie, T.	21		21
Walmsley, A.	27	1	28
Whittaker, A.	23	1	24
Wilson, J.	10		10
Wolstenholme, S.	9		9
Wombwell, R.	10		10

Goalscorers

PLAYER	LEAGUE	CUP COMPETITION FA CUP	TOTAL
Davies, W.	11		11
Latheron, E.G.	8		8
Martin, J.	8		8
Crompton, G.E.	5		5
Robertson, J.	5		5
Bradshaw, W.	2		2
Walmsley, A.	2		2
Whittaker, A.	2		2
Aitkenhead, W.A.C.	1		1
Anthony, W.	1		1
Bracegirdle, E.	1		1
Chadwick, M.	1		1
Crompton, R.	1		1
Ferguson, J.	1		1
Manson, R.	1		1
Opps' o.gs.	1		1

Fact File

In February 1908 the club raided Brighton & Hove Albion to sign Walter Anthony, Dick Wombwell and Joe Lumley.

SECRETARY: Robert Middleton

TOP SCORER: Billy Davies

BIGGEST WIN: 4-1, 11 April 1908, v Bristol City, Division 1

HIGHEST ATTENDANCE: 30,000, 19 October 1907, v Manchester United, Division 1; 1 January 1908, v Preston North End, Division 1

MAJOR TRANSFERS IN: Archie Kyle from Glasgow Rangers, Walter Anthony from Brighton & Hove Albion, James Ferguson from Airdrieonians

MAJOR TRANSFERS OUT: John Cameron to Chelsea

Final Division 1 Table

		P	W	D	L	F	A	Pts
1	MANCHESTER U	38	23	6	9	81	48	52
2	ASTON VILLA	38	17	9	12	77	59	43
3	MANCHESTER C	38	16	11	11	62	54	43
4	NEWCASTLE U	38	15	12	11	65	54	42
5	SHEFFIELD W	38	19	4	15	73	64	42
6	MIDDLESBROUGH	38	17	7	14	54	45	41
7	BURY	38	14	11	13	58	61	39
8	LIVERPOOL	38	16	6	16	68	61	38
9	NOTTINGHAM F	38	13	11	14	59	62	37
10	BRISTOL C	38	12	12	14	58	61	36
11	EVERTON	38	15	6	17	58	64	36
12	PRESTON NE	38	12	12	14	47	53	36
13	CHELSEA	38	14	8	16	53	62	36
14	BLACKBURN R	38	12	12	14	51	63	36
14	WOOLWICH ARSENAL	38	12	12	14	51	63	36
16	SUNDERLAND	38	16	3	19	78	75	35
17	SHEFFIELD U	38	12	11	15	52	58	35
18	NOTTS CO	38	13	8	17	39	51	34
19	BOLTON W	38	14	5	19	52	58	33
20	BIRMINGHAM	38	9	12	17	40	60	30

Season 1908-09

Football League Division 1

DATE	OPPONENTS	SCORE	GOALSCORERS	ATTENDANCE
Sep 1	BRISTOL CITY	D 1-1	Ellis	15,000
Sep 5	Manchester City	D 3-3	E. Crompton 2, Wombwell	30,000
Sep 12	LIVERPOOL	W 1-0	Davies	25,000
Sep 19	Bury	D 1-1	Crompton E.	12,000
Sep 26	SHEFFIELD UNITED	L 0-1		12,000
Oct 3	Aston Villa	D 1-1	Crompton E.	25,000
Oct 10	NOTTINGHAM FOREST	L 0-3		15,000
Oct 17	Sunderland	W 1-0	Latheron	15,000
Oct 24	CHELSEA	W 2-0	Davies, Kyle	15,000
Oct 31	SHEFFIELD WEDNESDAY	D 2-2	Latheron, Davies	15,000
Nov 7	Bradford City	W 2-0	Kyle, Davies	25,000
Nov 14	MANCHESTER UNITED	L 1-3	Crompton R. (pen)	25,000
Nov 21	Everton	D 4-4	Davies 4	20,000
Nov 28	LEICESTER FOSSE	W 3-0	Kyle 2, Davies	14,000
Dec 5	Woolwich Arsenal	W 1-0	Kyle	12,000
Dec 12	NOTTS COUNTY	L 0-2		10,000
Dec 19	Newcastle United	L 0-2		22,000
Dec 25	MIDDLESBROUGH	D 0-0		25,000
Dec 26	Preston North End	L 0-2		25,000
Jan 1	PRESTON NORTH END	D 1-1	Kyle	30,000
Jan 2	MANCHESTER CITY	W 3-2	Aitkenhead, Davies, Latheron	12,000
Jan 9	Liverpool	D 1-1	Aitkenhead	20,000
Jan 23	BURY	L 0-1		12,000
Jan 30	Sheffield United	D 0-0		10,000
Feb 13	Nottingham Forest	L 1-2	Davies	8,000
Feb 15	ASTON VILLA	W 3-1	Latheron 2, Aitkenhead	15,000
Feb 27	Chelsea	D 1-1	Crompton E.	10,000
Mar 13	BRADFORD CITY	D 1-1	Anthony	10,000
Mar 20	Manchester United	W 3-0	Holden o.g., Linkson o.g., Crompton E.	11,000
Mar 22	SUNDERLAND	W 8-1	Latheron, Garbutt, Crompton E. 3, Stevenson, Aitkenhead 2	8,000
Mar 27	EVERTON	D 0-0		10,000
Apr 3	Leicester Fosse	W 4-2	Garbutt, Latheron 2, Kyle	12,000
Apr 10	WOOLWICH ARSENAL	L 1-3	Latheron	5,000
Apr 12	Middlesbrough	L 0-1		12,000
Apr 13	Bristol City	W 4-1	Davies 4	8,000
Apr 17	Notts County	W 3-2	Chapman, Davies, Latheron	6,000
Apr 19	Sheffield Wednesday	W 2-1	Davies, Kyle	2,000
Apr 24	NEWCASTLE UNITED	L 2-4	Davies 2 (1 pen)	7,000

FA Cup

Jan 16	Notts County	(Rd1) W 1-0	Latheron	13,500
Feb 6	CHELSEA	(Rd2) W 2-1	Cameron, Latheron	31,897
Feb 20	Manchester United	(Rd3) L 1-6	Davies	38,500

League & Cup Appearances

PLAYER	LEAGUE	CUP COMPETITION FA CUP	TOTAL
Ashcroft, J.	38	3	41
Aitkenhead, W.A.C.	9	2	11
Anthony, W.	32	2	34
Bracegirdle, E.	2		2
Bradshaw, W.	27	3	30
Cameron, W.S.	17	3	20
Chapman, G.	36	3	39
Cowell, A.	19	3	22
Crompton, G.E.	11		11
Crompton, R.	31	3	34
Davies, W.	27	3	30
Ellis, R.	1		1
Ferguson, J.	17		17
Garbutt, W.	29		29
Heywood, J.	1		1
Houlker, A.E.	5		5
Kyle, A.	33	2	35
Latheron, E.G.	29	3	32
Lawrie, J.	2		2
Stevenson, H.	8		8
Suttie, T.	24		24
Walmsley, A.	15	3	18
Wombwell, R.	5		5

Goalscorers

PLAYER	LEAGUE	CUP COMPETITION FA CUP	TOTAL
Davies, W.	19	1	20
Latheron, E.G.	10	2	12
Crompton, G.E.	9		9
Kyle, A.	8		8
Aitkenhead, W.A.C.	5		5
Garbutt, W.	2		2
Anthony, W.	1		1
Chapman, G.	1		1
Crompton, R.	1		1
Ellis, R.	1		1
Stevenson, H.	1		1
Wombwell, R.	1		1
Cameron, W.S.		1	1
Opps' o.gs.	2		2

Fact File

Billy Davies, the leading marksman at Ewood Park, notched up four goals on two separate occasions during the league campaign.

SECRETARY: Robert Middleton
TOP SCORER: Billy Davies
BIGGEST WIN: 8-1, 22 March 1909, v Sunderland, Division 1
HIGHEST ATTENDANCE: 38,500, 20 February 1909, v Manchester United, FA Cup Round 3
MAJOR TRANSFERS IN: George Chapman from Raith Rovers, Billy Garbutt from Woolwich Arsenal

Final Division 1 Table

		P	W	D	L	F	A	Pts
1	NEWCASTLE U	38	24	5	9	65	41	53
2	EVERTON	38	18	10	10	82	57	46
3	SUNDERLAND	38	21	2	15	78	63	44
4	BLACKBURN R	38	14	13	11	61	50	41
5	SHEFFIELD W	38	17	6	15	67	61	40
6	WOOLWICH ARSENAL	38	14	10	14	52	49	38
7	ASTON VILLA	38	14	10	14	58	56	38
8	BRISTOL C	38	13	12	13	45	58	38
9	MIDDLESBROUGH	38	14	9	15	59	53	37
10	PRESTON NE	38	13	11	14	48	44	37
11	CHELSEA	38	14	9	15	56	61	37
12	SHEFFIELD U	38	14	9	15	51	59	37
13	MANCHESTER U	38	15	7	16	58	68	37
14	NOTTINGHAM F	38	14	8	16	66	57	36
15	NOTTS CO	38	14	8	16	51	48	36
16	LIVERPOOL	38	15	6	17	57	65	36
17	BURY	38	14	8	16	63	77	36
18	BRADFORD C	38	12	10	16	47	47	34
19	MANCHESTER C	38	15	4	19	67	69	34
20	LEICESTER FOSSE	38	8	9	21	54	102	25

Season 1909-10

Football League Division 1

DATE	OPPONENTS	SCORE	GOALSCORERS	ATTENDANCE
Sep 4	NEWCASTLE UNITED	W 2-0	Latheron, Davies	16,000
Sep 11	Liverpool	L 1-3	Davies	25,000
Sep 13	BRISTOL CITY	W 5-2	Anthony, Aitkenhead, Latheron, Bracegirdle, Clay o.g.	8,000
Sep 18	ASTON VILLA	W 3-2	Crompton E., Anthony, Chapman	25,000
Sep 25	Sheffield United	L 0-3		12,000
Oct 2	WOOLWICH ARSENAL	W 7-0	Chapman, Aitkenhead, Latheron, Sands o.g., Anthony, Davies, Walmsley	10,000
Oct 9	Bolton Wanderers	W 2-1	Davies, Aitkenhead	16,000
Oct 16	CHELSEA	W 1-0	Davies	10,000
Oct 23	Middlesbrough	W 3-1	Garbutt, Latheron, Davies	5,000
Oct 30	Nottingham Forest	W 4-0	Latheron, Chapman, Davies, Aitkenhead	2,000
Nov 6	SUNDERLAND	D 0-0		10,000
Nov 13	Everton	W 2-0	Aitkenhead, Latheron	30,000
Nov 20	MANCHESTER UNITED	W 3-2	Aitkenhead, Bradshaw 2 (2 pens)	40,000
Nov 27	Bradford City	L 0-2		35,000
Dec 4	SHEFFIELD WEDNESDAY	D 0-0		10,000
Dec 11	Bristol City	D 2-2	Bradshaw, Crompton E.	4,000
Dec 18	BURY	W 5-1	Cameron 2, Latheron 2, Aitkenhead	10,000
Dec 25	PRESTON NORTH END	D 2-2	Cameron, Latheron	30,000
Dec 27	Preston North End	L 2-3	Cameron 2	33,000
Dec 28	Notts County	D 2-2	Stevenson, Aitkenhead	18,000
Jan 1	TOTTENHAM HOTSPUR	W 2-0	Cameron, Aitkenhead	15,000
Jan 8	Newcastle United	L 1-4	Cameron	35,000
Jan 22	LIVERPOOL	D 1-1	Garbutt	15,000
Jan 29	Aston Villa	L 3-4	Crompton E. 2, Cameron	20,000
Feb 12	Woolwich Arsenal	W 1-0	Cameron	7,500
Feb 26	Chelsea	L 1-3	Latheron	30,000
Mar 5	MIDDLESBROUGH	D 1-1	Aitkenhead	15,000
Mar 12	NOTTINGHAM FOREST	D 2-2	Cameron, Walmsley	10,000
Mar 19	Sunderland	D 0-0		10,000
Mar 25	NOTTS COUNTY	W 2-0	Crompton E., Bradshaw (pen)	12,000
Mar 26	Bolton Wanderers	W 4-2	Orr 2, Crompton E., Aitkenhead	15,000
Mar 29	Tottenham Hotspur	L 0-4		23,000
Apr 2	Manchester United	L 0-2		20,000
Apr 9	BRADFORD CITY	W 2-0	Orr, Garbutt	10,000
Apr 11	EVERTON	W 2-1	Orr 2	3,000
Apr 16	Sheffield Wednesday	L 1-2	Anthony	4,000
Apr 23	SHEFFIELD UNITED	W 3-1	Chapman, Orr, Aitkenhead	5,000
Apr 30	Bury	L 1-2	Stevenson	8,000

FA Cup

Jan 15	Accrington*	(Rd1) W 7-1	Chapman 2, Aitkenhead 2, Latheron 2, Anthony	15,000
Feb 5	Bradford City	(Rd2) W 2-1	Aitkenhead 2	28,000
Feb 19	Newcastle United	(Rd3) L 1-3	Anthony	54,772

*Match played at Ewood Park, Blackburn.

League & Cup Appearances

PLAYER	LEAGUE	CUP COMPETITION	TOTAL
		FA CUP	
Aitkenhead, W.A.C.	38	3	41
Anthony, W.	29	3	32
Ashcroft, J.	35	3	38
Bracegirdle, E.	18		18
Bradshaw, W.	34	3	37
Cameron, W.S.	17	3	20
Chapman, G.	31	3	34
Cowell, A.	34	3	37
Crompton, G.E.	12	1	13
Crompton, R.	25	2	27
Davies, W.	12		12
Ferguson, J.	4		4
Garbutt, W.	29	3	32
Latheron, E.G.	27	2	29
Murray, R.W.	3		3
Orr, J.	11		11
Stevenson, H.	6		6
Suttie, T.	16	1	17
Walmsley, A.	37	3	40

Goalscorers

PLAYER	LEAGUE	CUP COMPETITION	TOTAL
		FA CUP	
Aitkenhead, W.A.C.	12	4	16
Latheron, E.G.	10	2	12
Cameron, W.S.	10		10
Davies, W.	7		7
Crompton, G.E.	6		6
Orr, J.	6		6
Anthony, W.	4	2	6
Chapman, G.	4	2	6
Bradshaw, W.	4		4
Garbutt, W.	3		3
Stevenson, H.	2		2
Walmsley, A.	2		2
Bracegirdle, E.	1		1
Opps' o.gs.	2		2

Fact File

Arthur Cowell won his only England cap on 12 February 1910 against Ireland in Belfast. Ironically, Bob Crompton was missing from the England side that day.

SECRETARY: Robert Middleton

TOP SCORER: Wattie Aitkenhead

BIGGEST WIN: 7-0, 2 October 1909, v Woolwich Arsenal, Division 1

HIGHEST ATTENDANCE: 54,772, 19 February 1910, v Newcastle United, FA Cup Round 3

Final Division 1 Table

		P	W	D	L	F	A	Pts
1	ASTON VILLA	38	23	7	8	84	42	53
2	LIVERPOOL	38	21	6	11	78	57	48
3	BLACKBURN R	38	18	9	11	73	55	45
4	NEWCASTLE U	38	19	7	12	70	56	45
5	MANCHESTER U	38	19	7	12	69	61	45
6	SHEFFIELD U	38	16	10	12	62	41	42
7	BRADFORD C	38	17	8	13	64	47	42
8	SUNDERLAND	38	18	5	15	66	51	41
9	NOTTS CO	38	15	10	13	67	59	40
10	EVERTON	38	16	8	14	51	56	40
11	SHEFFIELD W	38	15	9	14	60	63	39
12	PRESTON NE	38	15	5	18	52	58	35
13	BURY	38	12	9	17	62	66	33
14	NOTTINGHAM F	38	11	11	16	54	72	33
15	TOTTENHAM H	38	11	10	17	53	69	32
16	BRISTOL C	38	12	8	18	45	60	32
17	MIDDLESBROUGH	38	11	9	18	56	73	31
18	WOOLWICH ARSENAL	38	11	9	18	37	67	31
19	CHELSEA	38	11	7	20	47	70	29
20	BOLTON W	38	9	6	23	44	71	24

Season 1910-11

Football League Division 1

DATE	OPPONENTS	SCORE	GOALSCORERS	ATTENDANCE
Sep 1	NOTTS COUNTY	D 1-1	Aitkenhead	17,000
Sep 3	Manchester United	L 2-3	Davies, Latheron	40,000
Sep 10	LIVERPOOL	L 1-2	Garbutt	20,000
Sep 17	Bury	D 2-2	Aitkenhead 2	12,000
Sep 24	SHEFFIELD UNITED	L 1-2	Davies	14,000
Oct 1	Aston Villa	D 2-2	Aitkenhead, Orr	28,000
Oct 8	SUNDERLAND	L 0-1		18,000
Oct 15	Woolwich Arsenal	L 1-4	Bradshaw (pen)	11,500
Oct 22	BRADFORD CITY	W 3-0	Davies, Aitkenhead, Orr	14,000
Oct 29	OLDHAM ATHLETIC	W 1-0	Aitkenhead	14,000
Nov 5	Nottingham Forest	L 2-5	Aitkenhead, Davies	8,000
Nov 12	MANCHESTER CITY	W 2-0	Garbutt, Orr	10,000
Nov 19	Everton	L 1-6	Garbutt	12,000
Nov 26	SHEFFIELD WEDNESDAY	W 6-1	Latheron 3, Aitkenhead, Davies 2	10,000
Dec 3	Bristol City	L 0-1		10,000
Dec 10	NEWCASTLE UNITED	W 3-1	Davies 2, Garbutt	12,000
Dec 17	Tottenham Hotspur	D 2-2	Aitkenhead 2	16,000
Dec 24	MIDDLESBROUGH	W 5-1	Davies 2, Bradshaw (pen), Weir o.g., Latheron	12,000
Dec 26	Preston North End	D 0-0		30,000
Dec 31	MANCHESTER UNITED	W 1-0	Anthony	20,000
Jan 2	PRESTON NORTH END	L 0-1		unknown
Jan 7	Liverpool	D 2-2	Orr, Garbutt	6,000
Jan 21	BURY	W 6-2	Davies 2, Aitkenhead 2, Walmsley, Bradshaw (pen)	10,000
Jan 28	Sheffield United	D 1-1	Latheron	18,000
Feb 11	Sunderland	D 2-2	Bradshaw (pen), Davies	12,000
Feb 18	WOOLWICH ARSENAL	W 1-0	Latheron	20,000
Feb 28	Bradford City	L 0-1		20,000
Mar 4	Oldham Athletic	L 0-2		5,000
Mar 18	Manchester City	D 0-0		35,000
Mar 27	NOTTINGHAM FOREST	W 4-1	Davies 2, Latheron 2	unknown
Apr 1	Sheffield Wednesday	L 0-1		5,000
Apr 6	EVERTON	L 0-1		unknown
Apr 8	BRISTOL CITY	W 2-0	Bradshaw (pen), Cameron	7,000
Apr 14	Notts County	L 0-2		20,000
Apr 15	Newcastle United	D 2-2	Crompton R. (pen), Latheron	25,000
Apr 22	TOTTENHAM HOTSPUR	W 3-0	Aitkenhead, Davies 2	14,000
Apr 24	ASTON VILLA	D 0-0		20,000
Apr 29	Middlesbrough	W 3-2	Latheron, Clennell 2	6,000

FA Cup

Jan 14	Southend United†	(Rd1) W 5-1	Latheron 2, Bradshaw (pen), Aitkenhead, Thompson o.g.	10,278
Feb 4	TOTTENHAM HOTSPUR	(Rd2) D 0-0		25,000
Feb 9	Tottenham Hotspur	(R) W 2-0	Bradshaw, Simpson	29,464
Feb 25	Middlesbrough	(Rd3) W 3-0	Simpson 2, Smith	30,369
Mar 11	West Ham United	(Rd4) W 3-2	Latheron, Simpson, Davies	20,000
Mar 25	Bradford City*	(SF) L 0-3		40,000

†Played at Ewood Park, Blackburn. *Played at Bramall Lane, Sheffield.

League & Cup Appearances

PLAYER	LEAGUE	CUP COMPETITION FA CUP	TOTAL
Aitkenhead, W.A.C.	35	6	41
Anthony, W.	24	1	25
Ashcroft, J.	31	6	37
Bradshaw, W.	34	6	40
Cameron, W.S.	14	4	18
Clennell, J.	3		3
Cowell, A.	23	2	25
Crompton, G.E.	1		1
Crompton, R.	31	6	37
Davies, W.	33	6	39
Dennison, H.	1		1
Ferguson, J.	2		2
Garbutt, W.	22	1	23
Johnston, J.	4		4
Latheron, E.G.	30	6	36
McGhie, A.	1		1
Murray, R.W.	7		7
Orr, J.	12	1	13
Proctor, B.J.	1	1	2
Simpson, J.	11	3	14
Smethams, J.C.	3		3
Smith, P.J.	25	6	31
Stevenson, H.	19	3	22
Suttie, T.	18	4	22
Walmsley, A.	33	4	37

Goalscorers

PLAYER	LEAGUE	CUP COMPETITION FA CUP	TOTAL
Davies, W.	17	2	19
Aitkenhead, W.A.C.	13	1	14
Latheron, E.G.	11	3	14
Bradshaw, W.	5	2	7
Garbutt, W.	5		5
Orr, J.	4		4
Simpson, J.		3	3
Clennell, J.	2		2
Anthony, W.	1		1
Cameron, W.S.	1		1
Crompton, R.	1		1
Walmsley, A.	1		1
Smith, P.J.		1	1
Opps' o.gs.	1	1	2

Fact File

An end of season tour took Blackburn to Austria and Hungary where their itinerary included two games against Oldham Athletic.

SECRETARY: Robert Middleton

TOP SCORER: Billy Davies

BIGGEST WIN: 6-1, 26 November 1910, v Sheffield Wednesday, Division 1

HIGHEST ATTENDANCE: 40,000, 3 September 1910, v Manchester United, Division 1; 25 March 1911, v Bradford City, FA Cup semi-final

MAJOR TRANSFERS IN: Joe Clennell from Blackpool, Jock Simpson from Falkirk

MAJOR TRANSFERS OUT: Ellis Crompton to Tottenham Hotspur, George Chapman to Glasgow Rangers

Final Division 1 Table

		P	W	D	L	F	A	PTS
1	MANCHESTER U	38	22	8	8	72	40	52
2	ASTON VILLA	38	22	7	9	69	41	51
3	SUNDERLAND	38	15	15	8	67	48	45
4	EVERTON	38	19	7	12	50	36	45
5	BRADFORD C	38	20	5	13	51	42	45
6	SHEFFIELD W	38	17	8	13	47	48	42
7	OLDHAM ATH	38	16	9	13	44	41	41
8	NEWCASTLE U	38	15	10	13	61	43	40
9	SHEFFIELD U	38	15	8	15	49	43	38
10	WOOLWICH ARSENAL	38	13	12	13	41	49	38
11	NOTTS CO	38	14	10	14	37	45	38
12	BLACKBURN R	38	13	11	14	62	54	37
13	LIVERPOOL	38	15	7	16	53	53	37
14	PRESTON NE	38	12	11	15	40	49	35
15	TOTTENHAM H	38	13	6	19	52	63	32
16	MIDDLESBROUGH	38	11	10	17	49	63	32
17	MANCHESTER C	38	9	13	16	43	58	31
18	BURY	38	9	11	18	43	71	29
19	BRISTOL C	38	11	5	22	43	66	27
20	NOTTINGHAM F	38	9	7	22	55	75	25

Season 1911-12

Football League Division 1

DATE	OPPONENTS	SCORE	GOALSCORERS	ATTENDANCE
Sep 2	BURY	W 2-0	Aitkenhead 2	21,694
Sep 6	Sunderland	L 0-3		20,000
Sep 9	Middlesbrough	L 1-2	Aitkenhead	19,147
Sep 16	NOTTS COUNTY	D 0-0		16,568
Sep 23	Tottenham Hotspur	W 2-0	Davies, Aitkenhead	37,820
Sep 30	MANCHESTER UNITED	D 2-2	Orr 2	30,913
Oct 7	Liverpool	W 2-1	Aitkenhead, Orr	30,000
Oct 14	ASTON VILLA	W 3-1	Aitkenhead, Chapman, Latheron,	27,537
Oct 21	Newcastle United	L 2-4	Latheron, Davies	30,000
Oct 28	SHEFFIELD UNITED	W 1-0	Aitkenhead	17,297
Nov 4	Oldham Athletic	W 1-0	Smith	15,000
Nov 11	BOLTON WANDERERS	W 2-0	Latheron, Anthony	24,971
Nov 18	Bradford City	L 0-1		35,000
Nov 25	WOOLWICH ARSENAL	W 4-0	Latheron, Bradshaw (pen), Chapman, Aitkenhead	15,864
Dec 2	Manchester City	L 0-3		40,000
Dec 9	EVERTON	W 2-1	Bradshaw (pen), Chapman	13,724
Dec 16	West Bromwich Albion	L 0-2		13,176
Dec 23	SUNDERLAND	D 2-2	Orr, Aitkenhead	14,219
Dec 25	SHEFFIELD WEDNESDAY	D 0-0		27,069
Dec 26	Preston North End	D 2-2	Simpson, Clennell	25,000
Dec 30	Bury	W 2-1	Orr, Clennell	10,000
Jan 1	PRESTON NORTH END	W 3-0	Simpson, Chapman, Aitkenhead	36,195
Jan 6	MIDDLESBROUGH	W 2-1	Chapman, Aitkenhead	10,167
Jan 20	Notts County	W 3-1	Cameron, Aitkenhead, Orr	3,000
Jan 27	TOTTENHAM HOTSPUR	D 0-0		18,567
Feb 10	LIVERPOOL	W 1-0	Chapman	15,196
Feb 17	Aston Villa	W 3-0	Chapman 2, Orr	30,000
Mar 2	Sheffield United	D 1-1	Orr	25,000
Mar 16	Bolton Wanderers	L 0-2		30,000
Mar 23	BRADFORD CITY	W 3-1	Bradshaw (pen), Aitkenhead, Orr	15,335
Apr 6	MANCHESTER CITY	W 2-0	Clennell, Chapman	18,233
Apr 8	Sheffield Wednesday	D 1-1	Clennell	15,000
Apr 13	Everton	W 3-1	Clennell 2, Latheron	40,000
Apr 15	OLDHAM ATHLETIC	W 1-0	Latheron	7,159
Apr 22	Woolwich Arsenal	L 1-5	Ducat o.g.	7,000
Apr 25	WEST BROMWICH ALBION	W 4-1	Aitkenhead 2, Clennell 2	10,601
Apr 27	NEWCASTLE UNITED	D 1-1	Latheron	10,000
Apr 29	Manchester United	L 1-3	Clennell	20,000

FA Cup

Jan 13	NORWICH CITY	(Rd1)	W 4-1	Simpson 2, Chapman 2	22,947
Feb 3	Derby County	(Rd2)	W 2-1	Orr, Chapman	22,023
Feb 24	WOLVERHAMPTON W.	(Rd3)	W 3-2	Chapman, Aitkenhead 2	45,711
Mar 9	Manchester United	(Rd4)	D 1-1	Aitkenhead	59,296
Mar 14	MANCHESTER UNITED	(R)	W 4-2*	Simpson, Aitkenhead, Chapman 2	39,286
Mar 30	West Bromwich Albion†	(SF)	D 0-0		30,063
Apr 3	West Bromwich Albion‡	(R)	L 0-1		20,050

*After extra-time. †Played at Anfield, Liverpool. ‡Played at Hillsborough, Sheffield.

League & Cup Appearances

PLAYER	LEAGUE	CUP COMPETITION FA CUP	TOTAL
Aitkenhead, W.A.C.	29	7	36
Anthony, W.	27	4	31
Ashcroft, J.	8	3	11
Bradshaw, W.	36	7	43
Cameron, W.S.	13	2	15
Chapman, G.	23	7	30
Clennell, J.	18	1	19
Cowell, A.	31	7	38
Crompton, R.	33	7	40
Davies, W.	11		11
Dennison, H.	1		1
Garbutt, W.	1		1
Johnston, J.	5		5
Latheron, E.G.	22		22
Orr, J.	19	7	26
Proctor, B.J.	1		1
Robinson, A.	30	4	34
Simpson, J.	35	7	42
Smith, P.J.	31	7	38
Suttie, T.	7		7
Walmsley, A.	37	7	44

Goalscorers

PLAYER	LEAGUE	CUP COMPETITION FA CUP	TOTAL
Aitkenhead, W.A.C.	15	4	19
Chapman, G.	9	6	15
Orr, J.	9	1	10
Clennell, J.	9		9
Latheron, E.G.	7		7
Simpson, J.	2	3	5
Bradshaw, W.	3		3
Davies, W.	2		2
Anthony, W.	1		1
Cameron, W.S.	1		1
Smith, P.J.	1		1
Opps' o.gs.	1		1

Fact File

Blackburn Rovers captured the First Division title for the first time in the club's history.

SECRETARY: Robert Middleton

TOP SCORER: Wattie Aitkenhead

BIGGEST WIN: 4-0, 25 November 1911, v Woolwich Arsenal, Division 1

HIGHEST ATTENDANCE: 59,296, 9 March 1912, v Manchester United, FA Cup Round 4

MAJOR TRANSFERS IN: George Chapman from Glasgow Rangers

Final Division 1 Table

		P	W	D	L	F	A	Pts
1	BLACKBURN R	38	20	9	9	60	43	49
2	EVERTON	38	20	6	12	46	42	46
3	NEWCASTLE U	38	18	8	12	64	50	44
4	BOLTON W	38	20	3	15	54	43	43
5	SHEFFIELD W	38	16	9	13	69	49	41
6	ASTON VILLA	38	17	7	14	76	63	41
7	MIDDLESBROUGH	38	16	8	14	56	45	40
8	SUNDERLAND	38	14	11	13	58	51	39
9	WBA	38	15	9	14	43	47	39
10	WOOLWICH ARSENAL	38	15	8	15	55	59	38
11	BRADFORD C	38	15	8	15	46	50	38
12	TOTTENHAM H	38	14	9	15	53	53	37
13	MANCHESTER U	38	13	11	14	45	60	37
14	SHEFFIELD U	38	13	10	15	63	56	36
15	MANCHESTER C	38	13	9	16	56	58	35
16	NOTTS CO	38	14	7	17	46	63	35
17	LIVERPOOL	38	12	10	16	49	55	34
18	OLDHAM ATH	38	12	10	16	46	54	34
19	PRESTON NE	38	13	7	18	40	57	33
20	BURY	38	6	9	23	32	59	21

Season 1912-13

Football League Division 1

DATE	OPPONENTS	SCORE	GOALSCORERS	ATTENDANCE
Sep 2	Sheffield Wednesday	L 1-2	Simpson	15,000
Sep 7	Derby County	D 1-1	Bradshaw (pen)	7,000
Sep 9	SUNDERLAND	W 4-0	Simpson 2, Chapman 2	17,821
Sep 14	TOTTENHAM HOTSPUR	W 6-1	Aitkenhead 2, Simpson, Latheron 2, Chapman	21,837
Sep 18	Sunderland	W 4-2	Latheron 2, Anthony, Aitkenhead	18,000
Sep 21	Middlesbrough	D 0-0		18,577
Sep 28	NOTTS COUNTY	W 2-1	Bradshaw 2 (1 pen)	20,104
Oct 5	Manchester United	D 1-1	Latheron	45,000
Oct 12	ASTON VILLA	D 2-2	Aitkenhead 2	41,115
Oct 19	Liverpool	L 1-4	Aitkenhead	20,000
Oct 26	BOLTON WANDERERS	W 6-0	Cameron 4, Latheron, Aitkenhead	23,661
Nov 2	Sheffield United	D 0-0		17,000
Nov 9	NEWCASTLE UNITED	W 2-0	Aitkenhead, Cameron	32,485
Nov 23	CHELSEA	D 1-1	Simpson	15,000
Nov 30	Woolwich Arsenal	W 1-0	Aitkenhead	9,000
Dec 7	BRADFORD CITY	W 5-0	Orr, Latheron, Simpson 2, Bradshaw	15,000
Dec 14	Manchester City	L 1-3	Latheron	20,000
Dec 21	WEST BROMWICH ALBION	L 2-4	Simpson, Latheron	22,000
Dec 25	Everton	L 1-2	Anthony	30,000
Dec 26	EVERTON	L 1-2	Simpson	20,000
Dec 28	DERBY COUNTY	L 0-1		15,000
Jan 1	Oldham Athletic	D 0-0		20,000
Jan 4	Tottenham Hotspur	W 1-0	Cameron	33,000
Jan 25	Notts County	L 1-3	Shea	15,000
Feb 8	MANCHESTER UNITED	D 0-0		35,000
Feb 10	MIDDLESBROUGH	W 5-2	Aitkenhead 3, Shea, Anthony	15,000
Feb 15	Aston Villa	D 1-1	Shea	20,000
Mar 1	Bolton Wanderers	D 1-1	Latheron	27,000
Mar 10	LIVERPOOL	W 5-1	Shea 2, Orr 3	4,000
Mar 15	Newcastle United	W 1-0	Orr	25,000
Mar 21	SHEFFIELD WEDNESDAY	L 0-1		20,000
Mar 22	OLDHAM ATHLETIC	W 7-1	Shea 2, Latheron 2, Chapman 2, Bradshaw (pen)	18,000
Mar 29	Chelsea	W 6-1	Chapman 2, Shea 3, Latheron	30,000
Apr 5	WOOLWICH ARSENAL	D 1-1	Latheron	8,000
Apr 7	SHEFFIELD UNITED	W 3-1	Shea 2, Chapman	2,000
Apr 12	Bradford City	W 2-0	Hodkinson 2	16,000
Apr 19	MANCHESTER CITY	D 2-2	Bradshaw (pen), Chapman	8,000
Apr 26	West Bromwich Albion	D 1-1	Hodkinson	11,834

FA Cup

Jan 18	NORTHAMPTON TOWN	(Rd1) W 7-2	Simpson, Latheron, Aitkenhead 3, Orr 2	23,623
Feb 1	Barnsley	(Rd2) W 3-2	Shea, Bradshaw (pen), Aitkenhead	30,800
Feb 22	Reading	(Rd3) W 2-1	Latheron, Anthony	19,926
Mar 8	BURNLEY	(Rd4) L 0-1		42,778

League & Cup Appearances

PLAYER	LEAGUE	CUP COMPETITION FA CUP	TOTAL
Aitkenhead, W.A.C.	24	4	28
Anthony, W.	25	4	29
Ashcroft, J.	2		2
Bradshaw, W.	35	4	39
Cameron, W.S.	6		6
Chapman, G.	25	1	26
Clennell, J.	1		1
Cowell, A.	32	3	35
Crompton, R.	31	4	35
Hodkinson, J.	13		13
Jacques, T.E.	2		2
Johnston, J.	3		3
Latheron, E.G.	36	4	40
McGhie, A.	6		6
Orr, J.	11	1	12
Porteous, G.	5		5
Robinson, A.	36	4	40
Shea, D.	15	3	18
Simpson, J.	34	4	38
Smith, P.J.	33	3	36
Suttie, J.	7	1	8
Walmsley, A.	36	4	40

Goalscorers

PLAYER	LEAGUE	CUP COMPETITION FA CUP	TOTAL
Latheron, E.G.	14	2	16
Aitkenhead, W.A.C.	12	4	16
Shea, D.	12	1	13
Simpson, J.	9	1	10
Chapman, G.	9		9
Bradshaw, W.	6	1	7
Orr, J.	5	2	7
Cameron, W.S.	6		6
Anthony, W.	3	1	4
Hodkinson, J.	3		3

Fact File

Danny Shea made a sensational start to his Ewood career with 12 goals in just 15 games, following his move from West Ham United in January 1913.

SECRETARY: Robert Middleton

TOP SCORER: Eddie Latheron/Wattie Aitkenhead

BIGGEST WIN: 7-1, 22 March 1913, v Oldham Athletic, Division 1

HIGHEST ATTENDANCE: 45,000, 5 October 1912, v Manchester United, Division 1

MAJOR TRANSFERS IN: Danny Shea from West Ham United, Joe Hodkinson from Glossop

MAJOR TRANSFERS OUT: William Cameron to Bury

Final Division 1 Table

		P	W	D	L	F	A	Pts
1	SUNDERLAND	38	25	4	9	86	43	54
2	ASTON VILLA	38	19	12	7	86	52	50
3	SHEFFIELD W	38	21	7	10	75	55	49
4	MANCHESTER U	38	19	8	11	69	43	46
5	BLACKBURN R	38	16	13	9	79	43	45
6	MANCHESTER C	38	18	8	12	53	37	44
7	DERBY CO	38	17	8	13	69	66	42
8	BOLTON W	38	16	10	12	62	63	42
9	OLDHAM ATH	38	14	14	10	50	55	42
10	WBA	38	13	12	13	57	50	38
11	EVERTON	38	15	7	16	48	54	37
12	LIVERPOOL	38	16	5	17	61	71	37
13	BRADFORD C	38	12	11	15	50	60	35
14	NEWCASTLE U	38	13	8	17	47	47	34
15	SHEFFIELD U	38	14	6	18	56	70	34
16	MIDDLESBROUGH	38	11	10	17	55	69	32
17	TOTTENHAM H	38	12	6	20	45	72	30
18	CHELSEA	38	11	6	21	51	73	28
19	NOTTS CO	38	7	9	22	28	56	23
20	WOOLWICH ARSENAL	38	3	12	23	26	74	18

The Essential History of Blackburn Rovers

Season 1913-14

Football League Division 1

DATE	OPPONENTS	SCORE	GOALSCORERS	ATTENDANCE
Sep 1	NEWCASTLE UNITED	W 3-0	Chapman, Latheron 2	20,000
Sep 6	LIVERPOOL	W 6-2	Shea 4, Latheron, Bradshaw (pen)	30,000
Sep 8	Burnley	W 2-1	Smith, Chapman	36,000
Sep 13	Aston Villa	W 3-1	Bradshaw (pen), Shea, Chapman	40,000
Sep 20	MIDDLESBROUGH	W 6-0	Chapman 3, Shea 3	25,000
Sep 27	Sheffield United	D 1-1	Chapman	35,000
Oct 4	DERBY COUNTY	W 3-1	Latheron, Clennell, McGhie	25,000
Oct 11	Manchester City	W 2-1	Smith, Hughes o.g.	40,000
Oct 18	BRADFORD CITY	D 0-0		25,000
Oct 25	Tottenham Hotspur	D 3-3	Latheron, Shea, Hodkinson	40,000
Nov 1	Sunderland	L 1-2	Orr	40,000
Nov 8	EVERTON	W 6-0	Chapman, Latheron 3, Bradshaw (pen), McGhie	15,000
Nov 15	West Bromwich Albion	L 0-2		25,000
Nov 22	SHEFFIELD WEDNESDAY	W 3-2	Chapman, Shea, Latheron	25,000
Nov 29	Bolton Wanderers	L 0-1		40,000
Dec 6	CHELSEA	W 3-1	Shea 2, Hodkinson	10,000
Dec 13	Oldham Athletic	D 1-1	Shea	22,000
Dec 20	MANCHESTER UNITED	L 0-1		20,000
Dec 25	PRESTON NORTH END	W 5-0	Aitkenhead 3, Shea 2	25,000
Dec 26	Preston North End	W 5-1	Shea 3, Simpson, Aitkenhead	26,000
Dec 27	Liverpool	D 3-3	Shea 2, Aitkenhead	25,000
Jan 1	BURNLEY	D 0-0		48,000
Jan 3	ASTON VILLA	D 0-0		15,000
Jan 17	Middlesbrough	L 0-3		18,000
Jan 24	SHEFFIELD UNITED	W 3-2	Shea 2 (1 pen), Latheron	15,000
Feb 7	Derby County	W 3-2	Aitkenhead, Shea, Latheron	10,000
Feb 14	MANCHESTER CITY	W 2-1	Smith, Aitkenhead	10,000
Feb 25	Bradford City	W 2-0	Shea 2	17,000
Feb 28	TOTTENHAM HOTSPUR	D 1-1	Shea	30,000
Mar 14	Everton	D 0-0		35,000
Mar 21	WEST BROMWICH ALBION	W 2-0	McGhie, Dawson	22,126
Mar 23	SUNDERLAND	W 3-1	Orr, Walmsley, Ness o.g.	10,000
Mar 28	Sheffield Wednesday	L 1-3	Shea	12,000
Apr 4	BOLTON WANDERERS	W 3-2	Latheron, Dawson, Shea	25,000
Apr 10	Newcastle United	D 0-0		40,000
Apr 11	Chelsea	L 0-2		40,000
Apr 18	OLDHAM ATHLETIC	W 2-1	Latheron, Dawson	10,000
Apr 25	Manchester United	D 0-0		15,000

FA Cup

DATE	OPPONENTS		SCORE	GOALSCORERS	ATTENDANCE
Jan 10	MIDDLESBROUGH	(Rd1)	W 3-0	Aitkenhead 3	25,395
Jan 31	BURY	(Rd2)	W 2-0	Shea 2	29,098
Feb 21	MANCHESTER CITY	(Rd3)	L 1-2	Aitkenhead	41,250

League & Cup Appearances

PLAYER	LEAGUE	CUP COMPETITION FA CUP	TOTAL
Aitkenhead, W.A.C.	17	3	20
Anthony, W.	1		1
Bell, A.	8	1	9
Bradshaw, W.	27	2	29
Chapman, G.	19		19
Clennell, J.	4		4
Cowell, A.	38	3	41
Crabtree, J.J.	10		10
Crompton, R.	33	3	36
Dawson, P.H.	8		8
Hodkinson, J.	33	3	36
Johnston, J.	2		2
Latheron, E.G.	35	3	38
McGhie, A.	9		9
Orr, J.	5		5
Porteous, G.	1		1
Robinson, A.	28	3	31
Shea, D.	36	3	39
Simpson, J.	34	3	37
Smith, P.J.	33	3	36
Walmsley, A.	37	3	40

Goalscorers

PLAYER	LEAGUE	CUP COMPETITION FA CUP	TOTAL
Shea, D.	28	2	30
Latheron, E.G.	13		13
Aitkenhead, W.A.C.	7	4	11
Chapman, J.	9		9
Bradshaw, W.	3		3
Dawson, P.H.	3		3
McGhie, A.	3		3
Smith, P.J.	3		3
Hodkinson, J.	2		2
Orr, J.	2		2
Clennell, J.	1		1
Simpson, J.	1		1
Walmsley, A.	1		1
Opps' o.gs.	2		2

Fact File

Bob Crompton won the last of his 41 England caps against Scotland at Hampden Park on 4 April 1914.

SECRETARY: Robert Middleton

TOP SCORER: Danny Shea

BIGGEST WIN: 6-0, 20 September 1913, v Middlesbrough, Division 1; 8 November 1913, v Everton, Division 1

HIGHEST ATTENDANCE: 48,000, 1 January 1914, v Burnley, Division 1

MAJOR TRANSFERS IN: Percy Dawson from Heart of Midlothian

MAJOR TRANSFERS OUT: Joe Clennell to Everton

Final Division 1 Table

		P	W	D	L	F	A	PTS
1	BLACKBURN R	38	20	11	7	78	42	51
2	ASTON VILLA	38	19	6	13	65	50	44
3	MIDDLESBROUGH	38	19	5	14	77	60	43
4	OLDHAM ATH	38	17	9	12	55	45	43
5	WBA	38	15	13	10	46	42	43
6	BOLTON W	38	16	10	12	65	52	42
7	SUNDERLAND	38	17	6	15	63	52	40
8	CHELSEA	38	16	7	15	46	55	39
9	BRADFORD C	38	12	14	12	40	40	38
10	SHEFFIELD U	38	16	5	17	63	60	37
11	NEWCASTLE U	38	13	11	14	39	48	37
12	BURNLEY	38	12	12	14	61	53	36
13	MANCHESTER C	38	14	8	16	51	53	36
14	MANCHESTER U	38	15	6	17	52	62	36
15	EVERTON	38	12	11	15	46	55	35
16	LIVERPOOL	38	14	7	17	46	62	35
17	TOTTENHAM H	38	12	10	16	50	62	34
18	SHEFFIELD W	38	13	8	17	53	70	34
19	PRESTON NE	38	12	6	20	52	69	30
20	DERBY CO	38	8	11	19	55	71	27

Season 1914-15

Football League Division 1

DATE	OPPONENTS	SCORE	GOALSCORERS	ATTENDANCE
Sep 5	Bradford	W 2-1	Dawson, Shea	20,000
Sep 7	Bolton Wanderers	L 2-3	Latheron 2	30,000
Sep 12	OLDHAM ATHLETIC	W 4-1	Dawson 2, Shea, Latheron	8,000
Sep 19	Manchester United	L 0-2		20,000
Sep 21	LIVERPOOL	W 4-2	Shea 2, Latheron 2	15,000
Sep 26	BOLTON WANDERERS	D 2-2	Latheron, Shea	20,000
Oct 3	MANCHESTER CITY	L 0-1		20,000
Oct 10	Notts County	D 1-1	Shea	15,000
Oct 17	SUNDERLAND	W 3-1	Latheron, Shea, Dawson	20,000
Oct 24	Sheffield Wednesday	D 1-1	Shea	20,000
Oct 31	WEST BROMWICH ALBION	W 2-1	Dawson 2	20,000
Nov 7	Everton	W 3-1	Shea 2 (1 pen), Latheron	25,000
Nov 14	CHELSEA	W 3-2	Shea 2, Dawson	15,000
Nov 21	Bradford City	L 0-3		15,000
Nov 28	BURNLEY	W 6-0	Dawson 4, Taylor o.g., Latheron	21,700
Dec 5	Tottenham Hotspur	W 4-0	Collins o.g., Hodkinson 2, Latheron	12,000
Dec 12	NEWCASTLE UNITED	L 2-3	Dawson, Shea	6,000
Dec 19	Middlesbrough	W 4-1	Latheron 2, Dawson 2	9,000
Dec 25	ASTON VILLA	L 1-2	Dawson	25,000
Dec 26	Sheffield United	W 2-1	Chapman, Hodkinson	35,000
Jan 1	SHEFFIELD UNITED	L 1-2	Chapman	10,000
Jan 2	BRADFORD	D 2-2	Aitkenhead 2	20,000
Jan 16	Oldham Athletic	L 2-3	Aitkenhead 2	8,000
Jan 23	MANCHESTER UNITED	D 3-3	Orr, Crompton, Smith	10,000
Feb 6	Manchester City	W 3-1	Aitkenhead 2, Simpson	20,000
Feb 13	NOTTS COUNTY	W 5-1	Hodkinson, Bradshaw (pen), Aitkenhead, Latheron 2	3,000
Feb 20	Sunderland	L 1-5	Bradshaw	6,000
Feb 27	SHEFFIELD WEDNESDAY	D 1-1	Orr	7,000
Mar 6	West Bromwich Albion	D 0-0		10,000
Mar 13	EVERTON	W 2-1	Crompton (pen), Dawson	20,000
Mar 20	Chelsea	W 3-1	Byrom 2, Orr	20,000
Mar 29	BRADFORD CITY	W 2-1	Latheron, Simpson	5,000
Apr 2	Aston Villa	L 1-2	Dawson	10,000
Apr 3	Burnley	L 2-3	Latheron, Crompton (pen)	14,000
Apr 5	Liverpool	L 0-3		25,000
Apr 10	TOTTENHAM HOTSPUR	W 4-1	Crompton (pen), Dawson 2, Orr	10,000
Apr 17	Newcastle United	L 1-2	Latheron	12,000
Apr 24	MIDDLESBROUGH	W 4-0	Aitkenhead 2, Dawson, Simpson	7,000

FA Cup

Jan 9	Swansea Town	(Rd1) L 0-1		14,178

League & Cup Appearances

PLAYER	LEAGUE	CUP COMPETITION FA CUP	TOTAL
Aitkenhead, W.A.C.	35	1	36
Bell, H.	3		3
Bradshaw, W.	20	1	21
Byrom, T.	4		4
Chapman, G.	4		4
Cowell, A.	30		30
Crompton, R.	34	1	35
Dawson, P.H.	28		28
Edge, A.S.	9		9
Hodkinson, J.	38	1	39
Latheron, E.G.	37	1	38
McGhie, A.	1	1	2
Orr, J.	13	1	14
Robinson, A.	29	1	30
Simpson, J.	37		37
Shea, D.	21		21
Smith, P.J.	35	1	36
Suttie, T.	9	1	10
Walmsley, A.	31	1	32

Goalscorers

PLAYER	LEAGUE	CUP COMPETITION FA CUP	TOTAL
Dawson, P.H.	20		20
Latheron, E.G.	17		17
Shea, D.	13		13
Aitkenhead, W.A.C.	9		9
Crompton, R.	4		4
Hodkinson, J.	4		4
Orr, J.	4		4
Simpson, J.	3		3
Bradshaw, W.	2		2
Byrom, T.	2		2
Chapman, G.	2		2
Smith, P.J.	1		1
Opps' o.gs.	2		2

Fact File

Despite completing the double over Everton it was the Merseyside club that captured the championship crown from Ewood Park.

SECRETARY: Robert Middleton
TOP SCORER: Percy Dawson
BIGGEST WIN: 6-0, 28 November 1914, v Burnley, Division 1
HIGHEST ATTENDANCE: 35,000, 26 December 1914, v Sheffield United, Division 1

Final Division 1 Table

		P	W	D	L	F	A	Pts
1	EVERTON	38	19	8	11	76	47	46
2	OLDHAM ATH	38	17	11	10	70	56	45
3	BLACKBURN R	38	18	7	13	83	61	43
4	BURNLEY	38	18	7	13	61	47	43
5	MANCHESTER C	38	15	13	10	49	39	43
6	SHEFFIELD U	38	15	13	10	49	41	43
7	SHEFFIELD W	38	15	13	10	61	54	43
8	SUNDERLAND	38	18	5	15	81	72	41
9	BRADFORD PA	38	17	7	14	69	65	41
10	WBA	38	15	10	13	49	43	40
11	BRADFORD C	38	13	14	11	55	49	40
12	MIDDLESBROUGH	38	13	12	13	62	74	38
13	LIVERPOOL	38	14	9	15	65	75	37
14	ASTON VILLA	38	13	11	14	62	72	37
15	NEWCASTLE U	38	11	10	17	46	48	32
16	NOTTS CO	38	9	13	16	41	57	31
17	BOLTON W	38	11	8	19	68	84	30
18	MANCHESTER U	38	9	12	17	46	62	30
19	CHELSEA	38	8	13	17	51	65	29
20	TOTTENHAM H	38	8	12	18	57	90	28

Season 1919-20

Football League Division 1

DATE	OPPONENTS	SCORE	GOALSCORERS	ATTENDANCE
Aug 30	PRESTON NORTH END	W 4-0	Hawksworth, Dawson 2, Shea	20,000
Sep 3	Middlesbrough	D 2-2	Shea, Hawksworth	25,000
Sep 6	Preston North End	D 0-0		20,000
Sep 13	BURNLEY	L 2-3	Dawson, Thorpe o.g.	20,000
Sep 15	MIDDLESBROUGH	L 0-2		15,000
Sep 20	Burnley	L 1-3	Hawksworth	16,000
Sep 27	ARSENAL	D 2-2	Shea, Eddleston	5,000
Oct 4	Arsenal	W 1-0	Shea	30,000
Oct 11	Sheffield Wednesday	D 0-0		11,000
Oct 18	SHEFFIELD WEDNESDAY	W 1-0	Eddleston	8,000
Oct 20	Sheffield United	L 0-2		15,000
Oct 25	Everton	L 0-3		25,000
Nov 1	EVERTON	W 3-2	Holland, Hawksworth 2	6,000
Nov 8	Manchester City	L 2-8	Hawksworth, Byrom	25,000
Nov 15	MANCHESTER CITY	L 1-4	Fawcett	6,000
Nov 22	Bradford City	L 1-3	Eddleston	16,000
Dec 6	DERBY COUNTY	W 2-0	Dawson, Bradshaw (pen)	15,000
Dec 11	BRADFORD CITY	W 4-1	Dawson 3, Hawksworth	11,000
Dec 13	Derby County	D 0-0		10,000
Dec 20	BOLTON WANDERERS	D 2-2	Shea, Dawson	20,000
Dec 25	Notts County	L 0-5		17,000
Dec 27	Bolton Wanderers	L 1-2	Dawson	25,000
Jan 1	NOTTS COUNTY	D 1-1	Shea	25,000
Jan 3	WEST BROMWICH ALBION	L 1-5	Dawson	25,000
Jan 17	West Bromwich Albion	L 2-5	Dawson, Hawksworth	30,000
Jan 24	BRADFORD	D 3-3	Hawksworth 2, Dawson	8,000
Feb 7	LIVERPOOL	L 0-2		15,000
Feb 14	Liverpool	L 0-3		30,000
Feb 23	Bradford	L 2-5	Shea, Rodgers	10,000
Feb 27	Chelsea	L 1-2	Rodgers	45,000
Mar 6	Newcastle United	D 0-0		27,000
Mar 11	CHELSEA	W 3-1	Dawson, Rodgers, Reilly	12,000
Mar 13	NEWCASTLE UNITED	W 2-0	Rodgers 2	20,000
Mar 20	Aston Villa	W 2-1	Dawson, Rodgers (pen)	35,000
Apr 2	SUNDERLAND	W 3-0	Hawksworth 2, Rodgers (pen)	38,388
Apr 3	Oldham Athletic	D 0-0		14,000
Apr 5	Sunderland	L 0-2		25,000
Apr 10	OLDHAM ATHLETIC	L 0-1		12,000
Apr 15	ASTON VILLA	W 5-1	Hawksworth 2, Shea 2, Hodkinson	20,000
Apr 17	Manchester United	D 1-1	Healless	40,000
Apr 24	MANCHESTER UNITED	W 5-0	Rodgers 3 (1 pen), Hawksworth 2	20,000
May 1	SHEFFIELD UNITED	W 4-0	Rodgers 3 (1 pen), Hawksworth	40,000

FA Cup

Jan 10	WOLVERHAMPTON W.	(Rd1) D 2-2	Reilly, Dawson	22,310
Jan 15	Wolverhampton W.	(R) L 0-1		36,800

Fact File

Bob Crompton made his final league appearance for the club at Bradford on 23 February 1920.

SECRETARY: Robert Middleton

TOP SCORER: Ernest Hawksworth

BIGGEST WIN: 5-0, 24 April 1920, v Manchester United, Division 1

HIGHEST ATTENDANCE: 45,000, 28 February 1920, v Chelsea, Division 1

MAJOR TRANSFERS IN: David Rollo from Linfield, Frank Reilly from Falkirk, Ronnie Sewell from Burnley, Levy Thorpe from Burnley, Norman Rodgers from Stockport County

League & Cup Appearances

PLAYER	LEAGUE	CUP COMPETITION FA CUP	TOTAL
Barton, J.W.	1	1	2
Boothman, J.	2		2
Bradshaw, W.	22	2	24
Brooks, E.	3		3
Byrom, T.	9		9
Clough, A.E.	1		1
Cowell, A.	1		1
Crabtree, J.J.	2		2
Crompton, R.	2		2
Dawson, P.H.	23	2	25
Dennis, W.	5		5
Dennison, H.	1		1
Duckworth, F.	35	1	36
Duckworth, J.	5	2	7
Eddleston, J.	7		7
Faulkner, R.	9		9
Fawcett, W.F.	5		5
Hawksworth, E.	41	2	43
Healless, H.	6		6
Heaton, T.	4		4
Hodkinson, J.	37	2	39
Holland, P.B.	10		10
Kerr, J.	15		15
McDonald, J.	1		1
McGhie, A.	6	1	7
Orr, J.	3		3
Pearce, R.G.	1		1
Reilly, F.	26	2	28
Rigg, T.	12		12
Robinson, A.	20		20
Rodgers, W.N.	11		11
Rollo, D.	15	2	17
Sewell, W.R.	15		15
Shea, D.	25	2	27
Smith, P.J.	15		15
Thorpe, L.	14		14
Walmsley, A.	19	2	21
Walmsley, R.H.	31	1	32
Webster, M.V.	2		2

Goalscorers

PLAYER	LEAGUE	CUP COMPETITION FA CUP	TOTAL
Hawksworth, E.	17		17
Dawson, P.H.	14	1	15
Rodgers, W.N.	13		13
Shea, D.	9		9
Eddleston, J.	3		3
Reilly, F.	1	1	2
Bradshaw, W.	1		1
Byrom, T.	1		1
Fawcett, W.F.	1		1
Healless, H.	1		1
Hodkinson, J.	1		1
Holland, P.B.	1		1
Opps' o.gs.	1		1

Final Division 1 Table

		P	W	D	L	F	A	Pts
1	WBA	42	28	4	10	104	47	60
2	BURNLEY	42	21	9	12	65	59	51
3	CHELSEA	42	22	5	15	56	51	49
4	LIVERPOOL	42	19	10	13	59	44	48
5	SUNDERLAND	42	22	4	16	72	59	48
6	BOLTON W	42	19	9	14	72	65	47
7	MANCHESTER C	42	18	9	15	71	62	45
8	NEWCASTLE U	42	17	9	16	44	39	43
9	ASTON VILLA	42	18	6	18	75	73	42
10	THE ARSENAL	42	15	12	15	56	58	42
11	BRADFORD PA	42	15	12	15	60	63	42
12	MANCHESTER U	42	13	14	15	54	50	40
13	MIDDLESBROUGH	42	15	10	17	61	65	40
14	SHEFFIELD U	42	16	8	18	59	69	40
15	BRADFORD C	42	14	11	17	54	63	39
16	EVERTON	42	12	14	16	69	68	38
17	OLDHAM ATH	42	15	8	19	49	52	38
18	DERBY CO	42	13	12	17	47	57	38
19	PRESTON NE	42	14	10	18	57	73	38
20	BLACKBURN R	42	13	11	18	64	77	37
21	NOTTS CO	42	12	12	18	56	74	36
22	SHEFFIELD W	42	7	9	26	28	64	23

Season 1920-21

Football League Division 1

DATE	OPPONENTS	SCORE	GOALSCORERS	ATTENDANCE
Aug 28	Tottenham Hotspur	W 2-1	Hawksworth, Dawson	47,000
Aug 30	Oldham Athletic	L 0-1		23,000
Sep 4	TOTTENHAM HOTSPUR	D 1-1	Hawksworth	31,605
Sep 11	SUNDERLAND	W 2-0	Hawksworth, Holland	32,685
Sep 18	Sunderland	L 0-2		35,000
Sep 20	OLDHAM ATHLETIC	W 5-1	Holland 2, Dawson, Hodkinson, Hawksworth	30,000
Sep 25	EVERTON	D 0-0		30,000
Oct 2	Everton	L 1-2	Dawson	40,000
Oct 9	WEST BROMWICH ALBION	W 5-1	Dawson, Rodgers 2, Hawksworth 2	15,300
Oct 16	West Bromwich Albion	D 1-1	Dawson	35,025
Oct 23	MANCHESTER CITY	L 0-2		30,000
Oct 30	Manchester City	D 0-0		35,000
Nov 6	ARSENAL	D 2-2	Hawksworth, Dawson	20,000
Nov 13	Arsenal	L 0-2		40,000
Nov 20	BOLTON WANDERERS	D 2-2	Thorpe, Rollo (pen)	40,000
Nov 27	Bolton Wanderers	L 1-2	Holland	40,000
Dec 4	DERBY COUNTY	W 2-0	McDonald 2	25,000
Dec 11	Derby County	W 1-0	McDonald	14,000
Dec 18	MIDDLESBROUGH	W 3-2	Dawson 2, Rollo (pen)	15,000
Dec 25	PRESTON NORTH END	D 2-2	Dawson, Hawksworth	40,000
Dec 27	Preston North End	L 2-4	Dawson 2 (1 pen)	34,097
Jan 1	Middlesbrough	D 1-1	Hawksworth	30,000
Jan 15	Burnley	L 1-4	Sandham	41,534
Jan 22	BURNLEY	L 1-3	Hodkinson	43,000
Feb 5	Huddersfield Town	D 0-0		22,000
Feb 10	HUDDERSFIELD TOWN	L 1-2	Dawson	25,000
Feb 12	Sheffield United	D 1-1	Hawksworth	20,000
Feb 19	SHEFFIELD UNITED	D 1-1	Reilly	25,000
Feb 26	Bradford	D 1-1	Ralphs	16,000
Mar 5	BRADFORD	W 1-0	Robinson P.	25,000
Mar 12	Newcastle United	W 2-1	Hawksworth, Dawson	40,000
Mar 19	NEWCASTLE UNITED	D 3-3	Dawson 2, Hawksworth	25,000
Mar 25	BRADFORD CITY	L 2-3	Ralphs, Robinson P.	35,000
Mar 26	LIVERPOOL	D 1-1	Dawson	32,000
Mar 29	Bradford City	W 4-3	Dawson, Holland, Hawksworth 2	28,000
Apr 2	Liverpool	L 0-2		35,000
Apr 9	ASTON VILLA	L 0-1		20,000
Apr 16	Aston Villa	L 0-3		20,000
Apr 23	MANCHESTER UNITED	W 2-0	Healless 2 (1 pen)	18,000
Apr 30	Manchester United	W 1-0	Holland	20,000
May 2	CHELSEA	D 0-0		8,000
May 7	Chelsea	W 2-1	Reilly, McDonald	20,000

FA Cup

Jan 8	FULHAM	(Rd1) D 1-1	Dawson	45,000
Jan 13	Fulham	(R) L 0-1		23,219

League & Cup Appearances

PLAYER	LEAGUE	CUP COMPETITION FA CUP	TOTAL
Bibby, J.	8		8
Dawson, P.H.	33	2	35
Donnelly, J.	8	2	10
Duckworth, F.	25	2	27
Hawksworth, E.	37	2	39
Healless, H.	11		11
Heaton, T.	29	2	31
Hodkinson, J.	39	2	41
Holland, P.B.	18	1	19
Kerr, J.	1		1
McCall, W.	7		7
McDonald, J.	16	2	18
McKinnell, J.T.B.	10	1	11
Ralphs, B.	16		16
Reilly, F.	38	2	40
Robinson, A.	1		1
Robinson, P.	18		18
Rodgers, W.N.	6		6
Rollo, D.	31		31
Sandham, W.	4		4
Sewell, W.R.	41	2	43
Thorpe, L.	42	2	44
Watson, J.W.	11		11
Wylie, T.	12		12

Goalscorers

PLAYER	LEAGUE	CUP COMPETITION FA CUP	TOTAL
Dawson, P.H.	17	1	18
Hawksworth, E.	14		14
Holland, P.B.	6		6
McDonald, J.	4		4
Healless, H.	2		2
Hodkinson, J.	2		2
Ralphs, B.	2		2
Reilly, F.	2		2
Robinson, P.	2		2
Rodgers, W.N.	2		2
Rollo, D.	2		2
Sandham, W.	1		1
Thorpe, L.	1		1

Fact File

The Darwen end of the ground suffered damage on 18 January 1921, when a gale struck Ewood Park.

SECRETARY: Robert Middleton

TOP SCORER: Percy Dawson

BIGGEST WIN: 5-1, 20 September 1920, v Oldham Athletic, Division 1; 9 October 1920, v West Bromwich Albion, Division 1

HIGHEST ATTENDANCE: 47,000, 28 August 1920, v Tottenham Hotspur, Division 1

MAJOR TRANSFERS IN: Jimmy McKinnell and Tom Wylie from Queen of the South

Final Division 1 Table

		P	W	D	L	F	A	Pts
1	BURNLEY	42	23	13	6	79	36	59
2	MANCHESTER C	42	24	6	12	70	50	54
3	BOLTON W	42	19	14	9	77	53	52
4	LIVERPOOL	42	18	15	9	63	35	51
5	NEWCASTLE U	42	20	10	12	66	45	50
6	TOTTENHAM H	42	19	9	14	70	48	47
7	EVERTON	42	17	13	12	66	55	47
8	MIDDLESBROUGH	42	17	12	13	53	53	46
9	THE ARSENAL	42	15	14	13	59	63	44
10	ASTON VILLA	42	18	7	17	63	70	43
11	BLACKBURN R	42	13	15	14	57	59	41
12	SUNDERLAND	42	14	13	15	57	60	41
13	MANCHESTER U	42	15	10	17	64	68	40
14	WBA	42	13	14	15	54	58	40
15	BRADFORD C	42	12	15	15	61	63	39
16	PRESTON NE	42	15	9	18	61	65	39
17	HUDDERSFIELD T	42	15	9	18	42	49	39
18	CHELSEA	42	13	13	16	48	58	39
19	OLDHAM ATH	42	9	15	18	49	86	33
20	SHEFFIELD U	42	6	18	18	42	68	30
21	DERBY CO	42	5	16	21	32	58	26
22	BRADFORD PA	42	8	8	26	43	76	24

The Essential History of Blackburn Rovers

Football League Division 1

DATE	OPPONENTS	SCORE	GOALSCORERS	ATTENDANCE
Aug 27	CHELSEA	D 1-1	Reilly	15,000
Aug 29	Bradford City	D 1-1	McDonald	18,000
Sep 3	Chelsea	L 0-1		35,000
Sep 10	West Bromwich Albion	W 2-0	Ralphs, McDonald	20,000
Sep 12	Aston Villa	D 1-1	Holland	25,000
Sep 17	WEST BROMWICH ALBION	L 2-3	Heaton, Holland	30,000
Sep 19	BRADFORD CITY	W 3-1	Holland 2, McDonald	18,000
Sep 24	Manchester City	D 1-1	Ralphs	35,000
Oct 1	MANCHESTER CITY	W 3-1	Holland, Dawson, Hodkinson	25,000
Oct 8	Everton	L 0-2		30,000
Oct 15	EVERTON	D 2-2	Reilly 2	25,000
Oct 22	Sunderland	L 1-3	Ralphs	10,000
Oct 29	SUNDERLAND	L 1-2	Hawksworth	20,000
Nov 5	Huddersfield Town	L 0-3		8,000
Nov 12	HUDDERSFIELD TOWN	W 2-0	McKay, Hodkinson	24,000
Nov 19	BIRMINGHAM	D 1-1	Hodkinson	15,000
Nov 26	Birmingham	L 0-1		20,000
Dec 3	ARSENAL	L 0-1		25,000
Dec 10	Arsenal	D 1-1	McKay	35,000
Dec 17	BOLTON WANDERERS	L 1-2	Dawson	24,000
Dec 24	Bolton Wanderers	D 1-1	McKay	35,000
Dec 26	PRESTON NORTH END	W 3-0	McKay, Dawson, Aitken	52,656
Dec 27	Preston North End	L 1-2	Rodgers	33,000
Dec 31	Oldham Athletic	D 1-1	Grundy o.g.	15,385
Jan 2	CARDIFF CITY	L 1-3	Crawley	35,000
Jan 14	OLDHAM ATHLETIC	W 3-2	Rodgers, Dawson 2	20,000
Jan 21	SHEFFIELD UNITED	L 2-3	Holland, Hodkinson	18,000
Feb 4	BURNLEY	W 3-2	Rodgers 2, Dawson	20,000
Feb 11	Burnley	W 2-1	Dawson, Rodgers	35,000
Feb 25	Newcastle United	L 0-2		25,000
Feb 27	Sheffield United	W 1-0	Ralphs	14,000
Mar 4	LIVERPOOL	D 0-0		35,000
Mar 6	NEWCASTLE UNITED	L 0-2		20,000
Mar 11	Liverpool	L 0-2		35,000
Mar 18	Manchester United	W 1-0	Dawson	30,000
Mar 25	MANCHESTER UNITED	W 3-0	Rodgers, Dawson 2	15,000
Apr 1	ASTON VILLA	L 1-2	Dawson	15,000
Apr 15	Middlesbrough	W 1-0	Dawson	20,000
Apr 17	Cardiff City	W 3-1	Haworth, Reilly, McIntyre	30,000
Apr 22	MIDDLESBROUGH	D 2-2	Haworth, McIntyre	15,000
Apr 29	Tottenham Hotspur	L 1-2	Haworth	24,559
May 6	TOTTENHAM HOTSPUR	D 1-1	McKay	25,000

FA Cup

Jan 7	SOUTHPORT	(Rd1) D 1-1	Rodgers	24,000
Jan 12	Southport	(R) W 2-0	Rodgers 2	12,448
Jan 28	Swindon Town	(Rd2) W 1-0	Rollo (pen)	19,149
Feb 18	HUDDERSFIELD TOWN	(Rd3) D 1-1	Hodkinson	45,068
Feb 22	Huddersfield Town	(R) L 0-5		31,899

League & Cup Appearances

PLAYER	LEAGUE	CUP COMPETITION FA CUP	TOTAL
Aitken, F.M.	8		8
Crawley, F.	15		15
Dawson, P.H.	27	5	32
Forrest, J.H.	4	2	6
Hawksworth, E.	5		5
Haworth, R.	5		5
Healless, H.	20	2	22
Heaton, T.	23		23
Hodkinson, J.	36	5	41
Holland, P.B.	17		17
Longmuir, A.M.	17	5	22
McCall, W.	4		4
McDonald, J.	16		16
McIntyre, J.M.	16	3	19
McKay, J.R.	12		12
McKinnell, J.T.B.	7	1	8
Pool, A.	7	2	9
Ralphs, B.V.H.	24	1	25
Reilly, F.	34	4	38
Rodgers, W.N.	22	5	27
Rollo, D.	25	5	30
Sewell, W.R.	41	5	46
Simpson, W.	4		4
Thorpe, L.	29	5	34
Walmsley, R.H.	3		3
Wrigley, T.	1		1
Wylie, T.	40	5	45

Goalscorers

PLAYER	LEAGUE	CUP COMPETITION FA CUP	TOTAL
Dawson, P.H.	12		12
Rodgers, W.N.	6	3	9
Holland, P.B.	6		6
McKay, J.R.	5		5
Hodkinson, J.	4	1	5
Ralphs, B.V.H.	4		4
Reilly, F.	4		4
Haworth, R.	3		3
McDonald, J.	3		3
McIntyre, J.M.	2		2
Aitken, F.M.	1		1
Crawley, F.	1		1
Hawksworth, E.	1		1
Heaton, T.	1		1
Rollo, D.		1	1
Opps' o.gs.	1		1

Fact File

Jack Carr became the first manager of Blackburn Rovers when he moved to Ewood Park from the backroom staff at Newcastle United in February 1922.

MANAGER: Jack Carr

TOP SCORER: Percy Dawson

BIGGEST WIN: 3-0, 26 December 1921, v Preston North End, Division 1; 25 March 1922, v Manchester United, Division 1

HIGHEST ATTENDANCE: 52,656, 26 December 1921, v Preston North End, Division 1

MAJOR TRANSFERS IN: Fergie Aitken from Bury, John McIntyre from Sheffield Wednesday, Jock McKay from Celtic

Final Division 1 Table

		P	W	D	L	F	A	Pts
1	LIVERPOOL	42	22	13	7	63	36	57
2	TOTTENHAM H	42	21	9	12	65	39	51
3	BURNLEY	42	22	5	15	72	54	49
4	CARDIFF C	42	19	10	13	61	53	48
5	ASTON VILLA	42	22	3	17	74	55	47
6	BOLTON W	42	20	7	15	68	59	47
7	NEWCASTLE U	42	18	10	14	59	45	46
8	MIDDLESBROUGH	42	16	14	12	79	69	46
9	CHELSEA	42	17	12	13	40	43	46
10	MANCHESTER C	42	18	9	15	65	70	45
11	SHEFFIELD U	42	15	10	17	59	54	40
12	SUNDERLAND	42	16	8	18	60	62	40
13	WBA	42	15	10	17	51	63	40
14	HUDDERSFIELD T	42	15	9	18	53	54	39
15	BLACKBURN R	42	13	12	17	54	57	38
16	PRESTON NE	42	13	12	17	42	65	38
17	THE ARSENAL	42	15	7	20	47	56	37
18	BIRMINGHAM	42	15	7	20	48	60	37
19	OLDHAM ATH	42	13	11	18	38	50	37
20	EVERTON	42	12	12	18	57	55	36
21	BRADFORD C	42	11	10	21	48	72	32
22	MANCHESTER U	42	8	12	22	41	73	28

Season 1922-23

Football League Division 1

DATE	OPPONENTS	SCORE	GOALSCORERS	ATTENDANCE
Aug 26	Aston Villa	L 0-2		18,000
Sep 2	ASTON VILLA	W 4-2	Hodkinson, Moss o.g., McKay, Rollo (pen)	25,000
Sep 4	Sheffield United	D 1-1	Dawson	10,000
Sep 9	Everton	L 0-2		35,000
Sep 16	EVERTON	W 5-1	Healless, McIntyre 4	15,000
Sep 18	SHEFFIELD UNITED	W 1-0	McKay	20,000
Sep 23	SUNDERLAND	D 0-0		20,000
Sep 30	Sunderland	L 3-4	Bond (pen), Haworth, McIntyre	25,000
Oct 7	BIRMINGHAM	D 1-1	Haworth	25,000
Oct 14	Birmingham	D 1-1	Haworth	28,000
Oct 21	Burnley	L 1-3	McIntyre	30,000
Oct 28	BURNLEY	W 2-1	Dawson, Bond	23,000
Nov 4	Huddersfield Town	W 2-0	McIntyre, McKay	16,000
Nov 11	HUDDERSFIELD TOWN	D 0-0		30,000
Nov 18	Stoke	D 1-1	Dawson	30,000
Dec 2	MANCHESTER CITY	D 0-0		20,000
Dec 9	Manchester City	L 1-2	Haworth	26,000
Dec 16	BOLTON WANDERERS	W 1-0	McKay	20,000
Dec 23	Bolton Wanderers	L 0-3		20,000
Dec 25	PRESTON NORTH END	D 1-1	McKay	30,000
Dec 26	Preston North End	L 0-1		28,159
Dec 30	WEST BROMWICH ALBION	W 5-1	McKay 2, Dawson 2, Hodkinson	7,000
Jan 1	ARSENAL	L 0-5		20,000
Jan 6	West Bromwich Albion	L 0-3		17,000
Jan 20	CARDIFF CITY	W 3-1	Hawksworth, Reilly, Hodkinson	28,000
Jan 22	STOKE	L 1-5	McKay	12,000
Jan 27	Cardiff City	L 0-5		22,000
Feb 10	TOTTENHAM HOTSPUR	W 1-0	McKay	6,000
Feb 14	Tottenham Hotspur	L 0-2		10,000
Feb 17	Liverpool	L 0-3		25,000
Mar 3	Newcastle United	L 1-5	Longmuir	30,000
Mar 10	NEWCASTLE UNITED	D 1-1	Crisp	15,000
Mar 12	LIVERPOOL	W 1-0	Crisp	30,000
Mar 17	NOTTINGHAM FOREST	W 2-0	Longmuir, Crisp	20,000
Mar 24	Nottingham Forest	L 0-1		12,000
Mar 31	OLDHAM ATHLETIC	W 1-0	McIntyre	10,000
Apr 2	Arsenal	D 1-1	McIntyre	32,000
Apr 7	Oldham Athletic	L 0-1		9,000
Apr 14	MIDDLESBROUGH	W 2-0	McIntyre, McKay	15,000
Apr 21	Middlesbrough	W 2-1	Rollo (pen), McKay	12,000
Apr 28	CHELSEA	D 0-0		10,000
May 5	Chelsea	D 1-1	McKay	12,000

FA Cup

Jan 13	Aston Villa	(Rd1)	W 1-0	Bond (pen)	47,000
Feb 3	South Shields	(Rd2)	D 0-0		18,750
Feb 8	SOUTH SHIELDS	(R)	L 0-1		15,358

League & Cup Appearances

PLAYER	LEAGUE	CUP COMPETITION FA CUP	TOTAL
Bond, R.	24	2	26
Byers, J.E.	2		2
Campbell, A.F.	1		1
Crawley, F.	9	2	11
Crisp, J.	9		9
Dawson, P.H.	21	2	23
Davis, E.	22	1	23
Dixon, E.S.	11		11
Forrest, J.H.	1		1
Hardy, J.H.	1		1
Hawksworth, E.	6		6
Haworth, R.	18		18
Healless, H.	39	3	42
Heaton, T.	1		1
Hodkinson, J.	32	3	35
Holland, P.B.	9	2	11
Longmuir, A.M.	7		7
McIntyre, J.M.	31	3	34
McKinnell, J.T.B.	41	3	44
McKay, J.R.	38	3	41
Malcolm, W.	1		1
Pool, A.	6		6
Reilly, F.	29	3	32
Ritchie, G.T.	2		2
Rodgers, W.N.	4		4
Rollo, D.	29	1	30
Sewell, W.R.	20	2	22
Walmsley, R.H.	4		4
Watson, J.W.	1		1
Williamson, T.R.	4		4
Wylie, T.	39	3	42

Goalscorers

PLAYER	LEAGUE	CUP COMPETITION FA CUP	TOTAL
McKay, J.R.	12		12
McIntyre, J.M.	10		10
Dawson, P.H.	5		5
Haworth, R.	4		4
Crisp, J.	3		3
Hodkinson, J.	3		3
Bond, R.	2	1	3
Longmuir, A.M.	2		2
Rollo, D.	2		2
Hawksworth, E.	1		1
Healless, H.	1		1
Reilly, F.	1		1
Opps' o.gs.	1		1

Fact File

John McIntyre scored four goals in five minutes against Everton at Ewood Park in September 1922.

MANAGER: Jack Carr

TOP SCORER: Jock McKay

BIGGEST WIN: 5-1, 16 September 1922, v Everton, Division 1; 30 December 1922, v West Bromwich Albion, Division 1

HIGHEST ATTENDANCE: 47,000, 13 January 1923, v Aston Villa, FA Cup Round 1

MAJOR TRANSFERS IN: Jack Crisp from West Bromwich Albion, Jack Byers from Huddersfield Town

MAJOR TRANSFERS OUT: Levy Thorpe to Lincoln City

Final Division 1 Table

		P	W	D	L	F	A	Pts
1	LIVERPOOL	42	26	8	8	70	31	60
2	SUNDERLAND	42	22	10	10	72	54	54
3	HUDDERSFIELD T	42	21	11	10	60	32	53
4	NEWCASTLE U	42	18	12	12	45	37	48
5	EVERTON	42	20	7	15	63	59	47
6	ASTON VILLA	42	18	10	14	64	51	46
7	WBA	42	17	11	14	58	49	45
8	MANCHESTER C	42	17	11	14	50	49	45
9	CARDIFF C	42	18	7	17	73	59	43
10	SHEFFIELD U	42	16	10	16	68	64	42
11	PRESTON NE	42	16	10	16	61	62	42
12	TOTTENHAM H	42	17	7	18	50	50	41
13	BOLTON W	42	14	12	16	50	58	40
14	BLACKBURN R	42	14	12	16	47	62	40
15	BURNLEY	42	16	6	20	58	59	38
16	PRESTON NE	42	13	11	18	60	64	37
17	BIRMINGHAM	42	13	11	18	41	57	37
18	MIDDLESBROUGH	42	13	10	19	57	63	36
19	CHELSEA	42	9	18	15	45	53	36
20	NOTTINGHAM F	42	13	8	21	41	70	34
21	STOKE	42	10	10	22	47	67	30
22	OLDHAM ATH	42	10	10	22	35	65	30

The Essential History of Blackburn Rovers

Football League Division 1

DATE	OPPONENTS	SCORE	GOALSCORERS	ATTENDANCE
Aug 25	CHELSEA	W 3-0	Crisp, Harper, McKay	12,000
Aug 29	Newcastle United	L 1-2	Byers	11,000
Sep 1	Chelsea	L 0-2		40,000
Sep 8	Everton	D 0-0		35,000
Sep 15	EVERTON	W 2-0	McIntyre, Harper	28,000
Sep 17	NEWCASTLE UNITED	W 2-1	McIntyre 2	15,000
Sep 22	West Bromwich Albion	D 3-3	Williamson, Harper 2	20,000
Sep 29	WEST BROMWICH ALBION	W 4-0	Rollo (pen), Byers, McKay (pen), Harper	20,000
Oct 6	Birmingham	D 1-1	McIntyre	19,000
Oct 13	BIRMINGHAM	W 4-1	Holland, McIntyre 2, Harper	20,000
Oct 20	MANCHESTER CITY	L 0-1		25,000
Oct 27	Manchester City	L 1-3	Harper	30,000
Nov 3	BURNLEY	D 1-1	McKay	30,000
Nov 10	Burnley	W 2-1	Harper, McIntyre	30,000
Nov 17	Sunderland	L 1-5	Harper	20,000
Nov 24	SUNDERLAND	W 3-2	Crisp, McKay 2 (1 pen)	15,000
Dec 1	Arsenal	D 2-2	McKay (pen), Harper	20,000
Dec 8	ARSENAL	W 2-0	Harper, Crisp	20,000
Dec 15	Tottenham Hotspur	L 1-2	Crisp	22,000
Dec 22	TOTTENHAM HOTSPUR	L 0-1		15,000
Dec 25	PRESTON NORTH END	W 2-0	Hamilton o.g., McKay	35,000
Dec 26	Preston North End	W 1-0	McIntyre	36,465
Dec 29	HUDDERSFIELD TOWN	W 1-0	Harper	18,000
Jan 1	NOTTS COUNTY	W 4-1	McIntyre 2, McKay 2 (1 pen)	18,000
Jan 5	Huddersfield Town	L 0-1		16,300
Jan 19	WEST HAM UNITED	D 0-0		5,000
Jan 26	West Ham United	W 1-0	Roscamp	25,000
Feb 2	MIDDLESBROUGH	W 2-0	Crisp, McKay	15,000
Feb 9	Cardiff City	L 0-2		20,000
Feb 16	SHEFFIELD UNITED	D 1-1	Harper	17,000
Feb 23	Sheffield United	L 0-4		15,000
Mar 1	ASTON VILLA	W 3-1	Harper 2, Hawksworth	15,000
Mar 8	Middlesbrough	L 0-2		14,000
Mar 15	Liverpool	D 0-0		30,000
Mar 20	CARDIFF CITY	W 2-1	McKay, Harper	10,000
Mar 22	LIVERPOOL	D 0-0		17,000
Mar 29	Nottingham Forest	D 0-0		8,000
Apr 2	Aston Villa	L 0-1		20,000
Apr 5	NOTTINGHAM FOREST	D 1-1	Harper	15,000
Apr 12	BOLTON WANDERERS	W 3-1	Finney o.g., McKay, Harper	12,000
Apr 18	Notts County	L 0-3		16,000
Apr 19	Bolton Wanderers	L 0-3		16,000

FA Cup

Jan 12	Corinthians*	(Rd1) L 0-1		18,912

*Played at Crystal Palace.

League & Cup Appearances

PLAYER	LEAGUE	CUP COMPETITION FA CUP	TOTAL
Bateson, E.	2		2
Byers, J.E.	25	1	26
Campbell, A.F.	12		12
Crisp, J.	34	1	35
Davis, E.	2		2
Dixon, E.S.	14		14
Fairbrother, R.	1		1
Forrest, J.H.	2		2
Harper, E.C.	42	1	43
Hawksworth, E.	7		7
Haworth, R.	2		2
Healless, H.	36	1	37
Holland, P.B.	9		9
Hulme, J.H.A.	11		11
McIntyre, J.M.	40	1	41
McKay, J.R.	33	1	34
McKinnell, J.T.B.	27	1	28
Malcolm, W.	1		1
Rollo, D.	40	1	41
Roscamp, J.	25	1	26
Sewell, W.R.	40	1	41
Williamson, T.R.	15		15
Wylie, T.	42	1	43

Goalscorers

PLAYER	LEAGUE	CUP COMPETITION FA CUP	TOTAL
Harper, E.C.	18		18
McKay, J.R.	12		12
McIntyre, J.M.	10		10
Crisp, J.	5		5
Byers, J.E.	2		2
Hawksworth, E.	1		1
Holland, P.B.	1		1
Rollo, D.	1		1
Roscamp, J.	1		1
Williamson, T.R.	1		1
Opps' o.g.s	2		2

Fact File

Blackburn became victims of a sensational FA Cup upset when the amateurs of Corinthians snatched a 1-0 win at Crystal Palace in the first round.

MANAGER: Jack Carr

TOP SCORER: Ted Harper

BIGGEST WIN: 4-0, 29 September 1923, v West Bromwich Albion, Division 1

HIGHEST ATTENDANCE: 40,000, 1 September 1923, v Chelsea, Division 1

MAJOR TRANSFERS IN: Ted Harper from Sheppey United, Joe Hulme from York City

MAJOR TRANSFERS OUT: Jack Byers to West Bromwich Albion

Final Division 1 Table

		P	W	D	L	F	A	Pts
1	HUDDERSFIELD T	42	23	11	8	60	33	57
2	CARDIFF C	42	22	13	7	61	34	57
3	SUNDERLAND	42	22	9	11	71	54	53
4	BOLTON W	42	18	14	10	68	34	50
5	SHEFFIELD U	42	19	12	11	69	49	50
6	ASTON VILLA	42	18	13	11	52	37	49
7	EVERTON	42	18	13	11	62	53	49
8	BLACKBURN R	42	17	11	14	54	50	45
9	NEWCASTLE U	42	17	10	15	60	54	44
10	NOTTS CO	42	14	14	14	44	49	42
11	MANCHESTER C	42	15	12	15	54	71	42
12	LIVERPOOL	42	15	11	16	49	48	41
13	WEST HAM U	42	13	15	14	40	43	41
14	BIRMINGHAM	42	13	13	16	41	49	39
15	TOTTENHAM H	42	12	14	16	50	56	38
16	WBA	42	12	14	16	51	62	38
17	BURNLEY	42	12	12	18	55	60	36
18	PRESTON NE	42	12	10	20	52	67	34
19	THE ARSENAL	42	12	9	21	40	63	33
20	NOTTINGHAM F	42	10	12	20	42	64	32
21	CHELSEA	42	9	14	19	31	53	32
22	MIDDLESBROUGH	42	7	8	27	37	60	22

Season 1924-25

Football League Division 1

DATE	OPPONENTS	SCORE	GOALSCORERS	ATTENDANCE
Aug 30	Sheffield United	W 3-2	McIntyre, Harper, Hulme	20,000
Sep 1	NEWCASTLE UNITED	D 1-1	McKay	20,000
Sep 6	WEST HAM UNITED	L 0-1		18,000
Sep 10	Newcastle United	L 0-4		30,000
Sep 13	Burnley	W 5-3	McKay, McIntyre 3, Hulme	14,000
Sep 15	LIVERPOOL	W 3-1	McIntyre 2, Harper	20,000
Sep 20	Huddersfield Town	D 0-0		18,000
Sep 27	ASTON VILLA	D 1-1	McKay	20,000
Oct 4	Arsenal	L 0-1		30,000
Oct 11	MANCHESTER CITY	W 3-1	McCleery, Healless, Holland	18,000
Oct 15	Liverpool	D 0-0		15,000
Oct 18	Bury	D 1-1	Holland	25,000
Oct 25	LEEDS UNITED	L 2-3	McKay 2 (1 pen)	15,000
Nov 1	Birmingham	D 1-1	McKay	10,000
Nov 8	WEST BROMWICH ALBION	W 1-0	McCleery	16,000
Nov 15	Tottenham Hotspur	L 0-5		25,000
Nov 22	BOLTON WANDERERS	L 0-2		14,000
Nov 29	Notts County	D 0-0		15,000
Dec 6	EVERTON	W 3-0	McKay, Crisp 2	11,000
Dec 13	Sunderland	L 0-1		7,000
Dec 20	CARDIFF CITY	W 3-1	McKay 2, Harper	20,000
Dec 25	PRESTON NORTH END	L 0-1		30,000
Dec 26	Preston North End	L 2-3	Crisp, Healless	32,032
Dec 27	SHEFFIELD UNITED	D 2-2	McKay (pen), McCleery	5,000
Jan 3	West Ham United	L 0-2		16,000
Jan 17	BURNLEY	L 0-3		20,000
Jan 24	HUDDERSFIELD TOWN	L 2-3	McIntyre, Crisp	12,000
Feb 7	ARSENAL	W 1-0	Puddefoot	15,000
Feb 14	Manchester City	W 3-1	McIntyre 2, Puddefoot	35,000
Feb 28	Leeds United	D 1-1	Holland	10,000
Mar 14	West Bromwich Albion	D 1-1	McIntyre	17,000
Mar 19	BURY	L 0-1		10,000
Mar 21	TOTTENHAM HOTSPUR	D 1-1	McKay	16,000
Apr 2	BIRMINGHAM	W 7-1	Hulme 2 (1 pen), Puddefoot, Jones o.g., McCleery, Roscamp, McKay	3,000
Apr 4	NOTTS COUNTY	L 0-2		8,000
Apr 10	Nottingham Forest	W 2-0	McCleery, Puddefoot	11,000
Apr 11	Everton	L 0-1		25,000
Apr 13	NOTTINGHAM FOREST	D 0-0		8,000
Apr 15	Cardiff City	L 0-3		12,000
Apr 18	SUNDERLAND	D 1-1	Brayshaw	unknown
Apr 22	Bolton Wanderers	L 0-6		14,000
Apr 29	Aston Villa	L 3-4	McIntyre 2, Puddefoot	10,000

FA Cup

Jan 10	OLDHAM ATHLETIC	(Rd1) W 1-0	McKay	24,531
Jan 31	PORTSMOUTH	(Rd2) D 0-0		18,200
Feb 4	Portsmouth	(R) D 0-0		24,746
Feb 9	Portsmouth*	(2R) W 1-0	Crisp	22,837
Feb 21	Tottenham Hotspur	(Rd3) D 2-2	Hulme, McKay	54,521
Feb 26	TOTTENHAM HOTSPUR	(R) W 3-1	Campbell, Puddefoot, Hulme	48,170
Mar 7	BLACKPOOL	(Rd4) W 1-0	Puddefoot	60,011
Mar 28	Cardiff City†	(SF) L 1-3	McKay	20,100

*Played at Highbury Stadium, London. †Played at Meadow Lane, Nottingham.

Fact File

Syd Puddefoot made a goal-scoring debut for the club with the only goal in the 1-0 win over Arsenal at Ewood Park.

MANAGER: Jack Carr

TOP SCORER: Jock McKay

BIGGEST WIN: 7-1, 2 April 1925, v Birmingham, Division 1

HIGHEST ATTENDANCE: 60,011, 7 March 1925, v Blackpool, FA Cup Round 4

MAJOR TRANSFERS IN: Bob Roxburgh from Newcastle United, Syd Puddefoot from Falkirk, Jock Crawford from Alloa Athletic, Arthur Rigby from Bradford City

MAJOR TRANSFERS OUT: Ronald Haworth to Hull City

League & Cup Appearances

PLAYER	LEAGUE	CUP COMPETITION FA CUP	TOTAL
Brayshaw, W.	1		1
Campbell, A.F.	29	8	37
Crawford, J.C.	1		1
Crisp, J.	35	7	42
Dixon, E.S.	1		1
Harper, E.C.	14		14
Healless, H.	36	8	44
Holland, P.B.	10	2	12
Hope, P.	3		3
Hulme, J.H.A.	42	8	50
Low, D.	3		3
McCleery, W.	22	2	24
McIntyre, J.M.	30	8	38
McKay, J.R.	39	7	46
McKinnell, J.T.B.	20	7	27
Pool, A.	4		4
Puddefoot, S.C.	14	4	18
Rigby, A.	1		1
Rollo, D.	28	8	36
Roscamp, J.	35	3	38
Roxburgh, R.	13		13
Sewell, W.R.	41	8	49
Wylie, T.	40	8	48

Goalscorers

PLAYER	LEAGUE	CUP COMPETITION FA CUP	TOTAL
McKay, J.R.	12	3	15
McIntyre, J.M.	12		12
Puddefoot, S.C.	5	2	7
Hulme, J.H.A.	4	2	6
McCleery, W.	5		5
Crisp, J.	4	1	5
Harper, E.C.	3		3
Holland, P.B.	3		3
Healless, H.	2		2
Brayshaw, W.	1		1
Roscamp, J.	1		1
Campbell, A.F.		1	1
Opps' o.gs.	1		1

Final Division 1 Table

		P	W	D	L	F	A	Pts
1	HUDDERSFIELD T	42	21	16	5	69	28	58
2	WBA	42	23	10	9	58	34	56
3	BOLTON W	42	22	11	9	76	34	55
4	LIVERPOOL	42	20	10	12	63	55	50
5	BURY	42	17	15	10	54	51	49
6	NEWCASTLE U	42	16	16	10	61	42	48
7	SUNDERLAND	42	19	10	13	64	51	48
8	BIRMINGHAM	42	17	12	13	49	53	46
9	NOTTS CO	42	16	13	13	42	31	45
10	MANCHESTER C	42	17	9	16	76	68	43
11	CARDIFF C	42	16	11	15	56	51	43
12	TOTTENHAM H	42	15	12	15	52	43	42
13	WEST HAM U	42	15	12	15	62	60	42
14	SHEFFIELD U	42	13	13	16	55	63	39
15	ASTON VILLA	42	13	13	16	58	71	39
16	BLACKBURN R	42	11	13	18	53	66	35
17	EVERTON	42	12	11	19	40	60	35
18	LEEDS U	42	11	12	19	46	59	34
19	BURNLEY	42	11	12	19	46	75	34
20	THE ARSENAL	42	14	5	23	46	58	33
21	PRESTON NE	42	10	6	26	37	74	26
22	NOTTINGHAM F	42	6	12	24	29	65	24

Season 1925-26

Football League Division 1

DATE	OPPONENTS	SCORE	GOALSCORERS	ATTENDANCE
Aug 29	BURY	L 1-2	Campbell	29,600
Sep 2	Sunderland	L 2-6	Puddefoot 2	19,701
Sep 5	Birmingham	L 0-2		14,204
Sep 9	Newcastle United	W 7-1	Harper 5, Hulme, Rigby	21,582
Sep 12	WEST BROMWICH ALBION	L 1-2	Harper (pen)	24,199
Sep 19	Sheffield United	D 1-1	Harper	9,924
Sep 21	SUNDERLAND	W 3-0	Rigby, Harper 2	16,682
Sep 26	CARDIFF CITY	W 6-3	Rigby, Harper 3, Rigby, Hulme, McKay	18,042
Oct 3	Tottenham Hotspur	L 2-4	Harper, Rigby	35,645
Oct 10	MANCHESTER CITY	D 3-3	Puddefoot 2, Harper	25,935
Oct 12	NEWCASTLE UNITED	L 1-2	Rigby	12,094
Oct 17	Bolton Wanderers	D 2-2	Crisp, Puddefoot	19,468
Oct 24	NOTTS COUNTY	W 4-1	Rigby, Roscamp, Harper 2 (1 pen)	10,096
Oct 31	Burnley	W 3-1	Harper 3	26,181
Nov 7	LEEDS UNITED	D 2-2	Harper (pen), McIntyre	9,190
Nov 14	West Ham United	L 1-2	McIntyre	21,029
Nov 21	ARSENAL	L 2-3	Harper 2 (1 pen)	11,386
Nov 28	Manchester United	L 0-2		33,660
Dec 5	LIVERPOOL	D 1-1	Harper	13,278
Dec 12	Aston Villa	W 2-1	Puddefoot, Rigby	24,162
Dec 19	LEICESTER CITY	D 0-0		13,679
Dec 25	EVERTON	D 2-2	Harper 2	24,753
Dec 26	Everton	L 0-3		47,356
Jan 2	Bury	L 1-3	Harper	20,755
Jan 16	BIRMINGHAM	D 4-4	McIntrye, Crisp 2, Harper	14,742
Jan 23	West Bromwich Albion	D 1-1	Harper	11,061
Feb 6	Cardiff City	L 1-4	Dixon	16,484
Feb 11	HUDDERSFIELD TOWN	W 2-1	Crisp, Healless	21,434
Feb 13	TOTTENHAM HOTSPUR	W 4-2	Harper 2, Rigby, Crisp	21,584
Feb 20	Leicester City	L 1-2	Mitchell	23,612
Feb 27	BOLTON WANDERERS	W 3-0	Rigby, Puddefoot, Crisp	21,348
Mar 1	SHEFFIELD UNITED	W 3-1	Harper, Webster o.g., Rigby	10,949
Mar 6	Notts County	D 1-1	Mitchell	10,658
Mar 13	BURNLEY	W 6-3	Puddefoot 2, Rigby 3, Harper	29,991
Mar 17	Manchester City	W 1-0	Harper	18,793
Mar 20	Leeds United	L 1-2	Harper	22,419
Mar 27	WEST HAM UNITED	W 1-0	Mitchell	16,152
Apr 3	Arsenal	L 2-4	Harper 2	31,031
Apr 6	Huddersfield Town	L 1-3	Harper (pen)	34,821
Apr 10	MANCHESTER UNITED	W 7-0	Campbell, Harper 4, Mitchell, Puddefoot	15,870
Apr 17	Liverpool	D 2-2	Holland 2	14,699
Apr 24	ASTON VILLA	W 3-1	Harper 2 (1 pen), Mitchell	15,258

FA Cup

Jan 9	PRESTON NORTH END	(Rd3) D 1-1	Holland	41,088
Jan 14	Preston North End	(R) W 4-1	Dixon 2, Rigby 2	34,577
Jan 30	Arsenal	(Rd4) L 1-3	Harper	44,836

League & Cup Appearances

PLAYER	LEAGUE	CUP COMPETITION FA CUP	TOTAL
Brayshaw, W.	8		8
Campbell, A.F.	34	2	36
Crawford, J.C.	18	1	19
Crisp, J.	19	2	21
Dixon, E.S.	3	2	5
Forrest, J.H.	9		9
Harper, E.C.	37	3	40
Healless, H.	33	3	36
Holland, P.B.	3	1	4
Hope, P.	3	2	5
Hulme, J.H.A.	20	1	21
Jones, H.	17		17
McCleery, W.	1		1
McIntyre, J.M.	35	3	38
McKay, J.R.	11		11
McKinnell, J.T.B.	6		6
Mitchell, T.	15		15
Puddefoot, S.C.	37	1	38
Rigby, A.	42	3	45
Rollo, D.	37	1	38
Roscamp, J.	29	3	32
Roxburgh, R.	17	3	20
Sewell, W.R.	24	2	26
Smailes, M.	1		1
Walter, J.D.	2		2
Wylie, T.	1		1

Goalscorers

PLAYER	LEAGUE	CUP COMPETITION FA CUP	TOTAL
Harper, E.C.	43	1	44
Rigby, A.	13	2	15
Puddefoot, S.C.	10		10
Crisp, J.	6		6
Mitchell, T.	5		5
McIntyre, J.M.	3		3
Holland, P.B.	2	1	3
Dixon, E.S.	1	2	3
Campbell, A.F.	2		2
Hulme, J.H.A.	2		2
Healless, H.	1		1
McKay, J.R.	1		1
Roscamp, J.	1		1
Opps' o.gs.	1		1

Fact File

Ted Harper established a new club record with an amazing 43 goals in 37 league appearances.

MANAGER: Jack Carr

TOP SCORER: Ted Harper

BIGGEST WIN: 7-0, 10 April 1926, v Manchester United, Division 1

HIGHEST ATTENDANCE: 47,356, 26 December 1925, v Everton, Division 1

MAJOR TRANSFERS IN: Herbert Jones from Blackpool, Tom Mitchell from Stockport County

MAJOR TRANSFERS OUT: Joe Hulme to Arsenal

Final Division 1 Table

		P	W	D	L	F	A	Pts
1	HUDDERSFIELD T	42	23	11	8	92	60	57
2	THE ARSENAL	42	22	8	12	87	63	52
3	SUNDERLAND	42	21	6	15	96	80	48
4	BURY	42	20	7	15	85	77	47
5	SHEFFIELD U	42	19	8	15	102	82	46
6	ASTON VILLA	42	16	12	14	86	76	44
7	LIVERPOOL	42	14	16	12	70	63	44
8	BOLTON W	42	17	10	15	75	76	44
9	MANCHESTER U	42	19	6	17	66	73	44
10	NEWCASTLE U	42	16	10	16	84	75	42
11	EVERTON	42	12	18	12	72	70	42
12	BLACKBURN R	42	15	11	16	91	80	41
13	WBA	42	16	8	18	79	78	40
14	BIRMINGHAM	42	16	8	18	66	81	40
15	TOTTENHAM H	42	15	9	18	66	79	39
16	CARDIFF C	42	16	7	19	61	76	39
17	LEICESTER C	42	14	10	18	70	80	38
18	WEST HAM U	42	15	7	20	63	76	37
19	LEEDS U	42	14	8	20	64	76	36
20	BURNLEY	42	13	10	19	85	108	36
21	MANCHESTER C	42	12	11	19	89	100	35
22	NOTTS CO	42	13	7	22	54	74	33

Season 1926-27

Football League Division 1

DATE	OPPONENTS	SCORE	GOALSCORERS	ATTENDANCE
Aug 28	Birmingham	L 1-3	Puddefoot	24,091
Sep 4	TOTTENHAM HOTSPUR	W 1-0	Rigby	21,964
Sep 11	West Ham United	W 5-1	Rigby, Harper, Puddefoot 3	20,680
Sep 15	Bury	W 2-0	Harper (pen), Rigby	14,702
Sep 18	SHEFFIELD WEDNESDAY	D 2-2	Harper 2 (1 pen)	21,401
Sep 20	SUNDERLAND	L 0-2		24,464
Sep 25	Leicester City	L 0-4		26,087
Oct 2	EVERTON	D 3-3	Walter, Puddefoot 2	20,385
Oct 4	BURY	D 2-2	McKay (pen), Puddefoot	17,698
Oct 9	Leeds United	L 1-4	Robinson o.g.	16,304
Oct 16	BURNLEY	L 1-5	Puddefoot	42,000
Oct 23	Newcastle United	L 1-6	Harper	27,147
Oct 30	LIVERPOOL	W 2-1	Puddefoot, Harper	19,282
Nov 6	Arsenal	D 2-2	Harper 2	29,439
Nov 13	SHEFFIELD UNITED	L 3-4	Harper 2, Rigby	14,647
Nov 20	Derby County	W 5-4	Harper 2, Puddefoot, McKay, Shaw	12,795
Nov 27	MANCHESTER UNITED	W 2-1	Harper 2	17,280
Dec 4	Bolton Wanderers	L 1-5	Rigby	25,614
Dec 11	ASTON VILLA	L 0-2		15,701
Dec 18	Cardiff City	W 1-0	Rigby	12,254
Dec 25	HUDDERSFIELD TOWN	W 4-2	Mitchell, Harper 3	30,144
Dec 27	Huddersfield Town	L 0-5		34,758
Jan 1	Sunderland	W 5-2	Puddefoot, Harper 2 (1 pen), Mitchell, Holland	25,212
Jan 15	BIRMINGHAM	W 3-2	Harper, Puddefoot, Rigby	10,176
Jan 22	Tottenham Hotspur	D 1-1	Shaw	14,323
Jan 29	Aston Villa	L 3-4	Holland, Harper (pen), McIntyre	16,455
Feb 5	Sheffield Wednesday	W 3-0	Rigby, Harper, Holland	16,708
Feb 12	LEICESTER CITY	W 2-1	Harper 2	17,802
Feb 14	WEST HAM UNITED	W 4-1	Harper 4 (1 pen)	10,443
Feb 19	Everton	L 0-1		39,093
Feb 26	LEEDS UNITED	W 4-1	Harper 2, McKay 2	16,149
Mar 5	Burnley	L 1-3	Campbell	24,546
Mar 12	NEWCASTLE UNITED	L 1-2	Puddefoot	35,334
Mar 19	Liverpool	D 2-2	McLean, Harper	24,351
Apr 2	Sheffield United	L 3-5	Harper, Walter, Puddefoot	17,009
Apr 9	DERBY COUNTY	D 4-4	Harper 2, Mitchell 2	10,729
Apr 16	Manchester United	L 0-2		24,845
Apr 18	West Bromwich Albion	L 0-2		9,474
Apr 19	WEST BROMWICH ALBION	D 0-0		10,670
Apr 23	BOLTON WANDERERS	L 0-3		14,816
Apr 28	ARSENAL	L 1-2	Rankin	13,833
May 7	CARDIFF CITY	W 1-0	Harper	11,786

FA Cup

Jan 3	Southport	(Rd3) L 0-2		10,582

League & Cup Appearances

PLAYER	LEAGUE	CUP COMPETITION FA CUP	TOTAL
Campbell, A.F.	22		22
Cope, H.	14		14
Crawford, J.C.	23		23
Crisp, J.	1		1
Harper, E.C.	39	1	40
Healless, H.	35	1	36
Holland, P.B.	16	1	17
Hutton, J.	17		17
Jones, H.	39	1	40
Low, D.	10		10
McCulloch, S.S.	1		1
McIntyre, J.M.	21	1	22
McKay, J.R.	17		17
McLean, T.	10		10
Mitchell, T.	22	1	23
Puddefoot, S.C.	39	1	40
Rankin, W.	2		2
Rigby, A.	40	1	41
Rollo, D.	2		2
Roscamp, J.	25	1	26
Roxburgh, R.	26	1	27
Sewell, W.R.	5	1	6
Shaw, G.R.	4		4
Smailes, M.	3		3
Walter, J.D.	22		22
Whyte, J.	7		7

Goalscorers

PLAYER	LEAGUE	CUP COMPETITION FA CUP	TOTAL
Harper, E.C.	35		35
Puddefoot, S.C.	14		14
Rigby, A.	8		8
McKay, J.R.	4		4
Mitchell, T.	4		4
Holland, P.B.	3		3
Shaw, G.R.	2		2
Walter, J.D.	2		2
Campbell, A.F.	1		1
McIntyre, J.M.	1		1
McLean, T.	1		1
Rankin, W.	1		1
Opps' o.gs.	1		1

Final Division 1 Table

		P	W	D	L	F	A	Pts
1	NEWCASTLE U	42	25	6	11	96	58	56
2	HUDDERSFIELD T	42	17	17	8	76	60	51
3	SUNDERLAND	42	21	7	14	98	70	49
4	BOLTON W	42	19	10	13	84	62	48
5	BURNLEY	42	19	9	14	91	80	47
6	WEST HAM U	42	19	8	15	86	70	46
7	LEICESTER C	42	17	12	13	85	70	46
8	SHEFFIELD U	42	17	10	15	74	86	44
9	LIVERPOOL	42	18	7	17	69	61	43
10	ASTON VILLA	42	18	7	17	81	83	43
11	THE ARSENAL	42	17	9	16	77	86	43
12	DERBY CO	42	17	7	18	86	73	41
13	TOTTENHAM H	42	16	9	17	76	78	41
14	CARDIFF C	42	16	9	17	55	65	41
15	MANCHESTER U	42	13	14	15	52	64	40
16	SHEFFIELD W	42	15	9	18	75	92	39
17	BIRMINGHAM	42	17	4	21	64	73	38
18	BLACKBURN R	42	15	8	19	77	96	38
19	BURY	42	12	12	18	68	77	36
20	EVERTON	42	12	10	20	64	90	34
21	LEEDS U	42	11	8	23	69	88	30
22	WBA	42	11	8	23	65	86	30

Fact File

Jack Carr resigned as secretary-manager in December 1926. He was replaced by Bob Crompton who took the position of 'honorary manager' while retaining his place as a director of the club.

MANAGER: Jack Carr/Bob Crompton
TOP SCORER: Ted Harper
BIGGEST WIN: 5-1, 11 September 1926, v West Ham United, Division 1
HIGHEST ATTENDANCE: 42,000, 16 October 1926, v Burnley, Division 1
MAJOR TRANSFERS IN: Jock Hutton from Aberdeen, Tom McLean from St Johnstone, Bill Rankin from Dundee
MAJOR TRANSFERS OUT: Jack Crisp to Coventry City, Jock McKay to Middlesbrough

Season 1927-28

Football League Division 1

DATE	OPPONENTS	SCORE	GOALSCORERS	ATTENDANCE
Aug 27	BURNLEY	W 2-1	Puddefoot, McLean	32,441
Sep 3	Bolton Wanderers	L 1-3	Harper	25,711
Sep 5	CARDIFF CITY	D 0-0		14,343
Sep 10	SHEFFIELD WEDNESDAY	W 3-1	Whyte 2, McLean	17,877
Sep 12	Cardiff City	D 1-1	Harper	15,955
Sep 17	Middlesbrough	L 0-2		28,300
Sep 19	MANCHESTER UNITED	W 3-0	Puddefoot 2, Harper	18,243
Sep 24	BIRMINGHAM	D 4-4	Harper 3, Healless	15,331
Oct 1	Newcastle United	W 1-0	Harper	30,869
Oct 8	HUDDERSFIELD TOWN	D 1-1	Puddefoot	28,032
Oct 15	Tottenham Hotspur	D 1-1	Rigby	23,020
Oct 22	LEICESTER CITY	D 0-0		11,115
Oct 29	Liverpool	L 2-4	Puddefoot 2	28,489
Nov 5	ARSENAL	W 4-1	Mitchell 3, Rigby	9,656
Nov 12	Portsmouth	D 2-2	Mitchell, Puddefoot	18,078
Nov 19	WEST HAM UNITED	W 1-0	Mitchell	14,040
Nov 26	Aston Villa	L 0-2		27,281
Dec 3	SUNDERLAND	D 0-0		16,175
Dec 10	Derby County	L 0-6		10,612
Dec 17	SHEFFIELD UNITED	W 1-0	Healless	12,588
Dec 24	Bury	W 3-2	Roscamp, McLean, Mitchell	12,855
Dec 26	Manchester United	D 1-1	Rigby	38,131
Dec 31	Burnley	L 1-3	Mitchell	28,354
Jan 2	EVERTON	W 4-2	Puddefoot 2, Mitchell, Rigby	39,300
Jan 7	BOLTON WANDERERS	L 1-6	Mitchell	14,660
Jan 21	Sheffield Wednesday	L 1-4	Holland	36,094
Feb 4	Birmingham	L 1-2	Mitchell	21,425
Feb 11	NEWCASTLE UNITED	W 1-0	Mitchell	12,504
Feb 23	MIDDLESBROUGH	W 3-0	Puddefoot, Roscamp 2	12,855
Feb 25	TOTTENHAM HOTSPUR	W 2-1	Mitchell, Roscamp	20,890
Mar 10	LIVERPOOL	W 2-1	McLean, Roscamp	16,249
Mar 14	Huddersfield Town	L 1-3	Roscamp	10,890
Mar 17	Arsenal	L 2-3	Puddefoot, Rigby	33,446
Mar 31	West Ham United	L 3-4	Roscamp 2, Thornewell	17,917
Apr 6	Everton	L 1-4	Holland	48,521
Apr 7	ASTON VILLA	L 0-1		21,432
Apr 14	Sunderland	L 0-1		12,577
Apr 24	PORTSMOUTH	W 6-0	Rigby, Puddefoot 2, Campbell (pen), Roscamp 2	35,516
Apr 26	DERBY COUNTY	W 3-2	Campbell (pen), Rigby, Mitchell	21,438
Apr 28	Sheffield United	W 3-2	Roscamp, Mitchell 2	25,239
Apr 30	Leicester City	L 0-6		14,914
May 5	BURY	L 0-1		16,836

FA Cup

Jan 14	NEWCASTLE UNITED	(Rd1) W 4-1	Puddefoot, Mitchell 2, Thornewell	27,652
Jan 28	Exeter City	(Rd2) D 2-2	Roscamp, Rigby	17,300
Feb 2	EXETER CITY	(R) W 3-1*	Roscamp, Mitchell, Puddefoot	28,348
Feb 18	PORT VALE	(Rd3) W 2-1	Roscamp, Mitchell	43,700
Mar 3	MANCHESTER UNITED	(Rd4) W 2-0	Puddefoot 2	42,312
Mar 24	Arsenal†	(SF) W 1-0	Roscamp	25,563
Apr 21	Huddersfield Town‡	(F) W 3-1	Roscamp 2, McLean	92,041

*After extra-time. †Played at Filbert Street, Leicester. ‡Played at Wembley Stadium.

League & Cup Appearances

PLAYER	LEAGUE	CUP COMPETITION FA CUP	TOTAL
Campbell, A.F.	32	7	39
Cope, H.	2		2
Crawford, J.C.	40	7	47
Harper, E.C.	12		12
Healless, H.	38	7	45
Holland, P.B.	24	2	26
Hutton, J.	37	7	44
Jones, H.	35	4	39
McIntyre, J.M.	2		2
McLean, T.	33	5	38
Mitchell, T.	28	4	32
O'Dowd, J.P.	8		8
Puddefoot, S.C.	35	7	42
Rankin, W.	31	7	38
Rigby, A.	37	7	44
Roscamp, J.	20	6	26
Roxburgh, R.	12	3	15
Shaw, G.R.	1		1
Thornewell, G.	14	4	18
Walter, J.B.	3		3
Whyte, J.	18		18

Goalscorers

PLAYER	LEAGUE	CUP COMPETITION FA CUP	TOTAL
Mitchell, T.	15	4	19
Puddefoot, S.C.	13	4	17
Roscamp, J.	11	6	17
Rigby, A.	7	1	8
Harper, E.C.	7		7
McLean, T.	4	1	5
Campbell, A.F.	2		2
Healless, H.	2		2
Holland, P.B.	2		2
Whyte, J.	2		2
Thornewell, G.	1	1	2

Fact File

Robert Marshall died on 3 January 1928 from injuries received in a Central League game at Blackpool on Boxing Day. January also brought the death of John Forbes, a director and former FA Cup winner with the club.

Final Division 1 Table

		P	W	D	L	F	A	Pts
1	EVERTON	42	20	13	9	102	66	53
2	HUDDERSFIELD T	42	22	7	13	91	68	51
3	LEICESTER C	42	18	12	12	96	72	48
4	DERBY CO	42	17	10	15	96	83	44
5	BURY	42	20	4	18	80	80	44
6	CARDIFF C	42	17	10	15	70	80	44
7	BOLTON W	42	16	11	15	81	66	43
8	ASTON VILLA	42	17	9	16	78	73	43
9	NEWCASTLE U	42	15	13	14	79	81	43
10	ARSENAL	42	13	15	14	82	86	41
11	BIRMINGHAM	42	13	15	14	70	75	41
12	BLACKBURN R	42	16	9	17	66	78	41
13	SHEFFIELD U	42	15	10	17	79	86	40
14	SHEFFIELD W	42	13	13	16	81	78	39
15	SUNDERLAND	42	15	9	18	74	76	39
16	LIVERPOOL	42	13	13	16	84	87	39
17	WEST HAM U	42	14	11	17	81	88	39
18	MANCHESTER U	42	16	7	19	72	80	39
19	BURNLEY	42	16	7	19	82	98	39
20	PORTSMOUTH	42	16	7	19	66	90	39
21	TOTTENHAM H	42	15	8	19	74	86	38
22	MIDDLESBROUGH	42	11	15	16	81	88	37

HONORARY MANAGER: Bob Crompton

TOP SCORER: Tom Mitchell

BIGGEST WIN: 6-0, 24 April 1928, v Portsmouth, Division 1

HIGHEST ATTENDANCE: 92,041, 21 April 1928, v Huddersfield Town, FA Cup final

MAJOR TRANSFERS IN: George Thornewell from Derby County

MAJOR TRANSFERS OUT: Ted Harper to Sheffield Wednesday, John McIntyre to Blackpool, David Rollo to Port Vale

Season 1928-29

Football League Division 1

DATE	OPPONENTS	SCORE	GOALSCORERS	ATTENDANCE
Aug 25	Derby County	L 1-5	Rigby	19,435
Aug 29	Sunderland	L 1-3	Rigby	28,979
Sep 1	SHEFFIELD WEDNESDAY	W 4-1	Thornewell 2, Campbell, Roscamp	18,647
Sep 8	Bolton Wanderers	W 3-0	Roscamp 3	15,633
Sep 15	PORTSMOUTH	W 4-0	Thornewell, Rigby 2, Roscamp	17,891
Sep 17	SUNDERLAND	W 2-0	Roscamp, Rankin	20,270
Sep 22	Birmingham	L 0-4		23,047
Sep 24	NEWCASTLE UNITED	W 2-0	Hudspeth o.g., Roscamp	14,750
Sep 29	MANCHESTER CITY	D 2-2	Rigby 2	25,430
Oct 6	Huddersfield Town	W 2-0	Rigby 2	18,261
Oct 13	EVERTON	W 2-1	Rigby, Puddefoot	33,966
Oct 20	Burnley	D 2-2	McLean 2	35,694
Oct 27	WEST HAM UNITED	W 2-0	Roscamp, Puddefoot	18,496
Nov 3	Sheffield United	L 1-2	Roscamp	23,262
Nov 10	BURY	D 1-1	Bourton	11,431
Nov 17	Aston Villa	L 1-2	Bourton	31,212
Nov 24	LEICESTER CITY	D 1-1	Puddefoot	10,831
Dec 1	Manchester United	W 4-1	Bourton 4	19,587
Dec 8	LEEDS UNITED	L 0-1		17,333
Dec 15	Liverpool	D 1-1	McLean	21,364
Dec 22	CARDIFF CITY	W 2-0	Blackburn o.g., McLean	11,040
Dec 25	ARSENAL	W 5-2	Puddefoot 2, Bourton 2, Campbell (pen)	30,828
Dec 29	DERBY COUNTY	W 3-1	Puddefoot, Roscamp, Bourton	22,592
Jan 1	Newcastle United	W 2-0	Roscamp, Bourton	36,964
Jan 5	Sheffield Wednesday	L 0-1		28,136
Jan 19	BOLTON WANDERERS	L 1-3	Bourton	22,037
Feb 2	BIRMINGHAM	W 4-1	Mitchell, Roscamp 2, Bourton	13,387
Feb 9	Manchester City	W 2-1	Roscamp, Mitchell	33,801
Feb 23	Everton	L 2-5	Roscamp, McLean	29,006
Mar 9	West Ham United	D 3-3	Keating 3	24,379
Mar 13	Portsmouth	D 2-2	Roscamp, Puddefoot	11,973
Mar 16	SHEFFIELD UNITED	D 1-1	Healless	13,992
Mar 23	Bury	L 0-1		15,058
Mar 29	Arsenal	L 0-1		39,038
Mar 30	ASTON VILLA	L 2-5	Rigby, Healless	15,690
Apr 1	HUDDERSFIELD TOWN	D 1-1	Puddefoot	14,335
Apr 6	Leicester City	L 1-2	Rigby	19,328
Apr 13	MANCHESTER UNITED	L 0-3		8,193
Apr 20	Leeds United	W 1-0	Rigby	17,201
Apr 27	LIVERPOOL	W 2-1	Rigby, Keating	7,059
May 2	BURNLEY	D 1-1	Puddefoot	5,461
May 4	Cardiff City	D 1-1	Mitchell	5,738

FA Cup

Jan 12	BARNSLEY	(Rd3) W 1-0	Healless		31,697
Jan 26	DERBY COUNTY	(Rd4) D 1-1	Bourton		45,410
Jan 30	Derby County	(R) W 3-0	Roscamp, Bourton, McLean		28,551
Feb 16	BURY	(Rd5) W 1-0	Bourton		40,100
Mar 2	BOLTON WANDERERS	(Rd6) D 1-1	Hutton		62,522
Mar 6	Bolton Wanderers	(R) L 1-2	Campbell (pen)		65,295

Charity Shield

Oct 24	Everton†	L 1-2	Thornewell	4,000

†Played at Old Trafford, Manchester.

League & Cup Appearances

PLAYER	LEAGUE	CUP COMPETITION		TOTAL
		FA CUP	OTHER	
Baxter, T.T.	6		1	7
Bourton, C.F.T.	28	6		34
Campbell, A.F.	29	6		35
Cope, H.	2			2
Crawford, J.C.	40	6	1	47
Groves, A.	2			2
Healless, H.	35	6	1	42
Hutton, J.	14	6		20
Jones, H.	22		1	23
Keating, A.E.	16			16
McLean, T.	28	6	1	35
Mitchell, T.	8	4		12
O'Dowd, J.P.	22		1	23
Puddefoot, S.C.	40	6	1	47
Raitt, D.	4			4
Rankin, W.	33	6		39
Rigby, A.	33	1	1	35
Roscamp, J.	34	5	1	40
Roxburgh, R.	38	6	1	45
Thornewell, G.	27	2	1	30
Whyte, J.	1			1

Goalscorers

PLAYER	LEAGUE	CUP COMPETITION		TOTAL
		FA CUP	OTHER	
Roscamp, J.	16	1		17
Bourton, C.F.T.	12	3		15
Rigby, A.	13			13
Puddefoot, S.C.	9			9
McLean, T.	5	1		6
Keating, A.E.	4			4
Thornewell, G.	3		1	4
Mitchell, T.	3			3
Campbell, A.F.	2	1		3
Healless, H.	2	1		3
Rankin, W.	1			1
Hutton, J.		1		1
Opps' o.gs.	2			2

Fact File

The FA Cup-tie against Bolton Wanderers in the sixth round at Ewood Park produced match receipts of £4,722 13s 6d.

Final Division 1 Table

		P	W	D	L	F	A	Pts
1	SHEFFIELD W	42	21	10	11	86	62	52
2	LEICESTER C	42	21	9	12	96	67	51
3	ASTON VILLA	42	23	4	15	98	81	50
4	SUNDERLAND	42	20	7	15	93	75	47
5	LIVERPOOL	42	17	12	13	90	64	46
6	DERBY CO	42	18	10	14	86	71	46
7	BLACKBURN R	42	17	11	14	72	63	45
8	MANCHESTER C	42	18	9	15	95	86	45
9	ARSENAL	42	16	13	13	77	72	45
10	NEWCASTLE U	42	19	6	17	70	72	44
11	SHEFFIELD U	42	15	11	16	86	85	41
12	MANCHESTER U	42	14	13	15	66	76	41
13	LEEDS U	42	16	9	17	71	84	41
14	BOLTON W	42	14	12	16	73	80	40
15	BIRMINGHAM	42	15	10	17	68	77	40
16	HUDDERSFIELD T	42	14	11	17	70	61	39
17	WEST HAM U	42	15	9	18	86	96	39
18	EVERTON	42	17	4	21	63	75	38
19	BURNLEY	42	15	8	19	81	103	38
20	PORTSMOUTH	42	15	6	21	56	80	36
21	BURY	42	12	7	23	62	99	31
22	CARDIFF C	42	8	13	21	43	59	29

HONORARY MANAGER: Bob Crompton

TOP SCORER: Jack Roscamp

BIGGEST WIN: 4-0, 15 September 1928, v Portsmouth, Division 1

HIGHEST ATTENDANCE: 62,522, 2 March 1929, v Bolton Wanderers, FA Cup Round 6

MAJOR TRANSFERS IN: Albert Keating from Bristol City, David Raitt from Everton

MAJOR TRANSFERS OUT: Peter Holland to Watford

Season 1929-30

Football League Division 1

DATE	OPPONENTS	SCORE	GOALSCORERS	ATTENDANCE
Aug 31	WEST HAM UNITED	D 3-3	Earl o.g., McLean, Gilhespy	21,817
Sep 4	Newcastle United	L 1-5	Keating	36,263
Sep 7	Manchester United	L 0-1		23,262
Sep 14	GRIMSBY TOWN	W 4-1	Crompton, Groves 2, Turner	18,187
Sep 16	NEWCASTLE UNITED	W 4-2	Groves, Crompton, Bruton L. 2	19,163
Sep 21	Leicester City	D 1-1	Groves	22,793
Sep 28	BIRMINGHAM	W 7-5	Puddefoot 4, Groves 2, Rankin	18,942
Oct 5	Huddersfield Town	D 0-0		16,543
Oct 9	Liverpool	D 1-1	Bruton L.	15,434
Oct 12	SHEFFIELD UNITED	L 0-1		18,955
Oct 19	Bolton Wanderers	L 1-2	Puddefoot	25,756
Oct 26	EVERTON	W 3-1	Groves, Hutton (pen), Roscamp	18,249
Nov 2	Derby County	L 3-4	Roscamp, Hutton (pen), Crompton	12,161
Nov 9	BURNLEY	W 8-3	Groves 3, Roscamp 2, McLean 2, Imrie	22,647
Nov 16	Portsmouth	L 0-4		16,387
Nov 23	ARSENAL	D 1-1	Imrie (pen)	25,591
Nov 30	Aston Villa	L 0-3		25,910
Dec 7	LEEDS UNITED	W 2-1	Imrie (pen), Roscamp	13,504
Dec 14	Sheffield Wednesday	L 0-4		19,278
Dec 21	MANCHESTER CITY	L 1-3	Imrie (pen)	20,483
Dec 25	SUNDERLAND	W 5-3	Puddefoot, Bourton 2, McLean, Bruton J.	19,704
Dec 26	Sunderland	L 1-3	Puddefoot	25,109
Dec 28	West Ham United	W 3-2	Turner, Bourton 2	23,901
Jan 1	MIDDLESBROUGH	W 7-0	Crompton 2, Puddefoot 2, Bourton 2, McLean	24,370
Jan 4	MANCHESTER UNITED	W 5-4	Bourton, McLean, Cunliffe 2, Imrie (pen)	23,923
Jan 18	Grimsby Town	L 3-5	McLean, Cunliffe, Bourton	11,773
Jan 27	LEICESTER CITY	W 3-1	McLean, Cunliffe 2	10,444
Feb 1	Birmingham	W 2-1	Bourton, Imrie	18,521
Feb 8	HUDDERSFIELD TOWN	W 5-2	Cunliffe 3, McLean, Puddefoot	23,140
Feb 22	BOLTON WANDERERS	W 3-1	Cunliffe, Bourton 2	19,362
Mar 1	Everton	D 2-2	Bourton, Puddefoot	27,514
Mar 3	Sheffield United	W 7-5	Bourton 4, Bruton L., Puddefoot, Bruton J.	8,568
Mar 8	DERBY COUNTY	L 0-3		21,197
Mar 15	Burnley	L 2-3	McLean, Bourton	16,673
Mar 22	PORTSMOUTH	W 1-0	Bourton	12,876
Mar 29	Arsenal	L 0-4		40,459
Apr 5	ASTON VILLA	W 2-0	J. Bruton, Bruton L.	14,136
Apr 12	Leeds United	L 2-4	Roscamp, Bruton J.	15,451
Apr 19	SHEFFIELD WEDNESDAY	L 0-1		17,768
Apr 21	Middlesbrough	W 4-2	Cunliffe 2, Bourton, Hutton	18,146
Apr 26	Manchester City	D 1-1	Bourton	19,868
May 3	LIVERPOOL	W 1-0	Bourton	8,544

FA Cup

Jan 11	NORTHAMPTON TOWN	(Rd3) W 4-1	Cunliffe, Imrie (pen), McLean, Bruton J.	26,000
Jan 25	EVERTON	(Rd4) W 4-1	McLean, Bourton, Bruton J., Cunliffe	53,000
Feb 15	Aston Villa	(Rd5) L 1-4	Bourton	69,884

HONORARY MANAGER: Bob Crompton

TOP SCORER: Clarrie Bourton

BIGGEST WIN: 7-0, 1 January 1930, v Middlesbrough, Division 1

HIGHEST ATTENDANCE: 69,884, 15 February 1930, v Aston Villa, FA Cup Round 5

MAJOR TRANSFERS IN: Les Bruton and Thomas Turner from Raith Rovers, Jack Bruton from Burnley

MAJOR TRANSFERS OUT: Aussie Campbell to Huddersfield Town, Arthur Rigby to Everton, Peter O'Dowd to Burnley

League & Cup Appearances

PLAYER	LEAGUE	CUP COMPETITION FA CUP	TOTAL
Baxter, T.T.	19	3	22
Binns, C.H.	9		9
Bourton, C.F.T.	23	3	26
Bruton, J.	20	3	23
Bruton, L.H.R.	12		12
Campbell, A.F.	2		2
Cope, H.	7		7
Crawford, J.C.	26	3	29
Crompton, W.	16		16
Cunliffe, A.	18	3	21
Gilhespy, T.W.C.	5		5
Groves, A.	16		16
Heall018, H.	7		7
Hutton, J.	18		18
Imrie, W.N.	35	3	38
Jones, H.	39	3	42
Keating, A.E.	1		1
McLean, T.	26	3	29
Melville, J.	1		1
O'Dowd, J.P.	20		20
Puddefoot, S.C.	37	3	40
Rankin, W.	38	3	41
Rigby, A.	3		3
Roscamp, J.	33	3	36
Roxburgh, R.	8		8
Turner, T.S.	23		23

Goalscorers

PLAYER	LEAGUE	CUP COMPETITION FA CUP	TOTAL
Bourton, C.F.T.	21	2	23
Cunliffe, A.	11	2	13
Puddefoot, S.C.	12		12
McLean, T.	10	2	12
Groves, A.	10		10
Imrie, W.N.	6	1	7
Roscamp, J.	6		6
Bruton, J.	4	2	6
Bruton, L.H.R.	5		5
Crompton, W.	5		5
Hutton, J.	3		3
Turner, T.S.	2		2
Gilhespy, T.W.C.	1		1
Keating, A.E.	1		1
Rankin, W.	1		1
Opps' o.gs.	1		1

Fact File

Jack Bruton cost £6,500, a new club record, when he moved from Burnley to Blackburn Rovers.

Final Division 1 Table

		P	W	D	L	F	A	Pts
1	SHEFFIELD W	42	26	8	8	105	57	60
2	DERBY CO	42	21	8	13	90	82	50
3	MANCHESTER C	42	19	9	14	91	81	47
4	ASTON VILLA	42	21	5	16	92	83	47
5	LEEDS U	42	20	6	16	79	63	46
6	BLACKBURN R	42	19	7	16	99	93	45
7	WEST HAM U	42	19	5	18	86	79	43
8	LEICESTER C	42	17	9	16	86	90	43
9	SUNDERLAND	42	18	7	17	76	80	43
10	HUDDERSFIELD T	42	17	9	16	63	69	43
11	BIRMINGHAM	42	16	9	17	67	62	41
12	LIVERPOOL	42	16	9	17	63	79	41
13	PORTSMOUTH	42	15	10	17	66	62	40
14	ARSENAL	42	14	11	17	78	66	39
15	BOLTON W	42	15	9	18	74	74	39
16	MIDDLESBROUGH	42	16	6	20	82	84	38
17	MANCHESTER U	42	15	8	19	67	88	38
18	GRIMSBY T	42	15	7	20	73	89	37
19	NEWCASTLE U	42	15	7	20	71	92	37
20	SHEFFIELD U	42	15	6	21	91	96	36
21	BURNLEY	42	14	8	20	79	97	36
22	EVERTON	42	12	11	19	80	92	35

Season 1930-31

Football League Division 1

DATE	OPPONENTS	SCORE	GOALSCORERS	ATTENDANCE
Aug 30	Liverpool	L 1-2	Bruton J.	33,287
Sep 1	PORTSMOUTH	L 1-2	Puddefoot	13,447
Sep 6	BLACKPOOL	W 5-0	Watson o.g., Bourton, Groves, Cunliffe, Imrie	25,388
Sep 10	Arsenal	L 2-3	Bruton J., Puddefoot	20,863
Sep 13	Leeds United	L 2-4	Groves, Bourton	11,837
Sep 15	ARSENAL	D 2-2	Puddefoot, Cunliffe	25,572
Sep 20	SUNDERLAND	W 3-0	Bruton J., Groves, Imrie	18,081
Sep 27	Leicester City	L 1-3	Imrie (pen)	18,820
Oct 4	BIRMINGHAM	W 2-1	Bruton J., Imrie (pen)	14,728
Oct 11	Sheffield United	D 1-1	Bourton	22,801
Oct 18	West Ham United	L 3-4	Puddefoot 2, McLean	22,114
Oct 25	BOLTON WANDERERS	D 2-2	Bruton J., McLean	18,649
Nov 1	Aston Villa	L 2-5	Bruton L., McLean	29,032
Nov 8	CHELSEA	W 2-0	Bourton, Turner	21,008
Nov 15	Grimsby Town	L 0-2		9,715
Nov 22	HUDDERSFIELD TOWN	W 5-3	Bruton L. 3 (1 pen), Bruton J., Puddefoot	10,556
Nov 29	Newcastle United	W 3-2	Bruton L., Puddefoot, Bruton J.	20,271
Dec 6	MANCHESTER UNITED	W 4-1	Bruton L. 2 (1 pen), Puddefoot, Turner	10,802
Dec 13	Middlesbrough	L 1-4	Bruton J.	16,119
Dec 20	SHEFFIELD WEDNESDAY	W 5-2	Puddefoot 2, Bruton J. 2, Cunliffe	17,778
Dec 25	DERBY COUNTY	W 1-0	Bruton J.	29,734
Dec 26	Derby County	D 1-1	Bruton J.	17,305
Dec 27	LIVERPOOL	D 3-3	Puddefoot, Rankin, Bruton L. (pen)	20,494
Jan 1	MANCHESTER CITY	L 0-1		27,965
Jan 3	Blackpool	D 1-1	Bruton L.	16,294
Jan 17	LEEDS UNITED	W 3-1	Bruton L. (pen), Puddefoot, Cunliffe	11,975
Feb 4	Sunderland	L 2-8	Bruton L. 2 (1 pen)	10,635
Feb 7	Birmingham	L 1-4	McLean	23,642
Feb 19	SHEFFIELD UNITED	W 2-1	Bruton L. (pen), Bruton J.	7,687
Feb 21	WEST HAM UNITED	W 1-0	Puddefoot	9,680
Feb 28	Bolton Wanderers	D 1-1	Bruton L. (pen)	9,462
Mar 2	LEICESTER CITY	W 3-0	McLean, Cunliffe, Bruton L.	6,699
Mar 7	ASTON VILLA	L 0-2		11,222
Mar 14	Chelsea	L 2-3	Bruton L. 2	32,623
Mar 21	GRIMSBY TOWN	W 5-2	Puddefoot 2, Bruton J. 2, Cunliffe	8,890
Mar 28	Huddersfield Town	D 1-1	Cunliffe	8,144
Apr 3	Manchester City	L 0-3		24,392
Apr 4	NEWCASTLE UNITED	W 1-0	Bruton L.	12,381
Apr 11	Manchester United	W 1-0	McLean	6,414
Apr 18	MIDDLESBROUGH	L 4-5	McLean, Britton, Bruton J. 2	6,917
Apr 25	Sheffield Wednesday	W 3-1	Bruton J. 2, Britton	5,102
May 2	Portsmouth	L 0-3		12,984

FA Cup

Jan 10	WALSALL	(Rd3)	D 1-1	Bruton L.	18,819
Jan 15	Walsall	(R)	W 3-0	Puddefoot, Cunliffe, Bruton L.	18,170
Jan 24	BRISTOL ROVERS	(Rd4)	W 5-1	Puddefoot, Bruton J., Bruton L. 3	25,070
Feb 14	Chelsea	(Rd5)	L 0-3		61,170

Fact File

Boardroom and dressing room intrigue rocked Ewood Park and resulted in Bob Crompton stepping down from the position of honorary manager in February 1931.

HONORARY MANAGER/MANAGER: Bob Crompton/Arthur Barritt

TOP SCORER: Les Bruton

BIGGEST WIN: 5-0, 6 September 1930, v Blackpool, Division 1

HIGHEST ATTENDANCE: 61,170, 14 February 1931, v Chelsea, FA Cup Round 5

MAJOR TRANSFERS OUT: Harold Cope to Swindon Town, Albert Keating to Cardiff City

League & Cup Appearances

PLAYER	LEAGUE	CUP COMPETITION FA CUP	TOTAL
Baxter, T.T.	6		6
Binns, C.H.	42	4	46
Bourton, C.F.T.	12		12
Britton, F.	6		6
Bruton, J.	35	3	38
Bruton, L.H.R.	24	4	28
Carver, J.	7		7
Crompton, W.	4		4
Cunliffe, A.	34	4	38
Gorman, J.	15		15
Groves, A.	9		9
Healless, H.	30	3	33
Hutton, J.	21	4	25
Imrie, W.N.	39	3	42
Jones, H.	38	4	42
McLean, T.	33	4	37
Melville, J.	4		4
Puddefoot, S.C.	41	4	45
Rankin, W.	30	2	32
Richards, J.	1		1
Roscamp, J.	16	4	20
Talbot, F.L.	1		1
Turner, T.S.	10	1	11
Whyte, C.	4		4

Goalscorers

PLAYER	LEAGUE	CUP COMPETITION FA CUP	TOTAL
Bruton, L.H.R.	18	5	23
Bruton, J.	19	1	20
Puddefoot, S.C.	15	2	17
Cunliffe, A.	7	1	8
McLean, T.	7		7
Bourton, C.F.T.	4		4
Imrie, W.N.	4		4
Groves, A.	3		3
Britton, F.	2		2
Turner, T.S.	2		2
Rankin, W.	1		1
Opps' o.gs.	1		1

Final Division 1 Table

		P	W	D	L	F	A	Pts
1	ARSENAL	42	28	10	4	127	59	66
2	ASTON VILLA	42	25	9	8	128	78	59
3	SHEFFIELD W	42	22	8	12	102	75	52
4	PORTSMOUTH	42	18	13	11	84	67	49
5	HUDDERSFIELD T	42	18	12	12	81	65	48
6	DERBY CO	42	18	10	14	94	79	46
7	MIDDLESBROUGH	42	19	8	15	98	90	46
8	MANCHESTER C	42	18	10	14	75	70	46
9	LIVERPOOL	42	15	12	15	86	85	42
10	BLACKBURN R	42	17	8	17	83	84	42
11	SUNDERLAND	42	16	9	17	89	85	41
12	CHELSEA	42	15	10	17	64	67	40
13	GRIMSBY T	42	17	5	20	82	87	39
14	BOLTON W	42	15	9	18	68	81	39
15	SHEFFIELD U	42	14	10	18	78	84	38
16	LEICESTER C	42	16	6	20	80	95	38
17	NEWCASTLE U	42	15	6	21	78	87	36
18	WEST HAM U	42	14	8	20	79	94	36
19	BIRMINGHAM	42	13	10	19	55	70	36
20	BLACKPOOL	42	11	10	21	71	125	32
21	LEEDS U	42	12	7	23	68	81	31
22	MANCHESTER U	42	7	8	27	53	115	22

Season 1931-32

Football League Division 1

DATE	OPPONENTS	SCORE	GOALSCORERS	ATTENDANCE
Aug 29	SHEFFIELD WEDNESDAY	L 1-6	Thompson	15,819
Aug 31	ARSENAL	D 1-1	Cunliffe	22,138
Sep 5	Portsmouth	L 0-2		17,766
Sep 9	Blackpool	L 1-2	Bruton J.	23,444
Sep 12	DERBY COUNTY	W 3-2	Talbot 2, Groves	10,790
Sep 19	West Bromwich Albion	L 1-4	Bruton J.	26,147
Sep 21	BLACKPOOL	W 5-1	Groves, Imrie, Roscamp, Bruton J., Turner	15,149
Sep 26	BIRMINGHAM	L 1-2	Bruton J. (pen)	11,004
Oct 3	Sunderland	D 2-2	Thompson, Bruton J.	20,566
Oct 10	MANCHESTER CITY	D 2-2	Cunliffe, Talbot	12,313
Oct 17	NEWCASTLE UNITED	L 0-3		11,947
Oct 24	Chelsea	W 2-1	Bruton J., Thompson	35,688
Oct 31	GRIMSBY TOWN	W 3-2	Thompson, Hutton (pen), Talbot	8,102
Nov 7	Liverpool	L 2-4	Cunliffe, Talbot	21,272
Nov 14	MIDDLESBROUGH	W 4-2	Thompson 2, McLean T. 2	8,795
Nov 21	Bolton Wanderers	L 1-3	Cunliffe	18,164
Nov 28	WEST HAM UNITED	L 2-4	Imrie, Bruton J.	8,426
Dec 5	Huddersfield Town	D 1-1	Cunliffe	9,628
Dec 12	LEICESTER CITY	W 6-0	Osborne o.g., Bruton J., Thompson 2, Cunliffe, McLean T.	7,885
Dec 19	Aston Villa	W 5-1	Thompson 3, Cunliffe, McLean T.	9,263
Dec 25	EVERTON	W 5-3	Bruton J., McLean T. 2 (1 pen), Thompson, Groves	40,059
Dec 26	Everton	L 0-5		52,991
Jan 1	Sheffield United	L 2-3	Cunliffe 2	30,932
Jan 2	Sheffield Wednesday	L 1-5	Thompson	12,792
Jan 16	PORTSMOUTH	W 5-3	McLean T. 2, Imrie, Bruton J., Groves	9,895
Jan 27	Derby County	D 1-1	Bruton J.	7,765
Jan 30	WEST BROMWICH ALBION	W 2-0	Thompson 2	14,678
Feb 6	Birmingham	L 1-2	Imrie (pen)	19,506
Feb 13	SUNDERLAND	W 5-2	Healless, Bruton J., Thompson, Imrie (pen), Puddefoot	10,934
Feb 20	Manchester City	L 1-3	Bruton J.	24,438
Mar 2	Newcastle United	L 3-5	Cunliffe, Bruton J., Talbot	16,760
Mar 5	CHELSEA	D 2-2	Russell o.g., Cunliffe	13,961
Mar 12	Grimsby Town	L 3-4	Thompson, Groves, McLean T.	10,531
Mar 19	LIVERPOOL	L 1-3	Bruton J.	9,771
Mar 26	Middlesbrough	W 2-0	McLean T., Thompson	9,681
Mar 28	SHEFFIELD UNITED	L 1-2	Thompson	13,027
Apr 2	BOLTON WANDERERS	W 3-1	Thompson, Bruton J. (pen), Groves	12,100
Apr 9	West Ham United	W 3-1	Cunliffe 3	10,136
Apr 16	HUDDERSFIELD TOWN	W 3-0	Bruton J. 2 (1 pen), Cunliffe	10,782
Apr 23	Leicester City	L 0-1		15,645
Apr 30	ASTON VILLA	W 2-0	Thompson, Bruton J.	9,116
May 7	Arsenal	L 0-4		23,127

FA Cup

Jan 9	Burton Town	(Rd3) W 4-0	Bruton J. 2, Cunliffe 2	9,674
Jan 23	Derby County	(Rd4) L 2-3	Britton, Cunliffe	30,825

Fact File

Tom Baxter asked for his release from the club so that he could embark upon a new career in the Blackburn Police Force.

MANAGER: Arthur Barritt

TOP SCORER: Ernie Thompson

BIGGEST WIN: 6-0, 12 December 1931, v Leicester City, Division 1

HIGHEST ATTENDANCE: 52,991, 26 December 1931, v Everton, Division 1

MAJOR TRANSFERS OUT: Les Bruton to Liverpool, Syd Puddefoot to West Ham United, Bill Rankin to Charlton Athletic, Jack Roscamp to Bradford City

League & Cup Appearances

PLAYER	LEAGUE	CUP COMPETITION FA CUP	TOTAL
Baxter, T.T.	5		5
Binns, C.H.	30	2	32
Britton, F.	27	2	29
Bruton, J.	42	2	44
Bruton, L.H.R.	2		2
Carver, J.	13		13
Crawford, J.C.	7		7
Crook, W.	1		1
Cunliffe, A.	38	2	40
Gorman, J.J.	24	2	26
Gormlie, W.	5		5
Groves, A.	23	2	25
Healless, H.	32	2	34
Hutton, J.	20	2	22
Imrie, W.N.	33	2	35
Jones, H.	34		34
McLean, J.	2		2
McLean, T.	35	2	37
Melville, J.	5		5
Puddefoot, S.C.	7		7
Rankin, W.	10		10
Richards, J.	1		1
Roscamp, J.	6		6
Talbot, F.L.	16		16
Thompson, J.E.	35	2	37
Turner, T.S.	6		6
Wood, W.H.	3		3

Goalscorers

PLAYER	LEAGUE	CUP COMPETITION FA CUP	TOTAL
Thompson, J.E.	21		21
Bruton, J.	19	2	21
Cunliffe, A.	15	3	18
McLean, T.	10		10
Groves, A.	6		6
Talbot, F.L.	6		6
Imrie, W.N.	5		5
Healless, H.	1		1
Hutton, J.	1		1
Puddefoot, S.C.	1		1
Roscamp, J.	1		1
Turner, T.S.	1		1
Britton, F.		1	1
Opps' o.gs.	2		2

Final Division 1 Table

		P	W	D	L	F	A	Pts
1	EVERTON	42	26	4	12	116	64	56
2	ARSENAL	42	22	10	10	90	48	54
3	SHEFFIELD W	42	22	6	14	96	82	50
4	HUDDERSFIELD T	42	19	10	13	80	63	48
5	ASTON VILLA	42	19	8	15	104	72	46
6	WBA	42	20	6	16	77	55	46
7	SHEFFIELD U	42	20	6	16	80	75	46
8	PORTSMOUTH	42	19	7	16	62	62	45
9	BIRMINGHAM	42	18	8	16	78	67	44
10	LIVERPOOL	42	19	6	17	81	93	44
11	NEWCASTLE U	42	18	6	18	80	87	42
12	CHELSEA	42	16	8	18	69	73	40
13	SUNDERLAND	42	15	10	17	67	73	40
14	MANCHESTER C	42	13	12	17	83	73	38
15	DERBY CO	42	14	10	18	71	75	38
16	BLACKBURN R	42	16	6	20	89	95	38
17	BOLTON W	42	17	4	21	72	80	38
18	MIDDLESBROUGH	42	15	8	19	64	89	38
19	LEICESTER C	42	15	7	20	74	94	37
20	BLACKPOOL	42	12	9	21	65	102	33
21	GRIMSBY T	42	13	6	23	67	98	32
22	WEST HAM U	42	12	7	23	62	107	31

Season 1932-33

Football League Division 1

DATE	OPPONENTS	SCORE	GOALSCORERS	ATTENDANCE
Aug 27	Chelsea	D 2-2	Cunliffe, Bruton	32,657
Aug 31	Derby County	L 1-2	Cooper o.g.	17,509
Sep 3	LEEDS UNITED	D 1-1	Thompson	13,010
Sep 10	Sheffield Wednesday	D 1-1	Cunliffe	14,134
Sep 17	WEST BROMWICH ALBION	D 4-4	Groves 2, Thompson, Dix	21,081
Sep 19	DERBY COUNTY	D 3-3	Groves, Dix, Cunliffe	16,655
Sep 24	Birmingham	L 1-3	Bruton (pen)	19,883
Oct 1	SUNDERLAND	L 1-3	Thompson	10,545
Oct 8	Manchester City	W 3-2	Cunliffe, Cann o.g., Imrie	8,428
Oct 15	ARSENAL	L 2-3	Dix 2	28,799
Oct 22	Huddersfield Town	W 3-0	Bruton, Cunliffe 2	11,357
Oct 29	SHEFFIELD UNITED	W 3-0	McLean T., Thompson, Cunliffe	7,154
Nov 5	Bolton Wanderers	L 2-4	McLean T. (pen), Bruton	20,225
Nov 12	LIVERPOOL	D 2-2	Groves 2	11,785
Nov 19	Leicester City	D 1-1	Thompson	12,680
Nov 26	PORTSMOUTH	W 3-2	Thompson, Cunliffe, Groves	9,915
Dec 3	Wolverhampton W.	L 3-5	Turner, Dix, Thompson	20,716
Dec 10	NEWCASTLE UNITED	W 2-1	McLean T. (pen), Dix	10,028
Dec 17	Aston Villa	L 0-4		23,518
Dec 24	MIDDLESBROUGH	W 4-2	Thompson, Cunliffe 2, Groves	8,303
Dec 26	EVERTON	W 3-1	Thompson, Dix, Bruton	35,987
Dec 27	Everton	L 1-6	Thompson	35,576
Dec 31	CHELSEA	L 1-3	Bruton	10,583
Jan 2	BLACKPOOL	W 6-5	Britton 3, Dix, Imrie, Thompson	22,471
Jan 7	Leeds United	L 1-3	Cunliffe	14,043
Jan 21	SHEFFIELD WEDNESDAY	D 1-1	McLean T. (pen)	10,417
Feb 4	BIRMINGHAM	W 2-0	Britton, Thompson	7,448
Feb 8	West Bromwich Albion	W 3-1	Dix, Bruton, Cunliffe	10,890
Feb 11	Sunderland	L 2-4	Dix, Thompson	15,939
Feb 23	MANCHESTER CITY	W 1-0	Thompson	8,391
Feb 25	Arsenal	L 0-8		27,576
Mar 4	HUDDERSFIELD TOWN	W 4-2	Dix 2, Bruton, Cunliffe	7,788
Mar 11	Sheffield United	L 1-2	Dix	15,515
Mar 18	BOLTON WANDERERS	W 3-2	Cunliffe, Dix, Thompson	10,432
Mar 25	Liverpool	D 2-2	McLean T, Thompson	15,471
Apr 1	LEICESTER CITY	D 1-1	Thompson	7,562
Apr 8	Portsmouth	L 0-2		14,303
Apr 14	Blackpool	L 0-3		26,365
Apr 15	WOLVERHAMPTON W.	W 1-0	Britton (pen)	9,323
Apr 22	Newcastle United	L 1-2	Turner	12,247
Apr 29	ASTON VILLA	L 0-5		3,624
May 6	Middlesbrough	L 0-4		7,340

FA Cup

DATE	OPPONENTS		SCORE	GOALSCORERS	ATTENDANCE
Jan 14	Lincoln City	(Rd3)	W 5-1	Dix, McLean T. (pen), Cunliffe 2, Bruton	13,276
Jan 28	Birmingham	(Rd4)	L 0-3		25,617

League & Cup Appearances

PLAYER	LEAGUE	CUP COMPETITION FA CUP	TOTAL
Binns, C.H.	13	2	15
Britton, F.	11	1	12
Bruton, J.	42	2	44
Bryant, C.	1		1
Carver, J.	37	2	39
Crook, W.	2		2
Cunliffe, A.	39	2	41
Dix, R.W.	38	2	40
Gorman, J.J.	41	2	43
Gormlie, W.	28		28
Groves, A.	15	1	16
Healless, H.	2		2
Hughes, J.I.	1		1
Imrie, W.N.	26	2	28
Jones, H.	23	2	25
McLean, J.	6		6
McLean, T.	37	2	39
Melville, J.	15		15
Talbott, F.L.	3		3
Thompson, J.E.	40	2	42
Turner, T.S.	6		6
Whiteside, A.	14		14
Whyte, C.	18		18
Wood, W.H.	4		4

Goalscorers

PLAYER	LEAGUE	CUP COMPETITION FA CUP	TOTAL
Thompson, J.E.	17		17
Cunliffe, A.	14	2	16
Dix, R.W.	14	1	15
Bruton, J.	8	1	9
Groves, A.	7		7
McLean, T.	5	1	6
Britton, F.	5		5
Imrie, W.N.	2		2
Turner, T.S.	2		2
Opps' o.gs.	2		2

Fact File

Arthur Cunliffe won two England caps during the course of the season. In October 1932, he made his international debut against Ireland at Blackpool, and the following month he appeared against Wales at Wrexham.

MANAGER: Arthur Barritt

TOP SCORER: Ernie Thompson

BIGGEST WIN: 5-1, 14 January 1933, v Lincoln City, FA Cup Round 3

HIGHEST ATTENDANCE: 35,987, 26 December 1932, v Everton, Division 1

MAJOR TRANSFERS IN: Ronnie Dix from Bristol Rovers, Wally Halsall from Bolton Wanderers

MAJOR TRANSFERS OUT: Ronnie Dix and Arthur Cunliffe to Aston Villa

Final Division 1 Table

		P	W	D	L	F	A	Pts
1	ARSENAL	42	25	8	9	118	61	58
2	ASTON VILLA	42	23	8	11	92	67	54
3	SHEFFIELD W	42	21	9	12	80	68	51
4	WBA	42	20	9	13	83	70	49
5	NEWCASTLE U	42	22	5	15	71	63	49
6	HUDDERSFIELD T	42	18	11	13	66	53	47
7	DERBY CO	42	15	14	13	76	69	44
8	LEEDS U	42	15	14	13	59	62	44
9	PORTSMOUTH	42	18	7	17	74	76	43
10	SHEFFIELD U	42	17	9	16	74	80	43
11	EVERTON	42	16	9	17	81	74	41
12	SUNDERLAND	42	15	10	17	63	80	40
13	BIRMINGHAM	42	14	11	17	57	57	39
14	LIVERPOOL	42	14	11	17	79	84	39
15	BLACKBURN R	42	14	10	18	76	102	38
16	MANCHESTER C	42	16	5	21	68	71	37
17	MIDDLESBROUGH	42	14	9	19	63	73	37
18	CHELSEA	42	14	7	21	63	73	35
19	LEICESTER C	42	11	13	18	75	89	35
20	WOLVERHAMPTON W	42	13	9	20	80	96	35
21	BOLTON W	42	12	9	21	78	92	33
22	BLACKPOOL	42	14	5	23	69	85	33

Season 1933-34

Football League Division 1

DATE	OPPONENTS	SCORE	GOALSCORERS	ATTENDANCE
Aug 26	LEEDS UNITED	W 4-2	Thompson 3, Bruton	10,130
Sep 2	Derby County	D 1-1	Bruton	15,519
Sep 6	Newcastle United	L 1-3	Thompson	17,506
Sep 9	WEST BROMWICH ALBION	W 4-0	Turner 2, Thompson, Kennedy	12,883
Sep 16	Birmingham	L 0-2		20,779
Sep 18	NEWCASTLE UNITED	W 3-2	Bruton 2, Halsall	14,066
Sep 23	SHEFFIELD WEDNESDAY	W 3-1	Thompson, Bruton, Turner	15,622
Sep 30	Manchester City	L 1-3	Bruton	33,343
Oct 7	ARSENAL	D 2-2	Imrie, Kennedy	31,636
Oct 14	Everton	L 1-7	Turner	23,933
Oct 21	CHELSEA	W 4-2	Kennedy, Turner, Imrie (pen), Bruton	12,570
Oct 28	Liverpool	L 0-4		22,317
Nov 4	WOLVERHAMPTON W.	W 7-1	Kennedy, Thompson 3, Bruton, Turner, Imrie (pen)	12,429
Nov 11	Leicester City	W 2-1	Harper, Bruton	17,364
Nov 18	ASTON VILLA	W 2-1	Harper, Bruton	19,450
Nov 25	Sheffield United	L 0-1		11,451
Dec 2	PORTSMOUTH	W 3-2	Kennedy 2, Imrie	11,823
Dec 9	Stoke City	L 0-2		13,900
Dec 16	HUDDERSFIELD TOWN	D 2-2	Kennedy, McLean	10,779
Dec 23	Tottenham Hotspur	L 1-4	Bruton	28,001
Dec 25	MIDDLESBROUGH	D 0-0		27,273
Dec 26	Middlesbrough	L 1-3	Bruton	19,203
Dec 30	Leeds United	L 0-4		10,772
Jan 1	TOTTENHAM HOTSPUR	W 1-0	Harper	19,955
Jan 6	DERBY COUNTY	W 2-1	Imrie, Britton	16,965
Jan 20	West Bromwich Albion	W 1-0	Harper	16,297
Jan 29	BIRMINGHAM	W 3-1	Imrie (pen), Bruton, Kennedy	5,949
Feb 3	Sheffield Wednesday	L 0-4		19,303
Feb 10	MANCHESTER CITY	W 3-0	Milne 2, Harper	14,076
Feb 21	Arsenal	L 1-2	Milne	29,886
Feb 24	EVERTON	D 1-1	Harper	12,645
Mar 3	Chelsea	L 0-3		26,409
Mar 10	LIVERPOOL	W 3-1	Harper, Brennan, McLean	7,074
Mar 17	Wolverhampton W.	L 3-5	Milne 2, Harper	18,689
Mar 24	LEICESTER CITY	W 3-0	Harper 3	6,670
Mar 30	Sunderland	L 0-3		20,626
Mar 31	Aston Villa	D 1-1	Harper	30,966
Apr 2	SUNDERLAND	D 0-0		13,860
Apr 7	SHEFFIELD UNITED	W 3-1	Harper, Bruton, Talbot	8,321
Apr 14	Portsmouth	L 0-2		13,351
Apr 21	STOKE CITY	W 4-1	Harper 2, Carver, Bruton	9,929
Apr 28	Huddersfield Town	L 3-5	Talbot (pen), Milne 2	4,214

FA Cup

Jan 13	Manchester City	(Rd3) L 1-3	Bruton	54,336

League & Cup Appearances

PLAYER	LEAGUE	CUP COMPETITION FA CUP	TOTAL
Binns, C.H.	24	1	25
Brennan, T.J.	8		8
Britton, F.	1		1
Bruton, J.	41	1	42
Carver, J.	42	1	43
Coombs, E.H.	6		6
Crook, W.	1		1
Duncan, W.M.	2	1	3
Gorman, J.J.	38	1	39
Gormlie, W.J.	11		11
Halsall, W.G.	23		23
Harper, E.C.	22	1	23
Hughes, J.I.	7		7
Imrie, W.N.	32	1	33
Kennedy, F.	29		29
Lanceley, E.	4		4
McLean, T.	28	1	29
Milne, J.V.	17		17
Pryde, R.I.	10		10
Talbot, F.L.	17		17
Thompson, J.E.	13		13
Turner, T.S.	26	1	27
Whiteside, A.	19	1	20
Whyte, C.	41	1	42

Goalscorers

PLAYER	LEAGUE	CUP COMPETITION FA CUP	TOTAL
Bruton, J.	15	1	16
Harper, E.C.	15		15
Thompson, J.E.	9		9
Kennedy, F.	8		8
Milne, J.V.	7		7
Imrie, W.N.	6		6
Turner, T.S.	6		6
McLean, T.	2		2
Talbot, F.L.	2		2
Brennan, T.J.	1		1
Britton, F.	1		1
Carver, J.	1		1
Halsall, W.G.	1		1

Fact File

The Rovers lost 17 of their 21 away League games and also slipped out of the FA Cup away from home. However, the team remained undefeated at Ewood Park with 16 wins and five draws.

MANAGER: Arthur Barritt

TOP SCORER: Jack Bruton

BIGGEST WIN: 7-1, 4 November 1933, v Wolverhampton Wanderers, Division 1

HIGHEST ATTENDANCE: 54,336, 13 January 1934, v Manchester City, FA Cup Round 3

MAJOR TRANSFERS IN: Bob Pryde from St Johnstone, Fred Kennedy from Racing Club de Paris, Ted Harper from Preston North End

MAJOR TRANSFERS OUT: Bill Imrie to Newcastle United

Final Division 1 Table

		P	W	D	L	F	A	Pts
1	ARSENAL	42	25	9	8	75	47	59
2	HUDDERSFIELD T	42	23	10	9	90	61	56
3	TOTTENHAM H	42	21	7	14	79	56	49
4	DERBY CO	42	17	11	14	68	54	45
5	MANCHESTER C	42	17	11	14	65	72	45
6	SUNDERLAND	42	16	12	14	81	56	44
7	WBA	42	17	10	15	78	70	44
8	BLACKBURN R	42	18	7	17	74	81	43
9	LEEDS U	42	17	8	17	75	66	42
10	PORTSMOUTH	42	15	12	15	52	55	42
11	SHEFFIELD W	42	16	9	17	62	67	41
12	STOKE C	42	15	11	16	58	71	41
13	ASTON VILLA	42	14	12	16	78	75	40
14	EVERTON	42	12	16	14	62	63	40
15	WOLVERHAMPTON W	42	14	12	16	74	86	40
16	MIDDLESBROUGH	42	16	7	19	68	80	39
17	LEICESTER C	42	14	11	17	59	74	39
18	LIVERPOOL	42	14	10	18	79	87	38
19	CHELSEA	42	14	8	20	67	69	36
20	BIRMINGHAM	42	12	12	18	54	56	36
21	NEWCASTLE U	42	10	14	18	68	77	34
22	SHEFFIELD U	42	12	7	23	58	101	31

Season 1934-35

Football League Division 1

DATE	OPPONENTS	SCORE	GOALSCORERS	ATTENDANCE
Aug 25	Liverpool	L 0-2		31,615
Sep 1	LEEDS UNITED	D 1-1	Bruton	12,316
Sep 5	Arsenal	L 0-4		39,654
Sep 8	West Bromwich Albion	D 2-2	Milne, Thompson	19,002
Sep 15	SHEFFIELD WEDNESDAY	W 2-1	Pryde, Talbot	14,334
Sep 17	ARSENAL	W 2-0	Thompson 2	25,472
Sep 22	Birmingham	L 0-1		11,802
Sep 29	STOKE CITY	L 0-1		10,386
Oct 6	Manchester City	D 3-3	Bruton 2, Thompson	35,489
Oct 13	MIDDLESBROUGH	W 3-2	Turner, Talbot, Bruton	12,429
Oct 20	SUNDERLAND	D 0-0		14,034
Oct 27	Leicester City	W 1-0	Thompson	13,041
Nov 3	GRIMSBY TOWN	D 2-2	Turner, Thompson	13,308
Nov 10	Preston North End	L 1-3	Turner	32,306
Nov 17	CHELSEA	L 1-2	Benson	10,781
Nov 24	Wolverhampton W.	L 1-2	Bruton	16,625
Dec 1	HUDDERSFIELD TOWN	W 4-2	Talbot 3, Thompson	12,256
Dec 8	Everton	L 2-5	Talbot, Bruton	21,451
Dec 15	DERBY COUNTY	L 2-5	Bruton (pen), Thompson	12,543
Dec 22	Aston Villa	D 1-1	Thompson	25,633
Dec 25	PORTSMOUTH	D 0-0		25,261
Dec 26	Portsmouth	L 1-3	Bruton (pen)	27,199
Dec 29	LIVERPOOL	L 0-2		14,015
Jan 1	TOTTENHAM HOTSPUR	W 2-0	Bruton (pen), Talbot	12,083
Jan 5	Leeds United	L 1-5	Beattie	13,832
Jan 19	WEST BROMWICH ALBION	W 3-0	Bruton 2 (1 pen), Thompson	12,492
Jan 28	Sheffield Wednesday	D 2-2	Beattie 2	8,043
Feb 2	BIRMINGHAM	W 3-1	Milne, Bruton 2 (1 pen)	12,297
Feb 9	Stoke City	L 1-3	Milne	20,653
Feb 23	Middlesbrough	D 3-3	Bruton, Sharp, Milne	9,108
Mar 2	Sunderland	L 0-3		17,898
Mar 4	MANCHESTER CITY	W 1-0	Thompson	11,328
Mar 9	LEICESTER CITY	D 0-0		9,299
Mar 16	Grimsby Town	W 2-1	Bruton 2	10,778
Mar 23	PRESTON NORTH END	W 1-0	Pryde	14,661
Mar 30	Chelsea	L 2-4	Thompson, Beattie	34,470
Apr 6	WOLVERHAMPTON W.	W 4-2	Beattie, Thompson 3	7,716
Apr 13	Huddersfield Town	L 0-6		15,078
Apr 19	Tottenham Hotspur	L 0-1		31,101
Apr 20	EVERTON	W 6-2	Bruton 2, Thompson (pen), Talbot, Beattie, Whiteside	13,559
Apr 27	Derby County	D 1-1	Thompson (pen)	8,336
May 4	ASTON VILLA	W 5-0	Thompson, Milne 2, Talbot, Carver	5,921

FA Cup

Jan 12	Middlesbrough	(Rd3) D 1-1	Talbot	34,637
Jan 17	MIDDLESBROUGH	(R) W 1-0	Milne	32,783
Jan 26	LIVERPOOL	(Rd4) W 1-0	Milne	49,546
Feb 21	BIRMINGHAM	(Rd5) L 1-2	Beattie	33,500

League & Cup Appearances

PLAYER	LEAGUE	CUP COMPETITION FA CUP	TOTAL
Beattie, J.M.	23	4	27
Benson, J.R.	1		1
Binns, C.H.	37	1	38
Brennan, T.J.	5		5
Bruton, J.	42	4	46
Bryant, C.S.	3		3
Carver, J.	21		21
Christie, N.	16	4	20
Crawford, R.	2		2
Crook, W.	25	4	29
Gorman, J.J.	31	4	35
Halsall, W.G.	5	2	7
Harper, E.C.	5		5
Hughes, J.I.	5	3	8
Lanceley, E.	4		4
McLean, T.	17	4	21
Milne, J.V.	28	4	32
Pryde, R.I.	40	2	42
Sharp, A.	7		7
Talbot, F.L.	30	3	33
Thompson, J.E.	36	1	37
Turner, T.S.	15		15
Whiteside, A.	40	4	44
Whyte, C.	24		24

Goalscorers

PLAYER	LEAGUE	CUP COMPETITION FA CUP	TOTAL
Bruton, J.	18		18
Thompson, J.E.	18		18
Talbot, F.L.	9	1	10
Milne, J.V.	6	2	8
Beattie, J.M.	6	1	7
Turner, T.S.	3		3
Pryde, R.I.	2		2
Benson, J.R.	1		1
Carver, J.	1		1
Sharp, A.	1		1
Whiteside, A.	1		1

Fact File

Walter Crook appeared at right back on 22 October 1934 in what was to be the first of 208 consecutive Football League appearances for the club.

MANAGER: Arthur Barritt

TOP SCORER: Jack Bruton/Ernie Thompson

BIGGEST WIN: 5-0, 4 May 1935, v Aston Villa, Division 1

HIGHEST ATTENDANCE: 49,546, 26 January 1935, v Liverpool, FA Cup Round 4

MAJOR TRANSFERS IN: Jack Beattie from Wolverhampton Wanderers, Norman Christie from Huddersfield Town

MAJOR TRANSFERS OUT: Herbert Jones to Brighton & Hove Albion, Fred Kennedy to Racing Club de Paris

Final Division 1 Table

		P	W	D	L	F	A	Pts
1	ARSENAL	42	23	12	7	115	46	58
2	SUNDERLAND	42	19	16	7	90	51	54
3	SHEFFIELD W	42	18	13	11	70	64	49
4	MANCHESTER C	42	20	8	14	82	67	48
5	GRIMSBY T	42	17	11	14	78	60	45
6	DERBY CO	42	18	9	15	81	66	45
7	LIVERPOOL	42	19	7	16	85	88	45
8	EVERTON	42	16	12	14	89	88	44
9	WBA	42	17	10	15	83	83	44
10	STOKE C	42	18	6	18	71	70	42
11	PRESTON NE	42	15	12	15	62	67	42
12	CHELSEA	42	16	9	17	73	82	41
13	ASTON VILLA	42	14	13	15	74	88	41
14	PORTSMOUTH	42	15	10	17	71	72	40
15	BLACKBURN R	42	14	11	17	66	78	39
16	HUDDERSFIELD T	42	14	10	18	76	71	38
17	WOLVERHAMPTON W	42	15	8	19	88	94	38
18	LEEDS U	42	13	12	17	75	92	38
19	BIRMINGHAM	42	13	10	19	63	81	36
20	MIDDLESBROUGH	42	10	14	18	70	90	34
21	LEICESTER C	42	12	9	21	61	86	33
22	TOTTENHAM H	42	10	10	22	54	93	30

Season 1935-36

Football League Division 1

DATE	OPPONENTS	SCORE	GOALSCORERS	ATTENDANCE
Aug 31	GRIMSBY TOWN	W 1-0	Turner	14,035
Sep 5	Brentford	L 1-3	Thompson	25,047
Sep 7	Leeds United	W 4-1	Edwards o.g., Beattie, Turner, Bruton	14,514
Sep 14	WEST BROMWICH ALBION	W 3-1	Thompson (pen), Bruton, Beattie	13,625
Sep 16	CHELSEA	W 1-0	Thompson (pen)	14,610
Sep 21	Sunderland	L 2-7	Pryde, Bruton	29,704
Sep 28	BIRMINGHAM	L 1-2	Pryde	13,177
Oct 5	Arsenal	L 1-5	Hamill A.	45,981
Oct 12	MANCHESTER CITY	W 4-1	McGrogan, Hamill A. 2, Pryde	21,416
Oct 19	Derby County	L 0-1		18,573
Oct 26	EVERTON	D 1-1	Bruton	14,612
Nov 2	Bolton Wanderers	L 1-3	Pryde	28,981
Nov 9	HUDDERSFIELD TOWN	W 2-1	Whiteside, Thompson (pen)	16,745
Nov 16	Middlesbrough	L 1-6	Thompson	14,945
Nov 23	PRESTON NORTH END	D 1-1	Thompson	33,016
Nov 30	Wolverhampton W.	L 1-8	Halsall	18,282
Dec 7	SHEFFIELD WEDNESDAY	W 3-2	Talbot, Turner, Thompson (pen)	9,815
Dec 14	Portsmouth	L 1-3	Thompson	14,584
Dec 21	ASTON VILLA	W 5-1	Thompson 2 (1 pen), Turner 2, Hamill A.	5,664
Dec 25	STOKE CITY	L 0-1		22,692
Dec 26	Stoke City	L 0-2		22,905
Dec 28	Grimsby Town	D 1-1	Thompson	8,068
Jan 1	BRENTFORD	W 1-0	Beattie	24,724
Jan 4	LEEDS UNITED	L 0-3		13,110
Jan 18	West Bromwich Albion	L 1-8	Thompson	16,487
Feb 1	Birmingham	L 2-4	Astill, Talbot	23,684
Feb 8	ARSENAL	L 0-1		24,998
Feb 15	SUNDERLAND	D 1-1	Beattie	18,628
Feb 19	Manchester City	L 0-2		12,498
Feb 22	DERBY COUNTY	D 0-0		14,597
Feb 29	Huddersfield Town	D 1-1	Thompson	3,886
Mar 7	WOLVERHAMPTON W.	W 1-0	Turner	8,087
Mar 14	Everton	L 0-4		25,694
Mar 21	MIDDLESBROUGH	D 2-2	Talbot, Calladine	11,553
Mar 28	Preston North End	L 0-2		24,921
Apr 4	BOLTON WANDERERS	L 0-3		13,779
Apr 10	LIVERPOOL	D 2-2	Thompson (pen), Beattie	8,964
Apr 11	Sheffield Wednesday	D 0-0		14,560
Apr 13	Liverpool	L 1-4	Sale	24,547
Apr 18	PORTSMOUTH	W 3-1	Bruton, Turner 2	7,618
Apr 25	Aston Villa	W 4-2	Sale 2, Halsall, Thompson	27,378
May 2	Chelsea	L 1-5	Sale	18,078

FA Cup

Jan 11	BOLTON WANDERERS	(Rd3) D 1-1	Halsall	41,000
Jan 15	Bolton Wanderers*	(R) W 1-0	Thompson	40,800
Feb 3	Bradford City	(Rd4) L 1-3	Thompson	18,396

*After extra-time.

League & Cup Appearances

PLAYER	LEAGUE	CUP COMPETITION FA CUP	TOTAL
Astill, L.V.	3	1	4
Barron, J.	2		2
Baxendale, F.	3		3
Beattie, J.M.	33	1	34
Benson, J.R.	1		1
Binns, C.H.	28	3	31
Bruton, J.	35	3	38
Bryant, C.S.	1		1
Calladine, C.F.	10		10
Carver, J.	23		23
Christie, N.	13	1	14
Clark, S.J.H.	1		1
Crawford, R.	3		3
Crook, W.	42	3	45
Gorman, J.J.	41	3	44
Halsall, W.G.	15	3	18
Hamill, A.	16	3	19
Hamill, K.J.	1		1
Hughes, J.I.	9		9
Lapham, E.H.	2		2
McGrogan, F.	4		4
Pinkerton, J.R.	1		1
Pinxton, A.E.	3	1	4
Pratt, J.T.	2		2
Pryde, R.I.	36	3	39
Sale, T.	8		8
Sharp, A.	2		2
Talbot, F.L.	23	3	26
Thompson, J.E.	38	3	41
Turner, T.S.	27		27
Vause, P.G.	5		5
Whiteside, A.	32	1	33

Goalscorers

PLAYER	LEAGUE	CUP COMPETITION FA CUP	TOTAL
Thompson, J.E.	15	2	17
Turner, T.S.	8		8
Beattie, J.M.	5		5
Bruton, J.	5		5
Hamill, A.	4		4
Pryde, R.I.	4		4
Sale, T.	4		4
Talbot, F.L.	3		3
Halsall, W.G.	2	1	3
Astill, L.V.	1		1
Calladine, C.F.	1		1
McGrogan, F.	1		1
Whiteside, A.	1		1
Opps' o.gs.	1		1

Fact File

Blackburn Rovers slipped into the Second Division for the first time in the club's history. Aston Villa, another founder member of the Football League, also tasted relegation for the first time when they accompanied the Rovers out of the top flight.

MANAGER: Arthur Barrit

TOP SCORER: Ernie Thompson

BIGGEST WIN: 5-1, 21 December 1935, v Aston Villa, Division 1

HIGHEST ATTENDANCE: 45,981, 5 October 1935, v Arsenal, Division 1

MAJOR TRANSFERS IN: Charles Calladine from Birmingham, Tom Sale from Stoke City

MAJOR TRANSFERS OUT: Jackie Milne to Arsenal

Final Division 1 Table

		P	W	D	L	F	A	Pts
1	SUNDERLAND	42	25	6	11	109	74	56
2	DERBY CO	42	18	12	12	61	52	48
3	HUDDERSFIELD T	42	18	12	12	59	56	48
4	STOKE C	42	20	7	15	57	57	47
5	BRENTFORD	42	17	12	13	81	60	46
6	ARSENAL	42	15	15	12	78	48	45
7	PRESTON NE	42	18	8	16	67	64	44
8	CHELSEA	42	15	13	14	65	72	43
9	MANCHESTER C	42	17	8	17	68	60	42
10	PORTSMOUTH	42	17	8	17	54	67	42
11	LEEDS U	42	15	11	16	66	64	41
12	BIRMINGHAM	42	15	11	16	61	63	41
13	BOLTON W	42	14	13	15	67	76	41
14	MIDDLESBROUGH	42	15	10	17	84	70	40
15	WOLVERHAMPTON W	42	15	10	17	77	76	40
16	EVERTON	42	13	13	16	89	89	39
17	GRIMSBY T	42	17	5	20	65	73	39
18	WBA	42	16	6	20	89	88	38
19	LIVERPOOL	42	13	12	17	60	64	38
20	SHEFFIELD W	42	13	12	17	63	77	38
21	ASTON VILLA	42	13	9	20	81	110	35
22	BLACKBURN R	42	12	9	21	55	96	33

Season 1936-37

Football League Division 2

DATE	OPPONENTS	SCORE	GOALSCORERS	ATTENDANCE
Aug 29	Bury	D 1-1	Thompson	16,388
Aug 31	Sheffield United	W 1-0	Thompson	16,185
Sep 5	LEICESTER CITY	D 0-0		14,757
Sep 12	West Ham United	L 1-3	Bruton	22,520
Sep 19	NORWICH CITY	W 1-0	Bruton	13,284
Sep 21	SHEFFIELD UNITED	W 3-1	Bruton, Sale 2	14,452
Sep 26	Newcastle United	L 0-2		21,866
Oct 3	BRADFORD	D 1-1	Bruton	13,610
Oct 10	Barnsley	L 2-3	Beattie, Sale	13,826
Oct 17	FULHAM	L 0-2		8,574
Oct 24	Burnley	D 0-0		32,567
Oct 31	SOUTHAMPTON	W 1-0	Beattie	13,618
Nov 7	Swansea Town	L 0-1		7,234
Nov 14	BRADFORD CITY	W 3-0	Bruton 2, Sale	9,839
Nov 21	Aston Villa	D 2-2	Sale 2	32,153
Nov 28	CHESTERFIELD	W 5-2	Sale, Beattie, Rutherford, Bruton 2	10,954
Dec 5	Nottingham Forest	L 0-2		10,699
Dec 12	PLYMOUTH ARGYLE	L 2-3	Beattie 2 (1 pen)	8,756
Dec 19	Coventry City	W 1-0	Beattie	21,984
Dec 25	TOTTENHAM HOTSPUR	L 0-4		26,756
Dec 26	BURY	L 2-3	Baxendale, Smeaton	26,471
Dec 28	Tottenham Hotspur	L 1-5	Baxendale	16,135
Jan 1	DONCASTER ROVERS	W 2-0	Baxendale, Bruton	12,900
Jan 2	Leicester City	L 0-1		15,823
Jan 9	WEST HAM UNITED	L 1-2	Vause	9,240
Jan 23	Norwich City	D 0-0		15,229
Jan 30	NEWCASTLE UNITED	W 6-1	Guest 2, Bruton 2, Forbes, Calladine	7,928
Feb 6	Bradford	W 2-1	Guest, Bruton	11,419
Feb 13	BARNSLEY	D 1-1	Calladine	14,294
Feb 20	Fulham	D 1-1	Bruton	20,059
Feb 27	BURNLEY	W 3-1	Butt, Bruton, Guest	18,240
Mar 6	Southampton	D 2-2	Sale, Calladine	14,238
Mar 13	SWANSEA TOWN	W 2-1	Bruton, Sale	12,941
Mar 20	Bradford City	D 2-2	Butt, Calladine	11,536
Mar 26	Blackpool	L 0-2		29,059
Mar 27	Aston Villa	L 3-4	Bruton, Smeaton, Sale	25,394
Mar 29	BLACKPOOL	W 2-0	Butt, Smeaton	26,927
Apr 3	Chesterfield	W 4-0	Sale 2, Guest, Smeaton	11,361
Apr 10	NOTTINGHAM FOREST	W 9-1	Butt 2, Guest 4, Calladine, Sale 2	11,614
Apr 17	Plymouth Argyle	L 0-2		17,294
Apr 24	COVENTRY CITY	L 2-5	Butt 2 (1 pen)	10,640
May 1	Doncaster Rovers	W 1-0	Butt	6,832

FA Cup

Jan 16	ACCRINGTON STANLEY	(Rd3) D 2-2	Craven o.g., Fraser	31,080
Jan 20	Accrington Stanley*	(R) L 1-3	Calladine	11,636

*After extra-time.

League & Cup Appearances

PLAYER	LEAGUE	CUP COMPETITION FA CUP	TOTAL
Barron, J.	13		13
Baxendale, F.	9	1	10
Beattie, J.M.	20		20
Bruton, J.	39	2	41
Butt, L.	17		17
Calladine, C.F.	25	1	26
Christie, N.	14	2	16
Crook, W.	42	2	44
Forbes, G.P.	2		2
Fraser, N.J.		1	1
Gallacher, P.	10		10
Gorman, J.J.	23		23
Guest, W.	16		16
Hall, F.W.	2		2
Hamill, A.	5		5
Hughes, J.I.	25		25
Lanceley, E.	19	2	21
Lee, J.B.		1	1
Pratt, J.T.	4	2	6
Pryde, R.I.	41	2	43
Rutherford, S.	13	1	14
Sale, T.	37	2	39
Smeaton, J.R.	18		18
Thompson, J.E.	9		9
Vause, P.G.	2	1	3
Whiteside, A.	34	2	36
Wightman, J.R.	17		17
Young, W.	6		6

Goalscorers

PLAYER	LEAGUE	CUP COMPETITION FA CUP	TOTAL
Bruton, J.	16		16
Sale, T.	14		14
Guest, W.	9		9
Butt, L.	8		8
Beattie, J.M.	6		6
Calladine, C.F.	5	1	6
Smeaton, J.R.	4		4
Baxendale, F.	3		3
Thompson, J.E.	2		2
Forbes, G.P.	1		1
Rutherford, S.	1		1
Vause, P.G.	1		1
Fraser, N.J.		1	1
Opps' o.gs.		1	1

Fact File

Billy Guest marked his home debut with two goals in the 6-1 win over Newcastle United in January 1937.

MANAGER: Reg Taylor

TOP SCORER: Jack Bruton

BIGGEST WIN: 9-1, 10 April 1937, v Nottingham Forest, Division 2

HIGHEST ATTENDANCE: 32,567, 24 October 1936, v Burnley, Division 2

MAJOR TRANSFERS IN: Sep Rutherford from Portsmouth, Billy Hough from Preston North End, Billy Guest from Birmingham, Len Butt from Huddersfield Town, Jock Wightman from Huddersfield Town

MAJOR TRANSFERS OUT: Ernie Thompson to Manchester United, Jimmy Gorman to Sunderland, Jack Beattie to Birmingham

Final Division 2 Table

		P	W	D	L	F	A	Pts
1	LEICESTER C	42	24	8	10	89	57	56
2	BLACKPOOL	42	24	7	11	88	53	55
3	BURY	42	22	8	12	74	55	52
4	NEWCASTLE U	42	22	5	15	80	56	49
5	PLYMOUTH ARG	42	18	13	11	71	53	49
6	WEST HAM U	42	19	11	12	73	55	49
7	SHEFFIELD U	42	18	10	14	66	54	46
8	COVENTRY C	42	17	11	14	66	54	45
9	ASTON VILLA	42	16	12	14	82	70	44
10	TOTTENHAM H	42	17	9	16	88	66	43
11	FULHAM	42	15	13	14	71	61	43
12	BLACKBURN R	42	16	10	16	70	62	42
13	BURNLEY	42	16	10	16	57	61	42
14	BARNSLEY	42	16	9	17	50	64	41
15	CHESTERFIELD	42	16	8	18	84	89	40
16	SWANSEA T	42	15	7	20	50	65	37
17	NORWICH C	42	14	8	20	63	71	36
18	NOTTINGHAM F	42	12	10	20	68	90	34
19	SOUTHAMPTON	42	11	12	19	53	77	34
20	BRADFORD PA	42	12	9	21	52	88	33
21	BRADFORD C	42	9	12	21	54	94	30
22	DONCASTER R	42	7	10	25	30	84	24

Football League Division 2

DATE	OPPONENTS	SCORE	GOALSCORERS	ATTENDANCE
Aug 28	Swansea Town	L 2-3	Sale, Smeaton	18,577
Aug 30	PLYMOUTH ARGYLE	W 2-1	Sale, Butt	9,910
Sep 4	NORWICH CITY	W 5-3	Guest 2, Sale, Butt (pen), Smeaton	16,259
Sep 8	Plymouth Argyle	D 2-2	Butt 2	20,053
Sep 11	Aston Villa	L 1-2	Iverson o.g.	44,808
Sep 18	BRADFORD	D 0-0		15,167
Sep 20	FULHAM	D 2-2	Sale, Butt (pen)	12,504
Sep 25	West Ham United	L 0-2		27,699
Oct 2	SOUTHAMPTON	W 4-0	Smeaton 2, Mortimer 2	16,133
Oct 9	Sheffield United	D 1-1	Butt	21,071
Oct 16	MANCHESTER UNITED	D 1-1	Guest	19,580
Oct 23	Stockport County	W 1-0	Mortimer	13,766
Oct 30	BARNSLEY	W 5-3	Guest, Bruton 2, Butt, Wightman	12,353
Nov 6	Luton Town	L 1-4	Guest	16,776
Nov 13	NEWCASTLE UNITED	W 2-1	Mortimer, Butt	17,468
Nov 20	Bury	L 1-2	Sale	13,161
Nov 27	COVENTRY CITY	L 1-3	Butt	17,810
Dec 4	Nottingham Forest	L 1-3	Sale	5,409
Dec 11	BURNLEY	D 3-3	Butt 2, Bruton	15,136
Dec 18	Tottenham Hotspur	L 1-3	Guest	20,251
Dec 25	CHESTERFIELD	D 3-3	Bruton, Smeaton, Butt (pen)	26,810
Dec 27	Chesterfield	L 0-3		16,924
Jan 1	SWANSEA TOWN	W 3-1	Guest 2, Butt	19,855
Jan 15	Norwich City	L 2-3	Dickie, Halsall	10,073
Jan 27	ASTON VILLA	W 1-0	Guest	11,919
Jan 29	Bradford	L 1-7	Butt	11,730
Feb 5	WEST HAM UNITED	W 2-1	Butt 2	13,082
Feb 12	Southampton	L 0-1		16,293
Feb 19	SHEFFIELD UNITED	L 2-3	Butt, Sale	13,880
Feb 26	Manchester United	L 1-2	Hargreaves	30,892
Mar 5	STOCKPORT COUNTY	W 3-0	Guest, Hargreaves, Butt (pen)	14,980
Mar 12	Barnsley	D 0-0		11,136
Mar 19	LUTON TOWN	D 2-2	Luke, Butt	11,957
Mar 26	Newcastle United	L 0-2		14,422
Apr 2	BURY	W 2-1	Butt, Tyson	9,514
Apr 9	Coventry City	L 2-3	Tyson, Chivers	20,007
Apr 16	NOTTINGHAM FOREST	W 5-1	Luke, Chivers, Pryde, Guest 2	13,962
Apr 18	SHEFFIELD WEDNESDAY	W 1-0	Guest	14,978
Apr 19	Sheffield Wednesday	D 1-1	Pryde	28,207
Apr 23	Burnley	L 1-3	Guest	14,139
Apr 30	TOTTENHAM HOTSPUR	W 2-1	Guest 2 (1 pen)	7,088
May 7	Fulham	L 1-3	Guest (pen)	11,765

FA Cup

Jan 8	Tottenham Hotspur	(Rd3) L 2-3	Sale, Guest	35,576

League & Cup Appearances

PLAYER	LEAGUE	CUP COMPETITION FA CUP	TOTAL
Barron, J.	20		20
Bruton, J.	27		27
Butt, L.	42	1	43
Calladine, C.F.	13		13
Chivers, F.C.	10		10
Crook, W.	42	1	43
Dickie, P.	17	1	18
Gallacher, P.	1		1
Guest, W.	42	1	43
Hall, F.W.	21	1	22
Halsall, W.G.	20	1	21
Hargreaves, T.	4		4
Hough, W.A.	18		18
Lanceley, E.	14		14
Luke, C.	10		10
McShane, H.	2		2
Matier, G.	19	1	20
Mortimer, R.	16		16
Pryde, R.I.	35	1	36
Sale, T.	20	1	21
Smeaton, J.R.	20		20
Tyson, W.G.	6		6
Westby, J.L.	2		2
Whiteside, A.	11	1	12
Wightman, J.R.	26	1	27
Wilson, R.	3		3
Woolley, G.H.A.	1		1

Goalscorers

PLAYER	LEAGUE	CUP COMPETITION FA CUP	TOTAL
Butt, L.	20		20
Guest, W.	17	1	18
Sale, T.	7	1	8
Smeaton, J.R.	5		5
Bruton, J.	4		4
Mortimer, R.	4		4
Chivers, F.C.	2		2
Hargreaves, T.	2		2
Luke, C.	2		2
Pryde, R.I.	2		2
Tyson, W.G.	2		2
Dickie, P.	1		1
Halsall, W.G.	1		1
Wightman, J.R.	1		1
Opps' o.gs.	1		1

Fact File

Bob Crompton returned to Ewood Park on 2 April 1938 as an unofficial assistant to Reg Taylor. Under the guidance of Crompton, the club avoided dropping into the Third Division North and, at the end of the season, Crompton was appointed manager while Taylor was retained as secretary.

MANAGER: Reg Taylor

TOP SCORER: Len Butt

BIGGEST WIN: April 16 1938, 5-1 v Nottingham Forest, Division 2

HIGHEST ATTENDANCE: 44,808, 11 September 1938, v Aston Villa, Division 2

MAJOR TRANSFERS IN: Percy Dickie from St Johnstone, Frank Chivers from Huddersfield Town

MAJOR TRANSFERS OUT: Tom Sale to Stoke City

Final Division 2 Table

		P	W	D	L	F	A	Pts
1	ASTON VILLA	42	25	7	10	73	35	57
2	MANCHESTER U	42	22	9	11	82	50	53
3	SHEFFIELD U	42	22	9	11	73	56	53
4	COVENTRY C	42	20	12	10	66	45	52
5	TOTTENHAM H	42	19	6	17	76	54	44
6	BURNLEY	42	17	10	15	54	54	44
7	BRADFORD PA	42	17	9	16	69	56	43
8	FULHAM	42	16	11	15	61	57	43
9	WEST HAM U	42	14	14	14	53	52	42
10	BURY	42	18	5	19	63	60	42
11	CHESTERFIELD	42	16	9	17	63	63	41
12	LUTON T	42	15	10	17	89	86	40
13	PLYMOUTH ARG	42	14	12	16	57	65	40
14	NORWICH C	42	14	11	17	56	75	39
15	SOUTHAMPTON	42	15	9	18	55	77	39
16	BLACKBURN R	42	14	10	18	71	80	38
17	SHEFFIELD W	42	14	10	18	49	56	38
18	SWANSEA T	42	13	12	17	45	73	38
19	NEWCASTLE U	42	14	8	20	51	58	36
20	NOTTINGHAM F	42	14	8	20	47	60	36
21	BARNSLEY	42	11	14	17	50	64	36
22	STOCKPORT CO	42	11	9	22	43	70	31

Season 1938-39

Football League Division 2

DATE	OPPONENTS	SCORE	GOALSCORERS	ATTENDANCE
Aug 27	TRANMERE ROVERS	W 3-2	Clarke 2, Guest	15,360
Aug 29	West Ham United	W 2-1	Rogers, Butt	15,222
Sep 3	Chesterfield	W 2-0	Crook, Rogers	9,085
Sep 8	Sheffield Wednesday	L 0-3		23,036
Sep 10	SWANSEA TOWN	W 4-0	Weddle, Clarke, Butt, Lawrence o.g.	14,272
Sep 17	Bradford	W 4-0	Rogers, Langton, Clarke 2 (1 pen)	13,608
Sep 19	WEST HAM UNITED	W 3-1	Weddle 2, Clarke	18,008
Sep 24	MANCHESTER CITY	D 3-3	Butt, Weddle, Clarke	26,457
Oct 1	Millwall	L 1-4	Butt	37,115
Oct 8	SHEFFIELD UNITED	L 1-2	Clarke (pen)	17,689
Oct 15	Burnley	L 2-3	Clarke 2	29,254
Oct 22	TOTTENHAM HOTSPUR	W 3-1	Buckingham o.g., Butt, Clarke	18,136
Oct 29	Luton Town	D 1-1	Clarke	16,819
Nov 5	COVENTRY CITY	L 0-2		15,787
Nov 12	Nottingham Forest	W 3-1	Weddle, Rogers, Butt	11,731
Nov 19	NEWCASTLE UNITED	W 3-0	Clarke 3	20,876
Nov 26	West Bromwich Albion	L 0-2		22,187
Dec 3	NORWICH CITY	W 6-0	Clarke 2, Rogers, Langton 2, Weddle	12,584
Dec 10	Southampton	W 3-1	Langton 2, Rogers	15,649
Dec 17	PLYMOUTH ARGYLE	W 4-0	Kirkwood o.g., Butt, Weddle 2	12,069
Dec 24	Tranmere Rovers	D 1-1	Langton	9,261
Dec 26	BURY	W 1-0	Weddle	25,548
Dec 27	Bury	W 4-2	Weddle, Rogers 2, Butt	21,190
Dec 31	CHESTERFIELD	W 3-0	McMillen o.g., Butt (pen), Clarke	16,872
Jan 2	SHEFFIELD WEDNESDAY	L 2-4	Langton 2	32,704
Jan 14	Swansea Town	L 1-2	Rogers	8,386
Jan 23	BRADFORD	W 6-4	Rogers 2, Clarke 2, Langton, Butt	7,547
Jan 28	Manchester City	L 2-3	Butt (pen), Langton	47,089
Feb 4	MILLWALL	W 3-1	Rogers, Butt 2 (1 pen)	17,071
Feb 18	BURNLEY	W 1-0	Rogers	30,223
Feb 25	Tottenham Hotspur	L 3-4	Rogers (pen), Langton, Pryde	22,709
Mar 11	Coventry City	W 1-0	Butt	24,717
Mar 16	LUTON TOWN	W 2-0	Weddle 2	8,872
Mar 18	NOTTINGHAM FOREST	W 3-2	Weddle 2, Whiteside	13,882
Mar 25	Newcastle United	D 2-2	Weddle, Rogers	40,237
Apr 1	WEST BROMWICH ALBION	W 3-0	Langton, Crook, Butt	22,360
Apr 7	Fulham	W 3-2	Rogers (pen), Clarke, Langton	28,532
Apr 8	Norwich City	L 0-4		18,547
Apr 10	FULHAM	W 2-1	Weddle, Langton	23,462
Apr 15	SOUTHAMPTON	W 3-0	Rogers 2 (1 pen), Butt	13,722
Apr 22	Plymouth Argyle	L 0-1		14,593
Apr 26	Sheffield United	D 0-0		42,216

FA Cup

DATE	OPPONENTS		SCORE	GOALSCORERS	ATTENDANCE
Jan 7	SWANSEA TOWN	(Rd3)	W 2-0	Clarke, Chivers	17,500
Jan 21	SOUTHEND UNITED	(Rd4)	W 4-2	Butt 2, Clarke, Weddle	21,200
Feb 11	Sunderland	(Rd5)	D 1-1	Butt	52,637
Feb 16	SUNDERLAND*	(R)	D 0-0		47,248
Feb 20	Sunderland†	(2R)	W 1-0*	Guest	30,000
Mar 4	Huddersfield Town	(Rd6)	D 1-1	Weddle	56,518
Mar 9	HUDDERSFIELD TOWN	(R)	L 1-2	Butt	54,400

*After extra time. †Played at Hillsborough, Sheffield.

League & Cup Appearances

PLAYER	LEAGUE	CUP COMPETITION FA CUP	TOTAL
Barron, J.	41	7	48
Bruton, J.	1		1
Butt, L.	41	6	47
Chivers, F.C.	38	7	45
Clarke, A.	38	4	42
Crook, W.	42	7	49
Dickie, P.	2	1	3
Guest, W.	8	3	11
Hall, F.W.	6		6
Hardy, G.G.	7		7
Hough, W.A.	31	7	38
Lanceley, E.	11		11
Langton, R.	37	7	44
Lee, W.R.	1		1
Matier, G.	1		1
Pryde, R.I.	41	7	48
Rogers, W.	41	7	48
Weddle, J.	42	7	49
Whiteside, A.	33	7	40

Goalscorers

PLAYER	LEAGUE	CUP COMPETITION FA CUP	TOTAL
Clarke, A.	21	2	23
Butt, L.	16	4	20
Rogers, W.	18		18
Weddle, J.	16	2	18
Langton, R.	14		14
Crook, W.	2		2
Guest, W.	1	1	2
Pryde, R.I.	1		1
Whiteside, A.	1		1
Chivers, F.C.		1	1
Opps' o.gs.	4		4

Fact File

Bob Crompton celebrated his return to managerial duties at Blackburn Rovers by leading the club to the Second Division championship.

Final Division 2 Table

		P	W	D	L	F	A	Pts
1	BLACKBURN R	42	25	5	12	94	60	55
2	SHEFFIELD U	42	20	14	8	69	41	54
3	SHEFFIELD W	42	21	11	10	88	59	53
4	COVENTRY C	42	21	8	13	62	45	50
5	MANCHESTER C	42	21	7	14	96	72	49
6	CHESTERFIELD	42	20	9	13	69	52	49
7	LUTON T	42	22	5	15	82	66	49
8	TOTTENHAM H	42	19	9	14	67	62	47
9	NEWCASTLE U	42	18	10	14	61	48	46
10	WBA	42	18	9	15	89	72	45
11	WEST HAM U	42	17	10	15	70	52	44
12	FULHAM	42	17	10	15	61	55	44
13	MILLWALL	42	14	14	14	64	53	42
14	BURNLEY	42	15	9	18	50	56	39
15	PLYMOUTH ARG	42	15	8	19	49	55	38
16	BURY	42	12	13	17	65	74	37
17	BRADFORD PA	42	12	11	19	61	82	35
18	SOUTHAMPTON	42	13	9	20	56	82	35
19	SWANSEA T	42	11	12	19	50	83	34
20	NOTTINGHAM F	42	10	11	21	49	82	31
21	NORWICH C	42	13	5	24	50	91	31
22	TRANMERE R	42	6	5	31	39	99	17

MANAGER: Bob Crompton

TOP SCORER: Albert Clarke

BIGGEST WIN: 6-0, 3 December 1938, v Norwich City, Division 2

HIGHEST ATTENDANCE: 56,518, 4 March 1939, v Huddersfield Town, FA Cup Round 6

MAJOR TRANSFERS IN: Jack Weddle from Portsmouth, Billy Rogers from Preston North End, Albert Clarke from Birmingham, George Hardy from Aston Villa

MAJOR TRANSFERS OUT: Wally Halsall to Birmingham

Season 1945-46

Football League North

DATE	OPPONENTS	SCORE	GOALSCORERS	ATTENDANCE
Aug 25	GRIMSBY TOWN	W 3-2	Coates 3	6,129
Sep 1	Grimsby Town	L 0-2		8,449
Sep 8	Blackpool	L 2-5	Coates, Fairweather	16,170
Sep 15	BLACKPOOL	D 1-1	Fairweather	6,951
Sep 17	CHESTERFIELD	L 0-7		4,806
Sep 22	LIVERPOOL	L 0-5		5,131
Sep 29	Liverpool	L 0-4		24,532
Oct 6	BURY	L 2-3	Butt, Bowden	7,682
Oct 13	Bury	L 2-3	Rogers, Wyles	8,076
Oct 20	BURNLEY	W 4-2	Stephan 2, Wyles (pen), Hall W.W.	8,228
Oct 27	Burnley	W 4-1	Wyles 4 (1 pen)	8,639
Nov 3	Bradford	L 1-2	Stephan	11,289
Nov 10	BRADFORD	L 1-2	Wyles (pen)	8,176
Nov 17	Manchester City	L 2-4	Wyles, Rawcliffe	22,277
Nov 24	MANCHESTER CITY	D 0-0		9,558
Dec 1	NEWCASTLE UNITED	L 1-2	Stephan	10,625
Dec 8	Newcastle United	L 1-8	Wyles (pen)	33,092
Dec 15	Sheffield Wednesday	D 1-1	Wyles	17,787
Dec 22	SHEFFIELD WEDNESDAY	W 2-1	Wyles (pen), Stephan	7,579
Dec 25	HUDDERSFIELD TOWN	L 1-6	Glaister	15,072
Dec 26	Huddersfield Town	W 2-0	Stephan, Glaister	17,657
Dec 29	Chesterfield	L 0-4		14,028
Jan 1	BARNSLEY	W 3-1	Glaister, Wyles 2	10,455
Jan 12	EVERTON	W 2-1	Fairweather, Glaister	9,055
Jan 19	Everton	L 1-4	Wyles	23,538
Feb 2	Bolton Wanderers	W 2-1	Glaister, Wyles	14,169
Feb 16	PRESTON NORTH END	L 0-2		11,616
Feb 20	BOLTON WANDERERS	L 0-1		4,444
Feb 23	LEEDS UNITED	D 0-0		6,048
Mar 2	Leeds United	W 4-1	Langton 2, Baldwin, Coates	10,752
Mar 9	Manchester United	L 2-6	Pryde (pen), Baldwin	31,422
Mar 16	MANCHESTER UNITED	L 1-3	Langton	8,000
Mar 21	Preston North End	L 1-3	Wyles	8,000
Mar 23	SUNDERLAND	W 2-1	Langton 2	7,600
Mar 30	Sunderland	D 2-2	Baldwin 2	15,000
Apr 6	Sheffield United	L 1-2	John Smith	25,000
Apr 13	SHEFFIELD UNITED	D 0-0		12,000
Apr 19	MIDDLESBROUGH	D 3-3	Stephan, Langton, John Smith	10,000
Apr 20	STOKE CITY	W 5-1	John Smith 3, Campbell 2	11,600
Apr 22	Middlesbrough	L 1-5	Langton	24,000
Apr 27	Stoke City	L 0-5		5,000
May 4	Barnsley	L 0-4		12,000

FA Cup

Jan 5	Bolton Wanderers	(Rd3/1L) L 0-1		26,307
Jan 9	BOLTON WANDERERS	(Rd3/2L) L 1-3	Wyles	16,800

Fact File

Eddie Hapgood became manager on 1 January 1946.

Final League North Table

		P	W	D	L	F	A	Pts
1	SHEFFIELD U	42	27	6	9	112	62	60
2	EVERTON	42	23	9	10	88	54	55
3	BOLTON W	42	20	11	11	67	45	51
4	MANCHESTER U	42	19	11	12	98	62	49
5	SHEFFIELD W	42	20	8	14	67	60	48
6	NEWCASTLE U	42	21	5	16	106	70	47
7	CHESTERFIELD	42	17	12	13	68	49	46
8	BARNSLEY	42	17	11	14	76	68	45
9	BLACKPOOL	42	18	9	15	94	92	45
10	MANCHESTER C	42	20	4	18	78	75	44
11	LIVERPOOL	42	17	9	16	80	70	43
12	MIDDLESBROUGH	42	17	9	16	75	87	43
13	STOKE C	42	18	6	18	88	79	42
14	BRADFORD PA	42	17	6	19	71	84	40
15	HUDDERSFIELD T	42	17	4	21	90	89	38
16	BURNLEY	42	13	10	19	63	84	36
17	GRIMSBY T	42	13	9	20	61	89	35
18	SUNDERLAND	42	15	5	22	55	83	35
19	PRESTON NE	42	14	6	22	70	77	34
20	BURY	42	12	10	20	60	85	34
21	BLACKBURN R	42	11	7	24	60	111	29
22	LEEDS U	42	9	7	26	66	118	25

League & Cup Appearances

PLAYER	LEAGUE	CUP COMPETITION FA CUP	TOTAL
Baldwin, J.	13	2	15
Baron, J.	19		19
Bell, J.E.	37		37
Bibby, J.J.	4		4
Boothway, J.	1		1
Bowden, N.H.	2		2
Boydell, R.	1		1
Butt, L.	2		2
Campbell, J.	20	2	22
Chapman, E.	1		1
Coates, F.	18		18
Cook, L.	14		14
Crook, W.	14		14
Dailey, H.	1		1
Dellow, R.W.	2		2
Egerton, F.	19		19
Fairweather, J.W.	5		5
Flinton, W.	2		2
Forbes, G.P.	25	1	26
Glaister, G.	16	2	18
Godwin, V.	17		17
Green, A.	23	2	25
Hacking, R.E.	1		1
Hall, F.W.	6		6
Hall, W.W.	3		3
Hapgood, E.A.	2		2
Hayhurst, S.	5		5
Hindle, F.J.	2		2
Langton, R.	21		21
Mansley, E.H.	1		1
Morson, M.	1		1
Patterson, J.G.	15	2	17
Peters, J.	3		3
Pryde, R.I.	25	2	27
Rawcliffe, F.	1		1
Rogers, W.	8		8
Smith, H.	2		2
Smith, James	1		1
Smith, John	9		9
Stephan, H.	28	2	30
Tattersall, A.	2		2
Taylor, W.	2		2
Tomlinson, R.W.	5	2	7
Whiteside, A.	19	2	21
Wightman, J.R.	22	2	24
Wyles, T.C.	22	2	24

Goalscorers

PLAYER	LEAGUE	CUP COMPETITION FA CUP	TOTAL
Wyles, T.C.	16	1	17
Langton, R.	7		7
Stephan, H.	7		7
Coates, F.	5		5
Glaister, G.	5		5
Smith, John	5		5
Baldwin, J.	4		4
Fairweather, J.W.	3		3
Campbell, J.	2		2
Bowden, N.H.	1		1
Butt, L.	1		1
Hall, W.W.	1		1
Pryde, R.I.	1		1
Rawcliffe, F.	1		1
Rogers, W.	1		1

MANAGER: Eddie Hapgood

TOP SCORER: Cec Wyles

BIGGEST WIN: 5-1, 20 April 1946, v Stoke City, Football League North

HIGHEST ATTENDANCE: 33,092, 8 December 1945, v Newcastle United, Football League North

MAJOR TRANSFERS IN: Jack Smith from Manchester United

Season 1946-47

Football League Division 1

DATE	OPPONENTS	SCORE	GOALSCORERS	ATTENDANCE
Aug 31	Portsmouth	L 1-3	Rogers	30,962
Sep 4	Arsenal	W 3-1	Pryde, Smith 2	25,137
Sep 7	EVERTON	W 4-1	Langton, Smith 3	25,678
Sep 14	Huddersfield Town	W 1-0	Smith	17,368
Sep 17	ARSENAL	L 1-2	Glaister	24,563
Sep 21	WOLVERHAMPTON W.	L 1-2	Smith	25,614
Sep 28	Sunderland	L 0-1		43,611
Oct 5	ASTON VILLA	L 0-1		22,619
Oct 12	Derby County	L 1-2	Campbell (pen)	25,050
Oct 19	SHEFFIELD UNITED	W 2-0	Rogers, Stephen	23,415
Oct 26	Leeds United	W 1-0	Campbell	28,683
Nov 2	LIVERPOOL	D 0-0		29,072
Nov 9	Bolton Wanderers	D 0-0		31,727
Nov 16	MIDDLESBROUGH	L 1-2	Campbell (pen)	23,797
Nov 23	Charlton Athletic	W 2-0	Campbell 2	27,726
Nov 30	GRIMSBY TOWN	D 1-1	Guest (pen)	22,677
Dec 7	Preston North End	L 0-4		32,238
Dec 14	MANCHESTER UNITED	W 2-1	Smith 2	21,455
Dec 21	Stoke City	D 0-0		23,641
Dec 25	BLACKPOOL	D 1-1	Langton	27,013
Dec 26	Blackpool	L 0-1		25,576
Dec 28	PORTSMOUTH	L 0-1		24,389
Jan 1	BRENTFORD	L 0-3		29,067
Jan 4	Everton	L 0-1		39,775
Jan 18	HUDDERSFIELD TOWN	D 2-2	Rogers, Smith	24,218
Feb 1	SUNDERLAND	L 1-2	Guest	24,194
Feb 15	DERBY COUNTY	D 1-1	Smith	31,509
Feb 22	Sheffield United	W 1-0	Weir	26,176
Mar 1	LEEDS UNITED	W 1-0	Weir	28,371
Mar 8	Liverpool	L 1-2	Oakes	49,378
Mar 15	BOLTON WANDERERS	W 2-1	Langton, Venters	31,262
Mar 22	Middlesbrough	W 1-0	Langton	31,001
Apr 4	Chelsea	W 2-0	Weir, Oakes	37,840
Apr 5	Grimsby Town	L 1-2	Smith	12,975
Apr 7	CHELSEA	L 1-2	Godwin	35,646
Apr 12	PRESTON NORTH END	L 1-2	Langton	34,688
Apr 19	Manchester United	L 0-4		46,390
Apr 26	STOKE CITY	L 0-2		26,323
May 3	Brentford	W 3-0	Weir, Rogers, Venters	18,022
May 10	Aston Villa	L 1-2	Guest	22,413
May 17	Wolverhampton W.	D 3-3	Weir 2, Venters	42,380
May 26	CHARLTON ATHLETIC	W 1-0	Wightman	18,129

FA Cup

Jan 11	HULL CITY	(Rd3) D 1-1	McClelland	23,500
Jan 16	Hull City	(R) W 3-0	McClelland, Rogers 2	30,501
Jan 25	PORT VALE	(Rd4) W 2-0	Rogers, Baldwin	32,900
Feb 8	Charlton Athletic	(Rd5) L 0-1		30,600

League & Cup Appearances

PLAYER	LEAGUE	CUP COMPETITION	TOTAL
		FA CUP	
Baldwin, J.	10	3	13
Bell, J.E.	28	3	31
Butt, L.	10		10
Campbell, J.	16	4	20
Cook, L.	39	4	43
Crook, W.	21	2	23
Glaister, G.	8		8
Godwin, V.	15		15
Guest, W.	22	2	24
Hayhurst, S.	6		6
Higgins, G.	12	2	14
Horton, H.	3		3
Langton, R.	32	2	34
McClelland, C.	2	2	4
McGorrighan, F.O.	4		4
Marks, W.G.	36	4	40
Oakes, J.	16		16
Pryde, R.I.	40	4	44
Rogers, W.	26	3	29
Smith, J.	30	4	34
Stephen, H.W.	12		12
Tomlinson, R.W.	1		1
Venters, A.	10		10
Webber, J.V.	2		2
Weir, J.B.	13		13
Whiteside, A.	25	3	28
Wightman, J.R.	23	2	25

Goalscorers

PLAYER	LEAGUE	CUP COMPETITION	TOTAL
		FA CUP	
Smith, J.	12		12
Rogers, W.	4	3	7
Weir, J.B.	6		6
Campbell, J.	5		5
Langton, R.	5		5
Guest, W.	3		3
Venters, A.	3		3
Oakes, J.	2		2
McClelland, C.		2	2
Glaister, G.	1		1
Godwin, V.	1		1
Pryde, R.I.	1		1
Stephen, H.W.	1		1
Wightman, J.R.	1		1
Baldwin, J.		1	1

Fact File

Walter Crook made his 208th consecutive league appearance
for Blackburn Rovers when he appeared at Deepdale on
7 December 1946.

MANAGER: Eddie Hapgood

TOP SCORER: Jack Smith

BIGGEST WIN: 4-1, 7 September 1946, v Everton, Division 1

HIGHEST ATTENDANCE: 49,378, 8 March 1947, v Liverpool, Division 1

MAJOR TRANSFERS IN: Jack Weir from Hibernian, Jackie Oakes from
Queen of the South, Alex Venters from Third Lanark

MAJOR TRANSFERS OUT: Len Butt to York City, Walter Crook to
Bolton Wanderers

Final Division 1 Table

		P	W	D	L	F	A	Pts
1	LIVERPOOL	42	25	7	10	84	52	57
2	MANCHESTER U	42	22	12	8	95	54	56
3	WOLVERHAMPTON W	42	25	6	11	98	56	56
4	STOKE C	42	24	7	11	90	53	55
5	BLACKPOOL	42	22	6	14	71	70	50
6	SHEFFIELD U	42	21	7	14	89	75	49
7	PRESTON NE	42	18	11	13	76	74	47
8	ASTON VILLA	42	18	9	15	67	53	45
9	SUNDERLAND	42	18	8	16	65	66	44
10	EVERTON	42	17	9	16	62	67	43
11	MIDDLESBROUGH	42	17	8	17	73	68	42
12	PORTSMOUTH	42	16	9	17	66	60	41
13	ARSENAL	42	16	9	17	72	70	41
14	DERBY CO	42	18	5	19	73	79	41
15	CHELSEA	42	16	7	19	69	84	39
16	GRIMSBY T	42	13	12	17	61	82	38
17	BLACKBURN R	42	14	8	20	45	53	36
18	BOLTON W	42	13	8	21	57	69	34
19	CHARLTON ATH	42	11	12	19	57	71	34
20	HUDDERSFIELD T	42	13	7	22	53	79	33
21	BRENTFORD	42	9	7	26	45	88	25
22	LEEDS U	42	6	6	30	45	90	18

The Essential History of Blackburn Rovers

Season 1947-48

Football League Division 1

DATE	OPPONENTS	SCORE	GOALSCORERS	ATTENDANCE
Aug 23	EVERTON	L 2-3	Webber, Rogers	24,536
Aug 27	Chelsea	L 0-1		36,375
Aug 30	Wolverhampton W.	L 1-5	Rogers	46,890
Sep 6	ASTON VILLA	D 0-0		24,772
Sep 8	Blackpool	L 0-1		28,137
Sep 13	Sunderland	W 1-0	Venters	36,039
Sep 15	BLACKPOOL	D 1-1	Godwin	27,790
Sep 20	GRIMSBY TOWN	W 4-0	Godwin 2, Oakes, Graham	24,254
Sep 27	Manchester City	W 3-1	Oakes (pen), Venters, Godwin	47,544
Oct 4	PRESTON NORTH END	L 2-3	Oakes, Graham	46,874
Oct 11	Stoke City	L 1-2	Langton (pen)	33,984
Oct 18	BURNLEY	L 1-2	Venters	41,635
Oct 25	Portsmouth	D 1-1	Graham	33,370
Nov 1	BOLTON WANDERERS	W 4-0	Oakes 2 (1 pen), Godwin, Langton	31,721
Nov 8	Charlton Athletic	W 1-0	Langton (pen)	37,634
Nov 15	ARSENAL	L 0-1		37,447
Nov 22	Liverpool	L 1-2	Graham	35,672
Nov 29	MIDDLESBROUGH	L 1-7	Oakes	26,506
Dec 6	Sheffield United	L 1-4	Venters	23,578
Dec 13	MANCHESTER UNITED	D 1-1	Weir	22,784
Dec 20	Everton	L 1-4	Oakes	32,655
Dec 25	DERBY COUNTY	L 3-4	Campbell, Graham, Langton	30,405
Dec 27	Derby County	L 0-5		25,366
Jan 1	CHELSEA	D 1-1	Graham	18,365
Jan 3	WOLVERHAMPTON W.	W 1-0	McClelland	26,203
Jan 31	SUNDERLAND	W 4-3	Graham, Campbell 2, Murphy	23,749
Feb 7	Grimsby Town	D 2-2	Crossan, Graham	14,231
Feb 14	MANCHESTER CITY	W 1-0	Graham	30,975
Feb 21	Preston North End	L 1-2	Crossan	31,735
Feb 28	STOKE CITY	W 2-0	Campbell (pen), Graham	24,346
Mar 6	Burnley	D 0-0		44,240
Mar 13	PORTSMOUTH	W 1-0	Langton	27,626
Mar 20	Bolton Wanderers	L 0-1		34,520
Mar 26	HUDDERSFIELD TOWN	L 1-2	Crossan	28,795
Mar 27	Charlton Athletic	D 0-0		26,750
Mar 29	Huddersfield Town	D 1-1	Pryde	19,928
Apr 3	Arsenal	L 0-2		45,801
Apr 10	LIVERPOOL	L 1-2	Graham	25,915
Apr 14	Aston Villa	L 2-3	Campbell (pen), Graham	19,394
Apr 17	Middlesbrough	D 1-1	Murphy	22,033
Apr 24	SHEFFIELD UNITED	W 4-0	Graham 3, McClelland	14,087
May 1	Manchester United	L 1-4	Murphy	45,711

FA Cup

Jan 10	WEST HAM UNITED*	(Rd3) D 0-0		32,500
Jan 17	West Ham United*	(R) W 4-2	McClelland 2, Murphy, Graham	30,000
Jan 24	Southampton	(Rd4) L 2-3	Campbell, McClelland	24,274
				*After extra-time.

League & Cup Appearances

PLAYER	LEAGUE	CUP COMPETITION FA CUP	TOTAL
Baldwin, J.	38	3	41
Bell, J.E.	27		27
Campbell, J.	21	1	22
Cook, L.	18	3	21
Crossan, E.	12		12
Eckersley, W.	1		1
Godwin, V.	12		12
Graham, L.	32	3	35
Hayhurst, S.	11		11
Higgins, G.	28		28
Holliday, K.J.	3		3
Horton, H.	22	3	25
Langton, R.	38	3	41
McClelland, C.	6	3	9
McGorrighan, F.O.	1		1
Marks, W.G.	31	3	34
Miller, A.B.	6		6
Mitchell, A.J.	3		3
Murphy, T.E.	20	3	23
Oakes, J.	19	2	21
Pryde, R.I.	40	3	43
Quinn, D.	1		1
Rogers, W.	6		6
Stephan, H.W.	1		1
Tomlinson, R.W.	24	3	27
Venters, A.	15		15
Webber, J.V.	6		6
Weir, J.B.V.	10		10
Wheeler, A.J.	1		1
Whiteside, A.	9		9

Goalscorers

PLAYER	LEAGUE	CUP COMPETITION FA CUP	TOTAL
Graham, L.	15	1	16
Oakes, J.	7		7
Campbell, J.	5	1	6
Godwin, V.	5		5
Langton, R.	5		5
McClelland, C.	2	3	5
Venters, A.	4		4
Murphy, T.E.	3	1	4
Crossan, E.	3		3
Rogers, W.	2		2
Pryde, R.I.	1		1
Webber, J.V.	1		1
Weir, J.B.V.	1		1

Fact File

One win in the last ten games consigned Blackburn Rovers to the Second Division at the end of a season that had seen manager Will Scott resign through ill health.

MANAGER: Will Scott/Jack Bruton

TOP SCORER: Les Graham

BIGGEST WIN: 4-0, 20 September 1947, v Grimsby Town, Division 1; 1 November 1947, v Bolton Wanderers, Division 1; 24 April 1948, v Sheffield United, Division 1

HIGHEST ATTENDANCE: 47,544, 27 September 1947, v Manchester City, Division 1

MAJOR TRANSFERS IN: Eddie Crossan from Derry City, Dennis Westcott from Wolverhampton Wanderers

MAJOR TRANSFERS OUT: Jack Weir to Celtic

Final Division 1 Table

		P	W	D	L	F	A	Pts
1	ARSENAL	42	23	13	6	81	32	59
2	MANCHESTER U	42	19	14	9	81	48	52
3	BURNLEY	42	20	12	10	56	43	52
4	DERBY CO	42	19	12	11	77	57	50
5	WOLVERHAMPTON W	42	19	9	14	83	70	47
6	ASTON VILLA	42	19	9	14	65	57	47
7	PRESTON NE	42	20	7	15	67	68	47
8	PORTSMOUTH	42	19	7	16	68	50	45
9	BLACKPOOL	42	17	10	15	57	41	44
10	MANCHESTER C	42	15	12	15	52	47	42
11	LIVERPOOL	42	16	10	16	65	61	42
12	SHEFFIELD U	42	16	10	16	65	70	42
13	CHARLTON ATH	42	17	6	19	57	66	40
14	EVERTON	42	17	6	19	52	66	40
15	STOKE C	42	14	10	18	41	55	38
16	MIDDLESBROUGH	42	14	9	19	71	73	37
17	BOLTON W	42	16	5	21	46	58	37
18	CHELSEA	42	14	9	19	53	71	37
19	HUDDERSFIELD T	42	12	12	18	51	60	36
20	SUNDERLAND	42	13	10	19	56	67	36
21	BLACKBURN R	42	11	10	21	54	72	32
22	GRIMSBY T	42	8	6	28	45	111	22

Season 1948-49

Football League Division 2

DATE	OPPONENTS	SCORE	GOALSCORERS	ATTENDANCE
Aug 21	Southampton	L 0-3		26,018
Aug 23	BRADFORD	L 2-3	Gray 2 (2 pens)	27,786
Aug 28	BARNSLEY	W 5-3	Graham, Crossan 2, Westcott 2	24,781
Sep 1	Bradford	L 0-2		17,749
Sep 4	Grimsby Town	W 2-1	Westcott, Wheeler	15,671
Sep 6	Luton Town	L 0-2		18,642
Sep 11	NOTTINGHAM FOREST	W 2-1	Gray (pen), Wharton	21,886
Sep 18	Fulham	D 1-1	Westcott	27,198
Sep 20	LUTON TOWN	W 4-1	Westcott 2, Gray (pen), Graham	24,533
Sep 25	PLYMOUTH ARGYLE	W 2-1	Westcott 2	20,719
Oct 2	Tottenham Hotspur	L 0-4		53,721
Oct 9	WEST HAM UNITED	D 0-0		24,037
Oct 16	Bury	L 1-3	Wheeler	28,456
Oct 23	WEST BROMWICH ALBION	D 0-0		28,107
Oct 30	Chesterfield	D 0-0		13,915
Nov 6	LINCOLN CITY	W 7-1	Wheeler, Wharton 2, Westcott 2, Murphy 2	25,603
Nov 13	Sheffield Wednesday	L 0-3		29,925
Nov 20	COVENTRY CITY	W 2-0	Wheeler, Westcott	22,910
Dec 4	LEICESTER CITY	W 2-0	Westcott 2	22,476
Dec 11	Brentford	W 1-0	Westcott	21,421
Dec 18	SOUTHAMPTON	L 1-2	Westcott	24,720
Dec 25	QUEENS PARK RANGERS	W 2-0	Graham, Wharton	31,526
Dec 27	Queens Park Rangers	L 2-4	Gray (pen), Westcott	17,091
Jan 1	Barnsley	D 1-1	Westcott	18,708
Jan 15	GRIMSBY TOWN	D 3-3	Murphy, Wharton, Bell	13,418
Jan 22	Nottingham Forest	L 0-1		25,624
Jan 29	Leeds United	L 0-1		32,963
Feb 5	FULHAM	W 1-0	Fenton	22,582
Feb 19	Plymouth Argyle	L 0-3		20,719
Feb 26	TOTTENHAM HOTSPUR	D 1-1	Graham	20,262
Mar 5	West Ham United	L 1-2	Westcott	18,245
Mar 12	BURY	L 1-2	Westcott	24,530
Mar 19	West Bromwich Albion	L 1-2	Wheeler	36,053
Mar 26	CHESTERFIELD	L 0-2		17,740
Apr 2	Lincoln City	L 0-3		11,749
Apr 9	SHEFFIELD WEDNESDAY	W 2-1	Bell, Priday	17,666
Apr 15	CARDIFF CITY	W 2-1	Crossan, Westcott	23,468
Apr 16	Coventry City	W 1-0	Fenton	23,452
Apr 18	Cardiff City	L 0-1		33,325
Apr 21	Leicester City	L 1-3	Eckersley (pen)	30,414
Apr 23	LEEDS UNITED	D 0-0		18,873
May 7	BRENTFORD	W 2-1	Bell, Westcott	15,453

FA Cup

Jan 3	Hull City*	(Rd3) L 1-2	Graham	33,200

*After extra-time.

League & Cup Appearances

PLAYER	LEAGUE	CUP COMPETITION FA CUP	TOTAL
Baldwin, J.	27		27
Bee, F.E.	4		4
Bell, J.E.	35	1	36
Campbell, J.	4		4
Carter, D.F.	2		2
Chadwick, F.R.	2		2
Cook, L.	19	1	20
Crossan, E.	31	1	32
Eckersley, W.	42	1	43
Fenton, W.H.	10		10
Graham, L.	27	1	28
Gray, D.	38	1	39
Hayhurst, S.	10		10
Holliday, K.J.	6		6
Holt, W.K.	1		1
Horton, H.	17		17
Hughes, W.A.	19	1	20
Jackson, H.	1	1	2
McCaig, R.A.M.	3		3
McClelland, C.	5		5
Murphy, T.E.	11		11
Patterson, J.G.	13		13
Priday, R.H.	10		10
Pryde, R.I.	37	1	38
Westcott, D.	36	1	37
Wharton, J.E.	30	1	31
Wheeler, A.J.	20		20
Whiteside, A.	1		1
Wilkinson, D.L.	1		1

Goalscorers

PLAYER	LEAGUE	CUP COMPETITION FA CUP	TOTAL
Westcott, D.	21		21
Gray, D.	5		5
Wharton, J.E.	5		5
Wheeler, A.J.	5		5
Graham, L.	4	1	5
Bell, J.E.	3		3
Crossan, E.	3		3
Murphy, T.E.	3		3
Fenton, W.H.	2		2
Eckersley, W.	1		1
Priday, R.H.	1		1

Fact File

Two pre-war favourites bowed out of Ewood Park when Bob Pryde and Arnold Whiteside ended their association with the club. Pryde made his final league appearance against Leeds United at Ewood Park on 23 April 1949 while Whiteside had made his final bow against Leicester City at Filbert Street two days earlier.

MANAGER: Jack Bruton
TOP SCORER: Dennis Westcott
BIGGEST WIN: 7-1, 6 November 1948, v Lincoln City, Division 2
HIGHEST ATTENDANCE: 53,721, 2 October 1948, v Tottenham Hotspur, Division 2
MAJOR TRANSFERS IN: Jackie Wharton from Manchester City, David Gray from Preston North End, Bill Hughes from Tottenham Hotspur, Bob Priday from Liverpool
MAJOR TRANSFERS OUT: Jackie Oakes to Manchester City, George Marks to Bristol City, Bob Langton to Preston North End, Stan Hayhurst to Tottenham Hotspur

Final Division 2 Table

		P	W	D	L	F	A	Pts
1	FULHAM	42	24	9	9	77	37	57
2	WBA	42	24	8	10	69	39	56
3	SOUTHAMPTON	42	23	9	10	69	36	55
4	CARDIFF C	42	19	13	10	62	47	51
5	TOTTENHAM H	42	17	16	9	72	44	50
6	CHESTERFIELD	42	15	17	10	51	45	47
7	WEST HAM U	42	18	10	14	56	58	46
8	SHEFFIELD W	42	15	13	14	63	56	43
9	BARNSLEY	42	14	12	16	62	61	40
10	LUTON T	42	14	12	16	55	57	40
11	GRIMSBY T	42	15	10	17	72	76	40
12	BURY	42	17	6	19	67	76	40
13	QPR	42	14	11	17	44	62	39
14	BLACKBURN R	42	15	8	19	53	63	38
15	LEEDS U	42	12	13	17	55	63	37
16	COVENTRY C	42	15	7	20	55	64	37
17	BRADFORD PA	42	13	11	18	65	78	37
18	BRENTFORD	42	11	14	17	42	53	36
19	LEICESTER C	42	10	16	16	62	79	36
20	PLYMOUTH ARG	42	12	12	18	49	64	36
21	NOTTINGHAM F	42	14	7	21	50	54	35
22	LINCOLN C	42	8	12	22	53	91	28

Season 1949-50

Football League Division 2

DATE	OPPONENTS	SCORE	GOALSCORERS	ATTENDANCE
Aug 20	CARDIFF CITY	W 1-0	Wharton	28,265
Aug 22	HULL CITY	W 4-2	Crossan, Bell, Wharton, Priday	30,982
Aug 27	Tottenham Hotspur	W 3-2	Ramsey o.g., Priday, Westcott	53,016
Sep 1	Hull City	L 1-3	Westcott	43,812
Sep 3	BURY	W 2-1	Westcott 2	30,482
Sep 10	Leicester City	D 3-3	Westcott 2, Bell	31,735
Sep 14	Brentford	L 0-2		19,889
Sep 17	BRADFORD	L 0-1		23,106
Sep 19	BRENTFORD	W 4-1	Crossan, Westcott 3	18,613
Sep 24	Chesterfield	L 1-2	Eckersley (pen)	15,255
Oct 1	PLYMOUTH ARGYLE	W 1-0	Priday	24,341
Oct 8	Swansea Town	L 0-2		20,143
Oct 15	LEEDS UNITED	L 0-1		22,038
Oct 22	Southampton	L 1-3	Wharton	21,406
Oct 29	COVENTRY CITY	L 0-1		15,204
Nov 5	Luton Town	L 2-5	Wharton, Westcott	9,513
Nov 12	BARNSLEY	W 4-0	Westcott 3, Priday	10,948
Nov 19	West Ham United	W 2-0	Crossan, Priday	19,687
Nov 26	SHEFFIELD UNITED	L 0-2		19,072
Dec 3	Grimsby Town	W 2-1	Westcott, Eckersley	15,005
Dec 10	QUEENS PARK RANGERS	D 0-0		16,808
Dec 17	Cardiff City	L 1-2	Graham	19,882
Dec 24	TOTTENHAM HOTSPUR	L 1-2	Westcott	33,078
Dec 26	Sheffield Wednesday	L 0-2		52,853
Dec 27	SHEFFIELD WEDNESDAY	D 0-0		30,636
Dec 31	Bury	L 0-3		21,708
Jan 14	LEICESTER CITY	W 3-0	Horton, Westcott, Graham	21,826
Jan 21	Bradford	D 2-2	Graham, Horsman o.g.	13,707
Feb 4	CHESTERFIELD	D 1-1	Graham	18,761
Feb 18	Plymouth Argyle	D 0-0		22,615
Feb 25	SWANSEA TOWN	W 2-0	Horton, Edds	14,092
Mar 11	SOUTHAMPTON	D 0-0		18,230
Mar 18	Coventry City	D 1-1	Edds	21,276
Mar 25	LUTON TOWN	D 0-0		17,255
Apr 1	Sheffield United	L 0-4		33,106
Apr 7	PRESTON NORTH END	L 2-3	Moore, Quigley o.g.	42,891
Apr 8	GRIMSBY TOWN	W 3-0	Eckersley 2 (2 pens), Horton	15,363
Apr 10	Preston North End	L 1-3	Edds	27,925
Apr 15	Barnsley	D 1-1	Campbell	12,323
Apr 22	WEST HAM UNITED	W 2-0	Crossan, Horton	17,375
Apr 26	Leeds United	L 1-2	Graham	12,538
Apr 29	Queens Park Rangers	W 3-2	McCaig 2, Crossan	10,352

FA Cup

Jan 7	LIVERPOOL	(Rd3) D 0-0		52,468
Jan 11	Liverpool	(R) L 1-2	Edds	52,221

League & Cup Appearances

PLAYER	LEAGUE	CUP COMPETITION FA CUP	TOTAL
Baldwin, J.	13		13
Bell, J.E.	42	2	44
Campbell, J.	28	2	30
Crossan, E.	27		27
Eckersley, W.	39	2	41
Edds, E.F.	14	1	15
Fenton, W.H.	6		6
Graham, L.	30	2	32
Gray, D.	38	2	40
Holt, W.K.	35	2	37
Horton, H.	33	2	35
Hughes, W.A.	8		8
McCaig, R.A.M.	20	2	22
Moore, N.W.	6		6
Patterson, J.G.	34	2	36
Priday, R.H.	18	1	19
Suart, R.	14		14
Westcott, D.	27	2	29
Wharton, J.E.	30		30

Goalscorers

PLAYER	LEAGUE	CUP COMPETITION FA CUP	TOTAL
Westcott, D.	16		16
Crossan, E.	5		5
Graham, L.	5		5
Priday, R.H.	5		5
Eckersley, W.	4		4
Horton, H.	4		4
Wharton, J.E.	4		4
Edds, E.F.	3	1	4
Bell, J.E.	2		2
McCaig, R.A.M.	2		2
Campbell, J.	1		1
Moore, N.W.	1		1
Opps' o.gs.	3		3

Fact File

Although Dennis Westcott was sold to Manchester City in February 1950, he remained the only player to take his goal-scoring tally for the season into double figures.

MANAGER: Jackie Bestall

TOP SCORER: Dennis Westcott

BIGGEST WIN: 4-0, 12 November 1949, v Barnsley, Division 2

HIGHEST ATTENDANCE: 53,016, 27 August 1949, v Tottenham Hotspur, Division 2

MAJOR TRANSFERS IN: Ron Suart from Blackpool

MAJOR TRANSFERS OUT: Leslie Cook to Coventry City, Jimmy Baldwin to Leicester City

Final Division 2 Table

		P	W	D	L	F	A	Pts
1	TOTTENHAM H	42	27	7	8	81	35	61
2	SHEFFIELD W	42	18	16	8	67	48	52
3	SHEFFIELD U	42	19	14	9	68	49	52
4	SOUTHAMPTON	42	19	14	9	64	48	52
5	LEEDS U	42	17	13	12	54	45	47
6	PRESTON NE	42	18	9	15	60	49	45
7	HULL C	42	17	11	14	64	72	45
8	SWANSEA T	42	17	9	16	53	49	43
9	BRENTFORD	42	15	13	14	44	49	43
10	CARDIFF C	42	16	10	16	41	44	42
11	GRIMSBY T	42	16	8	18	74	73	40
12	COVENTRY C	42	13	13	16	55	55	39
13	BARNSLEY	42	13	13	16	64	67	39
14	CHESTERFIELD	42	15	9	18	43	47	39
15	LEICESTER C	42	12	15	15	55	65	39
16	BLACKBURN R	42	14	10	18	55	60	38
17	LUTON T	42	10	18	14	41	51	38
18	BURY	42	14	9	19	60	65	37
19	WEST HAM U	42	12	12	18	53	61	36
20	QPR	42	11	12	19	40	57	34
21	PLYMOUTH ARG	42	8	16	18	44	65	32
22	BRADFORD PA	42	10	11	21	51	77	31

Season 1950-51

Football League Division 2

DATE	OPPONENTS	SCORE	GOALSCORERS	ATTENDANCE
Aug 19	Sheffield United	W 3-0	Eckersley (pen), Priday, Crossan	34,766
Aug 21	BRENTFORD	W 3-2	Graham 2, Priday	30,176
Aug 26	LUTON TOWN	W 1-0	Crossan	25,114
Aug 30	Brentford	L 2-3	Todd, Priday	12,122
Sep 2	Leeds United	W 1-0	Crossan	32,799
Sep 6	Southampton	D 1-1	Todd	22,561
Sep 9	WEST HAM UNITED	L 1-3	Graham (pen)	25,323
Sep 11	SOUTHAMPTON	W 1-0	Graham	17,515
Sep 16	Swansea Town	W 2-1	Priday, Campbell	18,166
Sep 23	HULL CITY	D 2-2	Graham (pen), Priday	28,904
Sep 30	Doncaster Rovers	W 1-0	Crossan	23,973
Oct 7	CARDIFF CITY	W 2-0	Campbell 2	24,831
Oct 14	Coventry City	L 1-6	Graham	34,918
Oct 21	GRIMSBY TOWN	W 2-0	Crossan, Todd	23,235
Oct 28	Birmingham City	L 2-3	Wharton, Graham	24,552
Nov 4	PRESTON NORTH END	W 2-1	Todd 2	44,612
Nov 11	Notts County	D 1-1	Graham	35,487
Nov 18	MANCHESTER CITY	W 4-1	Crossan, Graham, Leaver, Eckersley (pen)	37,594
Nov 25	Leicester City	L 0-2		22,361
Dec 2	CHESTERFIELD	D 1-1	Bell	22,284
Dec 9	Queens Park Rangers	L 1-3	Wharton	13,585
Dec 16	SHEFFIELD UNITED	L 0-2		15,451
Dec 23	Luton Town	D 1-1	Graham	11,632
Dec 25	BURY	L 2-4	Todd, Graham	32,741
Jan 1	Bury	W 3-1	Horton, Fenton, Graham	21,263
Jan 13	West Ham United	W 3-2	Crossan, Fenton, Harris	22,667
Jan 20	SWANSEA TOWN	W 3-0	Elwell o.g., Fenton, Harris	17,964
Feb 3	Hull City	D 2-2	Todd 2	38,786
Feb 10	LEEDS UNITED	W 2-1	Harris, Graham	25,496
Feb 17	DONCASTER ROVERS	W 4-2	Harris 2, Todd, Makepeace o.g.	21,605
Feb 24	Cardiff City	L 0-1		32,811
Mar 3	COVENTRY CITY	W 1-0	Eckersley (pen)	31,144
Mar 10	Grimsby Town	D 1-1	Harris	13,216
Mar 17	BIRMINGHAM CITY	L 2-3	Fenton, Todd	28,116
Mar 23	BARNSLEY	L 3-4	Fenton, Harris 2	31,060
Mar 24	Preston North End	L 0-3		39,122
Mar 26	Barnsley	L 0-3		15,125
Mar 31	NOTTS COUNTY	D 0-0		17,626
Apr 7	Manchester City	L 0-1		37,853
Apr 14	LEICESTER CITY	W 1-0	Leaver	10,867
Apr 21	Chesterfield	L 1-4	Harris	8,995
Apr 25	QUEENS PARK RANGERS	W 2-1	Harris, Anderson	9,770

FA Cup

Jan 6	Bristol City	(Rd3) L 1-2	Wharton		23,245

League & Cup Appearances

PLAYER	LEAGUE	CUP COMPETITION FA CUP	TOTAL
Anderson, C.S.	6		6
Bell, J.E.	36	1	37
Campbell, J.	35	1	36
Clayton, R.	1		1
Crossan, E.	36		36
Eckersley, W.	29		29
Edds, E.F.	4		4
Fenton, W.H.	17	1	18
Graham, L.	38	1	39
Gray, D.	12		12
Harris, J.	17		17
Higgins, G.	13	1	14
Holliday, K.J.	8	1	9
Holt, W.K.	34		34
Horton, H.	17	1	18
Leaver, D.	4		4
McCaig, R.A.M.	7		7
McKee, W.A.	1		1
Moore, N.W.	1		1
Patterson, J.G.	42	1	43
Priday, R.H.	16		16
Suart, R.	30	1	31
Todd, P.R.	39	1	40
Wharton, J.E.	19	1	20

Goalscorers

PLAYER	LEAGUE	CUP COMPETITION FA CUP	TOTAL
Graham, L.	13		13
Harris, J.	10		10
Todd, P.R.	10		10
Crossan, E.	7		7
Fenton, W.H.	5		5
Priday, R.H.	5		5
Campbell, J.	3		3
Eckersley, W.	3		3
Wharton, J.E.	2	1	3
Leaver, D.	2		2
Anderson, C.S.	1		1
Bell, J.E.	1		1
Horton, H.	1		1
Opps' o.gs.	2		2

Fact File

Ronnie Clayton made his debut against Queens Park Rangers on the final day of the season.

MANAGER: Jackie Bestall

TOP SCORER: Les Graham

BIGGEST WIN: 4-1, 18 November 1950, v Manchester City, Division 2

HIGHEST ATTENDANCE: 44,612, 4 November 1950, v Preston North End, Division 2

MAJOR TRANSFERS IN: Paul Todd from Doncaster Rovers

MAJOR TRANSFERS OUT: Bill Hughes to Rochdale

Final Division 2 Table

		P	W	D	L	F	A	Pts
1	PRESTON NE	42	26	5	11	91	49	57
2	MANCHESTER C	42	19	14	9	89	61	52
3	CARDIFF C	42	17	16	9	53	45	50
4	BIRMINGHAM C	42	20	9	13	64	53	49
5	LEEDS U	42	20	8	14	63	55	48
6	BLACKBURN R	42	19	8	15	65	66	46
7	COVENTRY C	42	19	7	16	75	59	45
8	SHEFFIELD U	42	16	12	14	72	62	44
9	BRENTFORD	42	18	8	16	75	74	44
10	HULL C	42	16	11	15	74	70	43
11	DONCASTER R	42	15	13	14	64	68	43
12	SOUTHAMPTON	42	15	13	14	66	73	43
13	WEST HAM U	42	16	10	16	68	69	42
14	LEICESTER C	42	15	11	16	68	58	41
15	BARNSLEY	42	15	10	17	74	68	40
16	QPR	42	15	10	17	71	82	40
17	NOTTS CO	42	13	13	16	61	60	39
18	SWANSEA T	42	16	4	22	54	77	36
19	LUTON T	42	9	14	19	57	70	32
20	BURY	42	12	8	22	60	86	32
21	CHESTERFIELD	42	9	12	21	44	69	30
22	GRIMSBY T	42	8	12	22	61	95	28

Season 1951-52

Football League Division 2

DATE	OPPONENTS	SCORE	GOALSCORERS	ATTENDANCE
Aug 18	SHEFFIELD UNITED	L 1-5	Todd	20,760
Aug 22	Doncaster Rovers	L 0-1		23,793
Aug 25	West Ham United	L 1-3	Harris	19,208
Aug 27	DONCASTER ROVERS	D 3-3	Graham 2, Todd	16,516
Sep 1	COVENTRY CITY	L 0-1		17,428
Sep 3	Queens Park Rangers	L 1-2	Wright	13,392
Sep 8	Swansea Town	L 1-5	Todd	22,047
Sep 15	BURY	L 1-2	Wharton	20,058
Sep 22	Luton Town	D 1-1	Harris	20,022
Sep 29	NOTTS COUNTY	W 2-0	Graham, Harris	25,560
Oct 6	Everton	W 2-0	Nightingale, Graham (pen)	39,756
Oct 13	SOUTHAMPTON	L 0-1		25,343
Oct 20	Sheffield Wednesday	L 0-2		31,439
Oct 27	LEEDS UNITED	L 2-3	Bell, Crossan	20,631
Nov 3	Rotherham United	L 0-3		18,254
Nov 10	CARDIFF CITY	L 0-1		22,477
Nov 17	Birmingham City	W 1-0	Quigley	22,337
Nov 24	LEICESTER CITY	W 2-1	Baldwin o.g., Quigley	24,931
Dec 1	Nottingham Forest	L 0-1		24,335
Dec 8	BRENTFORD	W 3-0	Crossan, Quigley 2	13,617
Dec 15	Sheffield United	D 1-1	Quigley	28,121
Dec 22	WEST HAM UNITED	W 3-1	Nightingale, Quigley, Glover	19,617
Dec 25	HULL CITY	W 1-0	Quigley	34,077
Dec 26	Hull City	L 0-3		36,689
Dec 29	Coventry City	W 2-1	Quigley 2	22,413
Jan 1	QUEENS PARK RANGERS	W 4-2	Holmes, Nightingale, Eckersley 2 (2 pens)	28,671
Jan 5	SWANSEA TOWN	W 3-1	Nightingale, Holmes, Eckersley (pen)	27,736
Jan 19	Bury	W 2-0	Holmes 2	25,577
Jan 26	LUTON TOWN	W 2-1	Nightingale, Wharton	25,156
Feb 9	Notts County	W 1-0	Holmes	26,177
Feb 16	EVERTON	W 1-0	Harris	30,434
Mar 1	Southampton	L 1-2	Quigley	22,095
Mar 12	SHEFFIELD WEDNESDAY	D 0-0		20,290
Mar 15	Leeds United	L 0-1		29,226
Mar 22	ROTHERHAM UNITED	D 1-1	Crossan	25,833
Apr 5	BIRMINGHAM CITY	L 1-4	Warhurst o.g.	19,151
Apr 11	BARNSLEY	W 2-1	Wright 2	25,183
Apr 12	Leicester City	L 1-2	Quigley	24,418
Apr 14	Barnsley	W 2-1	Holmes 2	18,251
Apr 19	NOTTINGHAM FOREST	W 3-2	Glover, Eckersley (pen), Wright	24,312
Apr 21	Cardiff City	L 1-3	Wright	31,169
Apr 26	Brentford	D 1-1	Crossan	16,195

FA Cup

Jan 12	Nottingham Forest	(Rd3)	D 2-2	Crossan, Holmes	24,976
Jan 16	NOTTINGHAM FOREST	(R)	W 2-0	Holmes, Nightingale	34,813
Feb 2	HULL CITY	(Rd4)	W 2-0	Nightingale, Wharton	45,320
Feb 23	WEST BROMWICH ALBION	(Rd5)	W 1-0	Eckersley (pen)	51,177
Mar 8	BURNLEY	(Rd6)	W 3-1	Nightingale, Holmes, Glover	52,920
Mar 29	Newcastle United†	(SF)	D 0-0		65,000
Apr 2	Newcastle United‡	(R)	L 1-2	Quigley	53,920

†Played at Hillsborough, Sheffield. ‡Played at Elland Road, Leeds.

League & Cup Appearances

PLAYER	LEAGUE	CUP COMPETITION FA CUP	TOTAL
Anderson, C.S.	7		7
Bell, J.E.	28	1	29
Campbell, J.	38	7	45
Clayton, R.	22	7	29
Crossan, E.	27	7	34
Eckersley, W.	37	7	44
Elvy, R.	27	7	34
Glover, A.	29	6	35
Graham, L.	12		12
Gray, D.	14	1	15
Harris, J.	18	1	19
Holliday, K.J.	12		12
Holmes, W.	8	4	12
Holt, W.K.	7		7
Johnson, A.	1		1
Kelly, W.M.	33	7	40
Leaver, D.	2		2
Nightingale, A.	27	7	34
Parker, H.	3		3
Patterson, J.G.	14		14
Quigley, E.	16	2	18
Roberts, T.	2		2
Suart, R.	23	6	29
Todd, P.R.	7		7
Wharton, J.E.	35	7	42
Wright, A.W.	13		13

Goalscorers

PLAYER	LEAGUE	CUP COMPETITION FA CUP	TOTAL
Quigley, E.	11	1	12
Holmes, W.	7	3	10
Nightingale, A.	5	3	8
Wright, A.W.	5		5
Crossan, E.	4	1	5
Eckersley, W.	4	1	5
Graham, L.	4		4
Harris, J.	4		4
Todd, P.R.	3		3
Glover, A.	2	1	3
Wharton, J.E.	2	1	3
Bell, J.E.	1		1
Opps' o.gs.	2		2

Fact File

Harry Healless returned in November 1951 as senior coach.

MANAGER: Jackie Bestall

TOP SCORER: Eddie Quigley

BIGGEST WIN: 3-0, 8 December 1951, v Brentford, Division 2

HIGHEST ATTENDANCE: 65,000, 29 March 1952, v Newcastle United, FA Cup semi-final

MAJOR TRANSFERS IN: Archie Wright from Falkirk, Alec Glover from Luton Town, Willie Kelly from Airdrieonians, Albert Nightingale from Huddersfield Town, Reg Elvy from Bolton Wanderers, Eddie Quigley from Preston North End

MAJOR TRANSFERS OUT: George Higgins to Bolton Wanderers, Henry Horton to Southampton, Paul Todd to Hull City

Final Division 2 Table

		P	W	D	L	F	A	Pts
1	SHEFFIELD W	42	21	11	10	100	66	53
2	CARDIFF C	42	20	11	11	72	54	51
3	BIRMINGHAM C	42	21	9	12	67	56	51
4	NOTTINGHAM F	42	18	13	11	77	62	49
5	LEICESTER C	42	19	9	14	78	64	47
6	LEEDS U	42	18	11	13	59	57	47
7	EVERTON	42	17	10	15	64	58	44
8	LUTON T	42	16	12	14	77	78	44
9	ROTHERHAM U	42	17	8	17	73	71	42
10	BRENTFORD	42	15	12	15	54	55	42
11	SHEFFIELD U	42	18	5	19	90	76	41
12	WEST HAM U	42	15	11	16	67	77	41
13	SOUTHAMPTON	42	15	11	16	61	73	41
14	BLACKBURN R	42	17	6	19	54	63	40
15	NOTTS CO	42	16	7	19	71	68	39
16	DONCASTER R	42	13	12	17	55	60	38
17	BURY	42	15	7	20	67	69	37
18	HULL C	42	13	11	18	60	70	37
19	SWANSEA T	42	12	12	18	72	76	36
20	BARNSLEY	42	11	14	17	59	72	36
21	COVENTRY C	42	14	6	22	59	82	34
22	QPR	42	11	12	19	52	81	34

Season 1952-53

Football League Division 2

DATE	OPPONENTS	SCORE	GOALSCORERS	ATTENDANCE
Aug 23	Nottingham Forest	W 2-1	Crossan, Glover	26,985
Aug 27	Lincoln City	L 1-4	Crossan	20,775
Aug 30	EVERTON	W 3-1	Holmes 3	27,134
Sep 1	LINCOLN CITY	L 0-2		25,118
Sep 6	Brentford	L 2-3	Crossan 2	21,904
Sep 8	HULL CITY	W 2-0	Graham, Holmes	21,146
Sep 13	DONCASTER ROVERS	W 2-1	Holmes 2	25,081
Sep 15	Hull City	L 0-3		24,849
Sep 20	Swansea Town	D 1-1	Wright	22,237
Sep 27	HUDDERSFIELD TOWN	D 1-1	Holmes	29,429
Oct 4	Sheffield United	L 0-3		29,029
Oct 11	WEST HAM UNITED	W 3-0	Wharton 2, Eckersley (pen)	22,545
Oct 18	Fulham	L 1-2	Quigley	29,078
Oct 25	ROTHERHAM UNITED	L 0-1		24,890
Nov 1	Plymouth Argyle	L 1-3	Quigley	24,552
Nov 8	LEEDS UNITED	D 1-1	Leaver	22,510
Nov 15	Luton Town	L 0-6		16,276
Nov 22	BIRMINGHAM CITY	L 1-2	McLuckie	18,533
Nov 29	Bury	L 0-1		17,478
Dec 6	SOUTHAMPTON	W 3-0	Briggs 2, Campbell	19,191
Dec 13	Notts County	L 0-5		10,222
Dec 20	NOTTINGHAM FOREST	W 2-1	Eckersley 2 (2 pens)	12,794
Dec 25	LEICESTER CITY	W 2-0	Quigley 2	29,410
Dec 27	Leicester City	L 1-2	Briggs	32,015
Jan 1	NOTTS COUNTY	W 3-2	Crossan, Quigley, Briggs	27,303
Jan 3	Everton	W 3-0	Quigley 2, Briggs	37,137
Jan 17	BRENTFORD	W 3-0	Chadwick, Quigley, Eckersley (pen)	21,489
Jan 24	Doncaster Rovers	D 3-3	Briggs 2, Crossan	15,010
Feb 7	SWANSEA TOWN	W 3-0	Quigley, McLuckie, Crossan	21,324
Feb 14	Huddersfield Town	W 3-0	Quigley 2, Eckersley (pen)	18,023
Feb 21	SHEFFIELD UNITED	L 1-2	Briggs	29,920
Feb 28	West Ham United	D 0-0		19,542
Mar 7	FULHAM	D 2-2	Briggs, Campbell	23,551
Mar 14	Rotherham United	D 0-0		14,439
Mar 21	PLYMOUTH ARGYLE	L 1-3	Quigley (pen)	21,465
Mar 28	Leeds United	W 3-0	Crossan, Holmes, Quigley	10,644
Apr 3	BARNSLEY	W 2-0	Crossan, Holmes	18,467
Apr 4	LUTON TOWN	D 1-1	Eckersley (pen)	23,920
Apr 6	Barnsley	W 4-1	Quigley 2, Wright 2	4,483
Apr 11	Birmingham City	W 2-1	Eckersley, Quigley	18,347
Apr 18	BURY	W 4-0	Crossan, Quigley 2, Wright	21,094
Apr 25	Southampton	L 1-6	Wright	15,850

FA Cup

Jan 10	Luton Town	(Rd3) L 1-6	McLuckie	21,034

League & Cup Appearances

PLAYER	LEAGUE	CUP COMPETITION FA CUP	TOTAL
Bean, A.	1		1
Bell, J.E.	34	1	35
Briggs, T.H.	17	1	18
Campbell, J.	42	1	43
Chadwick, F.R.	9		9
Clayton, K.	3		3
Clayton, R.	12	1	13
Crossan, E.	38	1	39
Eckersley, W.	39	1	40
Elvy, R.	42	1	43
Glover, A.	17		17
Graham, L.	11		11
Gray, D.	5		5
Holmes, W.	13		13
Holt, W.K.	1		1
Kelly, W.M.	37	1	38
Leaver, D.	4		4
McLuckie, G.R.	20	1	21
Nightingale, A.	8		8
Quigley, E.	33	1	34
Roberts, T.	3		3
Smith, W.H.	7		7
Suart, R.	42	1	43
Wharton, J.E.	15		15
Wright, A.W.	9		9

Goalscorers

PLAYER	LEAGUE	CUP COMPETITION FA CUP	TOTAL
Quigley, E.	18		18
Crossan, E.	10		10
Briggs, T.H.	9		9
Holmes, W.	9		9
Eckersley, W.	7		7
Wright, A.W.	5		5
McLuckie, G.R.	2	1	3
Campbell, J.	2		2
Wharton, J.E.	2		2
Chadwick, F.R.	1		1
Glover, A.	1		1
Graham, L.	1		1
Leaver, D.	1		1

Fact File

Jackie Bestall resigned as Blackburn manager in May 1953.

MANAGER: Jackie Bestall

TOP SCORER: Eddie Quigley

BIGGEST WIN: 4-0, 18 April 1953, v Bury, Division 2

HIGHEST ATTENDANCE: 37,137, 3 January 1953 v Everton, Division 2

MAJOR TRANSFERS IN: Tommy Briggs and Bill Smith from Birmingham City

MAJOR TRANSFERS OUT: Albert Nightingale to Leeds United, Les Graham to Newport County, Jackie Wharton to Newport County, Joe Harris to Oldham Athletic

Final Division 2 Table

		P	W	D	L	F	A	PTS
1	SHEFFIELD U	42	25	10	7	97	55	60
2	HUDDERSFIELD T	42	24	10	8	84	33	58
3	LUTON T	42	22	8	12	84	49	52
4	PLYMOUTH ARG	42	20	9	13	65	60	49
5	LEICESTER C	42	18	12	12	89	74	48
6	BIRMINGHAM C	42	19	10	13	71	66	48
7	NOTTINGHAM F	42	18	8	16	77	67	44
8	FULHAM	42	17	10	15	81	71	44
9	BLACKBURN R	42	18	8	16	68	65	44
10	LEEDS U	42	14	15	13	71	63	43
11	SWANSEA T	42	15	12	15	78	81	42
12	ROTHERHAM U	42	16	9	17	75	74	41
13	DONCASTER R	42	12	16	14	58	64	40
14	WEST HAM U	42	13	13	16	58	60	39
15	LINCOLN C	42	11	17	14	64	71	39
16	EVERTON	42	12	14	16	71	75	38
17	BRENTFORD	42	13	11	18	59	76	37
18	HULL C	42	14	8	20	57	69	36
19	NOTTS CO	42	14	8	20	60	88	36
20	BURY	42	13	9	20	53	81	35
21	SOUTHAMPTON	42	10	13	19	68	85	33
22	BARNSLEY	42	5	8	29	47	108	18

Season 1953-54

Football League Division 2

DATE	OPPONENTS	SCORE	GOALSCORERS	ATTENDANCE
Aug 20	Rotherham United	W 4-1	Briggs 2, Quigley 2	17,834
Aug 22	BRISTOL ROVERS	D 1-1	Campbell	26,145
Aug 27	Brentford	W 4-1	Quigley, Briggs 3	16,682
Aug 29	Lincoln City	L 0-8		12,246
Aug 31	BRENTFORD	D 2-2	Campbell, Quigley	11,793
Sep 5	NOTTS COUNTY	W 2-0	Quigley, Briggs	23,244
Sep 9	Derby County	D 2-2	Quigley, Briggs	15,675
Sep 12	Hull City	W 2-0	Crossan, Quigley	23,564
Sep 19	EVERTON	D 0-0		32,177
Sep 26	Oldham Athletic	L 0-1		30,832
Oct 3	BURY	W 4-2	Quigley 2, Briggs, Crossan	33,291
Oct 10	Stoke City	L 0-3		23,329
Oct 17	FULHAM	W 5-1	Briggs, Crossan 2, Glover, Langton	25,796
Oct 24	West Ham United	L 1-2	Quigley	22,814
Oct 31	LEEDS UNITED	D 2-2	Langton, Briggs	25,272
Nov 7	Birmingham City	D 0-0		24,604
Nov 14	NOTTINGHAM FOREST	W 2-0	Briggs 2	16,549
Nov 21	Luton Town	L 1-2	Briggs	16,269
Nov 28	PLYMOUTH ARGYLE	L 2-3	Leaver, Quigley	21,204
Dec 5	Swansea Town	L 1-2	Briggs	17,399
Dec 12	ROTHERHAM UNITED	W 3-0	Crossan 2, Briggs	17,248
Dec 19	Bristol Rovers	W 2-1	Quigley 2	22,314
Dec 25	DONCASTER ROVERS	W 2-0	Crossan, Quigley	27,337
Dec 26	Doncaster Rovers	W 2-0	Quigley 2	21,481
Jan 1	DERBY COUNTY	L 0-3		33,077
Jan 2	LINCOLN CITY	W 6-0	Briggs 4, Quigley, Smith	16,276
Jan 16	Notts County	W 5-0	Crossan 2, Briggs 3	15,044
Jan 23	HULL CITY	W 3-1	Langton (pen), Quigley, Briggs	24,196
Feb 6	Everton	D 1-1	Quigley	56,434
Feb 13	OLDHAM ATHLETIC	W 4-0	Langton (pen), Briggs 2, Smith	29,510
Feb 20	Bury	D 0-0		28,887
Feb 27	STOKE CITY	W 3-0	Mooney, Crossan, Briggs	27,164
Mar 6	Fulham	W 3-2	Langton 2 (1 pen), Crossan	29,076
Mar 13	WEST HAM UNITED	W 4-1	Briggs 2, Mooney 2	25,294
Mar 20	Leeds United	L 2-3	Briggs 2	24,915
Mar 27	LUTON TOWN	W 2-0	Briggs, Quigley	24,331
Apr 3	Plymouth Argyle	D 1-1	Langton	20,757
Apr 10	BIRMINGHAM CITY	W 3-0	Langton 2, Briggs	31,955
Apr 16	LEICESTER CITY	W 3-0	Quigley, Bell, Kelly	45,521
Apr 17	Nottingham Forest	W 1-0	Langton (pen)	29,154
Apr 19	Leicester City	L 0-4		40,040
Apr 24	SWANSEA TOWN	W 1-0	Quigley	31,202

FA Cup

Jan 9	Bristol Rovers	(Rd3) W 1-0	Quigley	25,017
Jan 30	HULL CITY	(Rd4) D 2-2	Berry o.g., Quigley	33,233
Feb 4	Hull City	(R) L 1-2	Briggs	23,439

League & Cup Appearances

PLAYER	LEAGUE	CUP COMPETITION FA CUP	TOTAL
Bell, J.E.	33		33
Bogan, T.	1		1
Briggs, T.H.	41	3	44
Campbell, J.	32	3	35
Clayton, R.	4	2	6
Crossan, E.	37	1	38
Eckersley, W.	41	3	44
Elvy, R.	42	3	45
Glover, A.	18	1	19
Kelly, W.M.	42	3	45
Langton, R.	32	3	35
Leaver, D.	2		2
McLean, W.	12	2	14
Mooney, F.	13		13
Quigley, E.	40	3	43
Roberts, T.	1		1
Smith, W.H.	29	3	32
Suart, R.	42	3	45

Goalscorers

PLAYER	LEAGUE	CUP COMPETITION FA CUP	TOTAL
Briggs, T.H.	32	1	33
Quigley, E.	22	2	24
Crossan, E.	11		11
Langton, R.	10		10
Mooney, F.	3		3
Campbell, J.	2		2
Smith, W.H.	2		2
Bell, J.E.	1		1
Glover, A.	1		1
Kelly, W.M.	1		1
Leaver, D.	1		1
Opps' o.gs.		1	1

Fact File

Bill Eckersley won his 17th and final England cap against Hungary at Wembley in November 1953.

MANAGER: Johnny Carey

TOP SCORER: Tommy Briggs

BIGGEST WIN: 6-0, 2 January 1954, v Lincoln City, Division 2

HIGHEST ATTENDANCE: 56,434, 6 February 1954 v Everton, Division 2

MAJOR TRANSFERS IN: Bobby Langton from Bolton Wanderers, Frank Mooney from Manchester United

MAJOR TRANSFERS OUT: Archie Wright to Grimsby Town, George McLuckie to Ipswich Town

Final Division 2 Table

		P	W	D	L	F	A	Pts
1	LEICESTER C	42	23	10	9	97	60	56
2	EVERTON	42	20	16	6	92	58	56
3	BLACKBURN R	42	23	9	10	86	50	55
4	NOTTINGHAM F	42	20	12	10	86	59	52
5	ROTHERHAM U	42	21	7	14	80	67	49
6	LUTON T	42	18	12	12	64	59	48
7	BIRMINGHAM C	42	18	11	13	78	58	47
8	FULHAM	42	17	10	15	98	85	44
9	BRISTOL R	42	14	16	12	64	58	44
10	LEEDS U	42	15	13	14	89	81	43
11	STOKE C	42	12	17	13	71	60	41
12	DONCASTER R	42	16	9	17	59	63	41
13	WEST HAM U	42	15	9	18	67	69	39
14	NOTTS CO	42	13	13	16	54	74	39
15	HULL C	42	16	6	20	64	66	38
16	LINCOLN C	42	14	9	19	65	83	37
17	BURY	42	11	14	17	54	72	36
18	DERBY CO	42	12	11	19	64	82	35
19	PLYMOUTH ARG	42	9	16	17	65	82	34
20	SWANSEA T	42	13	8	21	58	82	34
21	BRENTFORD	42	10	11	21	40	78	31
22	OLDHAM ATH	42	8	9	25	40	89	25

Season 1954-55

Football League Division 2

DATE	OPPONENTS	SCORE		GOALSCORERS	ATTENDANCE
Aug 21	Fulham	L	1-5	Quigley	31,148
Aug 23	WEST HAM UNITED	W	5-2	Crossan, Mooney, Quigley 2, Briggs	26,813
Aug 28	SWANSEA TOWN	W	4-1	Briggs 2, Langton (pen), Mooney	27,697
Aug 30	West Ham United	W	5-2	Briggs 2, Langton (pen), Quigley, Mooney	17,699
Sep 4	Notts County	L	1-3	Briggs	14,918
Sep 8	Derby County	W	3-0	Crossan, Quigley 2	15,936
Sep 11	LIVERPOOL	W	4-3	Mooney, Briggs, Quigley 2	29,421
Sep 13	DERBY COUNTY	W	5-2	Quigley, Upton o.g., Mooney, Briggs 2	24,742
Sep 18	Bristol Rovers	L	1-2	Quigley	26,742
Sep 25	PLYMOUTH ARGYLE	D	2-2	Crossan, Quigley	23,456
Oct 2	Port Vale	W	3-0	Briggs 2, Quigley	25,619
Oct 9	IPSWICH TOWN	W	4-1	Quigley, Crossan, Bell, Briggs	27,083
Oct 16	Nottingham Forest	W	2-1	Langton, Mooney	15,892
Oct 23	ROTHERHAM UNITED	W	4-1	Crossan 3, Briggs	28,605
Oct 30	Stoke City	D	1-1	Crossan	27,565
Nov 6	MIDDLESBROUGH	W	9-0	Quigley 3, Crossan 2, Mooney 3, Langton	29,189
Nov 13	Birmingham City	L	1-3	Langton (pen)	23,829
Nov 20	HULL CITY	W	4-0	Briggs, Crossan, Quigley, Mooney	26,873
Nov 27	Luton Town	L	3-7	Briggs, Langton, Quigley	17,314
Dec 4	LEEDS UNITED	L	1-2	Langton (pen)	26,187
Dec 11	Bury	L	1-2	Langton	26,030
Dec 18	FULHAM	W	3-1	Langton, Briggs 2	25,635
Dec 25	Doncaster Rovers	W	3-1	Crossan, Briggs, Quigley	15,754
Dec 27	DONCASTER ROVERS	W	7-2	Gavin o.g., Crossan, Briggs 2, Mooney 2, Langton (pen)	36,273
Jan 1	Swansea Town	W	3-2	Briggs 2, Quigley	26,930
Jan 15	NOTTS COUNTY	L	4-5	Quigley 3, Briggs	18,664
Jan 22	Liverpool	L	1-4	Mooney	45,544
Feb 5	BRISTOL ROVERS	W	8-3	Crossan, Briggs 7 (1 pen)	24,760
Feb 12	Plymouth Argyle	W	2-0	Crossan, Quigley	16,625
Feb 19	PORT VALE	W	2-1	Briggs, Clayton	24,965
Feb 26	Ipswich Town	D	1-1	Briggs	13,389
Mar 5	NOTTINGHAM FOREST	L	0-1		27,306
Mar 12	Rotherham United	L	1-5	Leaver	16,110
Mar 19	STOKE CITY	W	2-0	Quigley, Langton (pen)	27,077
Mar 26	Middlesbrough	L	3-4	Mooney 2, Clayton	19,426
Apr 2	BIRMINGHAM CITY	D	3-3	Langton, Quigley, Briggs	27,673
Apr 8	LINCOLN CITY	W	1-0	Quigley	29,700
Apr 9	Hull City	W	4-1	Langton (pen), Mooney, Crossan 2	17,347
Apr 11	Lincoln City	L	1-2	Crossan	14,745
Apr 16	LUTON TOWN	D	0-0		35,912
Apr 23	Leeds United	L	0-2		39,208
Apr 30	BURY	D	1-1	Quigley	17,469

FA Cup

Jan 8	SWANSEA TOWN	(Rd3) L	0-2		34,337

League & Cup Appearances

PLAYER	LEAGUE	CUP COMPETITION FA CUP	TOTAL
Bean, A.	1		1
Bell, J.E.	42	1	43
Briggs, T.H.	41	1	42
Campbell, J.	2		2
Clayton, R.	42	1	43
Crossan, E.	40	1	41
Douglas, B.	1		1
Eckersley, W.	41	1	42
Elvy, R.	41	1	42
Kelly, W.M.	38	1	39
Langton, R.	42	1	43
Leaver, D.	2		2
Mooney, F.	42	1	43
Patterson, J.G.	1		1
Quigley, E.	40	1	41
Smith, W.H.	20	1	21
Suart, R.	25		25
Taylor, K.G.	1		1

Goalscorers

PLAYER	LEAGUE	CUP COMPETITION FA CUP	TOTAL
Briggs, T.H.	33		33
Quigley, E.	28		28
Crossan, E.	18		18
Mooney, F.	16		16
Langton, R.	13		13
Clayton, R.	2		2
Bell, J.E.	1		1
Leaver, D.	1		1
Opps' o.gs.	2		2

Fact File

Tommy Briggs created a new club record when he scored seven goals in the 8-3 win over Bristol Rovers at Ewood Park in February 1955.

MANAGER: Johnny Carey

TOP SCORER: Tommy Briggs

BIGGEST WIN: 9-0, 6 November 1954, v Middlesbrough, Division 2

HIGHEST ATTENDANCE: 45,544, 22 January 1955, v Liverpool, Division 2

MAJOR TRANSFERS IN: Mick McGrath from Home Farm

MAJOR TRANSFERS OUT: Alec Glover to Barrow

Final Division 2 Table

		P	W	D	L	F	A	Pts
1	BIRMINGHAM C	42	22	10	10	92	47	54
2	LUTON T	42	23	8	11	88	53	54
3	ROTHERHAM U	42	25	4	13	94	64	54
4	LEEDS U	42	23	7	12	70	53	53
5	STOKE C	42	21	10	11	69	46	52
6	BLACKBURN R	42	22	6	14	114	79	50
7	NOTTS CO	42	21	6	15	74	71	48
8	WEST HAM U	42	18	10	14	74	70	46
9	BRISTOL R	42	19	7	16	75	70	45
10	SWANSEA T	42	17	9	16	86	83	43
11	LIVERPOOL	42	16	10	16	92	96	42
12	MIDDLESBROUGH	42	18	6	18	73	82	42
13	BURY	42	15	11	16	77	72	41
14	FULHAM	42	14	11	17	76	79	39
15	NOTTINGHAM F	42	16	7	19	58	62	39
16	LINCOLN C	42	13	10	19	68	79	36
17	PORT VALE	42	12	11	19	48	71	35
18	DONCASTER R	42	14	7	21	58	95	35
19	HULL C	42	12	10	20	44	69	34
20	PLYMOUTH ARG	42	12	7	23	57	82	31
21	IPSWICH T	42	11	6	25	57	92	28
22	DERBY CO	42	7	9	26	53	82	23

Season 1955-56

Football League Division 2

DATE	OPPONENTS	SCORE	GOALSCORERS	ATTENDANCE
Aug 20	LINCOLN CITY	L 0-2		22,397
Aug 24	Fulham	L 0-3		18,314
Aug 27	Leicester City	W 2-0	Briggs, Quigley	27,380
Aug 29	FULHAM	W 1-0	Briggs	24,383
Sep 3	LIVERPOOL	D 3-3	Langton, Crossan 2	30,013
Sep 10	Plymouth Argyle	L 0-1		20,500
Sep 17	STOKE CITY	W 3-0	Langton, Douglas, Briggs	22,875
Sep 24	Bristol Rovers	L 0-1		29,393
Oct 1	DONCASTER ROVERS	D 1-1	Quigley	24,493
Oct 8	Bury	W 4-0	Briggs 2, Douglas, Langton (pen)	16,946
Oct 15	BARNSLEY	W 5-1	Briggs 2, Douglas 2, Quigley	22,288
Oct 22	Notts County	W 2-1	Briggs 2	13,926
Oct 29	BRISTOL CITY	L 4-6	Briggs 2, Langton, Crossan	24,695
Nov 5	West Ham United	W 3-2	Quigley, Douglas, Briggs	22,990
Nov 12	PORT VALE	W 7-1	Briggs 2, Crossan 3, Quigley, Langton (pen)	25,464
Nov 19	Rotherham United	L 2-3	Clayton R., Langton (pen)	12,802
Nov 26	SWANSEA TOWN	W 3-0	Campbell, Langton (pen), Douglas	24,289
Dec 3	Middlesbrough	L 0-1		16,827
Dec 10	LEEDS UNITED	L 2-3	Quigley 2	18,898
Dec 17	Lincoln City	L 0-3		11,465
Dec 24	LEICESTER CITY	L 2-3	Briggs, Langton (pen)	22,771
Dec 26	SHEFFIELD WEDNESDAY	D 2-2	Briggs, Douglas	24,139
Dec 27	Sheffield Wednesday	L 1-5	Briggs	30,771
Dec 31	Liverpool	W 2-1	Smith 2	46,071
Jan 2	NOTTINGHAM FOREST	D 2-2	Briggs, Smith	33,582
Jan 14	PLYMOUTH ARGYLE	W 2-1	Smith, Crossan	18,344
Jan 21	Stoke City	W 2-1	Briggs, Smith	18,714
Feb 4	BRISTOL ROVERS	W 2-0	Briggs, O'Leary	19,099
Feb 11	Doncaster Rovers	D 2-2	Briggs, Crossan	9,503
Feb 25	Barnsley	L 1-2	Briggs	11,683
Mar 3	NOTTS COUNTY	W 2-0	Chatham o.g., Quigley	18,697
Mar 10	Leeds United	W 2-1	Vernon, Langton	28,380
Mar 17	WEST HAM UNITED	W 4-1	Briggs 2, Douglas, Quigley	21,581
Mar 24	Port Vale	L 1-4	Briggs (pen)	15,217
Mar 30	HULL CITY	W 2-0	Smith, Briggs (pen)	25,327
Mar 31	BURY	W 3-1	Quigley, Briggs, Crossan	26,983
Apr 2	Hull City	W 3-0	Briggs, Quigley 2	14,135
Apr 7	Swansea Town	L 1-2	Quigley	17,493
Apr 14	MIDDLESBROUGH	W 2-1	Williamson, Langton (pen)	21,070
Apr 21	Bristol City	L 0-2		20,554
Apr 28	Nottingham Forest	D 1-1	Briggs	10,214
Apr 30	ROTHERHAM UNITED	W 3-1	Briggs 2, Douglas	12,635

FA Cup

Jan 7	Northampton Town	(Rd3) W 2-1	Briggs 2	14,887
Jan 28	Barnsley	(Rd4) W 1-0	Smith	38,163
Feb 18	West Ham United	(Rd5) D 0-0		27,728
Feb 23	WEST HAM UNITED	(R) L 2-3*	Langton (pen), Smith	29,300

*After extra-time.

League & Cup Appearances

PLAYER	LEAGUE	CUP COMPETITION FA CUP	TOTAL
Bell, J.E.	14		14
Binns, E.	19		19
Briggs, T.H.	41	4	45
Cairns, R.	1		1
Campbell, J.	6		6
Clayton, K.	28	4	32
Clayton, R.	42	4	46
Clinton, T.	6	2	8
Crossan, E.	27	4	31
Douglas, B.	36	4	40
Eckersley, W.	39	3	42
Elvy, R.	40	4	44
Herron, A.	1		1
Kelly, W.M.	22	4	26
Langton, R.	31	2	33
McGrath, M.	2		2
Mooney, F.	3		3
O'Leary, D.P.	6	1	7
Patterson, J.G.	2		2
Quigley, E.	30		30
Smith, W.H.	33	4	37
Taylor, K.G.	16	3	19
Vernon, T.R.	12	1	13
Williamson, J.	4		4
Willis, J.J.	1		1

Goalscorers

PLAYER	LEAGUE	CUP COMPETITION FA CUP	TOTAL
Briggs, T.H.	31	2	33
Quigley, E.	13		13
Langton, R.	10	1	11
Crossan, E.	9		9
Douglas, B.	9		9
Smith, W.H.	6	2	8
Campbell, J.	1		1
Clayton, R.	1		1
O'Leary, D.P.	1		1
Vernon, T.R.	1		1
Williamson, J.	1		1
Opps' o.gs.	1		1

Fact File

Ronnie Clayton made his England debut in the 3-0 win over Northern Ireland at Wembley in November 1955.

MANAGER: Johnny Carey

TOP SCORER: Tommy Briggs

BIGGEST WIN: 7-1, 12 November 1955, v Port Vale, Division 2

HIGHEST ATTENDANCE: 46,071, 31 December 1955, v Liverpool, Division 2

MAJOR TRANSFERS IN: Eric Binns from Burnley, John Williamson from Manchester City

MAJOR TRANSFERS OUT: Derek Leaver to Bournemouth

Final Division 2 Table

		P	W	D	L	F	A	Pts
1	SHEFFIELD W	42	21	13	8	101	62	55
2	LEEDS U	42	23	6	13	80	60	52
3	LIVERPOOL	42	21	6	15	85	63	48
4	BLACKBURN R	42	21	6	15	84	65	48
5	LEICESTER C	42	21	6	15	94	78	48
6	BRISTOL R	42	21	6	15	84	70	48
7	NOTTINGHAM F	42	19	9	14	68	63	47
8	LINCOLN C	42	18	10	14	79	65	46
9	FULHAM	42	20	6	16	89	79	46
10	SWANSEA T	42	20	6	16	83	81	46
11	BRISTOL C	42	19	7	16	80	64	45
12	PORT VALE	42	16	13	13	60	58	45
13	STOKE C	42	20	4	18	71	62	44
14	MIDDLESBROUGH	42	16	8	18	76	78	40
15	BURY	42	16	8	18	86	90	40
16	WEST HAM U	42	14	11	17	74	69	39
17	DONCASTER R	42	12	11	19	69	96	35
18	BARNSLEY	42	11	12	19	47	84	34
19	ROTHERHAM U	42	12	9	21	56	75	33
20	NOTTS CO	42	11	9	22	55	82	31
21	PLYMOUTH ARG	42	10	8	24	54	87	28
22	HULL C	42	10	6	26	53	97	26

Season 1956-57

Football League Division 2

DATE	OPPONENTS	SCORE	GOALSCORERS	ATTENDANCE
Aug 18	Swansea Town	L 1-5	Briggs	20,513
Aug 20	West Ham United	W 3-1	Douglas 2, MacLeod	19,727
Aug 25	LINCOLN CITY	L 3-4	Smith, Briggs, Williamson	23,663
Aug 27	WEST HAM UNITED	L 0-2		15,003
Sep 1	Rotherham United	W 2-0	Crossan, Briggs	9,789
Sep 6	Nottingham Forest	L 1-2	Douglas	21,251
Sep 8	PORT VALE	L 2-4	Briggs (pen), Crossan	20,753
Sep 15	Barnsley	D 3-3	Douglas, Briggs 2	14,605
Sep 22	SHEFFIELD UNITED	W 3-1	Briggs 3	21,150
Sep 29	Bristol City	L 0-3		23,323
Oct 6	Liverpool	W 3-2	Vernon, Crossan, Douglas	41,538
Oct 13	LEYTON ORIENT	D 3-3	Briggs 2, Douglas	20,320
Oct 20	Leicester City	L 0-6		30,710
Oct 27	BURY	W 6-2	Vernon 2, Clayton R., Briggs 2, MacLeod	23,428
Nov 3	Grimsby Town	W 3-1	MacLeod, Briggs, Vernon	16,850
Nov 10	DONCASTER ROVERS	D 2-2	Dobing, MacLeod	16,588
Nov 17	Stoke City	L 1-4	Vernon	21,073
Nov 24	MIDDLESBROUGH	W 1-0	Briggs	21,066
Dec 1	Huddersfield Town	W 2-0	Vernon, Cairns	14,418
Dec 8	BRISTOL ROVERS	W 2-0	Briggs 2	20,478
Dec 15	SWANSEA TOWN	W 5-3	Briggs 2, Vernon, Dobing, Douglas	19,395
Dec 22	Lincoln City	W 2-1	Douglas, Briggs	7,396
Dec 25	FULHAM	W 2-0	Briggs, Vernon	23,884
Dec 26	Fulham	L 2-7	Dobing 2	8,230
Dec 29	ROTHERHAM UNITED	W 3-2	Dobing, Vernon, Clayton R.	24,442
Jan 1	NOTTINGHAM FOREST	D 2-2	Douglas, MacLeod	28,810
Jan 12	Port Vale	W 3-0	Douglas, Briggs 2	12,422
Jan 19	BARNSLEY	W 2-0	Briggs, Williamson	21,075
Feb 2	Sheffield United	W 2-0	Douglas, Briggs	22,058
Feb 9	BRISTOL CITY	W 3-1	MacLeod, Douglas, Clayton R.	25,986
Feb 16	LIVERPOOL	D 2-2	Briggs, Dobing	27,063
Feb 23	Leyton Orient	D 1-1	Vernon	9,843
Mar 2	LEICESTER CITY	D 1-1	Briggs	32,380
Mar 9	Bury	D 2-2	Briggs, Vernon	23,810
Mar 16	GRIMSBY TOWN	W 2-0	Eckersley, Briggs	23,195
Mar 23	Doncaster Rovers	D 1-1	Briggs	12,476
Mar 30	STOKE CITY	W 1-0	MacLeod	27,686
Apr 6	Middlesbrough	L 1-2	Dobing	20,716
Apr 13	HUDDERSFIELD TOWN	W 3-2	Briggs 2, Clayton R.	24,181
Apr 19	NOTTS COUNTY	D 1-1	Woods (pen)	24,367
Apr 20	Bristol Rovers	W 1-0	Briggs	20,783
Apr 23	Notts County	L 0-2		27,613

FA Cup

Jan 5	Everton	(Rd3) L 0-1		56,293

League & Cup Appearances

PLAYER	LEAGUE	CUP COMPETITION FA CUP	TOTAL
Bell, J.E.	4		4
Binns, E.	4		4
Briggs, T.H.	42	1	43
Cairns, R.	3		3
Clayton, K.	38	1	39
Clayton, R.	34	1	35
Crossan, E.	12		12
Dobing, P.A.	25	1	26
Douglas, B.	42	1	43
Eckersley, W.	34	1	35
Herron, A.	3		3
Kelly, W.M.	14		14
Leyland, H.K.	41	1	42
MacLeod, A.R.	41	1	42
McGrath, M.	7		7
Patterson, J.G.	1		1
Smith, W.H.	13		13
Taylor, K.G.	39	1	40
Vernon, T.R.	31	1	32
Whelan, D.	4		4
Williamson, J.	5		5
Woods, M.	25	1	26

Goalscorers

PLAYER	LEAGUE	CUP COMPETITION FA CUP	TOTAL
Briggs, T.H.	32		32
Douglas, B.	12		12
Vernon, T.R.	11		11
Dobing, P.A.	8		8
MacLeod, A.R.	7		7
Clayton, R.	4		4
Crossan, E.	3		3
Williamson, J.	2		2
Cairns, R.	1		1
Eckersley, W.	1		1
Smith, W.H.	1		1
Woods, M.	1		1

Fact File

Ken Clayton broke his leg in the game at Middlesbrough in April 1957.

MANAGER: Johnny Carey

TOP SCORER: Tommy Briggs

BIGGEST WIN: 6-2, 27 October 1956 6-2 v Bury, Division 2

HIGHEST ATTENDANCE: 56,293, 5 January 1957 v Everton, FA Cup Round 3

MAJOR TRANSFERS IN: Ally MacLeod from St Mirren, Harry Leyland from Tonbridge, Andy McEvoy from Bray Wanderers, Matt Woods from Everton

MAJOR TRANSFERS OUT: Frank Mooney to Carlisle United, Reg Elvy to Northampton Town, Jackie Campbell to Oldham Athletic, Eddie Quigley to Bury

Final Division 2 Table

		P	W	D	L	F	A	Pts
1	LEICESTER C	42	25	11	6	109	67	61
2	NOTTINGHAM F	42	22	10	10	94	55	54
3	LIVERPOOL	42	21	11	10	82	54	53
4	BLACKBURN R	42	21	10	11	83	75	52
5	STOKE C	42	20	8	14	83	58	48
6	MIDDLESBROUGH	42	19	10	13	84	60	48
7	SHEFFIELD U	42	19	8	15	87	76	46
8	WEST HAM U	42	19	8	15	59	63	46
9	BRISTOL R	42	18	9	15	81	67	45
10	SWANSEA T	42	19	7	16	90	90	45
11	FULHAM	42	19	4	19	84	76	42
12	HUDDERSFIELD T	42	18	6	18	68	74	42
13	BRISTOL C	42	16	9	17	74	79	41
14	DONCASTER R	42	15	10	17	77	77	40
15	LEYTON ORIENT	42	15	10	17	66	84	40
16	GRIMSBY T	42	17	5	20	61	62	39
17	ROTHERHAM U	42	13	11	18	74	75	37
18	LINCOLN C	42	14	6	22	54	80	34
19	BARNSLEY	42	12	10	20	59	89	34
20	NOTTS CO	42	9	12	21	58	86	30
21	BURY	42	8	9	25	60	96	25
22	PORT VALE	42	8	6	28	57	101	22

Season 1957-58

Football League Division 2

DATE	OPPONENTS	SCORE	GOALSCORERS	ATTENDANCE
Aug 24	IPSWICH TOWN	D 0-0		24,406
Aug 26	WEST HAM UNITED	W 2-1	Douglas, Vernon	18,845
Aug 31	Notts County	D 1-1	Dobing	17,927
Sep 2	West Ham United	D 1-1	Vernon	24,009
Sep 7	LINCOLN CITY	L 0-1		20,948
Sep 9	BARNSLEY	W 3-1	Vernon 2, Briggs	13,006
Sep 14	Bristol Rovers	L 0-4		22,811
Sep 18	Barnsley	W 2-0	Cairns, Douglas	12,814
Sep 21	DERBY COUNTY	W 3-1	Briggs, MacLeod, Vernon	18,331
Sep 28	Swansea Town	W 4-0	Cairns 2, Vernon 2	20,767
Oct 5	FULHAM	D 1-1	Cairns	25,802
Oct 12	Rotherham United	W 2-1	Dobing, Cairns	12,599
Oct 19	HUDDERSFIELD TOWN	D 1-1	Isherwood	20,606
Oct 26	Grimsby Town	W 4-3	Dobing 2, MacLeod, Cairns	14,873
Nov 2	STOKE CITY	W 1-0	Douglas	26,110
Nov 9	Bristol City	D 0-0		23,276
Nov 16	CARDIFF CITY	W 4-0	Dobing 2, Clayton, MacLeod	24,642
Nov 23	Liverpool	L 0-2		55,232
Nov 30	MIDDLESBROUGH	D 3-3	Vernon, MacLeod 2	29,248
Dec 7	Leyton Orient	L 1-5	Stephenson	11,038
Dec 14	CHARLTON ATHLETIC	D 1-1	Briggs	22,073
Dec 21	Ipswich Town	L 1-2	Douglas	16,023
Dec 25	SHEFFIELD UNITED	W 1-0	Dobing	23,283
Dec 26	Sheffield United	L 2-4	Stephenson, Dobing	25,445
Dec 28	NOTTS COUNTY	W 3-0	MacLeod 3	24,605
Jan 11	Lincoln City	D 1-1	Douglas (pen)	9,023
Jan 18	BRISTOL ROVERS	W 2-0	MacLeod, Stephenson	16,922
Feb 1	Derby County	W 3-0	MacLeod, Dobing 2	20,457
Feb 08	SWANSEA TOWN	D 2-2	Dobing, MacLeod	18,513
Feb 22	LIVERPOOL	D 3-3	Douglas, Stephenson, Dobing	41,789
Mar 5	Huddersfield Town	L 1-2	McGrath	6,431
Mar 8	GRIMSBY TOWN	W 3-0	Smith, Johnston 2	27,923
Mar 15	Stoke City	W 4-2	Johnston, Douglas, MacLeod, Vernon	24,107
Mar 24	BRISTOL CITY	W 5-0	Douglas, Dobing 4 (1 pen)	8,825
Mar 29	Cardiff City	L 3-4	Douglas 2, Johnston	10,335
Apr 4	Doncaster Rovers	W 5-1	Douglas 3, Johnston, MacLeod	14,487
Apr 5	ROTHERHAM UNITED	W 5-0	Vernon, Johnston 2, MacLeod, Douglas	22,074
Apr 7	DONCASTER ROVERS	W 3-2	MacLeod, Johnston, Douglas	23,853
Apr 12	Middlesbrough	W 3-2	Dobing 2, Vernon	31,771
Apr 19	LEYTON ORIENT	W 4-1	Vernon 3, MacLeod	24,961
Apr 23	Fulham	D 1-1	MacLeod	32,109
Apr 26	Charlton Athletic	W 4-3	Dobing 2, Vernon, Douglas (pen)	56,435

FA Cup

Jan 4	Rotherham United	(Rd3) W 4-1	Douglas, Dobing 3	11,716
Jan 29	Everton	(Rd4) W 2-1	Dobing, Meagan o.g.	75,818
Feb 15	Cardiff City	(Rd5) D 0-0		45,078
Feb 20	CARDIFF CITY	(R) W 2-1	McGrath, Douglas	37,400
Mar 1	LIVERPOOL	(Rd6) W 2-1	Clayton, MacLeod	51,000
Mar 22	Bolton Wanderers†	(SF) L 1-2	Dobing	74,800

†Played at Maine Road, Manchester.

League & Cup Appearances

PLAYER	LEAGUE	CUP COMPETITION FA CUP	TOTAL
Briggs, T.H.	12		12
Cairns, R.	15		15
Clayton, R.	36	6	42
Dobing, P.A.	34	6	40
Douglas, B.	40	6	46
Eckersley, W.	29	5	34
Isherwood, R.E.	1		1
Johnston, T.B.	11		11
Kennedy, P.A.	3		3
Leyland, H.K.	42	6	48
MacLeod, A.R.	38	6	44
McGrath, M.	42	6	48
Stephenson, R.A.	16	6	22
Smith, W.H.	11	1	12
Swindells, J.	5		5
Taylor, K.G.	35	6	41
Vernon, T.R.	37	6	43
Whelan, D.	13		13
Woods, M.	42	6	48

Goalscorers

PLAYER	LEAGUE	CUP COMPETITION FA CUP	TOTAL
Dobing, P.A.	20	5	25
MacLeod, A.R.	17	1	18
Douglas, B.	16	2	18
Vernon, T.R.	15		15
Johnston, T.B.	8		8
Cairns, R.	6		6
Stephenson, R.A.	4		4
Briggs, T.H.	3		3
Clayton, R.	1	1	2
McGrath, M.	1	1	2
Isherwood, R.E.	1		1
Smith, W.H.	1		1

Fact File

Blackburn clinched promotion on the final day of the season with a thrilling 4-3 win over promotion rivals Charlton Athletic.

Final Division 2 Table

		P	W	D	L	F	A	Pts
1	WEST HAM U	42	23	11	8	101	54	57
2	BLACKBURN R	42	22	12	8	93	57	56
3	CHARLTON ATH	42	24	7	11	107	69	55
4	LIVERPOOL	42	22	10	10	79	54	54
5	FULHAM	42	20	12	10	97	59	52
6	SHEFFIELD U	42	21	10	11	75	50	52
7	MIDDLESBROUGH	42	19	7	16	83	74	45
8	IPSWICH T	42	16	12	14	68	69	44
9	HUDDERSFIELD T	42	14	16	12	63	66	44
10	BRISTOL R	42	17	8	17	85	80	42
11	STOKE C	42	18	6	18	75	73	42
12	LEYTON ORIENT	42	18	5	19	77	79	41
13	GRIMSBY T	42	17	6	19	86	83	40
14	BARNSLEY	42	14	12	16	70	74	40
15	CARDIFF C	42	14	9	19	63	77	37
16	DERBY CO	42	14	8	20	60	81	36
17	BRISTOL C	42	13	9	20	63	88	35
18	ROTHERHAM U	42	14	5	23	65	101	33
19	SWANSEA T	42	11	9	22	72	99	31
20	LINCOLN C	42	11	9	22	55	82	31
21	NOTTS CO	42	12	6	24	44	80	30
22	DONCASTER R	42	8	11	23	56	88	27

MANAGER: Johnny Carey

TOP SCORER: Peter Dobing

BIGGEST WIN: 5-0, 24 March 24, 1958, Bristol City, Division 2;
5 April 1958, Rotherham United, Division 2

HIGHEST ATTENDANCE: 74,800, 22 March 1958, v Bolton Wanderers,
FA Cup semi-final

MAJOR TRANSFERS IN: Roy Stephenson from Rotherham United,
Tom Johnston from Leyton Orient

MAJOR TRANSFERS OUT: Eddie Crossan to Tranmere Rovers,
Tommy Briggs to Grimsby Town

Season 1958-59

Football League Division 1

DATE	OPPONENTS	SCORE	GOALSCORERS	ATTENDANCE
Aug 23	Newcastle United	W 5-1	Vernon, Johnston 2, Dobing, Douglas (pen)	52,497
Aug 25	LEICESTER CITY	W 5-0	McGrath, Johnston, Dobing 2, Vernon	36,451
Aug 30	TOTTENHAM HOTSPUR	W 5-0	Dobing 2, Johnston 2, Vernon	41,830
Sep 3	Leicester City	D 1-1	Vernon	30,669
Sep 6	Manchester United	L 1-6	Douglas	65,187
Sep 8	Blackpool	D 1-1	MacLeod	31,752
Sep 13	WOLVERHAMPTON W.	L 1-2	Dobing	43,192
Sep 15	BLACKPOOL	D 0-0		30,947
Sep 20	Portsmouth	L 1-2	Johnston	28,537
Sep 27	ASTON VILLA	L 2-3	Johnston 2	28,172
Oct 4	West Ham United	L 3-6	Vernon 2, Dobing	25,280
Oct 11	PRESTON NORTH END	W 4-1	Douglas, Vernon, Whelan 2	39,075
Oct 18	Burnley	D 0-0		41,961
Oct 25	ARSENAL	W 4-1	Dobing 3, MacLeod	37,747
Nov 1	Everton	D 2-2	Douglas, Vernon	52,733
Nov 8	BIRMINGHAM CITY	W 3-2	Dobing 2, Vernon	28,806
Nov 15	West Bromwich Albion	W 3-2	Dobing, Douglas, Johnston	31,540
Nov 22	LEEDS UNITED	L 2-4	MacLeod, Vernon	27,727
Nov 29	Manchester City	W 1-0	Johnston	16,405
Dec 6	BOLTON WANDERERS	D 1-1	Dobing	38,027
Dec 13	Luton Town	D 1-1	Johnston	13,475
Dec 20	NEWCASTLE UNITED	W 3-0	Johnston 3	25,207
Dec 25	CHELSEA	L 0-3		32,149
Dec 27	Chelsea	W 2-0	Dobing, Vernon	46,312
Jan 3	Tottenham Hotspur	L 1-3	Vernon	39,552
Jan 31	Wolverhampton W.	L 0-5		30,743
Feb 7	PORTSMOUTH	W 2-1	Dobing (pen), Swindells	22,587
Feb 18	Aston Villa	L 0-1		30,050
Feb 21	WEST HAM UNITED	L 1-2	MacLeod	17,613
Feb 28	Preston North End	W 2-1	Douglas, Vernon	22,700
Mar 2	MANCHESTER UNITED	L 1-3	Dobing	40,401
Mar 7	BURNLEY	W 4-1	Dobing, Stephenson, Airey, Vernon	27,071
Mar 14	Arsenal	D 1-1	Dougan	39,955
Mar 21	EVERTON	W 2-1	Dobing 2 (1 pen)	26,914
Mar 27	NOTTINGHAM FOREST	W 3-0	Vernon, Dobing 2	26,589
Mar 31	Nottingham Forest	D 1-1	Dobing	27,917
Apr 4	WEST BROMWICH ALBION	D 0-0		27,217
Apr 11	Leeds United	L 1-2	Isherwood	15,232
Apr 18	MANCHESTER CITY	W 2-1	Vernon, Clayton R.	24,616
Apr 20	LUTON TOWN	W 3-1	McEvoy 2, Hudson	18,092
Apr 22	Birmingham City	L 0-3		22,958
Apr 25	Bolton Wanderers	L 1-3	Dobing	18,268

FA Cup

Jan 10	LEYTON ORIENT	(Rd3)	W 4-2	Johnston, MacLeod, Vernon, Dobing	27,728
Jan 28	BURNLEY	(Rd4)	L 1-2	Dobing	43,752

League & Cup Appearances

PLAYER	LEAGUE	CUP COMPETITION	TOTAL
		FA CUP	
Airey, J.	1		1
Appleby, J.P.	1		1
Cairns, R.	7		7
Clayton, K.	3		3
Clayton, R.	40	2	42
Dobing, P.A.	40	2	42
Dougan, A.D.	4		4
Douglas, B.	30	1	31
Eckersley, W.	29	2	31
Hudson, G.A.	4		4
Isherwood, R.E.	13	1	14
Johnston, T.B.	25	2	27
Jones, R.W.	2		2
Leyland, H.K.	40	2	42
MacLeod, A.R.	40	2	42
McEvoy, M.A.	2		2
McGrath, M.	39	2	41
Smith, W.H.	2		2
Stephenson, R.A.	5		5
Swindells, J.	3		3
Taylor, K.G.	30	2	32
Vernon, T.R.	36	2	38
Whelan, D.	25		25
Woods, M.	41	2	43

Goalscorers

PLAYER	LEAGUE	CUP COMPETITION	TOTAL
		FA CUP	
Dobing, P.A.	24	2	26
Vernon, T.R.	16	1	17
Johnston, T.B.	14	1	15
Douglas, B.	6		6
MacLeod, A.R.	4	1	5
McEvoy, M.A.	2		2
Whelan, D.	2		2
Airey, J.	1		1
Clayton, R.	1		1
Dougan, A.D.	1		1
Hudson, G.A.	1		1
Isherwood, R.E.	1		1
McGrath, M.	1		1
Stephenson, R.A.	1		1
Swindells, J.	1		1

Fact File

Blackburn captured the FA Youth Cup with a 2-1 aggregate win over West Ham United. The Blackburn team included Fred Pickering, Keith Newton and Mike England.

MANAGER: Johnny Carey/Dally Duncan

TOP SCORER: Peter Dobing

BIGGEST WIN: 5-0, 25 August 1958, v Leicester City, Division 1; 30 August 1958, v Tottenham Hotspur, Division 1

HIGHEST ATTENDANCE: 65,187, 6 September 1958, v Manchester United, Division 1

MAJOR TRANSFERS IN: Derek Dougan from Portsmouth

MAJOR TRANSFERS OUT: Tom Johnston to Leyton Orient, Roy Stephenson to Leicester City

Final Division 1 Table

		P	W	D	L	F	A	Pts
1	WOLVERHAMPTON W	42	28	5	9	110	49	61
2	MANCHESTER U	42	24	7	11	103	66	55
3	ARSENAL	42	21	8	13	88	68	50
4	BOLTON W	42	20	10	12	79	66	50
5	WBA	42	18	13	11	88	68	49
6	WEST HAM U	42	21	6	15	85	70	48
7	BURNLEY	42	19	10	13	81	70	48
8	BLACKPOOL	42	18	11	13	66	49	47
9	BIRMINGHAM C	42	20	6	16	84	68	46
10	BLACKBURN R	42	17	10	15	76	70	44
11	NEWCASTLE U	42	17	7	18	80	80	41
12	PRESTON NE	42	17	7	18	70	77	41
13	NOTTINGHAM F	42	17	6	19	71	74	40
14	CHELSEA	42	18	4	20	77	98	40
15	LEEDS U	42	15	9	18	57	74	39
16	EVERTON	42	17	4	21	71	87	38
17	LUTON T	42	12	13	17	68	71	37
18	TOTTENHAM H	42	13	10	19	85	95	36
19	LEICESTER C	42	11	10	21	67	98	32
20	MANCHESTER C	42	11	9	22	64	95	31
21	ASTON VILLA	42	11	8	23	58	87	30
22	PORTSMOUTH	42	6	9	27	64	112	21

The Essential History of Blackburn Rovers

Football League Division 1

DATE	OPPONENTS	SCORE	GOALSCORERS	ATTENDANCE
Aug 22	FULHAM	W 4-0	Dougan 2, Vernon, Dobing	30,232
Aug 26	Bolton Wanderers	W 3-0	Vernon, Dobing 2	42,324
Aug 29	Nottingham Forest	D 2-2	Vernon, Dobing	26,027
Aug 31	BOLTON WANDERERS	W 1-0	Isherwood	39,039
Sep 5	SHEFFIELD WEDNESDAY	W 3-1	Dobing 2, Dougan	32,689
Sep 12	Wolverhampton W.	L 1-3	Dobing	39,900
Sep 16	Everton	L 0-2		41,813
Sep 19	ARSENAL	D 1-1	Isherwood	31,647
Sep 21	EVERTON	W 3-1	Douglas (pen), Dougan, MacLeod	27,012
Sep 26	Manchester City	L 1-2	MacLeod	41,687
Oct 3	PRESTON NORTH END	L 1-4	Dobing	41,694
Oct 10	Leicester City	W 3-2	McGrath, Dobing, McEvoy	26,107
Oct 17	BURNLEY	W 3-2	Dougan, Dobing, Vernon	33,316
Oct 24	Leeds United	W 1-0	Vernon	17,159
Oct 31	MANCHESTER UNITED	D 1-1	MacLeod	39,621
Nov 7	Chelsea	L 1-3	Dobing	27,677
Nov 14	WEST BROMWICH ALBION	W 3-2	MacLeod, Dobing, Whelan	18,449
Nov 21	Newcastle United	L 1-3	Dobing	31,368
Nov 28	BIRMINGHAM CITY	W 2-1	Dobing, MacLeod	20,549
Dec 5	Tottenham Hotspur	L 1-2	Bimpson	37,130
Dec 12	WEST HAM UNITED	W 6-2	Dougan 4, Dobing 2	22,261
Dec 19	Fulham	W 1-0	Dougan	17,536
Dec 25	BLACKPOOL	W 1-0	Dougan	27,502
Dec 26	Blackpool	L 0-1		30,071
Jan 2	NOTTINGHAM FOREST	L 1-2	Vernon (pen)	27,817
Jan 16	Sheffield Wednesday	L 0-3		27,025
Jan 23	WOLVERHAMPTON W.	L 0-1		30,145
Feb 6	Arsenal	L 2-5	MacLeod, Dobing	35,482
Feb 13	MANCHESTER CITY	W 2-1	Dougan, Clayton	23,731
Feb 27	TOTTENHAM HOTSPUR	L 1-4	MacLeod	29,228
Mar 1	Preston North End	L 3-5	MacLeod, Douglas 2 (1 pen)	26,781
Mar 5	Burnley	L 0-1		32,331
Mar 19	West Ham United	L 1-2	Bimpson	25,921
Mar 30	CHELSEA	W 1-0	Dougan	15,832
Apr 2	West Bromwich Albion	L 0-2		9,396
Apr 9	NEWCASTLE UNITED	D 1-1	McGrath	21,962
Apr 15	LUTON TOWN	L 0-2		22,714
Apr 16	Manchester United	L 0-1		46,071
Apr 18	Luton Town	D 1-1	Dobing	14,167
Apr 23	LEICESTER CITY	L 0-1		18,550
Apr 27	LEEDS UNITED	W 3-2	Isherwood 2, Dougan	19,295
Apr 30	Birmingham City	L 0-1		24,476

FA Cup

Jan 9	Sunderland	(Rd3) D 1-1	Dobing	34,129
Jan 13	SUNDERLAND	(R) W 4-1	Vernon 2, MacLeod, Bimpson	27,617
Jan 30	BLACKPOOL	(Rd4) D 1-1	McGrath	51,223
Feb 3	Blackpool	(R) W 3-0	Dobing 2, Dougan	31,975
Feb 20	Tottenham Hotspur	(Rd5) W 3-1	Woods, Bimpson 2	54,745
Mar 12	Burnley	(Rd6) D 3-3	Douglas (pen), Dobing, McGrath	51,501
Mar 16	BURNLEY	(R) W 2-0*	Dobing, MacLeod	53,839
Mar 26	Sheffield Wednesday†	(SF) W 2-1	Dougan 2	74,135
May 7	Wolverhampton Wanderers‡	(F) L 0-3		98,776

*After extra-time. †Played at Maine Road, Manchester. ‡Played at Wembley Stadium.

League & Cup Appearances

PLAYER	LEAGUE	CUP COMPETITION FA CUP	TOTAL
Airey, J.	2		2
Bimpson, J.L.	16	7	23
Bray, J.	31	9	40
Clayton, R.	38	9	47
Crowe, C.	5		5
Daly, P.J.	1		1
Dobing, P.A.	40	8	48
Dougan, A.D.	33	9	42
Douglas, B.	27	9	36
Eckersley, W.	2		2
England, H.M.	7		7
Griffiths, B.	1		1
Isherwood, R.E.	17		17
Jones, R.W.	9		9
Leyland, H.K.	32	9	41
McEvoy, M.A.	6		6
McGrath, M.	40	9	49
MacLeod, A.R.	39	9	48
Pickering, F.	3		3
Ratcliffe, J.B.	1		1
Smith, W.H.	4		4
Swindells, J.	1		1
Taylor, K.G.	11		11
Thomas, E.	4		4
Vernon, T.R.	15	3	18
Whelan, D.	36	9	45
Woods, M.	41	9	50

Goalscorers

PLAYER	LEAGUE	CUP COMPETITION FA CUP	TOTAL
Dobing, P.A.	18	5	23
Dougan, A.D.	14	3	17
MacLeod, A.R.	8	2	10
Vernon, T.R.	6	2	8
Bimpson, J.L.	2	3	5
Isherwood, R.E.	4		4
Douglas, B.	3	1	4
McGrath, M.	2	2	4
Clayton, R.	1		1
McEvoy, M.A.	1		1
Whelan, D.	1		1
Woods, M.		1	1

Fact File

The Wembley hoodoo struck Blackburn when Dave Whelan suffered a broken leg in the FA Cup final.

MANAGER: Dally Duncan

TOP SCORER: Peter Dobing

BIGGEST WIN: 6-2, 12 December 1959, v West Ham United, Division 1

HIGHEST ATTENDANCE: 98,776, 7 May 1960, v Wolverhampton Wanderers, FA Cup final

MAJOR TRANSFERS IN: Louis Bimpson from Liverpool, Eddie Thomas from Everton, Chris Crowe from Leeds United

MAJOR TRANSFERS OUT: Roy Vernon to Everton

Final Division 1 Table

		P	W	D	L	F	A	Pts
1	BURNLEY	42	24	7	11	85	61	55
2	WOLVERHAMPTON W	42	24	6	12	106	67	54
3	TOTTENHAM H	42	21	11	10	86	50	53
4	WBA	42	19	11	12	83	57	49
5	SHEFFIELD W	42	19	11	12	80	59	49
6	BOLTON W	42	20	8	14	59	51	48
7	MANCHESTER U	42	19	7	16	102	80	45
8	NEWCASTLE U	42	18	8	16	82	78	44
9	PRESTON NE	42	16	12	14	79	76	44
10	FULHAM	42	17	10	15	73	80	44
11	BLACKPOOL	42	15	10	17	59	71	40
12	LEICESTER C	42	13	13	16	66	75	39
13	ARSENAL	42	15	9	18	68	80	39
14	WEST HAM U	42	16	6	20	75	91	38
15	EVERTON	42	13	11	18	73	78	37
16	MANCHESTER C	42	17	3	22	78	84	37
17	BLACKBURN R	42	16	5	21	60	70	37
18	CHELSEA	42	14	9	19	76	91	37
19	BIRMINGHAM C	42	13	10	19	63	80	36
20	NOTTINGHAM F	42	13	9	20	50	74	35
21	LEEDS U	42	12	10	20	65	92	34
22	LUTON T	42	9	12	21	50	73	30

Season 1960-61

Football League Division 1

DATE	OPPONENTS	SCORE	GOALSCORERS	ATTENDANCE
Aug 20	Manchester United	W 3-1	Dougan 3	47,838
Aug 24	NOTTINGHAM FOREST	W 4-1	Dobing 2 (1 pen), Dougan, MacLeod	20,539
Aug 27	TOTTENHAM HOTSPUR	L 1-4	Dougan	26,819
Aug 31	Nottingham Forest	D 1-1	McGrath	19,317
Sep 3	Leicester City	W 4-2	Dobing 2 (1 pen), MacLeod, Douglas	17,455
Sep 7	Chelsea	L 2-5	Dobing 2	23,224
Sep 10	ASTON VILLA	W 4-1	Dobing (pen), Crowe, Dougan 2	22,112
Sep 17	Wolverhampton W.	D 0-0		28,781
Sep 19	CHELSEA	W 3-1	Dobing, Dougan, Douglas	21,508
Sep 24	BOLTON WANDERERS	W 3-1	Bimpson, Crowe, Douglas	29,236
Oct 1	West Ham United	L 2-3	MacLeod, Thomas	17,519
Oct 8	BURNLEY	L 1-4	Thomas	26,223
Oct 15	Preston North End	L 0-2		24,229
Oct 22	ARSENAL	L 2-4	Bimpson 2	21,348
Oct 29	Manchester City	L 0-4		33,641
Nov 5	BIRMINGHAM CITY	W 2-0	MacLeod, Thomas	13,463
Nov 12	West Bromwich Albion	W 2-1	Dobing, Thomas	18,701
Nov 19	CARDIFF CITY	D 2-2	Dobing, Crowe	15,132
Nov 26	Newcastle United	L 1-3	MacLeod	22,623
Dec 3	FULHAM	W 5-1	Dobing 2 (2 pens) Isherwood 2, Woods	12,916
Dec 10	Sheffield Wednesday	L 4-5	Douglas, Dougan, Isherwood, Crowe	20,462
Dec 17	MANCHESTER UNITED	L 1-2	MacLeod	17,285
Dec 24	Blackpool	L 0-2		19,379
Dec 27	BLACKPOOL	W 2-0	Dobing 2	18,170
Dec 31	Tottenham Hotspur	L 2-5	Douglas, Dobing	48,742
Jan 14	LEICESTER CITY	D 1-1	Dougan	14,762
Jan 21	Aston Villa	D 2-2	Douglas 2	31,113
Feb 4	WOLVERHAMPTON W.	W 2-1	Thomas, MacLeod	15,997
Feb 11	Bolton Wanderers	D 0-0		16,183
Feb 25	Burnley	D 1-1	MacLeod	26,492
Mar 4	PRESTON NORTH END	W 1-0	Dougan	23,270
Mar 11	Arsenal	D 0-0		34,030
Mar 18	MANCHESTER CITY	W 4-1	Pickering 2, Dobing, Thomas	19,733
Mar 20	WEST HAM UNITED	W 4-1	MacLeod 2, Dobing, McEvoy	13,953
Mar 25	Birmingham City	D 1-1	Pickering	19,301
Mar 31	EVERTON	L 1-3	Dobing	24,982
Apr 1	SHEFFIELD WEDNESDAY	D 1-1	McEvoy	21,355
Apr 3	Everton	D 2-2	Thomas, Pickering	41,991
Apr 8	Cardiff City	D 1-1	Pickering	16,192
Apr 15	WEST BROMWICH ALBION	W 2-1	Bray, Pickering	14,669
Apr 22	Fulham	D 1-1	Thomas	17,020
Apr 29	NEWCASTLE UNITED	L 2-4	Pickering, MacLeod	12,746

FA Cup

Jan 7	Chesterfield	(Rd3) D 0-0		14,225
Jan 11	CHESTERFIELD	(R) W 3-0	Douglas, Dobing 2	18,300
Jan 28	Bolton Wanderers	(Rd4) D 3-3	MacLeod 2, Dougan	29,804
Feb 1	BOLTON WANDERERS	(R) W 4-0	Dobing 2, Douglas 2	31,000
Feb 18	Sheffield United	(Rd 5) L 1-2	Crowe	43,987

League Cup

Oct 10	York City	(Rd1) W 3-1	Crowe, Dougan 2	10,933
Oct 18	Swansea Town	(Rd2) W 2-1	Thomas, Dougan	14,340
Nov 21	ROCHDALE	(Rd3) W 2-1	Crowe 2	6,316
Dec 5	WREXHAM	(Rd4) D 1-1	Crowe	8,061
Dec 14	Wrexham	(R) L 1-3*	Dougan	9,986

*After extra-time.

MANAGER: Jack Marshall

TOP SCORER: Peter Dobing

BIGGEST WIN: 5-1, 3 December 1960, v Fulham, Division 1

HIGHEST ATTENDANCE: 48,742, 31 December 1960, v Tottenham Hotspur, Division 1

MAJOR TRANSFERS OUT: Bill Smith to Accrington Stanley, Louis Bimpson to Bournemouth, Harry Leyland to Tranmere Rovers

League & Cup Appearances

PLAYER	LEAGUE	CUP COMPETITION		TOTAL
		FA CUP	LC	
Bimpson, J.L.	6			6
Bray, J.	27	5	4	36
Clayton, R.	41	5	5	51
Crowe, C.	30	5	3	38
Daly, P.J.	2		1	3
Dobing, P.A.	40	5	4	49
Dougan, A.D.	22	5	3	30
Douglas, B.	35	4	3	42
Eckersley, W.	4			4
England, H.M.	13		1	14
Isherwood, R.E.	9	1	5	15
Jones, R.W.	20		1	21
Leyland, H.K.	11		4	15
McEvoy, M.A.	28	5	4	37
McGrath, M.	12			12
MacLeod, A.R.	35	5	2	42
Newton, K.R.	8		1	9
Pickering, F.	21		2	23
Ratcliffe, J.B.			1	1
Reeves, T.B.	11	5		16
Taylor, K.G.	24	5	4	33
Thomas, E.	21		2	23
Woods, M.	42	5	5	52

Goalscorers

PLAYER	LEAGUE	CUP COMPETITION		TOTAL
		FA CUP	LC	
Dobing, P.A.	18	4		22
Dougan, A.D.	11	1	4	16
MacLeod, A.R.	11	2		13
Douglas, B.	7	3		10
Thomas, E.	8		1	9
Crowe, C.	4	1	4	9
Pickering, F.	7			7
Bimpson, J.L.	3			3
Isherwood, R.E.	3			3
McEvoy, M.A.	2			2
Bray, J.	1			1
McGrath, M.	1			1
Woods, M.	1			1

Fact File

Jack Marshall took over the managerial duties at Ewood Park in September 1960.

Final Division 1 Table

		P	W	D	L	F	A	Pts
1	TOTTENHAM H	42	31	4	7	115	55	66
2	SHEFFIELD W	42	23	12	7	78	47	58
3	WOLVERHAMPTON W	42	25	7	10	103	75	57
4	BURNLEY	42	22	7	13	102	77	51
5	EVERTON	42	22	6	14	87	69	50
6	LEICESTER C	42	18	9	15	87	70	45
7	MANCHESTER U	42	18	9	15	88	76	45
8	BLACKBURN R	42	15	13	14	77	76	43
9	ASTON VILLA	42	17	9	16	78	77	43
10	WBA	42	18	5	19	67	71	41
11	ARSENAL	42	15	11	16	77	85	41
12	CHELSEA	42	15	7	20	98	100	37
13	MANCHESTER C	42	13	11	18	79	90	37
14	NOTTINGHAM F	42	14	9	19	62	78	37
15	CARDIFF C	42	13	11	18	60	85	37
16	WEST HAM U	42	13	10	19	77	88	36
17	FULHAM	42	14	8	20	72	95	36
18	BOLTON W	42	12	11	19	58	73	35
19	BIRMINGHAM C	42	14	6	22	62	84	34
20	BLACKPOOL	42	12	9	21	68	73	33
21	NEWCASTLE U	42	11	10	21	86	109	32
22	PRESTON NE	42	10	10	22	43	71	30

Season 1961-62

Football League Division 1

DATE	OPPONENTS	SCORE	GOALSCORERS	ATTENDANCE
Aug 19	CARDIFF CITY	D 0-0		18,428
Aug 21	Blackpool	L 1-2	Douglas (pen)	21,680
Aug 26	Manchester United	L 1-6	Bray	45,302
Aug 28	BLACKPOOL	D 1-1	Pickering	22,439
Sep 2	WOLVERHAMPTON W.	W 2-1	Clayton, Haverty	15,379
Sep 5	Ipswich Town	L 1-2	Douglas (pen)	24,928
Sep 9	Nottingham Forest	W 2-1	Douglas, Crowe	22,649
Sep 16	ASTON VILLA	W 4-2	Lawther 2, Douglas 2	15,611
Sep 18	IPSWICH TOWN	D 2-2	Lawther, McEvoy	19,904
Sep 23	Chelsea	D 1-1	Crowe	23,301
Sep 30	SHEFFIELD UNITED	L 1-2	Lawther	16,677
Oct 14	ARSENAL	D 0-0		14,024
Oct 21	Sheffield Wednesday	L 0-1		24,510
Oct 28	LEICESTER CITY	W 2-1	McEvoy, Lawther	11,113
Nov 4	West Bromwich Albion	L 0-4		17,298
Nov 11	BIRMINGHAM CITY	W 2-0	Lawther, Pickering	12,083
Nov 18	Everton	L 0-1		40,359
Nov 25	FULHAM	L 0-2		12,893
Dec 2	Bolton Wanderers	D 1-1	Lawther	12,855
Dec 9	MANCHESTER CITY	W 4-1	Lawther, Byrom 2, Ratcliffe	13,892
Dec 16	Cardiff City	D 1-1	Lawther	13,799
Dec 26	West Ham United	W 3-2	Byrom 3	22,280
Jan 13	Wolverhampton W.	W 2-0	Lawther, Byrom	19,692
Jan 20	NOTTINGHAM FOREST	W 2-1	Clayton, Byrom	16,343
Feb 3	Aston Villa	L 0-1		28,718
Feb 10	CHELSEA	W 3-0	Pickering (pen), Clayton, Thomas	12,206
Feb 20	Sheffield United	D 0-0		21,417
Feb 24	BURNLEY	W 2-1	Lawther, Pickering	33,914
Mar 3	Arsenal	D 0-0		25,774
Mar 17	Leicester City	L 0-2		16,194
Mar 24	WEST BROMWICH ALBION	D 1-1	Pickering	11,644
Mar 28	WEST HAM UNITED	W 1-0	Byrom	8,876
Mar 30	Birmingham City	L 1-2	Lawther	17,431
Apr 7	EVERTON	D 1-1	Lawther	13,047
Apr 10	MANCHESTER UNITED	W 3-0	Clayton, Pickering, Ratcliffe	14,623
Apr 14	Fulham	L 0-2		20,512
Apr 17	Burnley	W 1-0	Ratcliffe	29,997
Apr 20	Tottenham Hotspur	L 1-4	Douglas	55,183
Apr 21	BOLTON WANDERERS	L 2-3	Douglas, Lawther	15,459
Apr 23	TOTTENHAM HOTSPUR	L 0-1		23,301
Apr 26	SHEFFIELD WEDNESDAY	L 0-2		12,171
Apr 28	Manchester City	L 1-3	Douglas (pen)	22,259

FA Cup

Jan 6	Brighton & Hove Albion	(Rd3) W 3-0	Byrom, Ratcliffe, Pickering	20,405
Jan 27	Stoke City	(Rd4) W 1-0	Douglas (pen)	49,500
Feb 17	MIDDLESBROUGH	(Rd 5) W 2-1	Pickering, Lawther	33,714
Mar 10	Fulham	(Rd 6) D 2-2	Thomas, Douglas	29,997
Mar 14	FULHAM	(R) L 0-1		34,045

League Cup

Sep 11	Peterborough United	(Rd1) W 3-1	Lawther 2, Douglas	15,094
Oct 2	Bristol Rovers	(Rd2) D 1-1	McGrath	15,686
Oct 16	BRISTOL ROVERS	(R) W 4-0	Thomas 4	5,157
Nov 14	Nottingham Forest	(Rd3) W 2-1	Ratcliffe, Lawther	9,512
Dec 11	IPSWICH TOWN	(Rd4) W 4-1	Lawther, Byrom, Pickering 2 (1 pen)	11,071
Feb 6	Rotherham United	(Rd5) W 1-0	Lawther	11,065
Mar 19	Rochdale	(SF/1L) L 1-3	Douglas	9,828
Apr 4	Rochdale	(SF/2L) W 2-1	Pickering (pen), Douglas	11,644

MANAGER: Jack Marshall

TOP SCORER: Ian Lawther

BIGGEST WIN: 4-0, 16 October 1961, v Bristol Rovers, Football League Cup Round 2 replay

HIGHEST ATTENDANCE: 55,183, 20 April 1962, v Tottenham Hotspur, Division 1

MAJOR TRANSFERS IN: Ian Lawther from Sunderland, Joe Haverty from Arsenal, Fred Else from Preston North End, Bobby Craig from Sheffield Wednesday

MAJOR TRANSFERS OUT: Peter Dobing to Manchester City, Derek Dougan to Aston Villa, Chris Crowe to Wolverhampton Wanderers

League & Cup Appearances

PLAYER	LEAGUE	CUP COMPETITION		TOTAL
		FA CUP	LC	
Appleby, J.P.	1			1
Bray, J.	13		2	15
Byrom, J.	18	3	5	26
Clayton, R.	38	5	7	50
Craig, R.M.	2			2
Crowe, C.	16		3	19
Douglas, B.	37	5	8	50
Else, F.	32	5	7	44
England, H.M.	14		2	16
Haverty, J.	23		4	27
Isherwood, R.E.	9		1	10
Jones, R.W.	9		1	10
Lawther, W.I.	37	5	6	48
McEvoy, M.A.	12		1	13
McGrath, M.	36	5	8	49
Newton, K.R.	41	5	8	54
Pickering, F.	29	5	5	39
Ratcliffe, J.B.	22	5	4	31
Reeves, T.B.	1			1
Taylor, K.G.	31	5	6	42
Thomas, E.	12	2	3	17
Woods, M.	29	5	7	41

Goalscorers

PLAYER	LEAGUE	CUP COMPETITION		TOTAL
		FA CUP	LC	
Lawther, W.I.	14	1	5	20
Douglas, B.	8	2	3	13
Pickering, F.	6	2	3	11
Byrom, J.	8	1	1	10
Thomas, E.	1	1	4	6
Ratcliffe, J.B.	3	1	1	5
Clayton, R.	4			4
Crowe, C.	2			2
McEvoy, M.A.	2			2
Bray, J.	1			1
Haverty, J.	1			1
McGrath, M.			1	1

Fact File

Eddie Thomas notched up all the goals in the 4-0 win over Bristol Rovers in the Football League Cup second-round replay at Ewood Park.

Final Division 1 Table

		P	W	D	L	F	A	Pts
1	IPSWICH T	42	24	8	10	93	67	56
2	BURNLEY	42	21	11	10	101	67	53
3	TOTTENHAM H	42	21	10	11	88	69	52
4	EVERTON	42	20	11	11	88	54	51
5	SHEFFIELD U	42	19	9	14	61	69	47
6	SHEFFIELD W	42	20	6	16	72	58	46
7	ASTON VILLA	42	18	8	16	65	56	44
8	WEST HAM U	42	17	10	15	76	82	44
9	WBA	42	15	13	14	83	67	43
10	ARSENAL	42	16	11	15	71	72	43
11	BOLTON W	42	16	10	16	62	66	42
12	MANCHESTER C	42	17	7	18	78	81	41
13	BLACKPOOL	42	15	11	16	70	75	41
14	LEICESTER C	42	17	6	19	72	71	40
15	MANCHESTER U	42	15	9	18	72	75	39
16	BLACKBURN R	42	14	11	17	50	58	39
17	BIRMINGHAM C	42	14	10	18	65	81	38
18	WOLVERHAMPTON W	42	13	10	19	73	86	36
19	NOTTINGHAM F	42	13	10	19	63	79	36
20	FULHAM	42	13	7	22	66	74	33
21	CARDIFF C	42	9	14	19	50	81	32
22	CHELSEA	42	9	10	23	63	94	28

Season 1962-63

Football League Division 1

DATE	OPPONENTS	SCORE	GOALSCORERS	ATTENDANCE
Aug 18	Ipswich Town	D 3-3	Craig 3	19,062
Aug 20	NOTTINGHAM FOREST	L 2-5	Douglas 2	17,408
Aug 25	LIVERPOOL	W 1-0	Douglas	21,974
Aug 28	Nottingham Forest	L 0-2		22,948
Sep 1	Wolverhampton W.	L 2-4	Ferguson, Bradshaw	26,883
Sep 5	Sheffield United	D 1-1	Ferguson	18,482
Sep 8	ASTON VILLA	W 4-1	Douglas 2, Pickering, Lawther	13,953
Sep 15	Tottenham Hotspur	L 1-4	Pickering	43,014
Sep 17	SHEFFIELD UNITED	L 1-2	Clayton	13,836
Sep 22	WEST HAM UNITED	L 0-4		15,545
Sep 29	Manchester City	W 1-0	Lawther	23,249
Oct 6	BURNLEY	L 2-3	Lawther, Douglas (pen)	26,626
Oct 13	Manchester United	W 3-0	McGrath, Harrison, Lawther	42,923
Oct 20	LEICESTER CITY	W 2-0	Douglas (pen), Pickering	14,197
Oct 27	Fulham	D 0-0		18,098
Nov 3	ARSENAL	D 5-5	Douglas 2, Pickering 2, Lawther	15,545
Nov 10	West Bromwich Albion	W 5-2	Ferguson, Pickering 3, Lawther	14,508
Nov 17	EVERTON	W 3-2	Lawther, Pickering, Douglas (pen)	30,243
Nov 24	Bolton Wanderers	D 0-0		26,868
Dec 1	LEYTON ORIENT	D 1-1	Harrison	15,593
Dec 8	Birmingham City	D 3-3	Ratcliffe, Pickering, Douglas	16,108
Dec 15	IPSWICH TOWN	L 0-1		8,564
Dec 22	Liverpool	L 1-3	Pickering	35,371
Jan 19	Aston Villa	D 0-0		18,276
Mar 2	MANCHESTER UNITED	D 2-2	Byrom, Pickering	27,924
Mar 9	Leicester City	L 0-2		25,624
Mar 16	FULHAM	L 0-1		9,891
Mar 23	Arsenal	L 1-3	Pickering	21,467
Mar 25	BLACKPOOL	D 3-3	Pickering, McEvoy, England	9,983
Mar 29	BOLTON WANDERERS	W 5-0	McEvoy, Byrom 2, Pickering 2	11,533
Apr 2	Burnley	L 0-1		25,746
Apr 6	Everton	D 0-0		39,790
Apr 12	SHEFFIELD WEDNESDAY	W 3-0	Byrom, McEvoy 2	14,361
Apr 13	WEST BROMWICH ALBION	W 3-1	Douglas 2 (1 pen), McGrath	11,451
Apr 15	Sheffield Wednesday	L 0-4		23,764
Apr 20	Leyton Orient	D 1-1	Pickering	8,274
Apr 23	Blackpool	L 1-4	Byrom	16,446
Apr 27	BIRMINGHAM CITY	W 6-1	England, Ferguson, Pickering 2, Smith o.g., Douglas	9,482
May 1	MANCHESTER CITY	W 4-1	Douglas, Byrom 2, Harrison	12,894
May 4	West Ham United	W 1-0	Pickering	18,898
May 13	WOLVERHAMPTON W.	W 5-1	Pickering 3, Byrom, Ferguson	12,143
May 20	TOTTENHAM HOTSPUR	W 3-0	Ferguson 2, Harrison	22,867

FA Cup

Mar 5	MIDDLESBROUGH	(Rd3) D 1-1	Pickering	16,375
Mar 11	Middlesbrough	(R) L 1-3	Byrom	39,596

League Cup

Sep 26	Derby County	(Rd2) D 1-1	Pickering	9,904
Oct 2	DERBY COUNTY	(R) W 3-1	Ratcliffe, Lawther 2	6,528
Oct 17	LEEDS UNITED	(Rd3) W 4-0	Ferguson, Lawther 2, Pickering	7,680
Nov 14	ROTHERHAM UNITED	(Rd4) W 4-1	Pickering 2, Douglas, Ratcliffe	7,391
Dec 5	Sunderland	(Rd5) L 2-3	Lawther, Ashurst o.g.	24,727

MANAGER: Jack Marshall

TOP SCORER: Fred Pickering

BIGGEST WIN: 6-1, 27 April 1963, v Birmingham City, Division 1

HIGHEST ATTENDANCE: 43,014, 15 September 1962, v Tottenham Hotspur, Division 1

MAJOR TRANSFERS IN: Mike Harrison from Chelsea

MAJOR TRANSFERS OUT: Eddie Thomas to Swansea Town, Joe Haverty to Millwall, Bobby Craig to Celtic, Dave Whelan to Crewe Alexandra

League & Cup Appearances

PLAYER	LEAGUE	CUP COMPETITION		TOTAL
		FA CUP	LC	
Bradshaw, A.	1			1
Bray, J.	38	2	5	45
Byrom, J.	19	2		21
Clayton, R.	35	1	5	41
Craig, R.M.	6		2	8
Douglas, B.	41	2	4	47
Else, F.	40	2	5	47
England, H.M.	17	1		18
Ferguson, M.K.	30	2	4	36
Griffiths, B.	1			1
Harrison, M.J.	31	2	1	34
Haverty, J.	4			4
Jones, R.W.	1			1
Lawther, W.I.	22		5	27
McEvoy, M.A.	13			13
McGrath, M.	25	2	4	31
Newton, K.R.	41	2	5	48
Pickering, F.	36	2	5	43
Ratcliffe, J.B.	10		4	14
Taylor, K.B.	11		1	12
Woods, M.	40	2	5	47

Goalscorers

PLAYER	LEAGUE	CUP COMPETITION		TOTAL
		FA CUP	LC	
Pickering, F.	23	1	4	28
Douglas, B.	15		1	16
Lawther, W.I.	7		5	12
Byrom, J.	8	1		9
Ferguson, M.K.	7		1	8
Harrison, M.J.	4			4
McEvoy, M.A.	4			4
Craig, R.M.	3			3
Ratcliffe, J.B.	1		2	3
England, H.M.	2			2
McGrath, M.	2			2
Bradshaw, A.	1			1
Clayton, R.	1			1
Opps' o.gs.	1		1	2

Fact File

George Eastham scored a last-minute goal to earn Arsenal a share of the spoils in a ten-goal thriller at Ewood Park in November 1962.

Final Division 1 Table

		P	W	D	L	F	A	Pts
1	EVERTON	42	25	11	6	84	42	61
2	TOTTENHAM H	42	23	9	10	111	62	55
3	BURNLEY	42	22	10	10	78	57	54
4	LEICESTER C	42	20	12	10	79	53	52
5	WOLVERHAMPTON W	42	20	10	12	93	65	50
6	SHEFFIELD W	42	19	10	13	77	63	48
7	ARSENAL	42	18	10	14	86	77	46
8	LIVERPOOL	42	17	10	15	71	59	44
9	NOTTINGHAM F	42	17	10	15	67	69	44
10	SHEFFIELD U	42	16	12	14	58	60	44
11	BLACKBURN R	42	15	12	15	79	71	42
12	WEST HAM U	42	14	12	16	73	69	40
13	BLACKPOOL	42	13	14	15	58	64	40
14	WBA	42	16	7	19	71	79	39
15	ASTON VILLA	42	15	8	19	62	68	38
16	FULHAM	42	14	10	18	50	71	38
17	IPSWICH T	42	12	11	19	59	78	35
18	BOLTON W	42	15	5	22	55	75	35
19	MANCHESTER U	42	12	10	20	67	81	34
20	BIRMINGHAM C	42	10	13	19	63	90	33
21	MANCHESTER C	42	10	11	21	58	102	31
22	LEYTON ORIENT	42	6	9	27	37	81	21

Season 1963-64

Football League Division 1

DATE	OPPONENTS	SCORE	GOALSCORERS	ATTENDANCE
Aug 24	LIVERPOOL	L 1-2	Harrison	34,390
Aug 28	Sheffield United	W 1-0	England	21,340
Aug 31	Aston Villa	W 2-1	McEvoy, Ferguson	23,629
Sep 4	SHEFFIELD UNITED	D 2-2	Harrison, Pickering	14,997
Sep 7	TOTTENHAM HOTSPUR	W 7-2	Douglas, McEvoy 4, England, Pickering	20,949
Sep 11	Chelsea	L 0-1		27,384
Sep 14	Wolverhampton W.	W 5-1	England, Pickering, McEvoy, Harrison, Ferguson	18,093
Sep 16	CHELSEA	D 2-2	Harrison 2	23,217
Sep 21	STOKE CITY	W 1-0	McEvoy	30,300
Sep 28	Nottingham Forest	D 1-1	Douglas	27,981
Oct 1	Burnley	L 0-3		24,345
Oct 5	FULHAM	W 2-0	McEvoy, England	13,610
Oct 9	BOLTON WANDERERS	W 3-0	Harrison 2, McEvoy	18,675
Oct 19	BURNLEY	L 1-2	Pickering	26,740
Oct 26	Leicester City	L 3-4	McEvoy 2, Douglas	24,278
Oct 28	Manchester United	D 2-2	Harrison, McEvoy	41,436
Nov 2	SHEFFIELD WEDNESDAY	D 1-1	Pickering	17,079
Nov 9	Everton	W 4-2	Pickering 3, Harrison	49,349
Nov 16	BIRMINGHAM CITY	W 3-0	Harrison, McEvoy, Douglas	14,813
Nov 23	West Bromwich Albion	W 3-1	McEvoy 3	16,441
Nov 30	ARSENAL	W 4-1	Pickering 3, McEvoy	21,060
Dec 7	Ipswich Town	D 0-0		15,500
Dec 14	Liverpool	W 2-1	McEvoy 2	45,182
Dec 21	ASTON VILLA	W 2-0	Pickering 2	17,095
Dec 26	West Ham United	W 8-2	Pickering 3, Douglas, McEvoy 3, Ferguson	20,500
Dec 28	WEST HAM UNITED	L 1-3	McEvoy	28,990
Jan 11	Tottenham Hotspur	L 1-4	Harrison	43,953
Jan 18	WOLVERHAMPTON W.	D 1-1	Pickering	18,928
Feb 1	Stoke City	L 1-3	Pickering	32,307
Feb 8	NOTTINGHAM FOREST	W 2-0	McEvoy 2	18,342
Feb 19	Fulham	D 1-1	Pickering	12,267
Feb 22	MANCHESTER UNITED	L 1-3	Pickering	37,526
Feb 29	Bolton Wanderers	W 5-0	Pickering 2, Ferguson, McEvoy, Harrison	18,343
Mar 7	LEICESTER CITY	W 5-2	McEvoy 4, Pickering	15,118
Mar 13	Birmingham City	D 2-2	Ferguson, Jones	15,809
Mar 21	EVERTON	L 1-2	Douglas	35,142
Mar 27	BLACKPOOL	L 1-2	England	23,039
Mar 28	Sheffield Wednesday	L 2-5	Harrison (pen), Byrom	20,002
Mar 30	Blackpool	L 2-3	McEvoy 2	20,165
Apr 4	WEST BROMWICH ALBION	L 0-2		12,052
Apr 11	Arsenal	D 0-0		26,164
Apr 18	IPSWICH TOWN	W 3-1	England, Harrison, Jones	10,341

FA Cup

Jan 4	GRIMSBY TOWN	(Rd3) W 4-0	Pickering, McEvoy 3	22,887
Jan 25	FULHAM	(Rd4) W 2-0	Pickering, McEvoy	24,314
Feb 15	Oxford United	(Rd5) L 1-3	Ferguson	21,300

League Cup

Sep 25	Notts County	(Rd2) L 1-2	Pickering	7,030

League & Cup Appearances

PLAYER	LEAGUE	CUP COMPETITION		TOTAL
		FA CUP	LC	
Blore, R.	4			4
Bray, J.	40	3	1	44
Byrom, J.	3			3
Clayton, R.	41	3	1	45
Douglas, B.	41	3	1	45
England, H.M.	41	3	1	45
Else, F.	42	3	1	46
Ferguson, M.K	40	3	1	44
Harrison, M.J.	41	3	1	45
Holden, A.	1			1
Jones, G.A.	8			8
Joyce, W.	9	1		10
McEvoy, M.A.	37	3	1	41
McGrath, M.	33	3		36
Newton, K.R.	31	2	1	34
Pickering, F.	34	3	1	38
Ratcliffe, J.B.	3			3
Sims, H.C.	11			11
Taylor, K.G.	2			2

Goalscorers

PLAYER	LEAGUE	CUP COMPETITION		TOTAL
		FA CUP	LC	
McEvoy, M.A.	32	4		36
Pickering, F.	23	2	1	26
Harrison, M.J.	14			14
Douglas, B.	6			6
England, H.M.	6			6
Ferguson, M.K	5	1		6
Jones, G.A.	2			2
Byrom, J.	1			1

Fact File

Andy McEvoy proved a revelation as a goal poacher with 32 goals in 37 First Division outings. Previously, he had scored just 11 goals in 61 league games.

MANAGER: Jack Marshall

TOP SCORER: Andy McEvoy

BIGGEST WIN: 8-2, 26 December 26, 1963, v West Ham United, Division 1

HIGHEST ATTENDANCE: 49,349, 9 November 1963 v Everton, Division 1

MAJOR TRANSFERS IN: Reg Blore from Southport, Walter Joyce from Burnley, George Jones from Bury

MAJOR TRANSFERS OUT: Ian Lawther to Scunthorpe United, Fred Pickering to Everton

Final Division 1 Table

		P	W	D	L	F	A	Pts
1	LIVERPOOL	42	26	5	11	92	45	57
2	MANCHESTER U	42	23	7	12	90	62	53
3	EVERTON	42	21	10	11	84	64	52
4	TOTTENHAM H	42	22	7	13	97	81	51
5	CHELSEA	42	20	10	12	72	56	50
6	SHEFFIELD W	42	19	11	12	84	67	49
7	BLACKBURN R	42	18	10	14	89	65	46
8	ARSENAL	42	17	11	14	90	82	45
9	BURNLEY	42	17	10	15	71	64	44
10	WBA	42	16	11	15	70	61	43
11	LEICESTER C	42	16	11	15	61	58	43
12	SHEFFIELD U	42	16	11	15	61	64	43
13	NOTTINGHAM F	42	16	9	17	64	68	41
14	WEST HAM U	42	14	12	16	69	74	40
15	FULHAM	42	13	13	16	58	65	39
16	WOLVERHAMPTON W	42	12	15	15	70	80	39
17	STOKE C	42	14	10	18	77	78	38
18	BLACKPOOL	42	13	9	20	52	73	35
19	ASTON VILLA	42	11	12	19	62	71	34
20	BIRMINGHAM C	42	11	7	24	54	92	29
21	BOLTON W	42	10	8	24	48	80	28
22	IPSWICH T	42	9	7	26	56	121	25

Season 1964-65

Football League Division 1

DATE	OPPONENTS	SCORE	GOALSCORERS	ATTENDANCE
Aug 22	Sheffield Wednesday	L 0-1		20,855
Aug 24	Blackpool	L 2-4	Jones G., England	22,381
Aug 29	LIVERPOOL	W 3-2	Byrom, Harrison (pen), McEvoy	26,865
Sep 2	BLACKPOOL	W 4-1	Harrison (pen), McEvoy 2, Byrom	20,315
Sep 5	Aston Villa	W 4-0	McEvoy 2, Byrom, Ferguson	21,785
Sep 8	Arsenal	D 1-1	Harrison	29,510
Sep 12	WOLVERHAMPTON W.	W 4-1	McEvoy 2, Byrom 2	16,745
Sep 16	ARSENAL	L 1-2	England	17,675
Sep 19	Sunderland	L 0-1		40,695
Sep 26	LEICESTER CITY	W 3-1	McEvoy, Ferguson, Byrom	14,964
Oct 3	Chelsea	L 1-5	McEvoy	34,913
Oct 7	STOKE CITY	D 1-1	Byrom	12,509
Oct 10	Burnley	D 1-1	Douglas (pen)	21,199
Oct 17	SHEFFIELD UNITED	W 4-0	McEvoy 3, England	14,169
Oct 24	Everton	W 3-2	McEvoy 2, Bradshaw	40,948
Oct 31	BIRMINGHAM CITY	W 3-1	Byrom, England, Newton	13,721
Nov 7	West Ham United	D 1-1	Harrison	22,725
Nov 14	WEST BROMWICH ALBION	W 4-2	McEvoy 2, Harrison (pen), Byrom	13,828
Nov 21	Manchester United	L 0-3		49,928
Nov 28	FULHAM	W 2-0	Byrom, Harrison (pen)	12,434
Dec 5	Nottingham Forest	W 5-2	Byrom, McEvoy 3, Byrom 2	17,705
Dec 19	Liverpool	L 2-3	McEvoy, England	33,316
Dec 26	Leeds United	D 1-1	McEvoy	45,341
Dec 28	LEEDS UNITED	L 0-2		24,511
Jan 2	ASTON VILLA	W 5-1	Byrom 3, McEvoy 2	18,292
Jan 16	Wolverhampton W.	L 2-4	Byrom, McEvoy	16,644
Jan 29	SHEFFIELD WEDNESDAY	L 0-1		12,202
Feb 6	Leicester City	W 3-2	McEvoy, Anderson, Byrom	18,001
Feb 13	CHELSEA	L 0-3		16,683
Feb 24	BURNLEY	L 1-4	McGrath	15,340
Feb 27	Sheffield United	D 1-1	Byrom	15,522
Mar 6	EVERTON	L 0-2		15,960
Mar 13	Stoke City	D 1-1	Byrom	19,282
Mar 20	WEST HAM UNITED	W 4-0	Byrom 3, Douglas (pen)	8,990
Mar 23	SUNDERLAND	W 3-2	Byrom, McEvoy, Joyce	10,119
Mar 26	West Bromwich Albion	D 0-0		15,414
Apr 3	MANCHESTER UNITED	L 0-5		29,363
Apr 9	Fulham	L 2-3	McEvoy, Douglas	11,653
Apr 16	Tottenham Hotspur	L 2-5	Douglas, McEvoy	36,497
Apr 19	TOTTENHAM HOTSPUR	W 3-1	Harrison (pen), Douglas, Byrom	14,026
Apr 24	Birmingham City	D 5-5	McEvoy, Ferguson, Hennessey o.g. Douglas 2	8,877
Apr 27	NOTTINGHAM FOREST	D 1-1	Douglas	9,590

FA Cup

Jan 9	Leicester City	(Rd3) D 2-2	Harrison, Douglas	23,067
Jan 14	LEICESTER CITY	(R) L 1-2	Byrom	25,875

League Cup

Sep 23	Bolton Wanderers	(Rd2) W 5-1	McEvoy 2, Byrom, Harrison (pen), Ferguson	17,335
Oct 14	Workington	(Rd3) D 0-0		11,763
Oct 22	WORKINGTON	(R) L 1-5	McEvoy	6,282

League & Cup Appearances

PLAYER	LEAGUE	CUP COMPETITION		TOTAL
		FA CUP	LC	
Anderson, B.C.	2			2
Blore, R.	1			1
Bradshaw, A.	10			10
Bray, A.	4			4
Byrom, J.	40	2	3	45
Clayton, R.	39	2	3	44
Douglas, B.	42	2	3	47
Else, F.	35	2	2	39
England, H.M.	37	2	2	41
Ferguson, M.K.	38	2	3	43
Harrison, M.J.	31	2	2	35
Horrey, R.G.	1		1	2
Jones, G.A.	3			3
Jones, R.W.	7		1	8
Joyce, W.	42	2	3	47
McEvoy, M.A.	40	2	3	45
McGrath, M.	31	2	3	36
Mulvaney, R.	7		1	8
Newton, K.R.	37	2	3	42
Sharples, G.F.V.	5			5
Sims, H.C.	2			2
Wilson, W.	8			8

Goalscorers

PLAYER	LEAGUE	CUP COMPETITION		TOTAL
		FA CUP	LC	
McEvoy, M.A.	29		3	32
Byrom, J.	25	1	1	27
Douglas, B.	8	1		9
Harrison, M.J.	6	1	1	8
England, H.M.	5			5
Ferguson, M.K.	3		1	4
Anderson, B.C.	1			1
Bradshaw, A.	1			1
Jones, G.A.	1			1
Joyce, W.	1			1
McGrath, M.	1			1
Newton, K.R.	1			1
Opps' o.gs.	1			1

Fact File

Andy McEvoy and Jimmy Greaves of Tottenham Hotspur were the leading goalscorers in the First Division with 29 goals each.

Final Division 1 Table

		P	W	D	L	F	A	Pts
1	MANCHESTER U	42	26	9	7	89	39	61
2	LEEDS U	42	26	9	7	83	52	61
3	CHELSEA	42	24	8	10	89	54	56
4	EVERTON	42	17	15	10	69	60	49
5	NOTTINGHAM F	42	17	13	12	71	67	47
6	TOTTENHAM H	42	19	7	16	87	71	45
7	LIVERPOOL	42	17	10	15	67	73	44
8	SHEFFIELD W	42	16	11	15	57	55	43
9	WEST HAM U	42	19	4	19	82	71	42
10	BLACKBURN R	42	16	10	16	83	79	42
11	STOKE C	42	16	10	16	67	66	42
12	BURNLEY	42	16	10	16	70	70	42
13	ARSENAL	42	17	7	18	69	75	41
14	WBA	42	13	13	16	70	65	39
15	SUNDERLAND	42	14	9	19	64	74	37
16	ASTON VILLA	42	16	5	21	57	82	37
17	BLACKPOOL	42	12	11	19	67	78	35
18	LEICESTER C	42	11	13	18	69	85	35
19	SHEFFIELD U	42	12	11	19	50	64	35
20	FULHAM	42	11	12	19	60	78	34
21	WOLVERHAMPTON W	42	13	4	25	59	89	30
22	BIRMINGHAM C	42	8	11	23	64	96	27

MANAGER: Jack Marshall

TOP SCORER: Andy McEvoy

BIGGEST WIN: 5-1, 23 September 1964, v Bolton Wanderers, Football League Cup Round 2; 2 January 1965, v Aston Villa, Division 1

HIGHEST ATTENDANCE: 49,928, 21 November 1964, v Manchester United, Division 1

MAJOR TRANSFERS IN: George Sharples from Everton

MAJOR TRANSFERS OUT: John Bray to Bury

Season 1965-66

Football League Division 1

DATE	OPPONENTS	SCORE	GOALSCORERS	ATTENDANCE
Aug 25	Fulham	L 2-5	Sharples, McEvoy	14,480
Sep 1	FULHAM	W 3-2	Byrom, McEvoy 2	10,497
Sep 4	ASTON VILLA	L 0-2		9,367
Sep 8	Stoke City	L 2-3	McEvoy 2	12,505
Sep 11	Sunderland	L 0-1		35,357
Sep 15	STOKE CITY	L 0-1		9,565
Sep 18	WEST HAM UNITED	L 1-2	Jones G.	10,178
Sep 25	Leeds United	L 0-3		31,098
Oct 2	SHEFFIELD UNITED	D 0-0		11,418
Oct 5	Everton	D 2-2	Ferguson, Newton	34,694
Oct 9	Burnley	W 4-1	England, Harrison, McEvoy, Douglas	23,198
Oct 16	CHELSEA	L 0-1		16,167
Oct 23	Arsenal	D 2-2	Court o.g., England	27,519
Oct 30	EVERTON	L 1-2	McEvoy	15,096
Nov 6	Manchester United	D 2-2	Harrison 2 (1 pen)	39,093
Nov 13	NEWCASTLE UNITED	W 4-2	England 2, Darling, Byrom	12,293
Nov 17	Liverpool	L 2-5	Jones G., Anderson	36,450
Nov 20	West Bromwich Albion	L 1-2	Jones G.	17,334
Nov 27	NOTTINGHAM FOREST	W 5-0	Darling, England, Jones G. 2, Ferguson	9,834
Dec 4	Sheffield Wednesday	L 1-2	Jones G.	13,905
Dec 11	NORTHAMPTON TOWN	W 6-1	Ferguson, Jones G 3, England, Harrison (pen)	10,685
Dec 25	Blackpool	L 2-4	Jones G., England	20,851
Jan 1	BURNLEY	L 0-2		28,013
Jan 8	Northampton Town	L 1-2		15,820
Jan 15	ARSENAL	W 2-1	Skirton o.g., McEvoy	12,532
Jan 29	Tottenham Hotspur	L 0-4		34,573
Feb 5	LIVERPOOL	L 1-4	Harrison (pen)	30,414
Feb 19	Aston Villa	L 1-3	Byrom	15,117
Feb 26	SUNDERLAND	W 2-0	Harrison, Sharples	14,025
Mar 12	West Ham United	L 1-4	McEvoy	18,686
Mar 19	LEEDS UNITED	L 2-3	Harrison (pen), Darling	25,398
Mar 29	Sheffield United	L 0-2		12,479
Apr 8	LEICESTER CITY	L 0-2		13,712
Apr 9	Newcastle United	L 1-2	Darling	21,607
Apr 12	Leicester City	L 0-2		21,224
Apr 16	WEST BROMWICH ALBION	L 0-1		7,637
Apr 23	Nottingham Forest	W 3-0	Douglas, Ferguson, England	17,742
Apr 30	SHEFFIELD WEDNESDAY	L 1-2	McEvoy	7,683
May 2	BLACKPOOL	L 1-3	Harrison	7,487
May 4	Chelsea	L 0-1		10,024
May 7	MANCHESTER UNITED	L 1-4	Harrison	14,513
May 9	TOTTENHAM HOTSPUR	L 0-1		7,256

FA Cup

Jan 22	ARSENAL	(Rd3)	W 3-0	McEvoy 2, Byrom	22,951
Feb 12	West Ham United	(Rd4)	D 3-3	Byrom 3	32,350
Feb 16	WEST HAM UNITED	(R)	W 4-1	McEvoy 3, Byrom	25,547
Mar 5	Norwich City	(Rd5)	D 2-2	Byrom, Jones G.	30,751
Mar 9	NORWICH CITY	(R)	W 3-2	McEvoy, Darling, Harrison	33,135
Mar 26	SHEFFIELD WEDNESDAY	(Rd6)	L 1-2	Byrom	33,000

League Cup

Sep 21	NORTHAMPTON TOWN	(Rd2)	L 0-1	8,814

Fact File

The second half of the First Division programme brought just three wins and 18 defeats.

MANAGER: Jack Marshall

TOP SCORER: Andy McEvoy

BIGGEST WIN: 6-1, 11 December 1965, v Northampton Town, Division 1

HIGHEST ATTENDANCE: 39,093, 6 November 1965, v Manchester United, Division 1

MAJOR TRANSFERS IN: Martin Britt from West Ham United

MAJOR TRANSFERS OUT: Mick McGrath to Bradford, Reg Blore to Oldham Athletic

League & Cup Appearances

PLAYER	LEAGUE	CUP COMPETITION		TOTAL
		FA CUP	LC	
Anderson, B.C.	0 (1)			0 (1)
Blore, R.	6			6
Britt, M.C.	8			8
Byrom, J.	26 (2)	5	1	32 (2)
Clayton, R.	39	5	1	45
Darling, M.	17 (2)	4		21 (2)
Douglas, B.	16	1	1	18
Else, F.	38	6	1	45
England, H.M.	36	6	1	43
Ferguson, M.K.	42	6		48
Harrison, M.J.	32	6	1	39
Holt, D.E.	5			5
Horrey, R.G.	2			2
Jones, G.A.	18 (1)	2	1	21 (1)
Jones, R.W.	1			1
Joyce, W.	23	6		29
McEvoy, M.A.	31	6	1	38
McGrath, M.	1			1
Mulvaney, R.	23			23
Newton, K.R.	32	6	1	39
Roberts, J.T.	3			3
Rogers, E.	2			2
Sharples, G.F.V.	28 (1)	1	1	30 (1)
Wilson, K.	33	6	1	40

Goalscorers

PLAYER	LEAGUE	CUP COMPETITION		TOTAL
		FA CUP	LC	
McEvoy, M.A.	10	6		16
Jones, G.A.	10	1		11
Harrison, M.J.	9	1		10
Byrom, J.	3	7		10
England, H.M.	8			8
Darling, M.	4	1		5
Ferguson, M.K.	4			4
Sharples, G.F.V.	3			3
Douglas, B.	2			2
Anderson, B.C.	1			1
Newton, K.R.	1			1
Opps' o.gs.	2			2

Final Division 1 Table

		P	W	D	L	F	A	PTS
1	LIVERPOOL	42	26	9	7	79	34	61
2	LEEDS U	42	23	9	10	79	38	55
3	BURNLEY	42	24	7	11	79	47	55
4	MANCHESTER U	42	18	15	9	84	59	51
5	CHELSEA	42	22	7	13	65	53	51
6	WBA	42	19	12	11	91	69	50
7	LEICESTER C	42	21	7	14	80	65	49
8	TOTTENHAM H	42	16	12	14	75	66	44
9	SHEFFIELD U	42	16	11	15	56	59	43
10	STOKE C	42	15	12	15	65	64	42
11	EVERTON	42	15	11	16	56	62	41
12	WEST HAM U	42	15	9	18	70	83	39
13	BLACKPOOL	42	14	9	19	55	65	37
14	ARSENAL	42	12	13	17	62	75	37
15	NEWCASTLE U	42	14	9	19	50	63	37
16	ASTON VILLA	42	15	6	21	69	80	36
17	SHEFFIELD W	42	14	8	20	56	66	36
18	NOTTINGHAM F	42	14	8	20	56	72	36
19	SUNDERLAND	42	14	8	20	51	72	36
20	FULHAM	42	14	7	21	67	85	35
21	NORTHAMPTON T	42	10	13	19	55	92	33
22	BLACKBURN R	42	8	4	30	57	88	20

Season 1966-67

Football League Division 2

DATE	OPPONENTS	SCORE	GOALSCORERS	ATTENDANCE
Aug 20	Derby County	W 3-1	Harrison 2, Gilliver	14,318
Aug 24	CHARLTON ATHLETIC	W 2-1	Gilliver, McEvoy	17,156
Aug 27	CRYSTAL PALACE	W 2-1	McEvoy 2	15,015
Aug 30	Charlton Athletic	D 0-0		6,504
Sep 3	Huddersfield Town	L 1-3	Harrison	15,685
Sep 7	PRESTON NORTH END	W 2-0	Sharples, Douglas	23,529
Sep 10	CARDIFF CITY	W 4-1	Jones, McEvoy 2, Hole	12,805
Sep 17	Wolverhampton W.	L 0-4		18,261
Sep 24	IPSWICH TOWN	L 1-2	Gilliver	16,523
Sep 26	Preston North End	L 0-3		24,173
Oct 1	Bristol City	D 2-2	McEvoy 2	12,824
Oct 8	BURY	W 2-1	Connelly, Harrison (pen)	15,391
Oct 15	Coventry City	L 0-2		21,017
Oct 22	NORWICH CITY	D 0-0		12,029
Oct 29	Birmingham City	D 1-1	Connelly	17,626
Nov 5	PORTSMOUTH	D 2-2	Connelly, Douglas	10,097
Nov 12	Hull City	W 3-2	Hole, Douglas, Darling	22,887
Nov 19	PLYMOUTH ARGYLE	W 3-0	Harrison, Joyce 2	12,187
Nov 26	Northampton Town	L 1-2	Hole	9,470
Dec 3	MILLWALL	W 1-0	Rogers	12,293
Dec 10	Rotherham United	L 1-2	Lord	9,788
Dec 17	DERBY COUNTY	D 0-0		10,904
Dec 26	Carlisle United	W 2-1	Hole 2	17,523
Dec 27	CARLISLE UNITED	W 2-0	Hole, Connelly	20,219
Dec 31	Crystal Palace	L 1-2	Connelly	17,703
Jan 14	Cardiff City	D 1-1	Connelly	11,322
Jan 21	WOLVERHAMPTON W.	D 0-0		15,489
Feb 4	Ipswich Town	D 1-1	Connelly	16,292
Feb 11	BRISTOL CITY	W 1-0	Connelly	12,089
Feb 18	HUDDERSFIELD TOWN	W 2-0	Douglas, Darling	19,647
Feb 25	Bury	W 2-1	Douglas (pen), Hole	15,922
Mar 4	BIRMINGHAM CITY	W 1-0	Harrison	14,908
Mar 18	Norwich City	W 1-0	Connelly	13,015
Mar 25	COVENTRY CITY	L 0-1		26,380
Mar 27	Bolton Wanderers	W 1-0	Douglas	21,740
Apr 1	Portsmouth	D 1-1	Hole	13,788
Apr 8	HULL CITY	W 4-1	Ferguson 2, Joyce, Connelly	11,622
Apr 15	Plymouth Argyle	L 0-4		12,217
Apr 22	NORTHAMPTON TOWN	W 3-0	Newton, Connelly, Douglas (pen)	9,883
Apr 25	BOLTON WANDERERS	D 0-0		12,403
Apr 29	Millwall	D 1-1	Anderson	12,397
May 6	ROTHERHAM UNITED	D 1-1	Douglas	8,567

FA Cup

Jan 28	CARLISLE UNITED	(Rd3) L 1-2	Connelly	23,312

League Cup

Sep 14	BARROW	(Rd2) W 4-1	Rogers, Ferguson 2, McEvoy	4,655
Oct 4	York City	(Rd3) W 2-0	Douglas, Newton	8,593
Oct 26	Carlisle United	(Rd4) L 0-4		14,054

League & Cup Appearances

PLAYER	LEAGUE	CUP COMPETITION		TOTAL
		FA CUP	LC	
Anderson, B.C.	8			8
Barton, J.B.	42	1	3	46
Britt, M.C.			1	1
Clayton, R.	41	1	3	45
Connelly, J.M.	34	1		35
Coxon, E.G.	1			1
Darling, M.	18 (2)			18 (2)
Douglas, B.	37	1	3	41
Ferguson, M.K.	31	1	3	35
Gilliver, A.H.	9		1	10
Harrison, M.J.	21	1	2	24
Helliwell, D.	1			1
Hole, B.G.	39	1	3	43
Holt, D.E.	5		1	6
Jones, G.A.	7 (2)			7 (2)
Joyce, W.	41		3	44
Lord, F.	10			10
McEvoy, M.A.	14	1	3	18
Mulvaney, R.	7 (1)		1	8 (1)
Newton, K.R.	33	1	2	36
Rogers, E.	5 (1)		1	6 (1)
Sharples, G.F.V.	26 (3)	1	1	28 (3)
Wilson, W.	32	1	2	35

Goalscorers

PLAYER	LEAGUE	CUP COMPETITION		TOTAL
		FA CUP	LC	
Connelly, J.M.	11	1		12
Douglas, B.	8		1	9
Hole, B.G.	8			8
McEvoy, M.A.	7		1	8
Harrison, M.J.	6			6
Ferguson, M.K.	2		2	4
Gilliver, A.H.	3			3
Joyce, W.	3			3
Darling, M.	2			2
Newton, K.R.	1		1	2
Rogers, E.	1		1	2
Anderson, B.C.	1			1
Jones, G.A.	1			1
Lord, F.	1			1
Sharples, G.F.V.	1			1

Fact File

Eddie Quigley returned to Ewood Park as assistant manager in October 1966. When Jack Marshall resigned Quigley acted as caretaker-manager until his appointment as manager in April 1967.

Final Division 2 Table

		P	W	D	L	F	A	Pts
1	COVENTRY C	42	23	13	6	74	43	59
2	WOLVERHAMPTON W	42	25	8	9	88	48	58
3	CARLISLE U	42	23	6	13	71	54	52
4	BLACKBURN R	42	19	13	10	56	46	51
5	IPSWICH T	42	17	16	9	70	54	50
6	HUDDERSFIELD T	42	20	9	13	58	46	49
7	CRYSTAL PALACE	42	19	10	13	61	55	48
8	MILLWALL	42	18	9	15	49	58	45
9	BOLTON W	42	14	14	14	64	58	42
10	BIRMINGHAM C	42	16	8	18	70	66	40
11	NORWICH C	42	13	14	15	49	55	40
12	HULL C	42	16	7	19	77	72	39
13	PRESTON NE	42	16	7	19	65	67	39
14	PORTSMOUTH	42	13	13	16	59	70	39
15	BRISTOL C	42	12	14	16	56	62	38
16	PLYMOUTH ARG	42	14	9	19	59	58	37
17	DERBY CO	42	12	12	18	68	72	36
18	ROTHERHAM U	42	13	10	19	61	70	36
19	CHARLTON ATH	42	13	9	20	49	53	35
20	CARDIFF C	42	12	9	21	61	87	33
21	NORTHAMPTON T	42	12	6	24	47	84	30
22	BURY	42	11	6	25	49	83	28

MANAGER: Jack Marshall/Eddie Quigley

TOP SCORER: John Connelly

BIGGEST WIN: 4-1, 10 September 1966, v Cardiff City, Division 2; 14 September 1966, v Barrow, Football League Cup Round 2; 8 April 1967, v Hull City, Division 2

HIGHEST ATTENDANCE: 26,380, 25 March 1967, v Coventry City, Division 2

MAJOR TRANSFERS IN: Allan Gilliver from Huddersfield Town, John Barton from Preston North End, Barrie Hole from Cardiff City, John Connelly from Manchester United, Frank Lord from Stockport County

MAJOR TRANSFERS OUT: John Byrom to Bolton Wanderers, Mike England to Tottenham Hotspur, George Jones to Bury

Season 1967-68

Football League Division 2

DATE	OPPONENTS	SCORE	GOALSCORERS	ATTENDANCE
Aug 19	Millwall	W 2-1	Anderson, Hole	13,725
Aug 23	CARLISLE UNITED	W 1-0	Anderson	17,740
Aug 26	HULL CITY	W 2-0	Anderson, Harrison (pen)	16,240
Aug 29	Carlisle United	L 0-1		11,668
Sep 2	Middlesbrough	D 0-0		23,757
Sep 6	IPSWICH TOWN	W 2-1	Coddington, Newton	13,610
Sep 9	BRISTOL CITY	W 2-0	Connelly, Ferguson (pen)	14,621
Sep 16	Birmingham City	D 1-1	Newton	28,972
Sep 23	BOLTON WANDERERS	W 2-1	Rogers, Anderson	19,393
Sep 30	Huddersfield Town	L 1-2	Ferguson (pen)	15,216
Oct 7	Norwich City	L 0-1		18,080
Oct 23	Crystal Palace	L 0-1		23,771
Nov 18	Preston North End	W 5-3	Hole 2, Gilliver, Darling, Ferguson (pen)	20,039
Nov 25	PORTSMOUTH	D 2-2	Gilliver, Connelly	13,081
Dec 2	Cardiff City	L 2-3	Newton, Hole	9,829
Dec 9	ROTHERHAM UNITED	W 3-1	Rogers 2, Darling	10,055
Dec 12	Queens Park Rangers	L 1-3	Connelly	12,917
Dec 16	MILLWALL	W 2-0	Darling, Gilliver	10,340
Dec 22	Hull City	D 1-1	Ferguson (pen)	18,662
Dec 26	DERBY COUNTY	W 3-0	Ferguson, Darling, Gilliver	17,902
Dec 30	Derby County	D 2-2	Darling, Connelly	19,064
Jan 6	MIDDLESBROUGH	W 3-0	Darling, Gilliver, Rogers	14,420
Jan 13	Bristol City	D 0-0		19,900
Jan 20	BIRMINGHAM CITY	L 1-2	Connelly	17,934
Feb 3	Bolton Wanderers	L 1-2	Hatton o.g.	17,334
Feb 14	HUDDERSFIELD TOWN	D 0-0		11,796
Feb 17	Plymouth Argyle	L 1-2	Newton	7,926
Feb 24	NORWICH CITY	D 0-0		12,803
Mar 1	Charlton Athletic	L 0-3		11,759
Mar 9	CHARLTON ATHLETIC	W 3-2	Connelly, Rogers, Ferguson	9,256
Mar 13	ASTON VILLA	W 2-1	Ferguson, Darling	10,026
Mar 16	CRYSTAL PALACE	W 2-1	Rogers (pen), Ferguson	10,204
Mar 23	Aston Villa	W 2-1	Martin 2	14,111
Mar 30	QUEENS PARK RANGERS	L 0-1		16,141
Apr 3	BLACKPOOL	W 2-1	Armfield o.g., Martin	13,655
Apr 13	PRESTON NORTH END	L 0-1		20,225
Apr 15	Blackpool	L 1-2	Martin	21,865
Apr 20	Portsmouth	L 1-2	Gilliver	19,943
Apr 24	PLYMOUTH ARGYLE	D 1-1	Rogers (pen)	7,465
Apr 27	CARDIFF CITY	D 1-1	Hole	7,195
May 4	Rotherham United	L 0-1		8,625
May 11	Ipswich Town	D 1-1	Martin	27,855

FA Cup

Jan 27	Swindon Town	(Rd3) L 0-1		20,830

League Cup

Sep 13	BRIGHTON & HOVE ALBION	(Rd2) W 3-1	Ferguson (pen), Rogers 2	10,257
Oct 11	MIDDLESBROUGH	(Rd3) W 3-2	Hole 2, Ferguson	10,442
Nov 1	Arsenal	(Rd4) L 1-2	Rogers	20,044

League & Cup Appearances

PLAYER	LEAGUE	CUP COMPETITION		TOTAL
		FA CUP	LC	
Anderson, B.C.	11 (6)			11 (6)
Barton, J.B.	13			13
Beardall, J.T.	1			1
Blacklaw, A.S.	29	1	3	33
Calloway, L.J.	3			3
Clayton, R.	23		3	26
Coddington, J.W.	38	1	3	42
Connelly, J.M.	40	1	3	44
Coxon, E.G.	9			9
Darling, M.	25 (1)	1	1	27 (1)
Douglas, B.	6		2	8
Ferguson, M.K.	39	1	3	43
Gilliver, A.H.	23 (2)	1	3	27 (2)
Harrison, M.J.	4			4
Helliwell, D.	5		1	6
Hole, B.G.	33	1	2	36
Joyce, W.	4 (1)			4 (1)
Martin, D.	15			15
Metcalfe, S.M.	3			3
Mulvaney, R.	6 (4)			6 (4)
Newton, K.R.	34	1	3	38
Rogers, E.	34 (2)	1	3	38 (2)
Sharples, G.F.V.	22	1		23
Wilson, W.	42	1	3	46

Goalscorers

PLAYER	LEAGUE	CUP COMPETITION		TOTAL
		FA CUP	LC	
Ferguson, M.K.	8		2	10
Rogers, E.	7		3	10
Darling, M.	7			7
Hole, B.G.	5		2	7
Connelly, J.M.	6			6
Gilliver, A.H.	6			6
Martin, D.	5			5
Anderson, B.C.	4			4
Newton, K.R.	4			4
Coddington, J.W.	1			1
Harrison, M.J.	1			1
Opps' o.gs.	2			2

Fact File

Stuart Metcalfe, who was still 17, made his senior debut against Cardiff City in April 1968.

MANAGER: Eddie Quigley

TOP SCORER: Mike Ferguson/Eamonn Rogers

BIGGEST WIN: 3-0, 26 December 1967, v Derby County, Division 2; 6 January 1968, v Middlesbrough, Division 2

HIGHEST ATTENDANCE: 28,972, 16 September 1967, v Birmingham City, Division 2

MAJOR TRANSFERS IN: John Coddington from Huddersfield Town, Adam Blacklaw from Burnley, Don Martin from Northampton Town

MAJOR TRANSFERS OUT: Andy McEvoy to Limerick, Walter Joyce to Oldham Athletic

Final Division 2 Table

		P	W	D	L	F	A	Pts
1	IPSWICH T	42	22	15	5	79	44	59
2	QPR	42	25	8	9	67	36	58
3	BLACKPOOL	42	24	10	8	71	43	58
4	BIRMINGHAM C	42	19	14	9	83	51	52
5	PORTSMOUTH	42	18	13	11	68	55	49
6	MIDDLESBROUGH	42	17	12	13	60	54	46
7	MILLWALL	42	14	17	11	62	50	45
8	BLACKBURN R	42	16	11	15	56	49	43
9	NORWICH C	42	16	11	15	60	65	43
10	CARLISLE U	42	14	13	15	58	52	41
11	CRYSTAL PALACE	42	14	11	17	56	56	39
12	BOLTON W	42	13	13	16	60	63	39
13	CARDIFF C	42	13	12	17	60	66	38
14	HUDDERSFIELD T	42	13	12	17	46	61	38
15	CHARLTON ATH	42	12	13	17	63	68	37
16	ASTON VILLA	42	15	7	20	54	64	37
17	HULL C	42	12	13	17	58	73	37
18	DERBY CO	42	13	10	19	71	78	36
19	BRISTOL C	42	13	10	19	48	62	36
20	PRESTON NE	42	12	11	19	43	65	35
21	ROTHERHAM U	42	10	11	21	42	76	31
22	PLYMOUTH ARG	42	9	9	24	38	72	27

Season 1968-69

Football League Division 2

DATE	OPPONENTS	SCORE	GOALSCORERS	ATTENDANCE
Aug 10	DERBY COUNTY	D 1-1	Rogers (pen)	13,686
Aug 17	Hull City	W 3-1	Martin 2, Darling	13,345
Aug 21	Portsmouth	W 1-0	Tindall o.g.	28,642
Aug 24	ASTON VILLA	W 2-0	Darling, Connelly	12,666
Aug 28	BLACKPOOL	D 1-1	Craven o.g.	21,062
Aug 31	Bristol City	L 0-1		19,787
Sep 7	MILLWALL	L 2-4	Martin 2	9,923
Sep 14	Bolton Wanderers	D 1-1	Darling	16,097
Sep 18	OXFORD UNITED	W 1-0	Rogers (pen)	10,895
Sep 21	SHEFFIELD UNITED	W 1-0	Martin	7,736
Sep 28	Fulham	D 1-1	Martin	12,934
Oct 5	Preston North End	D 1-1	Connelly	20,711
Oct 7	Blackpool	W 1-0	Darling	21,154
Oct 12	CARLISLE UNITED	L 0-2		12,101
Oct 19	Bury	W 3-1	Sharples, Connelly, Darling	11,711
Oct 26	NORWICH CITY	W 3-0	Coddington, Newton (pen), Rogers	11,516
Nov 2	Cardiff City	L 1-2	Martin	11,672
Nov 9	BIRMINGHAM CITY	W 3-2	Fryatt 2, Darling	11,721
Nov 16	Crystal Palace	L 0-1		13,505
Nov 23	CHARLTON ATHLETIC	L 0-1		8,914
Nov 30	Middlesbrough	L 0-2		16,423
Dec 7	HUDDERSFIELD TOWN	D 0-0		9,312
Dec 14	Carlisle United	L 1-4	Douglas (pen)	9,160
Dec 21	BURY	W 3-0	Martin, Darling, Helliwell	9,068
Dec 26	PRESTON NORTH END	W 1-0	Darling	21,224
Jan 11	CARDIFF CITY	W 1-0	Connelly	12,100
Jan 18	Birmingham City	L 1-3	Fryatt	27,161
Mar 1	Derby County	L 2-4	Darling, Connelly	24,930
Mar 8	HULL CITY	D 1-1	Connelly	9,018
Mar 15	Aston Villa	D 1-1	Connelly	27,644
Mar 22	BRISTOL CITY	L 1-3	Martin	7,566
Mar 25	MIDDLESBROUGH	D 1-1	Beardall	7,193
Mar 28	Millwall	D 2-2	Rogers, Connelly	10,227
Apr 4	Oxford United	L 1-2	Rogers	13,852
Apr 5	FULHAM	D 2-2	Coddington, Rogers	7,863
Apr 7	PORTSMOUTH	W 3-1	Connelly 2, Rogers	6,432
Apr 12	Sheffield United	L 0-3		9,645
Apr 15	Charlton Athletic	L 0-4		12,862
Apr 19	BOLTON WANDERERS	L 2-3	Metcalfe, Martin	8,178
Apr 23	Norwich City	L 1-3	Rogers	7,861
Apr 28	CRYSTAL PALACE	L 1-2	Rogers	4,777
Apr 30	Huddersfield Town	L 1-2	Darling	5,843

FA Cup

Jan 4	STOCKPORT COUNTY	(Rd3) W 2-0	Connelly, Fryatt	17,604
Jan 25	PORTSMOUTH	(Rd4) W 4-0	Fryatt, Darling 3	17,551
Feb 24	MANCHESTER CITY	(Rd5) L 1-4	Fryatt	42,315

League Cup

Sep 4	STOKE CITY	(Rd2) D 1-1	Rogers (pen)	12,464
Sep 11	Stoke City	(R) W 1-0	Metcalfe	13,848
Sep 24	Swindon Town	(Rd3) L 0-1		15,402

League & Cup Appearances

PLAYER	LEAGUE	CUP COMPETITION		TOTAL
		FA CUP	LC	
Atherton, D.	0 (1)			0 (1)
Barton, J.B.	3			3
Beardall, J.T.	3 (2)			3 (2)
Blacklaw, A.S.	39	3	3	45
Calloway, L.J.	10 (6)	1	1 (1)	12 (7)
Chappell, L.A.	7			7
Clayton, R.	11 (2)	1		12 (2)
Coddington, J.W.	31 (1)	3	2	36 (1)
Connelly, J.M.	39	3	3	45
Darling, M.	33 (3)	3	3	39 (3)
Douglas, B.	7	0 (1)		7 (1)
Fryatt, J.E.	24	3		27
Helliwell, D.	9			9
Hole, B.G.	7		2	9
Kopel, F.	4 (2)			4 (2)
Martin, D.	38	3	3	44
Metcalfe, S.M.	38 (1)	3	3	44 (1)
Mulvaney, R.	23 (1)	2	2	27 (1)
Newton, K.R.	32	2	3	37
Rogers, E.	41	2	3	46
Sharples, G.F.V.	18	2	2 (1)	22 (1)
Whittle, M.	5 (2)			5 (2)
Wilson, W.	40	2	3	45

Goalscorers

PLAYER	LEAGUE	CUP COMPETITION		TOTAL
		FA CUP	LC	
Darling, M.	10	3		13
Connelly, J.M.	10	1		11
Martin, D.	10			10
Rogers, E.	9		1	10
Fryatt, J.E.	3	3		6
Coddington, J.W.	2			2
Metcalfe, S.M.	1		1	2
Beardall, J.T.	1			1
Douglas, B.	1			1
Helliwell, D.	1			1
Newton, K.R.	1			1
Sharples, G.F.V.	1			1
Opps' o.gs.	2			2

Fact File

Bryan Douglas and Ronnie Clayton both made their final appearances for the club. Douglas made his exit against Fulham on 5 April 1969, while Clayton made his final bow against Huddersfield Town on the last day of the season.

MANAGER: Eddie Quigley

TOP SCORER: Malcom Darling

BIGGEST WIN: 4-0, 25 January 1969, v Portsmouth, FA Cup Round 4

HIGHEST ATTENDANCE: 42,315, 24 February 1969, v Manchester City, FA Cup Round 5

MAJOR TRANSFERS IN: Jim Fryatt from Stockport County, Frank Kopel from Manchester United

MAJOR TRANSFERS OUT: Mike Ferguson to Aston Villa, Barrie Hole to Aston Villa

Final Division 2 Table

		P	W	D	L	F	A	Pts
1	DERBY CO	42	26	11	5	65	32	63
2	CRYSTAL PALACE	42	22	19	8	70	47	56
3	CHARLTON ATH	42	18	14	10	61	52	50
4	MIDDLESBROUGH	42	19	11	12	58	49	49
5	CARDIFF C	42	20	7	15	67	54	47
6	HUDDERSFIELD T	42	17	12	13	53	46	46
7	BIRMINGHAM C	42	18	8	16	73	59	44
8	BLACKPOOL	42	14	15	13	51	41	43
9	SHEFFIELD U	42	16	11	15	61	50	43
10	MILLWALL	42	17	9	16	57	49	43
11	HULL C	42	13	16	13	59	52	42
12	CARLISLE U	42	16	10	16	46	49	42
13	NORWICH C	42	15	10	17	53	56	40
14	PRESTON NE	42	12	15	15	38	44	39
15	PORTSMOUTH	42	12	14	16	58	58	38
16	BRISTOL C	42	11	16	15	46	53	38
17	BOLTON W	42	12	14	16	55	67	38
18	ASTON VILLA	42	12	14	16	37	48	38
19	BLACKBURN R	42	13	11	18	52	63	37
20	OXFORD U	42	12	9	21	34	55	33
21	BURY	42	11	8	23	51	80	30
22	FULHAM	42	7	11	24	40	81	25

The Essential History of Blackburn Rovers

Season 1969-70

Football League Division 2

DATE	OPPONENTS	SCORE	GOALSCORERS	ATTENDANCE
Aug 9	SWINDON TOWN	W 2-0	Martin, Connelly	12,953
Aug 16	Cardiff City	D 0-0		19,745
Aug 18	Blackpool	D 0-0		21,053
Aug 23	HULL CITY	W 2-1	Martin, Rogers	11,627
Aug 26	Huddersfield Town	W 1-0	Martin	15,586
Aug 30	Portsmouth	L 0-2		18,348
Sep 6	MIDDLESBROUGH	W 4-0	Mulvaney, Newton (pen), Martin, Hill	12,120
Sep 13	Preston North End	D 0-0		17,125
Sep 17	QUEENS PARK RANGERS	L 0-1		15,945
Sep 20	MILLWALL	W 4-0	Connelly, Martin 3	10,638
Sep 27	Watford	W 2-0	Connelly 2	18,478
Oct 4	NORWICH CITY	W 3-1	Knighton, Mulvaney, Fryatt	12,139
Oct 8	CARDIFF CITY	W 1-0	Hill	15,062
Oct 11	Birmingham City	L 0-3		25,602
Oct 18	Charlton Athletic	D 0-0		11,560
Oct 25	LEICESTER CITY	W 3-1	Knighton, Hill, Darling	15,362
Nov 1	Sheffield United	L 0-4		20,064
Nov 8	BOLTON WANDERERS	W 3-1	Martin, Darling, Knighton	13,175
Nov 15	BLACKPOOL	W 2-1	Rogers, Connelly	17,393
Nov 15	Carlisle United	W 1-0	Darling	14,481
Nov 22	BRISTOL CITY	D 3-3	Darling, Rogers, Martin (pen)	13,307
Nov 29	Oxford United	L 0-1		7,406
Dec 6	ASTON VILLA	W 2-0	Martin, Fryatt	12,008
Dec 13	PRESTON NORTH END	W 4-2	Martin, Connelly 3	16,216
Dec 26	Hull City	L 0-3		11,486
Dec 27	PORTSMOUTH	L 0-3		13,411
Jan 13	Middlesbrough	L 1-4	Connelly	21,950
Jan 17	WATFORD	W 1-0	Rogers	8,441
Jan 20	Millwall	L 1-3	Calloway	11,434
Jan 31	Norwich City	W 1-0	Mulvaney	9,661
Feb 28	SHEFFIELD UNITED	L 1-2	Martin (pen)	15,795
Mar 4	BIRMINGHAM CITY	D 1-1	Darling	8,639
Mar 7	Bristol City	L 0-4		12,683
Mar 14	OXFORD UNITED	W 2-0	Darling, Goodwin	7,890
Mar 17	Leicester City	L 1-2	Metcalfe	20,225
Mar 21	Aston Villa	D 1-1	Goodwin	18,840
Mar 28	CARLISLE UNITED	W 1-0	Knighton	8,394
Mar 30	Bolton Wanderers	L 0-1		18,032
Apr 4	HUDDERSFIELD TOWN	L 0-2		15,125
Apr 8	CHARLTON ATHLETIC	W 3-0	Knighton 2, Martin	7,339
Apr 14	Queens Park Rangers	W 3-2	Knighton, Darling, Rogers	11,161
Apr 20	Swindon Town	L 0-1		10,716

FA Cup

Jan 3	SWINDON TOWN	(Rd3) L 0-4		11,538

League Cup

Aug 13	Stockport County	(Rd1) W 2-0	Knighton, Connelly	5,925
Sep 3	DONCASTER ROVERS	(Rd2) W 4-2	Hill, Martin 2, Rogers	10,024
Sep 24	Carlisle United	(Rd3) L 1-2	Rogers	11,748

League & Cup Appearances

PLAYER	LEAGUE	CUP COMPETITION		TOTAL
		FA CUP	LC	
Barton, J.B.	9			9
Blacklaw, A.S.	28	1	3	32
Calloway, L.J.	4 (2)	1		5 (2)
Charter, R.	9			9
Coddington, J.W.	3	1	1	5
Connelly, J.M.	35 (1)	1	3	39 (1)
Darling, M.	21 (6)		0 (1)	21 (7)
Eccles, T.S.	4			4
Fryatt, J.E.	5 (8)	1		6 (8)
Goodwin, F.J.	11			11
Hill, B.	22 (2)	1	3	26 (2)
Hunter, A.	37	1	2	40
Jones, R.	5			5
Knighton, K.	41	1	3	45
Kopel, F.	5			5
Martin, D.	42	1	3	46
Metcalfe, S.M.	39	1	3	43
Mulvaney, R.	41		3	44
Newton, K.R.	17		3	20
Rogers, E.	35		3	38
Whalley, J.H.	1			1
Wilson, W.	42	1	3	46
Wood, M.J.	6 (1)	0 (1)		6 (2)

Goalscorers

PLAYER	LEAGUE	CUP COMPETITION		TOTAL
		FA CUP	LC	
Martin, D.	13		2	15
Connelly, J.M.	9		1	10
Knighton, K.	7		1	8
Darling, M.	7			7
Rogers, E.	5		2	7
Hill, B.	3		1	4
Mulvaney, R.	3			3
Fryatt, J.E.	2			2
Goodwin, F.J.	2			2
Calloway, L.J.	1			1
Metcalfe, S.M.	1			1
Newton, K.R.	1			1

Fact File

Keith Newton left Ewood Park in December 1969 to join Everton for a fee of £80,000. Five months later he had won a First Division championship medal.

MANAGER: Eddie Quigley

TOP SCORER: Don Martin

BIGGEST WIN: 4-0, 6 September 1969, v Middlesbrough, Division 2; 20 September 1969, v Millwall, Division 2

HIGHEST ATTENDANCE: 25,602, 11 October 1969, v Birmingham City, Division 2

MAJOR TRANSFERS IN: Allan Hunter from Oldham Athletic, Brian Hill from Huddersfield Town, Ken Knighton from Preston North End, Roger Jones from Bournemouth, Fred Goodwin from Stockport County

MAJOR TRANSFERS OUT: Keith Newton to Everton, Jim Fryatt to Oldham Athletic, John Coddington to Stockport County

Final Division 2 Table

		P	W	D	L	F	A	PTS
1	HUDDERSFIELD T	42	24	12	6	68	37	60
2	BLACKPOOL	42	20	13	9	56	45	53
3	LEICESTER C	42	19	13	10	64	50	51
4	MIDDLESBROUGH	42	20	10	12	55	45	50
5	SWINDON T	42	17	16	9	57	47	50
6	SHEFFIELD U	42	22	5	15	73	38	49
7	CARDIFF C	42	18	13	11	61	41	49
8	BLACKBURN R	42	20	7	15	54	50	47
9	QPR	42	17	11	14	66	57	45
10	MILLWALL	42	15	14	13	56	56	44
11	NORWICH C	42	16	11	15	49	46	43
12	CARLISLE U	42	14	13	15	58	56	41
13	HULL C	42	15	11	16	72	70	41
14	BRISTOL C	42	13	13	16	54	50	39
15	OXFORD U	42	12	15	15	35	42	39
16	BOLTON W	42	12	12	18	54	61	36
17	PORTSMOUTH	42	13	9	20	66	80	35
18	BIRMINGHAM C	42	11	11	20	51	78	33
19	WATFORD	42	9	13	20	44	57	31
20	CHARLTON ATH	42	7	17	18	35	76	31
21	ASTON VILLA	42	8	13	21	36	62	29
22	PRESTON NE	42	8	12	22	43	63	28

Season 1970-71

Football League Division 2

DATE	OPPONENTS	SCORE	GOALSCORERS	ATTENDANCE
Aug 15	Watford	L 1-2	Martin	15,589
Aug 22	ORIENT	D 0-0		9,306
Aug 29	Sheffield Wednesday	D 1-1	Rogers	14,988
Sep 2	QUEENS PARK RANGERS	L 0-2		7,783
Sep 5	SWINDON TOWN	W 1-0	Conlon	6,330
Sep 12	Middlesbrough	D 1-1	Goodwin	15,083
Sep 19	BOLTON WANDERERS	L 0-2		10,421
Sep 21	OXFORD UNITED	D 0-0		6,220
Sep 26	Bristol City	D 1-1	Conlon	14,019
Oct 3	LEICESTER CITY	D 2-2	Rogers, Manley o.g.	9,061
Oct 10	Millwall	L 0-2		8,279
Oct 17	WATFORD	L 2-3	Rogers, Conlon	7,331
Oct 20	Luton Town	L 0-2		16,372
Oct 24	NORWICH CITY	W 2-1	Mulvaney, Knighton (pen)	7,161
Oct 31	Portsmouth	L 1-4	Knighton	9,936
Nov 7	SHEFFIELD UNITED	L 1-3	Russell	8,281
Nov 14	Cardiff City	L 1-4	Knighton	17,213
Nov 21	Carlisle United	L 0-1		7,305
Nov 28	SUNDERLAND	L 0-1		7,020
Dec 5	Charlton Athletic	W 4-2	Russell, Reeves o.g., Conlon, Dunning	11,546
Dec 12	HULL CITY	L 0-1		7,490
Dec 19	Orient	D 1-1	Knighton	5,931
Dec 26	BIRMINGHAM CITY	D 2-2	Hill, Dunning	8,787
Jan 9	Oxford United	L 1-2	Eccles	9,540
Jan 16	LUTON TOWN	W 1-0	Russell	8,385
Jan 30	Sunderland	L 2-3	Eccles, Rogers	10,354
Feb 6	CHARLTON ATHLETIC	W 1-0	Eccles	8,278
Feb 20	CARLISLE UNITED	L 0-2		9,195
Feb 23	Hull City	D 0-0		23,976
Feb 27	PORTSMOUTH	D 1-1	Eccles	7,259
Mar 6	Norwich City	L 1-2	Russell	8,111
Mar 13	CARDIFF CITY	D 1-1	Goodwin	10,458
Mar 20	Sheffield United	L 0-5		20,050
Mar 27	Swindon Town	L 0-3		11,508
Apr 3	SHEFFIELD WEDNESDAY	W 3-2	Parkes, Rogers, Conlon	6,820
Apr 9	MIDDLESBROUGH	D 1-1	Pickering	11,210
Apr 10	Birmingham City	L 0-1		25,572
Apr 13	Leicester City	D 1-1	Pickering	32,749
Apr 17	MILLWALL	L 0-2		7,939
Apr 24	Bolton Wanderers	D 1-1	Conlon	7,195
Apr 27	Queens Park Rangers	L 0-2		9,343
May 1	BRISTOL CITY	D 2-2	Hunter, Rogers	3,971

FA Cup

Jan 2	Everton	(Rd3) L 0-2		40,471

League Cup

Sep 9	Bolton Wanderers	(Rd2) L 0-1		12,000

League & Cup Appearances

PLAYER	LEAGUE	CUP COMPETITION		TOTAL
		FA CUP	LC	
Atherton, D.L.	9			9
Charter, R.	4 (5)	0 (1)		4 (6)
Conlon, B.	30	1	1	32
Dunning, W.S.	8 (1)			8 (1)
Eccles, T.S.	15 (5)	1		16 (5)
Fazackerley, D.W.	14			14
Goodwin, F.J.	39 (1)	1	1	41 (1)
Hill, B.	12 (1)	1	1	14 (1)
Hunter, A.	42	1	1	44
Jones, R.	42	1	1	44
Kerr, J.P.	11			11
Knighton, K.	29	1	1	31
Kopel, F.	11			11
Martin, D.	7			7
Metcalfe, S.M.	32 (1)	1	0 (1)	33 (2)
Mulvaney, R.	28		1	29
Parkes, T.	12		1	13
Pickering, F.	11			11
Rogers, E.	35 (1)	1	1	37 (1)
Russell, A.	22 (2)	1	1	24 (2)
Whalley, J.H.	1			1
Wilson, W.	35	1	1	37
Wood, M.J.	13 (1)			13 (1)

Goalscorers

PLAYER	LEAGUE	CUP COMPETITION		TOTAL
		FA CUP	LC	
Conlon, B.	6			6
Rogers, E.	6			6
Eccles, T.S.	4			4
Knighton, K.	4			4
Russell, A.	4			4
Dunning, W.S.	2			2
Goodwin, F.J.	2			2
Pickering, F.	2			2
Hill, B.	1			1
Hunter, A.	1			1
Martin, D.	1			1
Mulvaney, R.	1			1
Parkes, T.	1			1
Opps' o.gs.	2			2

Fact File

The season with three managers on the Ewood Park staff. Eddie Quigley was in charge of first-team affairs while former Ewood boss Johnny Carey was employed as administrative manager. Jack Marshall completed the unique trio when he returned to Ewood Park in July 1970 to take over as physiotherapist.

MANAGER: Eddie Quigley/Johnny Carey

TOP SCORER: Bryan Conlon/Eamonn Rogers

BIGGEST WIN: 4-2, 5 December 1970, v Charlton Athletic, Division 2

HIGHEST ATTENDANCE: 40,471, 2 January 1971, v Everton, FA Cup Round 3

MAJOR TRANSFERS IN: Bryan Conlon from Norwich City, Jimmy Kerr from Bury, Alex Russell from Southport, Fred Pickering from Blackpool

MAJOR TRANSFERS OUT: Malcolm Darling to Norwich City, John Connelly to Bury, Adam Blacklaw to Blackpool, Ken Knighton to Hull City

Final Division 2 Table

		P	W	D	L	F	A	Pts
1	LEICESTER C	42	23	13	6	57	30	59
2	SHEFFIELD U	42	21	14	7	73	39	56
3	CARDIFF C	42	20	13	9	64	41	53
4	CARLISLE U	42	20	13	9	65	43	53
5	HULL C	42	19	13	10	54	41	51
6	LUTON T	42	18	13	11	62	43	49
7	MIDDLESBROUGH	42	17	14	11	60	43	48
8	MILLWALL	42	19	9	14	59	42	47
9	BIRMINGHAM C	42	17	12	13	58	48	46
10	NORWICH C	42	15	14	13	54	52	44
11	QPR	42	16	11	15	58	53	43
12	SWINDON T	42	15	12	15	61	51	42
13	SUNDERLAND	42	15	12	15	52	54	42
14	OXFORD U	42	14	14	14	41	48	42
15	SHEFFIELD W	42	12	12	18	51	69	36
16	PORTSMOUTH	42	10	14	18	46	61	34
17	ORIENT	42	9	16	17	29	51	34
18	WATFORD	42	10	13	19	38	60	33
19	BRISTOL C	42	10	11	21	46	64	31
20	CHARLTON ATH	42	8	14	20	41	65	30
21	BLACKBURN R	42	6	15	21	37	69	27
22	BOLTON W	42	7	10	25	35	74	24

The Essential History of Blackburn Rovers

Season 1971-72

Football League Division 3

DATE	OPPONENTS	SCORE	GOALSCORERS	ATTENDANCE
Aug 14	ROTHERHAM UNITED	W 2-1	Rogers, McDonald	7,801
Aug 21	Plymouth Argyle	L 0-1		10,280
Aug 28	WREXHAM	W 2-1	Martin, Parkes	7,716
Aug 31	AFC Bournemouth	L 0-1		13,280
Sep 4	Chesterfield	L 0-2		9,041
Sep 11	BOLTON WANDERERS	L 0-3		13,938
Sep 18	Walsall	D 0-0		4,235
Sep 25	SWANSEA CITY	L 1-2	Rogers	6,695
Sep 27	Port Vale	D 0-0		4,963
Oct 2	Shrewsbury Town	L 1-7	Price	4,519
Oct 9	ROCHDALE	W 3-0	Shanahan 2, McDonald	8,492
Oct 16	Rotherham United	L 1-2	Arentoft	7,508
Oct 20	NOTTS COUNTY	L 0-2		6,935
Oct 23	MANSFIELD TOWN	D 1-1	Arentoft	7,103
Oct 30	Aston Villa	L 1-4	Field	25,588
Nov 6	BRADFORD CITY	W 1-0	Price	7,169
Nov 13	Torquay United	L 1-3	Price	4,554
Nov 26	Tranmere Rovers	W 3-1	Price, Field, Conlon	3,937
Dec 4	OLDHAM ATHLETIC	L 0-1		7,593
Dec 11	Oldham Athletic	D 1-1	Field	7,538
Dec 18	CHESTERFIELD	W 1-0	Parkes	5,643
Dec 27	Halifax Town	W 1-0	McNamee	7,218
Jan 1	WALSALL	D 1-1	Parkes	10,113
Jan 8	Wrexham	D 1-1	McNamee	4,550
Jan 15	YORK CITY	W 3-0	McNamee, Field, Eccles	7,273
Jan 22	PORT VALE	W 3-0	Field (pen), Eccles, Price	8,495
Jan 29	Notts County	L 0-1		12,375
Feb 5	BARNSLEY	W 4-0	Field 3, McNamee	7,678
Feb 12	Mansfield Town	L 0-1		5,155
Feb 19	ASTON VILLA	D 1-1	Garbett	15,562
Feb 26	Bradford City	W 2-1	Martin, Field	4,775
Mar 4	TORQUAY UNITED	W 1-0	Parkes	8,333
Mar 11	Rochdale	L 1-2	Field	6,542
Mar 14	Bristol Rovers	L 0-3		7,501
Mar 18	PLYMOUTH ARGYLE	W 3-2	Field 2, Farrell	7,610
Mar 25	Bolton Wanderers	L 0-1		11,330
Mar 27	BRISTOL ROVERS	L 1-2	Price	5,740
Mar 31	SHREWSBURY TOWN	W 1-0	Martin	8,928
Apr 4	Swansea City	W 1-0	Field	3,367
Apr 8	Barnsley	D 0-0		4,509
Apr 12	BRIGHTON & HOVE ALBION	D 2-2	McNamee 2	8,558
Apr 15	TRANMERE ROVERS	W 4-1	Martin 2, Price, Field	7,676
Apr 19	Brighton & Hove Albion	L 0-3		23,269
Apr 26	AFC BOURNEMOUTH	W 2-1	Field (pen), Bradford	8,941
Apr 29	York City	W 1-0	Price	5,636
May 8	HALIFAX TOWN	W 2-0	Field 2	5,899

FA Cup

Nov 20	PORT VALE	(Rd1) D 1-1	Fazackerley	6,947
Nov 22	Port Vale	(R) L 1-3	Field (pen)	5,717

League Cup

Aug 18	WORKINGTON	(Rd1) W 2-0	Eccles, Rogers	7,692
Sep 8	LINCOLN CITY	(Rd2) D 0-0		6,457
Sep 15	Lincoln City	(R) L 1-4	Rogers	7,638

Fact File

Bobby Bell joined the Rovers as part of the deal that took Allan Hunter to Ipswich Town. Although he was installed as captain, he was sold to Crystal Palace a fortnight later at a £30,000 profit.

MANAGER: Ken Furphy

TOP SCORER: Tony Field

BIGGEST WIN: 4-0, 5 February 1972, v Barnsley, Division 3

HIGHEST ATTENDANCE: 25,588, 30 October 1971, v Aston Villa, Division 3

MAJOR TRANSFERS IN: Mick Heaton from Sheffield United, Bobby Bell from Ipswich Town, Terry Garbett from Watford, Ben Arentoft from Newcastle United, Tony Field from Southport, Barry Endean from Charlton Athletic, John McNamee from Newcastle United

MAJOR TRANSFERS OUT: Dick Mulvaney to Oldham Athletic

League & Cup Appearances

PLAYER	LEAGUE	CUP COMPETITION		TOTAL
		FA CUP	LC	
Arentoft, P.	12	2		14
Atherton, D.L.			1	1
Barton, J.B.	1			1
Bell, R.C.	2			2
Bradford, D.W.	29		2	31
Conlon, B.	13 (2)	1	2 (1)	16 (3)
Dunning, W.S.	2 (2)			2 (2)
Eccles, T.S.	13 (8)		2	15 (8)
Endean, B.	12 (2)			12 (2)
Farrell, G.W.	14 (1)	2		16 (1)
Fazackerley, D.W.	39	2	2	43
Field, A.	33	2		35
Garbett, T.G.	40	2		42
Goodwin, F.J.	13		3	16
Heaton, J.M.	35	2		37
Hunter, A.	5		2	7
Jones, R.	45	2	3	50
Kopel, F.	3			3
McDonald, G.	19 (2)	0 (2)	3	22 (4)
McNamee, J.	27			27
Martin, D.	25 (1)		0 (1)	25 (2)
Metcalfe, S.M.	6 (2)		3	9 (2)
Parkes, T.	27	1	1	29
Pickering, F.			1	1
Price, J.	38	2		40
Rogers, E.	7 (2)		3	10 (2)
Shanahan, T.C.	6			6
Whalley, J.C.			1	1
Wilson, W.	14 (1)	2	3	19 (1)
Wood, M.J.	26	2	1 (1)	29 (1)

Goalscorers

PLAYER	LEAGUE	CUP COMPETITION		TOTAL
		FA CUP	LC	
Field, A.	17	1		18
Price, J.	8			8
McNamee, J.	6			6
Martin, D.	5			5
Parkes, T.	4			4
Rogers, E.	2		2	4
Eccles, T.S.	2		1	3
Arentoft, P.	2			2
McDonald, G.	2			2
Shanahan, T.C.	2			2
Bradford, D.W.	1			1
Conlon, B.	1			1
Farrell, G.W.	1			1
Garbett, T.G.	1			1
Fazackerley, D.W.		1		1

Final Division 3 Table

		P	W	D	L	F	A	Pts
1	ASTON VILLA	46	32	6	8	85	32	70
2	BRIGHTON & HA	46	27	11	8	82	47	65
3	BOURNEMOUTH	46	23	16	7	73	37	62
4	NOTTS CO	46	25	12	9	74	44	62
5	ROTHERHAM U	46	20	15	11	69	52	55
6	BRISTOL R	46	21	12	13	75	56	54
7	BOLTON W	46	17	16	13	51	41	50
8	PLYMOUTH ARG	46	20	10	16	74	64	50
9	WALSALL	46	15	18	13	62	57	48
10	BLACKBURN R	46	19	9	18	54	57	47
11	OLDHAM ATH	46	17	11	18	59	63	45
12	SHREWSBURY T	46	17	10	19	73	65	44
13	CHESTERFIELD	46	18	8	20	57	57	44
14	SWANSEA C	46	17	10	19	46	59	44
15	PORT VALE	46	13	15	18	43	59	41
16	WREXHAM	46	16	8	22	59	63	40
17	HALIFAX T	46	13	12	21	48	61	38
18	ROCHDALE	46	12	13	21	57	83	37
19	YORK C	46	12	12	22	57	66	36
20	TRANMERE R	46	10	16	20	50	71	36
21	MANSFIELD T	46	8	20	18	41	63	36
22	BARNSLEY	46	9	18	19	32	64	36
23	TORQUAY U	46	10	12	24	41	69	32
24	BRADFORD C	46	11	10	25	45	77	32

Season 1972-73

Football League Division 3

DATE	OPPONENTS	SCORE	GOALSCORERS	ATTENDANCE
Aug 12	Bristol Rovers	L 0-3		10,735
Aug 19	ROCHDALE	D 1-1	Endean	6,172
Aug 26	Brentford	L 0-4		9,427
Aug 29	Oldham Athletic	W 2-1	Parkes, Field	6,239
Sep 2	BOLTON WANDERERS	L 0-3		9,546
Sep 9	Shrewsbury Town	L 0-2		2,722
Sep 16	WATFORD	D 0-0		6,484
Sep 20	PLYMOUTH ARGYLE	W 3-1	O'Mara 2, Napier	6,326
Sep 23	Chesterfield	L 1-3	Endean	7,731
Sep 26	Grimsby Town	L 0-2		12,994
Sep 30	SCUNTHORPE UNITED	W 3-0	O'Mara 2, Field	5,764
Oct 7	Wrexham	D 0-0		6,517
Oct 9	York City	L 0-1		3,607
Oct 14	PORT VALE	L 0-1		6,500
Oct 21	Swansea City	D 2-2	Jones P. o.g., Field	3,060
Oct 25	WALSALL	W 2-0	Field (pen), O'Mara	5,943
Oct 28	CHARLTON ATHLETIC	W 3-1	McNamee, O'Mara, Field	7,095
Nov 4	GRIMSBY TOWN	D 0-0		7,676
Nov 11	Plymouth Argyle	W 2-1	Napier, Saxton o.g.	5,812
Nov 24	Tranmere Rovers	D 1-1	Bradford	5,703
Dec 2	HALIFAX TOWN	W 3-0	O'Mara, Metcalfe, Price	7,402
Dec 16	SOUTHEND UNITED	W 2-1	Field 2	5,710
Dec 23	Rotherham United	D 1-1	Field (pen)	3,856
Dec 30	Rochdale	W 1-0	Field	5,116
Jan 6	BRENTFORD	W 2-1	Endean, Napier	6,534
Jan 13	Walsall	W 2-0	Parkes, Field	3,834
Jan 27	SHREWSBURY TOWN	D 0-0		8,279
Feb 3	YORK CITY	W 2-0	Hutchins, Napier	8,259
Feb 10	Watford	W 3-1	Endean, Field, Napier	7,217
Feb 17	BRISTOL ROVERS	D 0-0		12,378
Feb 24	Southend United	W 1-0	Arentoft	6,794
Mar 3	WREXHAM	D 1-1	Napier	10,536
Mar 7	NOTTS COUNTY	W 2-0	Field 2 (1 pen)	13,626
Mar 10	Port Vale	L 1-2	Field	7,854
Mar 14	CHESTERFIELD	L 0-1		12,344
Mar 17	SWANSEA CITY	W 3-0	Field, McNamee, Hutchins	8,388
Mar 20	AFC Bournemouth	L 0-3		12,389
Mar 24	Charlton Athletic	W 2-1	Curtis o.g., Price	5,770
Mar 28	Bolton Wanderers	W 1-0	Fazackerley	33,309
Mar 31	TRANMERE ROVERS	D 2-2	Field, Endean	11,159
Apr 7	Halifax Town	D 2-2	Fazackerley, Parkes	4,838
Apr 14	AFC BOURNEMOUTH	W 2-1	Endean 2	15,114
Apr 20	ROTHERHAM UNITED	W 2-1	Endean, Field (pen)	16,346
Apr 21	Notts County	D 0-0		22,712
Apr 24	Scunthorpe United	D 1-1	Endean	2,706
Apr 28	OLDHAM ATHLETIC	D 1-1	McNamee	14,346

FA Cup

Nov 18	Lincoln City	(Rd1) D 2-2	Napier, Field	5,128
Nov 27	LINCOLN CITY	(R) W 4-1	McNamee, Field 3	9,036
Dec 9	CREWE ALEXANDRA	(Rd2) L 0-1		9,523

League Cup

Aug 16	ROCHDALE	(Rd1) L 0-1		6,292

League & Cup Appearances

PLAYER	LEAGUE	CUP COMPETITION		TOTAL
		FA CUP	LC	
Arentoft, P.	45	3	1	49
Bradford, D.W.	13 (3)	3	1	17 (3)
Eccles, T.S.	1			1
Endean, B.	26 (2)		1	27 (2)
Farrell, G.W.	7			7
Fazackerley, D.W.	46	3	1	50
Field, A.	43	3	1	47
Garbett, T.G.	25	2	1	28
Heaton, J.M.	45	2	1	48
Hutchins, D.	14 (2)		1	15 (2)
Jones, R.	46	3	1	50
Kenyon, J.F.	0 (1)			0 (1)
McNamee, J.	29	1		30
Martin, D.	9 (2)	2 (1)	1	12 (3)
Metcalfe, S.M.	34 (2)	2	0 (1)	36 (3)
Napier, C.R.A.	33	2		35
O'Mara, J.	21 (3)	3		24 (3)
Parkes, T.	29 (2)			29 (2)
Price, J.	14 (11)	2 (1)	1	17 (12)
Turner, D.J.	20 (1)	1		21 (1)
Wilkinson, N.	1	1		2
Wood, M.J.	5 (1)			5 (1)

Goalscorers

PLAYER	LEAGUE	CUP COMPETITION		TOTAL
		FA CUP	LC	
Field, A.	17	4		21
Endean, B.	9			9
O'Mara, J.	7			7
Napier, C.R.A.	6	1		7
McNamee, J.	3	1		4
Parkes, T.	3			3
Fazackerley, D.W.	2			2
Hutchins, D.	2			2
Price, J.	2			2
Arentoft, P.	1			1
Bradford, D.W.	1			1
Metcalfe, S.M.	1			1
Opps' o.gs.	3			3

Fact File

A crowd of 33,309 saw Derek Fazackerley snatch the points for the Rovers in a thrilling promotion battle at Burnden Park in March 1973.

MANAGER: Ken Furphy

TOP SCORER: Tony Field

BIGGEST WIN: 4-1, 27 November 1972, v Lincoln City, FA Cup Round 1 replay

HIGHEST ATTENDANCE: 33,309, 28 March 1973, v Bolton Wanderers, Division 3

MAJOR TRANSFERS IN: Don Hutchins from Plymouth Argyle, Kit Napier from Brighton & Hove Albion, John O'Mara from Brentford

Final Division 3 Table

		P	W	D	L	F	A	Pts
1	BOLTON W	46	25	11	10	73	39	61
2	NOTTS CO	46	23	11	12	67	47	57
3	BLACKBURN R	46	20	15	11	57	47	55
4	OLDHAM ATH	46	19	16	11	72	54	54
5	BRISTOL R	46	20	13	13	77	56	53
6	PORT VALE	46	21	11	14	56	69	53
7	BOURNEMOUTH	46	17	16	13	66	44	50
8	PLYMOUTH ARG	46	20	10	16	74	66	50
9	GRIMSBY T	46	20	8	18	67	61	48
10	TRANMERE R	46	15	16	15	56	52	46
11	CHARLTON ATH	46	17	11	18	69	67	45
12	WREXHAM	46	14	17	15	55	54	45
13	ROCHDALE	46	14	17	15	48	54	45
14	SOUTHEND U	46	17	10	19	61	54	44
15	SHREWSBURY T	46	15	14	17	46	54	44
16	CHESTERFIELD	46	17	9	20	57	61	43
17	WALSALL	46	18	7	21	56	66	43
18	YORK C	46	13	15	18	42	46	41
19	WATFORD	46	12	17	17	43	48	41
20	HALIFAX T	46	13	15	18	43	53	41
21	ROTHERHAM U	46	17	7	22	51	65	41
22	BRENTFORD	46	15	7	24	51	69	37
23	SWANSEA C	46	14	9	23	51	73	37
24	SCUNTHORPE U	46	10	10	26	33	72	30

Season 1973-74

Football League Division 3

DATE	OPPONENTS	SCORE	GOALSCORERS	ATTENDANCE
Aug 25	SOUTHEND UNITED	W 1-0	Endean	8,684
Sep 1	Hereford United	L 0-1		9,483
Sep 8	YORK CITY	W 4-0	Garbett, Napier 2, Field (pen)	8,057
Sep 11	Charlton Athletic	L 3-4	Hutchins, Garbett 2	4,785
Sep 15	Chesterfield	L 0-3		5,618
Sep 19	GRIMSBY TOWN	W 1-0	Parkes	7,971
Sep 22	BRISTOL ROVERS	L 0-2		8,424
Sep 29	Walsall	L 0-2		4,896
Oct 2	Grimsby Town	L 2-4	Fazackerley, Endean	7,782
Oct 6	BRIGHTON & HOVE ALBION	W 3-1	Price, Field, Endean	6,516
Oct 12	Tranmere Rovers	D 1-1	Kenyon	5,379
Oct 20	CAMBRIDGE UNITED	W 2-0	Parkes, Kenyon	6,327
Oct 24	Charlton Athletic	D 1-1	O'Mara	7,521
Oct 27	Wrexham	D 2-2	O'Mara, Waddington	6,569
Nov 3	PLYMOUTH ARGYLE	W 2-0	Garbett, Parkes	7,756
Nov 10	AFC Bournemouth	W 2-1	Field 2	10,559
Nov 12	Port Vale	W 2-1	Parkes, Napier	3,633
Nov 17	WATFORD	W 5-0	Parkes, Field 2, Endean, Metcalfe	8,991
Dec 8	Rochdale	W 2-1	Field 2 (1 pen)	3,660
Dec 22	WALSALL	L 0-2		7,323
Dec 26	Oldham Athletic	W 3-2	O'Mara, Field, Napier	10,130
Dec 29	York City	L 0-1		6,479
Jan 1	HEREFORD UNITED	L 1-2	Hutchins	9,720
Jan 12	CHESTERFIELD	W 2-1	Kenyon, Garbett	6,996
Jan 19	Southend United	D 1-1	Field	5,540
Jan 27	SHREWSBURY TOWN	W 2-0	Field, Price	10,989
Jan 29	Huddersfield Town	L 0-1		5,204
Feb 3	SOUTHPORT	W 2-1	Martin, Bradford	10,614
Feb 17	TRANMERE ROVERS	D 0-0		10,077
Feb 23	Brighton & Hove Albion	L 0-3		12,102
Mar 2	OLDHAM ATHLETIC	L 0-1		10,204
Mar 12	Bristol Rovers	L 0-3		14,034
Mar 16	Cambridge United	W 2-0	Parkes, Martin	4,655
Mar 23	AFC BOURNEMOUTH	W 4-3	Endean 2, Fazackerley, Kenyon	5,929
Mar 27	HUDDERSFIELD TOWN	W 1-0	Kenyon	6,671
Mar 30	Plymouth Argyle	L 1-2	Endean	5,799
Apr 2	Shrewsbury Town	L 0-3		1,392
Apr 6	PORT VALE	D 1-1	Martin	5,298
Apr 8	Southport	D 2-2	Endean, Parkes	2,255
Apr 13	Watford	D 0-0		7,125
Apr 15	HALIFAX TOWN	D 1-1	Endean	4,808
Apr 16	Halifax Town	D 1-1	Martin	2,446
Apr 20	ROCHDALE	W 3-1	Hutchins, Martin 2	4,517
Apr 24	ALDERSHOT	L 1-2	Hutchins	4,016
Apr 27	Aldershot	L 0-4		5,047
May 1	WREXHAM	L 1-2	Martin	3,520

FA Cup

Nov 24	Willington	(Rd1) D 0-0		4,600
Dec 3	WILLINGTON	(R) W 6-1	Field, O'Mara 2, Garbett, Napier, Parkes	4,025
Dec 15	ALTRINCHAM	(Rd2) D 0-0		8,701
Dec 19	Altrincham	(R) W 2-0	Napier, Field (pen)	5,021
Jan 5	Everton	(Rd3) L 0-3		31,940

League Cup

Aug 29	Southport	(Rd1) D 1-1	Field (pen)	5,292
Sep 5	SOUTHPORT	(R) W 3-1*	Endean, Parkes, Field	8,691
Oct 9	ORIENT	(Rd2) L 0-2		7,384

*After extra-time.

League & Cup Appearances

PLAYER	LEAGUE	CUP COMPETITION		TOTAL
		FA CUP	LC	
Arentoft, P.	37	5	3	45
Bradford, D.W.	16 (3)	2	1	19 (3)
Bradshaw, P.W.	18			18
Endean, B.	25 (5)	5	2	31 (5)
Fazackerley, D.W.	46	5	3	54
Field, A.	28 (2)	5	3	36 (2)
Garbett, T.G.	25	5	3	33
Heaton, J.M.	36	2	2	40
Hird, K.	6			6
Hutchins, D.	23 (1)	1 (1)	1 (1)	25 (3)
Jones, R.	28	5	3	36
Kenyon, J.F.	20 (4)			20 (4)
Martin, D.	32	1	2	35
Metcalfe, S.M.	27 (1)	1	1	29 (1)
Napier, C.R.A.	20 (1)	5	3	28 (1)
O'Mara, J.	9 (2)	2 (1)	1	12 (3)
Parkes, T.	45	5	2	52
Price, J.	11 (2)	0 (1)	0 (1)	11 (4)
Turner, D.J.	3 (1)			3 (1)
Waddington, J.	30	4	1	35
Wilkinson, N.	4	1	1	6
Wood, M.J.	16	1	1	18
Wright, G.M.	1			1

Goalscorers

PLAYER	LEAGUE	CUP COMPETITION		TOTAL
		FA CUP	LC	
Field, A.	11	2	2	15
Endean, B.	9		1	10
Parkes, T.	7	1	1	9
Martin, D.	7			7
Garbett, T.G.	5	1		6
Napier, C.R.A.	4	2		6
Kenyon, J.F.	5			5
O'Mara, J.	3	2		5
Hutchins, D.	4			4
Fazackerley, D.W.	2			2
Price, J.	2			2
Bradford, D.W.	1			1
Metcalfe, S.M.	1			1
Waddington, J.	1			1

Fact File

Ken Furphy resigned as manager on 7 December 1973 to take charge of First Division Sheffield United.

Final Division 3 Table

		P	W	D	L	F	A	Pts
1	OLDHAM ATH	46	25	12	9	83	47	62
2	BRISTOL R	46	22	17	7	65	33	61
3	YORK C	46	21	19	6	67	38	61
4	WREXHAM	46	22	12	12	63	43	56
5	CHESTERFIELD	46	21	14	11	55	42	56
6	GRIMSBY T	46	18	15	13	67	50	51
7	WATFORD	46	19	12	15	64	56	50
8	ALDERSHOT	46	19	11	16	65	52	49
9	HALIFAX T	46	14	21	11	48	51	49
10	HUDDERSFIELD T	46	17	13	16	56	55	47
11	BOURNEMOUTH	46	16	15	15	54	58	47
12	SOUTHEND U	46	16	14	16	62	62	46
13	BLACKBURN R	46	18	10	18	62	64	46
14	CHARLTON ATH	46	19	8	19	66	73	46
15	WALSALL	46	16	13	17	57	48	45
16	TRANMERE R	46	15	15	16	50	44	45
17	PLYMOUTH ARG	46	17	10	19	59	54	44
18	HEREFORD U	46	14	15	17	53	57	43
19	BRIGHTON & HA	46	16	11	19	52	58	43
20	PORT VALE	46	14	14	18	52	58	42
21	CAMBRIDGE U	46	13	9	24	48	81	35
22	SHREWSBURY T	46	10	11	25	41	62	31
23	SOUTHPORT	46	6	16	24	35	82	28
24	ROCHDALE	46	2	17	27	38	94	21

MANAGER: Ken Furphy/Gordon Lee

TOP SCORER: Tony Field

BIGGEST WIN: 6-1, 3 December 1973, v Willington, FA Cup Round 1 replay

HIGHEST ATTENDANCE: 31,940, 5 January 1974, v Everton, FA Cup Round 3

MAJOR TRANSFERS OUT: Terry Garbett to Sheffield United, Johnny Price to Stockport County, Tony Field to Sheffield United

Season 1974-75

Football League Division 3

DATE	OPPONENTS	SCORE	GOALSCORERS	ATTENDANCE
Aug 17	Grimsby Town	W 2-1	Beamish, Oates	7,483
Aug 24	COLCHESTER UNITED	W 3-2	Martin, Oates, Hawkins	8,390
Aug 31	Swindon Town	L 0-2		5,130
Sep 7	BRIGHTON & HOVE ALBION	W 1-0	Martin	5,858
Sep 14	Preston North End	D 0-0		18,042
Sep 21	HALIFAX TOWN	W 1-0	Oates (pen)	7,884
Sep 25	SOUTHEND UNITED	W 1-0	Oates	9,159
Sep 27	Tranmere Rovers	D 1-1	Mathias o.g.	4,156
Oct 2	GILLINGHAM	W 4-1	Martin 3 (1 pen), Hilton	8,587
Oct 5	AFC BOURNEMOUTH	W 1-0	Oates	10,671
Oct 12	Chesterfield	W 2-1	Hilton, Beamish	6,547
Oct 19	PORT VALE	D 2-2	Beamish 2	9,777
Oct 22	Crystal Palace	L 0-1		17,910
Oct 26	Walsall	W 3-1	Beamish, Martin, Waddington (pen)	6,618
Nov 2	BURY	W 1-0	Beamish	12,454
Nov 6	CRYSTAL PALACE	D 1-1	Waddington	13,623
Nov 9	Peterborough United	L 0-1		11,778
Nov 16	ALDERSHOT	W 2-0	Martin 2	10,584
Nov 25	Wrexham	D 1-1	Waddington (pen)	5,963
Nov 30	WATFORD	D 0-0		10,021
Dec 7	Charlton Athletic	L 1-2	Oates	8,975
Dec 21	Hereford United	L 3-6	Burgin, Beamish, Waddington (pen)	7,288
Dec 26	PRESTON NORTH END	W 3-0	Martin 2 (1 pen), Parkes	24,007
Dec 28	Huddersfield Town	W 2-1	Beamish, Dolan o.g.	8,122
Jan 11	CHARLTON ATHLETIC	W 3-1	Fazackerley, Metcalfe, Beamish	12,999
Jan 18	Watford	D 0-0		5,828
Feb 1	PETERBOROUGH UNITED	L 0-1		12,323
Feb 4	Plymouth Argyle	L 1-2	Fazackerley	28,744
Feb 8	Bury	W 2-1	Hickman, Martin	11,963
Feb 15	PLYMOUTH ARGYLE	W 5-2	Beamish, Martin 2, Hickman 2	17,818
Feb 22	Aldershot	D 1-1	Metcalfe	5,498
Mar 1	SWINDON TOWN	W 2-0	Parkes, Martin	13,621
Mar 8	Southend United	D 2-2	Metcalfe (pen), Beamish	5,031
Mar 15	TRANMERE ROVERS	W 2-1	Fazackerley, Heaton	12,398
Mar 19	GRIMSBY TOWN	D 1-1	Martin	12,962
Mar 22	Brighton & Hove Albion	W 1-0	Kenyon	13,497
Mar 28	HUDDERSFIELD TOWN	D 1-1	Parkes	16,746
Mar 29	HEREFORD UNITED	W 1-0	Hickman	13,003
Apr 1	Halifax Town	D 1-1	Parkes	8,689
Apr 5	WALSALL	D 3-3	Parkes, Hickman, Metcalfe	12,002
Apr 9	Gillingham	D 1-1	Metcalfe	7,567
Apr 12	AFC Bournemouth	D 0-0		7,282
Apr 19	CHESTERFIELD	W 2-0	Metcalfe (pen), Hickman	14,780
Apr 22	Colchester United	L 0-2		4,183
Apr 26	Port Vale	W 4-1	Fazackerley, Harris o.g., Metcalfe, Hickman	9,135
Apr 28	WREXHAM	D 0-0		21,290

FA Cup

Nov 23	Matlock Town	(Rd1) W 4-1	Martin, Beamish 2, Parkes	5,180
Dec 14	DARLINGTON	(Rd2) W 1-0	Oates	9,096
Jan 4	BRISTOL ROVERS	(Rd3) L 1-2	Martin	12,876

League Cup

Aug 21	Stockport County	(Rd1) W 2-0	Metcalfe, Beamish	4,028
Sep 10	Northampton Town	(Rd2) D 2-2	Martin, Beamish	5,706
Sep 18	NORTHAMPTON TOWN	(R) W 1-0	Beamish	8,566
Oct 9	Hartlepool	(Rd3) D 1-1	Martin	5,995
Oct 16	HARTLEPOOL	(R) L 1-2	Parkes	11,121

MANAGER: Gordon Lee

TOP SCORER: Don Martin

BIGGEST WIN: 5-2, 15 February 1975, v Plymouth Argyle, Division 3

HIGHEST ATTENDANCE: 28,744, 4 February 1975, v Plymouth Argyle, Division 3

MAJOR TRANSFERS IN: Ken Beamish from Brighton & Hove Albion, Graham Hawkins from Preston North End, Graham Oates from Bradford City, Andy Burgin from Halifax Town, Mike Hickman from Grimsby Town

MAJOR TRANSFERS OUT: Don Hutchins to Bradford City, David Bradford to Sheffield United, Barry Endean to Huddersfield Town

League & Cup Appearances

PLAYER	LEAGUE	CUP COMPETITION		TOTAL
		FA CUP	LC	
Beamish, K.G.	43	3	5	51
Burgin, A.	40	3		43
Endean, B.	2 (5)		0 (1)	2 (6)
Fazackerley, D.W.	22 (1)	1	2	25 (1)
Hawkins, G.N.	42	3	4	49
Heaton, J.M.	40 (2)	2	5	47 (2)
Hickman, M.F.T.	18 (1)			18 (1)
Hilton, P.J.	16		5	21
Hird, K.	1 (1)		1	2 (1)
Hoy, R.	6 (1)			6 (1)
Jones, R.	46	3	5	54
Kenyon, J.F.	9 (3)			9 (3)
Martin, D.	42 (1)	3	5	50 (1)
Metcalfe, S.M.	42 (1)	3	5	50 (1)
Mullen, J.	5 (4)	1		6 (4)
Oates, G.	45	3	5	53
Parkes, T.	46	3	5	54
Waddington, J.	21	2	3	26
Wilkinson, N.	2		4	6
Wood, M.J.	18	3	1	22

Goalscorers

PLAYER	LEAGUE	CUP COMPETITION		TOTAL
		FA CUP	LC	
Martin, D.	15	2	2	19
Beamish, K.G.	11	2	3	16
Metcalfe, S.M.	7		1	8
Hickman, M.F.T.	7			7
Oates, G.	6	1		7
Parkes, T.	5	1	1	7
Fazackerley, D.W.	4			4
Waddington, J.	4			4
Hilton, P.J.	2			2
Burgin, A.	1			1
Hawkins, G.N.	1			1
Heaton, J.M.	1			1
Kenyon, J.F.	1			1
Opps' o.gs.	3			3

Fact File

Within weeks of guiding the club to the Third Division championship Gordon Lee left Ewood Park to become manager of Newcastle United.

Final Division 3 Table

		P	W	D	L	F	A	Pts
1	BLACKBURN R	46	22	16	8	68	45	60
2	PLYMOUTH ARG	46	24	11	11	79	58	59
3	CHARLTON ATH	46	22	11	13	76	61	55
4	SWINDON T	46	21	11	14	64	58	53
5	CRYSTAL PALACE	46	18	15	13	66	57	51
6	PORT VALE	46	18	15	13	61	54	51
7	PETERBOROUGH U	46	19	12	15	47	53	50
8	WALSALL	46	18	13	15	67	52	49
9	PRESTON NE	46	19	11	16	63	56	49
10	GILLINGHAM	46	17	14	15	65	60	48
11	COLCHESTER U	46	17	13	16	70	63	47
12	HEREFORD U	46	16	14	16	64	66	46
13	WREXHAM	46	15	15	16	65	55	45
14	BURY	46	16	12	18	53	50	44
15	CHESTERFIELD	46	16	12	18	62	66	44
16	GRIMSBY T	46	15	13	18	55	64	43
17	HALIFAX T	46	13	17	16	49	65	43
18	SOUTHEND U	46	13	16	17	46	51	42
19	BRIGHTON & HA	46	16	10	20	56	64	42
20	ALDERSHOT	46	14	11	21	53	63	38
21	BOURNEMOUTH	46	13	12	21	44	58	38
22	TRANMERE R	46	14	9	23	55	57	37
23	WATFORD	46	17	19	52	75	37	
24	HUDDERSFIELD T	46	11	10	25	47	76	32

ALDERSHOT ONE POINT DEDUCTED FOR FIELDING AN INELIGIBLE PLAYER.

Season 1975-76

Football League Division 2

DATE	OPPONENTS	SCORE	GOALSCORERS	ATTENDANCE
Aug 16	Orient	D 1-1	Beamish	6,054
Aug 23	OLDHAM ATHLETIC	W 4-1	Beamish, Martin, Metcalfe (pen), Parkes	12,688
Aug 30	Carlisle United	W 1-0	Hickman	8,721
Sep 6	BRISTOL CITY	L 1-2	Parkes	10,381
Sep 13	Southampton	L 1-2	Hird (pen)	13,279
Sep 20	SUNDERLAND	L 0-1		15,773
Sep 24	BLACKPOOL	L 0-2		11,088
Sep 27	Luton Town	D 1-1	Kenyon	8,458
Oct 4	FULHAM	L 0-1		10,190
Oct 11	WEST BROMWICH ALBION	D 0-0		9,973
Oct 18	Oxford United	D 0-0		5,595
Oct 21	Plymouth Argyle	D 2-2	Beamish, Hutt	14,371
Oct 25	CHELSEA	D 1-1	Metcalfe	12,168
Nov 1	Bristol Rovers	D 1-1	Svarc	10,533
Nov 4	HULL CITY	W 1-0	Oates	8,816
Nov 8	BOLTON WANDERERS	D 1-1	Oates	24,430
Nov 15	Portsmouth	W 1-0	Beamish	7,323
Nov 22	OXFORD UNITED	D 0-0		9,373
Nov 29	CHARLTON ATHLETIC	W 2-0	Metcalfe (pen), Svarc	8,776
Dec 6	Notts County	L 0-3		10,252
Dec 13	Oldham Athletic	L 1-2	Beamish	10,289
Dec 20	ORIENT	D 1-1	Metcalfe	7,263
Dec 26	York City	L 1-2	Svarc	7,295
Dec 27	NOTTINGHAM FOREST	L 1-4	Parkes	10,720
Jan 17	Bristol City	L 0-1		12,168
Jan 28	SOUTHAMPTON	D 1-1	Svarc	8,786
Jan 31	PLYMOUTH ARGYLE	W 3-1	Svarc 2, Hird	8,515
Feb 6	Hull City	W 1-0	Oates	6,205
Feb 21	PORTSMOUTH	L 0-3		8,067
Feb 24	Blackpool	D 1-1	Parkes	8,772
Feb 28	Chelsea	L 1-3	Oates	14,855
Mar 6	BRISTOL ROVERS	L 1-2	Hawkins	6,765
Mar 13	West Bromwich Albion	D 2-2	Fazackerley, Parkes	17,746
Mar 20	Charlton Athletic	L 1-2	Beamish	9,775
Mar 23	Bolton Wanderers	W 1-0	Waddington	25,621
Mar 27	NOTTS COUNTY	W 2-1	Hird 2 (2 pens)	8,472
Apr 3	LUTON TOWN	W 3-0	Parkes, Waddington, Beamish	7,911
Apr 10	Sunderland	L 0-3		33,253
Apr 16	CARLISLE UNITED	W 1-0	Hird (pen)	11,225
Apr 17	YORK CITY	W 4-0	Hird, Parkes, Metcalfe, Waddington	8,941
Apr 20	Nottingham Forest	L 0-1		13,006
Apr 24	Fulham	D 1-1	Taylor	5,914

FA Cup

Jan 3	Luton Town	(Rd3) L 0-2		11,195

League Cup

Aug 19	Preston North End	(Rd1/1L) L 0-2		11,503
Aug 27	PRESTON NORTH END	(Rd1/2L) D 0-0		14,077

Anglo-Scottish Cup

Aug 2	Sheffield United	L 1-3	Beamish	9,633
Aug 6	MANCHESTER CITY	W 1-0	Oates	10,612
Aug 9	BLACKPOOL	W 3-2	Oates, Beamish, Metcalfe	9,774
Sep 17	MOTHERWELL	(QF/1L) D 0-0		8,647
Sep 29	Motherwell	(QF/2L) L 1-2	Beamish	5,962

MANAGER: Jim Smith

TOP SCORER: Ken Beamish

BIGGEST WIN: 4-0, 17 April 1976, v York City, Division 2

HIGHEST ATTENDANCE: 33,253, 10 April 1976 v Sunderland, Division 2

MAJOR TRANSFERS IN: Bobby Svarc from Colchester United, Dave Wagstaffe from Wolverhampton Wanderers, Gordon Taylor from Birmingham City

MAJOR TRANSFERS OUT: Mike Hickman to Torquay United, Graham Oates to Newcastle United, Roger Jones to Newcastle United

League & Cup Appearances

PLAYER	LEAGUE	CUP COMPETITION			TOTAL
		FA CUP	LC	ASC	
Bailey, J.A.	4 (2)		1		5 (2)
Beamish, K.G.	37		2	5	44
Bradshaw, P.W.	12				12
Burgin, A.	5		2	3	10
Downes, S.F.	6				6
Fazackerley, D.W.	42	1	2	5	50
Hawkins, G.N.	29 (1)		2	5	36 (1)
Heaton, J.M.	13	1	2	4	20
Hickman, M.F.T.	5 (2)		2	4	11 (2)
Hindson, G.	10				10
Hird, K.	20 (1)		1	1	22 (1)
Hoy, R.	7 (5)		0 (2)	1 (1)	9 (8)
Hutt, G.	10			2	12
Jones, R.	30	1	2	5	38
Kenyon, J.F.	3 (6)			1	4 (6)
Martin, D.	8 (2)		2	3	13 (2)
Metcalfe, S.M.	38	1	1	4	44
Mullen, J.	1		1		2
Oates, G.	31	1	1	5	38
Parkes, T.	41	1	1	5	48
Svarc, R.L.	19	1			20
Taylor, G.	10				10
Waddington, J.	25 (1)	1		1	28 (1)
Wagstaffe, D.	9				9
Wilkinson, N.	19 (2)			1	20 (2)
Wood, M.J.	28 (1)	1			29 (1)

Goalscorers

PLAYER	LEAGUE	CUP COMPETITION			TOTAL
		FA CUP	LC	ASC	
Beamish, K.G.	7			3	10
Parkes, T.	7				7
Hird, K.	6				6
Svarc, R.L.	6				6
Metcalfe, S.M.	5			1	6
Oates, G.	4			2	6
Waddington, J.	3				3
Fazackerley, D.W.	1				1
Hawkins, G.N.	1				1
Hickman, M.F.T.	1				1
Hutt, G.	1				1
Kenyon, J.F.	1				1
Martin, D.	1				1
Taylor, G.	1				1

Fact File

The £25,000 that Blackburn paid to Colchester United for Bobby Svarc was a record fee for the Layer Road club.

Final Division 2 Table

		P	W	D	L	F	A	Pts
1	SUNDERLAND	42	24	8	10	67	36	56
2	BRISTOL C	42	19	15	8	59	35	53
3	WBA	42	20	13	9	50	33	53
4	BOLTON W	42	20	12	10	64	38	52
5	NOTTS CO	42	19	11	12	60	41	49
6	SOUTHAMPTON	42	21	7	14	66	50	49
7	LUTON T	42	19	10	13	61	51	48
8	NOTTINGHAM F	42	17	12	13	55	40	46
9	CHARLTON ATH	42	15	12	15	61	72	42
10	BLACKPOOL	42	14	14	14	40	49	42
11	CHELSEA	42	12	16	14	53	54	40
12	FULHAM	42	13	14	15	45	47	40
13	ORIENT	42	13	14	15	37	39	40
14	HULL C	42	14	11	17	45	49	39
15	BLACKBURN R	42	12	14	16	45	50	38
16	PLYMOUTH ARG	42	13	12	17	48	54	38
17	OLDHAM ATH	42	13	12	17	57	68	38
18	BRISTOL R	42	11	16	15	38	50	38
19	CARLISLE U	42	12	13	17	45	59	37
20	OXFORD U	42	11	11	20	39	59	33
21	YORK C	42	10	8	24	39	71	28
22	PORTSMOUTH	42	9	7	26	32	61	25

Season 1976-77

Football League Division 2

DATE	OPPONENTS	SCORE	GOALSCORERS	ATTENDANCE
Aug 21	BOLTON WANDERERS	W 3-1	Svarc (pen), Parkes, Wagstaffe	14,330
Aug 24	Plymouth Argyle	L 0-4		13,553
Aug 28	Cardiff City	L 1-2	Mitchell	11,845
Sep 4	BLACKPOOL	L 0-1		10,131
Sep 11	Oldham Athletic	L 0-2		9,528
Sep 18	BRISTOL ROVERS	D 0-0		7,751
Sep 25	Sheffield United	D 1-1	Franks o.g.	15,951
Oct 2	Orient	W 1-0	Svarc	5,082
Oct 9	NOTTS COUNTY	W 6-1	Mitchell, Parkes 2, Svarc 2, Hawkins	7,993
Oct 16	Millwall	W 1-0	Svarc	9,201
Oct 23	CHELSEA	L 0-2		14,984
Oct 30	LUTON TOWN	W 1-0	Silvester	8,674
Nov 6	Nottingham Forest	L 0-3		12,972
Nov 13	HULL CITY	W 1-0	Mitchell (pen)	8,807
Nov 20	Wolverhampton W.	W 2-1	Byrom 2	19,302
Nov 27	HEREFORD UNITED	W 1-0	Wagstaffe	9,040
Dec 4	Charlton Athletic	L 0-4		7,943
Dec 14	Fulham	L 0-2		8,543
Dec 27	BURNLEY	D 2-2	Byrom 2	22,189
Dec 29	Carlisle United	D 1-1	Svarc	8,852
Jan 1	NOTTINGHAM FOREST	L 1-3	Alcock	14,524
Jan 22	Bolton Wanderers	L 1-3	Waddington	29,643
Feb 5	CARDIFF CITY	W 2-1	Waddington (pen), Svarc	9,516
Feb 12	Blackpool	D 1-1	Byrom	14,922
Feb 15	Luton Town	L 0-2		9,044
Feb 19	OLDHAM ATHLETIC	W 2-0	Mitchell, Parkes	11,372
Mar 2	PLYMOUTH ARGYLE	W 2-0	Waddington (pen), Svarc	7,734
Mar 5	SHEFFIELD UNITED	W 1-0	Mitchell	9,630
Mar 8	Bristol Rovers	D 0-0		5,690
Mar 12	ORIENT	D 2-2	Hawkins, Hird	7,707
Mar 19	Notts County	D 0-0		9,343
Mar 26	MILLWALL	W 2-0	Svarc, Round	8,457
Apr 2	Chelsea	L 1-3	Waddington	20,769
Apr 6	CARLISLE UNITED	L 1-3	Parkes	6,851
Apr 8	Burnley	L 1-3	Svarc	17,372
Apr 12	Hull City	L 0-1		4,800
Apr 16	WOLVERHAMPTON W.	L 0-2		11,358
Apr 20	SOUTHAMPTON	W 3-0	Waddington 2, Blyth o.g.	5,923
Apr 23	Hereford United	L 0-1		5,853
Apr 30	CHARLTON ATHLETIC	D 0-0		6,350
May 7	Southampton	L 0-2		16,138
May 14	FULHAM	W 1-0	Mitchell	9,406

FA Cup

Jan 8	Charlton Athletic	(Rd3) D 1-1	Svarc	10,569
Jan 12	CHARLTON ATHLETIC	(R) W 2-0	Byrom, Parkes	11,465
Jan 29	ORIENT	(Rd4) W 3-0	Waddington, Parkes, Byrom	12,367
Feb 26	Derby County	(Rd5) L 1-3	Todd o.g.	30,439

League Cup

Aug 14	Rochdale	(Rd1/1L) W 1-0	Svarc	3,547
Aug 18	ROCHDALE	(Rd1/2L) W 4-1	Hird, Beamish, Svarc 2	5,225
Sep 1	STOCKPORT COUNTY	(Rd2) L 1-3	Beamish	6,264

Anglo-Scottish Cup

Aug 7	BURNLEY	D 1-1	Wagstaffe	11,012
Aug 9	BLACKPOOL	W 1-0	Svarc	6,600
Aug 10	Bolton Wanderers	L 0-2		7,054

MANAGER: Jim Smith

TOP SCORER: Bobby Svarc

BIGGEST WIN: 6-1, 9 October 1976, v Notts County, Division 2

HIGHEST ATTENDANCE: 30,439, 26 February 1977, v Derby County, FA Cup Round 5

MAJOR TRANSFERS IN: Bobby Mitchell from Sunderland, Andy Needham from Birmingham City, Glenn Keeley from Newcastle United, John Byrom from Bolton Wanderers

MAJOR TRANSFERS OUT: Ken Beamish to Port Vale

League & Cup Appearances

PLAYER	LEAGUE	CUP COMPETITION			TOTAL
		FA CUP	LC	ASC	
Alcock, T.	3	2			5
Bailey, J.A.	31 (3)	3	3	2	39 (3)
Beamish, K.G.			2	1	9
Bradshaw, P.W.	41	4	3	3	51
Butcher, J.M.	1				1
Byrom, J.	15 (1)	4			19 (1)
Crompton, A.	2 (2)				2 (2)
Fazackerley, D.W.	37 (1)	4	3	3	47 (1)
Hawkins, G.N.	31	1		2	34
Hird, K.	38 (1)	4	3	1 (2)	46 (3)
Keeley, G.M.	33	2	1		36
Metcalfe, S.M.	35	4	3	3	45
Mitchell, R.	13 (8)			1	15 (8)
Needham, A.P.	4 (1)		1 (1)	2	7 (2)
Parkes, T.	42	4	3	2	51
Parkin, T.J.	1				1
Round, P.G.	2				2
Silvester, P.	5				5
Svarc, R.L.	23 (8)	3	2 (1)	2	30 (9)
Taylor, G.	22	0 (1)	2	3	27 (1)
Waddington, J.	23 (1)	4	1	2	30 (1)
Wagstaffe, D.	31 (1)	3	3	2	39 (1)
Wilkinson, N.	1 (1)		0 (1)	2	3 (2)
Wood, M.J.	22 (2)	1	3	2	28 (2)

Goalscorers

PLAYER	LEAGUE	CUP COMPETITION			TOTAL
		FA CUP	LC	ASC	
Svarc, R.L.	10	1	3	1	15
Waddington, J.	6	1			7
Byrom, J.	5	2			7
Parkes, T.	5	2			7
Mitchell, R.	6				6
Wagstaffe, D.	2			1	3
Hawkins, G.N.	2				2
Hird, K.	1		1		2
Beamish, K.G.			2		2
Alcock, T.	1				1
Round, P.G.	1				1
Silvester, P.	1				1
Opps' o.gs.	2	1			3

Fact File

Dave Wagstaffe became the first player to have a red card shown to him in a Football League game when he was sent off against Orient on 2 October 1976.

Final Division 2 Table

		P	W	D	L	F	A	Pts
1	WOLVERHAMPTON W	42	22	13	7	84	45	57
2	CHELSEA	42	21	13	8	73	53	55
3	NOTTINGHAM F	42	21	10	11	77	43	52
4	BOLTON W	42	20	11	11	74	54	51
5	BLACKPOOL	42	17	17	8	58	42	51
6	LUTON T	42	23	6	15	67	48	48
7	CHARLTON ATH	42	16	16	10	71	58	48
8	NOTTS CO	42	19	10	13	65	60	48
9	SOUTHAMPTON	42	17	10	15	72	67	44
10	MILLWALL	42	17	13	14	57	53	43
11	SHEFFIELD U	42	14	12	16	54	63	40
12	BLACKBURN R	42	15	9	18	42	54	39
13	OLDHAM ATH	42	14	10	18	52	64	38
14	HULL C	42	10	17	15	45	53	37
15	BRISTOL R	42	12	13	17	53	68	37
16	BURNLEY	42	11	14	17	46	64	36
17	FULHAM	42	11	13	18	54	61	35
18	CARDIFF C	42	12	10	20	56	67	34
19	ORIENT	42	9	16	17	37	55	34
20	CARLISLE U	42	11	12	19	49	75	34
21	PLYMOUTH ARG	42	8	16	18	46	65	32
22	HEREFORD U	42	8	15	19	57	78	31

Season 1977-78

Football League Division 2

DATE	OPPONENTS	SCORE	GOALSCORERS	ATTENDANCE
Aug 20	Notts County	D 1-1	Parkes	8,237
Aug 24	TOTTENHAM HOTSPUR	D 0-0		9,540
Aug 27	CARDIFF CITY	W 3-0	Lewis, Metcalfe, Brotherston	7,088
Sep 3	Fulham	D 0-0		10,095
Sep 10	BLACKPOOL	L 1-2	Brotherston	8,211
Sep 17	Luton Town	D 0-0		9,149
Sep 24	ORIENT	W 1-0	Wagstaffe	6,316
Oct 1	Oldham Athletic	W 2-0	Lewis, Brotherston	7,795
Oct 4	Bolton Wanderers	L 2-4	Taylor, Waddington	19,913
Oct 8	CHARLTON ATHLETIC	W 2-1	Hird, Parkes	6,888
Oct 15	Bristol Rovers	L 1-4	Brotherston	6,436
Oct 22	STOKE CITY	W 2-1	Round 2	10,221
Oct 29	Hull City	W 1-0	Hird	7,932
Nov 5	SOUTHAMPTON	W 2-1	Brotherston, Waddington (pen)	9,930
Nov 12	Millwall	D 1-1	Lewis	5,745
Nov 19	MANSFIELD TOWN	W 3-1	Metcalfe, Bailey, Brotherston	8,796
Nov 26	Brighton & Hove Albion	D 2-2	Wagstaffe (pen), Lewis	26,467
Dec 3	CRYSTAL PALACE	W 3-0	Wood 2, Hird	12,119
Dec 10	Sheffield United	L 0-2		17,888
Dec 17	MILLWALL	W 2-1	Wagstaffe, Lewis	10,295
Dec 26	Burnley	W 3-2	Wagstaffe, Fear, Brotherston	27,427
Dec 27	SUNDERLAND	D 1-1	Parkes	22,660
Dec 31	Tottenham Hotspur	L 0-4		30,520
Jan 2	NOTTS COUNTY	W 1-0	Fear	14,394
Jan 14	Cardiff City	D 1-1	Metcalfe	7,025
Feb 4	Blackpool	L 2-5	Waddington, Hird (pen)	12,416
Feb 11	LUTON TOWN	W 2-0	Round, Brotherston	11,511
Feb 25	OLDHAM ATHLETIC	W 4-2	Radford, Parkes, Brotherston, Hicks o.g	15,574
Mar 4	Charlton Athletic	D 2-2	Hird (pen), Taylor	7,496
Mar 11	BRISTOL ROVERS	L 0-1		11,780
Mar 15	FULHAM	W 4-0	Hird 2 (2 pens), Metcalfe, Radford	8,499
Mar 18	Stoke City	L 2-4	Radford, Lewis	16,989
Mar 24	HULL CITY	D 1-1	Brotherston	11,561
Mar 25	Sunderland	W 1-0	Brotherston	16,900
Mar 27	BURNLEY	L 0-1		24,379
Apr 1	Southampton	L 0-5		21,087
Apr 4	Orient	D 0-0		7,072
Apr 8	BRIGHTON & HOVE ALBION	L 0-1		10,178
Apr 15	Mansfield Town	D 2-2	Parkes, Wagstaffe	5,859
Apr 22	SHEFFIELD UNITED	D 1-1	Radford	8,990
Apr 26	BOLTON WANDERERS	L 0-1		27,835
Apr 29	Crystal Palace	L 0-5		13,021

FA Cup

Jan 7	SHREWSBURY TOWN	(Rd3) W 2-1	Mitchell, Brotherston	12,712
Jan 28	Orient	(Rd4) L 1-3	Metcalfe	9,547

League Cup

Aug 31	COLCHESTER UNITED	(Rd2) D 1-1	Metcalfe	6,193
Sep 7	Colchester United	(R) L 0-4		5,843

Anglo-Scottish Cup

Aug 2	Burnley	L 1-2	Mitchell	8,092
Aug 6	BLACKPOOL	W 3-1	Wood, Brotherston 2	5,074
Aug 10	BOLTON WANDERERS	W 2-0	Wood, Wagstaffe	6,757
Sep 14	Hibernian	(QF/1L) L 1-2	Brotherston	5,349
Sep 28	HIBERNIAN	(QF/2L) L 0-1		6,154

MANAGER: Jim Smith/Jim Iley

TOP SCORER: Noel Brotherston

BIGGEST WIN: 4-0, 15 March 1978, v Fulham, Division 2

HIGHEST ATTENDANCE: 30,520, 31 December 1977, v Tottenham Hotspur, Division 2

MAJOR TRANSFERS IN: Noel Brotherston from Tottenham Hotspur, John Curtis from Blackpool, Jack Lewis from Grimsby Town, John Radford from West Ham United

MAJOR TRANSFERS OUT: Paul Bradshaw to Wolverhampton Wanderers, Graham Hawkins to Port Vale, Mick Wood to Bradford City

League & Cup Appearances

PLAYER	LEAGUE	CUP COMPETITION			TOTAL
		FA CUP	LC	ASC	
Bailey, J.A.	41	2	2	5	50
Bradshaw, P.W.	7		2	4	13
Brotherston, N.	38 (2)	2	2	5	47 (2)
Butcher, J.M.	35	2		1	38
Curtis, J.	7 (1)		2	4	13 (1)
Fazackerley, D.W.	28	2	2	2	34
Fear, K.W.	5	1			6
Hargreaves, D.	2				2
Hawkins, G.N.	6		2	3	11
Hird, K.	42	2	1 (1)	5	50 (1)
Keeley, G.M.	26 (1)	1	1	5	33 (1)
Lewis, F.J.	24 (4)		2	2	28 (4)
Metcalfe, S.M.	41		2	4 (1)	49 (1)
Mitchell, R.	4 (4)	1		3 (2)	8 (6)
Parkes, T.	37	1	2	3	43
Radford, J.	13				13
Round, P.G.	9 (4)				9 (4)
Svarc, R.L.		1		1 (1)	2 (1)
Taylor, G.	30 (2)	2			32 (2)
Waddington, J.	29 (5)	1	0 (1)	1	31 (6)
Wagstaffe, D.	32 (2)	1	1	5	39 (2)
Wood, M.J.	6 (2)	2		2	10 (2)

Goalscorers

PLAYER	LEAGUE	CUP COMPETITION			TOTAL
		FA CUP	LC	ASC	
Brotherston, N.	11	1		3	15
Hird, K.	7				7
Lewis, F.J.	6				6
Wagstaffe, D.	5			1	6
Metcalfe, S.M.	4	1	1		6
Parkes, T.	5				5
Radford, J.	4				4
Wood, M.J.	2			2	4
Round, P.G.	3				3
Waddington, J.	3				3
Fear, K.W.	2				2
Taylor, G.	2				2
Mitchell, R.		1		1	2
Bailey, J.A.	1				1
Opps' o.gs.	1				1

Fact File

Jim Smith resigned on 13 March 1978 to become manager of Birmingham City.

Final Division 2 Table

		P	W	D	L	F	A	Pts
1	BOLTON W	42	24	10	8	63	33	58
2	SOUTHAMPTON	42	22	13	7	70	39	57
3	TOTTENHAM H	42	20	16	6	83	49	56
4	BRIGHTON & HA	42	22	12	8	63	38	56
5	BLACKBURN R	42	16	13	13	56	60	45
6	SUNDERLAND	42	14	16	12	67	59	44
7	STOKE C	42	16	10	16	53	49	42
8	OLDHAM ATH	42	13	16	13	54	58	42
9	CRYSTAL PALACE	42	13	15	14	50	47	41
10	FULHAM	42	14	13	15	49	49	41
11	BURNLEY	42	15	10	17	56	64	40
12	SHEFFIELD U	42	16	8	18	62	73	40
13	LUTON T	42	14	10	18	54	52	38
14	ORIENT	42	10	18	14	43	49	38
15	NOTTS CO	42	11	16	15	54	62	38
16	MILLWALL	42	12	14	16	49	57	38
17	CHARLTON ATH	42	13	12	17	55	68	38
18	BRISTOL R	42	13	12	17	61	77	38
19	CARDIFF C	42	13	12	17	51	71	38
20	BLACKPOOL	42	12	13	17	59	60	37
21	MANSFIELD T	42	10	11	21	49	69	31
22	HULL C	42	8	12	22	34	52	28

Season 1978-79

Football League Division 2

DATE	OPPONENTS	SCORE	GOALSCORERS	ATTENDANCE
Aug 19	CRYSTAL PALACE	D 1-1	Metcalfe	9,393
Aug 22	Preston North End	L 1-4	Gregory	15,412
Aug 26	Notts County	L 1-2	Radford	7,774
Sep 2	ORIENT	W 3-0	Radford, Gregory, Hird (pen)	6,781
Sep 9	Newcastle United	L 1-3	Gregory	23,751
Sep 16	LEICESTER CITY	D 1-1	Radford	7,908
Sep 23	Cardiff City	L 0-2		6,234
Sep 30	CHARLTON ATHLETIC	L 1-2	Radford	8,341
Oct 7	Bristol Rovers	L 1-4	Craig	7,111
Oct 14	LUTON TOWN	D 0-0		7,450
Oct 21	Cambridge United	W 1-0	Hird	5,240
Oct 28	WREXHAM	D 1-1	Craig	9,906
Nov 3	Fulham	W 2-1	Garner 2	12,583
Nov 11	Crystal Palace	L 0-3		16,937
Nov 18	NOTTS COUNTY	L 3-4	Hird (pen), Craig, Radford	7,893
Nov 21	Orient	L 0-2		4,415
Nov 25	STOKE CITY	D 2-2	Hird, Garner	10,841
Dec 9	BRIGHTON & HOVE ALBION	D 1-1	Radford	8,046
Dec 16	Millwall	D 1-1	Hird	6,070
Dec 26	Burnley	L 1-2	Hird	23,133
Dec 30	West Ham United	L 0-4		21,269
Jan 17	SUNDERLAND	D 1-1	Garner	8,130
Jan 20	Leicester City	D 1-1	Garner	13,234
Feb 10	Charlton Athletic	L 0-2		5,480
Feb 24	Luton Town	L 1-2	Garner	6,247
Feb 28	CARDIFF CITY	L 1-4	Garner	7,158
Mar 10	Wrexham	L 1-2	Brotherston	9,407
Mar 14	OLDHAM ATHLETIC	L 0-2		8,367
Mar 24	PRESTON NORTH END	L 0-1		17,790
Mar 28	CAMBRIDGE UNITED	W 1-0	Fazackerley (pen)	6,448
Mar 31	Stoke City	W 2-1	Craig, Brotherston	17,020
Apr 4	BRISTOL ROVERS	L 0-2		8,554
Apr 7	SHEFFIELD UNITED	W 2-0	Aston, Craig	10,762
Apr 13	Oldham Athletic	L 0-5		10,056
Apr 14	BURNLEY	L 1-2	Garner	14,761
Apr 16	Sunderland	W 1-0	Fazackerley (pen)	35,005
Apr 21	MILLWALL	D 1-1	Waddington	5,819
Apr 25	NEWCASTLE UNITED	L 1-3	McKenzie	4,902
Apr 28	Brighton & Hove Albion	L 1-2	Aston	26,094
May 2	Sheffield United	W 1-0	Round	16,012
May 5	WEST HAM UNITED	W 1-0	McKenzie	7,585
May 9	FULHAM	W 2-1	Taylor, Fazackerley (pen)	4,684

FA Cup

Jan 10	Millwall*	(Rd3) W 2-1	Brotherston, Radford	8,354
Jan 27	Liverpool	(Rd4) L 0-1		43,432

*Played at Ewood Park, Blackburn.

League Cup

Aug 29	Exeter City	(Rd2) L 1-2	Gregory	4,005

Anglo-Scottish Cup

Aug 5	Blackpool	W 1-0	Round	6,554
Aug 9	PRESTON NORTH END	W 1-0	Brotherston	9,538
Aug 12	BURNLEY	D 1-1	Brotherston	9,791

MANAGER: Jim Iley/John Pickering

TOP SCORER: Simon Garner

BIGGEST WIN: 3-0, 2 September 1978, v Orient, Division 2

HIGHEST ATTENDANCE: 43,432, 27 January 1979, v Liverpool, FA Cup Round 4

MAJOR TRANSFERS IN: Martin Fowler from Huddersfield Town, John Aston from Mansfield Town, Alan Birchenall from Memphis Rogues, Joe Craig from Celtic, Dave Wagstaffe from Blackpool, Russell Coughlin from Manchester City, Mick Rathbone from Birmingham City, Duncan McKenzie from Chelsea

MAJOR TRANSFERS OUT: Gordon Taylor to Bury, Jack Lewis to Doncaster Rovers, Dave Wagstaffe to Blackpool, Kevin Hird to Leeds United

League & Cup Appearances

PLAYER	LEAGUE	CUP COMPETITION			TOTAL
		FA CUP	LC	ASC	
Aston, J.	10 (3)		1	3	14 (3)
Bailey, J.A.	39	2	1	3	45
Birchenall, A.J.	17 (1)	2			19 (1)
Brotherston, N.	34 (1)	1 (1)		3	38 (2)
Butcher, J.M.	32	2	1	3	38
Coughlin, R.J.	11				11
Craig, J.	28 (2)	1			29 (2)
Curtis, J.	2				2
Fazackerley, D.W.	37	2	1		40
Fowler, M.	32 (2)	1	1	3	37 (2)
Garner, S.	20 (5)	2	1	1 (1)	24 (6)
Gregory, D.W.	5		1		6
Hird, K.	22	2	1	3	28
Keeley, G.M.	26	1	1	3	31
McKenzie, D.	13				13
Metcalfe, S.M.	24 (1)	2		3	29 (1)
Morley, B.J.	3				3
Morris, P.A.	2 (2)	1 (1)			3 (3)
Parkes, T.	12			3	15
Parkin, T.J.	12				12
Radford, J.	23	1	1	1	26
Ramsbottom, N.	10				10
Rathbone, M.J.	15				15
Round, P.G.	17 (2)	2		1 (1)	20 (3)
Taylor, R.	3				3
Waddington, J.	11 (2)		1	3	15 (2)
Wagstaffe, D.	2				2

Goalscorers

PLAYER	LEAGUE	CUP COMPETITION			TOTAL
		FA CUP	LC	ASC	
Garner, S.	8				8
Radford, J.	6	1			7
Hird, K.	6				6
Craig, J.	5				5
Brotherston, N.	2	1		2	5
Gregory, D.W.	3		1		4
Fazackerley, D.W.	3				3
Aston, J.	2				2
McKenzie, D.	2				2
Round, P.G.	1			1	2
Metcalfe, S.M.	1				1
Taylor, R.	1				1
Waddington, J.	1				1

Fact File

Jim Iley was sacked as manager after just 172 days at the helm at Ewood Park.

Final Division 2 Table

		P	W	D	L	F	A	Pts
1	CRYSTAL PALACE	42	19	19	4	51	24	57
2	BRIGHTON & HA	42	23	10	9	72	39	56
3	STOKE C	42	20	16	6	58	31	56
4	SUNDERLAND	42	22	11	9	70	44	55
5	WEST HAM U	42	18	14	10	70	39	50
6	NOTTS CO	42	14	16	12	48	60	44
7	PRESTON NE	42	12	18	12	59	57	42
8	NEWCASTLE U	42	17	8	17	51	55	42
9	CARDIFF C	42	16	10	16	56	70	42
10	FULHAM	42	13	15	14	50	47	41
11	ORIENT	42	15	10	17	51	51	40
12	CAMBRIDGE U	42	12	16	14	44	52	40
13	BURNLEY	42	14	12	16	51	62	40
14	OLDHAM ATH	42	13	13	16	52	61	39
15	WREXHAM	42	12	14	16	45	42	38
16	BRISTOL R	42	14	10	18	48	60	38
17	LEICESTER C	42	10	17	15	43	52	37
18	LUTON T	42	13	10	19	60	57	36
19	CHARLTON ATH	42	11	13	18	60	69	35
20	SHEFFIELD U	42	11	12	19	52	69	34
21	MILLWALL	42	11	10	21	42	61	32
22	BLACKBURN R	42	10	10	22	41	72	30

Season 1979-80

Football League Division 3

DATE	OPPONENTS	SCORE	GOALSCORERS	ATTENDANCE
Aug 18	MILLWALL	D 1-1	Craig	8,232
Aug 21	Carlisle United	D 1-1	McKenzie	5,726
Aug 25	Sheffield Wednesday	W 3-0	Craig, Fazackerley, McKenzie	14,405
Sep 1	GRIMSBY TOWN	D 0-0		8,877
Sep 8	Wimbledon	L 0-1		3,786
Sep 15	SOUTHEND UNITED	D 1-1	Craig	6,603
Sep 19	BARNSLEY	L 0-1		7,582
Sep 22	Blackpool	L 1-2	Kendall	10,193
Sep 29	ROTHERHAM UNITED	L 0-3		7,435
Oct 2	Barnsley	D 1-1	Parker	12,460
Oct 6	Gillingham	W 2-1	Stonehouse 2	7,851
Oct 10	CARLISLE UNITED	L 1-2	Crawford	7,114
Oct 13	PLYMOUTH ARGYLE	W 1-0	Brotherston	6,026
Oct 20	Brentford	L 0-2		7,970
Oct 24	Chester	D 0-0		4,211
Oct 27	COLCHESTER UNITED	W 3-0	Crawford, Keeley, Brotherston	6,436
Nov 3	Millwall	L 0-1		6,386
Nov 7	CHESTER	W 2-0	Crawford, Keeley	5,757
Nov 14	CHESTERFIELD	W 1-0	Crawford	5,955
Nov 17	Swindon Town	L 0-2		7,307
Dec 1	Reading	D 1-1	Crawford	6,010
Dec 8	OXFORD UNITED	W 2-1	McKenzie, Brotherston	6,714
Dec 21	Hull City	W 1-0	Keeley	3,720
Dec 26	MANSFIELD TOWN	D 0-0		8,491
Jan 1	Sheffield United	L 1-2	McKenzie (pen)	20,620
Jan 12	Grimsby Town	W 2-1	McKenzie 2	10,965
Jan 19	WIMBLEDON	W 3-0	Crawford, McKenzie, Rathbone	7,954
Feb 2	Southend United	W 1-0	Crawford	4,518
Feb 5	Rotherham United	W 3-1	Branagan, Garner 2	4,663
Feb 9	BLACKPOOL	W 2-0	Brotherston, Kendall	14,446
Feb 23	Plymouth Argyle	W 1-0	Garner	6,918
Feb 27	EXETER CITY	D 1-1	Brotherston	10,601
Mar 1	BRENTFORD	W 3-0	McKenzie, Crawford, Brotherston	10,227
Mar 8	Colchester United	W 1-0	Crawford	4,957
Mar 14	GILLINGHAM	W 3-1	Crawford, McKenzie 2	11,636
Mar 22	Chesterfield	W 1-0	Garner	14,480
Mar 29	SWINDON TOWN	W 2-0	Crawford 2	11,571
Apr 4	HULL CITY	W 1-0	McKenzie	14,571
Apr 5	Mansfield Town	W 1-0	McKenzie	7,385
Apr 7	SHEFFIELD UNITED	W 1-0	Crawford	18,140
Apr 12	Exeter City	L 0-2		5,407
Apr 19	READING	W 4-2	Crawford 3, Parkes (pen)	10,916
Apr 22	SHEFFIELD WEDNESDAY	L 1-2	Brotherston	26,130
Apr 26	Oxford United	W 1-0	Garner	5,476
Apr 29	Bury	W 2-1	Crawford 2	13,369
May 3	BURY	L 1-2	Garner	15,741

FA Cup

Nov 24	Kidderminster Harriers	(Rd1) W 2-0	Crawford, Craig	4,500
Dec 17	STAFFORD RANGERS	(Rd2) W 2-0	Crawford, McKenzie	5,422
Jan 8	FULHAM	(Rd3) D 1-1	Crawford	9,826
Jan 15	Fulham	(R) W 1-0	Crawford	5,684
Jan 26	COVENTRY CITY	(Rd4) W 1-0	Crawford	20,785
Feb 16	ASTON VILLA	(Rd 5) D 1-1	Evans o.g.	29,468
Feb 20	Aston Villa	(R) L 0-1		42,161

League Cup

Aug 11	Bury	(Rd 1/1L) W 3-0	Brotherston 2, McKenzie	6,143
Aug 14	BURY	(Rd 1/2L) W 3-2	McKenzie 2 (1 pen), Kendall	5,753
Aug 29	NOTTINGHAM FOREST	(Rd 2/1L) D 1-1	Parkes	20,458
Sep 5	Nottingham Forest	(Rd 2/2L) L 1-6	Craig	21,244

Anglo-Scottish Cup

Aug 1	Blackpool	D 2-2	Parker, Brotherston	6,348
Aug 4	BURNLEY	D 2-2	Brotherston, Craig	7,749
Aug 7	PRESTON NORTH END	D 1-1	Parker	8,175

PLAYER-MANAGER: Howard Kendall

TOP SCORER: Andy Crawford

BIGGEST WIN: 3-0, 11 August 1979, v Bury; 25 August 1979, v Sheffield Wednesday; 27 October 1979, v Colchester United; 19 January 1980, v Wimbledon; 1 March 1980, v Brentford

HIGHEST ATTENDANCE 42,161, 20 February 1980 v Aston Villa, FA Cup Round 5 replay

League & Cup Appearances

PLAYER	LEAGUE	CUP COMPETITION			TOTAL
		FA CUP	LC	ASC	
Arnold, J.A.	38	7		2	47
Aston, J.	2			1 (1)	3 (1)
Branagan, J.P.S.	31	7			38
Brotherston, N.	41	7	3	3	54
Butcher, J.M.	8		4	1	13
Coughlin, R.J.	8 (2)		1 (1)	1	10 (3)
Craig, J.	16 (1)	2	3	2	23 (1)
Crawford, A.	36				43
Fazackerley, D.W.	46	7	4	3	60
Fowler, M.	4		2	0 (1)	6 (1)
Garner, S.	25 (3)	5	1 (2)	1	32 (5)
Keeley, G.M.	45	7	4	3	59
Kendall, H.	41	6	4	2	53
McKenzie, D.	42	7	4	2	55
Metcalfe, S.M.	16 (2)	3	1	2	22 (2)
Morley, B.J.	17		4	2	23
Parker, S.J.	5 (4)		1	2	8 (4)
Parkes, T.	38 (1)	5	4	2	49 (1)
Rathbone, M.J.	27 (1)	5		2	34 (1)
Round, P.G.	12 (3)	2	4	2	20 (3)
Stonehouse, K.	6 (1)				6 (1)
Thorley, D.	2 (2)				2 (2)

Goalscorers

PLAYER	LEAGUE	CUP COMPETITION			TOTAL
		FA CUP	LC	ASC	
Crawford, A.	18	5			23
McKenzie, D.	12	1	3		16
Brotherston, N.	7		2	2	11
Garner, S.	6				6
Craig, J.	3	1	1	1	6
Keeley, G.M.	3				3
Kendall, H.	2		1		3
Parker, S.J.	1			2	3
Stonehouse, K.	2				2
Parkes, T.	1		1		2
Branagan, J.P.S.	1				1
Fazackerley, D.W.	1				1
Rathbone, M.J.	1				1
Opps' o.gs.		1			1

Fact File

The 15 games between the 12 January 1980 and 7 April 1980 produced 14 wins and one draw as Howard Kendall led the club to promotion in his first season at Ewood Park.

Final Division 3 Table

		P	W	D	L	F	A	Pts
1	GRIMSBY T	46	26	10	10	73	42	62
2	BLACKBURN R	46	25	9	12	58	36	59
3	SHEFFIELD W	46	21	16	9	81	47	58
4	CHESTERFIELD	46	23	11	12	71	46	57
5	COLCHESTER U	46	20	12	14	64	56	52
6	CARLISLE U	46	18	12	16	66	56	48
7	READING	46	16	16	14	66	65	48
8	EXETER C	46	19	10	17	60	68	48
9	CHESTER	46	17	13	16	49	57	47
10	SWINDON T	46	19	8	19	71	63	46
11	BARNSLEY	46	16	14	16	53	56	46
12	SHEFFIELD U	46	18	10	18	60	66	46
13	ROTHERHAM U	46	18	10	18	58	66	46
14	MILLWALL	46	16	13	17	65	59	45
15	PLYMOUTH ARG	46	16	12	18	59	55	44
16	GILLINGHAM	46	14	14	18	49	51	42
17	OXFORD U	46	14	13	19	57	62	41
18	BLACKPOOL	46	15	11	20	62	74	41
19	BRENTFORD	46	15	11	20	59	73	41
20	HULL C	46	12	16	18	51	69	40
21	BURY	46	16	7	23	45	59	39
22	SOUTHEND U	46	14	10	22	47	58	38
23	MANSFIELD T	46	10	16	20	47	58	36
24	WIMBLEDON	46	10	14	22	52	81	34

Season 1980-81

Football League Division 2

DATE	OPPONENTS	SCORE	GOALSCORERS	ATTENDANCE
Aug 16	Cardiff City	W 2-1	Brotherston, Crawford	6,810
Aug 20	OLDHAM ATHLETIC	W 1-0	Keeley	10,831
Aug 23	Orient	D 1-1	Speight	5,059
Aug 30	SHREWSBURY TOWN	W 2-0	Kendall (pen), Garner	8,465
Sep 6	Derby County	D 2-2	Kendall (pen), Garner	18,159
Sep 13	LUTON TOWN	W 3-0	Garner 2, Stonehouse	9,076
Sep 20	GRIMSBY TOWN	W 2-0	Garner, Stonehouse	10,338
Sep 27	Wrexham	W 1-0	McKenzie	10,913
Oct 4	QUEENS PARK RANGERS	W 2-1	Stonehouse 2 (1 pen)	12,209
Oct 7	Sheffield Wednesday	L 1-2	Stonehouse	16,944
Oct 11	West Ham United	L 0-2		32,402
Oct 18	CHELSEA	D 1-1	Stonehouse	15,483
Oct 22	CAMBRIDGE UNITED	W 2-0	Garner, Kendall	9,438
Oct 25	Notts County	L 0-2		13,500
Nov 1	SWANSEA CITY	D 0-0		10,846
Nov 8	Bristol City	L 0-2		9,026
Nov 11	Oldham Athletic	L 0-1		7,748
Nov 15	CARDIFF CITY	L 2-3	Stonehouse (pen), Keeley	7,855
Nov 22	Watford	D 1-1	McKenzie	13,673
Nov 29	BRISTOL ROVERS	W 2-0	Brotherston, Stonehouse	8,025
Dec 13	WEST HAM UNITED	D 0-0		13,279
Dec 20	Cambridge United	D 0-0		4,389
Dec 26	PRESTON NORTH END	D 0-0		17,726
Dec 27	Bolton Wanderers	W 2-1	Stonehouse, Burke	18,184
Jan 10	WATFORD	D 0-0		9,466
Jan 17	Shrewsbury Town	D 1-1	Burke	5,212
Jan 31	ORIENT	W 2-0	Burke, Lowey	9,091
Feb 7	Luton Town	L 1-3	Burke	9,350
Feb 14	DERBY COUNTY	W 1-0	Brotherston	12,533
Feb 21	WREXHAM	D 1-1	Garner	10,147
Feb 28	Grimsby Town	D 0-0		12,210
Mar 7	Queens Park Rangers	D 1-1	Speight	9,513
Mar 14	SHEFFIELD WEDNESDAY	W 3-1	Speight, Kendall, Busby	19,222
Mar 21	Chelsea	D 0-0		14,314
Mar 28	NOTTS COUNTY	D 0-0		14,391
Apr 4	Swansea City	L 0-2		12,011
Apr 11	BRISTOL CITY	W 1-0	Burke	9,970
Apr 15	Newcastle United	D 0-0		13,128
Apr 18	BOLTON WANDERERS	D 0-0		16,357
Apr 21	Preston North End	D 0-0		18,777
Apr 25	NEWCASTLE UNITED	W 3-0	Lowey (pen), Burke, Speight	10,609
May 2	Bristol Rovers	W 1-0	Stonehouse	9,078

FA Cup

Jan 3	Notts County	(Rd3) L 1-2	Burke	7,885

League Cup

Aug 9	HUDDERSFIELD TOWN	(Rd1/1L) D 0-0		8,670
Aug 12	Huddersfield Town	(Rd1/2L) D 1-1*†Garner		9,500
Aug 27	GILLINGHAM	(Rd2/1L) D 0-0		7,316
Sep 2	Gillingham	(Rd2/2L) W 2-1*	McKenzie, Stonehouse (pen)	6,315
Sep 23	Birmingham City	(Rd3) L 0-1		14,580

*After extra-time. †Blackburn won on the away-goals rule.

Anglo-Scottish Cup

Jul 30	Blackpool	L 0-2		7,522
Aug 2	Preston North End	W 1-0	Stonehouse	5,560
Aug 5	Carlisle United	W 4-1	Speight, Garner 2, Parkes	2,499

PLAYER-MANAGER: Howard Kendall

TOP SCORER: Kevin Stonehouse

BIGGEST WIN: 3-0, 13 September 1980, v Luton Town, Division 2; 25 April 1980, v Newcastle United, Division 2

HIGHEST ATTENDANCE: 32,402, 11 October 1980 v West Ham United, Division 2

MAJOR TRANSFERS IN: Mick Speight from Sheffield United, Roger De Vries from Hull City, John Lowey from Sheffield Wednesday, Marshall Burke from Leeds United, Viv Busby from Tulsa Roughnecks

MAJOR TRANSFERS OUT: Stuart Metcalfe to Carlisle United, Russell Coughlin to Carlisle United, Duncan McKenzie to Tulsa Roughnecks, Joe Craig to Hamilton Academicals

League & Cup Appearances

PLAYER	LEAGUE	CUP COMPETITION			TOTAL
		FA CUP	LC	ASC	
Arnold, J.A.	20		3	2	25
Butcher, J.M.	22	1	2	1	26
Branagan, J.P.S.	42	1	5	1	49
Brotherston, N.	33	1	5	3	42
Burke, M.	18 (2)	1			19 (2)
Busby, V.D.	8				8
Cornstive, P.T.	2 (1)				2 (1)
Coughlin, R.J.	3			1	4
Craig, J.	0 (1)		0 (1)	1 (1)	1 (3)
Crawford, A.	12	1	4	3	20
De Vries, R.S.	13	1	3	2	19
Fazackerley, D.W.	38	1	5	2	46
Garner, S.	31 (2)	0 (1)	5	1 (1)	37 (4)
Hall J.			1		1
Hamilton, D.	0 (3)				0 (3)
Keeley, G.M.	42	1	5	1	49
Kendall, H.	38		3	2	43
Lowey, J.A.	19				19
McKenzie, D.	19	1	4	2	26
Morley A.				0 (1)	0 (1)
Morley B.J.			1		1
Parkes, T.	16	1	2	2	21
Rathbone, M.J.	26 (1)		2	2	30 (1)
Round, R.G.	1 (1)		1	2	4 (1)
Speight, M.	37 (1)		5	2 (1)	44 (2)
Stonehouse, K.	22 (4)	1	1 (1)	1	25 (5)

Goalscorers

PLAYER	LEAGUE	CUP COMPETITION			TOTAL
		FA CUP	LC	ASC	
Stonehouse, K.	10		1	1	12
Garner, S.	7		1	2	10
Burke, M.	6				6
Speight, M.	4			1	5
Kendall, H.	4				4
Brotherston, N.	3				3
McKenzie, D.	2		1		3
Parkes, T.	2			1	3
Keeley, G.M.	2				2
Lowey, J.A.	2				2
Busby, V.D.	1				1
Crawford, A.	1				1

Fact File

Five goalless draws in the last nine matches proved costly as only goal difference prevented Howard Kendall from winning a second successive promotion with Blackburn.

Final Division 2 Table

		P	W	D	L	F	A	Pts
1	WEST HAM U	42	28	10	4	79	29	66
2	NOTTS CO	42	18	17	7	49	38	53
3	SWANSEA C	42	18	14	10	64	44	50
4	BLACKBURN R	42	16	18	8	42	29	50
5	LUTON T	42	18	12	12	61	46	48
6	DERBY CO	42	15	15	12	57	52	45
7	GRIMSBY T	42	15	15	12	44	42	45
8	QPR	42	15	13	14	56	46	43
9	WATFORD	42	16	11	15	50	45	43
10	SHEFFIELD W	42	17	8	17	53	51	42
11	NEWCASTLE U	42	14	14	14	30	45	42
12	CHELSEA	42	14	12	16	46	41	40
13	CAMBRIDGE U	42	17	6	17	53	65	40
14	SHREWSBURY T	42	11	17	14	46	47	39
15	OLDHAM ATH	42	12	15	15	39	48	39
16	WREXHAM	42	12	14	16	43	45	38
17	ORIENT	42	13	12	17	52	56	38
18	BOLTON W	42	14	10	18	61	66	38
19	CARDIFF C	42	12	12	18	44	60	36
20	PRESTON NE	42	11	14	17	41	62	36
21	BRISTOL C	42	7	16	19	29	51	30
22	BRISTOL R	42	5	13	24	34	65	23

The Essential History of Blackburn Rovers

Season 1981-82

Football League Division 2

DATE	OPPONENTS	SCORE	GOALSCORERS	ATTENDANCE
Aug 29	SHEFFIELD WEDNESDAY	L 0-1		15,182
Sep 1	Shrewsbury Town	W 2-1	Lowey, Brotherson	4,219
Sep 5	Charlton Athletic	L 0-2		6,140
Sep 12	ORIENT	W 2-0	Keeley, Crawford	7,043
Sep 19	Cardiff City	W 3-1	Stonehouse 2, Pontin o.g.	4,248
Sep 23	CAMBRIDGE UNITED	W 1-0	Crawford	7,518
Sep 26	LEICESTER CITY	L 0-2		8,925
Oct 3	Queens Park Rangers	L 0-2		9,541
Oct 10	BARNSLEY	W 2-1	Garner 2	10,522
Oct 17	Derby County	D 1-1	Keeley	10,572
Oct 24	Grimsby Town	D 1-1	Garner	7,235
Oct 31	WREXHAM	D 0-0		8,159
Nov 7	Crystal Palace	W 2-1	Garner 2	9,650
Nov 14	LUTON TOWN	L 0-1		9,862
Nov 21	Watford	L 2-3	Burke, Stonehouse (pen)	11,822
Nov 25	SHREWSBURY TOWN	D 0-0		6,892
Nov 28	NORWICH CITY	W 3-0	Garner 2, Miller	8,152
Dec 5	Newcastle United	D 0-0		18,775
Dec 19	Chelsea	D 1-1	Miller	11,768
Dec 26	Oldham Athletic	W 3-0	Garner, Stonehouse, Bell	15,845
Dec 28	Bolton Wanderers	D 2-2	Arnott, Stonehouse (pen)	16,577
Jan 1	CHARLTON ATHLETIC	L 0-2		5,825
Jan 16	Sheffield Wednesday	D 2-2	Stonehouse, Keeley	13,381
Jan 23	ROTHERHAM UNITED	W 2-0	Stonehouse, Arnott	7,656
Jan 30	CARDIFF CITY	W 1-0	Garner	6,121
Feb 6	Orient	D 0-0		3,990
Feb 16	QUEENS PARK RANGERS	W 2-1	Stonehouse, Brotherston	6,884
Feb 20	Leicester City	L 0-1		11,667
Feb 27	Barnsley	W 1-0	Garner	13,150
Mar 6	DERBY COUNTY	W 4-1	Miller, Stonehouse (pen), Bell, Garner	8,364
Mar 13	GRIMSBY TOWN	W 2-0	Stonehouse (pen), Garner	8,676
Mar 20	Wrexham	L 0-1		5,780
Mar 27	CRYSTAL PALACE	W 1-0	Bell	8,358
Apr 3	Luton Town	L 0-2		10,721
Apr 9	OLDHAM ATHLETIC	D 0-0		11,044
Apr 12	BOLTON WANDERERS	L 0-2		11,912
Apr 17	WATFORD	L 1-2	Stonehouse (pen)	7,284
Apr 24	Norwich City	L 0-2		16,309
May 1	NEWCASTLE UNITED	W 4-1	Bell, Branagan, Rathbone, Garner	5,207
May 4	Cambridge United	L 0-1		3,203
May 8	Rotherham United	L 1-4	Fazackerley	8,333
May 15	CHELSEA	D 1-1	Garner	5,833

FA Cup

Jan 2	West Bromwich Albion	(Rd3)	L 2-3	Garner 2	17,540

League Cup

Oct 7	SHEFFIELD WEDNESDAY	(Rd2)	D 1-1	Garner	7,900
Oct 27	Sheffield Wednesday	(R)	W 2-1	Lowey, Garner	13,099
Nov 11	NOTTINGHAM FOREST	(Rd3)	L 0-1		14,752

League & Cup Appearances

PLAYER	LEAGUE	CUP COMPETITION		TOTAL
		FA CUP	LC	
Arnott, K.W.	17	1		18
Bell, N.	25	1		26
Branagan, J.P.S.	40	1	3	44
Brotherston, N.	38	1	3	42
Burke, M.	16 (3)		3	19 (3)
Butcher, J.M.	6			6
Comstive, P.T.	1 (1)			1 (1)
Crawford, A.	8			8
Fazackerley, D.W.	39	1	3	43
Garner, S.	35 (1)	1	3	39 (1)
Gennoe, T.W.	35	1	3	39
Hamilton, D.	16 (1)		1	17 (1)
Keeley, G.M.	41	1	3	45
Lowey, J.A.	12 (2)		3	15 (2)
Miller, I.	42	1	3	46
Murphy, D.P.	1 (2)			1 (2)
Rathbone, M.J.	41	1	3	45
Salmon, M.B.	1			1
Speight, M.	13		1	14
Stonehouse, K.	35 (2)	1	1	37 (2)
Williamson, P.J.	0 (1)			0 (1)

Goalscorers

PLAYER	LEAGUE	CUP COMPETITION		TOTAL
		FA CUP	LC	
Garner, S.	14	2	2	18
Stonehouse, K.	11			11
Bell, N.	4			4
Keeley, G.M.	3			3
Miller, I.	3			3
Arnott, K.W.	2			2
Brotherston, N.	2			2
Crawford, A.	2			2
Lowey, J.A.	1		1	2
Branagan, J.P.S.	1			1
Burke, M.	1			1
Fazackerley, D.W.	1			1
Rathbone, M.J.	1			1
Opps' o.gs.	1			1

Fact File

Two wins in the last 11 matches saw the Rovers slip from third to tenth position in the table.

MANAGER: Bob Saxton

TOP SCORER: Simon Garner

BIGGEST WIN: 4-1, 6 March 1982, v Derby County, Division 2; 1 May 1982, v Newcastle United, Division 2

HIGHEST ATTENDANCE: 18,775, 5 December 1981, v Newcastle United, Division 2

MAJOR TRANSFERS IN: Ian Miller from Swindon Town, Terry Gennoe from Southampton, Norman Bell from Wolverhampton Wanderers

MAJOR TRANSFERS OUT: Jim Arnold to Everton, Andy Crawford to AFC Bournemouth

Final Division 2 Table

		P	W	D	L	F	A	Pts
1	LUTON T	42	25	13	4	86	46	88
2	WATFORD	42	23	11	8	76	42	80
3	NORWICH C	42	22	5	15	64	50	71
4	SHEFFIELD W	42	20	10	12	55	51	70
5	QPR	42	21	6	15	65	43	69
6	BARNSLEY	42	19	10	13	59	41	67
7	ROTHERHAM U	42	20	7	15	66	54	67
8	LEICESTER C	42	18	12	12	56	48	66
9	NEWCASTLE U	42	18	8	16	52	50	62
10	BLACKBURN R	42	16	11	15	47	43	59
11	OLDHAM ATH	42	15	14	13	50	51	59
12	CHELSEA	42	15	12	15	60	60	57
13	CHARLTON ATH	42	13	12	17	50	65	51
14	CAMBRIDGE U	42	13	9	20	48	53	48
15	CRYSTAL PALACE	42	13	9	20	34	45	48
16	DERBY CO	42	12	12	18	53	68	48
17	GRIMSBY T	42	11	13	18	53	65	46
18	SHREWSBURY T	42	11	3	18	37	57	46
19	BOLTON W	42	13	7	22	39	61	46
20	CARDIFF C	42	12	8	22	45	61	44
21	WREXHAM	42	11	11	20	40	56	44
22	ORIENT	42	10	9	23	36	61	39

Season 1982-83

Football League Division 2

DATE	OPPONENTS	SCORE	GOALSCORERS	ATTENDANCE
Aug 28	Wolverhampton W.	L 1-2	Garner	15,605
Sep 1	NEWCASTLE UNITED	L 1-2	Bell	14,021
Sep 4	CAMBRIDGE UNITED	W 3-1	Garner 2, Bell	4,488
Sep 7	Grimsby Town	L 0-5		7,567
Sep 11	Crystal Palace	L 0-2		7,508
Sep 18	LEICESTER CITY	W 3-1	Garner, Bell, Barton	4,963
Sep 25	Derby County	W 2-1	Garner, Hamilton	9,361
Oct 2	SHEFFIELD WEDNESDAY	L 2-3	Garner, Stonehouse (pen)	10,362
Oct 9	Fulham	L 1-3	Brotherston	5,698
Oct 16	CHELSEA	W 3-0	Garner 2, Stonehouse	6,062
Oct 23	LEEDS UNITED	D 0-0		12,040
Oct 30	Charlton Athletic	L 0-3		5,726
Nov 6	CARLISLE UNITED	W 3-2	Garner 2, Hamilton	5,204
Nov 13	Queens Park Rangers	D 2-2	Miller, Bell	9,149
Nov 20	BOLTON WANDERERS	D 1-1	Stonehouse (pen)	7,428
Nov 27	Middlesbrough	W 5-1	Stonehouse, Brotherston 2 Bell, Randell	10,821
Dec 4	BARNSLEY	D 1-1	Brotherston	6,769
Dec 11	Shrewsbury Town	D 0-0		4,833
Dec 18	ROTHERHAM UNITED	W 3-0	Garner, Miller, Randell	6,333
Dec 27	Burnley	W 1-0	Garner	20,439
Dec 29	OLDHAM ATHLETIC	D 2-2	Garner 2	10,121
Jan 1	Bolton Wanderers	L 0-1		11,481
Jan 3	Cambridge United	L 0-2		3,471
Jan 15	WOLVERHAMPTON W.	D 2-2	Branagan, Keeley	7,401
Jan 22	Leicester City	W 1-0	Lowey	8,361
Feb 5	GRIMSBY TOWN	W 2-1	Arnott, Miller	4,724
Feb 15	Sheffield Wednesday	D 0-0		11,823
Feb 19	FULHAM	D 0-0		6,154
Feb 26	Chelsea	L 0-2		6,982
Mar 5	Leeds United	L 1-2	Lowey	12,280
Mar 13	CHARLTON ATHLETIC	W 2-0	Lowey, Miller	5,493
Mar 19	Carlisle United	L 1-3	Brotherston	4,756
Mar 26	QUEENS PARK RANGERS	L 1-3	Garner (pen)	5,317
Apr 1	Oldham Athletic	D 0-0		7,866
Apr 4	BURNLEY	W 2-1	Garner 2 (2 pens)	13,431
Apr 9	Newcastle United	L 2-3	Keeley 2	17,839
Apr 16	CRYSTAL PALACE	W 3-0	Garner 2, Lowey	4,635
Apr 23	Barnsley	D 2-2	Garner, Keeley	7,617
Apr 30	MIDDLESBROUGH	D 1-1	Lowey	4,083
May 2	DERBY COUNTY	W 2-0	Garner, Brotherston	5,619
May 7	Rotherham United	L 1-3	Bell	5,871
May 14	SHREWSBURY TOWN	W 1-0	Garner	3,797

FA Cup

Jan 8	LIVERPOOL	(Rd3) L 1-2	Garner	21,966

Milk Cup

Oct 5	Brentford	(Rd2/1L) L 2-3	Fazackerley, Stonehouse	6,201
Oct 27	BRENTFORD	(Rd2/2L) D 0-0		4,137

League & Cup Appearances

PLAYER	LEAGUE	CUP COMPETITION		TOTAL
		FA CUP	MILK	
Arnott, K.W.	11 (1)	1		12 (1)
Barton, D.	8			8
Bell, N.	31 (4)	1	2	34 (4)
Branagan, J.P.S.	36 (1)	1	2	39 (1)
Brotherston, N.	39	1	2	42
Comstive, P.T.	0 (1)			0 (1)
Devine, P.	1			1
Fazackerley, D.W.	38	1	2	41
Garner, S.	40 (1)	1	2	43 (1)
Gennoe, T.W.	33	1	2	36
Hamilton, D.	30 (2)		2	32 (2)
Keeley, G.M.	10 (4)			10 (4)
Lowey, J.A.	22			22
Mail, D.	34	1	2	37
Metcalfe, S.M.	1			1
Miller, I.	31 (1)	1	1 (1)	33 (2)
O'Keefe, J.V.	9			9
Randell, C.W.	32	1	2	35
Rathbone, M.J.	42	1	2	45
Stonehouse, K.	14 (1)		1	15 (1)

Goalscorers

PLAYER	LEAGUE	CUP COMPETITION		TOTAL
		FA CUP	MILK	
Garner, S.	22	1		23
Bell, N.	6			6
Brotherston, N.	6			6
Lowey, J.A.	5			5
Stonehouse, K.	4		1	5
Keeley, G.M.	4			4
Miller, I.	4			4
Hamilton, D.	2			2
Randell, C.W.	2			2
Arnott, K.W.	1			1
Barton, D.	1			1
Branagan, J.P.S.	1			1
Fazackerley, D.W.			1	1

Fact File

Kevin Arnott returned to Ewood Park in November 1982 for a second loan spell having spent four months with Blackburn in 1981-82.

MANAGER: Bob Saxton
TOP SCORER: Simon Garner
BIGGEST WIN: 5-1, 27 November 1982, v Middlesbrough, Division 2
HIGHEST ATTENDANCE: 21,966, 8 January 1983, v Liverpool, FA Cup Round 3
MAJOR TRANSFERS IN: Colin Randell from Plymouth Argyle, Vince O'Keefe from Torquay United
MAJOR TRANSFERS OUT: John Butcher to Oxford United, Mick Speight to Grimsby Town, Kevin Stonehouse to Huddersfield Town

Final Division 2 Table

		P	W	D	L	F	A	Pts
1	QPR	42	26	7	9	77	36	85
2	WOLVERHAMPTON W	42	20	15	7	68	44	75
3	LEICESTER C	42	20	10	12	72	44	70
4	FULHAM	42	20	9	13	64	47	69
5	NEWCASTLE U	42	18	13	11	75	53	67
6	SHEFFIELD W	42	16	15	11	60	47	63
7	OLDHAM ATH	42	14	19	9	64	47	61
8	LEEDS U	42	13	21	8	51	46	60
9	SHREWSBURY T	42	15	14	13	48	48	59
10	BARNSLEY	42	14	15	13	57	55	57
11	BLACKBURN R	42	15	12	15	58	58	57
12	CAMBRIDGE U	42	13	12	17	42	60	51
13	DERBY CO	42	10	19	13	49	58	49
14	CARLISLE U	42	12	12	18	68	70	48
15	CRYSTAL PALACE	42	12	12	18	43	52	48
16	MIDDLESBROUGH	42	11	15	16	46	67	48
17	CHARLTON ATH	42	13	9	20	63	86	48
18	CHELSEA	42	11	14	17	51	61	47
19	GRIMSBY T	42	12	11	19	45	70	47
20	ROTHERHAM U	42	10	15	17	45	68	45
21	BURNLEY	42	12	8	22	56	66	44
22	BOLTON W	42	11	11	20	42	61	44

DERBY V FULHAM ABANDONED AFTER 88 MINUTES BUT 1-0 RESULT ALLOWED TO STAND.

Football League Division 2

DATE	OPPONENTS	SCORE	GOALSCORERS	ATTENDANCE
Aug 27	HUDDERSFIELD TOWN	D 2-2	Keeley, Thompson	7,739
Aug 29	Carlisle United	W 1-0	Randell	4,470
Sep 3	Cambridge United	L 0-2		2,636
Sep 7	CHELSEA	D 0-0		5,873
Sep 10	DERBY COUNTY	W 5-1	Garner 5 (1 pen)	5,837
Sep 17	Manchester City	L 0-6		25,433
Sep 24	BRIGHTON & HOVE ALBION	D 2-2	Thompson, Garner (pen)	5,085
Oct 1	Sheffield Wednesday	L 2-4	Thompson 2	17,112
Oct 8	Middlesbrough	W 2-1	Keeley, Garner	7,062
Oct 16	SHREWSBURY TOWN	D 1-1	Garner	5,772
Oct 22	OLDHAM ATHLETIC	W 3-1	Randell, Miller, Thompson	6,178
Oct 29	Swansea City	W 1-0	Garner	7,610
Nov 5	Charlton Athletic	L 0-2		4,563
Nov 12	LEEDS UNITED	D 1-1	Devine	9,554
Nov 19	PORTSMOUTH	W 2-1	Devine, Garner	5,600
Nov 26	Fulham	W 1-0	Miller	5,647
Dec 4	GRIMSBY TOWN	D 1-1	Patterson	6,409
Dec 10	Cardiff City	W 1-0	Patterson	5,200
Dec 17	CRYSTAL PALACE	W 2-1	Garner, Mail	4,798
Dec 26	Newcastle United	D 1-1	Barker	33,622
Dec 28	BARNSLEY	D 1-1	Garner	8,960
Dec 31	CAMBRIDGE UNITED	W 1-0	Miller	5,675
Jan 2	Brighton & Hove Albion	D 1-1	Garner	9,829
Jan 14	Huddersfield Town	W 2-0	Patterson, Thompson	8,203
Jan 21	MANCHESTER CITY	W 2-1	Brotherston, Fazackerley (pen)	18,201
Feb 4	SHEFFIELD WEDNESDAY	D 0-0		16,146
Feb 11	Derby County	D 1-1	Keeley	13,020
Feb 25	Oldham Athletic	D 0-0		6,855
Mar 7	SWANSEA CITY	W 4-1	Fazackerley, Evans o.g., Thompson, Patterson	5,556
Mar 10	Leeds United	L 0-1		12,856
Mar 16	Chelsea	L 1-2	Garner	18,905
Mar 21	CHARLTON ATHLETIC	D 1-1	Thompson	4,784
Mar 24	CARLISLE UNITED	W 4-1	Garner, Barker, Hamilton, Fazackerley (pen)	6,191
Mar 30	Shrewsbury Town	L 0-1		3,352
Apr 7	MIDDLESBROUGH	W 1-0	Patterson	4,914
Apr 14	Portsmouth	W 4-2	Garner 3, Patterson	8,915
Apr 20	NEWCASTLE UNITED	D 1-1	Fazackerley (pen)	19,199
Apr 23	Barnsley	D 0-0		7,123
Apr 29	FULHAM	L 0-1		4,301
May 5	Grimsby Town	L 2-3	Garner, Barker	4,826
May 7	CARDIFF CITY	D 1-1	Patterson	3,107
May 12	Crystal Palace	W 2-0	Hamilton, Keeley	5,076

FA Cup

Jan 6	CHELSEA	(Rd3) W 1-0	Brotherston	10,940
Jan 28	Swindon Town	(Rd4) W 2-1	Garner, Batty o.g.	11,143
Feb 17	SOUTHAMPTON	(Rd5) L 0-1		15,357

Milk Cup

Oct 5	Ipswich Town	(Rd2/1L) L 3-4	Garner 2, Miller	11,537
Oct 26	IPSWICH TOWN	(Rd2/2L) L 1-2	Garner	9,000

League & Cup Appearances

PLAYER	LEAGUE	FA CUP	MILK	TOTAL
Barker, S.	28	2		30
Bell, N.	1			1
Branagan, J.P.S.	41	3	2	46
Brotherston, N.	18 (3)	3	2	23 (3)
Devine, P.	7			7
Fazackerley, D.W.	39	3	2	44
Garner, S.	42	3	2	47
Gennoe, T.W.	30	3	2	35
Glenn, D.A.	21 (1)	3		24 (1)
Hamilton, D.	24 (2)	1		27 (2)
Keeley, G.M.	35	1 (1)	2	38 (1)
Lowey, J.A.	42	3	2	47
Mail, D.	8 (3)	2	0 (1)	10 (4)
Miller, I.	35 (1)	1	2	38 (1)
O'Keefe, J.V.	12			12
Patterson, M.A.	27 (2)	2		29 (2)
Randell, C.W.	10 (1)		2	12 (1)
Rathbone, M.J.	11			11
Thompson, C.D.	31 (2)	3	2	36 (2)

Goalscorers

PLAYER	LEAGUE	FA CUP	MILK	TOTAL
Garner, S.	19	1	3	23
Thompson, C.D.	8			8
Patterson, M.A.	7			7
Fazackerley, D.W.	4			4
Keeley, G.M.	4			4
Miller, I.	3		1	4
Barker, S.	3			3
Devine, P.	2			2
Hamilton, D.	2			2
Randell, C.W.	2			2
Brotherston, N.	1	1		2
Mail, D.	1			1
Opps' o.gs.	1	1		2

Fact File

Norman Bell suffered a serious knee injury on the opening day of the season which was to force him into premature retirement.

MANAGER: Bob Saxton
TOP SCORER: Simon Garner
BIGGEST WIN: 5-1, 10 September 1983, v Derby County, Division 2
HIGHEST ATTENDANCE: 33,622, 26 December 1983, v Newcastle United, Division 2
MAJOR TRANSFERS IN: Chris Thompson from Bolton Wanderers

Final Division 2 Table

		P	W	D	L	F	A	PTS
1	CHELSEA	42	25	13	4	90	40	89
2	SHEFFIELD W	42	26	10	6	72	34	89
3	NEWCASTLE U	42	24	8	10	85	53	80
4	MANCHESTER C	42	20	10	12	66	48	70
5	GRIMSBY T	42	19	13	10	60	47	70
6	BLACKBURN R	42	17	16	9	57	46	67
7	CARLISLE U	42	16	16	10	48	41	64
8	SHREWSBURY T	42	17	10	15	49	53	61
9	BRIGHTON & HA	42	17	9	16	69	60	60
10	LEEDS U	42	16	12	14	55	56	60
11	FULHAM	42	15	12	15	60	53	57
12	HUDDERSFIELD T	42	14	15	13	56	49	57
13	CHARLTON ATH	42	16	9	17	53	64	57
14	BARNSLEY	42	15	7	20	57	53	52
15	CARDIFF C	42	15	6	21	53	66	51
16	PORTSMOUTH	42	14	7	21	73	64	49
17	MIDDLESBROUGH	42	12	13	17	41	47	49
18	CRYSTAL PALACE	42	12	11	19	42	52	47
19	OLDHAM ATH	42	13	8	21	47	73	47
20	DERBY CO	42	11	9	22	36	72	42
21	SWANSEA C	42	7	8	27	36	85	29
22	CAMBRIDGE U	42	4	12	26	28	77	24

Season 1984-85

Football League Division 2

DATE	OPPONENTS	SCORE	GOALSCORERS	ATTENDANCE
Aug 25	Crystal Palace	D 1-1	Thompson	6,709
Sep 1	CARLISLE UNITED	W 4-0	Garner, Miller, Thompson 2	5,121
Sep 4	Huddersfield Town	D 1-1	Brotherston	6,177
Sep 8	Fulham	L 2-3	Keeley, Brotherston	4,541
Sep 15	GRIMSBY TOWN	W 3-1	Garner 2, Miller	5,203
Sep 18	CARDIFF CITY	W 2-1	Barker, Thompson	5,922
Sep 22	Notts County	W 3-0	Garner, Lowey, Thompson	5,241
Sep 29	WIMBLEDON	W 2-0	Garner, Thompson	5,911
Oct 6	SHREWSBURY TOWN	W 3-1	Fazackerley (pen), Garner, Thompson	6,226
Oct 13	Birmingham City	W 2-0	Thompson 2	12,758
Oct 20	OLDHAM ATHLETIC	D 1-1	Branagan	7,300
Oct 27	Manchester City	L 1-2	Brotherston	23,798
Nov 3	Oxford United	L 1-2	Garner	9,292
Nov 10	BRIGHTON & HOVE ALBION	W 2-0	Garner, Randell	7,341
Nov 17	Middlesbrough	W 2-1	Thompson, Nattrass o.g.	4,815
Nov 24	CHARLTON ATHLETIC	W 3-0	Brotherston, Garner, Thompson	7,156
Dec 1	Portsmouth	D 2-2	Blake o.g., Tait o.g.	16,284
Dec 8	SHEFFIELD UNITED	W 3-1	Quinn 2, Thompson	9,284
Dec 15	Wolverhampton W.	W 3-0	Quinn 2, Randell	7,538
Dec 23	Carlisle United	W 1-0	Fazackerley (pen)	10,730
Dec 26	LEEDS UNITED	W 2-1	Brotherston, Randell	20,150
Dec 29	HUDDERSFIELD TOWN	L 1-3	Brotherston	15,524
Jan 1	Barnsley	D 1-1	Brotherston	10,628
Jan 12	Grimsby Town	D 1-1	Thompson	7,856
Feb 2	Wimbledon	D 1-1	Quinn	4,011
Feb 9	FULHAM	W 2-1	Quinn, Thompson	11,023
Feb 23	OXFORD UNITED	D 1-1	Quinn	12,006
Mar 2	MANCHESTER CITY	L 0-1		22,137
Mar 6	Brighton & Hove Albion	L 1-3	Fazackerley (pen)	11,117
Mar 9	Oldham Athletic	L 0-2		6,992
Mar 16	BIRMINGHAM CITY	W 2-1	Barker, Lowey	10,596
Mar 23	Shrewsbury Town	L 0-3		4,979
Mar 30	NOTTS COUNTY	W 1-0	Garner	7,132
Apr 6	Leeds United	D 0-0		15,843
Apr 8	BARNSLEY	D 0-0		9,322
Apr 13	Cardiff City	W 2-1	Garner, Miller	3,387
Apr 20	MIDDLESBROUGH	W 3-0	Garner, Miller, Thompson	8,216
Apr 23	CRYSTAL PALACE	L 0-1		9,725
Apr 27	Charlton Athletic	L 0-1		4,327
May 4	PORTSMOUTH	L 0-1		7,747
May 6	Sheffield United	W 3-1	Quinn 3	7,697
May 11	WOLVERHAMPTON W.	W 3-0	Fazackerley (pen), Lowey, Keeley	9,543

FA Cup

Jan 4	Portsmouth	(Rd3) D 0-0		14,966
Jan 26	PORTSMOUTH	(R) W 2-1	Quinn 2	12,017
Jan 30	Oxford United	(Rd4) W 1-0	Quinn	11,132
Feb 15	MANCHESTER UNITED	(Rd5) L 0-2		22,692

Milk Cup

Sep 25	OXFORD UNITED	(Rd1/1L) D 1-1	Garner	6,441
Oct 10	Oxford United	(Rd1/2L) L 1-3*	Garner	8,316

*After extra-time.

League & Cup Appearances

PLAYER	LEAGUE	CUP COMPETITION		TOTAL
		FA CUP	MILK	
Barker, S.	38	4	2	44
Branagan, J.P.S.	40	4	2	46
Brotherston, N.	32 (1)	4	2	38 (1)
Fazackerley, D.W.	39	4	2	45
Garner, S.	37	0 (2)	2	39 (2)
Gennoe, T.W.	37	4	1	42
Glenn, D.	2			2
Hamilton, D.	3	0 (1)		3 (1)
Keeley, G.M.	41	3	2	46
Lowey, J.A.	18 (3)		2	20 (3)
Mail, D.	4	1		5
Miller, I.	38	4	2	44
O'Keefe, J.V.	5		1	6
Patterson, M.A.	9			9
Quinn, J.A.	14 (11)	4	0 (1)	18 (12)
Randell, C.W.	30	4		34
Rathbone, M.J.	42	4	2	48
Thompson, C.D.	33 (2)	4	2	39 (2)

Goalscorers

PLAYER	LEAGUE	CUP COMPETITION		TOTAL
		FA CUP	MILK	
Thompson, C.D.	15			15
Garner, S.	12		2	14
Quinn, J.A.	10	3		13
Brotherston, N.	7			7
Fazackerley, D.W.	4			4
Miller, I.	4			4
Lowey, J.A.	3			3
Randell, C.W.	3			3
Barker, S.	2			2
Keeley, G.M.	2			2
Branagan, J.P.S.	1			1
Opps' o.gs.	3			3

Fact File

Blackburn held a four-point lead at the top of the Second Division at Christmas but won only seven out of 21 games after that point to end the season out of the promotion places.

MANAGER: Bob Saxton

TOP SCORER: Chris Thompson

BIGGEST WIN: 4-0, 1 September 1984, v Carlisle United, Division 2

HIGHEST ATTENDANCE: 23,798, 27 October 1984, v Manchester City, Division 2

MAJOR TRANSFERS IN: Jimmy Quinn from Swindon Town

Final Division 2 Table

		P	W	D	L	F	A	PTS
1	OXFORD U	42	25	9	8	84	36	84
2	BIRMINGHAM C	42	25	7	10	59	33	82
3	MANCHESTER C	42	21	11	10	66	40	74
4	PORTSMOUTH	42	20	14	8	69	50	74
5	BLACKBURN R	42	21	10	11	66	41	73
6	BRIGHTON & HA	42	20	12	10	54	34	72
7	LEEDS U	42	19	12	11	66	43	69
8	SHREWSBURY T	42	18	11	13	66	53	65
9	FULHAM	42	19	8	15	68	64	65
10	GRIMSBY T	42	18	8	16	72	64	62
11	BARNSLEY	42	14	16	12	42	42	58
12	WIMBLEDON	42	16	10	16	71	75	58
13	HUDDERSFIELD T	42	15	10	17	52	64	55
14	OLDHAM ATH	42	15	8	19	49	67	53
15	CRYSTAL PALACE	42	12	12	18	46	65	48
16	CARLISLE U	42	13	8	21	50	67	47
17	CHARLTON ATH	42	11	12	19	51	63	45
18	SHEFFIELD U	42	10	14	18	54	66	44
19	MIDDLESBROUGH	42	10	10	22	41	57	40
20	NOTTS CO	42	10	7	25	45	73	37
21	CARDIFF C	42	9	8	25	47	79	35
22	WOLVERHAMPTON W	42	8	9	25	37	79	33

Season 1985-86

Football League Division 2

DATE	OPPONENTS	SCORE	GOALSCORERS	ATTENDANCE
Aug 17	Sunderland	W 2-0	Patterson, Quinn	21,202
Aug 20	NORWICH CITY	W 2-1	Fazackerley (pen), Garner	6,581
Aug 24	SHREWSBURY TOWN	D 1-1	Garner	6,072
Aug 26	Hull City	D 2-2	Patterson, Barker	7,288
Aug 31	CARLISLE UNITED	W 2-0	Garner, Patterson	5,955
Sep 3	Huddersfield Town	D 0-0		9,060
Sep 7	Brighton & Hove Albion	L 1-3	Keeley	8,151
Sep 14	WIMBLEDON	W 2-0	Patterson 2	5,006
Sep 21	FULHAM	W 1-0	Patterson	5,241
Sep 28	Portsmouth	L 0-3		16,870
Oct 5	BRADFORD CITY	W 3-0	Quinn, Keeley, Garner	7,728
Oct 12	Millwall	W 1-0	Garner	6,050
Oct 19	OLDHAM ATHLETIC	D 0-0		9,666
Oct 26	Crystal Palace	L 0-2		5,408
Nov 2	Middlesbrough	D 0-0		5,140
Nov 9	BARNSLEY	L 0-3		5,927
Nov 16	Sheffield United	D 3-3	Keeley, Barker, Lowey	13,610
Nov 23	CHARLTON ATHLETIC	D 0-0		5,320
Nov 30	Grimsby Town	L 2-5	Lowey 2	5,012
Dec 7	Norwich City	L 0-3		12,156
Dec 14	SUNDERLAND	W 2-0	Barker (pen), Garner	6,072
Dec 20	Shrewsbury Town	L 0-2		3,174
Dec 26	LEEDS UNITED	W 2-0	Brotherston, Barker	8,666
Jan 1	Stoke City	D 2-2	Garner, Barker (pen)	11,875
Jan 18	Carlisle United	L 1-2	Garner	3,801
Feb 1	HULL CITY	D 2-2	Ainscow 2	5,414
Feb 8	Oldham Athletic	L 1-3	Barker	5,314
Feb 15	CRYSTAL PALACE	L 1-2	Keeley	4,825
Mar 1	PORTSMOUTH	W 1-0	Garner	4,980
Mar 8	Bradford City	L 2-3	Quinn, Hamilton	5,263
Mar 11	Fulham	D 3-3	Patterson, Garner, Quinn	2,564
Mar 15	MILLWALL	L 1-2	Barker	4,336
Mar 18	BRIGHTON & HOVE ALBION	L 1-4	Barker (pen)	3,587
Mar 22	Wimbledon	D 1-1	Miller	3,271
Mar 29	STOKE CITY	L 0-1		5,408
Mar 31	Leeds United	D 1-1	Mail	9,911
Apr 5	MIDDLESBROUGH	L 0-1		4,049
Apr 12	Barnsley	D 1-1	Hamilton	4,256
Apr 15	HUDDERSFIELD TOWN	L 0-1		5,183
Apr 19	SHEFFIELD UNITED	W 6-1	Garner, Patterson 3, Thompson, Barker	4,736
Apr 26	Charlton Athletic	L 0-3		5,766
May 5	GRIMSBY TOWN	W 3-1	Garner, Hamilton, Barker (pen)	7,600

FA Cup

Jan 4	Nottingham Forest	(Rd3) D 1-1	Thompson	15,772
Jan 13	NOTTINGHAM FOREST	(R) W 3-2	Lowey, Brotherston, Thompson	11,710
Jan 25	Everton	(Rd4) L 1-3	Van den Hauwe o.g.	41,831

Milk Cup

Sep 24	Wimbledon	(Rd2/1L) L 0-5		2,110
Oct 8	WIMBLEDON	(Rd2/2L) W 2-1	Patterson, Quinn	2,161

League & Cup Appearances

PLAYER	LEAGUE	CUP COMPETITION		TOTAL
		FA CUP	MILK	
Ainscow, A	5			5
Barker, S.	41	3	1	45
Branagan, J.P.S.	32 (1)	3	1	36 (1)
Brotherston, N.	18 (1)	3		21 (1)
Fazackerley, D.W.	36 (1)	3	2	41 (1)
Garner, S.	36 (2)	3	2	41 (2)
Gennoe, T.W.	32	3	1	36
Hamilton, D.	31 (2)		2	33 (2)
Keeley, G.M.	31	1	2	34
Lowey, J.A.	23	3	2	28
Mail, D.	17 (1)	2		19 (1)
Miller, I.	38	3	1	42
O'Keefe, J.V.	10		1	11
Patterson, M.A.	24 (2)		2	26 (2)
Quinn, J.M.	29 (2)		2	31 (2)
Rathbone, M.J.	42	3	2	47
Thompson, C.D.	17	3	1	21

Goalscorers

PLAYER	LEAGUE	CUP COMPETITION		TOTAL
		FA CUP	MILK	
Garner, S.	12			12
Patterson, M.A.	10		1	11
Barker, S.	10			10
Quinn, J.M.	4		1	5
Keeley, G.M.	4			4
Lowey, J.A.	3	1		4
Hamilton, D.	3			3
Thompson, C.D.	1	2		3
Ainscow, A.	2			2
Brotherston, N.	1	1		2
Fazackerley, D.W.	1			1
Mail, D.	1			1
Miller, I.	1			1
Opps' o.gs.	1			1

Fact File

Only a last day win over Grimsby Town prevented Blackburn Rovers from being relegated to the Third Division.

MANAGER: Bob Saxton

TOP SCORER: Simon Garner

BIGGEST WIN: 6-1, 19 April 1986, v Sheffield United, Division 2

HIGHEST ATTENDANCE: 41,831, 25 January 1986, v Everton, FA Cup Round 4

MAJOR TRANSFERS IN: Alan Ainscow from Wolverhampton Wanderers

MAJOR TRANSFERS OUT: Colin Randell to Swansea City, David Glenn to Chester City

Final Division 2 Table

		P	W	D	L	F	A	PTS
1	NORWICH C	42	25	9	8	84	37	84
2	CHARLTON ATH	42	22	11	9	78	45	77
3	WIMBLEDON	42	21	13	8	58	37	76
4	PORTSMOUTH	42	22	7	13	69	41	73
5	CRYSTAL PALACE	42	19	9	14	57	52	66
6	HULL C	42	17	13	12	65	55	64
7	SHEFFIELD U	42	17	11	14	64	63	62
8	OLDHAM ATH	42	17	9	16	62	61	60
9	MILLWALL	42	17	8	17	64	65	59
10	STOKE C	42	14	15	13	48	50	57
11	BRIGHTON & HA	42	16	8	18	64	64	56
12	BARNSLEY	42	14	14	14	47	50	56
13	BRADFORD C	42	16	6	20	51	63	54
14	LEEDS U	42	15	8	19	56	72	53
15	GRIMSBY T	42	14	10	18	58	62	52
16	HUDDERSFIELD T	42	14	10	18	51	67	52
17	SHREWSBURY T	42	14	9	19	52	64	51
18	SUNDERLAND	42	13	11	18	47	61	50
19	BLACKBURN R	42	12	13	17	53	62	49
20	CARLISLE U	42	13	7	22	47	71	46
21	MIDDLESBROUGH	42	12	9	21	44	53	45
22	FULHAM	42	10	6	26	45	69	36

Season 1986-87

Football League Division 2

DATE	OPPONENTS	SCORE	GOALSCORERS	ATTENDANCE
Aug 23	LEEDS UNITED	W 2-1	Quinn (pen), Barker	8,346
Aug 30	Shrewsbury Town	W 1-0	Sellars	3,186
Sep 6	SUNDERLAND	W 6-1	Garner 4, Barker, Quinn	7,115
Sep 13	Portsmouth	L 0-1		8,773
Sep 20	CRYSTAL PALACE	L 0-2		5,921
Sep 27	Millwall	D 2-2	Steven o.g., Patterson	3,025
Sep 30	PLYMOUTH ARGYLE	L 1-2	Fazackerley	5,300
Oct 4	Reading	L 0-4		6,781
Oct 11	WEST BROMWICH ALBION	L 0-1		5,701
Oct 18	Stoke City	L 0-1		7,715
Nov 1	Barnsley	D 1-1	Sellars (pen)	4,861
Nov 8	SHEFFIELD UNITED	L 0-2		5,869
Nov 15	HULL CITY	L 0-2		4,149
Nov 22	Brighton & Hove Albion	W 2-0	Young o.g., Quinn	7,362
Nov 29	IPSWICH TOWN	D 0-0		4,951
Dec 2	Grimsby Town	L 0-1		3,483
Dec 6	Birmingham City	D 1-1	Keeley	6,428
Dec 21	Sunderland	L 0-3		11,843
Dec 26	HUDDERSFIELD TOWN	L 1-2	Garner	7,144
Dec 27	Hull City	D 0-0		5,789
Jan 3	PORTSMOUTH	W 1-0	Sellars	6,582
Jan 17	GRIMSBY TOWN	D 2-2	Barker 2	4,654
Jan 24	Leeds United	D 0-0		14,458
Jan 31	OLDHAM ATHLETIC	W 1-0	Diamond	7,643
Feb 7	SHREWSBURY TOWN	W 2-1	Branagan, Diamond	5,598
Feb 14	Plymouth Argyle	D 1-1	Ainscow	9,884
Feb 21	MILLWALL	W 1-0	Barker (pen)	5,422
Feb 28	Crystal Palace	L 0-2		5,891
Mar 7	Bradford City	L 0-2		8,521
Mar 14	STOKE CITY	W 2-1	Price, Berry o.g.	10,073
Mar 18	Derby County	L 2-3	Barker (pen), Hendry	15,576
Mar 21	West Bromwich Albion	W 1-0	Hendry	8,565
Mar 24	BRADFORD CITY	W 2-1	Barker 2 (1 pen)	8,683
Apr 4	Sheffield United	L 1-4	Barker (pen)	7,762
Apr 11	BARNSLEY	W 4-2	Barker 2 (1 pen), Curry, Ainscow	7,320
Apr 14	READING	D 0-0		6,609
Apr 17	DERBY COUNTY	W 3-1	Garner 2, Curry	13,019
Apr 20	Huddersfield Town	W 2-1	Garner 2	7,731
Apr 25	BRIGHTON & HOVE ALBION	D 1-1	Sellars	6,509
May 2	Ipswich Town	L 1-3	Hendry	10,703
May 5	BIRMINGHAM CITY	W 1-0	Garner	8,844
May 9	Oldham Athletic	L 0-3		7,504

FA Cup

Jan 10	Portsmouth	(Rd3) L 0-2		10,679

Littlewoods Cup

Aug 26	Wigan Athletic	(Rd1/1L) W 3-1	Ainscow, Barker, Thompson o.g.	2,368
Sep 2	WIGAN ATHLETIC	(Rd1/2L) W 2-0	Barker 2	2,831
Sep 23	Queens Park Rangers	(Rd2/1L) L 1-2	Garner	6,512
Oct 7	QUEENS PARK RANGERS	(Rd2/2L) D 2-2	Barker, Quinn (pen)	5,100

Full Members' Cup

Sep 16	Huddersfield Town	(Rd1) W 2-1*	Quinn, Brotherston	1,947
Nov 4	SHEFFIELD UNITED	(Rd2) W 1-0	Garner	2,220
Jan 20	OXFORD UNITED	(Rd3) W 3-1	Garner, Keeley, Barker (pen), Ainscow	2,843
Mar 3	CHELSEA	(QF) W 3-0	Curry, Garner, Miller	7,298
Mar 11	IPSWICH TOWN	(SF) W 3-0	Garner, Barker (pen), Patterson	12,060
Mar 29	Charlton Athletic†		W 1-0	Hendry	40,000

*After extra-time. †Played at Wembley Stadium.

MANAGER: Bob Saxton/Don Mackay

TOP SCORER: Simon Barker

BIGGEST WIN: 6-1, 6 September 1986, v Sunderland, Division 2

HIGHEST ATTENDANCE: 40,000, 29 March 1987 v Charlton Athletic, Full Members' Cup final

MAJOR TRANSFERS IN: Scott Sellars from Leeds United, Chris Price from Hereford United, Chris Sulley from Dundee United, Colin Hendry from Dundee

MAJOR TRANSFERS OUT: Chris Thompson to Wigan Athletic, John Lowey to Wigan Athletic, Jimmy Quinn to Swindon Town, Derek Fazackerley to Chester City

League & Cup Appearances

PLAYER	LEAGUE	CUP COMPETITION			TOTAL
		FA CUP	LITTLEWOODS	FMC	
Ainscow, A.	15 (2)		1(1)	3 (1)	19 (4)
Barker, S.	42	1	4	6	53
Branagan, J.P.S.	28 (2)		3	5	36 (2)
Brotherston, N.	16 (2)	1	3	2 (1)	22 (3)
Curry, S.P.	9 (2)			1	10 (2)
Diamond, A.J.	6 (2)			1	7 (2)
Fazackerley, D.W.	7		2		9
Garner, S.	39 (1)	1	4	6	50 (1)
Gennoe, T.W.	11			1	12
Hendry, E.C.J.	12 (1)		2		14 (1)
Keeley, G.M.	35	1	2	5	43
McKinnon, P.	5		1	1	7
Mail, D.	38	1	4	6	49
Miller, I.	28	0 (1)		4 (1)	32 (2)
Mimms, R.A.	6				6
O'Keefe, J.V.	25	1	4	5	35
Patterson, M.A.	18 (6)	1	2	1 (4)	22 (10)
Price, C.J.	40	1	4	5	50
Quinn, J.M.	15		4	2	21
Rathbone, M.J.	24 (1)	1	3	4	32 (1)
Sellars, S.	30 (2)	1	4	4	39 (2)
Sulley, C.S.	13			2	15

Goalscorers

PLAYER	LEAGUE	CUP COMPETITION			TOTAL
		FA CUP	LITTLEWOODS	FMC	
Barker, S.	11		4	2	17
Garner, S.	10		1	4	15
Quinn, J.M.	3		1	1	5
Sellars, S.	4				4
Hendry, E.C.J.	3			1	4
Ainscow, A.	2		1	1	4
Curry, S.P.	2			1	3
Diamond, A.J.	2				2
Keeley, G.M.	1			1	2
Patterson, M.A.	1			1	2
Branagan, J.P.S.	1				1
Fazackerley, D.W.	1				1
Price, C.J.	1				1
Brotherston, N.				1	1
Miller, I.				1	1
Opps' o.gs.	3		1		4

Fact File

Simon Barker won the Man of the Match award at Wembley in the Full Members' Cup final.

Final Division 2 Table

		P	W	D	L	F	A	PTS
1	DERBY CO	42	25	9	8	64	38	84
2	PORTSMOUTH	42	23	9	10	53	28	78
3	OLDHAM ATH	42	22	9	11	65	44	75
4	LEEDS U	42	19	11	12	58	44	68
5	IPSWICH T	42	17	13	12	59	43	64
6	CRYSTAL PALACE	42	19	5	18	51	53	62
7	PLYMOUTH ARG	42	16	13	13	62	57	61
8	STOKE C	42	16	10	16	63	53	58
9	SHEFFIELD U	42	15	13	14	50	49	58
10	BRADFORD C	42	15	10	17	62	62	55
11	BARNSLEY	42	14	13	15	49	52	55
12	BLACKBURN R	42	15	10	17	45	55	55
13	READING	42	14	11	17	52	59	53
14	HULL C	42	13	14	15	41	55	53
15	WBA	42	13	12	17	51	49	51
16	MILLWALL	42	14	9	19	39	45	51
17	HUDDERSFIELD T	42	13	12	17	54	61	51
18	SHREWSBURY T	42	15	6	21	41	53	51
19	BIRMINGHAM C	42	11	17	14	47	59	50
20	SUNDERLAND	42	12	12	18	49	59	48
21	GRIMSBY T	42	10	14	18	39	59	44
22	BRIGHTON & HA	42	9	12	21	37	54	39

Season 1987-88

Football League Division 2

DATE	OPPONENTS	SCORE	GOALSCORERS	ATTENDANCE
Aug 15	Hull City	D 2-2	Garner, Patterson	6,427
Aug 18	BARNSLEY	L 0-1		6,708
Aug 22	WEST BROMWICH ALBION	W 3-1	Curry, Garner, Hendry	5,619
Aug 29	Sheffield United	L 1-3	Garner	8,540
Sep 1	IPSWICH TOWN	W 1-0	Hendry	6,074
Sep 5	Manchester City	W 2-1	Patterson, Curry	20,372
Sep 12	HUDDERSFIELD TOWN	D 2-2	Barker (pen), Gayle	7,109
Sep 15	Birmingham City	L 0-1		6,032
Sep 19	Bradford City	L 1-2	Curry	12,037
Sep 26	MIDDLESBROUGH	L 0-2		6,879
Sep 30	Aston Villa	D 1-1	Barker	11,772
Oct 3	LEEDS UNITED	D 1-1	Garner	7,675
Oct 10	AFC Bournemouth	D 1-1	Price	6,789
Oct 17	STOKE CITY	W 2-0	Sellars, Garner	7,280
Oct 24	PLYMOUTH ARGYLE	D 1-1	Sellars (pen)	6,014
Oct 31	Leicester City	W 2-1	Garner, Hendry	8,650
Nov 7	OLDHAM ATHLETIC	W 1-0	Reid	7,521
Nov 14	Shrewsbury Town	W 2-1	Curry, Price	3,165
Nov 21	CRYSTAL PALACE	W 2-0	Barker, Price	6,371
Nov 28	Reading	D 0-0		4,755
Dec 5	MILLWALL	W 2-1	Sellars, Hendry	6,140
Dec 12	West Bromwich Albion	W 1-0	Price	7,413
Dec 19	BIRMINGHAM CITY	W 2-0	Hendry, Sellars	8,542
Dec 26	Middlesbrough	D 1-1	Garner	23,406
Dec 28	BRADFORD CITY	D 1-1	Hendry	14,123
Jan 1	SHEFFIELD UNITED	W 4-1	Price, Garner, Barker (pen), Hendry	10,493
Jan 2	Huddersfield Town	W 2-1	Garner, Barker	10,735
Jan 16	HULL CITY	W 2-1	Archibald, Price	9,682
Jan 30	Ipswich Town	W 2-0	Sellars, Ainscow	12,849
Feb 6	MANCHESTER CITY	W 2-1	Garner, Price	13,508
Feb 13	Barnsley	W 1-0	Sellars	8,972
Feb 20	ASTON VILLA	W 3-2	Garner, Archibald 2	17,356
Feb 27	Leeds United	D 2-2	Garner, Hendry	24,350
Mar 5	Stoke City	L 1-2	Price	14,103
Mar 12	AFC BOURNEMOUTH	W 3-1	Barker, Price, Archibald	10,807
Mar 19	LEICESTER CITY	D 3-3	Walsh o.g., Sellars, Hendry	12,506
Mar 26	Plymouth Argyle	L 0-3		12,359
Apr 1	Oldham Athletic	L 2-4	Hendry, Barker	14,853
Apr 4	SHREWSBURY TOWN	D 2-2	Hendry, Barker	13,741
Apr 9	Swindon Town	W 2-1	Archibald 2	9,373
Apr 25	SWINDON TOWN	D 0-0		13,563
Apr 30	Crystal Palace	L 0-2		13,059
May 2	READING	D 1-1	Hendry	11,373
May 7	Millwall	W 4-1	Price, Garner 2, Barker	15,467

Play-offs

May 15	CHELSEA	(SF/1L) L 0-2		16,598
May 18	Chelsea	(SF/2L) L 1-4	Sellars	23,509

FA Cup

Jan 9	PORTSMOUTH	(Rd3) L 1-2	Garner	10,352

Littlewoods Cup

Sep 23	LIVERPOOL	(Rd2/1L) D 1-1	Sellars	13,924
Oct 6	Liverpool	(Rd2/2L) L 0-1		28,994

Simod Cup

Nov 10	SWINDON TOWN	(Rd1) L 1-2	Reid	3,638

MANAGER: Don Mackay

TOP SCORER: Simon Garner

BIGGEST WIN: 4-1, 1 January 1988, v Sheffield United, Division 2; 7 May 1988, v Millwall, Division 2

HIGHEST ATTENDANCE: 28,994, 6 October 1987, v Liverpool, Littlewoods Cup Round 2 second leg

MAJOR TRANSFERS IN: Nicky Reid from Manchester City, Ally Dawson from Rangers, Howard Gayle from Stoke City, Steve Archibald on loan from Barcelona, Ossie Ardiles on loan from Tottenham Hotspur

MAJOR TRANSFERS OUT: Noel Brotherston to Bury, Mick Rathbone to Preston North End, Glenn Keeley to Oldham Athletic

League & Cup Appearances

PLAYER	LEAGUE	CUP COMPETITION				TOTAL
		FA CUP	LITTLEWOODS	SIMOD	OTHER	
Ainscow, A.	16 (12)				1 1	18 (12)
Archibald, S.	20	1			1	22
Ardiles, O.C.	5				1 (1)	6 (1)
Barker, S.	31 (2)	1	2		2	36 (2)
Curry, S.P.	15 (5)	0 (1)	2	1		18 (6)
Dawson, A.J.	20 (2)	1	1	0 (1)		22 (3)
Diamond, A.J.	2 (5)			0 (1)		2 (6)
Garner, S.	40	1	2		2	45
Gayle, H.A.	10 (3)		1		2	13 (3)
Gennoe, T.W.	39	1	2	1	2	45
Hendry, E.C.J.	44		1	1	2	48
Hill, K.J.	1	1	1		0 (2)	3 (2)
Johnrose, L.	0 (1)					0 (1)
Mail, D.	34 (2)	1	2	1	2	40 (2)
Millar, J.	13 (2)		0 (1)		2	15 (3)
Miller, I.	19 (4)		0 (1)	1		20 (5)
O'Keefe, J.V.	5					5
Patterson, M.A.	11 (2)	0 (1)				12 (3)
Price, C.J.	43	1	2	1	1	48
Reid, N.S.	44	1	2	1	2	50
Sellars, S.	38 (4)	1	2	1	2	44 (4)
Sulley, C.S.	34	1	2	1		38

Goalscorers

PLAYER	LEAGUE	CUP COMPETITION				TOTAL
		FA CUP	LITTLEWOODS	SIMOD	OTHER	
Garner, S.	14	1				15
Hendry, E.C.J.	12					12
Price, C.J.	10					10
Barker, S.	9					9
Sellars, S.	7		1		1	9
Archibald, S.	6					6
Curry, S.P.	4					4
Patterson, M.A.	2					2
Reid, N.S.	1		1			2
Ainscow, A.	1					1
Gayle, H.A.	1					1
Opps' o.gs.	1					1

Fact File

Blackburn rocked the world of football in December 1987 when Steve Archibald agreed to leave Barcelona and spend six months on loan at Ewood Park.

Final Division 2 Table

		P	W	D	L	F	A	Pts
1	MILLWALL	44	25	7	12	72	52	82
2	ASTON VILLA	44	22	12	10	68	41	78
3	MIDDLESBROUGH	44	22	12	10	63	36	78
4	BRADFORD C	44	22	11	11	74	54	77
5	BLACKBURN R	44	21	14	9	68	52	77
6	CRYSTAL PALACE	44	22	9	13	86	59	75
7	LEEDS U	44	19	12	13	61	51	69
8	IPSWICH T	44	19	9	16	61	52	66
9	MANCHESTER C	44	19	8	17	80	60	65
10	OLDHAM ATH	44	18	11	15	72	64	65
11	STOKE C	44	17	11	16	50	57	62
12	SWINDON T	44	16	11	17	73	60	59
13	LEICESTER C	44	16	11	17	62	61	59
14	BARNSLEY	44	15	12	17	61	62	57
15	HULL C	44	14	15	15	54	60	57
16	PLYMOUTH ARG	44	16	8	20	65	67	56
17	BOURNEMOUTH	44	13	10	21	56	68	49
18	SHREWSBURY T	44	11	16	17	42	54	49
19	BIRMINGHAM C	44	11	15	18	41	66	48
20	WBA	44	12	11	21	50	69	47
21	SHEFFIELD U	44	13	7	24	45	74	46
22	READING	44	10	12	22	44	70	42
23	HUDDERSFIELD T	44	6	10	28	41	100	28

Season 1988-89

Football League Division 2

DATE	OPPONENTS	SCORE	GOALSCORERS	ATTENDANCE
Aug 27	Chelsea	W 2-1	Gayle 2 (1 pen)	8,772
Sep 3	OLDHAM ATHLETIC	W 3-1	Garner 3	9,992
Sep 10	Stoke City	W 1-0	Hendry	8,625
Sep 17	SWINDON TOWN	D 0-0		7,622
Sep 20	Hull City	W 3-1	Hendry, Garner 2	6,681
Sep 24	BIRMINGHAM CITY	W 3-0	Garner 2, Hendry	7,562
Oct 1	Manchester City	L 0-1		22,111
Oct 5	Bradford City	D 1-1	Hendry	13,022
Oct 8	CRYSTAL PALACE	W 5-4	Gayle 2 (1 pen), Garner 2, Hendry	8,022
Oct 15	BARNSLEY	W 2-1	Kennedy, Gayle (pen)	9,316
Oct 22	Oxford United	D 1-1	Garner	6,498
Oct 25	Sunderland	L 0-2		16,601
Oct 29	WEST BROMWICH ALBION	L 1-2	Hill	9,503
Nov 5	Plymouth Argyle	L 3-4	Reid, Garner, Kennedy	7,823
Nov 12	BRIGHTON & HOVE ALBION	W 2-1	Kennedy 2	6,980
Nov 19	Walsall	W 2-1	Kennedy 2	5,848
Nov 22	SHREWSBURY TOWN	L 0-1		6,898
Nov 26	PORTSMOUTH	W 3-1	Hendry, Gayle 2	8,146
Dec 3	AFC Bournemouth	L 1-2	Garner	8,418
Dec 10	IPSWICH TOWN	W 1-0	Gayle (pen)	7,262
Dec 17	WATFORD	W 2-1	Hildersley, Gayle	8,808
Dec 26	Leeds United	L 0-2		31,595
Dec 31	Leicester City	L 0-4		10,820
Jan 2	STOKE CITY	W 4-3	Atkins, Gayle (pen), Kennedy, Hildersley	11,629
Jan 14	Shrewsbury Town	D 1-1	Hildersley	3,879
Jan 21	CHELSEA	D 1-1	Hill	11,713
Feb 4	BRADFORD CITY	W 2-1	Gayle, Atkins	9,571
Feb 11	Crystal Palace	D 2-2	Gayle, Miller	11,270
Feb 21	OXFORD UNITED	W 3-1	Hendry, Slatter o.g., Diamond	5,724
Feb 25	Barnsley	W 1-0	Garner	8,777
Feb 28	SUNDERLAND	D 2-2	Atkins, Gray o.g.	8,288
Mar 4	Brighton & Hove Albion	L 0-3		8,075
Mar 11	PLYMOUTH ARGYLE	L 1-2	Hildersley	7,462
Mar 15	West Bromwich Albion	L 0-2		12,821
Mar 18	HULL CITY	W 4-0	Garner, Gayle 2 (1 pen), Kennedy	5,864
Mar 24	Oldham Athletic	D 1-1	Garner	11,752
Mar 27	LEEDS UNITED	W 2-0	Kennedy, Gayle	11,533
Apr 1	Swindon Town	D 1-1	Gayle	8,220
Apr 4	Watford	D 2-2	Atkins, Gayle	8,667
Apr 8	LEICESTER CITY	D 0-0		8,103
Apr 15	MANCHESTER CITY	W 4-0	Kennedy, Garner 3	16,927
Apr 22	Birmingham City	L 0-2		5,813
Apr 29	Portsmouth	W 2-1	Gayle 2 (2 pens)	6,057
May 1	AFC Bournemouth	W 2-0	Atkins, Gayle	9,345
May 6	WALSALL	W 3-0	Garner, Sellars 2	8,229
May 13	Ipswich Town	L 0-2		11,081

Play-offs

May 21	Watford	(SF/1L) D 0-0		14,008
May 24	WATFORD	(SF/2L) D 1-1*†	Garner	13,854
May 31	CRYSTAL PALACE	(F/1L) W 3-1	Gayle 2, Garner	16,421
Jun 3	Crystal Palace	(F/2L) L 0-3		26,358

*After extra-time. †Blackburn won on the away-goals rule.

FA Cup

Jan 7	Welling United	(Rd3) W 1-0	Hildersley	3,850
Jan 28	SHEFFIELD WEDNESDAY	(Rd4) W 2-1	Garner, Finnigan	16,235
Feb 18	BRENTFORD	(Rd5) L 0-2		15,280

Littlewoods Cup

Sep 27	BRENTFORD	(Rd1/1L) W 3-1	Gayle, Sellars, Garner	4,606
Oct 12	Brentford	(Rd2/2L) L 3-4	Garner, Atkins, Sellars	3,844
Nov 1	Tottenham Hotspur	(Rd3) D 0-0		18,814
Nov 9	TOTTENHAM HOTSPUR	(R) L 1-2*	Butters o.g.	12,965

*After extra-time.

Simod Cup

Dec 13	MANCHESTER CITY	(Rd1) W 3-2*	Atkins, Kennedy 2 (1 pen)	5,763
Dec 22	SUNDERLAND	(Rd2) W 2-1	Gayle (pen), Finnigan	4,457
Jan 10	Ipswich Town	(Rd3) L 0-1		8,155

*After extra-time.

MANAGER: Don Mackay

TOP SCORER: Simon Garner

BIGGEST WIN: 4-0, 18 March 1989, v Hull City, Division 2;
15 April 1989, v Manchester City, Division 2

League & Cup Appearances

PLAYER	LEAGUE	CUP COMPETITION				TOTAL
		FA CUP	LITTLEWOODS	SIMOD	OTHER	
Ainscow, A.	6 (9)		1	0 (1)	0 (2)	7 (12)
Atkins, M.N.	46	3	4	3	4	60
Byrne, D.S.	4					4
Collier, D.J.	1					1
Curry, S.P.	1 (6)		1 (2)	0 (1)	0 (2)	2 (11)
Dawson, A.J.	3 (3)	2	1			6 (3)
Diamond, A.J.	1 (10)					1 (10)
Finnigan, A.	13 (4)	3	1	3		20 (4)
Gayle, H.A.	45	3	4	2	4	58
Garner, S.	43 (1)	3	4	2	4	56 (1)
Gennoe, T.W.	43	3	3	2	4	55
Hendry, E.C.J.	38	3	3	3	4	51
Hildersley, R.	23 (2)	3		3		29 (2)
Hill, K.J.	13 (2)	1 (1)	1	1		16 (3)
Kennedy, A.J.	23 (2)	1	2	3		29 (2)
Mail, D.	40	2	4	2	4	52
May, D.	1					1
Millar, J.	37 (1)		4	1	4	46 (1)
Miller, I.	21 (10)	2	1	0 (2)	4	28 (12)
O'Keefe, J.V.	2		1	1		4
Reid, N.S.	37	0 (1)	4	2	4	47 (1)
Sellars, S.	46	3	4	3	4	60
Sulley, C.S.	19	3		1	4	27

Goalscorers

PLAYER	LEAGUE	CUP COMPETITION				TOTAL
		FA CUP	LITTLEWOODS	SIMOD	OTHER	
Garner, S.	20	1	2		2	25
Gayle, H.A.	19		1	1	2	23
Kennedy, A.J.	10			2		12
Hendry, E.C.J.	7					7
Atkins, M.N.	5		1	1		7
Hildersley, R.	4	1				5
Sellars, S.	2		2			4
Hill, K.J.	2					2
Finnigan, A.	1		1			2
Diamond, A.J.	1					1
Miller, I.	1					1
Reid, N.S.	1					1
Opps' o.gs.	2		1			3

Fact File

The second goal that Simon Garner scored against Manchester City in April 1989 broke Tommy Briggs's club record of 140 league goals.

Final Division 2 Table

		P	W	D	L	F	A	Pts
1	CHELSEA	46	29	12	5	96	50	99
2	MANCHESTER C	46	23	13	10	77	53	82
3	CRYSTAL PALACE	46	23	12	11	71	49	81
4	WATFORD	46	22	12	12	74	48	78
5	BLACKBURN R	46	22	11	13	74	59	77
6	SWINDON T	46	20	16	10	68	53	76
7	BARNSLEY	46	20	14	12	66	58	74
8	IPSWICH T	46	22	7	17	71	61	73
9	WBA	46	18	18	10	65	41	72
10	LEEDS U	46	17	16	13	59	50	67
11	SUNDERLAND	46	16	15	15	60	60	63
12	BOURNEMOUTH	46	18	8	20	53	62	62
13	STOKE C	46	15	14	17	57	72	59
14	BRADFORD C	46	13	17	16	52	59	56
15	LEICESTER C	46	13	16	17	56	63	55
16	OLDHAM ATH	46	11	21	14	75	72	54
17	OXFORD U	46	14	12	20	62	70	54
18	PLYMOUTH ARG	46	14	12	20	55	66	54
19	BRIGHTON & HA	46	14	9	23	57	66	51
20	PORTSMOUTH	46	13	12	21	53	62	51
21	HULL C	46	11	14	21	52	68	47
22	SHREWSBURY T	46	8	18	20	40	67	42
23	BIRMINGHAM C	46	8	11	27	31	76	35
24	WALSALL	46	5	16	25	41	80	31

Season 1989-90

Football League Division 2

DATE	OPPONENTS	SCORE	GOALSCORERS	ATTENDANCE
Aug 19	OLDHAM ATHLETIC	W 1-0	Garner	9,939
Aug 23	Leicester City	W 1-0	Sellars	11,411
Aug 26	Leeds United	D 1-1	Atkins	25,045
Sep 2	OXFORD UNITED	D 2-2	Sellars, Gayle	7,578
Sep 9	Port Vale	D 0-0		7,601
Sep 16	SUNDERLAND	D 1-1	Millar	10,329
Sep 23	AFC Bournemouth	W 4-2	Kennedy, Stapleton, Reid, Sellars	7,000
Sep 27	West Bromwich Albion	D 2-2	Garner, Sellars	9,269
Sep 30	BARNSLEY	W 5-0	Garner 3, Sellars, Kennedy	8,415
Oct 14	Portsmouth	D 1-1	Kennedy (pen)	7,004
Oct 18	Newcastle United	L 1-2	Kennedy	20,702
Oct 21	WATFORD	D 2-2	Kennedy (pen), Garner	7,950
Oct 28	Plymouth Argyle	D 2-2	Gayle, Sellars	6,876
Oct 31	HULL CITY	D 0-0		7,456
Nov 4	Brighton & Hove Albion	W 2-1	Garner, Sellars	7,445
Nov 11	IPSWICH TOWN	D 2-2	Johnrose, Atkins (pen)	7,913
Nov 18	Wolverhampton W.	W 2-1	Garner, Reid	14,695
Nov 21	MIDDLESBROUGH	L 2-4	Stapleton, Johnrose	8,317
Nov 25	WEST HAM UNITED	W 5-4	Sellars 2, Garner, Stapleton, Johnrose	10,215
Dec 1	Oldham Athletic	L 0-2		10,635
Dec 9	LEICESTER CITY	L 2-4	Garner, Gayle	7,538
Dec 26	Swindon Town	L 3-4	Garner, Kennedy (pen), Gayle	8,426
Dec 30	Sheffield United	W 2-1	Kennedy, Garner	17,279
Jan 1	BRADFORD CITY	D 2-2	Kennedy 2 (1 pen)	9,957
Jan 13	LEEDS UNITED	L 1-2	Garner	14,485
Jan 20	Oxford United	D 1-1	Atkins	5,973
Jan 27	STOKE CITY	W 3-0	Kennedy, Gayle (pen), Sellars	9,132
Feb 3	AFC BOURNEMOUTH	D 1-1	Atkins	7,947
Feb 10	Sunderland	W 1-0	Reid	16,043
Feb 17	PORT VALE	W 1-0	Garner	9,240
Feb 24	West Ham United	D 1-1	Sellars	20,054
Mar 3	WOLVERHAMPTON W.	L 2-3	Garner, Kennedy	12,064
Mar 10	WEST BROMWICH ALBION	W 2-1	Atkins, Reid	8,148
Mar 17	Middlesbrough	W 3-0	Garner, Kennedy, Moran	15,259
Mar 20	PORTSMOUTH	W 2-0	Atkins, Garner	8,047
Mar 24	NEWCASTLE UNITED	W 2-0	Moran, Sellars	13,285
Mar 31	Watford	L 1-3	Irvine	9,096
Apr 3	Barnsley	D 0-0		8,713
Apr 7	PLYMOUTH ARGYLE	W 2-0	Sellars 2	7,492
Apr 10	Hull City	L 0-2		5,327
Apr 14	Bradford City	W 1-0	Oliver o.g.	9,082
Apr 16	SWINDON TOWN	W 2-1	Garner, Atkins	10,689
Apr 21	Stoke City	W 1-0	Mail (pen)	9,305
Apr 28	Ipswich Town	L 1-3	Mail (pen)	11,007
May 1	SHEFFIELD UNITED	D 0-0		15,633
May 5	BRIGHTON & HOVE ALBION	D 1-1	Kennedy	9,283

Play-offs

May 13	SWINDON TOWN	(SF/1L) L 1-2	Kennedy	15,636
May 16	Swindon Town	(SF/2L) L 1-2	Gayle	12,416

FA Cup

Jan 6	ASTON VILLA	(Rd3) D 2-2	Stapleton, Sellars	14,456
Jan 10	Aston Villa	(R) L 1-3	Kennedy	31,169

Littlewoods Cup

Sep 20	Exeter City	(Rd2/1L) L 0-3		4,808
Oct 3	EXETER CITY	(Rd2/2L) W 2-1	Atkins 2	6,608

Zenith Data Systems Cup

Nov 7	Leeds United	(Rd1) L 0-1		5,070

MANAGER: Don Mackay

TOP SCORER: Simon Garner

BIGGEST WIN: 5-0, 30 September 1989, v Barnsley, Division 2

HIGHEST ATTENDANCE: 31,169, 10 January 1990, v Aston Villa, FA Cup Round 3 replay

MAJOR TRANSFERS IN: Frank Stapleton from Le Havre, Alan Irvine from Dundee United, Kevin Moran from Sporting Gijon

MAJOR TRANSFERS OUT: Colin Hendry to Manchester City

League & Cup Appearances

PLAYER	LEAGUE	CUP COMPETITION				TOTAL
		FA CUP	LITTLEWOODS	ZENITH	OTHER	
Atkins, M.N.	41		2	1	2	46
Collier, D.J.	16		1	1		18
Dawson, A.J.	9 (3)				1 (1)	10 (4)
Finnigan, A.	8 (11)	2	2	0 (1)		12 (12)
Garner, S.	42 (1)	2	1	1	1 (1)	47 (2)
Gayle, H.A.	19 (11)	0 (2)	0 (1)	0 (1)	2	21 (15)
Gennoe, T.W.	28	2	1	2		33
Hendry, E.C.J.	5 (2)			1		6 (2)
Hildersley, R.	2 (3)		0 (1)			2 (4)
Hill, K.J.	25	1	2	1		29
Irvine, J.A.	13 (12)					13 (12)
Johnrose, L.	4 (4)	0 (1)				4 (5)
Kennedy, A.J.	26 (8)	2	2		1 (1)	31 (9)
Mail, D.	25	2			2	29
Marriott, A.	2					2
May, D.	17	1	2			20
Millar, J.	38 (1)	2	2	1	2	45 (1)
Moran, K.B.	19				2	21
Oliver, N.	3			1		4
Reid, N.S.	42	2	2	1	2	49
Sellars, S.	43	2	2	1	2	50
Skinner, C.R.		0 (1)	1		1	(1)
Stapleton, F.A.	42 (1)	2	2	1	2	49 (1)
Sulley, C.S.	36	2	1		1	40
Wilcox, J.M.	1					1

Goalscorers

PLAYER	LEAGUE	CUP COMPETITION				TOTAL
		FA CUP	LITTLEWOODS	ZENITH	OTHER	
Garner, S.	18					18
Sellars, S.	14	1				15
Kennedy, A.J.	13	1			1	15
Atkins, M.N.	7		2			9
Gayle, H.A.	5			1		6
Reid, N.S.	4					4
Stapleton, F.A.	3	1				4
Johnrose, L.	3					3
Mail, D.	2					2
Moran, K.B.	2					2
Irvine, J.A.	1					1
Millar, J.	1					1
Opps' o.gs.	1					1

Fact File

Blackburn Rovers reached the play-offs for the third successive season but once again failed to win promotion.

Final Division 2 Table

		P	W	D	L	F	A	Pts
1	LEEDS U	46	24	13	9	79	52	85
2	SHEFFIELD U	46	24	13	9	78	58	85
3	NEWCASTLE U	46	22	14	10	80	55	80
4	SWINDON T	46	20	14	12	79	59	74
5	BLACKBURN R	46	19	17	10	74	59	74
6	SUNDERLAND	46	20	14	12	70	64	74
7	WEST HAM U	46	20	12	14	80	57	72
8	OLDHAM ATH	46	19	14	13	70	57	71
9	IPSWICH T	46	19	12	15	67	66	69
10	WOLVERHAMPTON W	46	18	13	15	67	60	67
11	PORT VALE	46	15	16	15	62	57	61
12	PORTSMOUTH	46	15	16	15	62	65	61
13	LEICESTER C	46	15	14	17	67	79	59
14	HULL C	46	14	16	16	58	65	58
15	WATFORD	46	14	15	17	58	60	57
16	PLYMOUTH ARG	46	14	13	19	58	63	55
17	OXFORD U	46	15	9	22	57	66	54
18	BRIGHTON & HA	46	15	9	22	56	72	54
19	BARNSLEY	46	13	15	18	49	71	54
20	WBA	46	12	15	19	67	71	51
21	MIDDLESBROUGH	46	13	11	22	52	63	50
22	BOURNEMOUTH	46	12	12	22	57	76	48
23	BRADFORD C	46	9	14	23	44	68	41
24	STOKE C	46	6	19	21	35	63	37

Season 1990-91

Football League Division 2

DATE	OPPONENTS	SCORE	GOALSCORERS	ATTENDANCE
Aug 25	Bristol City	L 2-4	Gayle 2	13,755
Aug 28	HULL CITY	W 2-1	Stapleton, Gayle	7,337
Sep 1	NEWCASTLE UNITED	L 0-1		11,329
Sep 8	Ipswich Town	L 1-2	Richardson	10,953
Sep 15	BARNSLEY	L 1-2	Stapleton	7,665
Sep 18	LEICESTER CITY	W 4-1	Irvine, Atkins, Reid, Starbuck	5,682
Sep 22	Portsmouth	L 2-3	Hill, Johnrose	7,801
Sep 29	BRIGHTON & HOVE ALBION	L 1-2	Johnrose	6,027
Oct 3	Bristol Rovers	W 2-1	Johnrose, Reid	5,110
Oct 6	Oldham Athletic	D 1-1	Johnrose	12,093
Oct 13	WATFORD	L 0-2		7,060
Oct 20	PLYMOUTH ARGYLE	D 0-0		6,267
Oct 24	West Ham United	L 0-1		20,003
Oct 27	Wolverhampton W.	W 3-2	Stapleton 3	17,776
Nov 3	MILLWALL	W 1-0	Johnrose	7,336
Nov 10	SHEFFIELD WEDNESDAY	W 1-0	Hill	13,437
Nov 17	West Bromwich Albion	L 0-2		10,985
Nov 23	PORT VALE	D 1-1	Johnrose	8,061
Dec 1	Swindon Town	D 1-1	Stapleton	8,091
Dec 8	Hull City	L 1-3	Atkins	4,166
Dec 15	BRISTOL CITY	L 0-1		7,072
Dec 22	Middlesbrough	W 1-0	Moran (pen)	17,206
Dec 26	NOTTS COUNTY	L 0-1		8,648
Dec 29	OXFORD UNITED	L 1-3	Johnrose	6,428
Jan 1	Charlton Athletic	D 0-0		5,558
Jan 12	Newcastle United	L 0-1		16,382
Jan 19	IPSWICH TOWN	L 0-1		8,256
Jan 26	Leicester City	W 3-1	Livingstone, Gayle, Sulley (pen)	8,167
Feb 9	PORTSMOUTH	D 1-1	Sulley (pen)	7,348
Feb 16	WEST BROMWICH ALBION	L 0-3		7,695
Mar 2	SWINDON TOWN	W 2-1	Garner, Livingstone	6,506
Mar 9	Port Vale	L 0-3		7,004
Mar 12	BRISTOL ROVERS	D 2-2	Livingstone, Stapleton	5,969
Mar 16	Brighton & Hove Albion	L 0-1		6,468
Mar 19	Watford	W 3-0	Livingstone 2, Stapleton	6,913
Mar 23	OLDHAM ATHLETIC	W 2-0	Livingstone 2	12,175
Mar 30	Notts County	L 1-4	Stapleton	6,831
Apr 1	MIDDLESBROUGH	W 1-0	Shepstone	8,925
Apr 6	Oxford United	D 0-0		4,767
Apr 10	Sheffield Wednesday	L 1-3	Irvine	23,139
Apr 13	CHARLTON ATHLETIC	D 2-2	Atkins, Livingstone	6,714
Apr 20	Plymouth Argyle	L 1-4	Stapleton	5,122
Apr 23	Barnsley	W 1-0	Sulley	8,648
Apr 27	WEST HAM UNITED	W 3-1	Richardson, Atkins, Sellars	10,808
May 4	WOLVERHAMPTON W.	D 1-1	Livingstone	9,560
May 11	Millwall	L 1-2	May	11,318

FA Cup

Jan 5	LIVERPOOL	(Rd3) D 1-1	Garner	18,524
Jan 8	Liverpool	(R) L 0-3		34,175

Rumbelows Cup

Sep 25	Rotherham United	(Rd2/1L) D 1-1	Johnrose	4,213
Oct 9	ROTHERHAM UNITED	(Rd2/2L) W 1-0	Stapleton	4,884
Oct 31	Queens Park Rangers	(Rd3) L 1-2	Hill	8,396

Zenith Data Systems Cup

Dec 18	Everton	(Rd2) L 1-4	Skinner	5,410

MANAGER: Don Mackay

TOP SCORER: Frank Stapleton

BIGGEST WIN: 4-1, 18 September 1990, v Leicester City, Division 2

HIGHEST ATTENDANCE: 34,175, 8 January 1991, v Liverpool, FA Cup Round 3 replay

MAJOR TRANSFERS IN: Mike Duxbury from Manchester United, Lee Richardson from Watford, Bobby Mimms from Tottenham Hotspur, Tony Dobson from Coventry City, Steve Livingstone from Coventry City

MAJOR TRANSFERS OUT: Tony Finnigan to Hull City, David Mail to Hull City, Andy Kennedy to Watford

League & Cup Appearances

PLAYER	LEAGUE	CUP COMPETITION			TOTAL
		FA CUP	RUMBELOWS	ZENITH	
Atkins, M.N.	35 (7)	2	3	1	41 (7)
Beckford, J.N.	3 (1)				3 (1)
Beglin, J.M.	6				6
Collier, D.J.	10	2			12
Dewhurst, R.M.	13		1	1	15
Dobson, A.J.	17				17
Donnelly, D.	1 (1)				1 (1)
Duxbury, M.	20 (2)	2	1	0 (1)	23 (3)
Gallacher, B.	4				4
Garner, S.	11 (1)	2	1		14 (1)
Gayle, H.W.	22 (2)	2	1		25 (2)
Gennoe, T.W.	1				1
Grew, M.S.	13		1		14
Hill, K.J.	19 (3)		2		21 (3)
Irvine, J.A.	23 (4)	2			25 (4)
Johnrose, L.	9 (17)	0 (2)	2 (1)	1	12 (20)
Livingstone, S.	18				18
May, D.	19	2		1	22
Millar, J.	34	2	3		39
Mimms, R.A.	22	2			24
Moran, K.B.	32	2	3	1	38
Oliver, N.	2 (1)		1 (1)		3 (2)
Reid, N.S.	29 (1)	2	3	1	35 (1)
Reitmaier, C.				1	1
Richardson, L.J.	32 (6)		1 (1)		33 (7)
Sellars, S.	9	2			11
Shepstone, P.T.A.	15 (10)	0 (1)		1	16 (11)
Skinner, C.R.	4 (3)			1	5 (3)
Stapleton, F.A.	38	2	3		43
Starbuck, P.M.	5 (1)				5 (1)
Sulley, C.S.	25		1	1	27
Wilcox, J.M.	15 (3)		2	1	18 (3)

Goalscorers

PLAYER	LEAGUE	CUP COMPETITION			TOTAL
		FA CUP	RUMBELOWS	ZENITH	
Stapleton, F.A.	10		1		11
Livingstone, S.	9				9
Johnrose, L.	7		1		8
Atkins, M.N.	4				4
Gayle, H.W.	4				4
Sulley, C.S.	3				3
Hill, K.J.	2		1		3
Irvine, J.A.	2				2
Reid, N.S.	2				2
Richardson, L.J.	2				2
Garner, S.	1	1			2
May, D.	1				1
Moran, K.B.	1				1
Sellars, S.	1				1
Shepstone, P.T.A.	1				1
Skinner, C.R.				1	1
Starbuck, P.M.	1				1

Final Division 2 Table

		P	W	D	L	F	A	Pts
1	OLDHAM ATH	46	25	13	8	83	53	88
2	WEST HAM U	46	24	15	7	60	34	87
3	SHEFFIELD W	46	22	16	7	80	51	82
4	NOTTS CO	46	23	11	12	76	55	80
5	MILLWALL	46	20	13	13	70	51	73
6	BRIGHTON & HA	46	21	7	18	63	69	70
7	MIDDLESBROUGH	46	20	9	17	66	47	69
8	BARNSLEY	46	19	12	15	63	48	69
9	BRISTOL C	46	20	7	19	68	71	67
10	OXFORD U	46	14	19	13	69	66	61
11	NEWCASTLE U	46	14	17	15	49	56	59
12	WOLVERHAMPTON W	46	13	19	14	63	63	58
13	BRISTOL R	46	15	13	18	56	59	58
14	IPSWICH T	46	13	18	15	60	68	57
15	PORT VALE	46	15	12	19	56	64	57
16	CHARLTON ATH	46	13	17	16	57	61	56
17	PORTSMOUTH	46	14	11	21	58	70	53
18	PLYMOUTH ARG	46	12	17	17	54	68	53
19	BLACKBURN R	46	14	10	22	51	66	52
20	WATFORD	46	12	15	19	45	59	51
21	SWINDON T	46	12	14	20	65	73	50
22	LEICESTER C	46	14	8	24	60	83	50
23	WBA	46	10	18	18	52	61	48
24	HULL C	46	10	15	21	57	85	45

Season 1991-92

Football League Division 2

DATE	OPPONENTS	SCORE	GOALSCORERS	ATTENDANCE
Aug 17	PORTSMOUTH	D 1-1	Moran	11,118
Aug 24	Bristol City	L 0-1		11,317
Aug 31	IPSWICH TOWN	L 1-2	Speedie	8,898
Sep 4	Derby County	W 2-0	Wilcox, Speedie	12,078
Sep 7	Sunderland	D 1-1	Speedie	17,043
Sep 14	PORT VALE	W 1-0	Speedie	10,225
Sep 17	WATFORD	W 1-0	Richardson	9,542
Sep 21	Leicester City	L 0-3		13,278
Sep 28	TRANMERE ROVERS	D 0-0		11,449
Oct 5	Millwall	W 3-1	Speedie, Johnrose, Garner	8,026
Oct 12	PLYMOUTH ARGYLE	W 5-2	Moran, Garner 2, Speedie 2 (1 pen)	10,830
Oct 19	Swindon Town	L 1-2	Speedie	10,717
Oct 26	GRIMSBY TOWN	W 2-1	Garner, Atkins	11,096
Nov 2	BRIGHTON & HOVE ALBION	W 1-0	Livingstone (pen)	9,877
Nov 5	Southend United	L 0-3		4,860
Nov 9	Charlton Athletic	W 2-0	Sellars, Speedie	7,114
Nov 16	BARNSLEY	W 3-0	Speedie, Wilcox, Newell	13,797
Nov 23	Newcastle United	D 0-0		23,639
Nov 30	MIDDLESBROUGH	W 2-1	Newell (pen), Atkins	15,541
Dec 7	Oxford United	W 3-1	Sellars, Cowans, Garner	5,924
Dec 14	BRISTOL ROVERS	W 3-0	Atkins 2, Sellars	12,295
Dec 26	Wolverhampton W.	D 0-0		18,277
Dec 28	Ipswich Town	L 1-2	Wright	17,675
Jan 1	CAMBRIDGE UNITED	W 2-1	Speedie, Reid	15,001
Jan 11	BRISTOL CITY	W 4-0	Newell 2, Speedie, Scott o.g.	12,964
Jan 18	Portsmouth	D 2-2	Speedie 2	20,106
Feb 1	SWINDON TOWN	W 2-1	Hendry, Speedie	14,887
Feb 8	Grimsby Town	W 3-2	Price, Sellars, Wilcox	10,014
Feb 11	DERBY COUNTY	W 2-0	Price, Atkins	15,350
Feb 15	NEWCASTLE UNITED	W 3-1	Speedie 3	19,511
Feb 22	Middlesbrough	D 0-0		19,353
Feb 25	Cambridge United	L 1-2	Hendry	7,857
Feb 29	OXFORD UNITED	D 1-1	Sellars (pen)	13,917
Mar 7	Bristol Rovers	L 0-3		6,313
Mar 10	SOUTHEND UNITED	D 2-2	Price, Speedie	14,404
Mar 14	Brighton & Hove Albion	W 3-0	Speedie, Hendry, Wegerle	10,845
Mar 21	CHARLTON ATHLETIC	L 0-2		13,844
Mar 28	Barnsley	L 1-2	Shearer	13,346
Mar 31	Port Vale	L 0-2		10,384
Apr 11	Watford	L 1-2	Wegerle	10,522
Apr 14	WOLVERHAMPTON W.	L 1-2	Sellars	14,114
Apr 18	LEICESTER CITY	L 0-1		18,075
Apr 20	Tranmere Rovers	D 2-2	Wilcox, Newell (pen)	13,705
Apr 25	MILLWALL	W 2-1	Newell, Atkins	12,820
Apr 29	SUNDERLAND	D 2-2	Hendry, Sellars	15,079
May 2	Plymouth Argyle	W 3-1	Speedie 3	17,459

Play-offs

May 10	DERBY COUNTY	(SF/1L)	W 4-2	Sellars, Newell, Speedie 2	19,677
May 13	Derby County	(SF/2L)	L 1-2	Moran	22,920
May 25	Leicester City	(F)	W 1-0	Newell (pen)	68,147

FA Cup

Jan 4	KETTERING TOWN	(Rd3)	W 4-1	Newell 2, Speedie, Cowans	13,821
Feb 4	Notts County	(Rd4)	L 1-2	Newell	12,173

Rumbelows Cup

Aug 20	HULL CITY	(Rd1/1L)	D 1-1	Buckley o.g.	6,300
Aug 27	Hull City	(Rd1/2L)	L 0-1		3,227

Zenith Data Systems Cup

Oct 1	Port Vale	(Rd1)	L 0-1	2,355

MANAGER: Don Mackay/Kenny Dalglish

TOP SCORER: David Speedie

BIGGEST WIN: 4-0, 11 January 1992, v Bristol City, Division 2

HIGHEST ATTENDANCE: 68,147, 25 May 1992, v Leicester City, play-off final

---

Fact File

Kenny Dalglish asked Tony Parkes to lead the players out at Wembley for the play-off final in recognition of his loyal service to the Rovers.

League & Cup Appearances

PLAYER	LEAGUE	CUP COMPETITION				TOTAL
		FA CUP	RUMBELOWS	ZENITH	OTHER	
Agnew, S.M.	2		2			4
Atkins, M.N.	40 (4)	2	2		3	47 (4)
Baah, P.H.	1					1
Beardsmore, R.P.	1 (1)					1 (1)
Brown, R.A.	24 (2)	2		1		27 (2)
Cowans, G.S.	26		2		3	31
Dickens, M.J.	1					1
Dobson, A.J.	4 (1)		2	1		7 (1)
Duxbury, M.	5					5
Garner, S.	14 (11)	0 (2)	2	1		17 (13)
Gayle, H.A.	1 (3)		0 (2)	1		2 (5)
Hendry, E.C.J.	26 (4)	0 (1)			3	29 (5)
Hill, K.J.	31 (1)	2		1		34 (1)
Irvine, J.A.	4 (2)		1	0 (1)		5 (3)
Johnrose, L.	7			1		8
Livingstone, S.	6 (4)		1			7 (4)
May, D.	12		1	1	3	17
Mimms, R.A.	45	2	2	1	3	53
Moran, K.B.	37 (4)	2	2		3	44 (4)
Munro, S.	1					1
Newell, M.C.	18 (2)	2			3	23 (2)
Price, C.J.	11 (2)				2	13 (2)
Reid, N.S.	8 (13)	1 (1)	2	0 (1)		11 (15)
Richardson, L.J.	18 (6)		0 (1)	1	1 (2)	20 (9)
Sellars, S.	28 (2)	2			3	33 (2)
Shearer, D.N.	5 (1)				0 (1)	5 (2)
Sherwood, T.A.	7 (4)					7 (4)
Shepstone, P.T.A.	1		1			2
Skinner, C.R.	7 (2)	1		1		9 (2)
Speedie, D.R.	34 (2)	2	2		3	41 (2)
Sulley, C.S.	7		2			9
Wegerle, R.C.	9 (3)					9 (3)
Wilcox, J.M.	33 (5)		1			34 (5)
Wright, A.G.	32 (1)	2			3	37 (1)

Goalscorers

PLAYER	LEAGUE	CUP COMPETITION				TOTAL
		FA CUP	RUMBELOWS	ZENITH	OTHER	
Speedie, D.R.	23	1			2	26
Newell, M.C.	6	3			2	11
Sellars, S.	7				1	8
Atkins, M.N.	6					6
Garner, S.	5					5
Hendry, E.C.J.	4					4
Wilcox, J.M.	4					4
Price, C.J.	3					3
Moran, K.B.	2			1		3
Wegerle, R.C.	2					2
Cowans, G.S.	1	1				2
Opps' o.gs.	1		1			2

Also scored one goal: L. Johnrose, S. Livingstone, N.S. Reid, L.J. Richardson, D.N. Shearer, A.G. Wright.

Final Division 2 Table

		P	W	D	L	F	A	Pts
1	IPSWICH T	46	24	12	10	70	50	84
2	MIDDLESBROUGH	46	23	11	12	58	41	80
3	DERBY CO	46	23	9	14	69	51	78
4	LEICESTER C	46	23	8	15	62	55	77
5	CAMBRIDGE U	46	19	17	10	65	47	74
6	BLACKBURN R	46	21	11	14	70	53	74
7	CHARLTON ATH	46	20	11	15	54	48	71
8	SWINDON T	46	18	15	13	69	55	69
9	PORTSMOUTH	46	19	12	15	65	51	69
10	WATFORD	46	18	11	17	51	48	65
11	WOLVERHAMPTON W	46	18	10	18	61	54	64
12	SOUTHEND U	46	17	11	18	63	63	62
13	BRISTOL R	46	16	14	16	60	63	62
14	TRANMERE R	46	14	19	13	56	56	61
15	MILLWALL	46	17	10	19	64	71	61
16	BARNSLEY	46	16	11	19	46	57	59
17	BRISTOL C	46	13	15	18	55	71	54
18	SUNDERLAND	46	14	11	21	61	65	53
19	GRIMSBY T	46	14	11	21	47	62	53
20	NEWCASTLE U	46	13	13	20	66	84	52
21	OXFORD U	46	13	11	22	66	73	50
22	PLYMOUTH ARG	46	13	9	24	42	64	48
23	BRIGHTON & HA	46	12	11	23	56	77	47
24	PORT VALE	46	10	15	21	42	59	45

Season 1992-93

Premier League

DATE	OPPONENTS	SCORE	GOALSCORERS	ATTENDANCE
Aug 15	Crystal Palace	D 3-3	Ripley, Shearer 2	17,086
Aug 18	ARSENAL	W 1-0	Shearer	16,454
Aug 22	MANCHESTER CITY	W 1-0	Newell	19,433
Aug 26	Chelsea	D 0-0		19,575
Aug 29	Coventry City	W 2-0	Shearer (pen), Atkins	14,541
Sep 5	NOTTINGHAM FOREST	W 4-1	Shearer 2 (1 pen), Atkins, Crossley o.g.	16,180
Sep 12	Arsenal	W 1-0	Newell	28,643
Sep 15	EVERTON	L 2-3	Shearer 2 (1 pen)	19,563
Sep 19	Wimbledon	D 1-1	Shearer	6,117
Sep 26	OLDHAM ATHLETIC	W 2-0	Shearer, Ripley	18,383
Oct 3	NORWICH CITY	W 7-1	Wegerle 2, Shearer 2, Sherwood, Cowans, Ripley	16,312
Oct 19	Aston Villa	D 0-0		30,398
Oct 24	MANCHESTER UNITED	D 0-0		20,305
Oct 31	Sheffield Wednesday	D 0-0		31,044
Nov 7	TOTTENHAM HOTSPUR	L 0-2		17,305
Nov 22	Southampton	D 1-1	Moran	16,626
Nov 28	QUEENS PARK RANGERS	W 1-0	Shearer	15,850
Dec 5	Middlesbrough	L 2-3	Wilcox, Phillips o.g.	20,096
Dec 13	Liverpool	L 1-2	Shearer	43,668
Dec 19	SHEFFIELD UNITED	W 1-0	Moran	16,057
Dec 26	LEEDS UNITED	W 3-1	Wilcox, Shearer 2	19,910
Dec 28	Ipswich Town	L 1-2	Wegerle	21,431
Jan 9	WIMBLEDON	D 0-0		14,504
Jan 16	Oldham Athletic	W 1-0	Ripley	13,742
Jan 26	COVENTRY CITY	L 2-5	Newell, Hendry	15,215
Jan 30	Manchester City	L 2-3	Newell, Phelan o.g.	29,122
Feb 2	CRYSTAL PALACE	L 1-2	Wegerle	14,163
Feb 21	CHELSEA	W 2-0	Newell 2	14,780
Feb 28	Norwich City	D 0-0		15,821
Mar 3	Everton	L 1-2	May	18,086
Mar 9	SOUTHAMPTON	D 0-0		13,556
Mar 20	MIDDLESBROUGH	D 1-1	Atkins	14,041
Mar 24	Queens Park Rangers	W 3-0	Ripley, Moran, Atkins	10,677
Apr 3	LIVERPOOL	W 4-1	Newell, Moran, Gallacher, Wilcox	15,032
Apr 7	Nottingham Forest	W 3-1	Wilcox, Ripley, Newell	20,467
Apr 10	Leeds United	L 2-5	Gallacher, Atkins	31,791
Apr 12	IPSWICH TOWN	W 2-1	Ripley, Whelan o.g.	14,071
Apr 17	Sheffield United	W 3-1	Gallacher, Newell, Sherwood	18,186
Apr 21	ASTON VILLA	W 3-0	Newell 2, Gallacher	15,127
May 3	Manchester United	L 1-3	Gallacher	40,447
May 5	Tottenham Hotspur	W 2-1	Newell 2	23,097
May 8	SHEFFIELD WEDNESDAY	W 1-0	Sherwood	14,956

FA Cup

Jan 2	AFC BOURNEMOUTH	(Rd3) W 3-1	Ripley 2, Newell	13,773
Jan 23	Crewe Alexandra	(Rd4) W 3-0	Wegerle, Newell, Moran	7,054
Feb 13	NEWCASTLE UNITED	(Rd5) W 1-0	Wegerle	19,972
Mar 6	SHEFFIELD UNITED	(Rd6) D 0-0		15,107
Mar 16	Sheffield United	(R) D 2-2*†	Livingstone, Newell	23,920

*After extra-time. †Lost on penalties.

Coca-Cola Cup

Sep 23	Huddersfield Town	(Rd2/1L) D 1-1	Shearer	11,071
Oct 06	HUDDERSFIELD TOWN	(Rd2/2L) W 4-3*	Shearer 2, Wegerle, Newell	15,038
Oct 28	NORWICH CITY	(Rd3) W 2-0	Shearer, May	14,216
Dec 9	WATFORD	(Rd4) W 6-1	Atkins, Wegerle, Moran, Newell 2, Wegerle	13,187
Jan 6	CAMBRIDGE UNITED	(Rd5) W 3-2	Newell 2, Wegerle	14,165
Feb 10	SHEFFIELD WEDNESDAY	(SF/1L) L 2-4	Wegerle, Palmer o.g.	17,283
Mar 14	Sheffield Wednesday	(SF/2L) L 1-2	Andersson	30,048

*After extra-time.

MANAGER: Kenny Dalglish

TOP SCORER: Alan Shearer

BIGGEST WIN: 7-1, 3 October 1992, v Norwich City, Premier League

HIGHEST ATTENDANCE: 43,668, 13 December 1992 v Liverpool, Premier League

MAJOR TRANSFERS IN: Alan Shearer from Southampton, Henning Berg from Lillestrom, Graeme Le Saux from Chelsea

MAJOR TRANSFERS OUT: David Speedie to Southampton, Simon Garner to West Bromwich Albion, Roy Wegerle to Coventry City

---

League & Cup Appearances

PLAYER	LEAGUE	CUP COMPETITION		TOTAL
		FA CUP	COCA-COLA	
Andersson, P.J.	6 (5)	1	2	9 (5)
Atkins, M.N.	24 (7)	2 (2)	5 (2)	31 (11)
Berg, H.	2 (2)		2	4 (2)
Brown, R.A.	2		1 (1)	3 (1)
Cowans, G.S.	23 (1)	3	4	30 (1)
Dobson, A.J.	15 (4)	2	3	20 (4)
Gallacher, K.W.	9			9
Hendry, E.C.J.	41	5	7	53
Hill, K.J.	0 (1)			0 (1)
Ireland, S.	0 (1)			0 (1)
Le Saux, G.P.	9			9
Livingstone, S.	1 (1)	1	1	3 (1)
Makel, L.R.	1		0 (2)	1 (2)
Marker, N.R.T.	12 (3)	2		14 (3)
May, D.	34	5	5 (1)	44 (1)
Mimms, R.A.	42	5	7	54
Moran, K.B.	36	4	2 (1)	42 (1)
Newell, M.C.	40	5	6 (1)	51 (1)
Price, C.J.	2 (4)		1	3 (4)
Ripley, S.E.	38 (2)	4	6	48 (2)
Shearer, A.	21	5		26
Sherwood, T.A.	38 (1)	4 (1)	6	48 (2)
Wegerle, R.C.	11 (11)	4 (1)	3 (3)	18 (15)
Wilcox, J.M.	31 (2)	5	5 (1)	41 (3)
Wright, A.	24	3	6	33

Goalscorers

PLAYER	LEAGUE	CUP COMPETITION		TOTAL
		FA CUP	COCA-COLA	
Shearer, A.	16		6	22
Newell, M.C.	13	3	5	21
Wegerle, R.C.	4	2	4	10
Ripley, S.E.	7	2		9
Atkins, M.N.	5		1	6
Gallacher, K.W.	5			5
Moran, K.B.	4	1		5
Wilcox, J.M.	4			4
Sherwood, T.A.	3			3
May, D.	1		1	2
Cowans, G.S.	1			1
Hendry, E.C.J.	1			1
Livingstone, S.		1		1
Andersson, P.J.			1	1
Opps' o.gs.	4		1	5

Fact File

Blackburn Rovers broke the British transfer record when Alan Shearer was signed from Southampton for a fee of £3.3 million.

Final Premier League Table

		P	W	D	L	F	A	Pts
1	MANCHESTER U	42	24	12	6	67	31	84
2	ASTON VILLA	42	21	11	10	57	40	74
3	NORWICH CITY	42	21	9	12	61	65	72
4	BLACKBURN R	42	20	11	11	68	46	71
5	QPR	42	17	12	13	63	56	63
6	LIVERPOOL	42	16	11	15	62	55	59
7	SHEFFIELD W	42	15	14	13	55	51	59
8	TOTTENHAM H	42	16	11	15	60	66	59
9	MANCHESTER C	42	15	12	15	56	51	57
10	ARSENAL	42	15	11	16	40	38	56
11	CHELSEA	42	14	14	14	51	54	56
12	WIMBLEDON	42	14	12	16	57	47	54
13	EVERTON	42	15	8	19	53	55	53
14	SHEFFIELD U	42	14	10	18	54	53	52
15	COVENTRY C	42	13	13	16	52	57	52
16	IPSWICH T	42	12	16	14	50	55	52
17	LEEDS UNITED	42	12	15	15	57	62	51
18	SOUTHAMPTON	42	13	11	18	54	61	50
19	OLDHAM A	42	13	10	19	63	74	49
20	CRYSTAL P	42	11	16	15	48	61	49
21	MIDDLESBROUGH	42	11	11	20	54	75	44
22	NOTTINGHAM F	42	10	10	22	41	62	40

Season 1993-94

Premier League

DATE	OPPONENTS	SCORE	GOALSCORERS	ATTENDANCE
Aug 14	Chelsea	W 2-1	Ripley, Newell	29,189
Aug 18	NORWICH CITY	L 2-3	Atkins, Wilcox	14,260
Aug 21	OLDHAM ATHLETIC	W 1-0	Moran	14,397
Aug 24	Manchester City	W 2-0	Newell, Gallacher	25,185
Aug 29	Newcastle United	D 1-1	Shearer	34,272
Sep 1	ARSENAL	D 1-1	Gallacher	14,410
Sep 12	Liverpool	W 1-0	Newell	37,355
Sep 18	WEST HAM UNITED	L 0-2		14,437
Sep 25	SHEFFIELD WEDNESDAY	D 1-1	Shearer	14,495
Oct 2	Swindon Town	W 3-1	Shearer 2, Ripley	15,224
Oct 18	SHEFFIELD UNITED	D 0-0		14,276
Oct 23	Leeds United	D 3-3	Shearer 3	37,827
Oct 30	TOTTENHAM HOTSPUR	W 1-0	Shearer	17,462
Nov 6	Queens Park Rangers	L 0-1		17,636
Nov 20	SOUTHAMPTON	W 2-0	Shearer 2 (1 pen)	17,343
Nov 23	COVENTRY CITY	W 2-1	Shearer 2	16,376
Nov 27	Ipswich Town	L 0-1		14,582
Dec 5	CHELSEA	W 2-0	Le Saux, Shearer	16,756
Dec 11	Oldham Athletic	W 2-1	Shearer 2	13,887
Dec 18	MANCHESTER CITY	W 2-0	Gallacher, Shearer	19,479
Dec 26	Manchester United	D 1-1	Gallacher	44,511
Dec 29	EVERTON	W 2-0	Shearer 2	22,061
Jan 1	Aston Villa	W 1-0	Shearer	40,903
Jan 15	Sheffield United	W 2-1	Shearer 2	19,124
Jan 23	LEEDS UNITED	W 2-1	Shearer 2	17,475
Feb 5	WIMBLEDON	W 3-0	Shearer (pen), Wilcox, Ripley	17,264
Feb 12	Tottenham Hotspur	W 2-0	Shearer, Gallacher	30,236
Feb 19	NEWCASTLE UNITED	W 1-0	May	20,798
Feb 22	Norwich City	D 2-2	Gallacher 2	15,193
Feb 26	Arsenal	L 0-1		35,030
Mar 5	LIVERPOOL	W 2-0	Wilcox, Sherwood	20,831
Mar 20	Sheffield Wednesday	W 2-1	Wilcox, Newell	24,699
Mar 26	SWINDON TOWN	W 3-1	Shearer 2 (1 pen), Sherwood	20,046
Mar 29	Wimbledon	L 1-4	Wilcox	10,537
Apr 2	MANCHESTER UNITED	W 2-0	Shearer 2	20,866
Apr 4	Everton	W 3-0	Newell 2, Wilcox	27,427
Apr 11	ASTON VILLA	W 1-0	Shearer	19,287
Apr 16	Southampton	L 1-3	Ripley	19,105
Apr 24	QUEENS PARK RANGERS	D 1-1	Shearer	19,913
Apr 27	West Ham United	W 2-1	Berg, Pearce	22,186
May 2	Coventry City	L 1-2	Le Saux	16,653
May 7	IPSWICH TOWN	D 0-0		20,633

FA Cup

Jan 8	PORTSMOUTH	(Rd3) D 3-3	Shearer, Gallacher, Sherwood	17,219
Jan 19	Portsmouth	(R) W 3-1	Shearer, May, Wilcox	23,035
Jan 29	Charlton Athletic	(Rd4) D 0-0		8,352
Feb 8	CHARLTON ATHLETIC	(R) L 0-1		15,438

Coca-Cola Cup

Sep 21	AFC BOURNEMOUTH	(Rd2/1L) W 1-0	Shearer	10,733
Oct 5	AFC Bournemouth	(Rd2/2L) D 0-0		10,321
Oct 26	SHREWSBURY TOWN	(Rd3) D 0-0		10,603
Nov 9	Shrewsbury Town	(R) W 4-3*	Newell 2 (1 pen), May, Pearce	7,330
Dec 4	Tottenham Hotspur	(Rd4) L 0-1		22,295

*After extra-time.

MANAGER: Kenny Dalglish

TOP SCORER: Alan Shearer

BIGGEST WIN: 3-0, 5 February 1994, v Wimbledon, Premier League; 4 April 1994, v Everton, Premier League

HIGHEST ATTENDANCE: 44,511, 26 December 1993, v Manchester United, Premier League

MAJOR TRANSFERS IN: Paul Warhurst from Sheffield Wednesday, Ian Pearce from Chelsea, David Batty from Leeds United, Tim Flowers from Southampton

MAJOR TRANSFERS OUT: Tony Dobson to Portsmouth, Patrik Andersson to Borussia Mönchengladbach

League & Cup Appearances

PLAYER	LEAGUE	FA CUP	COCA-COLA	TOTAL
Andersson, P.J.	1			1
Atkins, M.N.	8 (7)	0 (1)	1 (2)	9 (10)
Batty, D.	26	4	2	32
Berg, H.	38 (3)	4	3	45 (3)
Flowers, T.D.	29	4		33
Gallacher, K.W.	27 (3)	4	4	35 (3)
Hendry, E.C.J.	22 (1)	2	5	29 (1)
Le Saux, G.P.	40 (1)	4	4	48 (1)
Makel, L.R.	0 (2)		0 (1)	0 (3)
Marker, N.R.T.	16 (7)	2	3	21 (7)
May, D.	40	2	4	46
Mimms, R.A.	13		5	18
Moran, K.B.	19	2 (1)	1	22 (1)
Morrison, A.C.	1 (4)	1		2 (4)
Newell, M.C.	27 (1)		4	31 (1)
Pearce, I.A.	1 (4)	0 (2)	0 (2)	1 (8)
Ripley, S.E.	40	4	5	49
Shearer, A.	34 (6)	4	4	42 (6)
Sherwood, T.A.	38	3	5	46
Warhurst, P.	4 (5)		1	5 (5)
Wilcox, J.M.	31 (2)	4	2	37 (2)
Wright, A.G.	7 (5)		2	9 (5)

Goalscorers

PLAYER	LEAGUE	FA CUP	COCA-COLA	TOTAL
Shearer, A.	31	2	1	34
Gallacher, K.W.	7	1		8
Newell, M.C.	6		2	8
Wilcox, J.M.	6	1		7
Ripley, S.E.	4			4
Sherwood, T.A.	2	1		3
May, D.	1	1	1	3
Le Saux, G.P.	2			2
Pearce, I.A.	1		1	2
Atkins, M.N.	1			1
Berg, H.	1			1
Moran, K.B.	1			1

Fact File

Blackburn Rovers qualified for the UEFA Cup after finishing second in the Premier League with 84 points. This was the first time that the club had qualified for a European competition.

Final Premier League Table

		P	W	D	L	F	A	Pts
1	MANCHESTER U	42	27	11	4	80	38	92
2	BLACKBURN R	42	25	9	8	63	36	84
3	NEWCASTLE U	42	23	8	11	82	41	77
4	ARSENAL	42	18	17	7	53	28	71
5	LEEDS UNITED	42	18	16	8	65	39	70
6	WIMBLEDON	42	18	11	13	56	53	65
7	SHEFFIELD W	42	16	16	10	76	54	64
8	LIVERPOOL	42	17	9	16	59	55	60
9	QPR	42	16	12	14	62	61	60
10	ASTON VILLA	42	15	12	15	46	50	57
11	COVENTRY C	42	14	14	14	43	45	56
12	NORWICH CITY	42	12	17	13	65	61	53
13	WEST HAM U	42	13	13	16	47	58	52
14	CHELSEA	42	13	12	17	49	53	51
15	TOTTENHAM H	42	11	12	19	54	59	45
16	MANCHESTER C	42	9	18	15	38	49	45
17	EVERTON	42	12	8	22	42	63	44
18	SOUTHAMPTON	42	12	7	23	49	66	43
19	IPSWICH T	42	9	16	17	35	58	43
20	SHEFFIELD U	42	8	18	16	42	60	42
21	OLDHAM A	42	9	13	20	42	68	40
22	SWINDON T	42	5	15	22	47	100	30

Season 1994-95

Premier League

DATE	OPPONENTS	SCORE	GOALSCORERS	ATTENDANCE
Aug 20	Southampton	D 1-1	Shearer	14,209
Aug 23	LEICESTER CITY	W 3-0	Sutton, Berg, Shearer	21,050
Aug 27	COVENTRY CITY	W 4-0	Sutton 3, Wilcox	21,657
Aug 31	Arsenal	D 0-0		37,629
Sep 10	EVERTON	W 3-0	Shearer 2 (1 pen), Wilcox	26,538
Sep 18	Chelsea	W 2-1	Johnsen o.g., Sutton	17,513
Sep 24	ASTON VILLA	W 3-1	Shearer 2 (1 pen), Sutton	22,694
Oct 1	Norwich City	L 1-2	Sutton	18,146
Oct 9	Newcastle United	D 1-1	Shearer (pen)	34,344
Oct 15	LIVERPOOL	W 3-2	Atkins, Sutton 2	30,263
Oct 23	MANCHESTER UNITED	L 2-4	Warhurst, Hendry	30,260
Oct 29	Nottingham Forest	W 2-0	Sutton 2	22,131
Nov 2	Sheffield Wednesday	W 1-0	Shearer	24,207
Nov 5	TOTTENHAM HOTSPUR	W 2-0	Wilcox, Shearer (pen)	26,933
Nov 19	Ipswich Town	W 3-1	Sutton, Sherwood, Shearer	17,607
Nov 26	QUEENS PARK RANGERS	W 4-0	Sutton, Shearer 3 (1 pen)	21,302
Dec 3	Wimbledon	W 3-0	Atkins, Wilcox, Shearer	12,341
Dec 10	SOUTHAMPTON	W 3-2	Atkins, Shearer 2	23,372
Dec 17	Leicester City	D 0-0		20,559
Dec 26	Manchester City	W 3-1	Shearer, Atkins, Le Saux	23,387
Dec 31	Crystal Palace	W 1-0	Sherwood	14,232
Jan 2	WEST HAM UNITED	W 4-2	Shearer 3 (2 pens), Le Saux	25,503
Jan 14	NOTTINGHAM FOREST	W 3-0	Warhurst, Wilcox, Chettle o.g.	27,510
Jan 22	Manchester United	L 0-1		43,742
Jan 28	IPSWICH TOWN	W 4-1	Shearer 3 (1 pen), Sherwood	21,325
Feb 1	LEEDS UNITED	D 1-1	Shearer (pen)	28,561
Feb 5	Tottenham Hotspur	L 1-3	Sherwood	28,124
Feb 12	SHEFFIELD WEDNESDAY	W 3-1	Sherwood, Atkins, Shearer	22,223
Feb 22	WIMBLEDON	W 2-1	Shearer, Atkins	20,586
Feb 25	NORWICH CITY	D 0-0		25,579
Mar 4	Aston Villa	W 1-0	Hendry	40,114
Mar 8	ARSENAL	W 3-1	Shearer 2 (1 pen), Le Saux	23,452
Mar 11	Coventry City	D 1-1	Shearer	18,556
Mar 18	CHELSEA	W 2-1	Shearer, Sherwood	25,490
Apr 1	Everton	W 2-1	Sutton, Shearer	37,905
Apr 4	Queens Park Rangers	W 1-0	Sutton	16,508
Apr 15	Leeds United	D 1-1	Hendry	39,426
Apr 17	MANCHESTER CITY	L 2-3	Shearer, Hendry	27,851
Apr 20	CRYSTAL PALACE	W 2-1	Kenna, Gallacher	28,005
Apr 30	West Ham United	L 0-2		24,202
May 8	NEWCASTLE UNITED	W 1-0	Shearer	30,545
May 14	Liverpool	L 1-2	Shearer	40,014

FA Cup

Jan 8	Newcastle United	(Rd3) D 1-1	Sutton	31,721
Jan 18	NEWCASTLE UNITED	(R) L 1-2	Sutton	22,658

Coca-Cola Cup

Sep 20	BIRMINGHAM CITY	(Rd2/1L) W 2-0	Wilcox, Sutton	14,517
Oct 4	Birmingham City	(Rd2/2L) D 1-1	Sutton	16,275
Oct 26	COVENTRY CITY	(Rd3) W 2-0	Shearer 2	14,538
Nov 30	LIVERPOOL	(Rd4) L 1-3	Sutton	30,115

UEFA Cup

Sep 13	TRELLEBORGS FF	(Rd1/1L) L 0-1		13,775
Sep 27	Trelleborgs FF	(Rd1/2L) D 2-2	Sutton, Shearer	6,730

Charity Shield

Aug 14	Manchester United†	L 0-2		60,402

†Played at Wembley Stadium.

MANAGER: Kenny Daglish

TOP SCORER: Alan Shearer

BIGGEST WIN: 4-0, 27 August 1994, v Coventry City, Premier League; 26 November 1994, v Queens Park Rangers, Premier League

HIGHEST ATTENDANCE: 60,402, 14 August 1994, v Manchester United, FA Charity Shield

MAJOR TRANSFERS IN: Chris Sutton from Norwich City, Robbie Slater from FC Lens, Tony Gale from West Ham United, Jeff Kenna from Southampton.

MAJOR TRANSFERS OUT: David May to Manchester United, Andy Morrison to Blackpool, Alan Wright to Aston Villa

League & Cup Appearances

PLAYER	LEAGUE	CUP COMPETITION				TOTAL
		FA CUP	COCA-COLA	UEFA	OTHER	
Atkins, M.N.	30 (4)	2	3	1 (1)	1	37 (5)
Batty, D.	4 (1)					4 (1)
Berg, H.	40	2	4	2	1	49
Flowers, T.D.	39	2	4	2	1	48
Gale, A.P.	15		2	2	1	20
Gallacher, K.W.	1					1
Hendry, E.C.J.	38	2	4	2	1	47
Kenna, J.J.	9					9
Le Saux, G.P.	39	2	4	2	1	48
Makel, L.R.				0 (1)		0 (1)
Mimms, R.A.	3 (1)					3 (1)
Newell, M.C.	2 (10)	0 (2)	0 (1)			2 (13)
Pearce, I.A.	22 (6)	1	0 (1)	0 (1)	1	24 (8)
Ripley, S.E.	36 (1)	1	4	2	1	44 (1)
Shearer, A.	42	2	3	2		49
Sherwood, T.A.	38	1	3	2	1	45
Slater, R.	12 (6)	1	1	1	1	16 (6)
Sutton, C.R.	40	2	4	2		48
Thorne, P.L.				0 (1)	0 (1)	0 (1)
Warhurst, P.	20 (7)	2	4	0 (1)		26 (8)
Wilcox, J.M.	27	2	4	2	1	36
Witschge, R.	1					1
Wright, A.G.	4 (1)	0 (1)				4 (2)

Goalscorers

PLAYER	LEAGUE	CUP COMPETITION				TOTAL
		FA CUP	COCA-COLA	UEFA	OTHER	
Shearer, A.	34		2	1		37
Sutton, C.R.	15	2	3	1		21
Atkins, M.N.	6					6
Sherwood, T.A.	6					6
Wilcox, J.M.	5		1			6
Hendry, E.C.J.	4					4
Le Saux, G.P.	3					3
Warhurst, P.	2					2
Berg, H.	1					1
Gallacher, K.W.	1					1
Kenna, J.J.	1					1
Opps' o.gs.	2					2

Fact File

Blackburn Rovers captured a league championship for the first time since 1913-14.

Final Premier League Table

		P	W	D	L	F	A	PTS
1	BLACKBURN R	42	27	8	7	80	39	89
2	MANCHESTER U	42	26	10	6	77	28	88
3	NOTTINGHAM F	42	22	11	9	72	43	77
4	LIVERPOOL	42	21	11	10	65	37	74
5	LEEDS UNITED	42	20	13	9	59	38	73
6	NEWCASTLE U	42	20	12	10	67	47	72
7	TOTTENHAM H	42	16	14	12	66	58	62
8	QPR	42	17	9	16	61	59	60
9	WIMBLEDON	42	15	11	16	48	65	56
10	SOUTHAMPTON	42	12	18	12	61	63	54
11	CHELSEA	42	13	15	14	50	55	54
12	ARSENAL	42	13	12	17	52	46	51
13	SHEFFIELD W	42	13	12	17	49	57	51
14	WEST HAM U	42	13	11	18	44	48	50
15	EVERTON	42	11	17	14	44	51	50
16	COVENTRY C	42	12	14	16	44	62	50
17	MANCHESTER C	42	12	13	17	53	64	49
18	ASTON VILLA	42	11	15	16	51	56	48
19	CRYSTAL P	42	11	12	19	34	49	45
20	NORWICH CITY	42	10	13	19	37	54	43
21	LEICESTER C	42	6	11	25	45	80	29
22	IPSWICH T	42	7	6	29	36	93	27

The Essential History of Blackburn Rovers

Season 1995-96

Premier League

DATE	OPPONENTS	SCORE	GOALSCORERS	ATTENDANCE
Aug 19	QUEENS PARK RANGERS	W 1-0	Shearer (pen)	25,932
Aug 23	Sheffield Wednesday	L 1-2	Shearer	25,544
Aug 26	Bolton Wanderers	L 1-2	Holmes	20,253
Aug 28	MANCHESTER UNITED	L 1-2	Shearer	29,843
Sep 9	ASTON VILLA	D 1-1	Shearer	27,084
Sep 16	Liverpool	L 0-3		39,502
Sep 23	COVENTRY CITY	W 5-1	Shearer 3, Hendry, Pearce	24,382
Sep 30	Middlesbrough	L 0-2		29,462
Oct 14	SOUTHAMPTON	W 2-1	Bohinen, Shearer	26,780
Oct 21	West Ham United	D 1-1	Shearer	21,776
Oct 28	CHELSEA	W 3-0	Sherwood, Shearer, Newell	27,733
Nov 5	Everton	L 0-1		30,097
Nov 8	Newcastle United	L 0-1		36,463
Nov 18	NOTTINGHAM FOREST	W 7-0	Shearer 3, Bohinen 2, Newell, Le Saux	27,660
Nov 26	Arsenal	D 0-0		37,695
Dec 2	WEST HAM UNITED	W 4-2	Shearer 3 (1 pen), Newell	26,638
Dec 9	Coventry City	L 0-5		13,376
Dec 16	MIDDLESBROUGH	W 1-0	Shearer	27,996
Dec 23	Wimbledon	D 1-1	Sherwood	7,105
Dec 26	MANCHESTER CITY	W 2-0	Shearer, Batty	28,915
Dec 30	TOTTENHAM HOTSPUR	W 2-1	Marker, Shearer	30,004
Jan 1	Leeds United	D 0-0		31,285
Jan 13	Queens Park Rangers	W 1-0	Shearer	13,957
Jan 20	SHEFFIELD WEDNESDAY	W 3-0	Shearer, Bohinen, Gallacher	24,732
Feb 3	BOLTON WANDERERS	W 3-1	Shearer 3	30,419
Feb 10	Manchester United	L 0-1		42,681
Feb 24	LIVERPOOL	L 2-3	Wilcox, Sherwood	30,895
Feb 28	Aston Villa	L 0-2		28,008
Mar 2	Manchester City	D 1-1	Shearer	29,078
Mar 13	LEEDS UNITED	W 1-0	Fenton	23,358
Mar 16	Tottenham Hotspur	W 3-2	Shearer 3 (1 pen)	32,387
Mar 30	EVERTON	L 0-3		29,468
Apr 6	Southampton	L 0-1		14,793
Apr 8	NEWCASTLE UNITED	W 2-1	Fenton 2	30,717
Apr 13	Nottingham Forest	W 5-1	Shearer, McKinlay, Wilcox 2, Fenton	25,273
Apr 17	WIMBLEDON	W 3-2	Shearer 2, Fenton	24,174
Apr 27	ARSENAL	D 1-1	Gallacher	29,834
May 5	Chelsea	W 3-2	Sherwood, McKinlay, Fenton	28,436

FA Cup

Jan 6	Ipswich Town	(Rd3)	D 0-0		21,236
Jan 16	IPSWICH TOWN	(R)	L 0-1*		19,606

*After extra-time.

Coca-Cola Cup

Sep 20	Swindon Town	(Rd2/1L)	W 3-2	Sutton, Shearer 2	14,740
Oct 4	SWINDON TOWN	(Rd2/2L)	W 2-0	Shearer 2	16,924
Oct 24	Watford	(Rd3)	W 2-1	Shearer, Newell	17,035
Nov 28	Leeds United	(Rd4)	L 1-2	Kelly o.g.	26,006

European Championship League

Sep 13	SPARTAK MOSCOW	L 0-1		20,940
Sep 27	Rosenborg	L 1-2	Newell	12,210
Oct 18	Legia Warsaw	L 0-1		15,000
Nov 1	LEGIA WARSAW	D 0-0		20,897
Nov 22	Spartak Moscow	L 0-3		35,000
Dec 6	ROSENBORG	W 4-1	Shearer (pen), Newell 3	20,677

Charity Shield

Aug 12	Everton†	L 0-1		40,149

†Played at Wembley Stadium.

MANAGER: Ray Harford
TOP SCORER: Alan Shearer
BIGGEST WIN: 7-0, 18 November 1995, v Nottingham Forest, Premier League
HIGHEST ATTENDANCE: 42,681, 10 February 1995, v Manchester United, Premier League
MAJOR TRANSFERS IN: Mattie Holmes from West Ham United, Lars Bohinen from Derby County, Billy McKinlay from Dundee United

League & Cup Appearances

PLAYER	LEAGUE	CUP COMPETITION				TOTAL
		FA CUP	COCA-COLA	EC	OTHER	
Atkins, M.N.	0 (4)			1	0 (1)	1 (5)
Batty, D.	23	1	4	5	1	34
Berg, H.	38	2	4	6		50
Bohinen, L.	17 (2)	1				18 (2)
Coleman, C.	19 (1)	2				21 (1)
Fenton, G.A.	4 (10)					4 (10)
Flitcroft, G.W.	3					3
Flowers, T.D.	37	2	3	6	1	49
Gallacher, K.W.	14 (2)	2		0 (1)	1	17 (3)
Gudmundsson, N.	1 (3)					1 (3)
Hendry, E.C.J.	33	2	4	5		44
Holmes, M.J.	8 (1)			2 (1)		10 (2)
Kenna, J.J.	32	2	4	5	1	44
Le Saux, G.P.	13 (1)		2	2 (1)	1	18 (2)
McKinlay, W.	13 (6)	1 (1)	1			15 (7)
Makel, L.R.	0 (3)			1 (1)	0 (1)	1 (5)
Marker, N.R.T.	8 (1)			1	0 (1)	9 (2)
Mimms, R.A.	1 (1)		1			2 (1)
Newell, M.C.	26 (4)	2	4	5 (1)	1	38 (5)
Pearce, I.A.	12		3	4	1	20
Ripley, S.E.	28	2	3	4 (1)	1	38 (1)
Shearer, A.	35	2	4	6	1	48
Sherwood, T.A.	33	1 (1)	4	6	1	45 (1)
Sutton, C.R.	9 (4)		2 (1)	3 (3)	1	15 (8)
Warhurst, P.	1 (9)		1(2)	4 (1)		6 (12)
Wilcox, J.M.	10					10

Goalscorers

PLAYER	LEAGUE	CUP COMPETITION				TOTAL
		FA CUP	COCA-COLA	EC	OTHER	
Shearer, A.	31		5	1		37
Newell, M.C.	3		1	4		8
Fenton, G.A.	6					6
Bohinen, L.	4					4
Sherwood, T.A.	4					4
Wilcox, J.M.	3					3
Gallacher, K.W.	2					2
McKinlay, W.	2					2
Batty, D.	1					1
Hendry, E.C.J.	1					1
Holmes, M.J.	1					1
Le Saux, G.P.	1					1
Marker, N.R.T.	1					1
Pearce, I.A.	1					1
Sutton, C.R.			1			1
Opps' o.gs.			1			1

Fact File

Blackburn celebrated the official opening of the rebuilt Ewood Park with a 7-0 win over Nottingham Forest on 18 November 1995.

Final Premier League Table

		P	W	D	L	F	A	Pts
1	MANCHESTER U	38	25	7	6	73	35	82
2	NEWCASTLE U	38	24	6	8	66	37	78
3	LIVERPOOL	38	20	11	7	70	34	71
4	ASTON VILLA	38	18	9	11	52	35	63
5	ARSENAL	38	17	12	9	49	32	63
6	EVERTON	38	17	10	11	64	44	61
7	BLACKBURN R	38	18	7	13	61	47	61
8	TOTTENHAM H	38	16	13	9	50	38	61
9	NOTTINGHAM F	38	15	13	10	50	54	58
10	WEST HAM U	38	14	9	15	43	52	51
11	CHELSEA	38	12	14	12	46	44	50
12	MIDDLESBROUGH	38	11	10	17	35	35	43
13	LEEDS UNITED	38	12	7	19	40	57	43
14	WIMBLEDON	38	10	11	17	55	70	41
15	SHEFFIELD W	38	10	10	18	48	61	40
16	COVENTRY C	38	8	14	16	42	60	38
17	SOUTHAMPTON	38	9	11	18	34	52	38
18	MANCHESTER C	38	9	11	18	33	58	38
19	QPR	38	9	6	23	38	57	33
20	BOLTON W	38	8	5	25	39	71	29

Season 1996-97

Premier League

DATE	OPPONENTS	SCORE	GOALSCORERS	ATTENDANCE
Aug 17	TOTTENHAM HOTSPUR	L 0-2		26,960
Aug 21	Aston Villa	L 0-1		32,457
Aug 25	Manchester United	D 2-2	Warhurst, Bohinen	54,178
Sep 4	LEEDS UNITED	L 0-1		23,226
Sep 9	DERBY COUNTY	L 1-2	Sutton	19,214
Sep 14	Newcastle United	L 1-2	Sutton	36,424
Sep 21	EVERTON	D 1-1	Donis	27,091
Sep 28	Coventry City	D 0-0		17,032
Oct 12	ARSENAL	L 0-2		24,303
Oct 19	Sheffield Wednesday	D 1-1	Bohinen	22,191
Oct 26	West Ham United	L 1-2	Berg	23,947
Nov 3	LIVERPOOL	W 3-0	Sutton 2 (1 pen), Wilcox	29,598
Nov 16	CHELSEA	D 1-1	Gallacher	27,229
Nov 25	Nottingham Forest	D 2-2	Gallacher, Wilcox	17,525
Nov 30	SOUTHAMPTON	W 2-1	Sherwood, Sutton	23,018
Dec 7	Leicester City	D 1-1	Sutton	19,306
Dec 14	Wimbledon	L 0-1		13,246
Dec 26	NEWCASTLE UNITED	W 1-0	Gallacher	30,398
Dec 28	Derby County	D 0-0		17,847
Jan 1	Everton	W 2-0	Sherwood, Sutton	30,427
Jan 11	COVENTRY CITY	W 4-0	Sutton 2, Gallacher, Donis	24,055
Jan 18	Sunderland	D 0-0		20,850
Jan 29	Tottenham Hotspur	L 1-2	Hendry	22,943
Feb 1	WEST HAM UNITED	W 2-1	Gallacher, Sutton	21,994
Feb 22	Liverpool	D 0-0		40,747
Mar 1	SUNDERLAND	W 1-0	Gallacher	24,208
Mar 5	Chelsea	D 1-1	Pedersen	25,784
Mar 11	NOTTINGHAM FOREST	D 1-1	Gallacher	20,485
Mar 15	WIMBLEDON	W 3-1	Gallacher 3	23,333
Mar 19	Middlesbrough	L 1-2	Sutton	29,891
Mar 22	ASTON VILLA	D 0-0		24,274
Apr 7	Leeds United	D 0-0		27,264
Apr 12	MANCHESTER UNITED	L 2-3	McKinlay, Warhurst	30,476
Apr 19	Arsenal	D 1-1	Flitcroft	38,086
Apr 22	SHEFFIELD WEDNESDAY	W 4-1	Berg, Sherwood, Le Saux, Flitcroft	20,845
May 3	Southampton	L 0-2		15,247
May 8	MIDDLESBROUGH	D 0-0		27,411
May 11	LEICESTER CITY	L 2-4	Flitcroft, Fenton	25,881

FA Cup

Jan 4	PORT VALE	(Rd3) W 1-0	Bohinen	19,891
Feb 15	COVENTRY CITY	(Rd4) L 1-2	Sherwood	21,123

Coca-Cola Cup

Sep 17	Brentford	(Rd2/1L) W 2-1	Flitcroft, Sutton	8,938
Sep 24	BRENTFORD	(Rd2/2L) W 2-0	Gallacher, Sherwood	9,599
Oct 22	STOCKPORT COUNTY	(Rd3) L 0-1		13,965

League & Cup Appearances

PLAYER	LEAGUE	CUP COMPETITION		TOTAL
		FA CUP	COCA-COLA	
Beattie, J.S.	1		1	2
Berg, H.	36	2	3	41
Bohinen, L.	17 (6)	1	2 (1)	20 (7)
Coleman, C.	8		1	9
Croft, G.	4 (1)		2	6 (1)
Donis, G.	11 (11)	0 (1)	3	14 (12)
Duff, D.A.	1			1
Fenton, G.A.	5 (8)	0 (1)	0 (2)	5 (11)
Flitcroft, G.W.	27 (1)	1	2	30 (1)
Flowers, T.D.	36	2	3	41
Gallacher, K.W.	34	3	3	40
Given, S.J.	2		0 (1)	2 (1)
Gudmundsson, N.	0 (2)			0 (2)
Hendry, E.C.J.	35	2	2	39
Kenna, J.J.	37	2	3	42
Le Saux, G.P.	26		2	28
McKinlay, W.J.A.	23 (2)	2		25 (2)
Marker, N.R.T.	5 (2)	0 (1)	0 (1)	5 (4)
Pearce, I.A.	7 (5)		1 (1)	8 (6)
Pedersen, P.W.	6 (5)			6 (5)
Ripley, S.E.	5 (8)			5 (8)
Sherwood, T.A.	37	2	3	42
Sutton, C.R.	24 (1)	2	2	28 (1)
Warhurst, P.	5 (6)	0 (1)		5 (7)
Wilcox, J.M.	26 (2)	2	2	30 (1)

Goalscorers

PLAYER	LEAGUE	CUP COMPETITION		TOTAL
		FA CUP	COCA-COLA	
Sutton, C.R.	11		1	12
Gallacher, K.W.	10		1	11
Sherwood, T.A.	3	1	1	5
Flitcroft, G.W.	3		1	4
Bohinen, L.	2	1		3
Berg, H.	2			2
Donis, G.	2			2
Warhurst, P.	2			2
Wilcox, J.M.	2			2
Fenton, G.A.	1			1
Hendry, E.C.J.	1			1
Le Saux, G.P.	1			1
McKinlay, W.J.A.	1			1
Pedersen, P.W.	1			1

Fact File

In December 1996, Sven Goran Eriksson agreed to become the new manager of Blackburn Rovers following the resignation of Ray Harford. Eriksson was due to take charge at Ewood Park in the summer but in February 1997 he announced that he would be staying in Italy.

MANAGER/CARETAKER MANAGER: Ray Harford/Tony Parkes
TOP SCORER: Chris Sutton
BIGGEST WIN: 4-0, 11 January 1997, v Coventry City, Premier League
HIGHEST ATTENDANCE: 54,178, 25 August 1996 v Manchester United, Premier League
MAJOR TRANSFERS IN: George Donis from Panathinaikos, Per Pedersen from Odense
MAJOR TRANSFERS OUT: Mike Newell to Birmingham City, Alan Shearer to Newcastle United

Final Premier League Table

		P	W	D	L	F	A	Pts
1	MANCHESTER U	38	21	12	5	76	44	75
2	NEWCASTLE U	38	19	11	8	73	40	68
3	ARSENAL	38	19	11	8	62	32	68
4	LIVERPOOL	38	19	11	8	62	37	68
5	ASTON VILLA	38	17	10	11	47	34	61
6	CHELSEA	38	16	11	11	58	55	59
7	SHEFFIELD W	38	14	15	9	50	51	57
8	WIMBLEDON	38	15	11	12	49	46	56
9	LEICESTER C	38	12	11	15	46	54	47
10	TOTTENHAM H	38	13	7	18	44	51	46
11	LEEDS U	38	11	13	14	28	38	46
12	DERBY CO	38	11	13	14	45	42	46
13	BLACKBURN R	38	9	15	14	42	43	42
14	WEST HAM U	38	10	12	16	39	48	42
15	EVERTON	38	10	12	16	44	57	42
16	SOUTHAMPTON	38	10	11	17	50	56	41
17	COVENTRY C	38	9	14	15	38	54	41
18	SUNDERLAND	38	10	10	18	35	53	40
19	MIDDLESBROUGH*	38	10	12	16	51	60	39
20	NOTTINGHAM F	38	6	16	16	31	59	34

*MIDDLESBROUGH HAD THREE POINTS DEDUCTED.

Season 1997-98

Premier League

DATE	OPPONENTS	SCORE	GOALSCORERS	ATTENDANCE
Aug 9	DERBY COUNTY	W 1-0	Gallacher	23,557
Aug 13	Aston Villa	W 4-0	Sutton 3, Gallacher	37,112
Aug 23	LIVERPOOL	D 1-1	Dahlin	30,187
Aug 25	SHEFFIELD WEDNESDAY	W 7-2	Gallacher 2, Hyde o.g., Wilcox, Sutton 2, Bohinen	19,618
Aug 30	Crystal Palace	W 2-1	Sutton, Gallacher	20,849
Sep 14	LEEDS UNITED	L 3-4	Gallacher, Sutton (pen), Dahlin	21,956
Sep 20	Tottenham Hotspur	D 0-0		26,573
Sep 24	Leicester City	D 1-1	Sutton	19,921
Sep 28	COVENTRY CITY	D 0-0		19,086
Oct 4	Wimbledon	W 1-0	Sutton	15,600
Oct 18	SOUTHAMPTON	W 1-0	Sherwood	24,130
Oct 25	Newcastle United	D 1-1	Sutton	36,716
Nov 1	Barnsley	D 1-1	Sherwood	18,665
Nov 8	EVERTON	W 3-2	Gallacher, Duff, Sherwood	25,397
Nov 22	CHELSEA	W 1-0	Croft	27,683
Nov 30	Manchester United	L 0-4		55,175
Dec 6	BOLTON WANDERERS	W 3-1	Gallacher, Sutton, Wilcox	25,503
Dec 13	Arsenal	W 3-1	Wilcox, Gallacher, Sherwood	38,147
Dec 20	WEST HAM UNITED	W 3-0	Ripley, Duff 2	21,653
Dec 26	Sheffield Wednesday	D 0-0		33,502
Dec 28	CRYSTAL PALACE	D 2-2	Gallacher, Sutton	23,872
Jan 11	Derby County	L 1-3	Sutton	27,823
Jan 17	ASTON VILLA	W 5-0	Sherwood, Gallacher 3, Ripley	24,834
Jan 31	Liverpool	D 0-0		43,890
Feb 7	TOTTENHAM HOTSPUR	L 0-3		30,388
Feb 21	Southampton	L 0-3		15,162
Feb 28	LEICESTER CITY	W 5-3	Dahlin, Sutton 3, Hendry	24,854
Mar 11	Leeds United	L 0-4		32,933
Mar 14	Everton	L 0-1		33,423
Mar 31	BARNSLEY	W 2-1	Dahlin, Gallacher	24,179
Apr 6	MANCHESTER UNITED	L 1-3	Sutton (pen)	30,547
Apr 11	Bolton Wanderers	L 1-2	Duff	25,000
Apr 13	ARSENAL	L 1-4	Gallacher	28,212
Apr 18	West Ham United	L 1-2	Wilcox	24,733
Apr 25	WIMBLEDON	D 0-0		24,848
Apr 29	Chelsea	W 1-0	Gallacher	33,311
May 2	Coventry City	L 0-2		18,794
May 10	NEWCASTLE UNITED	W 1-0	Sutton	29,300

FA Cup

Jan 3	WIGAN ATHLETIC	(Rd3)	W 4-2	McGibbon o.g., Gallacher 2, Sherwood	22,402
Jan 26	Sheffield Wednesday	(Rd4)	W 3-0	Sutton, Sherwood, Duff	15,940
Feb 14	West Ham United	(Rd5)	D 2-2	Gallacher, Sutton	25,729
Feb 25	WEST HAM UNITED	(R)	D 1-1*†	Ripley	21,972

*After extra-time. †Lost 5-4 on penalties.

Coca-Cola Cup

Sep 17	PRESTON NORTH END	(Rd2/1L)	W 6-0	Dahlin 2, Sutton, Gallacher, Andersson, Bohinen	22,564
Sep 30	Preston North End	(Rd2/2L)	L 0-1		11,472
Oct 15	Chelsea	(Rd3)	D 1-1*†	McKinlay	18,671

*After extra-time. † Lost 4-1 on penalties.

League & Cup Appearances

PLAYER	LEAGUE	CUP COMPETITION		TOTAL
		FA CUP	COCA-COLA	
Andersson, A.P.	1 (3)	0 (1)	3	4 (4)
Beattie, J.S.	0 (3)	0 (1)	1	1 (4)
Bohinen, L.	6 (10)	0 (1)	1 (1)	7 (12)
Broomes, M.C.	2 (2)		1	3 (2)
Coleman, C.			1	1
Croft, G.	19 (4)	2	3	24 (4)
Dahlin, M.	11 (10)	0 (1)	2	13 (11)
Davidson, C.I.	1			1
Duff, D.A.	17 (9)	3 (1)	2 (1)	22 (11)
Fettis, A.W.	7 (1)	1		8 (1)
Filan, J.R.	7			7
Flitcroft, G.W.	28 (5)	2 (1)	1 (1)	31 (7)
Flowers, T.D.	24 (1)	3	3	30 (1)
Gallacher, K.W.	31 (2)	4	0 (1)	35 (3)
Henchoz, S.	36	4	0 (1)	40 (1)
Hendry, E.C.J.	34	4	1	39
Johnson, D.M.			1	1
Kenna, J.J.	37	4	1	42
McKinlay, W.	26 (4)	3	2	31 (4)
Pearce, I.A.	1 (4)			1 (4)
Pedersen, P.W.			1 (1)	1 (1)
Pedersen, T.	3 (2)		3	6 (2)
Ripley, S.E.	25 (4)	3		28 (4)
Sherwood, T.A.	29 (2)	4	1 (1)	34 (3)
Sutton, C.R.	35	4	2	41
Valery, P.J.C.	14 (1)	1 (1)	2	17 (2)
Wilcox, J.M.	24 (7)	2 (2)	1	27 (9)

Goalscorers

PLAYER	LEAGUE	CUP COMPETITION		TOTAL
		FA CUP	COCA-COLA	
Sutton, C.R.	18	2	1	21
Gallacher, K.W.	16	3	1	20
Sherwood, T.A.	5	2		7
Dahlin, M.	4		2	6
Duff, D.A.	4	1		5
Wilcox, J.M.	4			4
Ripley, S.E.	2	1		3
Bohinen, L.	1		1	2
Croft, G.	1			1
Hendry, E.C.J.	1			1
McKinlay, W.			1	1
Andersson, A.P.			1	1
Opps' o.gs.	1	1		2

Fact File

Roy Hodgson led the club to European qualification in his first season at Ewood Park.

Final Premier League Table

		P	W	D	L	F	A	Pts
1	ARSENAL	38	23	9	6	68	33	78
2	MANCHESTER U	38	23	8	7	73	26	77
3	LIVERPOOL	38	18	11	9	68	42	65
4	CHELSEA	38	20	3	15	71	43	63
5	LEEDS U	38	17	8	13	57	46	59
6	BLACKBURN R	38	16	10	12	57	52	58
7	ASTON VILLA	38	17	6	15	49	48	57
8	WEST HAM U	38	16	8	14	56	57	56
9	DERBY CO	38	16	7	15	52	49	55
10	LEICESTER C	38	13	14	11	51	41	53
11	COVENTRY C	38	12	16	10	46	44	52
12	SOUTHAMPTON	38	14	6	18	50	55	48
13	NEWCASTLE U	38	11	11	16	35	44	44
14	TOTTENHAM H	38	11	11	16	44	56	44
15	WIMBLEDON	38	10	14	14	34	46	44
16	SHEFFIELD W	38	12	8	18	52	67	44
17	EVERTON	38	9	13	16	41	56	40
18	BOLTON W	38	9	13	16	41	61	40
19	BARNSLEY	38	10	5	23	37	82	35
20	CRYSTAL P	38	8	9	21	37	71	33

MANAGER: Roy Hodgson

TOP SCORER: Chris Sutton

BIGGEST WIN: 7-2, 25 August 1997, v Sheffield Wednesday, Premier League

HIGHEST ATTENDANCE: 55,175, 30 November 1997, v Manchester United, Premier League

MAJOR TRANSFERS IN: Stephane Henchoz from SV Hamburg, Patrick Valery from Bastia, Anders Andersson from FF Malmo, Martin Dahlin from AS Roma, John Filan from Coventry City

MAJOR TRANSFERS OUT: Henning Berg to Chelsea, Graeme Le Saux to Chelsea, Paul Warhurst to Crystal Palace, Shay Given to Newcastle United, Graham Fenton to Leicester City, Nicky Marker to Sheffield United, Niklas Gudmundsson to FF Malmo

Season 1998-99

Premier League

DATE	OPPONENTS	SCORE	GOALSCORERS	ATTENDANCE
Aug 15	DERBY COUNTY	D 0-0		24,007
Aug 24	Leeds United	L 0-1		30,652
Aug 29	LEICESTER CITY	W 1-0	Gallacher	22,544
Sep 9	Tottenham Hotspur	L 1-2	Gallacher	28,338
Sep 12	Sheffield Wednesday	L 0-3		20,846
Sep 21	CHELSEA	L 3-4	Sutton 2 (1 pen), Perez	23,113
Sep 26	Everton	D 0-0		36,404
Oct 3	WEST HAM UNITED	W 3-0	Flitcroft 2, Davidson	25,213
Oct 17	Middlesbrough	L 1-2	Sherwood	34,413
Oct 25	ARSENAL	L 1-2	Johnson	27,012
Oct 31	Wimbledon	D 1-1	Sutton (pen)	12,526
Nov 7	COVENTRY CITY	L 1-2	Sherwood	23,779
Nov 14	Manchester United	L 2-3	Marcolin, Blake	55,198
Nov 21	SOUTHAMPTON	L 0-2		22,812
Nov 29	Liverpool	L 0-2		41,753
Dec 5	CHARLTON ATHLETIC	W 1-0	Davies	22,568
Dec 12	NEWCASTLE UNITED	D 0-0		27,569
Dec 19	Nottingham Forest	D 2-2	Blake 2	22,013
Dec 26	ASTON VILLA	W 2-1	Gallacher, Sherwood	27,536
Dec 28	Leicester City	D 1-1	Gallacher	21,083
Jan 9	LEEDS UNITED	W 1-0	Gillespie	27,620
Jan 16	Derby County	L 0-1		27,386
Jan 30	TOTTENHAM HOTSPUR	D 1-1	Jansen	29,643
Feb 6	Aston Villa	W 3-1	Southgate o.g., Ward, Dunn	37,404
Feb 17	Chelsea	D 1-1	Ward	34,382
Feb 20	SHEFFIELD WEDNESDAY	L 1-4	McAteer	24,643
Feb 27	West Ham United	L 0-2		25,529
Mar 10	EVERTON	L 1-2	Ward	27,219
Mar 13	Coventry City	D 1-1	Wilcox	19,701
Mar 20	WIMBLEDON	W 3-1	Ward, Jansen 2	21,754
Apr 3	MIDDLESBROUGH	D 0-0		27,482
Apr 6	Arsenal	L 0-1		37,762
Apr 17	Southampton	D 3-3	Ward, Peacock, Wilcox	15,209
Apr 24	LIVERPOOL	L 1-3	Duff	29,944
May 1	Charlton Athletic	D 0-0		20,041
May 8	NOTTINGHAM FOREST	L 1-2	Gallacher	24,565
May 12	MANCHESTER UNITED	D 0-0		30,436
May 16	Newcastle United	D 1-1	Wilcox	36,623

FA Cup

Jan 2	CHARLTON ATHLETIC	(Rd3) W 2-0	Davies, Wilcox	16,631
Jan 23	SUNDERLAND	(Rd4) W 1-0	Gillespie	30,125
Feb 14	Newcastle United	(Rd 5) D 0-0		36,295
Feb 24	NEWCASTLE UNITED	(R) L 0-1		27,483

Worthington Cup

Oct 28	Crewe Alexandra	(Rd3) W 1-0	Sutton	5,403
Nov 11	Newcastle United	(Rd4) D 1-1*†	Sherwood	34,702
Dec 2	Leicester City	(Rd 5) L 0-1		19,442

*After extra-time. †Won 4-2 on penalties.

UEFA Cup

Sep 15	OLYMPIQUE LYONNAIS	(Rd1/1L) L 0-1		13,646
Sep 29	Olympique Lyonnais	(Rd1/2L) D 2-2	Perez, Flitcroft	24,558

Fact File

Roy Hodgson was relieved of his managerial duties immediately after the 2-0 home defeat by Southampton on 21 November 1998.

MANAGER: Roy Hodgson/Brian Kidd

TOP SCORER: Kevin Gallacher/Ashley Ward

BIGGEST WIN: 3-0, 3 October 1998, v West Ham United, Premier League

HIGHEST ATTENDANCE: 55,198, 14 November 1998, v Manchester United, Premier League

MAJOR TRANSFERS IN: Darren Peacock from Newcastle United, Christian Dailly from Derby County, Keith Gillespie from Newcastle United, Ashley Ward from Barnsley, Jason McAteer from Liverpool, Matt Jansen from Crystal Palace, Lee Carsley from Derby County

MAJOR TRANSFERS OUT: Stuart Ripley to Southampton, Patrick Valery to Bastia, James Beattie to Southampton, Colin Hendry to Rangers

League & Cup Appearances

PLAYER	LEAGUE	CUP COMPETITION			TOTAL
		FA CUP	WORTHINGTON	UEFA	
Blake, N.A.	9 (2)	1 (2)			10 (4)
Broomes, M.C.	8 (5)	4			12 (5)
Carsley, L.K.	7 (1)				7 (1)
Croft, G.	10 (2)	2 (2)	1		13 (4)
Dahlin, M.	2 (3)			0 (1)	2 (4)
Dailly, C.E.	14 (3)		2	2	18 (3)
Davidson, C.I.	34	2	2 (1)	1 (1)	39 (2)
Davies, K.C.	9 (12)	2	3	1	15 (12)
Duff, D.A.	18 (10)	3 (1)	3	1	25 (11)
Dunn, D.J.I.	10 (5)	2 (1)	1 (1)		13 (7)
Fettis, A.W.	2				2
Filan, J.R.	26	4	2		32
Flitcroft, G.W.	8			2	10
Flowers, T.D.	10 (1)	0 (1)	1	2	13 (2)
Gallacher, K.W.	13 (3)	1	1		15 (3)
Gillespie, K.R.	13 (3)	4			17 (3)
Henchoz, S.	34	2	3	2	41
Jansen, M.B.	10 (1)				10 (1)
Johnson, D.M.	14 (7)		3	0 (1)	17 (8)
Kenna, J.J.	22 (1)	3	3	1	29 (1)
Konde, O.		0 (1)			0 (1)
McAteer, J.W.	13				13
McKinlay, W.	14 (2)	1	1	1	17 (2)
Marcolin, D.	5 (5)	3	2		10 (5)
Peacock, D.	27 (3)	3	2	2	34 (3)
Perez, S.	4 (1)	1		2	7 (1)
Sherwood, T.A.	19		2	2	23
Sutton, C.R.	17	1	1	1	20
Taylor, M.	1 (2)			0 (1)	1 (3)
Ward, A.S.	17	2 (1)			19 (1)
Wilcox, J.M.	28 (1)	3		2	33 (2)

Goalscorers

PLAYER	LEAGUE	CUP COMPETITION			TOTAL
		FA CUP	WORTHINGTON	UEFA	
Gallacher, K.W.	5				5
Ward, A.S.	5				5
Sutton, C.R.	3		1		4
Wilcox, J.M.	3	1			4
Sherwood, T.A	3		1		4
Blake, N.A	3				3
Jansen, M.B	3				3
Flitcroft, G.W	2			1	3
Davies, K.C	1	1			2
Gillespie, K.R	1	1			2
Perez, S	1			1	2
Davidson, C.I	1				1
Duff, D.A	1				1
Dunn, D.J.I	1				1
Johnson, D.M	1				1
McAteer, J.W	1				1
Marcolin, D	1				1
Peacock, D	1				1
Opps' o.gs.	1				1

Final Premier League Table

		P	W	D	L	F	A	Pts
1	MANCHESTER U	38	22	13	3	80	37	79
2	ARSENAL	38	22	12	4	59	17	78
3	CHELSEA	38	20	15	3	57	30	75
4	LEEDS U	38	18	13	7	62	34	67
5	WEST HAM U	38	16	9	13	46	53	57
6	ASTON VILLA	38	15	10	13	51	46	55
7	LIVERPOOL	38	15	9	14	68	49	54
8	DERBY CO	38	13	13	12	40	45	52
9	MIDDLESBROUGH	38	12	15	11	48	54	51
10	LEICESTER C	38	12	13	13	40	46	49
11	TOTTENHAM H	38	11	14	13	47	50	47
12	SHEFFIELD W	38	13	7	18	41	36	46
13	NEWCASTLE U	38	11	13	14	48	54	46
14	EVERTON	38	11	10	17	42	47	43
15	COVENTRY C	38	11	9	18	39	51	42
16	WIMBLEDON	38	10	12	16	40	63	42
17	SOUTHAMPTON	38	11	8	19	37	64	41
18	CHARLTON A	38	8	12	18	41	56	36
19	BLACKBURN R	38	7	14	17	38	52	35
20	NOTTINGHAM F	38	7	9	22	35	69	30

Season 1999-2000

Football League Division 1

DATE	OPPONENTS	SCORE	GOALSCORERS	ATTENDANCE
Aug 7	PORT VALE	D 0-0		20,530
Aug 13	Huddersfield Town	L 2-3	Carsley, Broomes	13,670
Aug 21	BARNSLEY	L 1-2	Carsley (pen)	19,537
Aug 28	Norwich City	W 2-0	Ostenstad 2	15,407
Sep 11	TRANMERE ROVERS	W 2-0	Ward, Blake	17,899
Sep 18	West Bromwich Albion	D 2-2	Dailly, Jansen	16,902
Sep 25	WALSALL	W 2-0	Ward, Carsley	18,232
Sep 28	Swindon Town	L 1-2	Ostenstad	7,354
Oct 2	Queens Park Rangers	D 0-0		14,002
Oct 16	GRIMSBY TOWN	D 1-1	Carsley (pen)	17,575
Oct 20	CRYSTAL PALACE	D 1-1	Frandsen	15,819
Oct 23	Manchester City	L 0-2		33,027
Oct 26	Walsall	D 1-1	Carsley (pen)	6,484
Oct 30	QUEENS PARK RANGERS	L 0-2		17,491
Nov 6	IPSWICH TOWN	D 2-2	Carsley 2 (1 pen)	18,512
Nov 20	FULHAM	W 2-0	Ostenstad, Duff	18,543
Nov 23	Crewe Alexandra	D 0-0		6,495
Nov 27	STOCKPORT COUNTY	W 2-0	Frandsen, Ostenstad	17,592
Nov 30	Charlton Athletic	W 2-1	Ward 2	18,939
Dec 4	Port Vale	D 0-0		6,084
Dec 7	BOLTON WANDERERS	W 3-1	Ward, McAteer, Blake	21,046
Dec 19	Sheffield United	L 1-2	Ward	10,437
Dec 26	NOTTINGHAM FOREST	W 2-1	Frandsen, Carsley (pen)	23,406
Dec 28	Portsmouth	W 2-1	Dailly, Ostenstad	15,208
Jan 3	WOLVERHAMPTON W.	D 1-1	Ostenstad	24,743
Jan 15	HUDDERSFIELD TOWN	W 2-0	Duff, Johnson	21,420
Jan 22	Barnsley	L 1-5	Frandsen	18,088
Feb 5	Bolton Wanderers	L 1-3	Blake	17,687
Feb 12	SWINDON TOWN	D 0-0		16,938
Feb 15	Birmingham City	L 0-1		20,719
Feb 19	Stockport County	W 1-0	McAteer	7,902
Feb 26	WEST BROMWICH ALBION	W 2-1	Gillespie, Dailly	18,184
Feb 29	NORWICH CITY	D 1-1	Frandsen	15,671
Mar 4	Tranmere Rovers	L 1-2	Dailly	9,502
Mar 7	Ipswich Town	D 0-0		18,871
Mar 12	CREWE ALEXANDRA	L 0-1		16,057
Mar 18	Fulham	D 2-2	Dunn, Gillespie	15,108
Mar 22	BIRMINGHAM CITY	W 1-0	Dunn	18,096
Mar 25	Nottingham Forest	W 1-0	Ward	16,823
Apr 1	SHEFFIELD UNITED	W 5-0	Duff 2, Ward, Ostenstad, Jansen	17,769
Apr 8	Wolverhampton W.	L 1-2	Duff	22,286
Apr 15	PORTSMOUTH	D 1-1	Carsley (pen)	17,263
Apr 22	Grimsby Town	D 0-0		6,558
Apr 24	CHARLTON ATHLETIC	D 1-1	Carsley (pen)	18,587
Apr 29	Crystal Palace	L 1-2	Jansen	18,272
May 7	MANCHESTER CITY	L 1-4	Jansen	29,913

FA Cup

Dec 11	West Bromwich Albion	(Rd3) D 2-2	Frandsen, Blake	10,609
Dec 22	WEST BROMWICH ALBION	(R) W 2-0*	Duff, Carsley (pen)	11,766
Jan 10	LIVERPOOL	(Rd4) W 1-0	Blake	32,839
Jan 31	NEWCASTLE UNITED	(Rd5) L 1-2	Jansen	29,946

*After extra-time.

Worthington Cup

Sep 14	Portsmouth	(Rd2/1L) W 3-0	Cundy o.g., Jansen 2	8,542
Sep 22	PORTSMOUTH	(Rd2/2L) W 3-1	Duff, Dunn, Gallacher	7,512
Oct 13	Leeds United	(Rd3) L 0-1		24,353

MANAGER: Brian Kidd/Tony Parkes/Graeme Souness

TOP SCORER: Lee Carsley

BIGGEST WIN: 5-0, 1 April 2000, v Sheffield United, Division 1

HIGHEST ATTENDANCE: 33,027, 23 October 1999, v Manchester City, Division 1

MAJOR TRANSFERS IN: Simon Grayson from Aston Villa, Alan Kelly from Sheffield United, Craig Short from Everton, Egil Ostenstad from Southampton, Steve Harkness from Benfica, Per Frandsen from Bolton Wanderers

MAJOR TRANSFERS OUT: Chris Sutton to Chelsea, Tim Flowers to Leicester City, Kevin Davies to Southampton, Gary Croft to Ipswich Town, Kevin Gallacher to Newcastle United, Jason Wilcox to Leeds United

---

League & Cup Appearances

PLAYER	LEAGUE	CUP COMPETITION		TOTAL
		FA CUP	WORTHINGTON	
Blake, N.A.	17 (11)	4	2	23 (11)
Broomes, M.C.	13			13
Burgess, B.	1 (1)			1 (1)
Carsley, L.K.	30	4		34
Dailly, C.E.	43	4	1	48
Davidson, C.I.	28 (2)	4	1	33 (2)
Davies, K.C.	2			2
Duff, D.A.	33 (6)	3	2	38 (6)
Dunn, D.J.I.	17 (5)	0 (1)	3	20 (6)
Fettis, A.W.	0 (1)			0 (1)
Filan, J.R.	16	1	1	18
Flitcroft, G.W.	18 (1)			18 (1)
Frandsen, P.	26 (5)	4		30 (5)
Gallacher, K.W.	3 (2)		0 (1)	3 (3)
Gill, W.J.			3	3
Gillespie, K.R.	11 (11)	0 (1)	2	13 (12)
Grayson, S.N.	31 (3)	2 (1)	0 (1)	33 (5)
Harkness, S.	17	1	1 (1)	19 (1)
Jansen, M.B.	16 (14)	1	1 (1)	18 (15)
Johnson, D.M.	11 (5)	1 (3)	2 (1)	14 (9)
Kelly, A.T.	29 (1)	3	2	34 (1)
Kenna, J.J.	11	2	3	16
McAteer, J.W.	24 (4)	3		27 (4)
Miller, A.J.	1			1
Ostenstad, E.	21 (7)	1 (1)	1	23 (8)
Peacock, D.	15 (2)	3	2	20 (2)
Richardson, L.N.			1	1
Short, C.J.	17		1	18
Taylor, M.	4 (2)	1	2	7 (2)
Ward, A.S.	35 (2)	2	2	39 (2)
Wilcox, J.M.	16 (4)			16 (4)

Goalscorers

PLAYER	LEAGUE	CUP COMPETITION		TOTAL
		FA CUP	WORTHINGTON	
Carsley, L.K.	10	1		11
Ostenstad, E.	8			8
Ward, A.S.	8			8
Duff, D.A.	5	1	1	7
Jansen, M.B.	4	1	2	7
Frandsen, P.	5	1		6
Blake, N.A.	3	2		5
Dailly, C.E.	4			4
Dunn, D.J.I.	2		1	3
Gillespie, K.R.	2			2
McAteer, J.W.	2			2
Broomes, M.C.	1			1
Johnson, D.M.	1			1
Gallacher, K.W.			1	1
Opps' o.gs.			1	1

Final Division 1 Table

		P	W	D	L	F	A	Pts
1	CHARLTON A	46	27	10	9	79	45	91
2	MANCHESTER C	46	26	11	9	78	40	89
3	IPSWICH T	46	25	12	9	71	42	87
4	BARNSLEY	46	24	10	12	88	67	82
5	BIRMINGHAM C	46	22	11	13	65	44	77
6	BOLTON W	46	21	13	12	69	50	76
7	WOLVERHAMPTON W	46	21	11	14	64	48	74
8	HUDDERSFIELD T	46	21	11	14	62	49	74
9	FULHAM	46	17	16	13	49	41	67
10	QPR	46	16	18	12	62	53	66
11	BLACKBURN R	46	15	17	14	55	51	62
12	NORWICH C	46	14	15	17	45	50	57
13	TRANMERE R	46	15	12	19	57	68	57
14	NOTTINGHAM F	46	14	14	18	53	55	56
15	CRYSTAL PALACE	46	13	15	18	57	67	54
16	SHEFFIELD U	46	13	15	18	59	71	54
17	STOCKPORT CO	46	13	15	18	55	67	54
18	PORTSMOUTH	46	13	12	21	55	66	51
19	CREWE ALEX	46	14	9	23	46	67	51
20	GRIMSBY T	46	13	12	21	41	67	51
21	WBA	46	10	19	17	43	60	49
22	WALSALL	46	11	13	22	52	77	46
23	PORT VALE	46	7	15	24	48	69	36
24	SWINDON T	46	8	12	26	38	77	36

Season 2000-01

Football League Division 1

DATE	OPPONENTS	SCORE	GOALSCORERS	ATTENDANCE
Aug 12	CRYSTAL PALACE	W 2-0	Blake, Jansen	18,733
Aug 19	Crewe Alexandra	D 0-0		8,059
Aug 26	NORWICH CITY	W 3-2	Dunn (pen), Blake, Jansen	19,542
Aug 28	Sheffield Wednesday	D 1-1	Taylor	15,646
Sep 9	NOTTINGHAM FOREST	W 3-0	Jansen, Dunn, Blake	18,471
Sep 12	WATFORD	L 3-4	Dunn, Blake 2	17,258
Sep 15	Sheffield United	L 0-2		10,816
Sep 23	BOLTON WANDERERS	D 1-1	Thomas	23,660
Sep 30	West Bromwich Albion	L 0-1		16,791
Oct 15	Fulham	L 1-2	Jansen	15,247
Oct 18	Wimbledon	W 2-0	Willmott o.g., Flitcroft	6,019
Oct 21	GRIMSBY TOWN	W 2-0	Flitcroft, Jansen	16,397
Oct 25	TRANMERE ROVERS	W 3-2	Hughes 2, Ostenstad	17,010
Oct 28	Huddersfield Town	W 1-0	Ostenstad	12,837
Nov 4	STOCKPORT COUNTY	W 2-1	Hughes, Hignett	17,404
Nov 8	Barnsley	W 2-1	Jansen, Dunn	13,622
Nov 11	Portsmouth	D 2-2	Bjornebye, Jansen	14,141
Nov 18	WOLVERHAMPTON W.	W 1-0	Dunn (pen)	20,380
Nov 25	GILLINGHAM	L 1-2	Hughes	18,061
Dec 2	Tranmere Rovers	D 1-1	Dunn	10,063
Dec 9	QUEENS PARK RANGERS	D 0-0		16,886
Dec 17	Burnley	W 2-0	McAteer, Bent	21,369
Dec 22	Crystal Palace	W 3-2	Dunn 2 (1 pen), Taylor	15,010
Dec 26	BIRMINGHAM CITY	W 2-1	Jansen 2	24,899
Dec 30	CREWE ALEXANDRA	W 1-0	Jansen	18,554
Jan 1	Norwich City	D 1-1	Bent	16,695
Jan 10	PRESTON NORTH END	W 3-2	Jansen 2, Hughes	23,983
Jan 13	SHEFFIELD WEDNESDAY	W 2-0	Bent, Taylor	19,308
Feb 3	BARNSLEY	D 0-0		18,573
Feb 10	Nottingham Forest	L 1-2	Jansen	22,455
Feb 20	Watford	W 1-0	Bent	15,970
Feb 23	Bolton Wanderers	W 4-1	Bent, Dunn, Jansen, Hignett	20,017
Mar 3	WEST BROMWICH ALBION	W 1-0	Bent	23,926
Mar 14	Birmingham City	W 2-0	Bent, Duff	29,150
Mar 17	WIMBLEDON	D 1-1	Jansen	19,000
Apr 1	BURNLEY	W 5-0	Short, Davis o.g., Jansen 2, Hignett	23,515
Apr 4	SHEFFIELD UNITED	D 1-1	Berg	26,276
Apr 7	Queens Park Rangers	W 3-1	Dunn, Jansen, Berkovic	12,449
Apr 11	FULHAM	L 1-2	Jansen	21,578
Apr 14	Stockport County	D 0-0		9,705
Apr 16	HUDDERSFIELD TOWN	W 2-0	Flitcroft, Jansen	29,406
Apr 21	Wolverhampton W.	D 0-0		20,018
Apr 24	Grimsby Town	W 4-1	Dunn, Berkovic, Jansen 2	6,507
Apr 29	PORTSMOUTH	W 3-1	Hiley o.g., Dunn, Bent	24,257
May 2	Preston North End	W 1-0	Jansen	16,973
May 6	Gillingham	D 1-1	Blake	10,319

FA Cup

Jan 6	CHESTER CITY	(Rd3) W 2-0	Taylor, Bent	15,223
Jan 27	DERBY COUNTY	(Rd4) D 0-0		18,585
Feb 7	Derby County	(R) W 5-2	Flitcroft, Bent 2, Dunn (pen), Jansen	15,203
Feb 17	Bolton Wanderers	(Rd5) D 1-1	Dunn	22,048
Mar 7	BOLTON WANDERERS	(R) W 3-0	Flitcroft, Hignett 2 (1 pen)	20,318
Mar 10	Arsenal	(Rd6) L 0-3		36,604

Worthington Cup

Aug 22	Rochdale	(Rd1/1L) D 1-1	Blake	4,873
Sep 6	ROCHDALE	(Rd1/2L) W 6-1	Duff 2, Dunn 3 (3 pens), Diawara	12,977
Sep 19	PORTSMOUTH	(Rd2/1L) W 4-0	Carsley, Thomas 2, Ostenstad	10,360
Sep 26	Portsmouth	(Rd2/2L) D 1-1	Dunn	2,731
Oct 31	West Ham United	(Rd3) L 0-2		21,863

MANAGER: Graeme Souness

TOP SCORER: Matt Jansen

BIGGEST WIN: 6-1, 6 September 2000, v Rochdale, Worthington Cup Round 2 second leg

HIGHEST ATTENDANCE: 36,604, 10 March 2001, v Arsenal, FA Cup Round 6

MAJOR TRANSFERS IN: Mark Hughes from Everton, Brad Friedel from Liverpool, Marcus Bent from Sheffield United

MAJOR TRANSFERS OUT: Lee Carsley to Coventry City, Christian Dailly to West Ham United

---

League & Cup Appearances

PLAYER	LEAGUE	CUP COMPETITION		TOTAL
		FA CUP	WORTHINGTON	
Bent, M.N.	21 (7)	5 (1)		26 (8)
Berg, H.	41	3	1	45
Berkovic, E.	4 (7)	3		7 (7)
Bjornebye, S.	30 (3)	2 (1)	2	34 (4)
Blake, N.A.	11 (1)	0 (1)	1	12 (2)
Broomes, M.C.	1		2	3
Carsley, L.K.	3 (5)		4	7 (5)
Curtis, J.C.	46	5	4	55
Dailly, C.E.	3 (7)		2 (1)	5 (8)
Diawara, K.	1 (4)		1	2 (4)
Douglas, J.		0 (1)	0 (1)	0 (2)
Duff, D.A.	31 (1)	3 (2)	2	36 (3)
Dunn, D.J.I.	41 (1)	5	3 (2)	49 (3)
Dunning, D.	1	1	1	3
Filan, J.R.	12 (1)		2	14 (1)
Flitcroft, G.W.	41	5	2 (1)	48 (1)
Friedel, B.H.	27	6		33
Gillespie, K.R.	12 (6)		1	13 (6)
Hignett, C.J.	15 (15)	2 (3)		17 (18)
Hughes, L.M.	21 (8)	3 (2)		24 (10)
Jansen, M.B.	31 (9)	3 (3)	2	36 (12)
Johnson, D.M.	12 (4)	0 (1)	3 (2)	15 (7)
Keller, M.	0 (2)	0 (3)		0 (5)
Kelly, A.T.	7		2	9
Kenna, J.J.	5 (1)		2 (2)	7 (3)
McAteer, J.W.	20 (7)	4	4	28 (7)
Mahon, A.J.	14 (4)	6		20 (4)
Ostenstad, E.	7 (6)	1	3 (1)	11 (7)
Short, C.J.	35	3		38
Taylor, M.	12 (4)	6	5	23 (4)
Thomas, J.A.	1 (3)		1	2 (3)

Also played one game: B. Burgess, S.N. Grayson, G. Hamilton, S. Harkness, A.J. Miller, B. O'Brien, M. Richards.

Goalscorers

PLAYER	LEAGUE	CUP COMPETITION		TOTAL
		FA CUP	WORTHINGTON	
Jansen, M.B.	23	1		24
Dunn, D.J.I.	12	2	4	18
Bent, M.N.	8	3		11
Blake, N.A.	6		1	7
Hughes, L.M.	5			5
Flitcroft, G.W.	3	2		5
Hignett, C.J.	3	2		5
Taylor, M.	3	1		4
Ostenstad, E.	2		1	3
Duff, D.A.	1		2	3
Thomas, J.A.	1		2	3
Berkovic, E.	2			2
Opps' o.gs.	3			3

Also scored one goal: H. Berg, S. Bjornebye, J.W. McAteer, C.J. Short, L.K. Carsley, K. Diawara

Final Division 1 Table

		P	W	D	L	F	A	Pts
1	FULHAM	46	30	11	5	90	32	101
2	BLACKBURN R	46	26	13	7	76	39	91
3	BOLTON W	46	24	15	7	76	45	87
4	PRESTON NE	46	23	9	14	64	52	78
5	BIRMINGHAM C	46	23	9	14	59	48	78
6	WBA	46	21	11	14	60	52	74
7	BURNLEY	46	21	9	16	50	54	72
8	WIMBLEDON	46	17	18	11	71	50	69
9	WATFORD	46	20	9	17	76	67	69
10	SHEFFIELD U	46	19	11	16	52	49	68
11	NOTTINGHAM F	46	20	8	18	55	53	68
12	WOLVERHAMPTON W	46	14	13	19	45	48	55
13	GILLINGHAM	46	13	16	17	61	66	55
14	CREWE A	46	15	10	21	47	62	55
15	NORWICH C	46	14	12	20	46	58	54
16	BARNSLEY	46	15	9	22	49	62	54
17	SHEFFIELD W	46	15	8	23	52	71	53
18	GRIMSBY T	46	14	10	22	43	62	52
19	STOCKPORT COU	46	11	18	17	58	65	51
20	PORTSMOUTH	46	10	19	17	47	59	49
21	CRYSTAL PALACE	46	12	13	21	57	70	49
22	HUDDERSFIELD TOWN	46	11	15	20	48	57	48
23	QPR	46	7	19	20	45	75	40
24	TRANMERE R	46	9	11	26	46	77	38

Complete Players' Career Records

Complete records for competitive first-team matches from 1888-89 to 2000-2001. 'Others' includes: Charity Shield, play-offs, test matches, Full Members' Cup, Simod Cup, Zenith Data Systems, Anglo-Scottish Cup, wartime. League Cup includes: Milk Cup, Littlewoods Cup, Rumbelows Cup, Coca-Cola Cup, Worthington Cup. Abandoned games, testimonials and

Player		Birthplace	From	Year Joined	Year Left	To	League Apps	Sub	Goals
Agnew	Steve	Shipley	Barnsley	1991	1993	Portsmouth	2	0	0
Ainscow	Alan	Bolton	Wolverhampton W.	1985	1989	Rochdale	42	23	5
Airey	Jack	Bedford	Juniors	1959	1963	Morecambe	3	0	1
Aitken	Fergie	Glasgow	Bury	1921	1923	Birmingham	8	0	1
Aitkenhead	Wattie	Maryhill, Glasgow	Partick Thistle	1906	1918	Retired	210	0	75
Alcock	Terry	Hanley	Blackpool	1976	1977	Blackpool	3	0	1
Almond	Willie	Blackburn	Witton	1888	1892	Accrington	58	0	3
Anderson	Ben	Aberdeen	Peterlee Juniors	1964	1968	Bury	21	7	7
Anderson	Chris	Wemyss	Lochore Welfare	1950	1953	Stockport County	13	0	1
Anderson	Geordie	Unknown	Leith Athletic	1892	1899	New Brighton Tower	178	0	19
Andersson	Anders	Tomelilla, Sweden	Malmo FF	1997	1998	Aalborg Boldspiklub	1	3	0
Andersson	Patrik	Borgeby, Sweden	Malmo FF	1993	1993	Borussia Mönchengladbach	7	5	0
Anthony	Walter	Nottingham	Brighton & HA	1908	1914	Stalybridge Celtic	149	0	11
Appleby	Jim	Shotton Colliery	Burnley	1958	1961	Southport	2	0	0
Archibald	Steve	Glasgow	Barcelona	1987	1988	Barcelona	20	0	6
Ardiles	Ossie	Argentina	Tottenham Hotspur	1988	1988	Tottenham Hotspur	5	0	0
Arentoft	Ben	Copenhagen, Denmark	Newcastle United	1971	1974	Retired	94	0	3
Arnold	Jim	Stafford	Stafford Rangers	1979	1981	Everton	58	0	0
Arnott	Kevin	Gateshead	Sunderland	1981	1982	Sunderland ⎫			
	(Two spells)		Sheffield United	1982	1983	Sheffield United ⎭	28	1	3
Arthur	Herbie	Blackburn	King's Own	1880	1890	Southport Central ⎫			
	(Two spells)		Southport Central	1891	1892	Retired ⎭	40	0	0
Ashcroft	Jimmy	Liverpool	Woolwich Arsenal	1908	1913	Tranmere Rovers	114	0	0
Astill	Len	Wolverhampton	Wolverhampton W.	1936	1937	Ipswich Town	3	0	1
Aston	John	Manchester	Mansfield Town	1978	1980	Retired	12	3	2
Atherton	Dewi	Bangor	Schoolboy	1968	1971	Bangor City	9	1	0
Atkins	Mark	Doncaster	Scunthorpe United	1988	1995	Wolverhampton W.	224	33	34
Avery	George	High Wycombe	Queens Own	1879	1884	Retired	0	0	0
Baah	Peter	Littleborough	YTS	1991	1992	Fulham	1	0	0
Bailey	John	Liverpool	Juniors	1975	1979	Everton	115	5	1
Baldwin	Jimmy	Blackburn	Mill Hill St Peter's	1943	1950	Leicester City	88	0	0
Ball	William	W. Derby, Liverpool	Rock Ferry	1897	1898	Everton ⎫			
	(Two spells)		Notts County	1901	1902	Manchester United ⎭	20	0	0
Barker	Simon	Farnsworth	Apprentice	1982	1988	Queens Park Rangers	180	2	35
Barron	Jim	Burnhope	Blyth Spartans	1935	1946	Darlington	76	0	0
Barton	Alfred	Blackburn	Unknown	1882	1885	Unknown	0	0	0
Barton	David	Bishop Auckland	Newcastle United	1982	1982	Newcastle United	8	0	1
Barton	John	Blackburn	Blackburn West End	1887	1891	Retired	40	0	2
Barton	John	Orrell	Preston North End	1966	1972	Retired	68	0	0
Barton	John	Southport	Rochdale	1919	1920	Merthyr Town	1	0	0
Bateson	Edward	Lundale	Unknown	1924	1925	Released	2	0	0
Batty	David	Leeds	Leeds United	1993	1996	Newcastle United	53	1	1
Baxendale	Frank	Leyland	Leyland Motors	1933	1937	Falkirk	12	0	3
Baxter	Tom	Blackburn	Unknown	1927	1932	Retired	36	0	0
Beamish	Ken	Bebington	Brighton & HA	1974	1976	Port Vale	86	0	18
Bean	Alan	Doncaster	Juniors	1952	1955	Released	2	0	0
Beardall	Jim	Salford	Juniors	1968	1969	Oldham Athletic	4	2	1
Beardsmore	Russell	Wigan	Manchester United	1991	1992	Manchester United	1	1	0
Beattie	Jack	Newhills	Wolverhampton W.	1934	1937	Birmingham	76	0	17
Beattie	James	Lancaster	Trainee	1995	1998	Southampton	1	3	0
Beckford	Jason	Manchester	Manchester City	1991	1991	Manchester City	3	1	0
Bee	Frank	Nottingham	Sunderland	1947	1950	Peterborough United	4	0	0
Beglin	Jim	Waterford	Leeds United	1990	1990	Leeds United	6	0	0
Bell	Alex	Cape Town	Manchester United	1913	1915	Retired	11	0	0
Bell	Bobby	Cambridge	Ipswich Town	1971	1971	Crystal Palace	2	0	0
Bell	Eric	Bedlington	Blyth Shipyard	1945	1957	Retired	323	0	9
Bell	Norman	Sunderland	Wolverhampton	1981	1984	Retired	57	4	10
Bennett	Jack	Unknown	Leicester Fosse	1905	1906	Released	1	0	0
Benson	James	Cowdenbeath	St Johnstone	1933	1936	East Fife	2	0	1
Bent	Marcus	Hammersmith	Crystal Palace	2000	Still at club		21	7	8
Beresford	James	Unknown	Unknown	1887	1889	Unknown	12	0	4

friendlies are not included in totals. Appearances and goalscorers are up to and including the 2000-2001 season. The 'Year Joined' column indicates the year in which the player signed for Blackburn Rovers as a professional. In alphabetical order, 'Mc' and 'Mac' are treated as the same and all come before names beginning with 'Ma' in the listing.

FAC			FLC			European			Others			Totals		
Apps	Sub	Goals	Apps	Sub	Goals	Apps	Sub	Goals	Apps	Sub	Goals	Apps	Sub	Goals
0	0	0	2	0	0	0	0	0	0	0	0	4	0	0
0	0	0	2	1	1	0	0	0	5	4	1	49	28	7
0	0	0	0	0	0	0	0	0	0	0	0	3	0	1
0	0	0	0	0	0	0	0	0	0	0	0	8	0	1
28	0	18	0	0	0	0	0	0	9	0	2	248	0	95
2	0	0	0	0	0	0	0	0	0	0	0	5	0	1
9	0	1	0	0	0	0	0	0	0	0	0	67	0	4
0	0	0	0	0	0	0	0	0	0	0	0	21	7	7
0	0	0	0	0	0	0	0	0	0	0	0	13	0	1
18	0	0	0	0	0	0	0	0	4	0	1	200	0	20
0	1	0	3	0	1	0	0	0	0	0	0	4	4	1
1	0	0	2	0	1	0	0	0	0	0	0	10	5	1
14	0	3	0	0	0	0	0	0	1	0	0	164	0	14
0	0	0	0	0	0	0	0	0	0	0	0	2	0	0
1	0	0	0	0	0	0	0	0	1	0	0	22	0	6
0	0	0	0	0	0	0	0	0	1	1	0	6	1	0
10	0	0	4	0	0	0	0	0	0	0	0	108	0	3
7	0	0	3	0	0	0	0	0	4	0	0	72	0	0
2	0	0	0	0	0	0	0	0	0	0	0	30	1	3
35	0	0	0	0	0	0	0	0	0	0	0	75	0	0
15	0	0	0	0	0	0	0	0	1	0	0	130	0	0
1	0	0	0	0	0	0	0	0	0	0	0	4	0	1
0	0	0	1	0	0	0	0	0	4	1	0	17	4	2
0	0	0	1	0	0	0	0	0	0	0	0	10	1	0
11	3	0	20	4	4	2	1	0	15	1	1	272	42	39
20	0	10	0	0	0	0	0	0	0	0	0	20	0	10
0	0	0	0	0	0	0	0	0	0	0	0	1	0	0
7	0	0	7	0	0	0	0	0	10	0	0	139	5	1
8	0	1	0	0	0	0	0	0	13	0	4	109	0	5
0	0	0	0	0	0	0	0	0	0	0	0	20	0	0
11	0	0	9	0	4	0	0	0	8	0	2	208	2	41
7	0	0	0	0	0	0	0	0	35	0	0	118	0	0
3	0	6	0	0	0	0	0	0	0	0	0	3	0	6
0	0	0	0	0	0	0	0	0	0	0	0	8	0	1
12	0	2	0	0	0	0	0	0	0	0	0	52	0	4
1	0	0	3	0	0	0	0	0	0	0	0	72	0	0
1	0	0	0	0	0	0	0	0	1	0	0	3	0	0
0	0	0	0	0	0	0	0	0	0	0	0	2	0	0
5	0	0	6	0	0	5	0	0	1	0	0	70	1	1
1	0	0	0	0	0	0	0	0	0	0	0	13	0	3
3	0	0	0	0	0	0	0	0	1	0	0	40	0	0
3	0	2	9	0	5	0	0	0	6	0	3	104	0	28
0	0	0	0	0	0	0	0	0	0	0	0	2	0	0
0	0	0	0	0	0	0	0	0	0	0	0	4	2	1
0	0	0	0	0	0	0	0	0	0	0	0	1	1	0
5	0	1	0	0	0	0	0	0	0	0	0	81	0	18
0	1	0	2	0	0	0	0	0	0	0	0	3	4	0
0	0	0	0	0	0	0	0	0	0	0	0	3	1	0
0	0	0	0	0	0	0	0	0	0	0	0	4	0	0
0	0	0	0	0	0	0	0	0	0	0	0	6	0	0
1	0	0	0	0	0	0	0	0	0	0	0	12	0	0
0	0	0	0	0	0	0	0	0	0	0	0	2	0	0
10	0	0	0	0	0	0	0	0	37	0	0	370	0	9
2	0	0	2	0	0	0	0	0	0	0	0	61	4	10
0	0	0	0	0	0	0	0	0	0	0	0	1	0	0
0	0	0	0	0	0	0	0	0	0	0	0	2	0	1
5	1	3	0	0	0	0	0	0	0	0	0	26	8	11
2	0	0	0	0	0	0	0	0	0	0	0	14	0	4

The Essential History of Blackburn Rovers

Player		Birthplace	From	Year Joined	Year Left	To	League Apps	Sub	Goals
Berg	Henning	Eidsvell, Norway	SK Lillestrom	1993	1997	Manchester United			
	(Two spells)		Manchester United	2000	Still at club		195	5	5
Berkovic	Eyal	Haifa, Israel	Celtic	2001	2001	Celtic	4	7	2
Beverley	Joe	Blackburn	Blackburn Olympic	1882	1884	Blackburn Olympic			
	(Two spells)		Blackburn Olympic	1886	1889	Retired	8	0	0
Bibby	Joseph	Rishton	Blackburn Trinity	1920	1921	Wigan Borough	8	0	0
Bimpson	Louis	Rainford	Liverpool	1959	1961	Bournemouth	22	0	5
Binns	Cliff	Cowling	Halifax Town	1930	1933	Workington			
	(Two spells)		Workington	1933	1936	Barnsley	183	0	0
Binns	Eric	Halifax	Burnley	1955	1957	Runcorn	23	0	0
Birchall	Jack	Prescott	Blackpool	1903	1907	Released	39	0	3
Birchenall	Alan	East Ham	Memphis Rogues, USA	1978	1979	Luton Town	17	1	0
Birtwistle	Alfred	Blackburn	Unknown	1875	1885	Unknown	0	0	0
Birtwistle	Richard	Great Harwood	Unknown	1875	1880	Unknown	0	0	0
Bjornebye	Stig Inge	Elverum, Norway	Liverpool	2000	Still at club		30	3	1
Blackburn	Arthur	Blackburn	Wellingborough	1899	1900	Southampton			
	(Two spells)		Southampton	1901	1902	Released	4	0	0
Blackburn	Fred	Mellor	Mellor	1897	1905	West Ham United	192	0	25
Blacklaw	Adam	Aberdeen	Burnley	1967	1970	Blackpool	96	0	0
Blackshaw	John	Blackburn	Blackburn Park Road	1900	1902	Darwen	2	0	0
Blake	Nathan	Cardiff	Bolton Wanderers	1998	Still at club		37	14	12
Blenkhorn	Bob	Unknown	Unknown	1881	1887	Unknown	0	0	0
Blore	Reg	Sesswick	Southport	1963	1965	Oldham Athletic	11	0	0
Bogan	Tommy	Glasgow	Southampton	1951	1954	Macclesfield Town	1	0	0
Bohinen	Lars	Vados, Norway	Nottingham Forest	1995	1998	Derby County	40	18	7
Bond	Dickie	Garstang	Bradford City	1922	1923	Lancaster Town	24	0	2
Booth	Tom	Ardwick	Ashton North End	1896	1900	Everton	111	0	10
Boothman	James	Blackburn	Blackburn Trinity	1917	1919	Lancaster Town	2	0	0
Bourton	Clarrie	Bristol	Bristol City	1928	1931	Coventry City	63	0	37
Bow	Billy	Edinburgh	St Bernard's	1902	1904	Darwen	20	0	2
Bowdler	Jack	Shrewsbury	Wolverhampton W.	1892	1893	Shrewsbury Town	22	0	5
Bowman	Adam	Forfar	Everton	1903	1907	Brentford	99	0	42
Bracegirdle	Ernest	Knutsford	Northwich Victoria	1906	1911	Crewe Alexandra	60	0	6
Bradbury	John	Normanby	Ashton North End	1897	1897	Ashton North End	2	0	0
Bradford	David	Manchester	Apprentice	1971	1974	Sheffield United	58	6	3
Bradshaw	Alan	Blackburn	Juniors	1960	1965	Crewe Alexandra	11	0	2
Bradshaw	Billy	Padiham	Accrington Stanley	1903	1920	Rochdale	386	0	36
Bradshaw	Paul	Altrincham	Apprentice	1973	1977	Wolverhampton	78	0	0
Branagan	Jim	Barton	Huddersfield Town	1979	1987	Preston North End	290	4	5
Brandon	Tom	Kirbirnie	St Mirren	1889	1891	Sheffield Wednesday			
	(Two spells)		Nelson	1893	1900	St Mirren	216	0	2
Bray	John	Rishton	Groundstaff	1954	1965	Bury	153	0	2
Brayshaw	Walter	Unknown	Denaby United	1925	1926	Southend United	9	0	1
Brennan	Tom	Calderbank	Tunbridge Wells Rangers	1933	1935	Stockport County	13	0	1
Briercliffe	Thomas	Blackburn	Clitheroe	1897	1900	Stalybridge Rovers	56	0	11
Briggs	Tommy	Chesterfield	Birmingham City	1952	1958	Grimsby Town	194	0	140
Britt	Martin	Leigh-on-Sea	West Ham United	1966	1967	Retired	8	0	0
Britton	Frank	Bristol	Bristol Rovers	1930	1934	Oldham Athletic	45	0	8
Brooks	Ernest	Brierley Hill	Brierley Hill Alliance	1920	1921	Wolverhampton W.	3	0	0
Broomes	Marlon	Birmingham	Trainee	1994	Still at club		24	7	1
Brotherston	Noel	Belfast	Tottenham Hotspur	1977	1987	Bury	307	10	40
Brown	Charles	Unknown	Leith Athletic	1898	1899	Mossend Swifts	1	0	0
Brown	Jimmy	Blackburn	Unknown	1876	1886	Retired			
	(Two spells)		Unknown	1888	1889	Retired	4	0	0
Brown	Richard	Nottingham	Kettering Town	1990	1995	Stockport County	26	2	0
Bruton	Jack	Westhoughton	Burnley	1929	1943	Retired	324	0	108
Bruton	Les	Foleshill	Raith Rovers	1929	1932	Liverpool	38	0	23
Bryant	Cliff	Bristol	Bristol Rovers	1932	1936	Wrexham	4	0	0
Bryant	Willie	Rotherham	Newton Heath	1900	1902	Released	25	0	8
Burgess	Ben	Buxton	Trainee	1998	Still at club		1	1	0
Burgin	Andy	Sheffield	Halifax Town	1974	1977	Retired	45	0	1
Burke	Marshall	Glasgow	Leeds United	1980	1982	Lincoln City	34	5	7
Burton	Jack	Grangetown	Grangetown	1906	1908	West Ham United	4	0	0
Busby	Viv	Slough	Tulsa Roughnecks	1981	1982	York City	8	0	1
Butcher	John	Newcastle	Juniors	1976	1982	Oxford United	104	0	0
Butt	Len	Wilmslow	Huddersfield Town	1937	1947	York City	110	0	44
Byers	Jack	Selby	Huddersfield Town	1923	1924	West Bromwich Albion	27	0	2
Byrne	David	Hammersmith	Millwall	1989	1989	Millwall	4	0	0
Byrom	John	Blackburn	School	1959	1966	Bolton Wanderers			
	(Two spells)		Bolton Wanderers	1976	1977	Retired	121	3	50
Byrom	Tom	Blackburn	Victoria Cross	1911	1920	Rochdale	13	0	3

FAC Apps	Sub	Goals	FLC Apps	Sub	Goals	European Apps	Sub	Goals	Others Apps	Sub	Goals	Totals Apps	Sub	Goals
13	0	0	17	0	0	8	0	0	1	0	0	234	5	5
3	0	0	0	0	0	0	0	0	0	0	0	7	7	2
14	0	0	0	0	0	0	0	0	0	0	0	22	0	0
0	0	0	0	0	0	0	0	0	0	0	0	8	0	0
7	0	3	0	0	0	0	0	0	0	0	0	29	0	8
13	0	0	0	0	0	0	0	0	0	0	0	196	0	0
0	0	0	0	0	0	0	0	0	0	0	0	23	0	0
1	0	0	0	0	0	0	0	0	0	0	0	40	0	3
2	0	0	0	0	0	0	0	0	0	0	0	19	1	0
5	0	1	0	0	0	0	0	0	0	0	0	5	0	1
4	0	1	0	0	0	0	0	0	0	0	0	4	0	1
2	1	0	2	0	0	0	0	0	0	0	0	34	4	1
0	0	0	0	0	0	0	0	0	0	0	0	4	0	0
12	0	5	0	0	0	0	0	0	2	0	1	206	0	31
5	0	0	9	0	0	0	0	0	0	0	0	110	0	0
0	0	0	0	0	0	0	0	0	0	0	0	2	0	0
5	3	2	3	0	1	0	0	0	0	0	0	45	17	9
3	0	0	0	0	0	0	0	0	0	0	0	3	0	0
0	0	0	0	0	0	0	0	0	0	0	0	11	0	0
0	0	0	0	0	0	0	0	0	0	0	0	1	0	0
2	1	1	3	2	1	0	0	0	0	0	0	45	21	9
2	0	1	0	0	0	0	0	0	0	0	0	26	0	3
9	0	1	0	0	0	0	0	0	3	0	0	123	0	11
0	0	0	0	0	0	0	0	0	50	0	2	52	0	2
9	0	5	0	0	0	0	0	0	0	0	0	72	0	42
3	0	0	0	0	0	0	0	0	0	0	0	23	0	2
4	0	2	0	0	0	0	0	0	0	0	0	26	0	7
5	0	1	0	0	0	0	0	0	0	0	0	104	0	43
5	0	1	0	0	0	0	0	0	0	0	0	65	0	7
0	0	0	0	0	0	0	0	0	0	0	0	2	0	0
5	0	0	4	0	0	0	0	0	0	0	0	67	6	3
0	0	0	0	0	0	0	0	0	0	0	0	11	0	2
39	0	3	0	0	0	0	0	0	31	0	12	457	0	51
4	0	0	5	0	0	0	0	0	0	0	0	87	0	0
20	0	0	18	0	0	0	0	0	6	0	0	334	4	5
26	0	0	0	0	0	0	0	0	3	0	0	245	0	2
19	0	0	12	0	0	0	0	0	0	0	0	184	0	2
0	0	0	0	0	0	0	0	0	0	0	0	9	0	1
0	0	0	0	0	0	0	0	0	0	0	0	13	0	1
4	0	0	0	0	0	0	0	0	1	0	1	61	0	12
10	0	3	0	0	0	0	0	0	0	0	0	204	0	143
0	0	0	1	0	0	0	0	0	0	0	0	9	0	0
3	0	1	0	0	0	0	0	0	0	0	0	48	0	9
0	0	0	0	0	0	0	0	0	0	0	0	3	0	0
4	0	0	3	0	0	0	0	0	0	0	0	31	7	1
24	1	4	22	0	2	0	0	0	16	1	8	369	12	54
0	0	0	0	0	0	0	0	0	0	0	0	1	0	0
32	0	29	0	0	0	0	0	0	0	0	0	36	0	29
2	0	0	1	1	0	0	0	0	1	0	0	30	3	0
20	0	7	0	0	0	0	0	0	1	0	2	345	0	117
4	0	5	0	0	0	0	0	0	0	0	0	42	0	28
1	0	0	0	0	0	0	0	0	0	0	0	5	0	0
0	0	0	0	0	0	0	0	0	0	0	0	25	0	8
0	0	0	1	0	0	0	0	0	0	0	0	2	1	0
3	0	0	2	0	0	0	0	0	3	0	0	53	0	1
1	0	1	3	0	0	0	0	0	0	0	0	38	5	8
0	0	0	0	0	0	0	0	0	0	0	0	4	0	0
0	0	0	0	0	0	0	0	0	0	0	0	8	0	1
5	0	0	7	0	0	0	0	0	6	0	0	122	0	0
7	0	4	0	0	0	0	0	0	74	0	48	191	0	96
1	0	0	0	0	0	0	0	0	0	0	0	28	0	2
0	0	0	0	0	0	0	0	0	0	0	0	4	0	0
16	0	12	9	0	2	0	0	0	0	0	0	146	3	64
0	0	0	0	0	0	0	0	0	6	0	2	19	0	5

The Essential History of Blackburn Rovers

Player		Birthplace	From	Year Joined	Year Left	To	League Apps	Sub	Goals
Cairns	Ronald	Chopwell	Conett	1953	1959	Rochdale	26	0	7
Calladine	Charlie	Wessington	Birmingham	1936	1938	Guildford City	48	0	6
Calloway	Laurie	Birmingham	Rochdale	1968	1970	Southport	17	8	1
Calvey	Michael	Unknown	Belfast Distillery	1893	1894	Manchester City	6	0	3
Cameron	Jock	Kirkwoodin	St Mirren	1904	1907	Chelsea	64	0	0
Cameron	William	Mossend	Bolton Wanderers	1908	1914	Bury	70	0	18
Campbell	Aussie	Hamsterley	Leadgate Park	1923	1929	Huddersfield Town	161	0	7
Campbell	Henry	Cardross	Renton	1889	1894	Unknown	98	0	22
Campbell	Jackie	Liverpool	Liverpool	1945	1956	Oldham Athletic	224	0	19
Campbell	John	Glasgow	Partick Thistle	1896	1898	Glasgow Rangers	55	0	10
Campbell	William	Inverness	Darwen	1893	1893	Newton Heath	1	0	0
Carsley	Lee	Birmingham	Derby County	1999	2000	Coventry City	40	6	10
Carter	Don	Midsomer Norton	Bury	1948	1948	New Brighton	2	0	0
Carter	James	Preston	Millwall Athletic	1897	1899	New Brompton	43	0	0
Carver	Jesse	Liverpool	Juniors	1928	1936	Newcastle United	143	0	2
Chadwick	Edgar	Blackburn	Blackburn Olympic	1887	1888	Everton	0	0	0
Chadwick	Frank	Blackburn	Juniors	1946	1955	York City	11	0	1
Chadwick	Miles	Blackburn	Darwen	1905	1908	Darwen	51	0	7
Chambers	Peter	Cockermouth	Black Diamonds	1897	1899	Bedminster	33	0	0
Chapman	George	Broxburn	Raith Rovers	1908	1910	Glasgow Rangers	}		
	(Two spells)		Glasgow Rangers	1911	1919	Accrington Stanley	138	0	34
Chappell	Les	Nottingham	Rotherham United	1968	1969	Reading	7	0	0
Charter	Ray	Ashton	Apprentice	1968	1971	Stockport County	13	5	0
Chippendale	Harry	Blackburn	Nelson	1891	1897	Retired	134	0	50
Chivers	Frank	Drybrook	Huddersfield Town	1938	1942	Died in 1942	48	0	2
Christie	Norman	Jarrow	Huddersfield Town	1934	1937	Macclesfield Town	43	0	0
Clark	Sam	Whitletts	Petershill	1933	1937	Halifax Town	1	0	0
Clarke	Albert	Sheffield	Birmingham	1938	1944	Died in 1944	38	0	21
Clayton	Ken	Preston	School	1949	1961	Ashton United	72	0	0
Clayton	Ronnie	Preston	School	1949	1969	Morecambe	579	2	15
Cleghorn	Thomas	Leith	Leith Athletic	1894	1896	Liverpool	45	0	3
Clennell	Joe	New Silksworth	Blackpool	1911	1914	Everton	26	0	12
Clinton	Tommy	Dublin	Everton	1955	1956	Tranmere Rovers	6	0	0
Clough	Albert	Blackburn	Accrington Stanley	1919	1921	Blackpool	1	0	0
Cockshutt	James	Darwen	Unknown	1890	1892	Brierfield	1	0	0
Coddington	John	Worksop	Huddersfield Town	1967	1970	Stockport County	72	1	3
Coleman	Chris	Swansea	Crystal Palace	1995	1997	Fulham	27	1	0
Collier	Darren	Stockton	Juniors	1988	1993	Darlington	27	0	0
Comstive	Paul	Southport	Juniors	1979	1983	Wigan Athletic	3	3	0
Conlon	Bryan	Shildon	Norwich City	1970	1972	Cambridge United	43	2	7
Connelly	John	St Helens	Manchester United	1966	1970	Bury	148	1	36
Cook	Leslie	Blackburn	School	1939	1949	Coventry City	76	0	0
Coombs	Ernest	Frome	Bath City	1933	1934	Bath City	6	0	0
Cope	Harold	Rawmarsh	Mexborough Town	1926	1930	Swindon Town	25	0	0
Coughlin	Russell	Swansea	Manchester City	1979	1980	Carlisle United	22	2	0
Coupe	Thomas	Rishton	Great Harwood	1899	1900	Accrington Stanley	1	0	0
Cowans	Gordon	Cornforth	Aston Villa	1991	1993	Aston Villa	49	1	2
Cowell	Arthur	Blackburn	Nelson	1905	Unknown	Retired	279	0	0
Coxon	Gary	Liverpool	Everton	1963	1969	Northwich Victoria	10	0	0
Crabtree	James	Clitheroe	Clitheroe Amateurs	1913	1920	Rochdale	12	0	0
Craig	Joe	Bridge of Allan	Celtic	1978	1981	Hamilton Academical	44	4	8
Craig	Bobby	Airdrie	Sheffield Wednesday	1962	1962	Celtic	8	0	3
Crawford	Andy	Filey	Derby County	1979	1981	AFC Bournemouth	56	0	21
Crawford	Bobby	Glespin	Blackpool	1934	1936	Southport	5	0	0
Crawford	Jock	Stirling	Alloa Athletic	1925	1932	East Stirling	155	0	0
Crawley	Frank	Paisley	Kirkintilloch Rob Roy	1921	1923	Lincoln City	24	0	1
Crisp	Jack	Hampstead	West Bromwich Albion	1923	1927	Coventry City	98	0	18
Croft	Garry	Burton-on-Trent	Grimsby Town	1996	1999	Ipswich Town	33	7	1
Crompton	Alan	Manchester	Sunderland	1976	1978	Wigan Athletic	2	2	0
Crompton	Bob	Blackburn	Blackburn Trinity	1896	1920	Retired	529	0	14
Crompton	Ellis	Ramsbottom	Padiham	1905	1910	Tottenham Hotspur	35	0	20
Crompton	Wilfred	Blackburn	Blackburn Parish School	1927	1932	Burnley	20	0	5
Crook	Albert	Darwen	Stalybridge Rovers	1899	1900	Stalybridge Rovers	9	0	2
Crook	Walter	Whittle-le-Woods	Blackburn Nomads	1931	1947	Bolton Wanderers	218	0	2
Crossan	Eddie	Londonderry	Derry City	1947	1957	Tranmere Rovers	287	0	73
Crowe	Chris	Newcastle-u-Tyne	Leeds United	1960	1962	Wolverhampton W.	51	0	6
Cunliffe	Arthur	Blackrod	Chorley	1928	1933	Aston Villa	129	0	47
Cunliffe	Thomas	Simms Lane, Wigan	Earlestown	1906	1908	Chorley	1	0	0
Curry	Sean	Liverpool	Liverpool	1987	1989	Hartlepool United	25	13	6
Curtis	John	Poulton-le-Flyde	Blackpool	1977	1979	Wigan Athletic	9	1	0
Curtis	John	Nuneaton	Manchester United	2000	Still at club		46	0	0

300

FAC Apps	Sub	Goals	FLC Apps	Sub	Goals	European Apps	Sub	Goals	Others Apps	Sub	Goals	Totals Apps	Sub	Goals
0	0	0	0	0	0	0	0	0	0	0	0	26	0	7
1	0	1	0	0	0	0	0	0	0	0	0	49	0	7
2	0	0	1	1	0	0	0	0	0	0	0	20	9	1
5	0	2	0	0	0	0	0	0	0	0	0	11	0	5
3	0	0	0	0	0	0	0	0	0	0	0	67	0	0
12	0	1	0	0	0	0	0	0	0	0	0	82	0	19
23	0	2	0	0	0	0	0	0	0	0	0	184	0	9
15	0	4	0	0	0	0	0	0	0	0	0	113	0	26
21	0	1	0	0	0	0	0	0	20	0	2	265	0	22
1	0	0	0	0	0	0	0	0	2	0	0	58	0	10
0	0	0	0	0	0	0	0	0	0	0	0	1	0	0
4	0	1	4	0	1	0	0	0	0	0	0	48	6	12
0	0	0	0	0	0	0	0	0	0	0	0	2	0	0
2	0	0	0	0	0	0	0	0	4	0	0	49	0	0
3	0	0	0	0	0	0	0	0	0	0	0	146	0	2
4	0	3	0	0	0	0	0	0	1	0	0	5	0	3
0	0	0	0	0	0	0	0	0	0	0	0	11	0	1
1	0	0	0	0	0	0	0	0	0	0	0	52	0	7
0	0	0	0	0	0	0	0	0	0	0	0	33	0	0
14	0	8	0	0	0	0	0	0	30	0	10	182	0	52
0	0	0	0	0	0	0	0	0	0	0	0	7	0	0
0	1	0	0	0	0	0	0	0	0	0	0	13	6	0
13	0	2	0	0	0	0	0	0	0	0	0	147	0	52
7	0	1	0	0	0	0	0	0	88	0	3	143	0	6
7	0	0	0	0	0	0	0	0	0	0	0	50	0	0
0	0	0	0	0	0	0	0	0	0	0	0	1	0	0
4	0	2	0	0	0	0	0	0	9	0	7	51	0	30
5	0	0	0	0	0	0	0	0	0	0	0	77	0	0
56	0	1	28	0	0	0	0	0	0	0	0	663	2	16
3	0	0	0	0	0	0	0	0	0	0	0	48	0	3
1	0	0	0	0	0	0	0	0	1	0	0	28	0	12
2	0	0	0	0	0	0	0	0	0	0	0	8	0	0
0	0	0	0	0	0	0	0	0	0	0	0	1	0	0
0	0	0	0	0	0	0	0	0	0	0	0	1	0	0
5	0	0	6	0	0	0	0	0	0	0	0	83	1	3
2	0	0	2	0	0	0	0	0	0	0	0	31	1	0
0	0	0	3	0	0	0	0	0	1	0	0	31	0	0
0	0	0	0	0	0	0	0	0	0	0	0	3	3	0
2	0	0	3	1	0	0	0	0	0	0	0	48	3	0
6	0	2	9	0	1	0	0	0	0	0	0	163	1	39
8	0	0	0	0	0	0	0	0	65	0	10	149	0	10
0	0	0	0	0	0	0	0	0	0	0	0	6	0	0
0	0	0	0	0	0	0	0	0	0	0	0	25	0	0
0	0	0	1	1	0	0	0	0	2	0	0	25	3	0
0	0	0	0	0	0	0	0	0	0	0	0	1	0	0
5	0	1	4	0	0	0	0	0	3	0	0	61	1	3
26	0	0	0	0	0	0	0	0	16	0	0	321	0	0
0	0	0	0	0	0	0	0	0	0	0	0	10	0	0
0	0	0	0	0	0	0	0	0	0	0	0	12	0	0
3	0	1	3	1	1	0	0	0	3	1	1	53	6	11
0	0	0	2	0	0	0	0	0	0	0	0	10	0	3
8	0	5	4	0	0	0	0	0	3	0	0	71	0	26
0	0	0	0	0	0	0	0	0	0	0	0	5	0	0
17	0	0	0	0	0	0	0	0	1	0	0	173	0	0
2	0	0	0	0	0	0	0	0	0	0	0	26	0	1
10	0	1	0	0	0	0	0	0	0	0	0	108	0	19
4	2	0	6	0	0	0	0	0	0	0	0	43	9	1
0	0	0	0	0	0	0	0	0	0	0	0	2	2	0
46	0	0	0	0	0	0	0	0	33	0	0	608	0	14
1	0	0	0	0	0	0	0	0	0	0	0	36	0	20
0	0	0	0	0	0	0	0	0	0	0	0	20	0	5
0	0	0	0	0	0	0	0	0	0	0	0	9	0	2
19	0	0	0	0	0	0	0	0	113	0	0	350	0	2
15	0	1	0	0	0	0	0	0	0	0	0	302	0	74
5	0	1	6	0	4	0	0	0	0	0	0	62	0	11
11	0	8	0	0	0	0	0	0	0	0	0	140	0	55
0	0	0	0	0	0	0	0	0	0	0	0	1	0	0
0	1	0	3	2	0	0	0	0	2	3	1	30	19	7
0	0	0	2	0	0	0	0	0	4	0	0	15	1	0
5	0	0	4	0	0	0	0	0	0	0	0	55	0	0

Player		Birthplace	From	Year Joined	Year Left	To	League Apps	Sub	Goals
Dahlin	Martin	Lund, Sweden	AS Roma	1997	1999	Retired	13	13	4
Dailly	Christian	Dundee	Derby County	1998	2001	West Ham United	60	10	4
Daly	Paddy	Manchester	School	1957	1962	Southport	3	0	0
Darling	Malcolm	Arbroath	Lucarty Juniors	1964	1970	Norwich City	114	14	30
Darroch	Jack	Alexandria	Bury	1901	1902	Dundee	17	0	0
Davidson	Callum	Stirling	St Johnstone	1998	2000	Leicester City	63	2	1
Davies	Billy	Wrexham	Wrexham	1905	1913	Retired	132	0	67
Davies	Kevin	Sheffield	Southampton	1998	1999	Southampton	11	12	1
Davis	Edwin	Bedminster	Huddersfield Town	1922	1925	Bristol City	24	0	0
Dawson	Ally	Johnstone	Glasgow Rangers	1987	1989	Airdrieonians	32	8	0
Dawson	Arthur	Blackburn	Blackburn Crosshill	1903	1907	Nelson	18	0	4
Dawson	Percy	Cullercoats	Heart of Midlothian	1914	1923	Preston Colliery	140	0	71
Dennis	William	Mossley	Stalybridge Celtic	1919	1920	Stalybridge Celtic	5	0	0
Dennison	Harry	Bradford	Blackburn Trinity	1911	1920	Rochdale	3	0	1
Derbyshire	James	Hawks Lane	Turton	1902	1903	Nelson	11	0	0
Devine	Peter	Blackburn	Bristol City	1982	1984	Chorley	8	0	2
Devlin	Hugh	Glasgow	Cambuslang	1896	1896	Unknown	1	0	0
De Vries	Roger	Willerby	Hull City	1980	1981	Scunthorpe United	13	0	0
Dewar	George	Dumbarton	Dumbarton	1889	1897	New Brighton Tower	174	0	7
Dewhurst	Bob	Keighley	Trainee	1990	1993	Hull City	13	0	0
Dewhurst	Jack	Padiham	Darwen	1899	1905	Brentford	169	0	43
Diamond	Tony	Rochdale	School	1984	1989	Blackpool	9	17	3
Diawara	Kaba	Toulon, France	Paris St Germain	2000	2000	Paris St Germain	1	4	0
Dickie	Percy	Aberdeen	St Johnstone	1937	1946	Aberdeen	19	0	1
Dickins	Matt	Sheffield	Lincoln City	1992	1995	Stockport County	1	0	0
Dix	Ronnie	Bristol	Bristol Rovers	1932	1933	Aston Villa	38	0	14
Dixon	Stan	Choppington	Newcastle United	1923	1926	Hull City	29	0	1
Dobing	Peter	Manchester	Crewe Rangers	1955	1961	Manchester City	179	0	88
Dobson	Tony	Coventry	Coventry City	1991	1993	Portsmouth	36	5	0
Doig	Ned	Letham	Arbroath	1889	1889	Arbroath	1	0	0
Donis	George	Frankfurt	Panathinaikos	1996	1997	Released	11	11	2
Donnelly	Darren	Liverpool	Trainee	1990	1993	Chester City	1	1	0
Donnelly	James	Mayo	Army football	1919	1922	Accrington Stanley	8	0	0
Dougan	Derek	Belfast	Portsmouth	1959	1961	Aston Villa	59	0	26
Douglas	Bryan	Blackburn	Groundstaff	1952	1969	Great Harwood	438	0	101
Douglas	Jimmy	Renfrew	Barrow Rangers	1880	1892	Retired	34	0	0
Douglas	Jonathan	Monaghan	Trainee	2000	Still at club		0	0	0
Downes	Steve	Leeds	Halifax Town	1976	1976	Halifax Town	6	0	0
Duckworth	Fred	Blackburn	Blackburn YMCA	1910	1922	Retired	60	0	0
Duckworth	John	Blackburn	Unknown	1878	1883	Unknown	0	0	0
Duckworth	Joseph	Blackburn	Accrington Stanley	1919	1921	Aberdare	5	0	0
Duckworth	Thomas	Blackpool	West Ham United	1903	1905	Blackpool	1	0	0
Duerden	James	Unknown	Livesey	1888	1889	Released	2	0	0
Duff	Damien	Dublin	Lourdes Celtic	1996	Still at club		100	26	11
Duncan	William	Dundee	Dundee Stobswell	1933	1935	Carlisle United	2	0	0
Dunkley	Albert	Northampton	Queens Park Rangers	1903	1904	Bristol Rovers	4	0	1
Dunn	David	Great Harwood	Trainee	1997	Still at club		68	11	15
Dunning	Bill	Bury	Apprentice	1972	1972	Released	10	3	2
Dunning	Darren	Scarborough	Trainee	1999	Still at club		1	0	0
Duxbury	Mike	Accrington	Manchester United	1990	1992	Bradford City	25	2	0
Eastham	Jack	Blackburn	St Peter's School	1901	1905	Glossop	48	0	0
Eccles	Terry	Leeds	Apprentice	1969	1973	Mansfield Town	33	13	6
Eckersley	Bill	Southport	High Park	1947	1961	Retired	406	0	20
Eddleston	Joe	Oswaldtwistle	St Mary's RC	1919	1921	Nelson	7	0	3
Edds	Ernie	Plymouth	Plymouth Argyle	1949	1951	Torquay United	18	0	3
Edge	Arthur	Freshfields	Cambridge University	1914	1915	Released	9	0	0
Ellis	Bob	Glasgow	Workington	1908	1910	Workington	1	0	1
Else	Fred	Golborne	Preston North End	1961	1966	Barrow	187	0	0
Elvy	Reg	Churwell	Bolton Wanderers	1951	1956	Northampton Town	192	0	0
Endean	Barry	Chester-le-Street	Charlton Athletic	1971	1975	Huddersfield Town	65	14	18
England	Mike	Greenfield	School	1957	1966	Tottenham Hotspur	165	0	21
Evans	Bob	Wrexham	Wrexham	1903	1908	Croydon Common	104	0	0
Evans	Lorenzo	Prestwich	Unknown	1898	1899	Glossop	2	0	0
Fairbrother	Ronald	Poulton-le-Fylde	Northern Nomads	1922	1929	Released	1	0	0
Farrell	Gerry	Liverpool	Unattached	1971	1973	Johannesburg Rovers	21	1	1
Faulkner	Robert	Paisley	Maryhill	1919	1920	Queens Park Rangers	9	0	0
Fawcett	William	Unknown	Unknown	1919	1920	Released	5	0	1
Fazackerley	Derek	Preston	School	1969	1987	Chester City	593	3	24
Fear	Keith	Bristol	Bristol City	1977	1978	Bristol City	5	0	2
Fecitt	Herbert	Blackburn	King's Own	1882	1887	Accrington	}		
	(Two spells)		Accrington	1888	1892	Northwich Victoria	21	0	13

FAC Apps	Sub	Goals	FLC Apps	Sub	Goals	European Apps	Sub	Goals	Others Apps	Sub	Goals	Totals Apps	Sub	Goals
0	1	0	2	0	2	0	1	0	0	0	0	15	15	6
4	0	0	5	1	0	2	0	0	0	0	0	71	11	4
0	0	0	1	0	0	0	0	0	0	0	0	4	0	0
8	0	4	4	1	0	0	0	0	0	0	0	126	15	34
1	0	0	0	0	0	0	0	0	0	0	0	18	0	0
6	0	0	3	1	0	1	1	0	0	0	0	73	4	1
11	0	3	0	0	0	0	0	0	2	0	0	145	0	70
2	0	1	3	0	0	1	0	0	0	0	0	17	12	2
1	0	0	0	0	0	0	0	0	0	0	0	25	0	0
1	0	0	3	0	0	0	0	0	2	2	0	38	10	0
0	0	0	0	0	0	0	0	0	0	0	0	18	0	4
11	0	2	0	0	0	0	0	0	4	0	3	155	0	76
0	0	0	0	0	0	0	0	0	0	0	0	5	0	0
0	0	0	0	0	0	0	0	0	0	0	0	3	0	0
0	0	0	0	0	0	0	0	0	0	0	0	11	0	0
0	0	0	0	0	0	0	0	0	0	0	0	8	0	2
0	0	0	0	0	0	0	0	0	0	0	0	1	0	0
1	0	0	3	0	0	0	0	0	2	0	0	19	0	0
22	0	3	0	0	0	0	0	0	0	0	0	196	0	10
0	0	0	1	0	0	0	0	0	1	0	0	15	0	0
13	0	4	0	0	0	0	0	0	0	0	0	182	0	47
0	0	0	0	0	0	0	0	0	1	1	0	10	18	3
1	0	1	0	0	0	0	0	0	0	0	0	2	4	1
2	0	0	0	0	0	0	0	0	28	0	0	49	0	1
0	0	0	0	0	0	0	0	0	0	0	0	1	0	0
2	0	1	0	0	0	0	0	0	0	0	0	40	0	15
2	0	2	0	0	0	0	0	0	0	0	0	31	0	3
22	0	16	4	0	0	0	0	0	0	0	0	205	0	104
2	0	0	5	0	0	0	0	0	1	0	0	44	5	0
0	0	0	0	0	0	0	0	0	0	0	0	1	0	0
0	1	0	3	0	0	0	0	0	0	0	0	14	12	2
0	0	0	0	0	0	0	0	0	0	0	0	1	1	0
2	0	0	0	0	0	0	0	0	0	0	0	10	0	0
14	0	4	3	0	4	0	0	0	0	0	0	76	0	34
39	1	9	25	0	5	0	0	0	0	0	0	502	1	115
42	0	8	0	0	0	0	0	0	0	0	0	76	0	8
0	1	0	0	1	0	0	0	0	0	0	0	0	2	0
0	0	0	0	0	0	0	0	0	0	0	0	6	0	0
3	0	0	0	0	0	0	0	0	60	0	1	123	0	1
13	0	7	0	0	0	0	0	0	0	0	0	13	0	7
2	0	0	0	0	0	0	0	0	0	0	0	7	0	0
1	0	0	0	0	0	0	0	0	0	0	0	2	0	0
0	0	0	0	0	0	0	0	0	0	0	0	2	0	0
12	4	2	9	1	3	1	0	0	0	0	0	122	31	16
1	0	0	0	0	0	0	0	0	0	0	0	3	0	0
0	0	0	0	0	0	0	0	0	0	0	0	4	0	1
7	2	2	7	3	5	0	0	0	0	0	0	82	16	22
0	0	0	0	0	0	0	0	0	0	0	0	10	3	2
1	0	0	1	0	0	0	0	0	0	0	0	3	0	0
2	0	0	1	0	0	0	0	0	0	1	0	28	3	0
4	0	0	0	0	0	0	0	0	0	0	0	52	0	0
1	0	0	2	0	1	0	0	0	0	0	0	36	13	7
26	0	1	0	0	0	0	0	0	0	0	0	432	0	21
0	0	0	0	0	0	0	0	0	0	0	0	7	0	3
1	0	1	0	0	0	0	0	0	0	0	0	19	0	4
0	0	0	0	0	0	0	0	0	0	0	0	9	0	0
0	0	0	0	0	0	0	0	0	0	0	0	1	0	1
18	0	0	16	0	0	0	0	0	0	0	0	221	0	0
16	0	0	0	0	0	0	0	0	0	0	0	208	0	0
5	0	0	3	1	1	0	0	0	0	0	0	73	15	19
12	0	0	7	0	0	0	0	0	0	0	0	184	0	21
9	0	0	0	0	0	0	0	0	0	0	0	113	0	0
0	0	0	0	0	0	0	0	0	0	0	0	2	0	0
0	0	0	0	0	0	0	0	0	0	0	0	1	0	0
2	0	0	0	0	0	0	0	0	0	0	0	23	1	1
0	0	0	0	0	0	0	0	0	0	0	0	9	0	0
0	0	0	0	0	0	0	0	0	0	0	0	5	0	1
40	0	1	38	0	1	0	0	0	15	0	0	686	3	26
1	0	0	0	0	0	0	0	0	0	0	0	6	0	2
23	0	13	0	0	0	0	0	0	0	0	0	44	0	26

The Essential History of Blackburn Rovers

Player		Birthplace	From	Year Joined	Year Left	To	League Apps	Sub	Goals
Fenton	Billy	West Hartlepool	Hordern Colliery Welfare	1948	1951	York City	33	0	7
Fenton	Graham	Wallsend	Aston Villa	1995	1997	Leicester City	9	18	7
Ferguson	James	Glasgow	Airdrieonians	1907	1912	St Johnstone	32	0	1
Ferguson	Mike	Burnley	Accrington Stanley	1962	1968	Aston Villa	220	0	29
Fettis	Alan	Belfast	Nottingham Forest	1997	2000	York City	9	2	0
Field	Tony	Halifax	Southport	1971	1974	Sheffield United	104	2	45
Filan	John	Sydney, Australia	Coventry City	1997	Still at club		61	1	0
Finnigan	Tony	Wimbledon	Crystal Palace	1988	1990	Hull City	21	15	0
Flitcroft	Garry	Bolton	Manchester City	1996	Still at club		125	7	8
Flowers	Tim	Kenilworth	Southampton	1993	1999	Leicester City	175	2	0
Forbes	George	Cheadle	Hyde United	1937	1946	Barrow	2	0	1
Forbes	John	Bonhill	Vale of Leven	1889	1894	Retired	106	0	1
Forrest	Jimmy (Snr)	Blackburn	Witton	1883	1895	Darwen	148	0	2
Forrest	Jimmy (Jnr)	Blackburn	Tramways	1920	1927	Released	16	0	0
Fowler	Martin	York	Huddersfield Town	1978	1980	Stockport County	36	2	0
France	Herbert	Stalybridge	Earlestown	1906	1907	St Helens Recreation	4	0	0
Frandsen	Per	Copenhagen	Bolton Wanderers	1999	2000	Bolton Wanderers	26	5	5
Fraser	Nathen	Kelvin, Glasgow	Ashfield	1935	1937	Wrexham	0	0	0
Friedel	Brad	Lakewood, USA	Liverpool	2000	Still at club		27	0	0
Fryatt	Jimmy	Swaythling	Stockport County	1968	1970	Oldham Athletic	29	8	5
Gale	Tony	Westminster	West Ham United	1994	1995	Crystal Palace	15	0	0
Gallacher	Bernard	Johnstone	Aston Villa	1990	1990	Aston Villa	4	0	0
Gallacher	Kevin	Clydebank	Coventry City	1993	1999	Newcastle United	132	12	46
Gallacher	Patrick	Glasgow	Third Lanark	1936	1938	Bournemouth	11	0	0
Garbett	Terry	Lanchester	Watford	1971	1974	Sheffield United	90	0	6
Garbutt	Billy	Stockport	Woolwich Arsenal	1908	1912	Retired	81	0	10
Garner	Simon	Boston	Boston United	1976	1992	West Bromwich Albion	455	29	168
Garstang	Harry	Preston	Unknown	1890	1891	Released	3	0	0
Garstang	John	Blackburn	Blackburn Etrurians	1897	1899	Chorley	4	0	0
Gate	William	Chorlton	Darwen	1901	1905	Darwen	4	0	1
Gayle	Howard	Liverpool	Stoke City	1987	1992	Halifax Town	97	19	29
Gennoe	Terry	Shrewsbury	Southampton	1981	1992	Retired	289	0	0
Gibson	Thomas	Blackburn	Blackburn Olympic	1880	1880	Blackburn Olympic	0	0	0
Gilhespy	Cyril	Fencehouses	Bristol City	1929	1930	Reading	5	0	1
Gill	Wayne	Chorley	YTS	1994	2000	Blackpool	0	0	0
Gillespie	Keith	Bangor, N. Ireland	Newcastle United	1998	Still at club		36	20	3
Gillespie	Matthew	Strathclyde	Glasgow Thistle	1892	1893	Leith Athletic	6	0	1
Gilliver	Allan	Swallownest	Huddersfield Town	1966	1968	Rotherham United	32	2	9
Given	Shay	Lifford	Celtic	1994	1997	Newcastle United	2	0	0
Glaister	George	Bywell	North Shields	1937	1947	Stockport County	8	0	1
Glenn	David	Wigan	Wigan Athletic	1983	1985	Chester City	23	1	0
Glover	Alec	Glasgow	Luton Town	1951	1954	Barrow	64	0	4
Glover	John	West Bromwich	West Bromwich Albion	1897	1899	New Brompton	25	0	0
Godwin	Verdi	Blackburn	Junior	1945	1948	Manchester City	27	0	6
Goodwin	Fred	Stockport	Stockport County	1970	1971	Southport	63	1	4
Gordon	Patrick	Scotland	Liverpool	1894	1895	Liverpool South End	12	0	2
Gorman	Jimmy	Liverpool	Burscough Rangers	1929	1937	Sunderland	213	0	0
Gormlie	William	Liverpool	Fleetwood Windsor Villa	1930	1935	Northampton Town	44	0	0
Gow	John	Unknown	Renton	1890	1891	Northwich Victoria	15	0	0
Graham	Les	Barton-on-Irwell	Urmston	1945	1953	Newport County	150	0	42
Gray	David	Dundee	Preston North End	1948	1954	Dundee	107	0	5
Grayson	Simon	Ripon	Aston Villa	1999	Still at club		31	3	0
Green	Alan	Unknown	Unknown	1945	1947	Released	0	0	0
Greenwood	Doc	Blackburn	Unknown	1875	1883	Corinthians	0	0	0
Gregory	David	Peterborough	Stoke City	1978	1978	Stoke City	5	0	3
Grew	Mark	Bilston	Port Vale	1990	1990	Port Vale	13	0	0
Griffiths	Barry	Manchester	Sheffield Wednesday	1958	1964	Altrincham	2	0	0
Groves	Arthur	Killamarsh	Halifax Town	1928	1933	Derby County	65	0	26
Gudmundsson	Niklas	Sweden	Halmstead	1995	1997	Malmo FF	1	5	0
Guest	Billy	Brierley Hill	Birmingham	1937	1947	Walsall	88	0	30
Hall	Coomb	North Leith	St Bernard's	1890	1895	St Bernard's	79	0	26
Hall	Fred	Chester-le-Street	Outston Juniors	1935	1946	Sunderland	29	0	0
Hall	George	Northern Ireland	Belfast Distillery	1897	1898	Released	1	0	1
Hall	Jim	Bootle	Blackpool	1980	1981	Released	0	0	0
Halsall	Wally	Liverpool	Bolton Wanderers	1932	1938	Birmingham	63	0	4
Hamill	Alex	Dumbarton	Cowdenbeath	1935	1936	Barnsley	21	0	4
Hamill	Kevin	Liverpool	Seaforth Social Club	1936	1936	Seaforth Social Club	1	0	0
Hamilton	David	South Shields	Sunderland	1981	1986	Wigan Athletic	104	10	7
Hamilton	Gary	Bambridge	Trainee	1998	2000	Released	0	0	0
Hand	John	Middlesbrough	Unknown	1906	1907	Hartlepool United	2	0	0
Hannah	Gardner	Old Monkland	Airdrieonians	1895	1896	Released	3	0	0

FAC Apps	Sub	Goals	FLC Apps	Sub	Goals	European Apps	Sub	Goals	Others Apps	Sub	Goals	Totals Apps	Sub	Goals
1	0	0	0	0	0	0	0	0	0	0	0	34	0	7
0	1	0	0	2	0	0	0	0	0	0	0	9	21	7
0	0	0	0	0	0	0	0	0	0	0	0	32	0	1
15	0	1	14	0	6	0	0	0	0	0	0	249	0	36
1	0	0	0	0	0	0	0	0	0	0	0	10	2	0
10	0	7	4	0	2	0	0	0	0	0	0	118	2	54
5	0	0	5	0	0	0	0	0	0	0	0	71	1	0
5	0	1	3	0	0	0	0	0	3	1	1	32	16	2
8	1	2	5	2	1	2	0	1	0	0	0	140	10	12
13	1	0	14	0	0	10	0	0	2	0	0	214	3	0
1	0	0	0	0	0	0	0	0	155	0	1	158	0	2
20	0	1	0	0	0	0	0	0	0	0	0	126	0	2
47	0	5	0	0	0	0	0	0	0	0	0	195	0	7
2	0	0	0	0	0	0	0	0	0	0	0	18	0	0
1	0	0	3	0	0	0	0	0	3	1	0	43	3	0
0	0	0	0	0	0	0	0	0	0	0	0	4	0	0
4	0	1	0	0	0	0	0	0	0	0	0	30	5	6
1	0	1	0	0	0	0	0	0	0	0	0	1	0	1
6	0	0	0	0	0	0	0	0	0	0	0	33	0	0
4	0	3	0	0	0	0	0	0	0	0	0	33	8	8
0	0	0	2	0	0	2	0	0	1	0	0	20	0	0
0	0	0	0	0	0	0	0	0	0	0	0	4	0	0
13	0	4	8	2	3	0	1	0	1	0	0	154	15	53
0	0	0	0	0	0	0	0	0	0	0	0	11	0	0
9	0	1	4	0	0	0	0	0	0	0	0	103	0	7
4	0	0	0	0	0	0	0	0	0	0	0	85	0	10
24	5	7	32	2	11	0	0	0	20	3	8	531	39	194
0	0	0	0	0	0	0	0	0	0	0	0	3	0	0
0	0	0	0	0	0	0	0	0	0	0	0	4	0	0
0	0	0	0	0	0	0	0	0	0	0	0	4	0	1
5	2	0	6	3	1	0	0	0	11	1	4	119	25	34
18	0	0	15	0	0	0	0	0	12	0	0	334	0	0
1	0	0	0	0	0	0	0	0	0	0	0	1	0	0
0	0	0	0	0	0	0	0	0	0	0	0	5	0	1
0	0	0	3	0	0	0	0	0	0	0	0	3	0	0
4	1	1	3	0	0	0	0	0	0	0	0	43	21	4
0	0	0	0	0	0	0	0	0	0	0	0	6	0	1
1	0	0	4	0	0	0	0	0	0	0	0	37	2	9
0	0	0	0	1	0	0	0	0	0	0	0	2	1	0
2	0	0	0	0	0	0	0	0	69	0	14	79	0	15
3	0	0	0	0	0	0	0	0	0	0	0	26	1	0
7	0	1	0	0	0	0	0	0	0	0	0	71	0	5
1	0	0	0	0	0	0	0	0	1	0	0	27	0	0
0	0	0	0	0	0	0	0	0	17	0	0	44	0	6
1	0	0	4	0	0	0	0	0	0	0	0	68	1	4
3	0	1	0	0	0	0	0	0	0	0	0	15	0	3
12	0	0	0	0	0	0	0	0	0	0	0	225	0	0
0	0	0	0	0	0	0	0	0	0	0	0	44	0	0
3	0	0	0	0	0	0	0	0	0	0	0	18	0	0
7	0	2	0	0	0	0	0	0	0	0	0	157	0	44
4	0	0	0	0	0	0	0	0	0	0	0	111	0	5
2	1	0	1	1	0	0	0	0	0	0	0	34	5	0
2	0	0	0	0	0	0	0	0	36	0	0	38	0	0
10	0	0	0	0	0	0	0	0	0	0	0	10	0	0
0	0	0	1	0	1	0	0	0	0	0	0	6	0	4
0	0	0	1	0	0	0	0	0	0	0	0	14	0	0
0	0	0	0	0	0	0	0	0	0	0	0	2	0	0
3	0	0	0	0	0	0	0	0	0	0	0	68	0	26
0	0	0	0	0	0	0	0	0	0	0	0	1	5	0
6	0	2	0	0	0	0	0	0	35	0	9	129	0	41
9	0	4	0	0	0	0	0	0	0	0	0	88	0	30
1	0	0	0	0	0	0	0	0	8	0	0	38	0	0
0	0	0	0	0	0	0	0	0	0	0	0	1	0	1
0	0	0	0	0	0	0	0	0	1	0	0	1	0	0
6	0	1	0	0	0	0	0	0	2	0	0	71	0	5
3	0	0	0	0	0	0	0	0	0	0	0	24	0	4
0	0	0	0	0	0	0	0	0	0	0	0	1	0	0
1	1	0	7	0	0	0	0	0	0	0	0	112	11	7
0	0	0	0	1	0	0	0	0	0	0	0	0	1	0
0	0	0	0	0	0	0	0	0	0	0	0	2	0	0
0	0	0	0	0	0	0	0	0	0	0	0	3	0	0

Player		Birthplace	From	Year Joined	Year Left	To	League Apps	Sub	Goals
Hardy	Allan	Ilkeston	Wigan County	1900	1903	Retired	42	0	0
Hardy	George	Newbold Verdun	Aston Villa	1938	1939	Released	7	0	0
Hardy	Jacob	Bishop Auckland	Shildon Athletic	1922	1923	Released	1	0	0
Haresnape	Bob	Preston	Darwen	1888	1889	Burnley	9	0	2
Hargreaves	A.	Unknown	Unknown	1892	1895	Released	2	0	0
Hargreaves	David	Accrington	Accrington Stanley	1977	1979	Accrington Stanley	2	0	0
Hargreaves	Fred	Blackburn	Malvern College	1877	1882	Retired	0	0	0
Hargreaves	John	Blackburn	Malvern College	1878	1884	Unknown	0	0	0
Hargreaves	Josh	Blackburn	Northwich Victoria	1893	1897	New Brighton Tower ⎫			
	(Two spells)		New Brighton Tower	1898	1898	New Brighton Tower ⎭	54	0	19
Hargreaves	Tom	Blackburn	Crosshill	1935	1946	Rochdale	4	0	2
Harkness	Steve	Carlisle	Benfica	1999	2000	Sheffield Wednesday	17	0	0
Harper	Ted	Sheerness	Sheppey United	1923	1927	Sheffield Wednesday ⎫			
	(Two spells)		Preston North End	1933	1935	Retired	171	0	121
Harris	Joe	Belfast	Larne	1951	1953	Oldham Athletic	35	0	14
Harrison	Mike	Ilford	Chelsea	1962	1967	Plymouth Argyle	160	0	40
Hartley	Dilworth	Clitheroe	Unknown	1890	1894	Darwen	6	0	0
Harvey	Arthur	Unknown	Shildon Athletic	1906	1907	Released	1	0	0
Haverty	Joe	Dublin	Arsenal	1961	1962	Millwall	27	0	1
Hawkins	Graham	Darlaston	Preston North End	1974	1978	Port Vale	108	1	4
Hawksworth	Ernie	Rochdale	Rochdale	1919	1925	Released	96	0	34
Haworth	George	Accrington	Accrington	1884	1885	Accrington	0	0	0
Haworth	Robert	Blackburn	Darwen	1897	1904	Fulham	122	0	5
Haworth	Ronald	Lower Darwen	Unknown	1922	1924	Hull City	25	0	7
Haydock	Jamie	Blackburn	Borough Road College	1890	1897	Retired	66	0	21
Hayhurst	Stan	Leyland	Royal Navy Football	1943	1948	Tottenham Hotspur	27	0	0
Healless	Harry	Blackburn	Blackburn Trinity	1915	1933	Retired	360	0	12
Heaton	Mick	Sheffield	Sheffield United	1971	1977	Retired	169	2	1
Heaton	Tom	Blackburn	Unknown	1915	1923	Oldham Athletic	57	0	1
Helliwell	David	Blackburn	Junior	1963	1969	Lincoln City	15	0	0
Henchoz	Stephane	Billens, Switz.	Hamburg	1997	1999	Liverpool	70	0	0
Hendry	Colin	Keith	Dundee	1987	1989	Manchester City ⎫			
	(Two spells)		Manchester City	1991	1998	Glasgow Rangers ⎭	328	8	34
Herron	Alan	Ashington	Newcastle United	1950	1959	Wigan Athletic	4	0	0
Heyes	Joe	Unknown	Unknown	1885	1889	Released	0	0	0
Heywood	Jimmy	Unknown	Stockport County	1907	1910	Glossop	15	0	0
Hickman	Mike	Elstead	Grimsby Town	1975	1975	Torquay United	23	3	8
Higgins	George	Dundee	Lochee Harp	1946	1951	Bolton Wanderers	53	0	0
Hildersley	Ronnie	Kirkcaldy	Preston North End	1988	1990	Wigan Athletic	25	5	4
Hignett	Craig	Prescot	Barnsley	2000	Still at club		15	15	3
Hill	Brian	Mansfield	Huddersfield Town	1969	1971	Torquay United	34	3	4
Hill	Keith	Bolton	School	1984	1992	Plymouth Argyle	89	7	4
Hilton	Pat	Aylesham	Brighton & HA	1974	1975	Gillingham	16	0	2
Hindle	Harry	Blackburn	Oswaldtwistle Rovers	1901	1903	Nelson	2	0	0
Hindson	Gordon	Quaking Houses	Luton Town	1975	1975	Luton Town	10	0	0
Hird	Kevin	Colne	School	1970	1979	Leeds United	129	3	20
Hodkinson	Joe	Lancaster	Glossop	1913	1923	Lancaster Town	228	0	19
Holden	Alan	Haslingden	Unknown	1959	1966	Stockport County	1	0	0
Holden	William	Darwen	Darwen	1888	1888	Darwen	1	0	0
Hole	Barrie	Swansea	Cardiff City	1966	1968	Aston Villa	79	0	13
Holland	Peter	Hindley	Unknown	1919	1928	Watford	116	0	24
Holliday	Ken	Darwen	Darwen Juniors	1946	1952	Accrington Stanley	29	0	0
Holmes	Bill	Hunslet	Morecambe	1952	1953	Morecambe	21	0	16
Holmes	Mattie	Unknown	West Ham United	1995	1997	Charlton Athletic	8	1	1
Holt	Bill	Boldon	Boldon Colliery Welfare	1949	1953	Weymouth	78	0	0
Holt	David	Whickham	Unknown	1963	1967	Retired	10	0	0
Hope	Philip	Kimblesworth	Norwich City	1924	1926	Southend United	6	0	0
Hopwood	W.	Unknown	Unknown	1884	1885	Unknown	0	0	0
Hornby	Albert	Blackburn	Unknown	1878	1880	Unknown	0	0	0
Horne	Jack	Huncoat	Accrington	1890	1890	Accrington	2	0	0
Horne	William	Huncoat	Accrington	1891	1892	Nelson	7	0	0
Horrey	Roland	Bishop Auckland	Ferryhill Athletic	1963	1966	York City	3	0	0
Horton	Henry	Malvern	Worcester City	1947	1951	Southampton	92	0	5
Hosie	James	Rutherglen	Reading	1900	1901	Manchester City	3	0	0
Hough	Billy	Greenfield, Wales	Preston North End	1936	1942	Retired	49	0	0
Houlker	Kelly	Blackburn	Blackburn Park Road	1894	1902	Portsmouth ⎫			
	(Two spells)		Southampton	1906	1907	Retired	151	0	2
Howorth	Roger	Blackburn	Unknown	1879	1884	Blackburn Olympic	0	0	0
Hoy	Bobby	Halifax	Huddersfield Town	1974	1976	Halifax Town	13	6	0
Hoyne	James	Sale	Sale Holmfield	1901	1903	Earlestown	2	0	0
Hudson	George	Manchester	Manchester jr football	1958	1960	Accrington Stanley	4	0	1

FAC Apps	Sub	Goals	FLC Apps	Sub	Goals	European Apps	Sub	Goals	Others Apps	Sub	Goals	Totals Apps	Sub	Goals
0	0	0	0	0	0	0	0	0	0	0	0	42	0	0
0	0	0	0	0	0	0	0	0	0	0	0	7	0	0
0	0	0	0	0	0	0	0	0	0	0	0	1	0	0
4	0	6	0	0	0	0	0	0	0	0	0	13	0	8
0	0	0	0	0	0	0	0	0	0	0	0	2	0	0
0	0	0	0	0	0	0	0	0	0	0	0	2	0	0
12	0	1	0	0	0	0	0	0	0	0	0	12	0	1
11	0	5	0	0	0	0	0	0	0	0	0	11	0	5
5	0	0	0	0	0	0	0	0	2	0	0	61	0	19
0	0	0	0	0	0	0	0	0	33	0	19	37	0	21
1	0	0	2	1	0	0	0	0	0	0	0	20	1	0
6	0	1	0	0	0	0	0	0	0	0	0	177	0	122
1	0	0	0	0	0	0	0	0	0	0	0	36	0	14
14	0	2	7	0	1	0	0	0	0	0	0	181	0	43
0	0	0	0	0	0	0	0	0	0	0	0	6	0	0
0	0	0	0	0	0	0	0	0	0	0	0	1	0	0
0	0	0	4	0	0	0	0	0	0	0	0	31	0	1
4	0	0	8	0	0	0	0	0	10	0	0	130	1	4
4	0	0	0	0	0	0	0	0	0	0	0	100	0	34
2	0	0	0	0	0	0	0	0	0	0	0	2	0	0
7	0	0	0	0	0	0	0	0	0	0	0	129	0	5
0	0	0	0	0	0	0	0	0	0	0	0	25	0	7
13	0	6	0	0	0	0	0	0	0	0	0	79	0	27
0	0	0	0	0	0	0	0	0	9	0	0	36	0	0
36	0	1	0	0	0	0	0	0	3	0	1	399	0	14
9	0	0	10	0	0	0	0	0	4	0	0	192	2	1
2	0	0	0	0	0	0	0	0	4	0	0	63	0	1
0	0	0	1	0	0	0	0	0	0	0	0	16	0	1
6	0	0	3	1	0	2	0	0	0	0	0	81	1	0
20	1	0	27	0	0	7	0	0	17	0	1	399	9	35
0	0	0	0	0	0	0	0	0	0	0	0	4	0	0
12	0	1	0	0	0	0	0	0	0	0	0	12	0	1
1	0	0	0	0	0	0	0	0	0	0	0	16	0	0
0	0	0	2	0	0	0	0	0	4	0	0	29	3	8
3	0	0	0	0	0	0	0	0	0	0	0	56	0	0
3	0	1	0	1	0	0	0	0	3	0	0	31	6	5
2	3	2	0	0	0	0	0	0	0	0	0	17	18	5
2	0	0	4	0	1	0	0	0	0	0	0	40	3	5
5	1	0	6	0	1	0	0	0	3	2	0	103	10	5
0	0	0	5	0	0	0	0	0	0	0	0	21	0	2
0	0	0	0	0	0	0	0	0	0	0	0	2	0	0
0	0	0	0	0	0	0	0	0	0	0	0	10	0	0
8	0	0	7	1	1	0	0	0	10	2	0	154	6	21
16	0	1	0	0	0	0	0	0	11	0	1	255	0	21
0	0	0	1	0	0	0	0	0	0	0	0	2	0	0
0	0	0	0	0	0	0	0	0	0	0	0	1	0	0
2	0	0	7	0	2	0	0	0	0	0	0	88	0	15
9	0	1	0	0	0	0	0	0	9	0	1	134	0	26
1	0	0	0	0	0	0	0	0	0	0	0	30	0	0
4	0	3	0	0	0	0	0	0	0	0	0	25	0	19
0	0	0	0	0	0	2	1	0	0	0	0	10	2	0
2	0	0	0	0	0	0	0	0	0	0	0	80	0	0
0	0	0	1	0	0	0	0	0	0	0	0	11	0	0
2	0	0	0	0	0	0	0	0	0	0	0	8	0	0
1	0	0	0	0	0	0	0	0	0	0	0	1	0	0
1	0	0	0	0	0	0	0	0	0	0	0	1	0	0
3	0	0	0	0	0	0	0	0	0	0	0	5	0	0
0	0	0	0	0	0	0	0	0	0	0	0	7	0	0
0	0	0	1	0	0	0	0	0	0	0	0	4	0	0
6	0	0	0	0	0	0	0	0	0	0	0	98	0	5
0	0	0	0	0	0	0	0	0	0	0	0	3	0	0
7	0	0	0	0	0	0	0	0	40	0	0	96	0	0
9	0	0	0	0	0	0	0	0	6	0	0	166	0	2
12	0	0	0	0	0	0	0	0	0	0	0	12	0	0
1	0	0	0	2	0	0	0	0	1	1	0	15	9	0
0	0	0	0	0	0	0	0	0	0	0	0	2	0	0
0	0	0	0	0	0	0	0	0	0	0	0	4	0	1

Player		Birthplace	From	Year Joined	Year Left	To	League Apps	Sub	Goals
Hughes	Bill	Colwyn Bay	Tottenham Hotspur	1948	1950	Rochdale	27	0	0
Hughes	Jack	Rhosllanerchrugog	Rhos FC	1933	1937	Mansfield Town	47	0	0
Hughes	Mark	Wrexham	Everton	2000	Still at club		21	8	5
Hulme	Joe	Stafford	York City	1924	1926	Arsenal	73	0	6
Hulse	Ben	Liverpool	Rock Ferry	1897	1900	New Brighton Tower	85	0	22
Hunter	Allan	Sion Mills	Oldham Athletic	1969	1971	Ipswich Town	84	0	1
Hurst	Daniel	Cockermouth	Black Diamonds	1897	1900	Workington	53	0	17
Hutchins	Don	Middlesbrough	Plymouth Argyle	1972	1974	Bradford City	37	3	6
Hutt	Geoff	Hazlewood	Huddersfield Town	1975	1975	Huddersfield Town	10	0	1
Hutton	Jock	Dalziel	Aberdeen	1926	1933	Retired	127	0	4
Imrie	Bill	Methil	St Johnstone	1929	1934	Newcastle United	165	0	23
Inglis	John	Scotland	Glasgow Rangers	1884	1884	Unknown	0	0	0
Ireland	Simon	Halifax	Huddersfield Town	1992	1994	Mansfield Town	0	1	0
Irvine	Alan	Glasgow	Dundee United	1989	1992	Retired	40	18	3
Isherwood	Roy	Blackburn	Unknown	1956	1962	Chelmsford City	49	0	9
Jackson	Harry	Blackburn	Preston North End	1948	1949	Chester	1	0	0
Jackson	Thomas	Unknown	Padiham	1897	1899	Released	26	0	10
Jacques	Thomas	Blackburn	Skipton	1912	1915	Nelson	2	0	0
Jansen	Matt	Carlisle	Crystal Palace	1999	Still at club		57	24	30
Jefferson	Thomas	Unknown	Unknown	1880	1882	Unknown	0	0	0
Johnrose	Lenny	Preston	School	1986	1992	Hartlepool United	20	22	11
Johnson	Arthur	Liverpool	Junior	1950	1955	Halifax Town	1	0	0
Johnson	Damien	Lisburn	Trainee	1996	Still at club		37	16	2
Johnston	James	Rothesay	Maryhill	1910	1914	Released	14	0	0
Johnston	Tommy	Loanhead	Leyton Orient	1958	1959	Leyton Orient	36	0	22
Jones	Bob	Liverpool	Chester	1958	1966	Great Harwood	49	0	0
Jones	George	Radcliffe	Bury	1964	1966	Bury	36	3	14
Jones	Herbert	Blackpool	Blackpool	1925	1934	Brighton & HA	247	0	0
Jones	Roger	Upton-on-Severn	Bournemouth	1970	1976	Newcastle United	242	0	0
Jones	Thomas	Unknown	Llandudno	1901	1903	Released	11	0	0
Joy	Billy	Preston	Preston North End	1896	1897	Darwen	3	0	0
Joyce	John	Burton-on-Trent	Burton United	1902	1903	Tottenham Hotspur	14	0	0
Joyce	Walter	Oldham	Burnley	1964	1967	Oldham Athletic	119	1	4
Keating	Albert	Swillington Common	Newcastle United	1928	1931	Cardiff City	17	0	5
Keeley	Glenn	Barking	Newcastle United	1976	1987	Oldham Athletic	365	5	23
Keller	Marc	Colmar, France	West Ham United	2001	2001	Strasbourg, France	0	2	0
Kelly	Alan	Preston	Sheffield United	1999	Still at club		36	1	0
Kelly	Michael	Unknown	Reading	1900	1901	Released	3	0	0
Kelly	Willie	Hill O'Beath	Airdrieonians	1951	1957	Mossley	186	0	1
Kendall	Howard	Ryton-on-Tyne	Stoke City	1979	1981	Everton	79	0	6
Kenna	Jeff	Dublin	Southampton	1995	Still at club		153	2	1
Kennedy	Andrew	Stirling	Birmingham City	1988	1990	Watford	49	10	23
Kennedy	Fred	Bury	Racing Club de Paris	1933	1934	Racing Club de Paris	29	0	8
Kennedy	Pat	Dublin	Manchester United	1956	1959	Southampton	3	0	0
Kenyon	John	Blackburn	Great Harwood	1972	1976	Wigan Athletic	32	14	7
Kerr	Jimmy	Glasgow	Bury	1970	1971	Retired	11	0	0
Kerr	John	Annfield	Queens Park	1919	1921	Brentford	16	0	0
Killean	Ted	Blackburn	3rd Coldstream Guards	1894	1898	Glossop	88	0	6
Knighton	Ken	Mexborough	Preston North End	1969	1971	Hull City	70	0	11
Knowles	Albert	Unknown	Whalley & District	1897	1900	Released	31	0	0
Konde	Oumar	Binnengen, Switz.	FC Basle, Switz.	1998	1999	Freiburg	0	0	0
Kopel	Frank	Falkirk	Manchester United	1969	1972	Dundee United	23	2	0
Kyle	Archie	Unknown	Glasgow Rangers	1908	1909	Bo'ness	36	0	8
Lanceley	Ernest	Mexborough	Dartford	1932	1941	Retired	52	0	0
Langton	Bobby	Burscough	Burscough Victoria	1937	1948	Preston North End			
	(Two spells)		Bolton Wanderers	1953	1956	Ards	212	0	57
Lapham	Edgar	Liverpool	Marine	1934	1936	Accrington Stanley	2	0	0
Latham	William	Unknown	Unknown	1879	1881	Unknown	0	0	0
Latheron	Eddie	Grangetown	Grangetown FC	1906	1917	Killed in World War I	256	0	94
Law	James	Unknown	Unknown	1899	1900	Released	3	0	1
Lawrie	Jack	Glasgow	Workington	1908	1909	Bristol Rovers	2	0	0
Lawther	Ian	Belfast	Sunderland	1961	1963	Scunthorpe United	59	0	21
Leaver	Derek	Blackburn	Unknown	1949	1955	Bournemouth	14	0	5
Leaver	William	Blackburn	Unknown	1897	1898	Released	0	0	0
Lee	Billy	Darwen	Pleasington	1936	1946	Barrow	1	0	0
Lee	Jack	Blackburn	Unknown	1937	1937	Corinthian Casuals	0	0	0
Le Saux	Graeme	Jersey	Chelsea	1993	1997	Chelsea	127	2	7
Lewis	Jack	Long Eaton	Grimsby Town	1977	1978	Doncaster Rovers	24	4	6
Lewis	John	Market Drayton	Unknown	1875	1880	Unknown	0	0	0
Leyland	Harry	Liverpool	Tonbridge	1956	1961	Tranmere Rovers	166	0	0
Livingstone	Steve	Middlesbrough	Coventry City	1991	1993	Chelsea	25	5	10

Complete Players' Career Records: Hughes – Livingstone

FAC Apps	Sub	Goals	FLC Apps	Sub	Goals	European Apps	Sub	Goals	Others Apps	Sub	Goals	Totals Apps	Sub	Goals
1	0	0	0	0	0	0	0	0	0	0	0	28	0	0
3	0	0	0	0	0	0	0	0	0	0	0	50	0	0
3	2	0	0	0	0	0	0	0	0	0	0	24	10	5
9	0	2	0	0	0	0	0	0	0	0	0	82	0	8
5	0	3	0	0	0	0	0	0	3	0	0	93	0	25
2	0	0	5	0	0	0	0	0	0	0	0	91	0	1
5	0	0	0	0	0	0	0	0	2	0	2	60	0	19
1	1	0	2	1	0	0	0	0	0	0	0	40	5	6
0	0	0	0	0	0	0	0	0	2	0	0	12	0	1
19	0	1	0	0	0	0	0	0	0	0	0	146	0	5
11	0	1	0	0	0	0	0	0	0	0	0	176	0	24
3	0	1	0	0	0	0	0	0	0	0	0	3	0	1
0	0	0	0	0	0	0	0	0	0	0	0	0	1	0
0	0	0	3	0	0	0	0	0	0	1	0	43	19	3
2	0	0	6	0	0	0	0	0	0	0	0	57	0	9
1	0	0	0	0	0	0	0	0	0	0	0	2	0	0
1	0	0	0	0	0	0	0	0	2	0	0	29	0	10
0	0	0	0	0	0	0	0	0	1	0	0	3	0	0
4	3	2	3	1	2	0	0	0	0	0	0	64	28	34
1	0	0	0	0	0	0	0	0	0	0	0	1	0	0
0	3	0	2	1	1	0	0	0	2	0	0	24	26	12
0	0	0	0	0	0	0	0	0	0	0	0	1	0	0
1	4	0	9	3	0	0	1	0	0	0	0	47	24	2
0	0	0	0	0	0	0	0	0	0	0	0	14	0	0
2	0	1	0	0	0	0	0	0	0	0	0	38	0	23
0	0	0	3	0	0	0	0	0	0	0	0	52	0	0
2	0	1	1	0	0	0	0	0	0	0	0	39	3	15
14	0	0	0	0	0	0	0	0	1	0	0	262	0	0
15	0	0	15	0	0	0	0	0	5	0	0	277	0	0
1	0	0	0	0	0	0	0	0	0	0	0	12	0	0
0	0	0	0	0	0	0	0	0	0	0	0	3	0	0
0	0	0	0	0	0	0	0	0	0	0	0	14	0	0
9	0	0	6	0	0	0	0	0	0	0	0	134	1	4
0	0	0	0	0	0	0	0	0	0	0	0	17	0	5
19	1	0	23	0	0	0	0	0	17	0	1	424	6	24
0	3	0	0	0	0	0	0	0	0	0	0	0	5	0
3	0	0	4	0	0	0	0	0	0	0	0	43	1	0
0	0	0	0	0	0	0	0	0	0	0	0	3	0	0
16	0	0	0	0	0	0	0	0	0	0	0	202	0	1
6	0	0	7	0	1	0	0	0	4	0	0	96	0	7
13	0	0	16	2	0	6	0	0	1	0	0	189	4	1
3	0	1	4	0	0	0	0	0	4	1	3	60	11	27
0	0	0	0	0	0	0	0	0	0	0	0	29	0	8
0	0	0	0	0	0	0	0	0	0	0	0	3	0	0
0	0	0	0	0	0	0	0	0	1	1	0	33	15	7
0	0	0	0	0	0	0	0	0	0	0	0	11	0	0
0	0	0	0	0	0	0	0	0	9	0	1	25	0	1
6	0	0	0	0	0	0	0	0	3	0	0	97	0	6
2	0	0	4	0	1	0	0	0	0	0	0	76	0	12
4	0	0	0	0	0	0	0	0	0	0	0	35	0	0
0	1	0	0	0	0	0	0	0	0	0	0	0	1	0
0	0	0	0	0	0	0	0	0	0	0	0	23	2	0
2	0	0	0	0	0	0	0	0	0	0	0	38	0	8
2	0	0	0	0	0	0	0	0	43	0	0	97	0	0
18	0	1	0	0	0	0	0	0	32	0	16	262	0	74
0	0	0	0	0	0	0	0	0	0	0	0	2	0	0
2	0	0	0	0	0	0	0	0	0	0	0	2	0	0
24	0	10	0	0	0	0	0	0	23	0	16	303	0	120
0	0	0	0	0	0	0	0	0	0	0	0	3	0	1
0	0	0	0	0	0	0	0	0	0	0	0	2	0	0
5	0	1	11	0	10	0	0	0	0	0	0	75	0	32
0	0	0	0	0	0	0	0	0	0	0	0	14	0	5
1	0	0	0	0	0	0	0	0	0	0	0	1	0	0
0	0	0	0	0	0	0	0	0	1	0	0	2	0	0
1	0	0	0	0	0	0	0	0	0	0	0	1	0	0
8	0	0	10	0	0	4	1	0	2	0	0	151	3	7
0	0	0	2	0	0	0	0	0	2	0	0	28	4	6
3	0	1	0	0	0	0	0	0	0	0	0	3	0	1
18	0	0	4	0	0	0	0	0	0	0	0	188	0	0
1	0	1	2	0	0	0	0	0	0	0	0	28	5	11

The Essential History of Blackburn Rovers

Player		Birthplace	From	Year Joined	Year Left	To	League Apps	Sub	Goals
Lofthouse	Joe	Blackburn	King's Own FC	1882	1887	Accrington	}		
	(Two spells)		Accrington	1889	1893	Darwen	51	0	18
Logan	Neil	Unknown	Swindon Town	1902	1903	Unknown	22	0	2
Longmuir	Archie	Ardrossan	Celtic	1921	1923	Oldham Athletic	24	0	2
Lord	Frank	Chadderton	Stockport County	1966	1967	Chesterfield	10	0	1
Low	David	New Herrington	New Herrington Swifts	1924	1927	Swindon Town	13	0	0
Lowe	John	Denton	Denton	1890	1891	Unknown	2	0	0
Lowey	John	Manchester	Sheffield Wednesday	1980	1986	Wigan Athletic	136	5	14
Luke	Charles	Esh Winning	Sheffield Wednesday	1938	1938	Chesterfield	10	0	2
McAllister	Tom	Govan	Castleford Town	1904	1906	Brentford	2	0	0
McAteer	Jason	Birkenhead	Liverpool	1999	Still at club		57	11	4
McCaig	Bob	Lockerbie	Carlisle United	1948	1951	Stockport County	30	0	2
McCall	William	Kirton	Queen of the South W	1920	1922	Wolverhampton W.	11	0	0
McCallum	Neil	Bonhill	Celtic	1890	1890	Celtic	2	0	0
McCleery	Willie	Belfast	Queens Island	1922	1927	Shelbourne	23	0	5
McClelland	Charlie	Manchester	Hyde United	1946	1949	Exeter City	13	0	2
McClure	Sam	Workington	Black Diamonds	1899	1906	Died in 1906	144	0	12
McCulloch	Sam	Glasgow	Petershill	1926	1929	Thames Association	1	0	0
McDonald	Gerry	Milnthorpe	School	1969	1973	Halifax Town	19	2	2
McDonald	John	Ayr	Ayr FC	1903	1905	Leeds City	1	0	0
McDonald	John	Glasgow	Linfield	1920	1922	Dundee	33	0	7
McEvoy	Andy	Dublin	Bray Wanderers	1956	1967	Limerick	183	0	89
MacFarlane	Robert	Unknown	St Mirren	1893	1893	Nelson	2	0	0
McGhie	Alex	Liverpool	Ashton Town	1910	1920	Unknown	23	0	3
McGorrighan	Frank	Easington	Hull City	1947	1947	Hull City	5	0	0
McGrath	Mick	Dublin	Home Farm	1954	1966	Bradford	268	0	8
McGrogan	Frank	Dumbarton	Renfrew	1934	1936	Dunfermline Athletic	4	0	1
McIntyre	Hugh	Glasgow	Glasgow Rangers	1879	1886	Retired	0	0	0
McIntyre	John	Glasgow	Sheffield Wednesday	1922	1928	Blackpool	175	0	38
McIver	Billy	Whittle-le-Woods	Darwen	1901	1908	Brentford	126	0	0
McKay	Jock	Glasgow	Celtic	1921	1927	Middlesbrough	150	0	46
McKee	Billy	Burtonwood	Earlestown	1949	1953	Released	1	0	0
McKenzie	Duncan	Grimsby	Chelsea	1979	1981	Tulsa Roughnecks	74	0	16
McKeown	Mick	Lugar	Celtic	1891	1892	Morton	19	0	0
McKinlay	Billy	Glasgow	Dundee United	1995	2000	Bradford City	76	14	3
McKinnell	Jimmy	Dalbeattie	Queen of the South	1920	1926	Darlington	111	0	0
McKinnon	Paul	Camberley	Sutton United	1986	1987	Orebro SK, Sweden	5	0	0
McLean	John	Busby	Kirkintilloch Rob Roy	1931	1933	Bristol Rovers	8	0	0
McLean	Tommy	Lochgelly	St Johnstone	1927	1935	Exeter City	247	0	44
McLean	Billy	Liverpool	Burscough	1953	1955	Released	12	0	0
MacLeod	Ally	Glasgow	St Mirren	1955	1961	Hibernian	193	0	47
McLuckie	George	Falkirk	Lochore Welfare	1952	1953	Ipswich Town	20	0	2
McNamee	John	Coatbridge	Newcastle United	1971	1972	Retired	56	0	9
McOwen	Billy	Darwen	Blackburn Olympic	1887	1890	Darwen	14	0	0
McShane	Harry	Holytown	Bellshill Athletic	1937	1946	Huddersfield Town	2	0	0
Mahon	Alan	Dublin	Sporting Lisbon, Portugal	2000	Still at club		14	4	0
Mail	David	Bristol	Aston Villa	1982	1990	Hull City	200	6	4
Makel	Lee	Sunderland	Newcastle United	1992	1995	Huddersfield Town	1	5	0
Malcolm	William	Alloa	Dunipace	1923	1924	Bo'ness	2	0	0
Mann	George	Unknown	East Stirlingshire	1892	1894	Manchester City	2	0	1
Manning	John	Unknown	Raith Rovers	1907	1908	Northampton Town	4	0	0
Manson	Robert	Unknown	Stockport County	1906	1908	Released	16	0	3
Marcolin	Dario	Brescia, Italy	Lazio	1998	1999	Lazio	5	5	1
Marker	Nicky	Budleigh Salterton	Plymouth Argyle	1992	1997	Sheffield United	41	13	1
Marks	George	Amesbury	Arsenal	1946	1948	Bristol City	67	0	0
Marriott	Andy	Sutton-in-Ashfield	Nottingham Forest	1989	1990	Nottingham Forest	2	0	0
Marshall	Harry	Portobello	Heart of Midlothian	1892	1896	Heart of Midlothian	53	0	2
Martin	Don	Corby	Northampton Town	1968	1975	Northampton Town	218	6	57
Martin	Jack	South Shields	Lincoln City	1906	1908	Brighton & HA	57	0	25
Matier	Gerry	Lisburn	Coleraine	1937	1939	Bradford City	20	0	0
May	David	Oldham	Trainee	1986	1994	Manchester United	123	0	3
Melville	Jim	Barrow-in-Furness	Barrow	1928	1933	Hull City	25	0	0
Metcalfe	Stuart	Blackburn	School	1966	1980	Carlisle United	}		
	(Two spells)		Carolina Lightning, USA	1982	1983	Retired	376	11	21
Millar	John	Coatbridge	Chelsea	1987	1991	Heart of Midlothian	122	4	1
Miller	Alan	Epping	West Bromwich Albion	2000	Still at club		1	0	0
Miller	Archie	Larkhall	Heart of Midlothian	1947	1948	Kilmarnock	6	0	0
Miller	Ian	Perth	Swindon Town	1981	1989	Port Vale	252	16	16
Mills	Andrew	Knighton	Knighton	1897	1898	Swindon Town	2	0	0
Milne	Jackie	Stirling	Glasgow Ashfield	1932	1935	Arsenal	45	0	13
Mimms	Bobby	York	Everton	1987	1987	Everton	}		
	(Two spells)		Tottenham Hotspur	1990	1996	Crystal Palace	132	2	0

FAC Apps	Sub	Goals	FLC Apps	Sub	Goals	European Apps	Sub	Goals	Others Apps	Sub	Goals	Totals Apps	Sub	Goals
32	0	12	0	0	0	0	0	0	0	0	0	83	0	30
0	0	0	0	0	0	0	0	0	0	0	0	22	0	2
5	0	0	0	0	0	0	0	0	0	0	0	29	0	2
0	0	0	0	0	0	0	0	0	0	0	0	10	0	1
0	0	0	0	0	0	0	0	0	0	0	0	13	0	0
0	0	0	0	0	0	0	0	0	0	0	0	2	0	0
6	0	1	9	0	1	0	0	0	0	0	0	151	5	16
0	0	0	0	0	0	0	0	0	0	0	0	10	0	2
0	0	0	0	0	0	0	0	0	0	0	0	2	0	0
7	0	0	4	0	0	0	0	0	0	0	0	68	11	4
2	0	0	0	0	0	0	0	0	0	0	0	32	0	2
0	0	0	0	0	0	0	0	0	0	0	0	11	0	0
0	0	0	0	0	0	0	0	0	0	0	0	2	0	0
2	0	0	0	0	0	0	0	0	0	0	0	25	0	5
5	0	5	0	0	0	0	0	0	0	0	0	18	0	7
8	0	0	0	0	0	0	0	0	0	0	0	152	0	12
0	0	0	0	0	0	0	0	0	0	0	0	1	0	0
0	2	0	3	0	0	0	0	0	0	0	0	22	4	2
0	0	0	0	0	0	0	0	0	0	0	0	1	0	0
2	0	0	0	0	0	0	0	0	0	0	0	35	0	7
17	0	10	13	0	4	0	0	0	0	0	0	213	0	103
0	0	0	0	0	0	0	0	0	0	0	0	2	0	0
2	0	0	0	0	0	0	0	0	42	0	1	67	0	3
0	0	0	0	0	0	0	0	0	0	0	0	5	0	0
29	0	3	15	0	1	0	0	0	0	0	0	312	0	12
0	0	0	0	0	0	0	0	0	0	0	0	4	0	1
34	0	4	0	0	0	0	0	0	0	0	0	34	0	4
19	0	0	0	0	0	0	0	0	0	0	0	194	0	38
6	0	0	0	0	0	0	0	0	22	0	0	154	0	0
11	0	3	0	0	0	0	0	0	0	0	0	161	0	49
0	0	0	0	0	0	0	0	0	0	0	0	1	0	0
8	0	1	8	0	4	0	0	0	4	0	0	94	0	21
2	0	0	0	0	0	0	0	0	0	0	0	21	0	0
7	1	0	4	0	1	1	0	0	0	0	0	88	15	4
13	0	0	0	0	0	0	0	0	0	0	0	124	0	0
1	0	0	0	0	0	0	0	0	1	0	0	7	0	0
0	0	0	0	0	0	0	0	0	0	0	0	8	0	0
27	0	5	0	0	0	0	0	0	1	0	0	275	0	49
2	0	0	0	0	0	0	0	0	0	0	0	14	0	0
23	0	6	2	0	0	0	0	0	0	0	0	218	0	53
1	0	1	0	0	0	0	0	0	0	0	0	21	0	3
1	0	1	0	0	0	0	0	0	0	0	0	57	0	10
1	0	0	0	0	0	0	0	0	0	0	0	15	0	0
0	0	0	0	0	0	0	0	0	19	0	14	21	0	14
6	0	0	0	0	0	0	0	0	0	0	0	20	0	0
12	0	0	12	1	0	0	0	0	17	0	0	241	7	4
0	0	0	0	3	0	1	2	0	0	1	0	2	11	0
0	0	0	0	0	0	0	0	0	0	0	0	2	0	0
0	0	0	0	0	0	0	0	0	0	0	0	4	0	0
0	0	0	0	0	0	0	0	0	0	0	0	16	0	3
3	0	0	2	0	0	0	0	0	0	0	0	10	5	1
4	1	0	3	1	0	1	0	0	0	1	0	49	16	1
7	0	0	0	0	0	0	0	0	0	0	0	74	0	0
0	0	0	0	0	0	0	0	0	0	0	0	2	0	0
9	0	0	0	0	0	0	0	0	4	0	0	66	0	2
10	1	2	16	1	4	0	0	0	3	0	0	247	8	63
5	0	2	0	0	0	0	0	0	0	0	0	62	0	27
1	0	0	0	0	0	0	0	0	0	0	0	21	0	0
10	0	1	12	1	2	0	0	0	5	0	0	150	1	6
0	0	0	0	0	0	0	0	0	0	0	0	25	0	0
23	0	1	22	2	3	0	0	0	16	1	1	437	14	26
4	0	0	9	1	0	0	0	0	10	0	0	145	5	1
0	0	0	1	0	0	0	0	0	0	0	0	2	0	0
0	0	0	0	0	0	0	0	0	0	0	0	6	0	0
12	1	0	10	2	1	0	0	0	9	3	1	283	22	18
0	0	0	0	0	0	0	0	0	1	0	0	3	0	0
4	0	2	0	0	0	0	0	0	0	0	0	49	0	15
9	0	0	15	0	0	0	0	0	4	0	0	160	2	0

The Essential History of Blackburn Rovers

Player		Birthplace	From	Year Joined	Year Left	To	League Apps	Sub	Goals
Mitchell	Albert	Cobridge	Stoke City	1948	1949	Kettering Town	3	0	0
Mitchell	Bobby	South Shields	Sunderland	1976	1978	Grimsby Town	17	12	6
Mitchell	T.	Unknown	Unknown	1889	1889	Unknown	1	0	2
Mitchell	Tom	Trimdon Grange	Stockport County	1926	1929	Lincoln City	73	0	27
Moir	Jimmy	Bonhill	Celtic	1900	1901	Celtic	}		
	(Two spells)		Celtic	1903	1906	Released	} 77	0	0
Monks	Albert	Unknown	Everton	1902	1904	Nelson	24	0	4
Mooney	Frank	Fauldhouse	Manchester United	1954	1956	Carlisle United	58	0	19
Moore	Norman	Grimsby	Hull City	1950	1951	Bury	7	0	1
Moran	Kevin	Dublin	Sporting Gijon, Spain	1990	1994	Retired	143	4	10
Moreland	John	Unknown	Nelson	1898	1899	Released	20	0	6
Morgan	Hugh	Shotts	Liverpool	1900	1903	Released	77	0	18
Morley	Andy	Unknown	Unknown	1979	1981	Released	0	0	0
Morley	Brian	Fleetwood	School	1977	1981	Tranmere Rovers	20	0	0
Morris	Peter	Farnworth	Preston North End	1978	1980	Released	2	2	0
Morrison	Andy	Inverness	Plymouth Argyle	1993	1994	Blackpool	1	4	0
Mortimer	Bob	Bolton	Accrington Stanley	1937	1938	York City	16	0	4
Mullen	Jimmy	Oxford	Rotherham United	1974	1976	Bury	6	4	0
Mulvaney	Dick	Sunderland	Merton Colliery	1964	1971	Oldham Athletic	135	6	4
Munro	Stuart	Falkirk	Glasgow Rangers	1991	1993	Bristol City	1	0	0
Murphy	Don	Dublin	Plymouth Argyle	1982	1983	Drogheda United	1	2	0
Murphy	Eddie	Middlesbrough	Middlesbrough	1947	1949	Halifax Town	31	0	6
Murray	Bobby	Alexandria	Darwen	1909	1912	Nelson	10	0	0
Murray	John	Strathblane	Sunderland	1892	1896	Retired	109	0	0
Napier	Kit	Dunblane	Brighton & HA	1972	1974	Released	53	1	10
Needham	Andy	Oldham	Birmingham City	1976	1977	Aldershot	4	1	0
Newell	Mike	Liverpool	Everton	1991	1996	Birmingham City	113	17	28
Newton	Keith	Manchester	Spurley Hey Youth Club	1958	1969	Everton	306	0	9
Nicol	Tom	Whitburn	Mossend Swifts	1896	1897	Southampton St Mary's	16	0	2
Nightingale	Albert	Thrybergh	Huddersfield Town	1948	1952	Leeds United	35	0	5
Oakes	Jackie	Hamilton	Queen of the South	1947	1948	Manchester City	35	0	9
Oates	Graham	Bradford	Bradford City	1974	1976	Newcastle United	76	0	10
O'Brien	Burton	South Africa	St Mirren	1999	Still at club		0	0	0
O'Brien	Joe	Glasgow	Reading	1900	1901	Aberdeen	3	0	0
O'Dowd	Peter	Halifax	Bradford	1926	1930	Burnley	50	0	1
Ogilvie	Adam	Scotland	Grimsby Town	1893	1897	Shrewsbury Town	108	0	0
O'Keefe	Vince	Birmingham	Torquay United	1982	1989	Wrexham	68	0	0
Oldham	Wilfred	Unknown	Everton	1900	1901	Released	9	0	1
O'Leary	Donal	Limehouse	Unknown	1954	1956	Released	6	0	1
Oliver	Alfred	Bangor	Bangor	1905	1906	Bangor	2	0	0
Oliver	Neil	Berwick-u-Tweed	Berwick Rangers	1989	1991	Falkirk	5	1	0
O'Mara	John	Bolton	Brentford	1972	1974	Chelmsford City	30	5	10
Orr	John	Leith	Unknown	1908	1920	Released	75	0	30
Ostenstad	Egil	Haugesund, Norway	Southampton	1999	Still at club		28	13	10
Parker	Harold	Blackburn	Lower Darwen Youth Club	1951	1953	Released	3	0	0
Parker	Stuart	Preston	Sparta Rotterdam	1979	1980	Frechville CA	5	4	1
Parkes	Tony	Sheffield	Buxton Town	1970	1982	Retired	345	5	38
Parkin	Tim	Penrith	School	1974	1980	FF Malmo	13	0	0
Parkinson	James	Unknown	Blackpool	1895	1896	Released	1	0	0
Patterson	Jack	East Cramlington	Nottingham Forest	1945	1956	Kettering Town	107	0	0
Patterson	Mark	Darwen	Apprentice	1983	1988	Preston North End	89	12	20
Paul	Arthur	Belfast	Unknown	1889	1890	Unknown	1	0	0
Peacock	Darren	Bristol	Newcastle United	1998	2000	Retired	42	5	1
Pearce	Ian	Bury St Edmunds	Chelsea	1993	1997	West Ham United	43	19	2
Pearce	Robert	Innerleithen	Vale of Leithen FC	1920	1920	Released	1	0	0
Pedersen	Per	Aalborg, Denmark	Odense Boldklub	1997	1998	Strasbourg, France	6	5	1
Pedersen	Tore	Fredrikstad, Norway	St Pauli, Germany	1997	1998	Eintracht Frankfurt	3	2	0
Pennington	Rowland	St Helens	Whiston	1890	1893	Northwich Victoria	8	0	0
Pentland	Fred	Wolverhampton	Blackpool	1903	1906	Brentford	51	0	9
Perez	Sebastian	St Chamond, France	Bastia	1998	1999	St Etienne	4	1	1
Pickering	Fred	Blackburn	School	1956	1964	Everton	}		
	(Two spells)		Blackpool	1971	1972	Released	} 134	0	61
Pinkerton	James	Rothsay	Partick Thistle	1936	1936	St Bernard's	1	0	0
Pinxton	Albert	Shelton	Nantwich	1933	1936	Cardiff City	3	0	0
Platt	Peter	Oldham	Oswaldtwistle Rovers	1901	1902	Liverpool	1	0	0
Pool	Alexander	Annan	Solway Star	1919	1925	Bristol City	17	0	0
Porteous	George	Unknown	St Anthony's FC	1910	1916	Clyde	6	0	0
Porter	Robert	Unknown	Unknown	1887	1889	Unknown	1	0	0
Porter	Walter	Mellor	St John's	1895	1896	Mellor	6	0	0
Pratt	John	Workington	Preston North End	1936	1937	Belfast Distillery	6	0	0
Price	Chris	Hereford	Hereford United	1986	1988	Aston Villa	}		
	(Two spells)		Aston Villa	1992	1993	Portsmouth	} 96	6	14

312

FAC Apps	Sub	Goals	FLC Apps	Sub	Goals	European Apps	Sub	Goals	Others Apps	Sub	Goals	Totals Apps	Sub	Goals
0	0	0	0	0	0	0	0	0	0	0	0	3	0	0
2	0	1	0	0	0	0	0	0	4	2	1	23	14	8
0	0	0	0	0	0	0	0	0	0	0	0	1	0	2
9	0	4	0	0	0	0	0	0	0	0	0	82	0	31
3	0	0	0	0	0	0	0	0	0	0	0	80	0	0
3	0	1	0	0	0	0	0	0	0	0	0	27	0	5
1	0	0	0	0	0	0	0	0	0	0	0	59	0	19
0	0	0	0	0	0	0	0	0	0	0	0	7	0	1
10	1	1	8	1	0	0	0	0	6	0	1	167	6	12
0	0	0	0	0	0	0	0	0	1	0	0	21	0	6
2	0	0	0	0	0	0	0	0	0	0	0	79	0	18
0	0	0	0	0	0	0	0	0	1	0	0	1	0	0
0	0	0	4	0	0	0	0	0	3	0	0	27	0	0
1	1	0	0	0	0	0	0	0	0	0	0	3	3	0
1	0	0	0	0	0	0	0	0	0	0	0	2	4	0
0	0	0	0	0	0	0	0	0	0	0	0	16	0	4
2	0	0	0	0	0	0	0	0	0	0	0	8	4	0
2	0	8	0	0	0	0	0	0	0	0	0	145	6	4
0	0	0	0	0	0	0	0	0	0	0	0	1	0	0
0	0	0	0	0	0	0	0	0	0	0	0	1	2	0
3	0	1	0	0	0	0	0	0	0	0	0	34	0	7
0	0	0	0	0	0	0	0	0	0	0	0	10	0	0
13	0	0	0	0	0	0	0	0	0	0	0	122	0	0
7	0	3	3	0	0	0	0	0	0	0	0	63	1	13
0	0	0	1	1	0	0	0	0	2	0	0	7	2	0
9	2	6	14	2	8	5	1	4	4	0	2	145	22	48
21	0	0	30	0	1	0	0	0	0	0	0	357	0	10
3	0	0	0	0	0	0	0	0	0	0	0	19	0	2
7	0	3	0	0	0	0	0	0	0	0	0	42	0	8
2	0	0	0	0	0	0	0	0	0	0	0	37	0	9
4	0	1	6	0	0	0	0	0	5	0	2	91	0	13
0	0	0	0	1	0	0	0	0	0	0	0	0	1	0
0	0	0	0	0	0	0	0	0	0	0	0	3	0	0
0	0	0	0	0	0	0	0	0	1	0	0	51	0	0
12	0	0	0	0	0	0	0	0	0	0	0	120	0	0
1	0	0	7	0	0	0	0	0	6	0	0	82	0	0
0	0	0	0	0	0	0	0	0	0	0	0	9	0	1
1	0	0	0	0	0	0	0	0	0	0	0	7	0	1
0	0	0	0	0	0	0	0	0	0	0	0	2	0	0
0	0	0	1	1	0	0	0	0	1	0	0	7	2	0
5	1	2	1	0	0	0	0	0	0	0	0	36	6	12
10	0	3	0	0	0	0	0	0	19	0	13	104	0	46
2	1	0	4	1	1	0	0	0	0	0	0	34	15	11
0	0	0	0	0	0	0	0	0	0	0	0	3	0	0
0	0	0	1	0	0	0	0	0	2	0	2	8	4	3
21	0	4	21	0	3	0	0	0	17	0	1	404	5	46
0	0	0	0	0	0	0	0	0	0	0	0	13	0	0
0	0	0	0	0	0	0	0	0	0	0	0	1	0	0
5	0	0	0	0	0	0	0	0	15	0	0	127	0	0
3	1	0	4	0	1	0	0	0	2	4	1	98	17	22
1	0	0	0	0	0	0	0	0	0	0	0	2	0	0
6	0	0	4	0	0	2	0	0	0	0	0	54	5	1
1	2	0	4	4	1	4	1	0	2	0	0	54	26	3
0	0	0	0	0	0	0	0	0	0	0	0	1	0	0
0	0	0	1	1	0	0	0	0	0	0	0	7	6	1
0	0	0	3	0	0	0	0	0	0	0	0	6	2	0
2	0	0	0	0	0	0	0	0	0	0	0	10	0	0
1	0	0	0	0	0	0	0	0	0	0	0	52	0	9
1	0	0	0	0	0	2	0	1	0	0	0	7	1	2
10	0	5	14	0	8	0	0	0	0	0	0	158	0	74
0	0	0	0	0	0	0	0	0	0	0	0	1	0	0
1	0	0	0	0	0	0	0	0	0	0	0	4	0	0
0	0	0	0	0	0	0	0	0	0	0	0	1	0	0
2	0	0	0	0	0	0	0	0	0	0	0	19	0	0
0	0	0	0	0	0	0	0	0	0	0	0	6	0	0
0	0	0	0	0	0	0	0	0	0	0	0	1	0	0
0	0	0	0	0	0	0	0	0	0	0	0	6	0	0
2	0	0	0	0	0	0	0	0	0	0	0	8	0	0
2	0	0	7	0	0	0	0	0	9	0	0	114	6	14

Player		Birthplace	From	Year Joined	Year Left	To	League Apps	Sub	Goals
Price	Johnny	Easington	Stockport County	1971	1974	Stockport County	63	13	12
Priday	Bob	Cape Town	Liverpool	1949	1951	Clitheroe	44	0	11
Proctor	Benjamin	Blackburn	Unknown	1909	1913	Stockport County	2	0	0
Proudfoot	John	Airdrie	Partick Thistle	1897	1898	Everton	36	0	14
Pryde	Bob	Methil	St Johnstone	1933	1949	Wigan Athletic	320	0	11
Puddefoot	Syd	West Ham	Falkirk	1925	1932	West Ham United	250	0	79
Quigley	Eddie	Bury	Preston North End	1951	1956	Bury	159	0	92
Quinn	Des	Tullyverry	Irish Fusiliers	1947	1949	Millwall	1	0	0
Quinn	Jimmy	Belfast	Swindon Town	1984	1986	Swindon Town	58	13	17
Radford	John	Hemsworth	West Ham United	1978	1979	Retired	36	0	10
Raitt	David	Buckhaven	Everton	1928	1929	Forfar Athletic	4	0	0
Ralphs	Bertram	Handsworth	Nuneaton	1921	1922	Stoke	40	0	6
Ramsbottom	Neil	Blackburn	Plymouth Argyle	1978	1979	Miami	10	0	0
Randell	Colin	Skewen, nr. Neath	Plymouth Argyle	1982	1985	Swansea City	72	1	7
Rankin	Bill	Dumbarton	Dundee	1927	1932	Charlton Athletic	144	0	4
Ratcliffe	Barrie	Blackburn	Bolton Wanderers	1958	1964	Scunthorpe United	36	0	4
Rathbone	Mick	Sheldon	Birmingham City	1979	1987	Preston North End	270	3	2
Reeves	Brian	Skelmersdale	Burscough	1960	1962	Scunthorpe United	12	0	0
Reid	Nicky	Urmston	Manchester City	1987	1992	West Bromwich Albion	160	14	9
Reilly	Frank	Perth	Falkirk	1919	1923	Llanelli	127	0	8
Reitmaier	Claus	Wurzburg, Germany	Wiener SK, Austria	1990	1990	Wiener SK, Austria	0	0	0
Richards	Jack	Rhosllanerchrugog	Wrexham	1929	1932	Chester	2	0	0
Richards	Marc	Wolverhampton	Trainee	1999	Still at club		0	0	0
Richardson	Leam	Leeds	YTS	1997	2000	Bolton Wanderers	0	0	0
Richardson	Lee	Halifax	Watford	1990	1992	Aberdeen	50	12	3
Rigby	Arthur	Chorlton	Bradford City	1925	1929	Everton	156	0	41
Rigg	Tweedale	Rochdale	Rochdale	1919	1921	Unknown	12	0	0
Riley	Tom	Blackburn	Chorley	1902	1905	Brentford	22	0	0
Ripley	Stuart	Middlesbrough	Middlesbrough	1992	1998	Southampton	172	15	13
Ritchie	George	Maryhill	Maryhill FC	1923	1924	Falkirk	2	0	0
Roberts	John	Cessnock, Australia	Apia Leichardt	1966	1968	Chesterfield	3	0	0
Roberts	Tommy	Liverpool	Skelmersdale United	1951	1954	Watford	6	0	0
Robertson	George	Glasgow	Clyde	1902	1903	Clyde	10	0	1
Robertson	Jimmy	Scotland	Vale of Leven	1905	1908	Brighton & HA	78	0	22
Robinson	Alfred	Manchester	Gainsborough Trinity	1911	1923	Darwen	144	0	0
Robinson	Patrick	Belfast	Belfast Distillery	1920	1921	Caerphilly	18	0	2
Rodgers	Norman	Hooley Hill	Stockport County	1920	1924	Retired	43	0	21
Rogers	Billy	Ulverston	Preston North End	1938	1947	Barrow	73	0	24
Rogers	Eamonn	Dublin	Larkview	1962	1971	Charlton Athletic	159	6	30
Rollo	David	Belfast	Linfield	1919	1927	Port Vale	207	0	5
Roscamp	Jack	Blaydon	Wallsend	1922	1932	Bradford City	223	0	37
Rostron	Tot	Darwen	Darwen	1885	1885	Darwen	0	0	0
Round	Paul	Blackburn	School	1975	1981	Le Havre (France)	41	10	5
Roxburgh	Bob	Morpeth	Newcastle United	1924	1931	Retired	114	0	0
Rushton	Walter	Unknown	Unknown	1885	1889	Unknown	0	0	0
Russell	Alex	Seaham	Southport	1970	1971	Tranmere Rovers	22	2	4
Russell	John	Unknown	Unknown	1902	1904	Released	1	0	0
Rutherford	Sep	Percy Main	Portsmouth	1936	1937	Retired	13	0	1
Sale	Tommy	Stoke-on-Trent	Stoke City	1936	1938	Stoke City	65	0	25
Salmon	Mike	Leyland	School	1981	1983	Stockport County	1	0	0
Sanderson	George	Unknown	Unknown	1891	1893	Released	4	0	0
Sandham	William	Unknown	Fleetwood	1920	1922	Rochdale	4	0	1
Sawers	Bill	Bridgetown, Glasgow	Clyde	1892	1893	Stoke	24	0	11
Sellars	Scott	Sheffield	Leeds United	1986	1992	Leeds United	194	8	35
Sewell	Ronnie	Middlesbrough	Burnley	1920	1927	Gainsborough Trinity	227	0	0
Shanahan	Terry	Paddington	Ipswich Town	1971	1971	Ipswich Town	6	0	2
Sharp	Alexander	Dundee	East Fife	1934	1935	Hull City	9	0	1
Sharples	George	Ellesmere Port	Everton	1965	1971	Southport	99	4	5
Sharples	Harold	Unknown	Unknown	1880	1883	Unknown	0	0	0
Shaw	Gilly	Pwllheli	Brierley Hill Alliance	1925	1928	Grimsby Town	5	0	2
Shea	Danny	Wapping	West Ham United	1913	1920	West Ham United	97	0	62
Shearer	Alan	Newcastle	Southampton	1992	1996	Newcastle United	132	6	112
Shearer	Duncan	Fort William	Swindon Town	1992	1992	Aberdeen	5	1	1
Shepstone	Paul	Coventry	Atherstone United	1990	1992	Motherwell	16	10	1
Sherrington	John	Unknown	Unknown	1895	1897	Released	1	0	0
Sherwood	Tim	St Albans	Norwich City	1992	1999	Tottenham Hotspur	239	7	26
Shorrock	F.	Unknown	Unknown	1883	1886	Unknown	0	0	0
Short	Craig	Bridlington	Everton	1999	Still at club		52	0	1
Silvester	Peter	Wokingham	Southend United	1976	1976	Southend United	5	0	1
Simpson	Jock	Pendleton	Falkirk	1911	1921	Retired	151	0	15
Simpson	William	Colzrum	Solway Star	1921	1922	Aberaman Athletic	4	0	0

FAC Apps	Sub	Goals	FLC Apps	Sub	Goals	European Apps	Sub	Goals	Others Apps	Sub	Goals	Totals Apps	Sub	Goals
4	2	0	1	1	0	0	0	0	0	0	0	68	16	12
1	0	0	0	0	0	0	0	0	0	0	0	45	0	11
1	0	0	0	0	0	0	0	0	0	0	0	3	0	0
1	0	0	0	0	0	0	0	0	1	0	0	38	0	14
25	0	0	0	0	0	0	0	0	180	0	11	525	0	22
26	0	8	0	0	0	0	0	0	1	0	0	277	0	87
7	0	3	0	0	0	0	0	0	0	0	0	166	0	95
0	0	0	0	0	0	0	0	0	0	0	0	1	0	0
4	0	3	6	1	2	0	0	0	2	0	1	70	14	23
1	0	1	1	0	0	0	0	0	1	0	0	39	0	11
0	0	0	0	0	0	0	0	0	0	0	0	4	0	0
1	0	0	0	0	0	0	0	0	0	0	0	41	0	6
0	0	0	0	0	0	0	0	0	0	0	0	10	0	0
5	0	0	4	0	0	0	0	0	0	0	0	81	1	7
18	0	0	0	0	0	0	0	0	0	0	0	162	0	4
5	0	1	9	0	3	0	0	0	0	0	0	50	0	8
15	0	0	14	0	0	0	0	0	8	0	0	307	3	2
5	0	0	0	0	0	0	0	0	0	0	0	17	0	0
6	2	0	13	0	0	0	0	0	13	1	1	192	17	10
11	0	1	0	0	0	0	0	0	0	0	0	138	0	9
0	0	0	0	0	0	0	0	0	1	0	0	1	0	0
0	0	0	0	0	0	0	0	0	0	0	0	2	0	0
0	0	0	1	0	0	0	0	0	0	0	0	1	0	0
0	0	0	1	0	0	0	0	0	0	0	0	1	0	0
0	0	0	1	2	0	0	0	0	2	2	0	53	16	3
12	0	3	0	0	0	0	0	0	0	0	0	169	0	44
0	0	0	0	0	0	0	0	0	0	0	0	12	0	0
2	0	0	0	0	0	0	0	0	0	0	0	24	0	0
14	0	3	18	0	0	6	1	0	2	0	0	212	16	16
0	0	0	0	0	0	0	0	0	0	0	0	2	0	0
0	0	0	0	0	0	0	0	0	0	0	0	3	0	0
0	0	0	0	0	0	0	0	0	0	0	0	6	0	0
3	0	0	0	0	0	0	0	0	0	0	0	13	0	1
7	0	0	0	0	0	0	0	0	0	0	0	85	0	22
12	0	0	0	0	0	0	0	0	14	0	0	170	0	0
0	0	0	0	0	0	0	0	0	0	0	0	18	0	2
5	0	3	0	0	0	0	0	0	0	0	0	48	0	24
10	0	3	0	0	0	0	0	0	72	0	26	155	0	53
4	0	0	14	0	9	0	0	0	0	0	0	177	6	39
18	0	1	0	0	0	0	0	0	0	0	0	225	0	6
26	0	7	0	0	0	0	0	0	1	0	0	250	0	44
1	0	1	0	0	0	0	0	0	0	0	0	1	0	1
4	0	0	5	0	0	0	0	0	5	1	1	55	11	6
13	0	0	0	0	0	0	0	0	1	0	0	128	0	0
4	0	1	0	0	0	0	0	0	0	0	0	4	0	1
1	0	0	1	0	0	0	0	0	0	0	0	24	2	4
0	0	0	0	0	0	0	0	0	0	0	0	1	0	0
1	0	0	0	0	0	0	0	0	0	0	0	14	0	1
3	0	1	0	0	0	0	0	0	0	0	0	68	0	26
0	0	0	0	0	0	0	0	0	0	0	0	1	0	0
1	0	0	0	0	0	0	0	0	0	0	0	5	0	0
0	0	0	0	0	0	0	0	0	0	0	0	4	0	1
4	0	3	0	0	0	0	0	0	0	0	0	28	0	14
11	0	1	12	0	3	0	0	0	20	0	2	237	8	41
21	0	0	0	0	0	0	0	0	0	0	0	248	0	0
0	0	0	0	0	0	0	0	0	0	0	0	6	0	2
0	0	0	0	0	0	0	0	0	0	0	0	9	0	1
5	0	0	4	1	0	0	0	0	0	0	0	108	5	5
4	0	1	0	0	0	0	0	0	0	0	0	4	0	1
0	0	0	0	0	0	0	0	0	0	0	0	5	0	2
8	0	3	0	0	0	0	0	0	3	0	4	108	0	69
8	0	2	16	0	14	8	0	2	1	0	0	165	6	130
0	0	0	0	0	0	0	0	0	0	1	0	5	2	1
0	1	0	1	0	0	0	0	0	1	0	0	18	11	1
0	0	0	0	0	0	0	0	0	0	0	0	1	0	0
15	2	4	24	1	2	10	0	0	2	0	0	290	10	32
1	0	0	0	0	0	0	0	0	0	0	0	1	0	0
3	0	0	1	0	0	0	0	0	0	0	0	56	0	1
0	0	0	0	0	0	0	0	0	0	0	0	5	0	1
17	0	7	0	0	0	0	0	0	1	0	0	169	0	22
0	0	0	0	0	0	0	0	0	0	0	0	4	0	0

Player		Birthplace	From	Year Joined	Year Left	To	League Apps	Sub	Goals
Sims	Chris	Liverpool	Groundstaff	1959	1966	Clitheroe	13	0	0
Skinner	Craig	Heywood	Trainee	1989	1992	Plymouth Argyle	11	5	0
Slater	Robbie	Ormskirk	Lens	1994	1995	West Ham United	12	6	0
Smailes	Matthew	Lancaster	Annfield Plain	1925	1927	West Ham United	4	0	0
Smeaton	Jock	Perth	St Johnstone	1936	1938	Sunderland	38	0	9
Smethams	John	Congleton	Burnley	1910	1911	Released	3	0	0
Smith	Albert	Unknown	Unknown	1891	1892	Released	7	0	0
Smith	Bill	Plymouth	Birmingham	1952	1960	Accrington Stanley	119	0	10
Smith	George	Preston	New Brompton	1903	1906	Plymouth Argyle	58	0	4
Smith	Jack	Batley	Manchester United	1946	1947	Port Vale	30	0	12
Smith	Percy	Burbage Spring	Preston North End	1910	1920	Fleetwood	172	0	5
Smith	William	Blackburn	Kearsley	1892	1893	Released	1	0	0
Somers	Peter	Avondale	Celtic	1900	1902	Celtic	76	0	13
Sorley	Jock	Scotland	Middlesbrough	1893	1895	Burton Swifts	26	0	9
Southworth	Jack	Blackburn	Blackburn Olympic	1887	1893	Everton	108	0	97
Southworth	James	Blackburn	Blackburn Olympic	1887	1892	Unknown	21	0	0
Sowerbutts	Joe	Blackburn	Unknown	1881	1887	Retired	0	0	0
Speedie	David	Glenrothes	Liverpool	1991	1992	Southampton	34	2	23
Speight	Micky	South Elmsall	Sheffield United	1980	1982	Grimsby Town	50	1	4
Stapleton	Frank	Dublin	Le Havre	1989	1991	Aldershot	80	1	13
Starbuck	Phil	Nottingham	Nottingham Forest	1990	1990	Nottingham Forest	5	1	1
Stephan	Harold	Farnworth	Unknown	1942	1948	Accrington Stanley	13	0	1
Stephenson	Roy	Crook	Rotherham United	1957	1959	Leicester City	21	0	5
Stevenson	Hugh	Unknown	Maryhill	1907	1912	St Mirren	58	0	3
Stonehouse	Kevin	Bishop Auckland	Shildon	1979	1983	Huddersfield Town	77	8	27
Stothert	James	unknown	Bohemians	1891	1892	Darwen Dimmocks	1	0	1
Strachan	Tot	Blackburn	Witton	1880	1886	Darwen	0	0	0
Stringfellow	John	Unknown	Unknown	1891	1893	Released	4	0	0
Stuart	James	Coatbridge	Albion Rovers	1894	1895	Rossendale United ⎫			
(Two spells)			Rossendale United	1896	1897	Woolwich Arsenal ⎭	15	0	5
Suart	Ron	Kendal	Blackpool	1949	1955	Wigan Athletic	176	0	0
Sulley	Chris	Camberwell	Dundee United	1987	1992	Port Vale	134	0	3
Suter	Fergie	Blythswood	Darwen	1880	1889	Retired	1	0	0
Suttie	Thomas	Lochgelly	Leith Athletic	1907	1915	Darwen	103	0	0
Sutton	Chris	Nottingham	Norwich City	1994	1999	Chelsea	125	5	47
Svarc	Bobby	Leicester	Colchester United	1975	1978	Retired	42	8	16
Swarbrick	James	Lytham St Annes	Blackpool Etrurians	1901	1903	Brentford	15	0	0
Swift	Edward	Unknown	Black Diamonds	1899	1900	Released	2	0	0
Swindells	Jack	Manchester	Manchester City	1957	1959	Accrington Stanley	9	0	1
Talbot	Les	Hednesford	Hednesford Town	1930	1936	Cardiff City	90	0	20
Taylor	Gordon	Ashton-under-Lyne	Birmingham City	1976	1978	Bury	62	2	20
Taylor	Ken	South Shields	Unknown	1950	1964	Morecambe	200	0	0
Taylor	Martin	Ashington	Trainee	1997	Still at club		17	8	3
Taylor	Royston	Blackpool	Sunderland	1976	1979	Barrow	3	0	1
Taylor	William	Edinburgh	Heart of Midlothian	1892	1893	Heart of Midlothian	10	0	1
Thomas	Eddie	Newton-le-Willows	Everton	1960	1962	Swansea Town	37	0	9
Thompson	Chris	Walsall	Bolton Wanderers	1983	1986	Wigan Athletic	81	4	24
Thompson	Ernie	New Biggin	Bath City	1931	1936	Manchester United	171	0	82
Thompson	Robert	Unknown	Whalley	1898	1900	Unknown	9	0	0
Thorley	Dennis	Stoke	Stoke City	1980	1980	Stoke City	2	2	0
Thorne	Peter	Manchester	YTS	1991	1995	Swindon Town	0	0	0
Thornewell	George	Romiley	Derby County	1927	1929	Chesterfield	41	0	4
Thorpe	Levy	Seaham Harbour	Burnley	1920	1922	Lincoln City	85	0	1
Tierney	Thomas	Northwich	Chorley	1895	1897	New Brighton Tower ⎫			
(Two spells)			New Brighton Tower	1898	1898	Chorley ⎭	21	0	3
Todd	Paul	Middlesbrough	Doncaster Rovers	1945	1951	Hull City	46	0	13
Tomlinson	Bob	Blackburn	Feniscowles	1943	1948	Accrington Stanley	25	0	0
Tomlinson	James	Blackburn	Unknown	1900	1902	Nelson	1	0	0
Townley	Billy	Blackburn	Blackburn Olympic	1886	1892	Stockton ⎫			
(Two spells)			Stockton	1893	1894	Darwen ⎭	97	0	37
Turnbull	Peter	Lanquhar	Burnley	1895	1896	Glasgow Rangers ⎫			
(Two spells)			Glasgow Rangers	1898	1898	Glasgow Rangers ⎭	26	0	7
Turner	David	Retford	Brighton & HA	1972	1974	Sheffield United	23	2	0
Turner	R.G.	Unknown	Unknown	1884	1886	Unknown	0	0	0
Turner	Thomas	Glasgow	Raith Rovers	1929	1936	Arbroath	113	0	24
Tyson	Billy	Skerton	Accrington Stanley	1937	1938	Boston United	6	0	2
Valery	Patrick	Brignoles, France	Bastia	1997	1998	Bastia	14	1	0
Vause	Peter	Chorley	Leyland Motors	1934	1938	Darwen	7	0	1
Venters	Alec	Cowdenbeath	Third Lanark	1947	1948	Raith Rovers	25	0	7
Vernon	Roy	Ffynnongroew	Mostyn YMCA	1954	1960	Everton	131	0	49
Waddington	John	Darwen	Darwen	1973	1979	Bury	139	9	18

Complete Players' Career Records: Sims – Waddington

FAC Apps	Sub	Goals	FLC Apps	Sub	Goals	European Apps	Sub	Goals	Others Apps	Sub	Goals	Totals Apps	Sub	Goals
0	0	0	0	0	0	0	0	0	0	0	0	13	0	0
1	0	0	0	1	0	0	0	0	3	0	1	15	6	1
1	0	0	1	0	0	1	0	0	1	0	0	16	6	0
0	0	0	0	0	0	0	0	0	0	0	0	4	0	0
0	0	0	0	0	0	0	0	0	0	0	0	38	0	9
0	0	0	0	0	0	0	0	0	0	0	0	3	0	0
0	0	0	0	0	0	0	0	0	0	0	0	7	0	0
9	0	2	0	0	0	0	0	0	0	0	0	128	0	12
3	0	0	0	0	0	0	0	0	0	0	0	61	0	4
4	0	0	0	0	0	0	0	0	9	0	5	43	0	17
20	0	1	0	0	0	0	0	0	42	0	3	234	0	9
0	0	0	0	0	0	0	0	0	0	0	0	1	0	0
2	0	0	0	0	0	0	0	0	0	0	0	78	0	13
1	0	0	0	0	0	0	0	0	0	0	0	27	0	9
24	0	24	0	0	0	0	0	0	0	0	0	132	0	121
6	0	0	0	0	0	0	0	0	0	0	0	27	0	0
20	0	16	0	0	0	0	0	0	0	0	0	20	0	16
2	0	1	2	0	0	0	0	0	3	0	2	41	2	26
0	0	0	6	0	0	0	0	0	2	1	1	58	2	5
4	0	1	5	0	1	0	0	0	3	0	0	92	1	15
0	0	0	0	0	0	0	0	0	0	0	0	5	1	1
2	0	0	0	0	0	0	0	0	82	0	35	97	0	36
6	0	0	0	0	0	0	0	0	0	0	0	27	0	5
4	0	0	0	0	0	0	0	0	2	0	0	64	0	3
2	0	0	3	1	2	0	0	0	1	0	1	83	9	30
0	0	0	0	0	0	0	0	0	0	0	0	1	0	1
21	0	6	0	0	0	0	0	0	0	0	0	21	0	6
0	0	0	0	0	0	0	0	0	0	0	0	4	0	0
0	0	0	0	0	0	0	0	0	0	0	0	15	0	5
11	0	0	0	0	0	0	0	0	0	0	0	187	0	0
6	0	0	6	0	0	0	0	0	10	0	0	156	0	3
38	0	3	0	0	0	0	0	0	0	0	0	39	0	3
7	0	0	0	0	0	0	0	0	0	0	0	110	0	0
9	0	4	11	1	7	6	3	1	1	0	0	152	9	59
4	0	1	3	1	3	0	0	0	3	1	1	52	10	21
1	0	0	0	0	0	0	0	0	0	0	0	16	0	0
0	0	0	0	0	0	0	0	0	0	0	0	2	0	0
0	0	0	0	0	0	0	0	0	0	0	0	9	0	1
6	0	1	0	0	0	0	0	0	0	0	0	96	0	21
2	1	0	2	0	0	0	0	0	3	0	0	69	3	3
22	0	0	11	0	0	0	0	0	0	0	0	233	0	0
7	0	1	7	0	0	0	1	0	0	0	0	31	9	4
0	0	0	0	0	0	0	0	0	0	0	0	3	0	1
3	0	1	0	0	0	0	0	0	0	0	0	13	0	2
2	0	1	5	0	5	0	0	0	0	0	0	44	0	15
10	0	2	5	0	0	0	0	0	0	0	0	96	4	26
8	0	2	0	0	0	0	0	0	0	0	0	179	0	84
0	0	0	0	0	0	0	0	0	0	0	0	9	0	0
0	0	0	0	0	0	0	0	0	0	0	0	2	2	0
0	0	0	0	0	0	0	0	0	0	1	0	0	1	0
6	0	1	0	0	0	0	0	0	1	0	1	48	0	6
7	0	0	0	0	0	0	0	0	0	0	0	92	0	1
0	0	0	0	0	0	0	0	0	0	0	0	21	0	3
1	0	0	0	0	0	0	0	0	0	0	0	47	0	13
4	0	0	0	0	0	0	0	0	7	0	0	36	0	0
0	0	0	0	0	0	0	0	0	0	0	0	1	0	0
26	0	14	0	0	0	0	0	0	0	0	0	123	0	51
1	0	1	0	0	0	0	0	0	0	0	0	27	0	8
1	0	0	0	0	0	0	0	0	0	0	0	24	2	0
9	0	0	0	0	0	0	0	0	0	0	0	9	0	0
2	0	0	0	0	0	0	0	0	0	0	0	115	0	24
0	0	0	0	0	0	0	0	0	0	0	0	6	0	2
1	1	0	2	0	0	0	0	0	0	0	0	17	2	0
1	0	0	0	0	0	0	0	0	0	0	0	8	0	1
0	0	0	0	0	0	0	0	0	0	0	0	25	0	7
13	0	3	0	0	0	0	0	0	0	0	0	144	0	52
12	0	2	7	1	0	0	0	0	7	0	0	165	10	20

Player		Birthplace	From	Year Joined	Year Left	To	League Apps	Sub	Goals
Wade	John	Lower Darwen	Darwen	1894	1896	Released	1	0	2
Wagstaffe	David	Manchester	Wolverhampton	1976	1978	Blackpool			
	(Two spells)		Blackpool	1979	1980	Retired	74	3	7
Walmsley	Albert	Blackburn	Darwen	1904	1902	Stockport County	272	0	6
Walmsley	Richard	Blackburn	Blackburn Trinity	1912	1923	Lancaster Town	38	0	1
Walter	Joseph	Bristol	Taunton United	1926	1928	Bristol Rovers	27	0	2
Walton	Nat	Preston	Witton FC	1884	1893	Nelson	110	0	37
Walton	William	Unknown	Fleetwood Rangers	1894	1896	Blackburn Park Road	5	0	1
Ward	Ashley	Manchester	Barnsley	1998	2000	Bradford City	52	2	13
Ward	Jimmy	Blackburn	Blackburn Olympic	1886	1887	Retired	0	0	0
Warhurst	Paul	Stockport	Sheffield Wednesday	1993	1997	Crystal Palace	30	27	4
Waring	Clement	Unknown	Unknown	1899	1900	Unknown	1	0	0
Waring	William	Unknown	Unknown	1889	1890	Darwen	1	0	0
Watson	Lionel	Southport	Manchester City	1902	1905	West Ham United	55	0	19
Watson	William	Darwen	Darwen Olympic	1920	1923	Accrington Stanley	12	0	0
Watts	Charlie	Middlesbrough	Middlesbrough Ironopolis	1893	1894	Burton Wanderers	9	0	0
Webber	Jack	Blackpool	Hyde United	1947	1948	Ashton United	8	0	1
Webster	Montague	Catford	Army football	1919	1920	Watford	2	0	0
Weddle	Jack	Sunderland	Portsmouth	1938	1943	Retired	42	0	16
Wegerle	Roy	Johannesburg	Queens Park Rangers	1992	1993	Coventry City	20	14	6
Weir	Jock	Fauldhouse	Hibernian	1947	1948	Celtic	23	0	7
Westby	Jack	Aintree	Burscough	1937	1944	Liverpool	2	0	0
Westcott	Dennis	Wallasey	Wolverhampton W.	1948	1950	Manchester City	63	0	37
Whalley	Jeff	Rossendale	Apprentice	1970	1972	Croatia, Australia	2	0	0
Wharton	Jackie	Bolton	Manchester City	1948	1953	Newport County	129	0	15
Wheeler	Alfred	Fareham	Portsmouth	1947	1949	Swindon Town	21	0	5
Whelan	Dave	Bradford	Wigan Boys Club	1953	1963	Crewe Alexandra	78	0	3
Whitehead	James	Church	Accrington	1893	1897	Manchester City	85	0	22
Whitehead	William	Unknown	Unknown	1886	1893	Released	3	0	1
Whiteside	Arnold	Calder Vale	Woodplumpton Juniors	1932	1949	Wigan Athletic	218	0	3
Whittaker	Arnold	Blackburn	Accrington Stanley	1899	1908	Accrington Stanley	250	0	57
Whittaker	Bernard	Liverpool	Unknown	1888	1889	Released	4	0	1
Whittaker	Walt	Manchester	Reading	1900	1901	Grimsby Town	52	0	0
Whittle	Maurice	Wigan	Apprentice	1966	1969	Oldham Athletic	5	2	0
Whyte	Crawford	Ryehope	Crawcrook Albion	1930	1935	Bradford	87	0	0
Whyte	John	Unknown	St Johnstone	1927	1929	Everton	26	0	2
Wightman	John	Duns	Huddersfield Town	1937	1947	Carlisle United	66	0	2
Wilcox	Jason	Farnworth	trainee	1989	1999	Leeds United	242	27	31
Wilkie	John	Unknown	Partick Thistle	1895	1898	Glasgow Rangers	75	0	17
Wilkie	T.	Glasgow	United Abstainers	1889	1889	Unknown	5	0	0
Wilkinson	David	Sunderland	North Shields	1948	1950	Bournemouth	1	0	0
Wilkinson	Neil	Blackburn	Apprentice	1973	1977	Cape Town	27	3	0
Williams	William	Unknown	Everton	1898	1901	Newton Heath	31	0	1
Williamson	John	Manchester	Manchester City	1956	1957	Released	9	0	3
Williamson	Philip	Macclesfield	Apprentice	1980	1982	Released	0	1	0
Williamson	Tom	Dalmuir	Kirkintilloch Rob Roy	1922	1924	Third Lanark	19	0	0
Willis	John	Boldon	Unknown	1954	1957	Accrington Stanley	1	0	0
Wilmington	Thomas	Unknown	Burnley	1896	1897	Nelson	9	0	0
Wilson	Billy	Seaton Delaval	Unknown	1963	1972	Portsmouth	246	1	0
Wilson	Joe	Westhoughton	Darwen	1904	1908	Brighton & HA	43	0	4
Wilson	Robert	Blantyre	Bellshill Athletic	1937	1938	Falkirk	3	0	0
Wilson	Tommy	Preston	Swindon Town	1898	1899	Swindon Town	1	0	0
Witschge	Richard	Amsterdam, Holland	Bordeaux	1995	1995	Bordeaux	1	0	0
Wolstenholme	Sam	Little Lever	Everton	1904	1908	Norwich City	98	0	1
Wombwell	Dick	Nottingham	Brighton & HA	1908	1910	Ilkeston Town	15	0	1
Wood	Mick	Bury	Apprentice	1970	1978	Bradford City	140	8	2
Wood	William	Unknown	Unknown	1927	1933	Burnley	7	0	0
Woods	Matt	Skelmersdale	Everton	1956	1963	Hakoah, Australia	260	0	2
Woolfall	Alfred	Blackburn	Unknown	1879	1883	Blackburn Olympic	0	0	0
Woolley	Horace	Rutherglen	Partick Thistle	1937	1938	East Kilbride Amateurs	1	0	0
Wright	Alan	Ashton-under-Lyne	Blackpool	1991	1995	Aston Villa	67	7	1
Wright	Archie	Glasgow	Falkirk	1951	1953	Grimsby Town	22	0	10
Wright*	Glenn	Liverpool	Apprentice	1972	1974	Released	1	0	0
Wrigley	Bernard	Clitheroe	Great Harwood	1921	1923	Released	1	0	0
Wyles	Cec	Bourne	Everton	1945	1946	Bury	0	0	0
Wylie	Tom	Darvel	Queen of the South	1921	1926	Darwen	174	0	0
Yarwood	John	Bacup	Accrington	1895	1896	Released	1	0	0
Young	William	Paisley	Clydebank Juniors	1934	1937	St Mirren	6	0	0

* Did not sign professional forms at the end of his apprenticeship.

FAC Apps	Sub	Goals	FLC Apps	Sub	Goals	European Apps	Sub	Goals	Others Apps	Sub	Goals	Totals Apps	Sub	Goals
0	0	0	0	0	0	0	0	0	0	0	0	1	0	2
4	0	0	4	0	0	0	0	0	7	0	2	89	3	9
28	0	0	0	0	0	0	0	0	35	0	0	335	0	6
0	0	0	0	0	0	0	0	0	21	0	0	60	0	0
0	0	0	0	0	0	0	0	0	0	0	0	27	0	2
29	0	12	0	0	0	0	0	0	0	0	0	139	0	49
0	0	0	0	0	0	0	0	0	0	0	0	5	0	1
4	1	0	2	0	0	0	0	0	0	0	0	58	3	13
2	0	0	0	0	0	0	0	0	0	0	0	2	0	0
2	1	0	6	2	0	4	2	0	0	0	0	42	32	4
0	0	0	0	0	0	0	0	0	0	0	0	1	0	0
0	0	0	0	0	0	0	0	0	0	0	0	1	0	0
6	0	1	0	0	0	0	0	0	0	0	0	61	0	20
0	0	0	0	0	0	0	0	0	0	0	0	12	0	0
0	0	0	0	0	0	0	0	0	0	0	0	9	0	0
0	0	0	0	0	0	0	0	0	0	0	0	8	0	1
0	0	0	0	0	0	0	0	0	0	0	0	2	0	0
7	0	2	0	0	0	0	0	0	42	0	14	91	0	32
4	1	2	3	3	4	0	0	0	0	0	0	27	18	12
0	0	0	0	0	0	0	0	0	0	0	0	23	0	7
0	0	0	0	0	0	0	0	0	18	0	0	20	0	0
3	0	0	0	0	0	0	0	0	0	0	0	66	0	37
0	0	0	1	0	0	0	0	0	0	0	0	3	0	0
9	0	2	0	0	0	0	0	0	30	0	3	168	0	20
0	0	0	0	0	0	0	0	0	0	0	0	21	0	5
9	0	0	0	0	0	0	0	0	0	0	0	87	0	3
8	0	2	0	0	0	0	0	0	0	0	0	93	0	24
1	0	0	0	0	0	0	0	0	0	0	0	4	0	1
21	0	0	0	0	0	0	0	0	177	0	0	416	0	3
15	0	0	0	0	0	0	0	0	0	0	0	265	0	57
0	0	0	0	0	0	0	0	0	0	0	0	4	0	1
1	0	0	0	0	0	0	0	0	0	0	0	53	0	0
0	0	0	0	0	0	0	0	0	0	0	0	5	2	0
1	0	0	0	0	0	0	0	0	0	0	0	88	0	0
0	0	0	0	0	0	0	0	0	0	0	0	26	0	2
5	0	0	0	0	0	0	0	0	57	0	2	128	0	4
18	2	2	16	1	1	4	0	0	3	0	0	283	30	34
5	0	1	0	0	0	0	0	0	2	0	0	82	0	18
0	0	0	0	0	0	0	0	0	0	0	0	5	0	0
0	0	0	0	0	0	0	0	0	0	0	0	1	0	0
2	0	0	5	1	0	0	0	0	0	0	0	34	4	0
0	0	0	0	0	0	0	0	0	0	0	0	31	0	1
0	0	0	0	0	0	0	0	0	0	0	0	9	0	3
0	0	0	0	0	0	0	0	0	0	0	0	0	1	0
0	0	0	0	0	0	0	0	0	0	0	0	19	0	0
0	0	0	0	0	0	0	0	0	0	0	0	1	0	0
0	0	0	0	0	0	0	0	0	0	0	0	9	0	0
14	0	0	16	0	0	0	0	0	0	0	0	276	1	0
3	0	0	0	0	0	0	0	0	0	0	0	46	0	4
0	0	0	0	0	0	0	0	0	4	0	0	7	0	0
0	0	0	0	0	0	0	0	0	0	0	0	1	0	0
0	0	0	0	0	0	0	0	0	0	0	0	1	0	0
7	0	1	0	0	0	0	0	0	0	0	0	105	0	2
0	0	0	0	0	0	0	0	0	0	0	0	15	0	1
10	1	0	6	1	0	0	0	0	4	0	2	160	10	4
0	0	0	0	0	0	0	0	0	0	0	0	7	0	0
30	0	1	17	0	0	0	0	0	0	0	0	307	0	3
3	0	0	0	0	0	0	0	0	0	0	0	3	0	0
0	0	0	0	0	0	0	0	0	0	0	0	1	0	0
5	1	0	8	0	0	0	0	0	3	0	0	83	8	1
0	0	0	0	0	0	0	0	0	0	0	0	22	0	10
0	0	0	0	0	0	0	0	0	0	0	0	1	0	0
0	0	0	0	0	0	0	0	0	0	0	0	1	0	0
2	0	1	0	0	0	0	0	0	24	0	17	26	0	18
17	0	0	0	0	0	0	0	0	0	0	0	191	0	0
0	0	0	0	0	0	0	0	0	0	0	0	1	0	0
0	0	0	0	0	0	0	0	0	0	0	0	6	0	0

The Essential History of Blackburn Rovers

Managers

February 1922-December 1926	Jack Carr
December 1926-February 1931	Bob Crompton (honorary manager)
February 1931-April 1936	Arthur Barritt (secretary-manager)
October 1936-May 1938	Reg Taylor (secretary-manager)
May 1938-March 1941	Bob Crompton
January 1946-February 1947	Eddie Hapgood
April 1947-December 1947	Will Scott
December 1947-May 1949	Jack Bruton
June 1949-May 1953	Jackie Bestall
June 1953-October 1958	Johnny Carey
October 1958-June 1960	Dally Duncan
September 1960-February 1967	Jack Marshall
April 1967-October 1970	Eddie Quigley
October 1970-June 1971	Johnny Carey
July 1971-December 1973	Ken Furphy
January 1974-June 1975	Gordon Lee
June 1975-March 1978	Jim Smith
April 1978-October 1978	Jim Iley
February 1979-May 1979	John Pickering
June 1979-May 1981	Howard Kendall (player-manager)
June 1981-December 1986	Bob Saxton
February 1987-September 1991	Don Mackay
October 1991-June 1995	Kenny Dalglish
June 1995-October 1996	Ray Harford
July 1997-November 1998	Roy Hodgson
December 1998-November 1999	Brian Kidd
December 1999-March 2000	Tony Parkes
March 2000 to date	Graeme Souness

Chairmen

1875-88	J. Lewis	1956-60	G.N. Forbes
1888-1901	E.S. Morley	1960-64	J. Wilkinson
1901-05	R. Birtwistle	1964-68	D. Hull
1905-19	L. Cotton	1968-70	C.R. Davies
1919-21	C. Cotton	1970-71	A.L. Fryars
1921-33	J.W. Walsh	1971-79	W.H. Bancroft
1933-38	W. Tempest	1979	D.T. Keighley
1938-43	J. Cotton	1979-82	D. Brown
1944-48	J. Caton	1982-91	W. Fox
1948-52	F. Wood	1991 to date	R.D. Coar
1952-56	T. Blackshaw		

Players with 50 or more goals in league football

168	Simon Garner	79	Syd Puddefoot
140	Tommy Briggs	75	Wattie Aitkenhead
121	Ted Harper	73	Eddie Crossan
112	Alan Shearer	71	Percy Dawson
108	Jack Bruton	67	Billy Davies
101	Bryan Douglas	62	Danny Shea
97	Jack Southworth	61	Fred Pickering
94	Eddie Latheron	57	Bobby Langton
92	Eddie Quigley	57	Don Martin
89	Andy McEvoy	57	Arnold Whittaker
88	Peter Dobing	50	John Byrom
82	Ernie Thompson	50	Harry Chippendale

Players with 300 or more league appearances

596	Derek Fazackerley	360	Harry Healless
581	Ronnie Clayton	350	Tony Parkes
529	Bob Crompton	336	Colin Hendry
484	Simon Garner	324	Jack Bruton
438	Bryan Douglas	323	Eric Bell
406	Bill Eckersley	320	Bob Pryde
387	Stuart Metcalfe	317	Noel Brotherston
386	Billy Bradshaw	306	Keith Newton
370	Glenn Keeley		

Players with 20 or more Football League Cup appearances

38	Derek Fazackerley	25	Tim Sherwood
34	Simon Garner	24	Mark Atkins
30	Keith Newton	24	Stuart Metcalfe
28	Ronnie Clayton	23	Glenn Keeley
27	Colin Hendry	22	Noel Brotherston
25	Bryan Douglas	21	Tony Parkes

Players with 30 or more FA Cup appearances

56	Ronnie Clayton	38	Fergie Suter
47	Jimmy Forrest	36	Harry Healless
46	Bob Crompton	35	Herbie Arthur
42	Jimmy Douglas	34	Hugh McIntyre
40	Bryan Douglas	32	Jimmy Brown
40	Derek Fazackerley	32	Joe Lofthouse
39	Billy Bradshaw	30	Matt Woods

Full International Appearances

England: Herbie Arthur (7), John Barton (1), David Batty (3), Joe Beverley (3), Fred Blackburn (3), Tom Booth (1), Billy Bradshaw (4), Jimmy Brown (5), Aussie Campbell (2), Harry Chippendale (1), Ronnie Clayton (35), Arthur Cowell (1), Bob Crompton (41), Arthur Cunliffe (2), Bryan Douglas (36), Bill Eckersley (17), Tim Flowers (10), Jimmy Forrest (11), Doc Greenwood (2), Fred Hargreaves (3), John Hargreaves (2), Ted Harper (1), Harry Healless (2), Joe Hodkinson (1), Kelly Houlker (1), Herbert Jones (6), Bobby Langton (7), Eddie Latheron (2), Graeme Le Saux (20), Joe Lofthouse (6), Keith Newton (19), Syd Puddefoot (2), Arthur Rigby (5), Stuart Ripley (2), Ronnie Sewell (1), Danny Shea (2), Alan Shearer (25), Jock Simpson (8), Jack Southworth (3), Chris Sutton (1), Billy Townley (2), Nat Walton (1), James Whitehead (1), Jason Wilcox (2), Sam Wolstenholme (2)

Ireland: Patrick Robinson (1), David Rollo (7)

Northern Ireland: Noel Brotherston (27), Eddie Crossan (3), Derek Dougan (5), Alan Fettis (7), Keith Gillespie (12), Allan Hunter (6), Damien Johnson (12), Ian Lawther (2), Jimmy Quinn (13), David Rollo (5)

Republic of Ireland: Lee Carlsey (7), Damien Duff (20), Shay Given (9), Joseph Haverty (2), Alan Kelly (11), Jeff Kenna (27), Jason McAteer (13), Andy McEvoy (17), Mike McGrath (18), Eamonn Rogers (14), Kevin Moran (24), Frank Stapleton (2)

Scotland: Wattie Aitkenhead (1), Thomas Brandon (1), Christian Dailly (13), Callum Davidson (12), Kevin Gallacher (30), Colin Hendry (35), John Hutton (3), John McKay (1), Billy McKinlay (15)

Wales: Nathan Blake (10), Chris Coleman (5), Billy Davies (9), Mike England (20), Bob Evans (1), Barrie Hole (7), John Hughes (1), Bill Hughes (5), Alfred Oliver (1), Roy Vernon (9)

Denmark: Per Frandsen (1), Per Werner Pedersen (3)

Greece: Georgios Donis (7)

Norway: Henning Berg (45), Stig-Inge Bjornebye (2), Lars Bohinen (4)

Sweden: Anders Andersson (2), Patrik Andersson (7), Martin Dahlin (4)

Switzerland: Stephane Henchoz (15)

USA: Brad Friedel (3), Roy Wegerle (4)